Frommer's

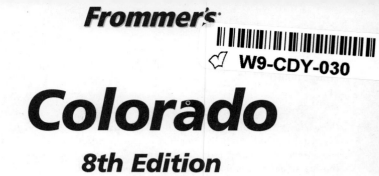

Colorado

8th Edition

by Don & Barbara Laine
& Eric Peterson

Here's what the critics say about Frommer's:

"Amazingly easy to use. Very portable, very complete."

—*Booklist*

"Detailed, accurate, and easy-to-read information for all price ranges."
—*Glamour Magazine*

"Hotel information is close to encyclopedic."

—*Des Moines Sunday Register*

"Frommer's Guides have a way of giving you a real feel for a place."
—*Knight Ridder Newspapers*

WILEY
Wiley Publishing, Inc.

Published by:

Wiley Publishing, Inc.

111 River St.
Hoboken, NJ 07030-5774

ISBN 0-7645-7431-0

Editor: Jennifer Reilly
With thanks to Cate Latting
Production Editor: Bethany André
Cartographer: Nick Trotter
Photo Editor: Richard Fox
Production by Wiley Indianapolis Composition Services

Front cover photo: A rancher and his horse
Back cover photo: Telluride: Skier crouches as he takes a leap in the air

Manufactured in the United States of America

5 4 3 2 1

Contents

List of Maps

About the Authors

Residents of northern New Mexico since 1970, **Don and Barbara Laine** have traveled extensively throughout the Rocky Mountains and the Southwest, spending as much time as possible in the outdoors, and especially in the region's national parks and monuments. They have written Frommer's guides to Utah, Colorado, Rocky Mountain National Park, and the National Parks of the American West. The Laines have also authored *Little-Known Southwest* and *New Mexico & Arizona State Parks* for The Mountaineers Books; and *The New Mexico Guide* for Fulcrum Publishing.

A Denver-based freelance writer, **Eric Peterson** has contributed to Frommer's guides to Colorado, Texas, and the National Parks of the American West, and has written *Frommer's Yellowstone & Grand Teton National Parks* and a coffee table book, *Roadside Americana* (www.roadsideamericanabook.com). When he's not on the road or writing about travel, Peterson covers Colorado's high-tech business scene and Denver's punk-rock underbelly. He's also an avid camper and hiker who enjoys long weekends in the Colorado Rockies with his antique boots, his campfire-cooked delicacies, and his faithful mutt, Giblet.

Acknowledgments

The authors wish to thank for their help Rich Grant and Jill Strunk with the Denver Metro Convention and Visitors Bureau, Nancy Kern with the Boulder Convention and Visitors Bureau, Elizabeth Youngquist with the Colorado Springs Convention and Visitors Bureau, Irene Carlow with the Grand Junction Visitor & Convention Bureau, and Patti Zink, Media Relations for Durango.

An Invitation to the Reader

In researching this book, we discovered many wonderful places—hotels, restaurants, shops, and more. We're sure you'll find others. Please tell us about them, so we can share the information with your fellow travelers in upcoming editions. If you were disappointed with a recommendation, we'd love to know that, too. Please write to:

Frommer's Colorado, 8th Edition
Wiley Publishing, Inc. • 111 River St. • Hoboken, NJ 07030-5774

An Additional Note

Please be advised that travel information is subject to change at any time—and this is especially true of prices. We therefore suggest that you write or call ahead for confirmation when making your travel plans. The authors, editors, and publisher cannot be held responsible for the experiences of readers while traveling. Your safety is important to us, however, so we encourage you to stay alert and be aware of your surroundings. Keep a close eye on cameras, purses, and wallets, all favorite targets of thieves and pickpockets.

Other Great Guides for Your Trip:

Frommer's Denver, Boulder & Colorado Springs
Frommer's National Parks of the American West
Frommer's Rocky Mountain National Park

Frommer's Star Ratings, Icons & Abbreviations

Every hotel, restaurant, and attraction listing in this guide has been ranked for quality, value, service, amenities, and special features using a **star-rating system.** In country, state, and regional guides, we also rate towns and regions to help you narrow down your choices and budget your time accordingly. Hotels and restaurants are rated on a scale of zero (recommended) to three stars (exceptional). Attractions, shopping, nightlife, towns, and regions are rated according to the following scale: zero stars (recommended), one star (highly recommended), two stars (very highly recommended), and three stars (must-see).

In addition to the star-rating system, we also use **seven feature icons** that point you to the great deals, in-the-know advice, and unique experiences that separate travelers from tourists. Throughout the book, look for:

Finds	Special finds—those places only insiders know about
Fun Fact	Fun facts—details that make travelers more informed and their trips more fun
Kids	Best bets for kids and advice for the whole family
Moments	Special moments—those experiences that memories are made of
Overrated	Places or experiences not worth your time or money
Tips	Insider tips—great ways to save time and money
Value	Great values—where to get the best deals

The following **abbreviations** are used for credit cards:

AE	American Express	DISC	Discover	V	Visa
DC	Diners Club	MC	MasterCard		

Frommers.com

Now that you have the guidebook to a great trip, visit our website at **www.frommers.com** for travel information on more than 3,000 destinations. With features updated regularly, we give you instant access to the most current trip-planning information available. At Frommers.com, you'll also find the best prices on airfares, accommodations, and car rentals—and you can even book travel online through our travel booking partners. At Frommers.com, you'll also find the following:

- Online updates to our most popular guidebooks
- Vacation sweepstakes and contest giveaways
- Newsletter highlighting the hottest travel trends
- Online travel message boards with featured travel discussions

What's New in Colorado

Colorado is a rich combination of the old and new, urban and rural, the civilized and the wild. The state's major cities lure us with their museums, galleries, performing arts, and historic sites, but just outside their boundaries await a vast array of outdoor recreation opportunities and some of America's most beautiful mountain scenery.

Growth, which Coloradans see as both a blessing and a curse, continues to be the main change occurring here. And for at least the next few years those who venture into the mountains will see not only the remnants of damage from dozens of forest fires that plagued the state in 2002, but also how quickly the forests begin to regenerate and heal themselves. Following are recent developments.

SETTLING INTO DENVER   Driving in Denver won't be much fun for the next few years while a huge **road construction** project continues into 2006. But at least you'll have some great places to stay while waiting for the traffic to ease up. The first hotel in the ritzy Cherry Creek area, the **JW Marriott,** 150 Clayton Lane (© **800/ 228-9290** or 303/316-2700), rivals Denver's best downtown luxury hotels and has a restaurant, **Mirepoix,** to match. Downtown Denver also boasts some fine new restaurants. These include the **Bistro Vendome,** 1424-H Larimer Sq. (© **303/825-3232**), serving what chef-owner Eric Roeder describes as "French soul food"; **Red Square Euro Bistro,** 1512 Larimer St. at Writer Square (© **303/595-8600**), with 100 brands of vodka behind the bar and excellent food that isn't purely Russian in lineage; **MAX Burgerworks,** 1512 Lawrence St. at Writer Square (© **303/534-0944**), which brings an upscale attitude to the art of burger making (20 varieties in all); and the **Tom Tom Room,** 1432 Market St. (© **303/534-5050**), a hip and romantic Japanese restaurant. See chapter 5 for details.

WHAT TO SEE & DO IN DENVER The **Vance Kirkland Museum,** 1311 Pearl St. (© **303/832-8576**), has greatly expanded its hours, and features remarkable collections of the work of Vance Kirkland (Colorado's most renowned painter) and other Colorado artists, as well as a superlative collection of decorative arts. The **Denver Museum of Nature and Science,** City Park, 2001 Colorado Blvd. (© **303/ 322-7009**), has added an exciting new "Space Odyssey" exhibit. Improvements have also been made at the **Butterfly Pavilion & Insect Center,** 6252 W. 104th Ave., Westminster (© **303/ 469-5441**), with a 31,000-square-foot expansion that was completed in 2004, housing "Shrunk!"—giant robotic insects and exhibits about the biomechanics of bugs. The south suburbs also have a new museum—**The Wildlife Experience,** 10035 S. Peoria St. (© **720/488-3300**), which specializes in art with a nature theme. The **Larimer Lounge,** 2721 Larimer St. (© **303/291-1007**), has been delivering punk and indie rock since 2003 in a barroom that's been open for more than a century. For more information see chapter 6.

COLORADO SPRINGS The former Antlers Adam's Mark is now the **Antlers Hilton,** 4 S. Cascade Ave. (© 877/754-9940 or 719/473-5600), after changing flags in fall 2004. It remains the cornerstone hotel of downtown Colorado Springs. **Walter's Bistro,** 136 E. Cheyenne Mountain Ave. (© 719/630-0201), relocated to a wonderful new space at the foot of Cheyenne Mountain and continues to deliver some of the best meals in town. See chapter 7 for details.

BOULDER The **St. Julien,** 900 Walnut St. (© 877/303-0900 or 720/406-9696), is the first hotel to open in downtown Boulder since the Boulderado in 1909. Elegant, with an excellent spa and incredible views, the hotel is Boulder's most upscale property. On the budget end of the spectrum, local entrepreneurs recycled a former "Holidome" into the colorful **Boulder Outlook,** 800 28th St. (© 800/542-0304 or 303/443-3322), with such unique perks as two bouldering rocks (one is 11 ft. high, the other a 4-footer) and a fenced, 4,000-square-foot dog run. Best of all, the rates are typically cheaper than its chain counterparts. On the culinary side of things, John Bizzarro handed the reins of **John's Restaurant,** 2328 Pearl St. (© 303/444-5232), to long-time Flagstaff House chef Corey Buck in 2004. The proprietors of **The Mediterranean** opened a French bistro across the street in **Brasserie Ten Ten,** 1011 Walnut St. (© 303/998-1010), which serves up delectable oysters as well as a nice selection of simple, fresh French stalwarts. See chapter 8 for details.

NORTHEASTERN COLORADO
Fort Morgan In 2003 we saw the completion of a major expansion and renovation project at the **Fort Morgan Museum** (© 970/867-6331), giving it more space for exhibits, gift shops, and educational programs.

Burlington The city **Swimming Pool** (© 719/346-8070) has a new 175-foot flume slide. See chapter 9 for all the details.

THE NORTHERN ROCKIES
Estes Park The community boasts a new outdoor entertainment venue, **Estes Park Performance Park,** on W. Elkhorn Avenue on the west side of town (© 970/586-9203).

In 2004 the **Stanley Hotel,** 333 Wonderview Ave. (© 800/976-1377 or 970/586-3371), opened a spa, plus several unattached one- to three-bedroom condo units that may be the most lavish in town.

Rocky Mountain National Park Trail Ridge Road (U.S. 36 between Estes Park and Grand Lake), will be undergoing repairs (© 970/586-1206) throughout the summer and fall seasons of 2005 and 2006. Be prepared for delays and night closures.

Steamboat Springs In summer 2004, **Strings in the Mountains** (© 970/879-5056) moved to its new home on 7 acres at the base of Mt. Werner, adjacent to the Village at Steamboat.

Amaze'n Steamboat Maze, 1255 U.S. 40 behind the chamber office (© 970/870-8682), has added bumper cars.

Winter Park   Devil's Thumb Ranch, Grand C.R. 83, Tabernash, 8 miles north of Winter Park (© 800/933-4339 or 970/726-5632), recently debuted several cabins, with hand-crafted and antique furniture. Summer 2004 saw the addition of a fly shop, while an ice-skating rink opened that winter.

Breckenridge A luxury three-bedroom house with private hot tub is now available at **The Lodge & Spa at Breckenridge,** 112 Overlook Dr. (© 800/736-1607 or 970/453-9300).

Vail For masterly pampering and comfort, you can't miss if you stay at

Vail Cascade Resort & Spa, 1300 Westhaven Dr. (✆ **800/420-2424** or 970/476-7111). Upon completion of a $5-million renovation project, Vail Cascade has gotten even better—and we didn't think that was possible.

Beaver Creek To help get you onto the mountain faster, **Beaver Creek Resort** (✆ **800/404-3535**) has added two new high-speed quad chairlifts.

Down the road at Edwards, **The Lodge & Spa at Cordillera,** 2205 Cordillera Way (✆ **800/877-3529** or 970/926-2200), has completed a $5-million renovation of all guest rooms, plus a spa expansion.

See chapter 10 for more information.

THE WESTERN SLOPE Glenwood Springs Glenwood Caverns Adventure Park, 51000 Two Rivers Plaza Rd. (✆ **800/530-1635** or 970/945-4228) opened in 2003, with eight six-person gondolas to take you up the side of Iron Mountain to visit the **Fairy Caves.** In the caves they've installed handrails and lighting, and added a few trails to the guided cave tour.

The popular Cajun eatery **The Bayou,** 919 Grand Ave. (✆ **970/945-1047**), moved from West Glenwood into a historic building in downtown Glenwood Springs in 2004.

See chapter 11 for more information.

SOUTHWESTERN COLORADO Mesa Verde National Park The **Far View Lodge** (✆ **800/449-2288** or 970/533-1944) recently renovated and upgraded their rooms, and added some upscale "Kiva" rooms with a king or two queen beds. See chapter 12 for details.

SOUTHERN ROCKIES Gunnison The **Wildwood Motel,** 1312 W. Tomichi Ave. (✆ **970/641-1663**),

has added two cabins, both with two bedrooms, two bathrooms, a washer and dryer, and private deck.

Lake City Intrigued with mining? Visit the new **Hard Tack Mine Tour & Museum,** about 3 miles west of town, via C.R. 20 (✆ **970/944-2506**) and see how miners lived and worked some 100 years ago.

Salida The **River Run Inn,** 8495 C.R. 160 (✆ **800/385-6925** or 719/539-3818), now offers private bathrooms with all five of its lovely rooms (occupants of the dorm room still share a bathroom).

Alamosa   Great Sand Dunes, 11999 Colo. 150, Mosca (✆ **719/378-2312**), has finally achieved national park status.

See chapter 13 for details.

SOUTHEASTERN COLORADO Pueblo The **El Pueblo History Museum,** 301 N. Union Ave. (✆ **719/583-0453**) opened its doors during the city's 2003 Chile and Frijoles Festival. Not only a splendid introduction to the history of the region, the museum also serves as the Scenic Byways Visitor Center, a gateway to the Arkansas Riverwalk, and the city's historic district.

Trinidad A great new biking, blading, and boarding park has opened here: the **Trinidad Skate Park,** Jefferson Street (✆ **719/846-9843**). It boasts 15,000 square feet of fast fun.

La Junta Just 35 miles east of town, **John Martin Reservoir State Park,** C.R. 24, Hasty (✆ **719/829-1801**), is Colorado's newest state park. It's a welcome oasis in the arid plains of southeastern Colorado. Boating, hiking, camping, birding, history—it has it all.

See chapter 14 for more information.

1

The Best of Colorado

The old and the new, the rustic and the sophisticated, the wild and the refined—all of these experiences exist practically side by side in Colorado, amid what is arguably the most breathtaking mountain scenery in America.

Colorado's booming cities—Boulder, Colorado Springs, and Denver—and its admittedly somewhat glitzy resorts—especially Vail and Aspen—offer much of the comfort and culture of New York or Los Angeles but at a slower, more relaxed pace. Throughout the state, you'll also find testaments to another time, when life was simpler but rougher, and only the strong survived: historic Victorian mansions, working turn-of-the-20th-century steam trains, thousand-year-old adobe-and-stone villages, and authentic Old West towns complete with false-fronted saloons and dusty streets.

Colorado truly comes alive for those who venture outdoors—among the towering Rocky Mountains, the western canyons, or the broad eastern plains. Atop Pikes Peak, you'll see what inspired Katharine Lee Bates to pen the lyrics to "America the Beautiful." Climb on a horse or mountain bike, take a hike or raft trip—or simply sit back and gaze at the mountains. Whatever you do, though, don't stay indoors. Enos Mills, an early-20th-century environmentalist and one of the driving forces behind the creation of Rocky Mountain National Park, said that knowledge of nature is the basis of wisdom. For many, that's the essence of Colorado.

The following are what we consider Colorado's best experiences—highlights that will help you begin planning your trip.

1 The Best Ski Resorts

- **Aspen:** Not only does Aspen have predictably superior ski terrain ranging from some of the most expert runs in Colorado to what *Ski* magazine has called the best mountain in America for beginners (Buttermilk), it's also one of the most fun, genuinely historic ski towns in Colorado. Although it might come off at first as somewhat glitzy and certainly expensive, Aspen is a real town, with longtime, year-round residents and a history that goes beyond the slopes. See chapter 10.
- **Breckenridge:** The lure of Breckenridge lies in its fabulous trails

for skiers of all abilities, its location in an old gold-prospecting settlement, and its abundance of ski-in/ski-out lodging. It's also less expensive than Aspen or Vail, more rustic in feel, and appealing to families for its variety of après-ski activities. See chapter 10.
- **Vail:** This is it, the big one, America's most popular ski resort as well as one of its largest, with 5,289 acres of skiable terrain, 193 trails, and 34 lifts. Every serious skier needs to ski Vail at least once. Its free bus system makes it easy to get around, but be prepared for steep prices, and don't look for

Colorado

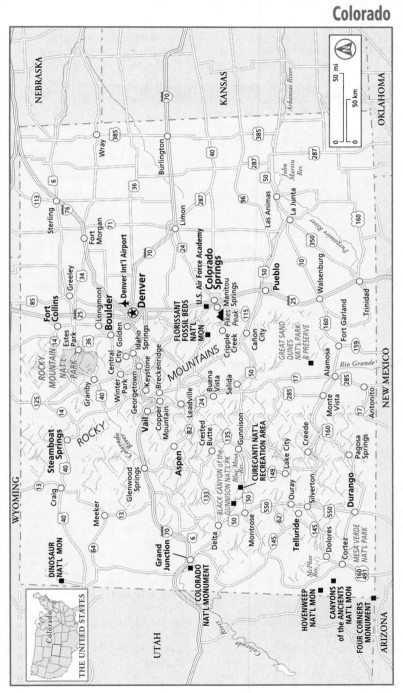

Victorian charm—all you'll find are rows of condominiums. See chapter 10.

• **Durango Mountain Resort:** One of Colorado's best-kept skiing secrets, this resort is known for its beautiful sunny days, heavy annual snowfall, and exceptionally friendly, easygoing atmosphere. See chapter 12.

2 The Best Active Vacations

• **Hiking in Rocky Mountain National Park:** There's something for everyone here, from short hikes around a lovely mountain lake to the difficult 8-mile trek to the top of 14,259-foot Longs Peak. Trail heads can be accessed with the park's shuttle bus, from campgrounds, and stops along Trail Ridge Road. However you do it, getting into the wilds is a treat in this beautiful setting. See chapter 10.

• **Cowpunching on a Cattle Drive:** To really step back into the West of the 1800s, join working cowboys on a genuine cattle drive. The **Saddleback Ranch** near Steamboat Springs (© **970/871-4697**) is a working cattle ranch, where you'll become just another cowpuncher, moving stock from one pasture to another, and performing other ranch duties. See p. 270.

• **Skiing the San Juan Hut System:** Ambitious cross-country skiers who want to put a few miles behind them and ski among 14,000-foot alpine peaks love the San Juan Hut System's trail and series of shelters between Telluride and Moab, Utah. Designed for intermediate skiers, the trail can be tackled in small sections or its entirety, with overnight stays in the well-equipped huts. See chapter 12.

3 The Best Hiking Trails

• **The Buttes Trail at Pawnee Buttes:** This easy day hike exposes you to some of the "other" Colorado: the prairie on the state's eastern plains. A 1.5-mile trail leads to Pawnee Buttes, the Rattlesnake Buttes made famous in James Michener's *Centennial.* Keep your eyes open for coyotes, a variety of birds, and other wildlife, and colorful wildflowers in the spring. See p. 232.

• **The Emerald Lake Trail at Rocky Mountain National Park:** If you like mountain lakes, this is the trail for you. Starting at Bear Lake, it's an easy .5-mile to Nymph Lake, then a moderate .5-mile climb to Dream Lake, and the last .8-mile brings you to Emerald Lake. Total elevation change is 605 feet over a little under 2 miles, with spectacular scenery all along the way. See p. 262.

• **The Colorado Trail at Kenosha Pass:** This easy section of the Colorado Trail near Breckenridge is a fun day's walk or can be the starting point for a serious backpacking trip. Pick up the trail off U.S. 285 where the highway crosses 10,001-foot Kenosha Pass. This access point provides opportunities for short or long hikes through the aspen and bristlecone forest. See p. 295.

• **Hiking the Dunes in Great Sand Dunes National Monument & Preserve:** This isn't a trail at all, but an opportunity to don your best French Foreign Legion hat and set out into the shifting sands in search of dramatic views from the top of a 750-foot dune. See p. 427.

4 The Best Mountain Biking

- **Tipperary Creek Trail:** Considered by many to be Colorado's very best mountain-biking trail, this 30-mile ride from Fraser to Winter Park runs through dense forest and wildflower-covered meadows, offering views of rugged snowcapped peaks. It's also strenuous, rising from an 8,600-foot elevation to more than 10,000 feet. See p. 286.

- **Crested Butte:** Crested Butte vies with Winter Park for the title of mountain-biking capital of Colorado. The highly skilled should try Trail 401, a strenuous single-track loop that combines scenic beauty with steep grades and rough terrain. See p. 418.

5 The Best Wilderness Experiences

- **Hiking the Colorado Trail:** For some 500 miles, this trail winds from Denver to Durango, through some of the state's most spectacular and rugged terrain, crossing the Continental Divide, eight mountain ranges, and six wilderness areas. Just to the west of Leadville, the trail passes through the Collegiate Peaks Wilderness with a view of some of Colorado's most prominent fourteeners (mountains at least 14,000 ft. high) and fields of wildflowers. The more hardy might take a side trip up Mount Elbert, the state's tallest peak at 14,433 feet. See chapters 4, 6, 10, and 12.

- **Hiking the Mills Lake Trail in Rocky Mountain National Park:** Although it's packed at first, this trail usually becomes much less crowded after you've logged a few miles. At trail's end (elevation 10,000 ft.), there's a gorgeous mountain lake ringed by towering peaks. See p. 262.

- **Rafting Glenwood Canyon:** Running the rapids of the Colorado River is one of the best and surely most exciting ways to see one of the most beautiful canyons in the West. Although a bit too popular to provide a genuine wilderness experience, this stretch of river has sections rated for experts during the high spring runoff as well as quieter areas appropriate for everyone. See chapter 11.

6 The Best Places to Discover American-Indian Culture

- **Ute Indian Museum (Montrose):** One of Colorado's few museums dedicated to an existing Indian tribe, this excellent collection, run by the Colorado Historical Society, shows how Utes lived in the 19th century, as they were being forced to reconcile their way of life with that of the invading white pioneers. There's a particularly good exhibit of Ute ceremonial items. See p. 362.

- **Mesa Verde National Park:** Home to the most impressive prehistoric cliff dwellings in the Southwest, Mesa Verde (Spanish for "green table") overwhelms you with its size and complexity. The first national park set aside to preserve works created by humans, it covers some 52,000 acres just outside Cortez. Among the most compelling sites are Spruce Tree House, Square Tower House, and Cliff Palace, a four-story apartment-style dwelling. See p. 388.

- **Ute Mountain Tribal Park:** These ruins differ from others in Colorado because they're located on the Ute Mountain Indian Reservation, and the only way to see it is on a guided tour conducted by members of the Ute tribe. You'll see ruins and petroglyphs similar to those in Mesa Verde, but with an informed personal guide and without the crowds. See p. 391.

7 The Best Places to Recapture the Old West

- **Old Town (Burlington):** On Colorado's eastern plains, right next door to Kansas, is this living-history museum, containing two dozen buildings (many from the 1880s). Watch a cancan, melodrama, or gunfight in a setting more reminiscent of Dodge City than Colorado's Victorian mountain towns. See chapter 9.
- **Creede, Lake City, and Leadville:** With extensive historic districts and false-fronted buildings, these mountain towns take you back to the time when Butch Cassidy, Doc Holliday, and other infamous dudes stalked the saloons in search of the next card game. See chapters 10 (Leadville) and 13 (Creede, Lake City).
- **Bent's Old Fort National Historic Site (La Junta):** Reconstructed to the way it appeared in the 1830s and 1840s, this adobe fort shows life as it really was, when pioneers spent their time either trading peaceably with or fighting off plains warriors. See p. 448.

8 The Most Scenic Views

- **Garden of the Gods:** There's nothing like sunrise at Garden of the Gods in Colorado Springs, with its fantastic and sometimes fanciful red-sandstone formations sculpted by wind and water over hundreds of thousands of years. It's worth spending some foot power to get away from the crowds on one of the park's many trails, to listen to the wind, and imagine the gods cavorting among the formations. See p. 162.
- **Trail Ridge Road:** Transversing Rocky Mountain National Park, Trail Ridge affords expansive and sometimes dizzying views in all directions. There are a dozen stops where you can take a short hike, possibly glimpse the unofficial mascots of the park (bighorn sheep), and get a close-up look at tundra. The drive rises above 12,000 feet and crosses the Continental Divide. See p. 258.
- **The Black Canyon of the Gunnison:** Among the steepest and most narrow canyons in North America, the Black Canyon of the Gunnison, near Montrose, offers breathtaking and sometimes eerie views into the darkness below or, for ambitious hikers, from the canyon depths to daylight above. The sheerness of its 2,500-foot-high walls, the narrowness of its 40-foot-wide base, and the resulting darkness at its core evoke a somber, almost religious mood. See p. 364.
- **Colorado National Monument:** Just west of Grand Junction are stunning vistas of red-rock canyons and sandstone monoliths. The monument's 23-mile Rim Rock Drive offers incredible views, and short walks and backcountry trails afford more solitude. You'll get the best light in the early morning or late afternoon, when the rocks glow

red and shadows dance among the stone sculptures. See p. 336.

- **The San Juan Skyway:** This 233-mile circle drive that goes through Durango, Telluride, and Ouray is among the most beautiful scenic drives in America, passing historic mining camps, fields of wildflowers, stately forests, snowcapped peaks, and cascading waterfalls; and crossing five mountain passes. It's not advisable for those who have difficulty with high elevation (Red Mountain Pass has an 11,008-ft. elevation) or steep, winding roads. Except in summer, it's wise to be sure the passes are open before heading out. See p. 384.

9 The Best Family Vacations

- **Playing Cowboy at Sylvan Dale Guest Ranch:** Nestled in the mountains outside Loveland, this is a real cattle-and-horse ranch where guests are encouraged to pitch in with chores when they're not horseback riding, swimming, fishing, or busy loafing. There's an outdoor pool, tennis and volleyball courts, indoor recreation room, children's programs, and square dancing. See chapter 9.
- **Riding an 1880s Narrow Gauge Steam Train:** There are two: the Durango & Silverton follows the Animas River from Durango up through the San Juan Mountains to historic Silverton; the Cumbres & Toltec chugs out of Antonito, Colorado, through the Toltec Gorge of the Los Piños River, over Cumbres Pass into Chama, New Mexico. Scenery is stupendous over both lines, and each fulfils every train buff's greatest dream of smoke in your eyes and cinders in your hair. See chapters 12 (Durango & Silverton) and 13 (Cumbres & Toltec).
- **Exploring Great Sand Dunes National Park and Preserve:** About 40 miles northeast of Alamosa, this huge pile of sand is a great place to explore, camp, hike, or just play in the 750-foot-tall dunes. Rangers provide guided nature walks and campfire programs in the summer, and a hiking/off-road-vehicle trail leads out the back of the monument into the national forest. See chapter 13.

10 The Best Luxury Hotels

- **Brown Palace Hotel** (Denver; ✆ **800/321-2599** or 303/297-3111): Denver's finest hotel, the Brown Palace has been open continuously since 1892, serving high society and celebrities—from President Dwight Eisenhower to the Beatles—with elegance and charm. Although most of the rooms are Victorian in decor, with Tiffany lamps and other accouterments, our favorites are the Art Deco rooms, which have an undeniable feel of the 1920s and 1930s. See p. 84.
- **The Broadmoor** (Colorado Springs; ✆ **800/634-7711** or 719/634-7711): Colorado's top-rated resort hotel has it all—excellent dining, golf courses, pools, tennis courts, a state-of-the-art fitness center, full-service spa, and shopping, plus extraordinary service—in a magnificently restored historic building set in immaculate grounds. Although extremely impressive, The Broadmoor is never pretentious, and it certainly knows how to pamper its guests. See p. 147.

- **The St. Regis Aspen** (Aspen; ✆ **888/454-9005** or 970/920-3300): At the base of Ajax Mountain, the St. Regis offers great views of the mountains or town, impeccable service, luxurious rooms, and all the services and amenities you'd expect in a fine hotel. Although a bit pricey, especially at Christmas, the hotel is supremely elegant in a comfortable, cozy way. See p. 331.

- **Park Hyatt Beaver Creek Resort and Spa** (Avon; ✆ **800/554-9288** or 970/949-1234): This plush ski-in/ski-out resort at the foot of the Beaver Creek lifts combines a casual, comfortable atmosphere with superb service in an elegant building. The rooms' decor is a quirky combination of Old West and French country that works. See p. 313.

11 The Best Moderately Priced Accommodations

- **Hearthstone Inn** (Colorado Springs; ✆ **800/521-1885** or 719/473-4413): This Colorado Springs gem, comprising two adjoining historic Victorian homes, is perfect for those who like the charm and amenities of a bed-and-breakfast but prefer the privacy of a hotel. Rooms are furnished with antiques, collectibles, and brass beds. A definite plus is the (included) scrumptious breakfast. See p. 151.

- **Boulder Outlook** (Boulder; ✆ **800/542-0304** or 303/443-3322): The Outlook is fun, fresh, and definitively Boulder, with two bouldering rocks, a huge dog run, and discounts on bike rentals and other activities. The rooms are larger than average and the indoor pool is superb, complete with a waterfall and a mural of a cloud-speckled sky. See p. 191.

- **Hotel Bristol** (Steamboat Springs; ✆ **800/851-0872** or 970/879-3083): Lodging with character, historic ambience, and unusual room layouts appeal to us at this reasonably priced 1940s hotel in downtown Steamboat. Rooms are small, but the family units easily accommodate four people. See p. 277.

- **Mid-Town Motel** (La Junta; ✆ **719/384-7741**): Those looking for a clean, quiet mom-and-pop motel at extremely good rates can't miss with the Mid-Town. Solo travelers get rooms with recliners, and pets are welcome. See p. 451.

12 The Best Bed & Breakfasts

- **Old Town GuestHouse** (Colorado Springs; ✆ **888/375-4210** or 719/632-9194): This three-story red-brick building looks like a 19th-century inn but was built in 1997 to offer all the modern amenities in a warm and inviting atmosphere. The overstuffed chairs in the library invite you to kick off your shoes and relax before the fireplace while enjoying a good book, or maybe a nap. See p. 150.

- **The Alps** (Boulder; ✆ **800/414-2577** or 303/444-5445): This historic log lodge on a mountainside west of Boulder is a delightful country bed-and-breakfast inn. The spacious rooms boast working Victorian fireplaces, British antiques, and views of the mountains and forests. Although only a few minutes from downtown, the inn is secluded and very quiet—a great getaway spot. See p. 187.

Planning Your Trip to Colorado

The beauty of a vacation here is that there's truly something for everyone. Depending on where you choose to go, you can have an affordable and fun time, or you can spend a bit more and have a truly world-class experience. The more expensive resorts—Vail, Aspen, Steamboat, and Telluride—tend to fill up quickly, especially during ski season. You'll want to book as far in advance as possible to stay there. The same is true for the state's most popular attractions, such as the national parks—especially busy over school vacations. This chapter gives you the information you need to get started.

1 Regions in Brief

This book is organized primarily geographically, and because this is a big state, many visitors will limit their Colorado vacation to one or two regions.

THE FRONT RANGE The state's three major cities—Denver, Boulder, and Colorado Springs—form a line along the eastern slope of the Rocky Mountains known as the **Front Range.** These cities are an intriguing blend of old and new; rustic and sophisticated; urban and rural. Founded in the mid–19th century by both East Coast gold-seekers and European and Asian immigrants in search of a better life, these cities became home to what we might call the more civilized pioneer—the mine owner instead of the prospector, the merchant rather than the gambler.

Today, these thoroughly modern cities have virtually all the amenities you'd expect to find in a major U.S. metropolis: opera, theater, dance, art, excellent restaurants, and sophisticated hotels and convention centers. You'll also find historic Victorian mansions, working steam trains, and old gold mines. You can go horseback riding, hiking, skiing, or shopping; do the Texas two-step to a live country band; or spend hours exploring museums, galleries, and shops. See chapters 5 through 8.

NORTHEASTERN COLORADO This region is quite different from the major cities and even more of a departure from the rugged mountain towns to the west. Northeastern Colorado contains the sparsely populated plains reminiscent of western Kansas, a place where buffalo once roamed and pioneer farmers endured drought, dust, snow, and wind to create farms and ranches.

Here is the relatively sophisticated college town of Fort Collins, home of the large Anheuser-Busch brewery; the town of Loveland, known primarily for its name and Valentine card remailing; plus smaller communities such as Fort Morgan, the boyhood home of famed big band leader Glenn Miller. This region is dotted with pioneer homes and museums, frontier forts, and preserved downtown districts, plus a surprising number of lakes and seemingly endless fields of wheat and corn. See chapter 9.

THE NORTHERN ROCKIES For many people, the northern Rockies epitomize Colorado. Here you'll find some of the West's most spectacular and inspiring scenery at Rocky Mountain National Park, as well as America's top ski resorts, including Vail and Aspen, both home and playground to many of Hollywood's beautiful people (at least they seem to think they're beautiful). But tucked away amid the ski slopes, overpriced boutiques, and towering peaks are delightful historic Old West towns such as Leadville and Steamboat Springs, where you can step back to a simpler, more rugged era. This region is an ideal spot for year-round outdoor activities, from skiing and snowboarding to hiking, mountain biking, fishing, boating, and four-wheeling. See chapter 10.

THE WESTERN SLOPE This region more closely resembles the canyon country of Utah than Colorado's famed Rocky Mountains. The area is defined in large part by its rivers—the Colorado, Gunnison, and Yampa—which over tens of thousands of years have carved ruggedly beautiful canyons that draw visitors from around the world. The Black Canyon of the Gunnison National Park encompasses an awe-inspiring narrow chasm, and colorful layers of rock define the canyon walls and unusual formations of the Colorado and Dinosaur national monuments. The latter also boasts one of the best dinosaur quarries you'll see anywhere. In addition, the western slope offers about a dozen wineries near the region's largest city, Grand Junction, and mineral hot springs and eye-opening caves in Glenwood Springs, where Old West gunfighter Doc Holliday is buried. See chapter 11.

SOUTHWESTERN COLORADO Those curious about the prehistoric peoples who once populated the West should head to this part of the state, where Mesa Verde National Park and a number of other sites preserve ancient cliff dwellings and other archaeological sites that help explain what life was like here 1,000 years ago. Also in this region is the historic community of Durango, with its main street (ca. 1880) and narrow-gauge steam railroad. Another Old West town, Telluride, retains its historic charm while emerging as a major ski and summer resort. In addition, the San Juan Mountains easily rival the vistas in Colorado's better-known northern Rockies. See chapter 12.

THE SOUTHERN ROCKIES An exciting mix of terrain and experiences await visitors to the southern Rockies, which contain 30 peaks soaring over 14,000 feet, as well as white-water rafting near the town of Salida, the historic picturesque mining town of Creede, and the tallest sand dunes in North America at Great Sand Dunes National Monument and Preserve. This area also contains splendid boating and fishing at Curecanti National Recreation Area, hunting in the nearby mountains, plus skiing and mountain biking, and a historic narrow-gauge steam train at Antonito, south of Alamosa. See chapter 13.

SOUTHEASTERN COLORADO History and a scenic stark beauty are the main draws of this region, which is probably best known for one of the world's most spectacular canyons—the deep, narrow Royal Gorge, which is carved by the Arkansas River as it makes its way down from the Rocky Mountains to the plains. The sector's largest city, Pueblo, offers outdoor recreation, several good museums, and a fine zoo. Boating and fishing opportunities abound on two lakes—Pueblo and Trinidad—both operated as state parks; and Bent's Old Fort is a national historic site that has re-created one of the West's most important frontier trading posts. The towns of Trinidad and La Junta also have a number of historic attractions, and you'll find dinosaur tracks in the Comanche National Grassland. See chapter 14.

Destination: Colorado—Red Alert Checklist

- Some attractions (such as the U.S. Mint and the top of the dome in the Colorado State Capitol in Denver or the U.S. Air Force Academy and Peterson Air & Space Museum in Colorado Springs) have been closed for security reasons, and are reopening slowly or with special restrictions. Call ahead for specifics.
- If you plan to drive through the mountains in winter, be sure to check on possible road closures first.
- If you purchased traveler's checks, have you recorded the check numbers, and stored the documentation separately from the checks?
- Did you pack your camera and an extra set of camera batteries, and purchase enough film? If you packed film in your checked baggage, did you invest in protective pouches to shield film from airport X-rays?
- Do you have a safe, accessible place to store money?
- Did you bring your ID cards that could entitle you to discounts such as AAA and AARP cards, student IDs, and so on?
- Did you bring emergency drug prescriptions and extra glasses and/or contact lenses?
- Do you have your credit card PINs?
- If you have an e-ticket, do you have documentation?
- If you want to attend a Denver Broncos game, call early—home games sell out months ahead.
- Did you leave a copy of your itinerary with someone at home?

2 Visitor Information

Start by contacting the **Colorado Tourism Office,** 1625 Broadway, Denver, CO 80202 (© **800/COL-ORADO;** www.colorado.com), for a free copy of the official state vacation guide, which includes a state map and describes attractions, activities, and lodgings throughout Colorado. Another good source for Colorado information is the website of the *Denver Post,* the state's major daily newspaper, at **www.denverpost.com.**

The **Colorado Hotel and Lodging Association,** 999 18th St., Suite 1240, Denver, CO 80202 (© **303/297-8335;** www.coloradolodging.com), offers a free guide to lodging across the state. The nonprofit **Bed and Breakfast Innkeepers of Colorado,** P.O. Box 38416, Colorado Springs, CO 80937 (© **800/265-7696;** www. innsofcolorado.org), distributes a free directory describing about 100 B&Bs across the state, including a number of historic inns in Denver, Boulder, and Colorado Springs.

Hostelling International-USA, 8401 Colesville Rd., Silver Spring, MD 20910 (© **301/495-1240;** www.hiayh.org), has a computerized system for making reservations in hostels worldwide, and also has a print directory of U.S. hostels.

A free copy of *Colorado State Parks,* which contains details on the state's 40 parks, is available from state park offices at 1313 Sherman St., Suite 618, Denver, CO 80203 (© **303/866-3437;** http://parks.state.co.us). State park offices can also provide information on boating and snowmobiling.

The **Colorado Directory,** 5101 Pennsylvania Ave., Boulder, CO 80303-2799 (© **888/222-4641** or

303/499-9343; www.coloradodirectory. com), will send you a free booklet describing commercial campgrounds, cabin facilities, resorts, country B&Bs, motels, and activities throughout the state; and the website has an especially useful search engine that allows you to use specific criteria to locate properties that accept pets, campgrounds with tent areas, and so on.

If it's a ranch vacation you're after, contact the **Colorado Dude & Guest Ranch Association,** P.O. Box 2120, Granby, CO 80446 (© **970/887-3128;** www.coloradoranch.com), which offers a free booklet of information on more than three dozen dude and guest ranches in the state.

3 Money

Generally, Colorado is not particularly expensive, especially compared to destinations on the East and West coasts. You'll find a wide range of prices for lodging and dining, and admission to most attractions is less than $10 (it's sometimes free, especially in Boulder). Prices in Denver and other major cities are mostly on a par with other Western cities, such as Albuquerque and Salt Lake City. Those traveling outside of the cities will discover that prices in small towns are usually quite reasonable, although ski resorts such as Vail and Aspen can be rather pricey—some cynics might say outrageously overpriced—especially during winter holidays. Traveler's checks and credit cards are accepted at almost all hotels, restaurants, shops, and attractions, plus many grocery stores; and ATMs for all the major national networks are practically everywhere, even in most small towns.

ATMs

The easiest and best way to get cash away from home is from an ATM (automated teller machine). The **Cirrus** (© **800/424-7787;** www.mastercard. com) and **PLUS** (© **800/843-7587;** www.visa.com) networks span the globe; look at the back of your bank card to see which network you're on, then call or check online for ATM locations at your destination. Be sure you know your personal identification number (PIN) before you leave home and be sure to find out your daily

withdrawal limit before you depart. Also keep in mind that many banks impose a fee every time a card is used at a different bank's ATM, and that fee can be higher for international transactions (up to $5 or more) than for domestic ones (where they're rarely more than $1.50). On top of this, the bank from which you withdraw cash may charge its own fee. To compare banks' ATM fees within the U.S., use www.bankrate.com. For international withdrawal fees, ask your bank.

You can also get cash advances on your credit card at an ATM. Keep in mind that credit card companies try to protect themselves from theft by limiting the funds someone can withdraw outside their home country, so call your credit card company before you leave home.

TRAVELER'S CHECKS

Traveler's checks are something of an anachronism from the days before the ATM made cash accessible at any time. Traveler's checks used to be the only sound alternative to traveling with dangerously large amounts of cash. They were as reliable as currency, but, unlike cash, could be replaced if lost or stolen.

These days, traveler's checks are less necessary because most cities have 24-hour ATMs that allow you to withdraw small amounts of cash as needed. However, keep in mind that you'll likely be charged an ATM withdrawal fee if the bank is not your own, so if you're withdrawing money every day, you might be better off with traveler's checks—provided that you don't mind showing identification every time you want to cash one.

You can get traveler's checks at almost any bank. **American Express** offers denominations of $20, $50, $100, $500, and (for cardholders only) $1,000. You'll pay a service charge ranging from 1% to 4%. You can also get American Express traveler's checks over the phone by calling ℂ **800/221-7282;** Amex gold and platinum cardholders who use this number are exempt from the 1% fee. AAA members can obtain checks without a fee at most AAA offices.

Visa offers traveler's checks at Citibank locations nationwide, as well as at several other banks. The service charge ranges between 1.5% and 2%; checks come in denominations of $20, $50, $100, $500, and $1,000. Call ℂ **800/732-1322** for information. **MasterCard** also offers traveler's checks. Call ℂ **800/223-9920** for a location near you.

If you choose to carry traveler's checks, be sure to keep a record of their serial numbers separate from your checks in the event that they are stolen or lost. You'll get a refund faster if you know the numbers.

CREDIT CARDS

Credit cards are a safe way to carry money, they provide a convenient record of all your expenses, and they generally offer good exchange rates. You can also withdraw cash advances from your credit cards at banks or ATMs, provided you know your PIN. If you've forgotten yours, or didn't even know you had one, call the number on the back of your credit card and ask the bank to send it to you. It usually takes 5 to 7 business days, though some banks will provide the number over the phone if you tell them your mother's maiden name or some other personal information.

For tips and telephone numbers to call if your wallet is stolen or lost, go to "Lost & Found" in the Fast Facts section of this chapter.

Practically all businesses in Colorado accept MasterCard and Visa, and many also accept American Express and Discover. Large hotels and restaurants also often take Diners Club.

4 When to Go

Colorado has two main tourist seasons: warm and cold. Those who want to see the state's parks and other scenic wonders, by hiking, mountain biking, or rafting, will usually visit from May through October; those who prefer skiing, snowboarding, and snowmobiling will obviously have to wait for winter, usually from late November through March or April, depending on snow levels. Although you can visit most museums year-round, some, especially those in smaller communities, close in winter.

The best way to avoid crowds at the more popular destinations, such as Rocky Mountain National Park, Garden of the Gods, and Pikes Peak, is to try to visit during the shoulder seasons of March through May and October through mid-December. Generally, those traveling without children will want to avoid visiting during school vacations.

To hear Coloradans tell it, the state has perfect weather all the time. Although they may be exaggerating just a bit, the weather here is usually quite pleasant, with an abundance of sun and relatively mild temperatures in most places—just avoid those winter snowstorms.

Along the Front Range, where Denver and Colorado Springs are located, summer days are hot and dry, and evenings pleasantly mild. Relative humidity is low, and temperatures

Average Monthly High/Low Temperatures (°F & °C) & Precipitation (in.):

		Jan	Feb	Mar	Apr	May	June	July	Aug	Sept	Oct	Nov	Dec
Denver	Temp. (°F)	43/16	47/20	52/26	62/35	71/44	81/52	88/59	86/57	77/48	66/36	53/25	45/17
	Temp. (°C)	6/–9	8/–7	11/–3	17/2	22/7	27/11	31/15	30/14	25/9	19/2	12/–4	7/–8
	Precip. (in.)	0.5	0.6	1.3	1.7	2.4	1.8	1.9	1.5	1.2	1.0	0.9	0.6
Elev. 5,280'													
Colorado Springs	Temp. (°F)	41/16	45/20	49/24	60/33	69/43	80/52	85/57	82/56	75/47	66/37	50/25	44/19
	Temp. (°C)	5/–9	7/–7	9/–4	16/1	21/6	27/11	29/14	28/13	24/8	19/3	10/–4	7/–7
	Precip. (in.)	0.3	0.4	0.9	1.2	2.2	2.3	2.9	3.0	1.3	0.8	0.5	0.5
Elev. 6,035'													
Grand Junction	Temp. (°F)	36/15	45/24	56/32	66/38	76/48	88/57	94/64	91/62	81/54	68/42	51/39	66/40
	Temp. (°C)	2/–9	7/–4	13/0	19/3	24/9	31/14	34/18	33/17	27/12	20/6	11/4	19/4
	Precip. (in.)	0.6	0.5	0.9	0.8	0.9	0.5	0.7	0.8	0.8	1.0	0.7	0.6
Elev. 4,586'													

seldom rise above the 90s (30s Celsius). Evenings start to get cooler by mid-September, but even as late as November the days are often warm. Surprisingly, winters here are warmer and less snowy than winters in the Great Lakes or New England.

Most of Colorado is considered semiarid, and overall the state has an average of 296 sunny days a year—more sunshine than San Diego or Miami Beach. The prairies average about 16 inches of precipitation annually; the Front Range, 14 inches; the western slope, only about 8 inches. Rain, when it falls, is commonly a short deluge—a summer afternoon thunderstorm. However, if you want to see snow, simply head to the mountains, where snowfall is measured in feet rather than inches, and mountain peaks may still be white in July. Mountain temperatures can be bitterly cold, especially if it's windy, but even at the higher elevations of some of the nation's top ski resorts, you'll find plenty of sunshine.

CALENDAR OF EVENTS

Below are some of the major annual events in Colorado. You'll find additional events on the Internet at www.colorado.com and www.coloradofestival.com, as well as on individual town and city websites. We strongly recommend that you confirm dates by telephone before you leave home.

January

- **Great Fruitcake Toss,** Colorado Springs. This zany event, where contestants compete to see who can throw a fruitcake the farthest, has been covered by national media and is among the most outlandish and festive spectacles of the year. It takes place in Manitou Springs' Memorial Park, 5 miles west of downtown Colorado Springs. Call © **800/642-2567** or 719/685-5089 for more information. Early January.

- **National Western Stock Show and Rodeo,** Denver. This is the world's largest livestock show and indoor rodeo, with about two dozen rodeo performances, a trade exposition, Western food and crafts booths, and livestock auctions. Call © **303/297-1166** for details. Second and third weeks in January.

- **International Snow Sculpture Championships,** Breckenridge. Four-person teams transform 20-ton blocks of snow into works of art. Call © **970/453-6018.** Late January.

- **Wintersköl Carnival,** Aspen and Snowmass. A 5-day event that includes a parade, fireworks, and torchlight descent. Call © **970/925-1940.** Mid- to late January.

- **Boulder Bach Festival,** Boulder. Music of the master baroque composer. Call ℂ **303/652-9101** or visit www.boulderbachfest.org for details. Last weekend in January.

February

- **Steamboat Springs Winter Carnival,** Steamboat Springs. Festivities include races, jumping, broomball, and skijoring street events. Call ℂ **970/879-0695.** First full week in February.

- **Leadville Valentine's Day Wine Tasting,** Leadville. Wine tasting and related activities cosponsored by the National Mining Hall of Fame and Museum. Call ℂ **888/ LEADVILLE** for information. Mid-February.

- **Loveland Valentine Remailing Program,** Loveland. More than 200,000 valentines are remailed annually from Loveland. Call ℂ **970/667-6311** for details. Before February 14.

- **Buffalo Bill's Birthday Celebration,** Golden. Ceremonies and live entertainment that commemorate the life of the legendary scout and entertainer take place at the Buffalo Bill Memorial Museum. Call ℂ **303/526-0744** or 303/526-0747 or check www. buffalobill.org for further information. Late February.

March

- **Colorado Springs Dance Theatre Wine Festival,** Colorado Springs. Sample the best wines at this 3-day benefit for the Colorado Springs Dance Theatre. Call ℂ **719/630-7434** for further information. Early March.

- **Pow Wow,** Denver. More than 1,500 American Indians (as well as 60 drum groups), representing some 85 tribes from 32 states, perform traditional music and dances. Arts and crafts are also sold. Call ℂ **303/934-8045** for details. Mid-March.

- **Saint Patrick's Day,** Denver. Among the largest Irish holiday parades in the United States, with floats, marching bands, and more than 5,000 horses. Call ℂ **303/ 892-1112** for further information. Saturday before March 17.

April

- **Easter Sunrise Service,** Colorado Springs and Denver. Worshippers watch the rising sun light red sandstone formations in the Garden of the Gods in Colorado Springs. For details, call ℂ **719/ 634-3144.** Denver's Easter Sunrise Service takes place at Red Rocks Amphitheatre, also in the midst of stunning geological formations. Call ℂ **303/295-4444** or visit www.redrocksonline.com for further information. Easter Sunday.

May

- **Cinco de Mayo,** Denver and Colorado Springs. More than 250,000 people from around the Denver metro area celebrate this annual Hispanic event with mariachi bands, dancers, Mexican food, and other activities. Call ℂ **303/ 534-8342** for information. Memorial Park is the site for the Colorado Springs celebration. Call ℂ **719/ 635-5001** for information. May 5.

- **Boulder Kinetic Fest,** Boulder. A wacky event that's a real crowd pleaser. Most years an average of 70 teams race over land and water at Boulder Reservoir in a variety of imaginative human-powered conveyances. Activities include the kinetic parade, kinetic concerts, the kinetic ball, and a hot-air-balloon launch. Call ℂ **303/ 444-5600** for details. Early May.

- **Iron Horse Bicycle Classic,** Durango. Mountain bikers race against a steam train from Durango to Silverton. Call ℂ **970/ 259-4621** or see www.ironhorse bicycleclassic.com. Memorial Day weekend.

- **Taste of Creede,** Creede. A festival of fine arts, with live music, artists' demonstrations, food, and an art auction. Call **800/327-2102** or see www.creede.com for information. Memorial Day weekend.
- **Bolder Boulder,** Boulder. This footrace attracts some 40,000 entrants each year, plus numerous spectators. Participants walk, jog, or run the 10K course. Call ℂ **303/444-RACE** or visit www.bolderboulder.com for details. Memorial Day.

June

- **FIBArk Whitewater Festival,** Salida. North America's longest and oldest downriver kayak race highlights this festival, which includes carnival rides, a parade, a white-water rodeo, and live entertainment. Call ℂ **877/772-5432** or visit www.fibark.net. Mid-June.
- **Strawberry Days,** Glenwood Springs. One of Colorado's oldest civic celebrations, with a rodeo, talent show, music, dancing, an arts-and-crafts fair, parade, carnival, and footraces. Call ℂ **970/945-6589** or visit www.glenscape.com. Third full weekend in June.
- **Glenn Miller Festival,** Fort Morgan. A big-band music extravaganza in the hometown of the legendary big band leader. Call ℂ **800/354-8660** or see www.fortmorganchamber.org for information. Mid-June.
- **International Buskerfest,** Denver. An international street performers' festival featuring amazing shows by world-class jugglers, sword swallowers, magicians, tightrope artists, mimes, and acrobats. Call ℂ **303/478-7878** or go to www.buskerfest.com for more information. Mid-June.
- **Wool Market,** Estes Park. This huge natural-fiber show boasts contests, demonstrations, a children's tent, and sale of animals, plus products made from their wool. Kids love it. Call ℂ **800/44-ESTES** or go to www.estespark resort.com for details. Mid-June.
- **Aspen Music Festival,** Aspen. Considered one of the finest summer music festivals in the country, featuring world-renowned artists in classical, chamber, and opera performances. Call ℂ **970/925-9042** or see www.aspenmusicfestival. com. Mid-June through August.
- **Strings in the Mountains Festival of Music,** Steamboat Springs. Top-notch classical, jazz, country, and pop musicians perform. Call ℂ **970/879-5056** or see www.stringsinthemountains.org. Mid-June through August.
- **Greeley's Rocky Mountain Stampede,** Greeley. One of the West's biggest rodeos, with top national entertainers, plus concerts, kids' events, art exhibits, fireworks, and more. Call ℂ **800/982-2855** or go to www.rocky mountainstampede.com for details. Late June to early July.
- **Telluride Bluegrass Festival,** Telluride. Featuring bluegrass, folk, and country music. Call ℂ **800/624-2422** or see www.planetbluegrass.com. Late June.
- **Colorado Shakespeare Festival,** Boulder. Considered among the top Shakespeare festivals in the country, with most performances in an outdoor theater. Call ℂ **303/492-0554** for details. Late June through late August.

July

- **Brush Rodeo,** Brush. Billed as the world's largest open (both amateurs and professionals compete) rodeo, with hundreds of participants, it offers traditional rodeo events, wild-cow milking, a parade, footrace, dance, and fireworks. Call ℂ **800/354-8659** or see www.brushcolo.com. First 4 days in July.

- **Colorado State Mining Championship,** Creede. Entrants from six states compete in old-style hand steeling, hand mucking, spike driving, and newer methods of machine drilling and machine mucking. Call ✆ **800/327-2102** or visit www.creede.com. July 4th weekend.

- **Pikes Peak Auto Hill Climb,** Colorado Springs. This "race to the clouds," held annually since 1916, takes drivers to the top of 14,110-foot Pikes Peak. Call ✆ **719/685-4400** for additional information. Saturday closest to July 4th.

- **Rooftop Rodeo & Parade,** Estes Park. Award-winning rodeos Tuesday through Sunday evenings. A grand parade kicks it all off on Tuesday morning. Call ✆ **970/586-6104** or visit www.estespark resort.com for details. Mid-July.

- **Buffalo Bill Days,** Golden. A parade, kids' rides, burro race, arts-and-crafts displays, petting zoo, car show, and a pancake breakfast mark Golden's largest event. Call ✆ **303/384-0003** or visit www.buffalobilldays.com for more information. Late July.

August

- **Boom Days,** Leadville. Events include a parade, carnival, gunslinger reenactments, minedrilling competition, and a burro race. Call ✆ **800/933-3901** or see www.leadville.com/boomdays. First weekend in August.

- **Pikes Peak or Bust Rodeo,** Colorado Springs. Colorado's largest outdoor rodeo, and a popular stop on the professional rodeo circuit. Call ✆ **719/635-3547** or visit www.coloradospringsrodeo.org for details. Early August.

- **Colorado State Fair,** Pueblo. National professional rodeo, carnival rides, food booths, industrial displays, horse shows, animal exhibits, and entertainment by top-name performers. Call ✆ **800/876-4567,** ext. 2028, or visit www.coloradostatefair.com for additional information. Mid-August through Labor Day.

September

- **Telluride Film Festival,** Telluride. This influential festival within the film industry has premiered some of the finest independent films. Call ✆ **603/433-9202** or see www.telluridefilmfestival.com. Early September.

- **A Taste of Colorado,** Denver. This is Denver's largest celebration, with an annual attendance of about 400,000. Local restaurants serve house specialties; there are also crafts exhibits and free concerts. Call ✆ **303/295-6330** or visit www.atasteofcolorado.com for details. Labor Day weekend.

- **Oktoberfest Vail,** Vail. A traditional village-wide weekend celebration, it features street entertainment, German beer and food, dancing, games, and singalongs. Call ✆ **800/525-3875** or go to www.visitvailvalley.com. Mid-September.

- **Colorado Performing Arts Festival,** Denver. This celebration of performing arts, which takes place at the Denver Performing Arts Complex, includes dance, music, theater, and storytelling. Call ✆ **303/640-6943** or visit www. denvergov.org/performingartsfest for information. Mid-September.

- **Fall Festival,** Boulder. An Oktoberfest celebration in downtown Boulder, this festival includes polka bands, food, carnival rides, and an art fair. Call ✆ **303/449-3774** or visit www.boulder downtown.com for more information. Late September or early October.

October

- **Great American Beer Festival,** Denver. Hundreds of American beers are available for sampling, and seminars are presented at what is considered the largest and most prestigious beer event in the United States. Call ℂ **303/447-0816** or visit www.beertown.org for information. Early October.
- **Cowboy Gathering,** Durango. Cowboy poetry, Western art, motorless parade, historical lectures, and demonstrations. Call ℂ **970/385-8904** or go to www.durangocowboygathering.org. Early October.
- **Pumpkin Festival,** Denver. This family event, sponsored by Denver Botanic Gardens and held at Chatfield Nature Preserve southwest of town, includes pumpkin picking, food, crafts, hayrides, and other activities. Call ℂ **720/865-3500** or visit www.botanicgardens.org for details. Mid-October.

November

- **Holiday Gift & Garden Market,** Denver. Handmade Christmas ornaments, gifts, dried-flower arrangements, and food items are among the unique merchandise at this annual sale at Denver Botanic Gardens. Call ℂ **720/865-3500** or visit www.botanicgardens.org for information. Mid-November.
- **Christmas Mountain USA,** Salida. More than 3,000 lights outline a huge tree; it also boasts a parade of lights and a visit from Santa Claus. Call ℂ **877/772-5432.** Day after Thanksgiving.

December

- **World's Largest Christmas Lighting Display,** Denver. Some 40,000 colored floodlights illuminate the Denver City and County Building. All month.
- **Blossoms of Light,** Denver. Over 12,000 sparkling lights cascade through the Botanic Gardens. Grand topiaries, nightly entertainment, "kissing spots," whimsical displays, and warm treats make for an unforgettable winter evening. Call ℂ **303/865-3500** or visit www.botanicgardens.org for information. All month.
- **Parade of Lights,** Denver. A holiday parade winds through downtown Denver, with floats, balloons, and marching bands. Call ℂ **303/478-7878** or visit www.denverparadeoflights.com for information. Early December.
- **Country Christmas Jubilee at Old Town,** Burlington. Victorian carolers and Christmas music, historic buildings decorated in individual themes, bell-ringing, plus other Victorian Christmas activities. Call ℂ **800/288-1334.** Early December.
- **Festival of Lights Parade,** Colorado Springs. A nighttime parade kicks off this month-long celebration of the holidays. Features include decorated live trees and holiday scenes from cultures around the world. Call ℂ **719/634-5581** or visit www.csfineartscenter.org for information. Early December.
- **Christmas with Cody,** Golden. Buffalo Bill Cody playing Santa? He sure did, and a reenactor continues the tradition, with gifts for the kids at the Buffalo Bill Memorial Museum. Call ℂ **303/526-0744** or 303/526-0747 or check www.buffalobill.org for further information. First Sunday in December.
- **Pikes Peak Summit Fireworks,** Colorado Springs. A wondrous fireworks display to ring in the New Year. Call ℂ **800/888-4748** or 719/635-7506 or check out www.coloradosprings-travel.com. December 31.

5 Travel Insurance

Check your existing insurance policies and credit card coverage before you buy travel insurance. You may already be covered for lost luggage, canceled tickets, or medical expenses. The cost of travel insurance varies widely, depending on the cost and length of your trip, your age, health, and the type of trip you're taking.

TRIP-CANCELLATION INSUR- ANCE Trip-cancellation insurance helps you get your money back if you have to back out of a trip, if you have to go home early, or if your travel supplier goes bankrupt. Allowed reasons for cancellation can range from sickness to natural disasters to the State Department declaring your destination unsafe for travel. Insurers usually won't cover vague fears, though, as many travelers discovered who tried to cancel their trips in October 2001 because they were wary of flying. In this unstable world, trip-cancellation insurance is a good buy if you're getting tickets well in advance—who knows what the state of the world, or your airline, will be in 9 months? Insurance policy details vary, so read the fine print—and especially make sure that your airline or cruise line is on the list of carriers covered in case of bankruptcy. For information, contact one of the following insurers: **Access America** (© 866/807-3982; www. accessamerica.com); **Travel Guard International** (© 800/826-4919; www.travelguard.com); **Travel Insured International** (© 800/243-3174;

www.travelinsured.com); and **Travelex Insurance Services** (© 888/457-4602; www.travelex-insurance.com).

MEDICAL INSURANCE Most health insurance policies cover you if you get sick away from home—but check, particularly if you're insured by an HMO.

LOST-LUGGAGE INSURANCE On domestic flights, checked baggage is covered up to $2,500 per ticketed passenger. On international flights (including U.S. portions of international trips), baggage is limited to approximately $9.07 per pound, up to approximately $635 per checked bag. If you plan to check items more valuable than the standard liability, see if your valuables are covered by your homeowner's policy, get baggage insurance as part of your comprehensive travel-insurance package, or buy Travel Guard's "BagTrak" product. Don't buy insurance at the airport, as it's usually overpriced. Be sure to take any valuables or irreplaceable items with you in your carry-on luggage, as many valuables (including books, money, and electronics) aren't covered by airline policies.

If your luggage is lost, immediately file a lost-luggage claim at the airport, detailing the luggage contents. For most airlines, you must report delayed, damaged, or lost baggage within 4 hours of arrival. The airlines are required to deliver luggage, once found, directly to your house or destination free of charge.

6 Health & Safety

STAYING HEALTHY

About two-thirds of Colorado is more than a mile above sea level, which means there is less oxygen and lower humidity than many travelers are accustomed to. This creates a unique set of problems for short-term visitors, such as the possibility of shortness of breath, fatigue, and other physical concerns.

Those not used to higher elevations should get sufficient rest, avoid large meals, and drink plenty of nonalcoholic fluids, especially water. Individuals with heart or respiratory problems should consult their personal physicians before planning a trip to the Colorado mountains. Those in generally good health need not take any special precautions, but it is best to ease the transition to high elevations by changing altitude gradually. For instance, spend a night or two in Denver (elevation 5,280 ft.) or Colorado Springs (elevation 6,035 ft.) before driving or taking the cog railway to the top of Pikes Peak (elevation 14,110 ft.).

Lowlanders can also help their bodies adjust to higher elevations by taking it easy for their first few days in the mountains, cutting down on cigarettes and alcohol, and avoiding sleeping pills and other drugs. Your doctor can provide prescription drugs to help prevent and relive symptoms of altitude sickness.

Because the sun's rays are more direct in the thinner atmosphere, they cause sunburn more quickly. The potential for skin damage increases when the sun reflects off snow or water. A good sunblock is strongly recommended, as are good-quality ultraviolet-blocking sunglasses. Remember that children need more protection than adults.

State health officials warn outdoor enthusiasts to take precautions against the hantavirus, a rare but often fatal respiratory disease first recognized in 1993. About half of the country's confirmed cases have been reported in the Four Corners states of Colorado, New Mexico, Arizona, and Utah. The disease is usually spread by the urine and droppings of deer mice and other rodents, and health officials recommend that campers avoid areas with signs of rodent droppings. Symptoms of hantavirus are similar to the flu and lead to breathing difficulties and shock.

Colorado is also one of the worst places in the United States for the West Nile virus, reporting more than 3,000 of the 9,800 cases of infection in the U.S. during 2003. The best prevention is mosquito repellent and keeping mosquito populations across the state in check. The virus can be fatal, but typically isn't. Symptoms include fever, headache, and body aches.

WHAT TO DO IF YOU GET SICK AWAY FROM HOME

You'll find excellent hospitals in all of Colorado's major cities and even in many smaller towns, and in most cases your existing health plan will provide the coverage you need. But double-check; you may want to buy **travel medical insurance** instead. (See the section on insurance, above.) Bring your insurance ID card with you when you travel.

If you suffer from a chronic illness, consult your doctor before your departure. For conditions like epilepsy, diabetes, or heart problems, wear a **MedicAlert Identification Tag** (© **800/825-3785;** www.medicalert. org), which will immediately alert doctors to your condition and give them access to your records through MedicAlert's 24-hour hot line.

Pack **prescription medications** in your carry-on luggage, and carry prescription medications in their original containers, with pharmacy labels—otherwise they won't make it through airport security. Also bring along copies of your prescriptions in case you lose your pills or run out. Don't

High and Mighty

Colorado boasts 75% of the land in the continental United States above 10,000 feet in elevation.

forget an extra pair of contact lenses or prescription glasses.

STAYING SAFE

While there are many reasons to visit Colorado, two of the reasons most often cited are its historic sites and magnificent outdoor activities. However, visiting historic sites and participating in outdoor activities can lead to accidents.

When visiting such historic sites as ghost towns, gold mines, and railroads, keep in mind that they were probably built more than 100 years ago, at a time when safety standards were extremely lax, if they existed at all. Never enter abandoned buildings, mines, or railroad equipment on your own. When you're visiting commercially operated historic tourist attractions, use common sense and don't be afraid to ask questions.

Walkways in mines are often uneven and poorly lit, and are sometimes slippery due to seeping groundwater that can also stain your clothing with its high iron content. When entering old buildings, be prepared for steep, narrow stairways, creaky floors, and low ceilings and doorways. Steam trains are a wonderful experience as long as you remember that steam is very hot, and that oil and grease can ruin your clothing.

When heading into the great outdoors, keep in mind that injuries often occur when people fail to follow instructions. Pay attention when the experts tell you to stay on established ski trails, hike only in designated areas, carry rain gear, and wear a life jacket when rafting. Mountain weather can be fickle, and many of the most beautiful spots are in remote areas. Be prepared for extreme changes in temperature at any time of year, and watch out for sudden summer-afternoon thunderstorms that can leave you drenched and shivering in minutes.

7 Specialized Travel Resources

TRAVELERS WITH DISABILITIES

Most disabilities shouldn't stop anyone from traveling. There are more options and resources out there than ever before. Travelers with disabilities will find the cities of Colorado fairly accessible, although some historic buildings are not wheelchair accessible, so you should check before going.

The U.S. National Park Service offers a **Golden Access Passport** that gives free lifetime entrance to all properties administered by the National Park Service—national parks, monuments, historic sites, recreation areas, and national wildlife refuges—for persons who are blind or permanently disabled, regardless of age. You may pick up a Golden Access Passport at any NPS entrance fee area by showing proof of medically determined disability and eligibility for receiving benefits under federal law. Besides free entry, the Golden Access Passport also offers a 50% discount on federal-use fees charged for such facilities as camping, swimming, parking, boat launching, and tours. For more information, go to www.nps.gov/fees_passes.htm or call ℂ **888/467-2757.**

Many travel agencies offer customized tours and itineraries for travelers with disabilities. **Flying Wheels Travel** (ℂ **507/451-5005;** www.flyingwheelstravel.com) offers escorted tours and cruises that emphasize sports and private tours in minivans with lifts. **Accessible Journeys** (ℂ **800/846-4537** or 610/521-0339; www.disabilitytravel.com) caters specifically to slow walkers and wheelchair travelers and their families and friends.

Organizations that offer assistance to disabled travelers include the **Moss-Rehab Hospital** (www.mossresource net.org), which provides a library of accessible-travel resources online; the

Society for Accessible Travel and Hospitality (© 212/447-7284; www.sath.org; annual membership fees: $45 adults, $30 seniors and students), which offers a wealth of travel resources for all types of disabilities and informed recommendations on destinations, access guides, travel agents, tour operators, vehicle rentals, and companion services; and the American Foundation for the Blind (© 800/232-5463; www.afb.org), which provides information on traveling with Seeing Eye dogs.

For more information specifically targeted to travelers with disabilities, the community website iCan (www.icanonline.net/channels/travel/index.cfm) has destination guides and several regular columns on accessible travel. Also check out the quarterly magazine Emerging Horizons ($14.95 per year, $19.95 outside the U.S.; www.emerginghorizons.com); Twin Peaks Press (© 360/694-2462), offering travel-related books for travelers with special needs; and Open World Magazine, published by the Society for Accessible Travel and Hospitality (see above; subscription: $18 per year, $35 outside the U.S.).

GAY & LESBIAN TRAVELERS

In general, gay and lesbian travelers will find they are treated just like any other travelers in Colorado. Even cities such as Colorado Springs, home of Focus on the Family and other conservative groups, have become somewhat more open-minded about alternative lifestyles recently. Those with specific concerns can contact Gay, Lesbian, Bisexual, and Transgender Community Services Center of Colorado (© 303/733-7743) in Denver; the organization can also provide information on events and venues of interest to gay and lesbian visitors.

The International Gay & Lesbian Travel Association (IGLTA) (© 800/448-8550 or 954/776-2626; www.iglta.org) is the trade association for the gay and lesbian travel industry, and offers an online directory of gay- and lesbian-friendly travel businesses.

Many agencies offer tours and travel itineraries specifically for gay and lesbian travelers. Above and Beyond Tours (© 800/397-2681; www.abovebeyondtours.com) is the exclusive gay and lesbian tour operator for United Airlines. Now, Voyager (© 800/255-6951; www.nowvoyager.com) is a well-known San Francisco–based gay-owned and operated travel service.

Frommer's Gay & Lesbian Europe is an excellent travel resource focused on gay and lesbian travel, as is Out and About (© 800/929-2268 or 415/644-8044; www.outandabout.com), which offers guidebooks and a newsletter 10 times a year packed with solid information on the global gay and lesbian scene.

We also recommend the Damron guides, with separate, annual books for gay men and lesbians; and Gay Travel A to Z: The World of Gay & Lesbian Travel Options at Your Fingertips by Marianne Ferrari (Ferrari Publications; Box 35575, Phoenix, AZ 85069), a very good gay and lesbian guidebook series.

SENIOR TRAVEL

Mention the fact that you're a senior citizen when you first make your travel reservations. Although all of the major U.S. airlines except America West have cancelled their senior discount and coupon book programs, many hotels still offer discounts for seniors. In most cities, people over the age of 60 (sometimes 62 or 65) qualify for reduced admission to theaters, museums, and other attractions, as well as discounted fares on public transportation.

Many Colorado hotels and motels offer special rates to senior citizens, and an increasing number of restaurants, attractions, and public transportation systems offer discounts as well, some for "oldsters" as young as 55. Members of **AARP** (formerly known as the American Association of Retired Persons), 601 E St. NW, Washington, DC 20049 (© **800/ 424-3410** or 202/434-2277; www. aarp.org), get discounts on hotels, airfares, and car rentals. AARP offers members a wide range of benefits, including a monthly magazine and a newsletter. Anyone over 50 can join.

The **U.S. National Park Service** offers a **Golden Age Passport** that gives seniors 62 years or older lifetime entrance to all properties administered by the National Park Service— national parks, monuments, historic sites, recreation areas, and national wildlife refuges—for a one-time processing fee of $10, which must be purchased in person at any NPS facility that charges an entrance fee. Besides free entry, a Golden Age Passport also offers a 50% discount on federal-use fees charged for such facilities as camping, swimming, parking, boat launching, and tours. For more information, go to www.nps.gov/fees_passes.htm or call © **888/467-2757.**

Elderhostel (© **877/426-8056;** www.elderhostel.org) arranges study programs for those aged 55 and over (and a spouse or companion of any age) in the U.S. and in more than 80 countries around the world. Most courses last 5 to 7 days in the U.S. (2–4 weeks abroad), and many include airfare, accommodations in university dormitories or modest inns, meals, and tuition. **ElderTreks** (© **800/741-7956;** www.eldertreks. com) offers small-group tours to off-the-beaten-path or adventure-travel locations, restricted to travelers 50 and older.

Recommended publications offering travel resources and discounts for seniors include: the quarterly magazine *Travel 50 & Beyond* (www.travel50 andbeyond.com); *Travel Unlimited: Uncommon Adventures for the Mature Traveler* (Avalon); *101 Tips for Mature Travelers,* available from Grand Circle Travel (© **800/221-2610** or 617/350-7500; www.gct.com); *The 50+ Traveler's Guidebook* (St. Martin's Press); and *Unbelievably Good Deals and Great Adventures That You Absolutely Can't Get Unless You're Over 50* (McGraw-Hill).

FAMILY TRAVEL

Colorado is generally a family-friendly state, with lots of things for all ages to enjoy. Throughout this book you'll find numerous attractions, lodgings, and even restaurants that are especially well suited to kids. These include places such as the Butterfly Pavilion & Insect Center in Denver, North Pole/Santa's Workshop in the Colorado Springs area, Dinosaur Journey Museum in Grand Junction, and Fairy Caves in Glenwood Springs.

Additionally, state and national parks are great places for family vacations, and the national parks usually have excellent children's programs (be sure to ask about Junior Ranger programs). The state's many ski resorts all have special programs for kids.

Frommer's Family Vacations in the National Parks (Wiley Publishing, Inc.) offers suggestions for family activities on a national park vacation.

TRAVELING WITH PETS

Many of us wouldn't dream of going on vacation without our pets. Under the right circumstances, it can be a wonderful experience for both you and your animals. Dogs and cats are accepted at many lodgings in Colorado, but not as universally in resorts and at the more expensive hotels. Throughout this book, we've tried to consistently note those lodgings that take pets. Some properties require you to pay a fee or damage deposit in advance, and most insist they be notified at check-in that you have a pet.

Be aware, however, that national parks and monuments and other federal lands administered by the National Park Service are not pet-friendly. Dogs are usually prohibited on all hiking trails, must always be leashed, and in some cases cannot be taken more than 100 feet from established roads. On the other hand, U.S. Forest Service and Bureau of Land Management areas and most state parks are pro-pet, allowing dogs on trails and just about everywhere except inside buildings. State parks require that dogs be leashed; regulations in national forests and BLM lands are generally looser.

Aside from regulations, though, you need to be concerned with your pet's well-being. Just as people need extra water in Colorado's dry climate, so do pets. And keep in mind that many trails are rough, and jagged rocks can cut the pads on your dog's feet.

An excellent resource is **www. petswelcome.com**, which dispenses medical tips, names of animal-friendly lodgings and campgrounds, and lists of kennels and veterinarians. If you plan to fly with your pet, the FAA has compiled a list of all requirements for transporting live animals at http://airconsumer.ost.dot.gov/publications/animals.htm.

8 Planning Your Trip Online

SURFING FOR AIRFARES

The "big three" online travel agencies—**Expedia.com, Travelocity,** and **Orbitz**—sell most of the air tickets bought on the Internet. (Canadian travelers should try expedia.ca and travelocity.ca; U.K. residents can go to expedia.co.uk and opodo.co.uk.) Each has different business deals with the airlines and may offer different fares on the same flights, so it's wise to shop around. Expedia and Travelocity will also send you an **e-mail notification** when a cheap fare becomes available to your favorite destination. Of the smaller travel agency websites, **Side-Step** (www.sidestep.com) has gotten the best reviews from Frommer's authors. It's a browser add-on that purports to "search 140 sites at once," but in reality only beats competitors' fares as often as other sites do.

Also remember to check **airline websites,** especially those for low-fare carriers such as Southwest, JetBlue, AirTran, WestJet, or Ryanair, whose fares are often misreported or simply missing from travel agency websites. Even with major airlines, you can often shave a few bucks from a fare by booking directly through the airline and avoiding a travel agency's transaction fee. But you'll get these discounts only by **booking online:** Most airlines now offer online-only fares that even their phone agents know nothing about. For the websites of airlines that fly to and from your destination, go to "Getting There," later in this chapter.

Great **last-minute deals** are available through free weekly e-mail services provided directly by the airlines. Most of these are announced on Tuesday or Wednesday and must be purchased online. Most are only valid for travel that weekend, but some (such as Southwest's) can be booked weeks or months in advance. Sign up for weekly e-mail alerts at airline websites or check megasites that compile comprehensive lists of last-minute specials, such as **Smarter Living** (smarterliving.com). For last-minute trips, **site59.com** in the U.S. and **lastminute.com** in Europe often have better deals than the major-label sites.

If you're willing to give up some control over your flight details, use an **opaque fare service** like **Priceline** (www.priceline.com; www.priceline.co.uk for Europeans) or **Hotwire** (www.hotwire.com). Both offer rock-bottom prices in exchange for travel on a "mystery airline" at a mysterious time

Travel in the Age of Bankruptcy

To protect yourself from airline bankruptcies, buy your tickets with a credit card, as the Fair Credit Billing Act guarantees that you can get your money back from the credit card company if a travel supplier goes under (and if you request the refund within 60 days of the bankruptcy). Travel insurance can also help, but make sure it covers against "carrier default" for your specific travel provider. And be aware that if a U.S. airline goes bust midtrip, a 2001 federal law requires other carriers to take you to your destination (albeit on a space-available basis) for a fee of no more than $25, provided you rebook within 60 days of the cancellation.

of day, often with a mysterious change of planes en route. The mystery airlines are all major, well-known carriers—and the possibility of being sent from Philadelphia to Chicago via Tampa is remote; the airlines' routing computers have gotten a lot better than they used to be. But your chances of getting a 6am or 11pm flight are pretty high. Hotwire tells you flight prices before you buy; Priceline usually has better deals than Hotwire, but you have to play their "name our price" game. If you're new at this, the helpful folks at **BiddingForTravel** (www.biddingfortravel.com) do a good job of demystifying Priceline's prices. Priceline and Hotwire are great for flights within North America and between the U.S. and Europe. But for flights to other parts of the world, consolidators will almost always beat their fares.

For much more about airfares and savvy air-travel tips and advice, pick up a copy of *Frommer's Fly Safe, Fly Smart* (Wiley Publishing, Inc.).

SURFING FOR HOTELS

Shopping online for hotels is much easier in the U.S., Canada, and certain parts of Europe than it is in the rest of the world. Of the "big three" sites, **Expedia.com** may be the best choice, thanks to its long list of special deals. **Travelocity** runs a close second. Hotel specialist sites **hotels.com** and **hotel discounts.com** are also reliable. An excellent free program, **TravelAxe**

(www.travelaxe.net), can help you search multiple hotel sites at once, even ones you may never have heard of.

Booking lodging online in Denver, Boulder, and Colorado Springs (and throughout Colorado, for that matter) is generally easy. Most of the chamber of commerce and visitor bureau websites are lodging links, and most B&B's in the area are members of Bed & Breakfast Innkeepers of Colorado, which has an excellent website: www.innsofcolorado.com.

Priceline and Hotwire are even better for hotels than for airfares; with both, you're allowed to pick the neighborhood and quality level of your hotel before offering up your money. Priceline's hotel product even covers Europe and Asia, though it's much better at getting five-star lodging for three-star prices than at finding anything at the bottom of the scale. *Note:* Hotwire overrates its hotels by one star—what Hotwire calls a four-star is a three-star anywhere else.

SURFING FOR RENTAL CARS

For booking rental cars online, the best deals are usually found at rental-car company websites, although all the major online travel agencies also offer rental-car reservations services. Priceline and Hotwire work well for rental cars, too; the only "mystery" is which major rental company you get, and for most travelers the difference between Hertz, Avis, and Budget is negligible.

Frommers.com: The Complete Travel Resource

For an excellent travel-planning resource, we highly recommend **Frommers. com** (www.frommers.com). We're a little biased, of course, but we guarantee that you'll find the travel tips, reviews, monthly vacation giveaways, and online-booking capabilities thoroughly indispensable. Among the special features are our popular **Message Boards,** where Frommer's readers post queries and share advice (sometimes even our authors show up to answer questions); **Frommers.com Newsletter,** for the latest travel bargains and insider travel secrets; and **Frommer's Destinations Section,** where you'll get expert travel tips, hotel and dining recommendations, and advice on the sights to see for more than 3,000 destinations around the globe. When your research is done, the **Online Reservations System** (www.frommers.com/book_a_trip) takes you to Frommer's preferred online partners for booking your vacation at affordable prices.

9 The 21st-Century Traveler

INTERNET ACCESS AWAY FROM HOME

Travelers have any number of ways to check their e-mail and access the Internet on the road. Of course, using your own laptop—or even a PDA (personal digital assistant) or electronic organizer with a modem—gives you the most flexibility. But even if you don't have a computer, you can still access your e-mail and even your office computer from cybercafes.

WITHOUT YOUR OWN COMPUTER

It's hard nowadays to find a city that *doesn't* have a few cybercafes. Although there's no definitive directory for cybercafes—these are independent businesses, after all—three places to start looking are at **www.cybercaptive. com**, **www.netcafeguide.com**, and **www.cybercafe.com**.

Aside from formal cybercafes, most **youth hostels** nowadays have at least one computer you can get to the Internet on. And most **public libraries** across the world offer Internet access free or for a small charge. Avoid **hotel business centers,** which often charge exorbitant rates.

Most major airports now have **Internet kiosks** scattered throughout their gates. These kiosks, which you'll also see in shopping malls, hotel lobbies, and tourist information offices around the world, give you basic Web access for a per-minute fee that's usually higher than cybercafe prices. The kiosks' clunkiness and high price means they should be avoided whenever possible.

To retrieve your e-mail, ask your **Internet Service Provider (ISP)** if it has a Web-based interface tied to your existing e-mail account. If your ISP doesn't have such an interface, you can use the free **mail2web** service (www.mail2web.com) to view (but not reply to) your home e-mail. For more flexibility, you may want to open a free, Web-based e-mail account with **Yahoo! Mail** (http://mail.yahoo.com). Microsoft's Hotmail is another popular option, but Hotmail has severe spam problems. Your home ISP may be able to forward your e-mail to the Web-based account automatically.

If you need to access files on your office computer, look into a service called **GoToMyPC** (www.gotomypc. com). The service provides a Web-based interface for you to access and manipulate a distant PC from anywhere—even a cybercafe—provided your "target" PC is on and has an always-on connection to the Internet (such as with Road Runner cable). The service offers top-quality security, but if you're worried about hackers, use your own laptop rather than a cybercafe to access the GoToMyPC system.

WITH YOUR OWN COMPUTER

Major Internet Service Providers (ISP) have **local access numbers** around the world, allowing you to go online by simply placing a local call. Check your ISP's website or call its toll-free number and ask how you can use your current account away from home, and how much it will cost.

Most business-class hotels offer dataports for laptop modems, and many properties in Colorado now offer high-speed Internet access using an Ethernet network cable. You'll have to bring your own cables either way, so **call your hotel in advance** to find out what the options are.

Many business-class hotels in the U.S. also offer a form of computer-free Web browsing through the room TV set. We've successfully checked Yahoo! Mail and Hotmail on these systems.

If you have an 802.11b/**Wi-Fi** card for your computer, several commercial companies have made wireless service available in airports, hotel lobbies, and coffee shops, primarily in the U.S. **T-Mobile Hotspot** (www.t-mobile.com/hotspot) serves up wireless connections at more than 1,000 Starbucks coffee shops nationwide. **Boingo** (www.boingo.com) and **Wayport** (www.wayport.com) have set up networks in airports and high-class hotel lobbies.

If you're traveling outside the reach of your ISP, the iPass network has dial-up numbers in most of the world's countries. IPass providers also give you access to a few hundred wireless hotel lobby setups. Best of all, you don't

need to stay at the Four Seasons to use the hotel's network; just set yourself up on a nice couch in the lobby. Unfortunately, the companies' pricing policies are byzantine, with a variety of monthly, per-connection, and per-minute plans. You'll have to sign up with an iPass provider, who will then tell you how to set up your computer for your destination(s). For a list of iPass providers, go to www.ipass.com. One solid provider is **i2roam** (www.i2roam.com; © **866/811-6209** or 920/235-0475).

Community-minded individuals have also set up **free wireless networks** in major cities around the world. These networks are spotty, but you get what you (don't) pay for. Each network has a home page explaining how to set up your computer for their particular system; start your explorations at www.personaltelco.net/index.cgi/WirelessCommunities.

USING A CELLPHONE
ACROSS THE U.S.

Just because your cellphone works at home doesn't mean it'll work elsewhere in the country (thanks to our nation's fragmented cellphone system). It's a good bet that your phone will work in major cities. But take a look at your wireless company's coverage map on its website before heading out—T-Mobile, Sprint, and Nextel are particularly weak in rural areas; Verizon works pretty well in many parts of Colorado, but it isn't perfect. If you need to stay in touch at a destination where you know your phone won't work, **rent** a phone that does from **InTouch USA** (© **800/872-7626**; www.intouchglobal.com) or a rental car location, but beware that you'll pay $1 a minute or more for airtime.

If you're venturing deep into the mountains or backcountry, you may want to consider renting a **satellite phone ("satphones"),** which are different from cellphones in that they connect to satellites rather than

Online Traveler's Toolbox

Veteran travelers usually carry some essential items to make their trips easier. Throughout this book you'll find websites pertinent to Colorado. Following are several other online tools to bookmark.

- **Visa ATM Locator** (www.visa.com), for locations of PLUS ATMs worldwide, or **MasterCard ATM Locator** (www.mastercard.com), for locations of Cirrus ATMs worldwide.
- **Intellicast** (www.intellicast.com) and **Weather.com** (www.weather. com). Gives weather forecasts for all 50 states and for cities around the world.
- **Mapquest** (www.mapquest.com). Lets you choose a specific address or destination, and in seconds, it will return a map and detailed directions.

ground-based towers. A satphone is more costly than a cellphone but works where there's no cellular signal and no towers. Unfortunately, you'll pay at least $2 per minute to use the phone, and it only works where you can see the horizon (i.e., usually not indoors). In North America, you can rent Iridium satellite phones from **RoadPost** (© **888/290-1606** or 905/272-5665; www.roadpost.com). InTouch USA (see above) offers a wider range of satphones but at higher rates. As of this writing, satphones were amazingly expensive to buy, so don't even think about it.

If you're not from the U.S., you'll be appalled at the poor reach of our **GSM (Global System for Mobiles) wireless network,** which is used by much of the rest of the world. Your phone will probably work in most major U.S. cities; it definitely won't work in many rural areas. (To see where GSM phones work in the U.S., check out www.t-mobile.com/coverage/national_popup.asp.) And you may or may not be able to send SMS (text messaging) home—something Americans tend not to do anyway, for various cultural and technological reasons. (International budget travelers like to send text messages home because it's much cheaper than making international calls.) Assume nothing—call your wireless provider and get the full scoop. In a worst-case scenario, you can always rent a phone; InTouch USA delivers to hotels.

10 Getting There

BY CAR

An excellent road system, connecting to interstate highways heading in all directions, makes driving in Colorado both a good and an economical choice. This is especially true for those planning excursions away from the major cities, where there is little or no public transportation and a car, either your own or a rental, will be practically mandatory.

Some 1,000 miles of interstate highways form a star on the map of Colorado, with its center at Denver. **I-25** crosses the state from south to north, extending from New Mexico to Wyoming; over its 300 miles, it goes through nearly every major city of the Front Range, including Pueblo, Colorado Springs, Denver, and Fort Collins.

I-70 crosses from west to east, extending from Utah to Baltimore, Maryland. It enters Colorado near Grand Junction, passes through Glenwood Springs, Vail, and Denver, and exits just east of Burlington, a distance of about 450 miles. **I-76** is an additional 190-mile spur that begins in Denver and extends northeast to Nebraska, joining **I-80** just beyond Julesburg. Visitors entering Colorado from the southwest may take **U.S. 160** (from Flagstaff, Arizona) or **U.S. 550** (from Farmington, New Mexico). Both routes enter the state near Durango.

Denver is about 1,025 miles from Los Angeles, 780 miles from Dallas, 600 miles from Kansas City, 510 miles from Salt Lake City, 440 miles from Albuquerque, 750 miles from Las Vegas, 820 miles from Phoenix, 1,010 miles from Chicago, and 1,800 miles from New York.

BY PLANE

Those flying to Colorado will probably land at Denver International Airport or Colorado Springs Airport. Both offer car rentals and shuttle services to their city's hotels.

Denver International Airport is 23 miles northeast of downtown Denver, about a 35- to 45-minute drive. It's the sixth-busiest airport in the nation, with six runways and 94 gates. An information line (© **800/AIR-2-DEN;** TDD 800/688-1333; www.flydenver.com) provides data on flight schedules and connections, parking, ground transportation, current weather conditions, and local accommodations. The local airport information and paging number is © **303/342-2300.**

Airlines serving Denver include **Air Canada** (© 888/247-2262; www.aircanada.ca), **Alaska Airlines** (© 877/502-5357; www.alaskaair.com), **American** (© 800/433-7300; www.aa.com), **America West** (© 800/235-9292; www.americawest.com), **British Airways** (© 800/AIRWAYS; www.britishairways.com), **Continental** (© 800/525-0280; www.continental.com), **Delta** (© 800/221-1212; www.delta.com), **Frontier** (© 800/432-1359; www.frontierairlines.com), **Korean Air** (© 800/438-5000; www.koreanair.com), **Lufthansa** (© 800/399-LUFT; www.lufthansa.com), **Martinair** (© 800/366-4655; www.martinair.com), **Mesa** (© 800/637-2247; www.mesa-air.com), **Mexicana** (© 800/531-7921; www.mexicana.com), **Midwest Airlines** (© 800/452-2022; www.midwestairlines.com), **Northwest** (© 800/225-2525; www.nwa.com), **Sun Country** (© 800/359-6786; www.suncountry.com), **United** and **United Express** (© 800/241-6522; www.ual.com), and **US Airways** (© 800/428-4322; www.usair.com).

Colorado Springs Airport (© **719/550-1900**), located in the southeast corner of Colorado Springs, has nearly 100 flights each day, with connections to most major U.S. cities. **American, America West, Continental, Mesa, Northwest,** and **United** serve Colorado Springs.

Those whose destination is western Colorado can make connections to Grand Junction's **Walker Field** (© **970/244-9100;** www.walkerfield.com) from Denver, Phoenix, or Salt Lake City.

(*Fun Fact* **Take the High Road**

The world's highest automobile tunnel, the Eisenhower Tunnel, crosses the Continental Divide 65 miles west of Denver, at an elevation of 11,000 feet.

GETTING THROUGH THE AIRPORT

With the federalization of airport security, security procedures at U.S. airports are more stable and consistent than ever. Generally, you'll be fine if you arrive at the airport **1 hour** before a domestic flight and **2 hours** before an international flight; if you show up late, tell an airline employee and he or she will probably whisk you to the front of the line.

Bring a **current, government-issued photo ID** such as a driver's license or passport, and if you've got an e-ticket, print out the **official confirmation page;** you'll need to show your confirmation at the security checkpoint, and your ID at the ticket counter or the gate. (Children under 18 do not need photo IDs for domestic flights, but the adults checking in with them will.)

Security lines are getting shorter than they were in the years following the September 11, 2001, terrorist attacks, but some doozies remain. If you have trouble standing for long periods of time, tell an airline employee; the airline will provide a wheelchair. Speed up security by **not wearing metal objects** such as big belt buckles or clanky earrings. If you've got metallic body parts, a note from your doctor can prevent a long chat with the security screeners. Keep in mind that only **ticketed passengers** are allowed past security, except for folks escorting disabled passengers or children.

Federalization has stabilized **what you can carry on** and **what you can't.** The general rule is that sharp things are out, nail clippers are okay, and food and beverages must be passed through the X-ray machine—but that security screeners can't make you drink from your coffee cup. Bring food in your carry-on rather than checking it, as explosive-detection machines used on checked luggage have been known to mistake food (especially chocolate, for some reason) for bombs. Travelers in the U.S. are allowed one carry-on bag, plus a "personal item" such as a purse, briefcase, or laptop bag. Carry-on hoarders can stuff all sorts of things into a laptop bag; as long as it has a laptop in it, it's still considered a personal item. The Transportation Security Administration (TSA) has issued a list of restricted items; check its website (www.tsa.gov/public/index.jsp) for details.

Passengers with e-tickets and without checked bags can beat the ticket-counter lines by using **electronic kiosks** or even **online check-in.** Ask your airline which alternatives are available, and if you're using a kiosk, bring the credit card you used to book the ticket. If you're checking bags, you will still be able to use most airlines' kiosks; again, call your airline for up-to-date information. **Curbside check-in** is also a good way to avoid lines, although a few airlines still ban curbside check-in entirely; call before you go.

FLYING FOR LESS: TIPS FOR GETTING THE BEST AIRFARE

Passengers sharing the same airplane cabin rarely pay the same fare. Travelers who need to purchase tickets at the last minute, change their itinerary at a moment's notice, or fly one-way often get stuck paying the premium rate. Here are some ways to keep your airfare costs down.

- Passengers who can book their ticket **long in advance,** who can **stay over Saturday night,** or who **fly midweek** or **at less-trafficked hours** will pay a fraction of the full fare. If your schedule is flexible, say so, and ask if you can secure a cheaper fare by changing your flight plans.
- You can also save on airfares by keeping an eye out in local newspapers for **promotional specials**

or **fare wars,** when airlines lower prices on their most popular routes. You rarely see fare wars offered for peak travel times, but if you can travel in the off-months, you may snag a bargain.

- Search **the Internet** for cheap fares (see "Planning Your Trip Online," earlier in this chapter).
- **Consolidators,** also known as bucket shops, are great sources for international tickets, although they usually can't beat the Internet on fares within North America. Start by looking in Sunday newspaper travel sections; U.S. travelers should focus on the *New York Times, Los Angeles Times,* and *Miami Herald.* For less-developed destinations, small travel agents who cater to immigrant communities in large cities often have the best deals. *Beware:* Bucket-shop tickets are usually nonrefundable or rigged with stiff cancellation penalties, often as high as 50% to 75% of the ticket price, and some put you on charter airlines with questionable safety records. Several reliable consolidators are worldwide and available on the Net. **STA Travel** is now the world's leader in student travel, thanks to its purchase of Council Travel. It also offers good fares for travelers of all ages. **Flights.com** (✆ 800/TRAV-800; www.flights.com) started in Europe and has excellent fares worldwide, but particularly to that continent. It also has "local" websites in 12 countries. **LowestFare** (✆ 800/FLY-CHEAP; www.lowestfare.com) has especially good access to fares for sunny destinations. **Air Tickets Direct** (✆ 800/778-3447; www.airticketsdirect.com) is based in Montreal and leverages the currently weak Canadian dollar for low fares.

- Join **frequent-flier clubs.** Accrue enough miles, and you'll be rewarded with free flights and elite status. It's free, and you'll get the best choice of seats, faster response to phone inquiries, and prompter service if your luggage is stolen, your flight is canceled or delayed, or if you want to change your seat. You don't need to fly to build frequent-flier miles—**frequent-flier credit cards** can provide thousands of miles for doing your everyday shopping.

- For many more tips about air travel, including a rundown of the major frequent-flier credit cards, pick up a copy of *Frommer's Fly Safe, Fly Smart* (Wiley Publishing, Inc.).

GETTING THERE BY TRAIN

Amtrak (✆ 800/USA-RAIL; www.amtrak.com) has two routes through Colorado. The California Zephyr, which links San Francisco and Chicago, passes through Grand Junction, Glenwood Springs, Granby, Fraser, Denver, and Fort Morgan en route to Omaha, Nebraska. The Southwest Chief, which runs between Los Angeles and Chicago, travels from Albuquerque, New Mexico, via Trinidad, La Junta, and Lamar before crossing the southeastern Colorado border into Kansas.

11 Packages for the Independent Traveler

Before you start your search for the lowest airfare, you may want to consider booking your flight as part of a travel package. Package tours are not the same thing as escorted tours. Package tours are simply a way to buy the airfare, accommodations, and other elements of your trip (such as car rentals, airport transfers, and sometimes even activities) at the same time and often at discounted prices—kind of like one-stop shopping. Packages are sold in bulk to tour operators—who resell them to the public at a cost that usually undercuts standard rates.

One good source of package deals is the airlines themselves. Most major airlines offer air/land packages, including **American Airlines Vacations** (© 800/ 321-2121; www.aavacations.com), **Delta Vacations** (© 800/221-6666; www.deltavacations.com), **Continental Airlines Vacations** (© 800/301-3800; www.coolvacations.com), and **United Vacations** (© 888/854-3899; www.unitedvacations.com). Several big **online travel agencies**— Expedia.com, Travelocity, Orbitz, Site59, and Lastminute.com—also do a brisk business in packages. If you're unsure about the pedigree of a smaller packager, check with the Better Business Bureau in the city where the company is based, or go online at www.bbb.org. If a packager won't tell you where it's based, don't fly with it.

One company that puts together packages for trips to several resort communities of Colorado, including Vail, Aspen, Steamboat Springs, and Durango, is **Mountain Vacations** (© **800/754-3704;** www.mountain vacations.com).

Travel packages are also listed in the travel section of your local Sunday newspaper. Or check ads in national travel magazines such as *Arthur Frommer's Budget Travel Magazine, Travel + Leisure, National Geographic Traveler,* and *Condé Nast Traveler.*

Package tours can vary by leaps and bounds. Some offer a better class of hotels than others. Some offer the same hotels for lower prices. Some offer flights on scheduled airlines, while others book charters. Some limit your choice of accommodations and travel days. You are often required to make a large payment upfront. On the plus side, packages can save you money, offering group prices but allowing for independent travel. Some even let you add on a few guided excursions or escorted day trips (also at prices lower than if you booked them yourself) without booking an entirely escorted tour.

Before you invest in a package tour, get some answers. Ask about the **accommodations choices** and prices for each. Then look up the hotels' reviews in a Frommer's guide and check their rates for your specific dates of travel online. Finally, look for **hidden expenses.** Ask whether airport departure fees and taxes, for example, are included in the total cost.

12 Escorted General-Interest Tours

Escorted tours are structured group tours, with a group leader. The price usually includes everything from airfare to hotels, meals, tours, admission costs, and local transportation. Below are some of the better companies that offer escorted tours in Colorado. These tour companies generally include your tour guide, admission costs, and local transportation.

Gray Line, 5855 E. 56th Ave. (P.O. Box 646), Denver, CO 80217 (© 303/289-2841; coloradograyline. com), provides traditional bus and van tours to the U.S. Air Force Academy, Pikes Peak, Rocky Mountain National Park, and historic sites of Denver.

Maupintour, 1515 St. Andrews Dr., Lawrence, KS 66047 (© **800/ 255-4266;** www.maupintour.com), offers a variety of tours, including well-planned multiday tours of Rocky Mountain National Park and other scenic and historic areas.

Sample Colorado Tour Company and Travel Club, P.O. Box 621906, Littleton, CO 80162-1906 (© **303/ 904-2376**), offers scheduled and custom tours with a historic theme throughout the state—both day trips from Denver and multiday excursions.

Many people derive a certain ease and security from escorted trips.

Escorted tours let travelers sit back and enjoy their trip without having to spend lots of time behind the wheel. All the little details are taken care of; you know your costs upfront; and there are few surprises. Escorted tours can take you to the maximum number of sights in the minimum amount of time with the least amount of hassle—you don't have to sweat over the plotting and planning of a vacation schedule. Escorted tours are also particularly convenient for people with limited mobility.

On the downside, an escorted tour often requires a big deposit upfront, and lodging and dining choices are predetermined. As part of a cloud of tourists, you'll get little opportunity for serendipitous interactions with locals. The tours can be jam-packed with activities, leaving little room for individual sightseeing, whim, or adventure—plus they also often focus only on the heavily touristed sites, so you miss out on the lesser-known gems.

Before you invest in an escorted tour, ask about the **cancellation policy:** Is a deposit required? Can they cancel the trip if they don't get enough people? Do you get a refund if they cancel? If *you* cancel? How late can you cancel if you are unable to go? When do you pay in full? *Note:* If you choose an escorted tour, think strongly about purchasing trip-cancellation insurance, especially if the tour operator asks you to pay upfront. See the section on "Travel Insurance," earlier in this chapter.

You'll also want to get a complete **schedule** of the trip to find out how much sightseeing is planned each day and whether enough time has been allotted for relaxing or wandering solo.

The **size** of the group is also important to know upfront. Generally, the smaller the group, the more flexible the itinerary, and the less time you'll spend waiting for people to get on and off the bus. Find out the **demographics** of the group as well. What is the age range? What is the gender breakdown? Is this mostly a trip for couples or singles?

Discuss what is included in the **price.** You may have to pay for transportation to and from the airport. A box lunch may be included in an excursion, but drinks might cost extra. Tips may not be included. Find out if you will be charged if you decide to opt out of certain activities or meals.

Before you invest in a package tour, get some answers. Ask about the **accommodations choices** and prices for each. Then look up the hotels' reviews in a Frommer's guide and check their rates for your specific dates of travel online.

Finally, if you plan to travel alone, you'll need to know if a **single supplement** will be charged and if the company can match you up with a roommate.

13 Getting Around

Cars are not really necessary for those visiting Denver, but for those going practically anywhere else in Colorado they're not only handy but in many cases essential.

Colorado law requires all drivers to carry proof of insurance, as well as a valid driver's license. Safety belts are required for drivers and all front-seat passengers; all children up to age 16 must wear safety belts or be in approved child seats, regardless of where they're seated in the vehicle. The minimum age for drivers is 16. Motorcyclists are not required to wear helmets (but are required to have protective eyewear); radar detectors are permitted.

The maximum speed limit is 75 mph on rural interstate highways and 65 mph on noninterstates, unless otherwise posted.

A state highway map can be obtained from visitor centers or by mail (see "Visitor Information," earlier in this chapter). Otherwise, maps can be purchased at bookstores, gas stations, and most supermarkets and discount stores. Maps are available free to members of the American Automobile Association. An excellent source for all kinds of maps and road atlases is **Mapsco Map and Travel Center,** 800 Lincoln St., Denver, CO 80203 (© **800/456-8703** or 303/830-2373; www.mapsco.com).

ROAD CONDITIONS

A recorded 24-hour hot line (© **303/639-1111;** www.cotrip.com) provides information on road conditions and possible delays due to road construction statewide.

Some of Colorado's roads and highways are closed during winter months. One is U.S. 34, the Trail Ridge Road through Rocky Mountain National Park. It's the highest continuous highway in the world, crossing the Continental Divide at 12,183 feet. Also, Colo. 82, over Independence Pass (elevation 12,095 ft.) east of Aspen, is the main route between Denver and Aspen in the summer months, but it's closed in winter. In addition, the Mount Evans Road (Colo. 103 and Colo. 5) is open from June to September only. It stretches from Idaho Springs (35 miles west of Denver) to the 14,264-foot summit of Mount Evans and is the highest paved road in North America. Among the world's highest tunnels at 11,000 feet, Eisenhower Tunnel carries I-70 beneath Loveland Pass, west of Denver, year-round, though this stretch of interstate is sometimes closed by winter storms. Snow tires or chains are often required when roads are snow-covered or icy.

ROAD EMERGENCIES

In case of an accident or road emergency, call © **911.** American Automobile Association members can get free emergency road service wherever they are, 24 hours a day, by calling AAA's emergency number (© **800/AAA-HELP**). In Colorado, AAA headquarters is at 4100 E. Arkansas Ave., Denver, CO 80222-3491, just off S. Colorado Boulevard (© **800/283-5222** or 303/753-8800; www.aaa.com).

RENTAL CARS

National rental agencies with offices in Colorado include **Advantage** (© 800/777-5500; www.arac.com), **Alamo** (© 800/462-5266; www.alamo.com), **Avis** (© 800/230-4898; www.avis.com), **Budget** (© 800/527-0700; www.budget.com), **Dollar** (© 800/800-4000; www.dollarcar.com), **Enterprise** (© 800/261-7331; www.enterprise.com), **Hertz** (© 800/654-3131; www.hertz.com), **National** (© 888/227-7368; www.nationalcar.com), and **Thrifty** (© 800/847-4389; www.thrifty.com). Campers, travel trailers, and motor homes are available in Denver from **Cruise America** (© 800/327-7799; www.cruiseamerica.com). Motorcycles can be rented in the Denver area at **Blue Sky Motorcycle Rentals** (© 866/971-5501; www.blueskymotorcyclerentals.com).

BY PLANE

Commuter flights are available from Denver to Grand Junction and several other cities year-round, as well as to some ski resort areas during winter. See the individual town and city listings for details.

BY TRAIN

Amtrak (© **800/USA-RAIL;** www.amtrak.com) has two routes through Colorado. One has stops in Grand Junction, Glenwood Springs, Granby, Winter Park, Denver, and Fort Morgan; while the other stops at Trinidad, La Junta, and Lamar. On winter weekends, the **Rio Grande Ski Train** (© **303/296-I-SKI**) runs to Winter Park Ski Resort, leaving Denver early in the morning and returning after the lifts close.

Colorado Driving Times & Distances

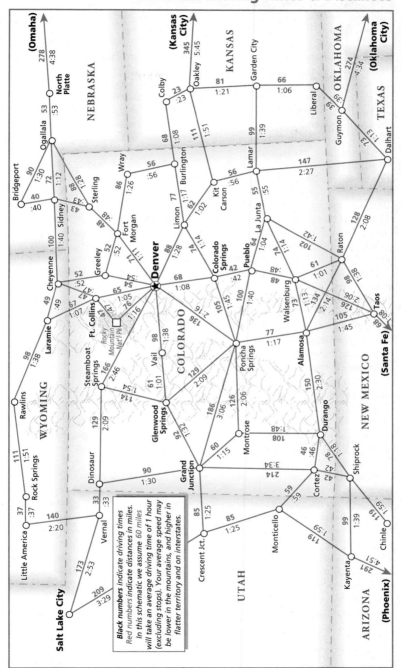

Black numbers indicate driving times. Red numbers indicate distances in miles. In this schematic we assume 60 miles will take an average driving time of 1 hour (excluding stops). Your average speed may be lower in the mountains, and higher in flatter territory and on interstates.

14 Tips on Accommodations

Colorado offers a variety of lodging options, from typical American chain motels to luxury hotels, Victorian bed-and-breakfasts, some pleasant and inexpensive mom-and-pop independent motels, cabins, ranch-style resorts, and magnificent historic hotels.

The chains here are the same ones you see everywhere else in America: Best Western, Comfort Inn, Days Inn, Embassy Suites, Hampton Inn, Hilton, Holiday Inn, Motel 6, Quality Inn, Sheraton, Sleep Inn, Super 8, Travelodge, and so on. They look just about the same as those found elsewhere, and have the same levels of service. In most cases their rooms are little more than boring boxes of various sizes, with beds and the appropriate plumbing and heating fixtures, and if you're lucky a decent view out the window. These chains, even the high-end ones like Hilton and Sheraton, are fine if you just want a place to sleep and plan to take advantage of their swimming pools, exercise rooms, and other facilities. However, they do very little to enhance your vacation experience, to let you know you're in Colorado.

To make your lodging an integral part of your Colorado experience we suggest choosing a historic property. There are numerous historic bed-and-breakfast inns discussed in the following pages, and especially when you take into consideration the wonderful breakfasts prepared at most of them, the rates are fairly reasonable. Why spend $90 for a boring motel room and then another $10 to $15 for breakfast when for just a bit more you can instead sleep in a handsome Victorian home, decorated with antiques, and be served a delightful home-cooked breakfast?

Colorado also has several magnificent yet pricey historic hotels, including the absolutely wonderful **Brown Palace** in Denver, the **Strater** in Durango, and the family-friendly **Broadmoor** in Colorado Springs. These hotels are just as much attractions as they are lodgings, and there's no better way to see them than to book a room for the night, just as others have done for the better part of a century.

Other lodging choices here include cabins and a handful of small independent motels. Both are usually fairly inexpensive, although they often lack the facilities, such as pools, spas, and exercise equipment, that you'll find in most chains. We still prefer the cabins and independents, though, because they're often a very good value and the rooms usually have at least some personality (can anybody actually describe the decor of the last Days Inn they stayed at?), and cabins, although sometimes a bit primitive, are often in beautiful settings.

SAVING ON YOUR HOTEL ROOM

The **rack rate** is the official rate, usually (but not always) the maximum rate that a hotel charges for a room. Hardly anybody pays these prices, however, and there are many ways around them.

- **Don't be afraid to bargain.** Most rack rates include commissions of 10% to 25% for travel agents, which some hotels may be willing to give you if you make your own reservations and haggle a bit. Always ask whether a room less expensive than the first one quoted is available, or whether any special rates apply to you. You may qualify for corporate, student, military, senior, or other discounts. Be sure to mention membership in AAA, AARP, frequent-flier programs, or trade unions, which may entitle you to special deals as well. Find out the hotel policy on children—do kids stay free in the room or is there a special rate?

- **Watch for coupon books and advertised discounts.** State welcome centers, community visitor centers, and a variety of businesses (but not hotels) distribute free booklets that contain nothing but discount lodging coupons. These are usually for chains, and usually are for walk-ins only, so you won't be able to make a reservation. They also do not generally apply during special events. But if you can use one of these coupons, you can often save 20% to 40% off the rack rate. These coupons are also available online; try www.hotel-coupons.com and www.room-saver.com. Also check ads in your local Sunday newspaper travel section, a good source for up-to-the-minute hotel deals, especially for lodging in resort areas.
- **Dial direct.** When booking a room in a chain hotel, you'll often get a better deal by calling the individual hotel's reservation desk instead of the chain's main number.
- **Book online.** Many hotels offer Internet-only discounts, or supply rooms to Priceline, Hotwire, or Expedia at rates much lower than the ones you can get through the hotel itself.
- **Remember the law of supply and demand.** Resort hotels are most crowded and therefore most expensive on weekends, so discounts are usually available for midweek stays. Business hotels in downtown locations are busiest during the week, so you can expect big discounts over the weekend. Many hotels have high-season and low-season prices, and booking the day after the high season ends can mean big discounts.
- **Look into group or long-stay discounts.** If you come as part of a large group, you should be able to negotiate a bargain rate, since the hotel can then guarantee occupancy in a number of rooms. Likewise, if you're planning a long stay (at least 5 days), you might qualify for a discount. As a general rule, expect 1 night free after a 7-night stay.
- **Avoid excess charges and hidden costs.** When you book a room, ask whether the hotel charges for parking. Use your own cellphone, pay phones, or prepaid phone cards instead of dialing direct from hotel phones, which usually have exorbitant rates. And don't be tempted by the room's minibar offerings: Most hotels charge through the nose for water, soda, and snacks. Finally, ask about local taxes and service charges, which can increase the cost of a room by 15% or more. If a hotel insists upon tacking on a surprise "energy surcharge" that wasn't mentioned at check-in or a "resort fee" for amenities you didn't use, you can often make a case for getting it removed.
- **Book an efficiency.** A room with a kitchenette allows you to shop for groceries and cook your own meals. This is a big money saver, especially for families on long stays.

LANDING THE BEST ROOM

Somebody has to get the best room in the house. It might as well be you. You can start by joining the hotel's frequent-guest program, which may make you eligible for upgrades. A hotel-branded credit card usually gives it owner "silver" or "gold" status in frequent-guest programs for free. Always ask about a corner room. They're often larger and quieter, with more windows and light, and they often cost the same as standard rooms. When you make your reservation, ask if the hotel is renovating; if it is, request a room away from the construction. Ask about nonsmoking rooms, rooms with views, rooms with twin, queen- or king-size beds. If you're a light sleeper, request a quiet room away from vending machines, elevators, restaurants, bars, and discos. Ask for one of the rooms that have been most recently renovated or redecorated.

If you aren't happy with your room when you arrive, say so. If another room is available, most lodgings will be willing to accommodate you.

15 Suggested Itineraries

At the risk of oversimplifying, let us suggest that there are essentially three activities for visitors to Colorado—viewing the scenery, visiting historic and cultural sites, and participating in outdoor sports such as skiing or hiking. While there are some visitors whose only goal is to explore prehistoric American-Indian sites or historic mining towns, and perhaps hard-core skiers or hikers who are interested solely in pursuing their preferred form of recreation, the vast majority of Colorado visitors want a smorgasbord of experiences: This might include a scenic drive over a mountain pass, a visit to a small-town museum in a Victorian mansion, and a hike to a picturesque lake.

The following suggested itineraries assume that you're looking for a mix of experiences; those interested primarily in outdoor activities should see chapter 4. All of the following start and end in Denver. Because of seasonal road closures, these driving tours are for summer use only, although parts of them can be adapted for winter use (see "Getting Around," earlier in this chapter).

IF YOU HAVE 1 WEEK

Day 1   Arrive in Denver, preferably in the late morning or early afternoon. Browse Larimer Square and the 16th Street Mall.

Day 2   In the morning, visit the Denver Art Museum, Colorado History Museum, and the State Capitol. (See chapter 6.) After lunch, take the short drive to Boulder, browse the Pearl Street Mall, where you might see a juggler or mime (or just a sleeping University of Colorado student), and settle in for the night.

Day 3   Follow U.S. 36 to Estes Park, eastern gateway to Rocky Mountain National Park. (See chapter 10.) From there, travel the spectacular Trail Ridge Road over the Continental Divide to Grand Lake (your destination for the night), watching for elk, deer, bighorn sheep, marmots, moose, and other wildlife along the way.

Day 4   Take U.S. 40 through the Winter Park resort community and over Berthoud Pass to Georgetown, a well-preserved Victorian mining town. I-70 goes west through the Eisenhower Tunnel to Frisco, where you can turn south on Colo. 9 to charming Breckenridge. (See chapter 10.)

Day 5   Colo. 9 runs southeast 100 miles in a near-straight line to Cañon City; see the magnificent Royal Gorge and the re-created Western film town of Buckskin Joe. (See chapter 14.) Proceed northeast to Colorado Springs for the evening.

Day 6   Spend a full day in Colorado Springs. Choose among the Pikes Peak Cog Railway, U.S. Olympic Training Center, the Garden of the Gods, and other sights. (See chapter 7.)

Day 7   Stop and visit the U.S. Air Force Academy on your way back to Denver, where your flight home awaits. (See chapter 7.)

IF YOU HAVE 2 WEEKS

Days 1 and 2   Same as above.

Day 3   Take Canyon Boulevard (Colo. 119) west to Nederland, then follow the foothills north on Colo. 72 and Colo. 7 to Estes Park.

Day 4   In the morning, enjoy spectacular Trail Ridge Road through Rocky Mountain National Park, across the Continental Divide to Grand Lake. After lunch, proceed south on U.S. 40 to Winter Park, Berthoud Pass, and Georgetown.

Day 5   I-70 and Colo. 91 will take you up to Leadville, Colorado's 2-mile-high city. See the historic district and National Mining Hall of Fame and Museum, then continue across Independence Pass to the famed resort town of Aspen.

Day 6   Give yourself a day in Aspen to shop, sightsee, hike, bike, or just enjoy the clean mountain air. (See chapter 10 for details about sights mentioned in days 3–6.)

Day 7   Drive to Montrose: The route follows the Roaring Fork River west to Carbondale, then south along scenic Colo. 133 over McClure Pass (elevation 8,755 ft.), and through the quaint historic village of Redstone. Try to complete the 140-mile drive by early afternoon, leaving time for a visit to the Ute Indian Museum and the wondrous deep, dark gorge at Black Canyon of the Gunnison National Park. (See chapter 11.)

Day 8   It's 98 miles via the Million Dollar Highway, U.S. 550, to Durango. En route, between the memorable old mining towns of Ouray and Silverton, you'll cross spectacular Red Mountain Pass in the San Juan Mountains. Durango's historic district is one of Colorado's largest and best preserved. (See chapter 12.)

Day 9   Visit the cliff dwellings of Mesa Verde National Park, about 40 miles west of Durango. (See chapter 12.)

Day 10   Get an early start for the 150-mile drive across Wolf Creek Pass on U.S. 160 to Alamosa. Spend part of the afternoon at Great Sand Dunes, 30 miles northeast of Alamosa. (See chapter 13.)

Day 11   Head north to the rafting capital of Salida, perhaps stopping for a dip in the hot springs pool, then head east on U.S. 50 to Cañon City. See the Royal Gorge, the re-created Old West town of Buckskin Joe, and the Territorial Prison Museum. (See chapter 14.)

Days 12 and 13   Spend two full days in Colorado Springs. (See day 6 in "If You Have 1 Week," above, as well as chapter 7.)

Day 14   See Day 7 in "If You Have 1 Week," above.

IF YOU HAVE 3 WEEKS

Day 1   Arrive in Denver, preferably in the late morning or early afternoon. Browse Larimer Square and the 16th Street Mall.

Day 2   Explore the State Capitol, Denver Art Museum, numerous other museums, and City Park. If there's time, visit nearby Golden, home of Coors Brewery and the historic buildings from Colorado's territorial days. (See chapter 6.)

Day 3   Enjoy a leisurely day in Boulder. Stroll the Pearl Street Mall and University of Colorado campus, or visit the Celestial Seasonings tea factory for a guided tour (the mint room will knock your socks off!). Another option is to rent a bike and explore the city's many bike paths. (See chapter 8.)

Day 4   Take Canyon Boulevard (Colo. 119) west to Nederland, then follow the foothills north on Colo. 72 and Colo. 7 to Estes Park.

Day 5 Spend the day in Rocky Mountain National Park, crossing the Continental Divide on Trail Ridge Road before enjoying the sunset on Grand Lake.

Day 6 Take U.S. 40 south through the Winter Park resort community, over Berthoud Pass, to Georgetown, an old Victorian mining town.

Day 7 Follow I-70 to Frisco, seat of Summit County, and detour on a 10-mile spur to Breckenridge. After lunch, return to I-70 and proceed west to Vail, America's most popular ski resort (and a booming summer resort as well).

Day 8 Take U.S. 24 south to Leadville, the state's highest city at over 10,000 feet elevation. See the historic district and National Mining Hall of Fame, then continue across Independence Pass to Aspen.

Day 9 Shop, sightsee, hike, bike, or just enjoy Aspen's clean mountain air. (See chapter 10 for details about sights mentioned in days 4–9.)

Day 10 Drive to Montrose via Carbondale, the historic villages of Redstone, Paonia, and Delta. Leave a few afternoon hours to visit Black Canyon of the Gunnison National Park. (See chapter 11.)

Day 11 The "Million Dollar Highway," U.S. 550 to Durango, passes through the picturesque historic mining towns of Ouray and Silverton and across Red Mountain Pass, an alpine locale worthy of Switzerland. You'll be in Durango 3 nights. (See chapter 12.)

Day 12 Durango's historic district is one of Colorado's largest and best preserved, and its Durango & Silverton Narrow Gauge Railroad traverses a magnificent route.

Day 13 This is a day for archaeological discovery. Spend most of it at Mesa Verde National Park, some 40 miles west, or at Ute Mountain Tribal Mountain Park, south of Cortez. Hovenweep National Monument and other sites are in the Cortez area. (See chapter 12.)

Day 14 It's 150 miles on U.S. 160 via Wolf Creek Pass to Alamosa. Spend the afternoon at the seemingly misplaced Great Sand Dunes National Park and Preserve, 30 miles northeast of Alamosa. (See chapter 13.)

Day 15 Continue east again on U.S. 160 over La Veta Pass to Walsenburg, then pick up Colo. 10 to La Junta. Visit the Koshare Indian Museum (a surprising find with wonderful early-20th-century art) and Bent's Old Fort National Historic Site, the reconstructed hub of a trading empire in the 1830s and 1840s. Proceed to Pueblo for dinner. (See chapter 14.)

Day 16 Browse Pueblo in the morning, including the impressive Victorian mansion that contains the Rosemount Museum, and then take a walk at the Greenway and Nature Center. Then take U.S. 50 west to Cañon City, the Royal Gorge, and the Western theme village of Buckskin Joe. (See chapter 14.)

Days 17, 18, and 19 Head north on I-25 to Colorado Springs, where there's plenty to do: the Pikes Peak Cog Railway, U.S. Air Force Academy, United States Olympic Complex, Garden of the God's rock formations, Cave of the Winds, and a variety of museums and historic sites. (See chapter 7.)

Day 20 Return to Denver for one last day. Catch up on some of the sites you may have missed earlier, or stop at the Tattered Cover Bookstore for some reading matter for the trip home.

Day 21 Have a great flight home!

16 Recommended Books & Films

Those planning vacations in Colorado can turn to a number of sources for background on the state and its major cities. Among our favorite books is *A Lady's Life in the Rocky Mountains,* a fascinating compilation of Isabella L. Bird's letters to her sister; they were written in the late 1800s as she traveled alone through the Rockies, usually on horseback. It's a bit wordy for us, but those who enjoy lengthy novels will want to get their hands on a copy of James Michener's 1,000-page *Centennial,* inspired by the northeastern plains of Colorado.

Aspiring bohemians should look no further than Jack Kerouac's classic, *On the Road,* while those seeking a gonzo take on Coloradan politics should turn to Hunter S. Thompson's account of his 1970 bid for sheriff of Aspen in *Fear and Loathing in America.* Also engrossing is Wallace Stegner's Pulitzer Prize–winning 1971 novel, *Angle of Repose.*

Horror fans will surely appreciate a pair of Stephen King classics with Colorado ties: *The Stand* is set in Boulder and *The Shining* was inspired by the writer's stay at the Stanley Hotel in Estes Park.

Travelers who want to see wildlife will likely be successful with help from the *Colorado Wildlife Viewing Guide,* by Mary Taylor Gray. You'll likely be seeing a lot of historical sights here, so it's good to first get some background from the short, easy-to-read *Colorado: A History,* by Marshall Sprague.

An excellent video introduction to the state is *Explore Colorado,* a 55-minute video tour that touches on most of the state's scenic and historic highlights. Videos, in both VHS and PAL formats, plus DVDs and interactive CD-ROMs, can be obtained from **Interpark,** 20596 C.R. P, Cortez, CO 81321 (✆ **800/687-5967;** www. petroglyphtrail.com).

FAST FACTS: Colorado

American Express The American Express Travel Agency in Denver is at 555 17th St. (✆ **303/383-5050**). It's open Monday through Friday from 8am to 5pm, offering full member services and currency exchange. To report a lost card, call ✆ **800/528-4800;** to report lost traveler's checks, call ✆ **800/221-7282.**

Area Codes Colorado uses four telephone area codes. Area codes in the immediate Denver and Boulder area are **303** and **720.** To make local calls in these cities, you will have to dial all 10 digits, starting with 303 or 720. The south-central and southeastern parts of the state, including Colorado Springs, use area code **719;** and the rest (west and north) use **970.** In 719 and 970 areas, local calls are reached by using only the seven-digit number. Long-distance calls in all areas of the state require dialing 1 plus the area code plus the seven-digit number.

Business Hours Banks are usually open weekdays from 9am to 5pm, occasionally a bit later on Friday, and sometimes on Saturday. There's 24-hour access to the automated teller machines (ATMs) at most banks, plus in many shopping centers and other outlets. Generally, business offices are open weekdays from 9am to 5pm and government offices are open from

8am until 4:30 or 5pm. Stores are open 6 days a week, with many also open on Sunday; department stores usually stay open until 9pm at least 1 day a week. Discount stores and supermarkets are often open later than other stores, and some supermarkets are open 24 hours a day.

Car Rentals See "Getting Around," earlier in this chapter.

Driving Rules See "Getting Around," earlier in this chapter.

Embassies & Consulates See chapter 3, "For International Visitors."

Emergencies For any emergency, dial © **911.** Coins are not required at pay phones.

Hot Lines For the **Rocky Mountain Poison Center,** call © **800/323-3073** or 303/739-1123. For the **Rape Crisis and Domestic Violence Hotline,** call © **303/318-9989.**

Information See "Visitor Information," earlier in this chapter.

Internet Access Easy Internet access is coming quickly to Colorado, with college towns such as Boulder and Fort Collins leading the way. You'll have more trouble in the smaller towns, although cybercafes are beginning to pop up even there, and most public libraries offer Internet access.

Legal Aid For lawyer referrals contact **Attorney Referral Service** (© **800/878-7485;** www.attorneyswest.com) or **Legal Aid–Colorado** (© **303/831-8000).**

Liquor Laws The legal age for purchase and consumption of alcoholic beverages is 21. Except for 3.2% beer (sold in supermarkets and convenience stores 7 days a week), alcoholic beverages, including full-strength beer, must be purchased in liquor stores in Colorado. These are open Monday through Saturday. Beverages may be served in licensed restaurants, lounges, and bars Monday through Saturday from 7am to 2am, Sunday from 8am to 2am, and Christmas Day from 8am to midnight, with the proper licenses. Incidentally, 3.2% beer, which is sold only in Colorado, Utah, Oklahoma, and Kansas, does have less alcohol than the same beer sold elsewhere despite what some storekeepers may tell you. According to the Budweiser people, 3.2% beer has about 4% alcohol by volume (which is equivalent to 3.2% alcohol by weight), while full-strength American beers have about 5% alcohol by volume. Some microbrews and specialty beers and ales have higher alcohol content.

Lost & Found Be sure to tell all of your credit card companies the minute you discover your wallet has been lost or stolen and file a report at the nearest police precinct. Your credit card company or insurer may require a police report number or record of the loss. Most credit card companies have an emergency toll-free number to call if your card is lost or stolen; they may be able to wire you a cash advance immediately or deliver an emergency credit card in a day or two. Visa's U.S. emergency number is © **800/847-2911** or 410/581-9994. American Express cardholders and traveler's check holders should call © **800/221-7282.** MasterCard holders should call © **800/307-7309** or 636/722-7111. For other credit cards, call the toll-free number directory at © **800/555-1212.**

Maps A state highway map can be obtained from visitor centers or by mail (see "Visitor Information," earlier in this chapter). Otherwise, maps can be purchased at bookstores, gas stations, and most supermarkets and discount stores. Maps are available free to members of the American Automobile Association. An excellent source for all kinds of maps and road atlases is **Mapsco Map and Travel Center,** 800 Lincoln St., Denver, CO 80203 (© **800/456-8703** or 303/830-2373; www.mapsco.com).

Newspapers & Magazines The state's largest daily newspaper is the *Denver Post* (www.denverpost.com), which is published in Denver and distributed statewide. Other cities and large towns, especially regional hubs, have daily newspapers, and many smaller towns publish weeklies. National newspapers such as *USA Today* and the *Wall Street Journal* can be purchased in cities and major hotels.

Police Dial 911 for emergencies.

Safety See "Health & Safety," earlier in this chapter.

Smoking Colorado has no statewide laws regarding smoking in restaurants, but most counties and/or towns require that at least the larger restaurants provide nonsmoking areas. The state's strictest laws are in Boulder, where a city ordinance prohibits smoking inside all restaurants. Smoking is also prohibited in most areas of the state in public places such as museums, galleries, and recreation centers, and in all public areas of government buildings.

Taxes Combined city and state sales taxes vary from place to place but are usually between 6% and 9% for purchases, and 9% to just over 14% for lodging.

Time Zone Colorado is on Mountain Standard Time (7 hr. behind Greenwich Mean Time), which is 1 hour ahead of the West Coast and 2 hours behind the East Coast. Daylight saving time is in effect from April through October.

Useful Telephone Numbers A recorded 24-hour hot line (© **303/639-1111;** www.cotrip.org) provides information on road conditions and possible delays due to road construction statewide.

3

For International Visitors

Whether it's your 1st visit or your 10th, a trip to the United States may require an additional degree of planning. This chapter will provide you with essential information, helpful tips, and advice for the more common problems that some visitors encounter.

1 Preparing for Your Trip

ENTRY REQUIREMENTS

Check at any U.S. embassy or consulate for current information and requirements. You can also obtain a visa application and other information online at the **U.S. State Department**'s website, at **www.travel.state.gov**.

VISAS The U.S. State Department has a **Visa Waiver Program** allowing citizens of certain countries to enter the United States without a visa for stays of up to 90 days. At press time these included Andorra, Australia, Austria, Belgium, Brunei, Denmark, Finland, France, Germany, Iceland, Ireland, Italy, Japan, Liechtenstein, Luxembourg, Monaco, the Netherlands, New Zealand, Norway, Portugal, San Marino, Singapore, Slovenia, Spain, Sweden, Switzerland, and the United Kingdom. Citizens of these countries need only a valid passport and a round-trip air or cruise ticket in their possession upon arrival. If they first enter the United States, they may also visit Mexico, Canada, Bermuda, and/or the Caribbean islands and return to the United States without a visa. Further information is available from any U.S. embassy or consulate. Canadian citizens may enter the United States without visas; they need only proof of residence.

Citizens of all other countries must have (1) a valid passport that expires at least 6 months later than the scheduled end of their visit to the United States, and (2) a tourist visa, which may be obtained without charge from any U.S. consulate.

To obtain a visa, the traveler must submit a completed application form (either in person or by mail) with a 1½-inch-square photo, and must demonstrate binding ties to a residence abroad. Usually you can obtain a visa at once or within 24 hours, but it may take longer during the summer rush from June through August. If you cannot go in person, contact the nearest U.S. embassy or consulate for directions on applying by mail. Your travel agent or airline office may also be able to provide you with visa applications and instructions. The U.S. consulate or embassy that issues your visa will determine whether you will be issued a multiple- or single-entry visa and any restrictions regarding the length of your stay.

British subjects can obtain up-to-date visa information by calling the **U.S. Embassy Visa Information Line** (*C* **0891/200-290**) or by visiting the American Embassy London's website at www.usembassy.org.uk.

Irish citizens can obtain up-to-date visa information through the **Embassy of USA Dublin,** 42 Elgin Rd., Dublin 4, Ireland (*C* **353/1-668-8777**) or by checking the "Consular Services" section of the website at http://dublin.usembassy.gov.

Australian citizens can obtain up-to-date visa information by contacting the **U.S. Embassy Canberra,** Moonah Place, Yarralumla, ACT 2600 (© 02/6214-5600) or by checking the U.S. Diplomatic Mission's website at http://usembassy-australia.state.gov/consular.

Citizens of **New Zealand** can obtain up-to-date visa information by contacting the **U.S. Embassy New Zealand,** 29 Fitzherbert Terrace, Thorndon, Wellington (© 644/472-2068), or get the information directly from the "For New Zealanders" section of the website at http://usembassy.org.nz.

MEDICAL REQUIREMENTS

Unless you're arriving from an area known to be suffering from an epidemic (particularly cholera or yellow fever), inoculations or vaccinations are not required for entry into the United States. If you have a medical condition that requires **syringe-administered medications**, carry a valid signed prescription from your physician—the Federal Aviation Administration (FAA) no longer allows airline passengers to pack syringes in their carry-on baggage without documented proof of medical need. If you have a disease that requires treatment with **narcotics**, you should also carry documented proof with you—smuggling narcotics aboard a plane is a serious offense that carries severe penalties in the U.S.

For **HIV-positive visitors,** requirements for entering the United States are somewhat vague and change frequently. According to the latest publication of *HIV and Immigrants: A Manual for AIDS Service Providers,* the Immigration and Naturalization Service (INS) doesn't require a medical exam for entry into the United States, but INS officials may stop individuals because they look sick or because they are carrying AIDS/HIV medicine.

If an HIV-positive noncitizen applies for a nonimmigrant visa, the question on the application regarding communicable diseases is tricky no matter which way it's answered. If the applicant checks "no," INS may deny the visa on the grounds that the applicant committed fraud. If the applicant checks "yes" or if INS suspects the person is HIV-positive, it will deny the visa unless the applicant asks for a special waiver for visitors. This waiver is for people visiting the United States for a short time, to attend a conference, for instance, or to visit close relatives or receive medical treatment. It can be a confusing situation. For up-to-the-minute information, contact the Centers for Disease Control's **National Center for HIV** (© 404/332-4559; www.hivatis.org) or the **Gay Men's Health Crisis** (© 212/367-1000; www.gmhc.org).

DRIVER'S LICENSES Foreign driver's licenses are mostly recognized in the U.S., although you may want to get an international driver's license if your home license is not written in English.

PASSPORT INFORMATION

Safeguard your passport in an inconspicuous, inaccessible place like a money belt. Make a copy of the critical pages, including the passport number, and store it in a safe place, separate from the passport itself. If you lose your passport, visit the nearest consulate of your native country as soon as possible for a replacement. Passport applications are downloadable from the websites listed below.

Note that the International Civil Aviation Organization (ICAO) has recommended a policy requiring that *every* individual who travels by air have his or her own passport. In response, many countries are now requiring that children must be issued their own passport to travel internationally, where before those under 16 or so may have been allowed to travel on a parent or guardian's passport.

FOR RESIDENTS OF CANADA

You can pick up a passport application at one of 28 regional passport offices or most travel agencies. Canadian children who travel must have their own passport. However, if you hold a valid Canadian passport issued before December 11, 2001, that bears the name of your child, the passport remains valid for you and your child until it expires. Passports cost C$85 for those 16 years and older (valid 5 years), C$35 for children 3 to 15 (valid 5 years), and C$20 for children under 3 (valid for 3 years). Applications, which must be accompanied by two identical passport-sized photographs and proof of Canadian citizenship, are available at travel agencies throughout Canada or from the central **Passport Office,** Department of Foreign Affairs and International Trade, Ottawa, ON K1A 0G3 (© **800/ 567-6868;** www.dfait-aeci.gc.ca/ passport). Processing takes 5 to 10 days if you apply in person, or about 3 weeks by mail.

FOR RESIDENTS OF THE UNITED KINGDOM

To pick up an application for a standard 10-year passport (5-year passport for children under 16), visit the nearest passport office, major post office, or travel agency. You can also contact the **United Kingdom Passport Service** at © **0870/571-0410** or visit its website at www.passport.gov.uk. Passports are £33 for adults and £19 for children under 16, with an additional £30 fee if you apply in person at a passport office. Processing takes about 2 weeks (1 week if you apply at the passport office).

FOR RESIDENTS OF IRELAND

You can apply for a 10-year passport, costing €57, at the **passport office,** Setanta Centre, Molesworth Street, Dublin 2 (© **01/671-1633;** www. irlgov.ie/iveagh). Those under age 18 and over 65 must apply for a €12 3-year passport. You can also apply at 1A South Mall, Cork (© **021/272-525**) or over the counter at most main post offices.

FOR RESIDENTS OF AUSTRALIA

You can pick up an application from your local post office or any branch of Passports Australia, but you must schedule an interview at the passport office to present your application materials. Call the **Australian Passport Information Service** at © **131-232,** or visit the government website at www.passports.gov.au. Passports for adults are A$144 and for those under 18 are A$72.

FOR RESIDENTS OF NEW ZEALAND

You can pick up a passport application at any New Zealand Passports Office or download it from their website. Contact the **Passports Office** at © **0800/225-050** in New Zealand or 04/474-8100, or log on to www. passports.govt.nz. Passports for adults are NZ$80 and are NZ$40 for children under 16.

CUSTOMS
WHAT YOU CAN BRING IN

Every visitor more than 21 years of age may bring in, free of duty, the following: (1) 1 liter of wine or hard liquor; (2) 200 cigarettes, 100 cigars (but not from Cuba), or 3 pounds of smoking tobacco; and (3) $100 worth of gifts. These exemptions are offered to travelers who spend at least 72 hours in the United States and who have not claimed them within the preceding 6 months. It is altogether forbidden to bring into the country foodstuffs (particularly fruit, cooked meats, and canned goods) and plants (vegetables, seeds, tropical plants, and the like). Foreign tourists may bring in or take out up to $10,000 in U.S. or foreign currency with no formalities; larger sums must be declared to U.S. Customs on entering or leaving, which includes filing form CM 4790. For more specific information regarding U.S. Customs, contact your nearest U.S. embassy or consulate, or the **U.S. Customs** office (© **202/927-1770** or www.customs.ustreas.gov).

WHAT YOU CAN TAKE HOME

U.K. citizens returning from a non-EU country have a Customs allowance of: 200 cigarettes; 50 cigars; 250g of smoking tobacco; 2 liters of still table wine; 1 liter of spirits or strong liqueurs (over 22% volume); 2 liters of fortified wine, sparkling wine or other liqueurs; 60cc (ml) perfume; 250cc (ml) of toilet water; and £145 worth of all other goods, including gifts and souvenirs. People under 17 cannot have the tobacco or alcohol allowance. For more information, contact HM Customs & Excise at © **0845/010-9000** (from outside the U.K., 020/8929-0152), or consult their website at www.hmce.gov.uk.

For a clear summary of **Canadian** rules, request the booklet *I Declare,* issued by the **Canada Customs and Revenue Agency** (© **800/461-9999** in Canada, or 204/983-3500; www.ccra-adrc.gc.ca). Canada allows its citizens a C$750 exemption, and you're allowed to bring back duty-free one carton of cigarettes, one can of tobacco, 40 imperial ounces of liquor, and 50 cigars. In addition, you're allowed to mail gifts to Canada valued at less than C$60 a day, provided they're unsolicited and don't contain alcohol or tobacco (write on the package

"Unsolicited gift, under $60 value"). All valuables should be declared on the Y-38 form before departure from Canada, including serial numbers of valuables you already own, such as expensive foreign cameras. *Note:* The $750 exemption can only be used once a year and only after an absence of 7 days.

The duty-free allowance in **Australia** is A$400 or, for those under 18, A$200. Citizens age 18 and over can bring in 250 cigarettes or 250 grams of loose tobacco, and 1,125 milliliters of alcohol. If you're returning with valuables you already own, such as foreign-made cameras, you should file form B263. A helpful brochure available from Australian consulates or Customs offices is *Know Before You Go.* For more information, call the **Australian Customs Service** at © **1300/363-263,** or log on to www.customs.gov.au.

The duty-free allowance for **New Zealand** is NZ$700. Citizens over 17 can bring in 200 cigarettes, 50 cigars, or 250 grams of tobacco (or a mixture of all three if their combined weight doesn't exceed 250g); plus 4.5 liters of wine and beer, or 1.125 liters of liquor. New Zealand currency doesn't carry import or export restrictions. Fill out a certificate of export, listing the valuables you are taking out of the country; that way, you can bring them back without paying duty. Most questions are answered in a free pamphlet available at New Zealand consulates and Customs offices: *New Zealand Customs Guide for Travellers, Notice no. 4.* For more information, contact **New Zealand Customs,** The Customhouse, 17–21 Whitmore St., Box 2218, Wellington (© **0800/428-786** or 04/473-6099; www.customs.govt.nz).

HEALTH INSURANCE

Although it's not required of travelers, health insurance is highly recommended. Unlike many European countries, the United States does not usually offer free or low-cost medical care to its citizens or visitors. Doctors and hospitals are expensive, and in most cases will require advance payment or proof of coverage before they render their services. Policies can cover everything from the loss or theft of your baggage and trip cancellation to the guarantee of bail in case you're arrested. Good policies will also cover the costs of an accident, repatriation, or death. See "Travel Insurance" and "Health & Safety" in chapter 2 for more information. Packages such as **Europ Assistance's "Worldwide Healthcare Plan"** are sold by European automobile clubs and travel agencies at attractive rates. **Worldwide Assistance Services**, Inc. (© **800/ 821-2828;** www.worldwideassistance. com) is the agent for Europ Assistance in the United States.

Though lack of health insurance may prevent you from being admitted to a hospital in nonemergencies, don't worry about being left on a street corner to die: The American way is to fix you now and bill the living daylights out of you later.

INSURANCE FOR BRITISH TRAVELERS Most big travel agents offer their own insurance and will probably try to sell you their package when you book a holiday. Think before you sign. **Britain's Consumers' Association** recommends that you insist on seeing the policy and reading the fine print before buying travel insurance. **The Association of British Insurers** (© **020/ 7600-3333;** www.abi.org.uk) gives advice by phone and publishes *Holiday*

Insurance, a free guide to policy provisions and prices. You might also shop around for better deals: Try **Columbus Direct** (© **020/7375-0011;** www. columbusdirect.net).

INSURANCE FOR CANADIAN TRAVELERS Canadians should check with their provincial health plan offices or call **Health Canada** (© **613/957-2991;** www.hc-sc.gc.ca) to find out the extent of their coverage and what documentation and receipts they must take home in case they are treated in the United States.

MONEY

CURRENCY The U.S. monetary system is very simple: The most common **bills** are the $1 (colloquially, a "buck"), $5, $10, and $20 denominations. There are also $2 bills (seldom encountered), $50 bills, and $100 bills (the last two are usually not welcome as payment for small purchases). All the paper money was recently redesigned, making the famous faces adorning them disproportionately large. The old-style bills are still legal tender.

There are seven denominations of coins: 1¢ (1 cent, or a penny); 5¢ (5 cents, or a nickel); 10¢ (10 cents, or a dime); 25¢ (25 cents, or a quarter); 50¢ (50 cents, or a half dollar); the gold "Sacagawea" coin worth $1; and, prized by collectors, the rare, older silver dollar.

Note: The "foreign-exchange bureaus" so common in Europe are rare even at airports in the United States, and nonexistent outside major cities. It's best not to change foreign money (or traveler's checks denominated in a currency other than U.S.

(Tips Small Change

When you change money, ask for some small bills or loose change. Petty cash will come in handy for tipping and public transportation. Consider keeping the change separate from your larger bills, so that it's readily accessible and you'll be less of a target for theft.

Travel Tip

Be sure to keep a copy of all your travel papers separate from your wallet or purse, and leave a copy with someone at home should you need it faxed in an emergency.

dollars) at a small-town bank, or even a branch in a big city; in fact, leave any currency other than U.S. dollars at home—it may prove a greater nuisance to you than it's worth.

TRAVELER'S CHECKS Though traveler's checks are widely accepted, make sure that they're denominated in U.S. dollars, as foreign-currency checks are often difficult to exchange. The three traveler's checks that are most widely recognized—and least likely to be denied—are **Visa, American Express,** and **Thomas Cook.** Be sure to record the numbers of the checks, and keep that information in a separate place in case they get lost or stolen. Most businesses are pretty good about taking traveler's checks, but you're better off cashing them in at a bank (in small amounts, of course) and paying in cash. *Remember:* You'll need identification, such as a driver's license or passport, to change a traveler's check.

CREDIT CARDS & ATMs Credit cards are the most widely used form of payment in the United States: **Visa** (Barclaycard in Britain), **MasterCard** (EuroCard in Europe, Access in Britain, Chargex in Canada), **American Express, Diners Club,** and **Discover.** There are, however, a handful of stores and restaurants that do not take credit cards, so be sure to ask in advance. Most businesses display a sticker near their entrance to let you know which cards they accept. *Note:* Businesses may require a minimum purchase, usually around $10, to use a credit card.

It is strongly recommended that you bring at least one major credit card—Visa and MasterCard are the most widely accepted in Colorado, with American Express and Discover next. You must have a credit or charge card to rent a car. Hotels and airlines usually require a credit card imprint as a deposit against expenses, and a credit card can be priceless in emergencies.

You'll find **automated teller machines (ATMs)** on just about every block—at least in almost every town—across the country. Some ATMs will allow you to draw U.S. currency against your bank and credit cards. Check with your bank before leaving home, and remember that you will need your personal identification number (PIN) to do so. Most accept Visa, MasterCard, and American Express, as well as ATM cards from other U.S. banks. Expect to be charged up to $3 per transaction, however, if you're not using your own bank's ATM.

One way around these fees is to ask for cash back at grocery stores that accept ATM cards and don't charge usage fees. Of course, you'll have to purchase something first.

ATM cards with major credit card backing, known as "debit cards," are now a commonly acceptable form of payment in most stores and restaurants. Debit cards draw money directly from your checking account. Some stores enable you to receive "cash back" on your debit-card purchases as well.

SAFETY
GENERAL SAFETY SUGGESTIONS Although tourist areas are generally safe, U.S. urban areas tend to be less safe than those in Europe or

Japan. You should always stay alert. This is particularly true of large American cities such as Denver. If you're in doubt about which neighborhoods are safe, don't hesitate to ask the hotel front-desk staff or the local tourist office.

Avoid deserted areas, especially at night, and don't go into public parks after dark unless there's a concert or similar occasion that will attract a crowd.

Avoid carrying valuables with you on the street, and keep expensive cameras or electronic equipment bagged up or covered when not in use. If you're using a map, try to consult it inconspicuously—or better yet, study it before you leave your room. Hold onto your pocketbook, and place your billfold in an inside pocket. In theaters, restaurants, and other public places, keep your possessions in sight.

Always lock your room door—don't assume that once you're inside the hotel you are automatically safe and no longer need to be aware of your surroundings. Hotels are open to the public, and in a large hotel, security may not be able to screen everyone who enters.

DRIVING SAFETY   Driving safety is important too, and carjacking is not unprecedented. Question your rental agency about personal safety and ask for a traveler-safety brochure when you pick up your car. Obtain written directions—or a map with the route clearly marked—from the agency showing how to get to your destination. (Many agencies now offer the option of renting a cellphone for the duration of your car rental; check with the rental agent when you pick up the car. Otherwise, contact **InTouch USA** at ✆ **800/872-7626** or www.intouch usa.com for short-term cellphone rental.) If possible, arrive and depart during daylight hours.

If you drive off a highway and end up in a dodgy-looking neighborhood, leave the area as quickly as possible. If you have an accident, even on the highway, stay in your car with the doors locked until you assess the situation or until the police arrive. If you're bumped from behind on the street or are involved in a minor accident with no injuries, and the situation appears to be suspicious, motion to the other driver to follow you. Never get out of your car in such situations. Go directly to the nearest police precinct, well-lit service station, or 24-hour store.

Park in well-lit and well-traveled areas whenever possible. Always keep your car doors locked, whether the vehicle is attended or unattended. Never leave any packages or valuables in sight. If someone attempts to rob you or steal your car, don't try to resist the thief/carjacker. Report the incident to the police department immediately by calling ✆ **911.**

2 Getting to the U.S.

Most international visitors will fly to **Denver International Airport** (✆ 800/AIR-2-DEN; www.flydenver. com). Airlines offering flights into Denver include **Air Canada** (✆ 888/247-2262; www.aircanada.ca), **Alaska Airlines** (✆ 877/502-5357; www.alaskaair.com), **American** (✆ 800/433-7300; www.aa.com), **America West** (✆ 800/235-9292; www.america west.com), **Continental** (✆ 800/ 525-0280; www.continental.com), **Delta** (✆ 800/221-1212; www.delta. com), **Frontier** (✆ 800/432-1359; www.frontierairlines.com), **Korean Air** (✆ 800/438-5000; www.korean air.com), **Martinair** (✆ 800/366-4655; www.martinair.com), **Mexicana** (✆ 800/531-7921; www.mexicana. com), **Midwest Airlines** (✆ 800/452-2022; www.midwestairlines.com), **Northwest** (✆ 800/225-2525; www.

nwa.com), **United** (☎ 800/241-6522; www.ual.com), and **US Airways** (☎ 800/428-4322; www.usair.com). International travelers can also take flights to O'Hare International Airport in Chicago, LAX in Los Angeles, and JFK International Airport in New York, and catch connecting flights to Denver from there.

British Airways (☎ **800/ 247-9297,** 0845/773-3377 in London; www.british-airways.com) offers one daily nonstop flight between London and Denver. Travelers from the United Kingdom can also take British Airways flights to such cities as Philadelphia or Chicago and make connecting flights to Denver.

AIRLINE DISCOUNTS The smart traveler can find numerable ways to reduce the price of a plane ticket simply by taking time to shop around. For example, overseas visitors can take advantage of the APEX (Advance Purchase Excursion) reductions offered by all major U.S. and European carriers. For the best rates, compare fares and be flexible with the dates and times of travel.

IMMIGRATION AND CUSTOMS CLEARANCE Visitors arriving by air, no matter what the port of entry, should cultivate patience and resignation before setting foot on U.S. soil. Getting through immigration control can take as long as 2 hours on some days, especially on summer weekends, so be sure to carry this guidebook or something else to read. This is especially true in the aftermath of the September 11, 2001, terrorist attacks, when security clearances have been considerably beefed up at U.S. airports.

People traveling by air from Canada, Bermuda, and certain countries in the Caribbean can sometimes clear Customs and Immigration at the point of departure, which is much quicker.

3 Getting Around the U.S.

BY PLANE Some large airlines (for example, Northwest and Delta) offer travelers on their transatlantic or transpacific flights special discount tickets under the name **Visit USA,** allowing mostly one-way travel from one U.S. destination to another at very low prices. These discount tickets are not on sale in the United States and must be purchased abroad in conjunction with your international ticket. This system is the best, easiest, and fastest way to see the United States at low cost. You should obtain information well in advance from your travel agent or the office of the airline concerned, since the conditions attached to these discount tickets can be changed without advance notice.

BY TRAIN Amtrak (☎ 800/USA-RAIL; www.amtrak.com) connects Denver, Grand Junction, and several other Colorado cities to both the East and West Coasts. International visitors (excluding Canada) can buy a **USA Rail Pass,** good for 15 or 30 days of unlimited travel on Amtrak. The pass is available through many foreign travel agents. Prices in 2004 for a 15-day pass were $295 off-peak and $440 peak; a 30-day pass costs $385 off-peak and $550 peak. With a foreign passport, you can also buy passes at some Amtrak offices in the United States, including locations in San Francisco, Los Angeles, Chicago, New York, Miami, Boston, and Washington, D.C. Reservations are generally required and should be made for each part of your trip as early as possible. Regional rail passes are also available.

BY BUS Although bus travel is often the most economical form of public transit for short hops between U.S. cities, it can also be slow and uncomfortable. It's certainly not an option for everyone, particularly when Amtrak, which is far more luxurious, offers similar rates. **Greyhound/ Trailways** (© 800/231-2222; www. greyhound.com), the sole nation-wide bus line, offers an **International Ameripass** that must be purchased before coming to the United States, or by phone through the Greyhound International Office at the Port Authority Bus Terminal in New York City (© 212/971-0492). The pass can be obtained from foreign travel agents and costs less than the domestic version. In 2004, options and prices were: 4 days ($135), 7 days ($183), 10 days ($223), 15 days ($271), 21 days ($319), 30 days ($367), 45 days ($407), or 60 days ($495). You can get more info on the pass at www. greyhound.com, or by calling © 212/ 971-0492 (14:00 to 21:00 GMT) or © 402/330-8552 (all other times). In addition, special rates are available for seniors and students.

BY CAR   Unless you plan to spend the bulk of your vacation time in a city where walking is the best and easiest way to get around (read: New York City, New Orleans, or maybe Denver), the most cost-effective, convenient, and comfortable way to travel around the United States is by car. The interstate highway system connects cities and towns all over the country; in addition to these high-speed, limited-access roadways, there's an extensive network of federal, state, and local highways and roads. Some of the major national car-rental companies with outlets in Denver and Colorado Springs include **Alamo** (© 800/ 462-5260; www.alamo.com), **Avis** (© 800/331-1212; www.avis.com), **Budget** (© 800/527-0700; www. budget.com), **Dollar** (© 800/800-4000; www.dollarcar.com), **Hertz** (© 800/654-3131; www.hertz.com), **National** (© 800/227-7368; www. nationalcar.com), and **Thrifty** (© 800/ 847-4389; www.thrifty.com).

If you plan to rent a car in the United States, you probably won't need the services of an additional automobile organization. If you're planning to buy or borrow a car, automobile-association membership is recommended. The **American Automobile Association (AAA)** (© 800/ 222-4357; www.aaa.com), the country's largest auto club, supplies its members with maps, insurance, and, most important, emergency road service. The cost of joining runs from $63 for singles to $95 for two members, but if you're a member of a foreign auto club with reciprocal arrangements, you can enjoy free AAA service in America. See "Getting There," in chapter 2, for more information.

FAST FACTS: **For the International Traveler**

Automobile Organizations Auto clubs will supply maps, suggested routes, guidebooks, accident and bail-bond insurance, and emergency road service. The **American Automobile Association (AAA),** the major auto club in the United States, has offices nationwide, and in Denver, Boulder, and Colorado Springs. If you belong to an auto club in your home country, inquire about AAA reciprocity before you leave. You may be able to join AAA even if you're not a member of a reciprocal club; to inquire, call AAA (© 800/222-4357; www.aaa.com). AAA is actually an organization of regional auto clubs; so look under "AAA Automobile Club" in the White Pages of the telephone directory.

Business Hours Offices are usually open weekdays from 9am to 5pm. Banks are open weekdays from 9am to 5pm or a bit later on Fridays, and sometimes Saturday morning. Stores typically open between 9 and 10am and close between 5 and 6pm from Monday through Saturday. Stores in shopping complexes or malls tend to stay open late, often until about 9pm, and many malls and larger department stores are open on Sundays. Discount stores and supermarkets are often open later than other stores, and some supermarkets are open 24 hours a day.

Currency & Currency Exchange See "Entry Requirements" and "Money" under "Preparing for Your Trip," earlier in this chapter.

Drinking Laws The legal age for purchase and consumption of alcoholic beverages is 21; proof of age is required and often requested at bars, nightclubs, and restaurants, so it's always a good idea to carry an ID when you go out. Except for 3.2% beer (sold in supermarkets and convenience stores 7 days a week), alcoholic beverages must be purchased in liquor stores in Colorado. These are open Monday through Saturday. Licensed restaurants, lounges, and bars may serve alcohol Monday through Saturday from 7am to 2am, Sunday from 8am to 2am, and Christmas Day from 8am to midnight. Incidentally, 3.2% beer, which is sold only in Colorado, Utah, Oklahoma, and Kansas, does have less alcohol than the same beer sold elsewhere, despite what some storekeepers may tell you. According to the Budweiser people, 3.2% beer has about 4% alcohol by volume (which is equivalent to 3.2% alcohol by weight), while full-strength American beers have about 5% alcohol by volume. Some microbrews and specialty beers and ales have much higher alcohol content, sometimes even 9 or 10%.

Do not carry open containers of alcohol in your car or any public area that isn't zoned for alcohol consumption. The police can fine you on the spot. And nothing will ruin your trip faster than getting a citation for DUI ("driving under the influence"), so don't even think about driving while intoxicated.

Electricity Like Canada, the United States uses 110 to 120 volts AC (60 cycles), compared to 220 to 240 volts AC (50 cycles) in most of Europe, Australia, and New Zealand. If your small appliances use 220 to 240 volts, you'll need a 110-volt transformer and a plug adapter with two flat parallel pins. Downward converters that change 220–240 volts to 110–120 volts are difficult to find in the United States, so bring one with you.

Embassies & Consulates All embassies are located in the nation's capital, Washington, D.C. Some consulates are located in major U.S. cities, and most nations have a mission to the United Nations in New York City. If your country isn't listed below, call for directory information in Washington, D.C. (© **202/555-1212**) or log on to **www.embassy.org/embassies**.

The embassy of **Australia** is at 1601 Massachusetts Ave. NW, Washington, DC 20036 (© **202/797-3000;** www.austemb.org). There are consulates in Denver, New York, Honolulu, Houston, Los Angeles, San Francisco, and other cities.

The embassy of **Canada** is at 501 Pennsylvania Ave. NW, Washington, DC 20001 (© **202/682-1740;** www.canadianembassy.org). Other Canadian consulates are in Buffalo (New York), Detroit, Los Angeles, New York, and other cities.

The embassy of **Ireland** is at 2234 Massachusetts Ave. NW, Washington, DC 20008 (© **202/462-3939;** www.irelandemb.org). Irish consulates are in Boston, Chicago, New York, and other cities.

The embassy of **Japan** is at 2520 Massachusetts Ave. NW, Washington, DC 20008 (② **202/238-6700**; www.embjapan.org). Japanese consulates are located in Denver, Atlanta, Kansas City, San Francisco, Washington D.C., and other cities.

The embassy of **New Zealand** is at 37 Observatory Circle NW, Washington, DC 20008 (② **202/328-4800**; www.nzemb.org). New Zealand consulates are in Los Angeles, Salt Lake City, San Francisco, and Seattle.

The embassy of the **United Kingdom** is at 3100 Massachusetts Ave. NW, Washington, DC 20008 (② **202/588-7800**; www.britainusa.com). Other British consulates are in Atlanta, Boston, Chicago, Cleveland, Denver, Houston, Los Angeles, New York, San Francisco, and other cities.

The following countries have consulates in the Denver area: **Australia,** 9200 W. Cross Dr. (② 303/321-2234); **Costa Rica,** 3356 S. Xenia (② 303/696-8211); **Denmark,** 5353 W. Dartmouth Ave., Lakewood (② 303/980-9100); **France,** 1420 Ogden St. (② 303/831-8616); **Germany,** 621 17th St. (② 303/279-1551); **Japan,** 1225 17th St. (② 303/534-1151); **Korea,** 1600 Broadway, Suite 500 (② 303/830-0500); **Mexico,** 48 Steele St. (② 303/331-1110); **Netherlands,** 1625 Broadway (② 303/592-5362); **Norway,** 370 17th St. (② 303/592-5930); **Sweden,** 4242 E. Amherst Ave. (② 303/758-0999); **Switzerland,** 2810 Iliff St., Boulder (② 303/499-5641); **Thailand,** 717 17th St. (② 303/312-1934); **United Kingdom** World Trade Center, 1675 Broadway, Ste. 1030 (② 303/592-5200). There are about 100 consulates in Denver.

Emergencies Call ② **911** to report a fire, call the police, or get an ambulance anywhere in the United States. This is a toll-free call. (No coins are required at public telephones.)

If you encounter serious problems, contact the **Traveler's Aid Society International** (② **202/546-1127;** www.travelersaid.org) to help direct you to a local branch, although at this time there are no branches in Colorado. This nationwide, nonprofit, social-service organization geared to helping travelers in difficult straits offers services that might include reuniting families separated while traveling, providing food and shelter to people stranded without cash, or even offering emotional counseling.

Gasoline (Petrol) Petrol is known as gasoline (or simply "gas") in the United States, and petrol stations are known as both gas stations and service stations. Gasoline costs about half as much here as it does in Europe (about $1.85–$2 per gallon at press time), and the printed price includes taxes. One U.S. gallon equals 3.8 liters or .85 imperial gallons.

Holidays Banks, government offices, post offices, and many stores, restaurants, and museums are closed on the following legal national holidays: January 1 (New Year's Day), the third Monday in January (Martin Luther King Jr. Day), the third Monday in February (Presidents' Day, Washington's Birthday), the last Monday in May (Memorial Day), July 4th (Independence Day), the first Monday in September (Labor Day), the second Monday in October (Columbus Day), November 11 (Veterans Day/Armistice Day), the fourth Thursday in November (Thanksgiving Day), and December 25 (Christmas). Also, the Tuesday following the first Monday in November is Election Day and is a federal-government holiday in presidential-election years (held every 4 years, and next in 2008).

Legal Aid If you are "pulled over" for a minor infraction (such as speeding), never attempt to pay the fine directly to a police officer; this could be construed as attempted bribery, a much more serious crime. Pay fines by mail, or directly into the hands of the clerk of the court. If accused of a more serious offense, say and do nothing before consulting a lawyer. Here the burden is on the state to prove a person's guilt beyond a reasonable doubt, and everyone has the right to remain silent, whether he or she is suspected of a crime or actually arrested. Once arrested, a person can make one telephone call to a party of his or her choice. Call your embassy or consulate.

Mail If you aren't sure what your address will be in the United States, mail can be sent to you, in your name, c/o General Delivery at the main post office of the city or region where you expect to be. Contact the U.S. Postal Service at ℭ **800/275-8777** or www.usps.com for information on the nearest post office. In Denver, the main downtown post office is at 951 20th St. The addressee must pick up mail in person and must produce proof of identity (driver's license, passport, or other ID). Most post offices will hold your mail for up to 1 month, and are open Monday to Friday from 8am to 6pm and Saturday from 9am to 3pm.

Generally found at intersections, mailboxes are blue with a red-and-white stripe and carry the inscription U.S. MAIL. If your mail is addressed to a U.S. destination, don't forget to add the five-digit postal code (or zip code), after the two-letter abbreviation of the state to which the mail is addressed (CO for Colorado). This is essential for prompt delivery.

At press time, domestic postage rates were 23¢ for a postcard and 37¢ for a letter. For international mail, a first-class letter of up to ½ ounce costs 80¢ (60¢ to Canada and Mexico), a first-class postcard costs 70¢ (50¢ to Canada and Mexico), and a preprinted postal aerogramme costs 70¢.

Measurements See the chart on the inside front cover of this book for details on converting metric measurements to U.S. equivalents.

Taxes The United States has no value-added tax (VAT) or other indirect tax at the national level. Every state, county, and city has the right to levy its own local tax on all purchases, including hotel and restaurant checks, airline tickets, and so on. Sales taxes in Colorado vary, but usually total about 7.5%. An exception is the tax on lodging, which often runs to 10%, and is 14% in Denver. Sales tax is not usually included in the price tags you'll see on merchandise or in the rates you're quoted for lodging. These taxes are not refundable.

Telephone, Telegraph, Telex & Fax Private corporations run the U.S. telephone system, so rates, especially for long-distance service and operator-assisted calls, can vary widely. Generally, hotel surcharges on long-distance and local calls are astronomical, so you're usually better off using a **public pay telephone,** which you'll find clearly marked in most public buildings and private establishments as well as on the street. Convenience (small grocery) stores and gas stations always have them. Many convenience stores and packaging services sell **prepaid calling cards** in denominations up to $50; these can be the least expensive way to call home. Many public phones at airports accept American Express, MasterCard, and Visa credit cards. **Local calls** made from public pay phones usually cost 50¢. Pay phones do not accept pennies, and few will take anything larger than a quarter.

You may want to look into leasing a cellphone for the duration of your trip.

Most long-distance and international calls can be dialed directly from any phone. **For calls within the United States and to Canada,** dial 1 followed by the area code and the seven-digit number. **For other international calls,** dial 011 followed by the country code, city code, and the telephone number of the person you are calling.

Calls to area codes **800, 888, 877,** and **866** are toll-free. However, calls to numbers in area codes **700** and **900** (chat lines, bulletin boards, "dating" services, and so on) can be very expensive—usually a charge of 95¢ to $3 or more per minute, and they sometimes have minimum charges that can run as high as $15 or more.

For **reversed-charge or collect calls,** and for person-to-person calls, dial 0 (zero, not the letter O) followed by the area code and number you want; an operator will then come on the line, and you should specify that you are calling collect, or person-to-person, or both. If your operator-assisted call is international, ask for the overseas operator.

For **local directory assistance** ("information"), dial ℂ **411;** for long-distance information, dial 1, then the appropriate area code and ℂ **555-1212.**

Telegraph and telex services are provided primarily by Western Union. You can bring your telegram into the nearest Western Union office (there are hundreds across the country) or dictate it over the phone (ℂ **800/ 325-6000**). You can also telegraph money, or have it telegraphed to you, very quickly over the Western Union system, but this service can cost as much as 15% to 20% of the amount sent.

Most hotels have **fax machines** available for guest use (be sure to ask about the charge to use it). Many hotel rooms are even wired for guests' fax machines. A less expensive way to send and receive faxes may be at stores such as Kinko's or The UPS Store. (Look in the Yellow Pages directory under "Fax Transmission Services" or "Packing Services.")

There are two kinds of telephone directories in the United States. The so-called **White Pages** list private households and business subscribers in alphabetical order. The inside front cover lists emergency numbers for police, fire, ambulance, the Coast Guard, poison-control center, crime-victims hot line, and so on. The first few pages usually will tell you how to make long-distance and international calls, complete with country codes and area codes. Government numbers are generally printed on blue paper within the White Pages. Printed on yellow paper, the so-called **Yellow Pages** list all local services, businesses, industries, and houses of worship according to activity, with an index at the front or back. (Drugstores/pharmacies and restaurants are also sometimes listed by geographic location.) The Yellow Pages often also include city maps, postal zip codes, and public transportation routes.

Time The continental United States is divided into **four time zones:** Eastern Standard Time (EST), Central Standard Time (CST), Mountain Standard Time (MST)—which includes all of Colorado—and Pacific Standard Time (PST).

Alaska and Hawaii have their own zones. For example, noon in New York City (EST) is 11am in Chicago (CST), 10am in Denver (MST), 9am in Los Angeles (PST), 8am in Anchorage (AST), and 7am in Honolulu (HST).

Daylight saving time is in effect in Colorado and most of the country from 1am on the first Sunday in April through 1am on the last Sunday in October. Note that Arizona (except for the Navajo Nation), Hawaii, much of Indiana, and Puerto Rico do not observe DST. Daylight saving time moves the clock 1 hour ahead of standard time.

Tipping Tipping is so ingrained in the American way of life that the annual income tax of tip-earning service personnel is based on how much they should have received in light of their employers' gross revenues. Accordingly, they may have to pay tax on a tip you didn't actually give them.

Here are some rules of thumb:

In hotels, tip **bellhops** at least $1 per bag ($2–$3 per bag if you have a lot of luggage) and tip the **chamber staff** $1 to $2 per day (more if you've left a disaster area, or if you're traveling with kids and/or pets). Tip the **doorman** or **concierge** only if he or she has provided you with some specific service (for example, calling a cab for you or obtaining difficult-to-get theater tickets). Tip the **valet-parking attendant** $1 every time you get your car.

In restaurants, bars, and nightclubs, tip **service staff** 15% to 20% of the check, tip **bartenders** 10% to 15%, tip **checkroom attendants** $1 per garment, and tip **valet-parking attendants** $1 per vehicle. Tip the **doorman** only if he has provided you with some specific service (such as calling a cab for you). Tipping is not expected in cafeterias and fast-food restaurants.

As for other service personnel, tip **cab drivers** 15% of the fare, tip **skycaps** at airports at least $1 per bag ($2–$3 per bag if you have a lot of luggage), and tip **hairdressers** and **barbers** 15% to 20%.

Tipping ushers at movies and theaters, and gas-station attendants, is not expected.

Toilets You won't find public toilets or "restrooms" on the streets in most U.S. cities, but they can be found in hotel lobbies, bars, restaurants, museums, department stores, railway and bus stations, and service stations. Large hotels, visitor centers, discount stores such as Wal-Mart and Target, and fast-food restaurants are probably the best bet for good, clean facilities. If possible, avoid the toilets at parks and beaches, which tend to be dirty; some may be unsafe. Restaurants and bars in resorts or heavily visited areas may reserve their restrooms for patrons. Some establishments display a notice indicating this. You can ignore this sign or, better yet, avoid arguments by paying for a cup of coffee or a soft drink, which will qualify you as a patron.

4

The Active Vacation Planner

The variety and sheer number of active sports and recreational activities Colorado has to offer is staggering. It's a place where you can easily arrange a weeklong, hard-core mountaineering expedition, but it's also a place where you can just as easily take one of the most scenic 2-hour bike rides of your life right in downtown Boulder—not to mention the superb winter activities, from skiing to snowshoeing to snowmobiling. This chapter outlines your choices and offers a few tips for planning everything from a guided, multisport vacation to an afternoon's outing.

1 Preparing for Your Active Vacation

Once you've picked the sport or activities you want to pursue, ask yourself a few questions: How physically fit am I really? How much skill in this particular activity do I have? How dangerous is this activity? How much money am I willing to spend? Answering these questions honestly can make the difference between a successful vacation and an unmitigated disaster. Some activities, such as cattle drives, require an outfitter, while others, such as biking, camping, or hiking, you can do on your own. Obviously, if you're attempting a dangerous sport in which you're inexperienced, such as rock or ice climbing, it's imperative to go with someone who (literally) knows the ropes.

If cost is an issue, prearranged escorted tour packages that include virtually everything can sometimes save you money. On the other hand, you'll be with a group, with limited freedom and flexibility to strike out on your own. Some people enjoy the company of their fellow tour members and the convenience of having everything arranged; others can't stand it. It's your choice.

Most outfitters and many tour operators keep their group size small and offer trips of different lengths and varying levels of ability. The best outfitters run well-organized trips and are willing to answer any and all questions, promptly and fully. They should have well-maintained equipment, possess appropriate land-use permits, and be fully insured. If you have any doubts, ask for the name and phone number of a satisfied former customer, and call that person and ask about their experience.

Several government agencies and other organizations provide maps and information that can be extremely useful for a variety of activities. These include **Colorado State Parks** (for state park, boating, RV, and snowmobile regulations), 1313 Sherman St., no. 618, Denver, CO 80203 (© **303/866-3437;** www.parks.state.co.us); the **Colorado Outfitters Association** (for a list of licensed guides and outfitters in the state), P.O. Box 1949, Rifle, CO 81650 (© **970/876-0543;** www.colorado-outfitters.com); the **U.S. Bureau of Land Management** (for topographical maps and information on activities on the vast amount of BLM land in the state), 2850 Youngfield St., Lakewood, CO 80215 (© **303/239-3600;** www.co.blm.gov); the **U.S. Forest Service,** Rocky Mountain

Region (for maps and information about activities and facilities in national forests), P.O. Box 25127, Lakewood, CO 80225 (© **303/275-5350;** www.fs.fed.us/r2); and the **National Park Service,** Intermountain Region (for information on national parks, monuments, historic sites, and recreation areas), 12795 Alameda Pkwy., Denver, CO 80225 (© **303/969-2500;** www.nps.gov). Another source for information on National Park Service properties is the **National Park Foundation**'s website, **www.nationalparks.org.**

Of the hundreds of outdoor recreation sites on the Internet, we usually like GORP (Great Outdoor Recreation Page), **www.gorp.com,** or you can go directly to the Colorado section at **www.gorp.com/gorp/location/co/co.htm,** which provides an abundance of detailed information about hiking trails, fishing accesses, watersports, and other activities on Colorado's public lands. Lately, however, that site has been getting a bit too cluttered and too commercial for us, so we've been checking out the very informative and user-friendly Public Lands Information Center website, **www.publiclands.org.**

The *Denver Post,* the state's major daily newspaper, has an especially good website (**www.denverpost.com**) with quite a bit of outdoor recreation information.

Those looking to buy or rent equipment will find shops practically everywhere in the state, particularly in resort towns. A convenient, statewide resource is **Gart Brothers,** the state's largest sporting-goods chain. For the location of the store nearest you, contact the **Gart Sports Castle,** a huge sales, repair, and rental facility, at 1000 Broadway in Denver (© **303/861-1122;** www.gartsports.com).

2 Visiting Colorado's National Parks & Monuments

Some of the most beautiful parts of Colorado have been preserved within the federal government's national park and monument system.

Rocky Mountain National Park, easily the most popular of the state's national parks in terms of number of visitors, is also the most spectacular. Because photos of its magnificent snowcapped peaks have graced so many calendars and coffee-table books, people often envision Rocky Mountain National Park when they think of Colorado. **Black Canyon of the Gunnison National Park** also offers fine scenery, but it's entirely different from Rocky. Black Canyon is an extremely narrow, rocky river canyon that's wild and beautiful, but difficult to explore because of its steep canyon walls. And then there's **Mesa Verde National Park.** Its reason for being is history, with the best-preserved ancient cliff dwellings in the Southwest.

The state's national monuments may not be as well known as Rocky Mountain National Park, but each has its own charm and is well worth a visit. For instance, **Colorado National Monument** is similar to the national parks of southern Utah—somewhat barren, with marvelous red-rock formations; and **Dinosaur National Monument** is really two parks—arid yet scenic canyons in Colorado and its namesake dinosaur quarry just across the border in Utah.

To get the most from your visit, try to avoid school-vacation periods and the dead of winter, when Rocky's high country and parts of Mesa Verde and Black Canyon of the Gunnison may be inaccessible. Although the parks are beautiful under a frosting of snow, you won't be able to see as much.

If you can, take a hike. Most park visitors tend to stay on the beaten track, stopping at the same scenic vistas before rushing to the next one. If you can spend even an hour or two on the trail, it's often possible to simply walk away from the crowds.

American parks and monuments are some of the biggest travel bargains in the world. If you plan to visit a number of national parks and monuments within a year, a **National Parks Pass,** which costs $50, will save you a bundle. The pass is good at all properties under the jurisdiction of the National Park Service, but not at sites administered by the Bureau of Land Management, U.S. Forest Service, or other federal or state agencies. The National Parks Pass provides free entrance for the pass holder and all vehicle occupants to National Park Service properties that charge vehicle entrance fees, and the pass holder, spouse, parents, and children for sites that charge per-person fees. The pass can be purchased at park entrance stations and visitor centers, or by mail order (© **888/GO-PARKS;** www. nationalparks.org). Because it's good for a full year from the date of purchase, and we're cheap and want to get as much use from the pass as possible, we prefer not buying the pass until we need it, usually at the first park or monument we visit.

Available in person at park service properties, as well as other federal recreation sites that charge entrance fees, is the **Golden Age Passport,** for those 62 and older, which has a one-time fee of $10 and provides free admission to all national parks and monuments, plus a 50% discount on camping fees. Be sure you have a photo ID with your date of birth. The **Golden Access Passport,** free for U.S. Citizens who are blind or have permanent disabilities, has the same benefits as the Golden Age Passport, and is available at all federal recreation sites that charge entrance fees. You'll need written proof of your disability.

Available from U.S. Forest Service, Bureau of Land Management, and Fish and Wildlife areas (such as wildlife refuges) is the **Golden Eagle Pass.** At a cost of $65 for 1 year from the date of purchase, the pass allows the bearer, plus everyone traveling with him or her in the same vehicle, free admission to all National Park Service properties plus other federal recreation sites that charge fees. The National Parks Pass discussed above can be upgraded to Golden Eagle status for $15.

3 Outdoor Activities A to Z

BALLOONING   You can take a hot-air balloon ride virtually anywhere in the state, but the most awe-inspiring scenery is in the mountains. Hot-air ballooning is expensive, and it's one sport where you don't want to cut corners. Choose an experienced and well-established balloon company, and if you have any qualms, ask about their safety record. And of course, you'll pay the highest rates at resorts.

BICYCLING   Road biking is popular throughout Colorado, but especially in Boulder, which has more bikes than people; in Fort Collins, public buses have bike racks. Our favorite city bike path is the **Boulder Creek Path,** which meanders through miles of Boulder parklands, with no cross streets or motor vehicle intrusion of any kind.

BOATING   Those who take their powerboats along on their visit to Colorado will find lakes scattered across the state. Most have boat ramps, some have fuel and supplies, and some of the larger lakes offer boat rentals. Popular choices include Bonny Lake near Burlington (known for water-skiing), Lake Pueblo, and Trinidad Lake. Because Colorado has been experiencing drought conditions in recent years, it's a good idea to call ahead to check on water conditions. In several instances lake levels have dropped well below the boat ramps, leaving boaters literally "high and dry."

> (*Fun Fact* **Elk, Elk & More Elk**
>
> There are more elk in Colorado than in any other state or Canadian province.

CAMPING   With so many acres of public land, Colorado offers practically unlimited opportunities for camping, especially in the mountains. There are over 400 public campgrounds in the national forests alone, plus sites in Bureau of Land Management areas, national parks, national monuments, and state parks. In addition, most communities have commercially operated campgrounds with RV hookups. If you plan to drive an RV in Colorado, a word of advice: Have the mechanical system checked out thoroughly first, as there are some extremely steep grades in the mountains.

One of the best places to camp in the state is Rocky Mountain National Park, but it can be crowded, especially in summer. Visit in late September or early October, if possible. Backpackers will find numerous camping opportunities along the Colorado Trail and in State Forest State Park west of Fort Collins. Mueller State Park, west of Colorado Springs, is tops for RV camping.

The **Colorado Directory, Inc.,** 5101 Pennsylvania Ave., Boulder, CO 80303-2799 (© **888/222-4641** or 303/499-9343; fax 303/499-9333; www.coloradodirectory.com), publishes a free annual booklet that describes commercial campgrounds, cabin facilities, and resorts throughout the state. For a free copy of *Colorado State Parks,* which contains details on the state's 40-plus parks, contact state park offices (see "Preparing for Your Active Vacation," earlier in this chapter).

CATTLE DRIVES   As elsewhere in the West, opportunities abound for city slickers to play cowboy by riding and roping cattle on actual drives that last from a day to a week or more. Each drive is different, so ask very specific questions about food, sleeping arrangements, and other conditions before plunking down your money. The best places for joining a drive are Steamboat Springs and Durango, with their beautiful mountain scenery and fun towns—perfect for relaxing at the end of the trail.

CROSS-COUNTRY SKIING   Practically every major downhill ski area also offers cross-country skiing, and there are thousands of miles of trails throughout Colorado's national forests—often over old mining and logging roads—that are perfect for cross-country skiing. Among top choices are Breckenridge, with trails winding through open meadows and a spruce forest, and the beautiful San Juan Mountains near Durango and Telluride. Information is available from the **Colorado Cross Country Ski Association,** P.O. Box 8937, Keystone, CO 80435 (www.colorado-xc.org), and from the **U.S. Forest Service** (see "Preparing for Your Active Vacation," earlier in this chapter).

DOGSLEDDING   If your fantasy is to be a Canadian Mountie mushing across the frozen Yukon, save the airfare and head to the mountains of Colorado instead. Dogsled rides are offered at several ski resorts, but we like Aspen best, where dog-power takes you far from the crowds into the rugged backcountry; some rides end with a fancy dinner. Incidentally, those movies you've seen are wrong: The dogs almost never bark while running, just before and after.

FISHING   Many cold-water species of fish live in the state's mountains, lakes, and streams, including seven kinds of trout (native cutthroat, rainbow, brown,

---

Fun Fact **A Wimpy State Fish**

Mistakenly believed to be extinct in 1937 and listed as an endangered species in the early 1970s, the greenback cutthroat trout has made a comeback, and in 1994 was named the official Colorado State Fish by the state legislature. It replaced the rainbow trout, a California transplant that had been listed on maps and other documents as the state fish, although state Division of Wildlife officials couldn't say why.

Known for its black spots and brilliant crimson color on its sides, the greenback cutthroat is one of four subspecies of cutthroat trout native to Colorado, one of the few species of fish that can truly be called the state's own. The greenback was abundant in Colorado waters during the early to mid–19th century, but pollution from silver and gold mining took its toll, and later the greenback was crowded out by the more aggressive rainbow, brown, and brook trout that had been imported to expand fishing opportunities.

Part of the greenback's problem is that it fails to live up to its cutthroat name, letting other trout invade its waters and practically jumping on any hook dropped into the water.

But rumors of its demise were premature, and two native populations were discovered just outside Rocky Mountain National Park in 1973. Efforts were begun to reintroduce the fish to its native waters, as government agencies and Trout Unlimited provided it with places to live that are free from more aggressive newcomers. By 1978 its status had improved from "endangered" to "threatened." State wildlife officials hope that if the greenback continues to prosper it can eventually be removed from the "threatened" list.

Today, the greenback cutthroat can be found in some four dozen bodies of water around the state, including several lakes in Rocky Mountain National Park. A good place in the national park to see the greenback cutthroat close-up is from the boardwalks through the Beaver Ponds on Trail Ridge Road.

Although the greenback's designation as official state fish does not provide any additional protection, Division of Wildlife officials say it strengthens the public's willingness to protect the fish, and encourages anglers to throw it back if they catch it, as should be the rule with any threatened species.

---

brook, lake, kokanee, and whitefish), walleye, yellow perch, northern pike, tiger muskie, and bluegill. Warm-water sport fish (especially in eastern Colorado and in large rivers) include catfish, crappie, and bass (largemouth, smallmouth, white, and wiper). Although you'll find good fishing throughout the state, among the best spots are the Arkansas River near Salida, the Roaring Fork River near Aspen, and the numerous streams and lakes in the mountains surrounding Steamboat Springs.

The fishing season is year-round, except in certain specified waters. A 1-year license costs $40 for a nonresident, and $20 for a resident. For both residents and nonresidents a 5-day license is $18 and 1-day license costs $5.25. The

Colorado Division of Wildlife, 6060 Broadway, Denver, CO 80216 (© **800/ 244-5613** or 303/297-1192; www.wildlife.state.co.us), can answer all your questions.

FOUR-WHEELING   For years, skiers have known that four-wheel-drive vehicles make getting to and from the slopes easier. But SUVs and 4WD trucks are also popular for exploring Colorado's backcountry in summer, especially its miles upon miles of old logging and mining roads. Top locations for four-wheeling include the San Juan Mountains around Ouray and Telluride. You can get information on events and tips on places to go from the **Colorado Association of Four-Wheel-Drive Clubs,** P.O. Box 1413, Wheat Ridge, CO 80034 (© **303/ 857-7992**); and **Colorado Off Highway Vehicle Coalition,** P.O. Box 620523, Littleton, CO 80162. Websites for both organizations, as well as other off-road groups, can be reached at **www.cohvco.org**.

GOLF   Clear blue skies and beautiful scenery are hallmarks of Colorado golf courses, but don't think they're merely pretty faces; these courses can be as challenging as any in the country. Balls travel farther here than at sea level, and golfers tend to tire more quickly, at least until they've adapted to the higher elevation. Be prepared for cool mornings and afternoon thunderstorms even at the height of summer. High-elevation courses, such as those in Steamboat Springs and Vail, are shut down by snow in winter, but those at lower elevations, such as along the western slope, in the southwest corner, and around Denver, are often open year-round.

Good golf resorts can be found in Crested Butte, Winter Park, Pueblo, and Alamosa; for high-altitude putting, try Leadville; and for what in our opinion is the absolutely best golf resort in the state, go to The Broadmoor in Colorado Springs. For information on the state's major golf courses, check out *Colorado Golf,* a small glossy annual magazine published jointly by several statewide golf organizations and available free at state welcome centers, or check its website, www.golfcolorado.com. The website of the **Colorado Golf Resort Association,** www.coloradogolfresorts.com, also has information on the state's courses. Serious (or should we say obsessed?) golfers may want to subscribe to *The Colorado Golfer,* a newspaper published seven times a year that carries articles on courses throughout the state. An annual subscription costs $6 (send check to 2110 S. Ash St., Denver, CO 80222; © **303/699-4653**), and includes an excellent guide to the state's courses that is published each spring.

HIKING, BACKPACKING & MOUNTAINEERING   Colorado is literally crisscrossed with hiking trails and dotted with mountains begging to be climbed. We especially like Rocky Mountain National Park's trails, but they can be crowded. The highly respected **Colorado Mountain School,** P.O. Box 1846, Estes Park, CO 80517 (© **970/586-5758;** www.cmschool.com), leads climbs up Longs Peak in the national park and can also provide advice on mountaineering in other parts of the state.

The 500-mile **Colorado Trail** ★★, which winds from Denver to Durango, crosses seven national forests and six designated wilderness areas, and is open to hikers, bikers, and equestrians. Scenery and terrain are varied, from grassy plains to snowcapped mountains. Although those in excellent physical condition can hike the entire trail in 6 to 8 weeks, most hikers make shorter excursions, and many enjoy day hikes. Most of the trail is above 10,000 feet elevation (the highest point is at 13,334 ft.), and hikes of more than a day or two will inevitably include some steep climbs. However, most of the trail has grades of no more

---

(Tips **Lightning—A Potential Killer**

Colorado is a wonderful place to explore the great outdoors, with some of America's most spectacular scenery and rugged terrain. But like most other places, outdoor activities here are not without risk. In the summer of 2004, Mary Wiper, an experienced hiker who was head of the Sierra Club in neighboring New Mexico, was struck and killed by lightning while hiking with friends near Breckenridge. Two of her companions were also struck by lightning and were knocked unconscious, but survived. The National Weather Service says that although the number of deaths from lightning is not high—an average of 67 each year in the U.S.—lightning does kill more people than either tornadoes or hurricanes, and injures hundreds more. The agency says that most people struck by lightning are not in the rain, and that lightning can travel sideways for up to 10 miles. It recommends that whenever people hear thunder they should immediately seek shelter in a building, cave, or hard-topped vehicle; if trapped by a thunderstorm, people should go to the lowest point in the area, stay out of the water, and avoid metal by dropping metal-frame backpacks and not leaning against cars. Of course, lightning is not the only outdoor hazard in Colorado. Also see "Health & Safety" in chapter 2.

---

than 10%. You'll find the easiest sections of the trail in the first 90 miles from Denver, but other sections, such as one 20-mile stretch near Salida, are also easy to moderate. In the Breckenridge and Winter Park areas, the trail is fairly rugged, and most sections below U.S. 50 are mountainous and at least somewhat strenuous. South of U.S. 50, where the trail winds through the San Juan Mountains, is serenely peaceful, but there are also fewer services, and if you're injured, it could be a long wait for help.

If it's serenity you seek, consider climbing one of the fourteeners—peaks over 14,000 feet—just off the Colorado Trail. Among the easiest is the climb to the summit of 14,420-foot Mount Harvard, the state's third-highest peak. The trail branches off the Colorado Trail about 8 miles north of Buena Vista.

Those planning multiday hikes on the Colorado Trail should carry maps or the official guidebook, which includes maps and details of the entire trail—elevation changes, trail conditions, vehicle access points, closest services, and general descriptions. Contact the **Colorado Trail Foundation,** American Mountaineering Center, 710 10th St. #210, Golden, CO 80401-5843 (© **303/ 384-3729;** www.coloradotrail.org).

Although the Colorado Trail may be the state's most famous hike, there are plenty of other opportunities. We particularly like the hike to **Long Lake** in the **Routt National Forest** outside Steamboat Springs, a moderately difficult 12-mile round-trip hike that leads through a forest and past several waterfalls to a peaceful, pristine alpine lake. Another pleasant hike in the Denver area is the easy 9-mile walk around **Barr Lake,** 18 miles northeast of the city, which offers excellent viewing of wildlife and birds. For the best city hike, try the **Boulder Creek Path,** a 16-mile trail leading from downtown Boulder into the nearby mountains, offering wildlife and bird-watching and good views of the mountains and city. Those in Colorado Springs can hike among the beautiful red sandstone formations in **Garden of the Gods,** or head west about 30 miles to **Mueller State Park,** with its 75 miles of trails through magnificent mountain scenery.

The **Continental Divide Trail Alliance (CDTA),** P.O. Box 628, Pine, CO 80470 (✆ **888/909-2382** or 303/838-3760; www.cdtrail.org), is building a trail—using volunteers—along the mountains of the Great Divide, from Canada to Mexico, and that means it shoots right through the middle of Colorado. Each year, the CDTA publishes a project schedule for the next summer, complete with volunteer needs, project descriptions, and difficulty ratings. This is an opportunity to experience some incredible backcountry, and to help create something your grandchildren will enjoy as well.

HORSEBACK RIDING   It's fun to see the Old West the way 19th-century pioneers did: from a horse's saddle. Plenty of stables and outfitters lead rides lasting from 1 hour to several days, but we recommend those near Estes Park, Steamboat Springs, Grand Junction, and Telluride. If you'd like to spend your entire vacation on horseback, the **Sylvan Dale Guest Ranch** (✆ **877/667-3999** or 970/667-3915; www.sylvandale.com) just outside of Loveland is among our top choices.

MOUNTAIN BIKING   The town of Crested Butte claims to be the mountain-biking capital of Colorado, but Telluride, Vail, and Durango are also top spots for fat-tire explorations. Those planning to go mountain biking in western Colorado can get current trail information from the **Colorado Plateau Mountain-Bike Trail Association,** P.O. Box 4602, Grand Junction, CO 81502 (www.copmoba.com).

The **Colorado Trail** (see above) is also open to mountain bikers. Riding the entire 500 miles—it takes at least 4 weeks—is easily the state's top mountain-bike adventure, but you can join or leave the trail at almost any point. One easily accessible stretch runs 24 miles from Copper Mountain Ski Resort to Tennessee Pass, crossing 12,280-foot Elk Ridge and descending into the ghost town of Camp Hale. On the trail, bikers yield to hikers and equestrians, and must detour around designated wilderness areas. For information, contact the **Colorado Trail Foundation** (see "Hiking, Backpacking & Mountaineering," above).

RAFTING & KAYAKING   Rivers swollen with melted snow lure rafters and kayakers from spring through midsummer, when rivers are at their fullest. Salida has become a famous rafting center; other popular destinations include Fort Collins, Estes Park, Grand Junction, and Glenwood Springs.

Rivers are classified from I to VI, depending on the roughness of their rapids. Class I is an easy float trip, practically calm; class II has some rapids alternating with calm; class III has some difficult rapids, with waves and boulders, and can be narrow in spots; class IV is considered very difficult, with long stretches of rough, raft-flipping rapids; class V is extremely difficult with violent rapids and steep drops; and class VI is considered unrunnable. The Arkansas River near Salida offers a variety of rapids from easy to almost unrunnable, and the Colorado River through Glenwood Canyon is a particularly scenic class II to III river, wild enough for some thrills but with enough calm stretches to let you catch your breath and enjoy the view.

Impressions

You can't see anything from your car. You've got to get out of the damn thing and walk!

—author Edward Abbey

You'll find a range of trips from numerous reliable outfitters. For a free directory of licensed river outfitters and tips on choosing a rafting company, contact the **Colorado River Outfitters Association,** P.O. Box 1662, Buena Vista, CO 81211 (© **303/280-2554;** www.croa.org).

ROCK CLIMBING   Although rock climbing is not as big here as in other parts of the West, Colorado does attract its share of climbers. One of the best spots is the Black Canyon of the Gunnison near Montrose, an extremely narrow chasm that sees little daylight; there are also several good spots near Durango. You can get information from the **Colorado Mountain Club,** American Mountaineering Center, 710 10th St., Golden, CO 80401 (© **303/279-3080;** www.cmc.org).

ROCKHOUNDING & GOLD PANNING   The state's mining heritage continues in many areas among rockhounders, who search for semiprecious gemstones, petrified woods, and agatized fossil bones. The Salida area has some of the best rockhounding opportunities in the state, and amateur gold panners should visit Idaho Springs (near Denver), Silverton, and Country Boy Mine in Breckenridge. Contact the **Colorado Geological Survey,** 1313 Sherman St., Room 715, Denver, CO 80203 (© **303/866-2611** or 303/866-4762 for publications; www.geosurvey.state.co.us), for information, maps, and a list of locations.

SKIING & SNOWBOARDING   The most popular winter sport in Colorado is, of course, downhill skiing. Since the state's first resort (Howelsen Hill in Steamboat Springs) opened in 1915, Colorado has been virtually synonymous with skiing in the western United States: It attracts more skiers per day, and its major resorts continue to win accolades.

The snowboarding craze hit Colorado just as hard as other winter-sports destinations, and after some initial resistance, has been welcomed with open arms. Many resorts have opened snowboarding parks and offer lessons and rentals.

For **current ski conditions** and general information, call **Colorado Ski Country USA,** 1507 Blake St., Denver, CO 80202 (© **303/837-0793** or 303/825-7669 for snow conditions; www.coloradoski.com). *Ski* magazine's website (**www.skimag.com**) is another useful tool. Colorado's slopes are most crowded over Christmas and New Year's, and on the Martin Luther King, Jr. and Presidents' Day holiday weekends, when lodging rates are at their highest. In good snow years, rates at Christmas can be outrageous. Those who can ski midweek will find more elbowroom on the slopes, and the beginning and end of the season are the best times to avoid crowds—assuming snow conditions are good.

Colorado's ski areas range from predominately day-use areas, with little beyond a mountain with trails and a few lifts, to full-fledged resorts, with a variety of accommodations, restaurants, and nightlife all within a half-hour of the slopes. The overview that follows describes the key mountains at these ski areas and resorts.

Arapahoe Basin (Summit County)   Arapahoe Basin, called "A-Basin" by its loyal fans, is the highest ski area in the state, and one of the oldest. Because of its elevation, it gets a bit more snow than elsewhere, so some prefer to ski it during spring's warmer temperatures.

Aspen Highlands (Aspen)   An intense mountain for only the most skilled and athletic of skiers. The views from the top are stupendous.

Aspen Mountain (Aspen)   With more than 100 restaurants and bars, Aspen is one of Colorado's most sophisticated resorts. Aspen Mountain was designed for advanced skiers and is the second most challenging of Aspen's four slopes.

Tips **A Word About Rates**

In the write-ups for each ski area in the regional chapters, we give the daily lift-ticket rates. Although handy for comparison, few people actually pay these prices. Most skiers buy packages that often include lift tickets for a given number of days, but they might also include transportation, rental equipment, lessons, lodging, meals, and lift tickets for nearby ski areas. The possibilities are almost endless.

In recent years some resorts have taken to charging more for lift tickets at busy times, and offering discounts at slow times, so it's impossible for us to guarantee the accuracy of even the daily lift-ticket prices. Certainly, the most expensive time to ski is between December 20 and January 1, followed by the Martin Luther King, Jr. and Presidents' Day holiday weekends. February through March is next; non-holiday times in January are generally cheaper; and the least expensive time is from Thanksgiving until mid-December and April until ski areas close. We generally prefer the last few weeks of the season—the snow's still great, the weather's nice, and the slopes are less crowded, because many skiers are turning their thoughts to golf and tennis.

Beaver Creek (Vail)   Beaver Creek is probably the most refined ski community in Colorado. The mountain has a good mix of runs for everyone but the superexpert, and lift lines are usually shorter than at Vail Mountain, especially on weekends.

Breckenridge (Summit County)   Colorado's second most popular resort, Breckenridge is the crown jewel of Summit County's ski areas. There's something for all levels of skiers, and it makes a great base camp for those who want to ski a different Summit County mountain every day.

Buttermilk (Aspen)   The usually uncrowded Buttermilk is a great place for affluent novices to practice their moves. It's located just outside the main village and is known for its great ski school.

Copper Mountain (Summit County)   With its four superb bowls and variety of trails for all levels, Copper is a fun place to ski, and the village is less expensive than nearby Breckenridge.

Crested Butte (Crested Butte)   Dependable snow, good beginner and intermediate trails, and lots of extreme skiing—but very little expert terrain—mark this area.

Durango Mountain (Durango)   This small, low-key ski area offers mostly intermediate, narrow, hilly trails meandering through the trees amid the breathtakingly beautiful San Juan Mountains.

Eldora (Nederland)   Just 21 miles from Boulder, Eldora is one of the state's smaller resorts, but has a good mix of terrain and is the closest ski area to the Denver-Boulder metropolitan area.

Howelsen Hill (Steamboat Springs)   The oldest ski area in continuous use in Colorado—it opened in 1915—Howelsen Hill is a fun little downtown ski area as well as a training facility for ski jumpers.

Keystone (Summit County)   Of Summit County's ski areas, Keystone is the closest to Denver, about 90 miles west of the airport. Its three separate mountains make it a good place for cruising, and night skiing draws locals from miles around.

Loveland (North of Denver)   Less than an hour from Denver by car, Loveland is an old-fashioned day-ski area: There's no village, but enough beginner and advanced trails to satisfy the average skier. If you're staying in Denver in winter, give it a whirl.

Monarch (Salida)   This family-oriented resort in southern Colorado has among the lowest rates, with good terrain and fewer crowds.

Powderhorn (Grand Junction)   This is a good mountain for groups of varying abilities, with half its slopes intermediate, and another 30% advanced or expert.

Silverton Mountain (Silverton)   This new ski/snowboard area plans to be less expensive than most of Colorado's resorts, and is geared to expert/advanced skiers and snowboarders only.

Ski Cooper (Leadville)   A small, inexpensive resort at a high elevation, Ski Cooper is known for its all-natural snow and beautiful mountain scenery. There's a good balance of trails for beginners, intermediates, and experts.

Snowmass (Aspen)   The highlight of Aspen, with plenty of wide-open spaces and trails for absolutely every level of ability. This is, by far, the largest mountain at Aspen. The base village has plenty of beds, but not much nightlife—most night owls hop the free shuttle bus to Aspen, 20 minutes down the road.

Solvista Golf & Ski Ranch (Near Winter Park)   Created by the merging of several smaller ski areas, Solvista is an all-season resort comprising two separate but interconnected mountains, with mostly beginner and intermediate runs, and just 20% expert.

Steamboat (Steamboat Springs)   One of Colorado's three largest mountains (the other two are Vail and Snowmass), Steamboat offers near-perfect skiing. It's well laid out and has gorgeous valley views, and the base village offers a wide choice of accommodations and restaurants. Another draw is the authentic old ranching town of Steamboat Springs, just a few miles away. Most of the mountain's trails are for intermediates, but there are beginner and expert trails as well.

Sunlight Mountain (Glenwood Springs)   Sunlight is family oriented, geared to intermediate skiers, and very affordable.

Telluride (Telluride)   Set at the top of a lovely box canyon, Telluride caters mainly to intermediate skiers, but also has novice trails some 2½ miles long and a number of steep expert trails.

Vail (Vail Valley)   Colorado's most popular resort, Vail mountain has a top-notch ski school and trails for everyone. The completely self-contained village at its base was created for skiers and is serviced by free shuttle buses.

Winter Park (Winter Park)   Young and athletic in spirit, Winter Park is unique—the focus is on value, with a variety of trails for all levels, plus well-regarded programs for children and skiers with disabilities.

Wolf Creek (Near Pagosa Springs)   One of the state's oldest ski areas, Wolf Creek is famous for consistently having the most snow in the state—an annual average of 465 inches (almost 39 ft.). There is terrain for skiers of all ability levels, but especially intermediates.

Tips **Ski Packages & Tours**

While many skiers enjoy planning their trips, others prefer making one phone call or sending an e-mail, and then letting someone else take care of all the details. Packages not only save time, but are sometimes cheaper than doing it yourself. The key is to make sure you get all the features you want, without paying for things you don't want. Packages often include air and ground transportation, lodging, and lift tickets, and sometimes include trip-cancellation insurance and some meals.

A good first step is to check with a ski club in your hometown. These nonprofit organizations often offer some of the best deals if they happen to be planning a trip to where you want to ski at a time you want to go. Many travel agents can arrange ski vacations, and the central reservations service for a particular resort and the reservations desks of nearby lodgings can give you the scoop on the latest packages. A good choice among the well-established companies that offer ski packages throughout Colorado is **Moguls Mountain Travel,** 6707 Winchester Circle, Suite 100, Boulder, CO 80301 (© **800/666-4857;** www.skimoguls.com).

SNOWMOBILING   If you've never been snowmobiling, the best places for a guided snowmobile tour are Steamboat Springs and Aspen. If you're an experienced snowmobiler and you plan to bring your rig with you, national forest trails are prime snowmobiling spots. Some of the state's best and most scenic rides are in Roosevelt National Forest, about 50 miles west of Fort Collins (via U.S. 287 and Colo. 14) at Chambers Lake. Because many of these trails are multiuse, snowmobilers should watch out for cross-country skiers and snowshoers, and slow down when passing. Colorado's light, dry snow is usually suitable for snowmobiling all winter long, although warm spring days can result in sticky snow, especially at lower elevations, which can gum up the works and make the going rough.

Information on snowmobiling in the state is available online from the **Colorado Snowmobile Association (www.sledcity.com);** for information on snowmobile regulations, contact **Colorado State Parks** (see "Preparing for Your Active Vacation," earlier in this chapter).

WILDLIFE & BIRD-WATCHING   There are numerous locations in Colorado to see animals and birds in the wild, including some that are close to the state's major cities. The South Platte River Greenway near Denver is a good spot to see ducks and other waterfowl, songbirds, deer, and beaver; and the U.S. Air Force Academy grounds in Colorado Springs offer opportunities to see deer, an occasional elk, peregrine falcons, and golden eagles. Other top spots to see wildlife include Durango, Glenwood Springs, Fort Collins, Vail, Rocky Mountain National Park, and Colorado National Monument.

5

Settling into Denver

It's no accident that Denver is called the Mile High City: When you climb up to the State Capitol, you're precisely 5,280 feet above sea level when you reach the 18th step. Denver's location at this altitude was purely coincidental; Denver is one of the few cities that was not built on an ocean, lake, navigable river, or even on an existing road or railroad.

In the summer of 1858, eager prospectors discovered a few flecks of gold where Cherry Creek empties into the shallow South Platte River, and a tent camp quickly sprang up on the site. (The first permanent structure was a saloon.) When militia Gen. William H. Larimer arrived in 1859, he claim-jumped the land on the east side of the Platte, laid out a city, and, hoping to gain political favors, named it after James Denver, governor of the Kansas Territory, which included this area. Larimer was not aware that Denver had recently resigned.

Larimer's was one of several settlements on the South Platte. Three others also sought recognition, but Larimer, a shrewd man, had a solution. For the price of a barrel of whisky, he bought out the other would-be town fathers, and the name "Denver" caught on.

Although the gold found in Denver was but a teaser for much larger strikes in the nearby mountains, the community grew as a shipping and trade center, in part because it had a milder climate than the mining towns it served. A devastating fire in 1863, a deadly flash flood in 1864, and American-Indian hostilities in the late 1860s created many hardships. But the establishment of rail links to the east and the influx of silver from the rich mines to the west kept Denver going. Silver from Leadville and gold from Cripple Creek made Denver a showcase city in the late 19th and early 20th centuries. The U.S. Mint, built in 1906, established Denver as a banking and financial center.

In the years following World War II, Denver mushroomed to become the largest city between the Great Plains and the Pacific Coast, with about 500,000 residents within the city limits and more than 2.5 million in the metropolitan area. Today, it's a sprawling and growing city, extending from the Rocky Mountain foothills on the west far into the plains to the south and east. Denver is noted for its dozens of tree-lined boulevards, 200 city parks that cover more than 20,000 acres, and architecture ranging from Victorian to sleek contemporary.

1 Orientation

ARRIVING

BY PLANE

Denver International Airport (DIA) is 23 miles northeast of downtown, usually a 35- to 45-minute drive. Covering 53 square miles (twice the size of Manhattan), DIA boasts one of the tallest flight-control towers in the world, at 327 feet. The airport, which has 94 gates and six full-service runways, can handle around 33 million passengers annually.

Major national airlines serving Denver include American, America West, Continental, Delta, Frontier, Northwest, Sun Country, JetBlue, United, and US Airways. **International airlines** include Air Canada, British Airways, Lufthansa, and Mexicana de Aviación.

Regional and **commuter airlines** connecting Denver with other points in the Rockies and Southwest include Alaska Airlines, Aspen Air, Mountain Air Express, and three United Express airlines: Air Wisconsin, Great Lakes Aviation, and Mesa.

For airlines' national reservations phone numbers and websites, see "Getting There," in chapter 2. For other information, call the Denver International Airport **information line** (✆ **800/AIR-2-DEN** or 303/342-2000; TDD 800/688-1333; www.flydenver.com). Other important airport phone numbers include: **administration,** ✆ 303/342-2200; **emergencies,** ✆ 303/342-4211; **ground transportation,** ✆ 303/342-4059; **vehicle assistance,** including emergency car start, ✆ 303/342-4650; **paging,** ✆ 303/342-2300; **parking,** ✆ 303/342-7275; and **police,** ✆ 303/342-4212.

GETTING TO & FROM THE AIRPORT   Bus, taxi, and limousine services shuttle travelers between the airport and downtown, and most major car-rental companies have outlets at the airport. Because many major hotels are some distance from the airport, travelers should check on the availability and cost of hotel shuttle services when making reservations.

The **city bus** fare from the airport to downtown Denver is $8; from the airport to Boulder and suburban Park-n-Ride lots it is about $10. The **Super-Shuttle** (✆ **800/525-3177** or 303/370-1300; www.supershuttledenver.com) provides transportation to and from a number of hotels downtown and in the Denver Tech Center. The SuperShuttle has frequent scheduled service between the airport and downtown hotels for $18 per person each way; door-to-door service is also available. **Taxi** companies (see "Getting Around," later in this chapter) are another option, with fares generally in the $30-to-$50 range, and you can often share a cab and split the fare by calling the cab company ahead of time. For instance, **Yellow Cab** (✆ **303/777-7777**) will take up to five people from DIA to most downtown hotels for a flat rate of $45.

Those who prefer a bit of luxury may prefer **Mile Hi City Limousine,** also known as White Dove Limousine (✆ **800/910-7433** or 303/355-5002; www.whitedovelimo.com). Rates to different parts of the Denver metro area start at $65 but vary, so call for prices. The company operates sedan and stretch limousines (as well as a minibus) built to accommodate 3 to 14 people. Charter services are also available.

BY CAR
The principal highway routes into Denver are **I-25** from the north (Fort Collins and Wyoming) and south (Colorado Springs and New Mexico); **I-70** from the east (Burlington and Kansas) and west (Grand Junction and Utah); and **I-76** from the northeast (Nebraska). If you're driving into Denver from Boulder, take **U.S. 36;** from Salida and southwest, **U.S. 285.**

BY TRAIN
Amtrak serves Union Station, 17th and Wynkoop streets (✆ **800/USA-RAIL** or 303/825-2583; www.amtrak.com), in the lower downtown historic district.

BY BUS

Greyhound, 19th and Arapahoe streets (© **800/231-2222;** www.greyhound.com), is the major bus service in Colorado, with about 60 daily arrivals and departures to communities in and out of the state.

VISITOR INFORMATION

The **Denver Metro Convention and Visitors Bureau** operates a visitor center on the 16th Street Mall at 918 16th St. (© **303/892-1505**). It's open Monday through Friday from 8am to 5pm and summer Saturdays from 9:30am to 1:30pm. Visitor information is also available in the Tabor and Cherry Creek shopping centers, and at the Colorado State Capitol and Denver International Airport. Ask for the *Official Visitors Guide,* a 150-plus-page full-color booklet with a comprehensive listing of accommodations, restaurants, and other visitor services in Denver and surrounding areas.

For advance information, contact the Denver Metro Convention and Visitors Bureau, 1555 California St., Suite 300, Denver, CO 80202-4264 (© **800/233-6837; www.denver.org**). Two other good Internet resources are **http://denver.citysearch.com** and **www.denvergov.org**.

CITY LAYOUT

It's difficult to get lost in Denver, as long as you remember that the mountains, nearly always visible, are to the west. All the same, getting around a city of half a million people can be perplexing. One element of confusion is that Denver has both an older grid system, which is oriented northeast-southwest to parallel the South Platte River, and a newer north-south grid system that surrounds the older one.

The *Official Visitors Guide,* available free of charge from the Denver Metro Convention and Visitors Bureau (see "Visitor Information," above), contains a good map.

MAIN ARTERIES & STREETS

It's probably easiest to get your bearings from Civic Center Park. From here, Colfax Avenue (U.S. 40) extends east and west as far as the eye can see. The same is true for Broadway, which reaches north and south.

DOWNTOWN DENVER   North of Colfax and west of Broadway is the center of downtown, where the streets follow the old grid pattern. A mile-long pedestrian mall, **16th Street,** cuts northwest off Broadway just above this intersection. (The numbered streets parallel 16th to the northeast, extending to 44th; and to the southwest, as far as 5th.) Intersecting the numbered streets at right angles are **Lawrence Street** (which runs one-way northeast) and **Larimer Street** (which runs one-way southwest), 12 and 13 blocks north, respectively, of the Colfax-Broadway intersection.

I-25 skirts downtown Denver to the west, with access from Colfax or **Speer Boulevard,** which winds diagonally along Cherry Creek past Larimer Square.

OUTSIDE DOWNTOWN   Outside the downtown sector, the pattern is a little less confusing. But keep in mind that the numbered *avenues* that parallel Colfax to the north and south (Colfax is equivalent to 15th Ave.) have nothing in common with the numbered *streets* of the downtown grid. In fact, any byway labeled an "avenue" runs east–west, never north–south.

FINDING AN ADDRESS

NORTH–SOUTH ARTERIES   The thoroughfare that divides avenues into east and west is **Broadway,** which runs one-way south between 19th Street and I-25. Each block east or west adds 100 to the avenue address; thus, if you wanted to find 2115 E. 17th Ave., it would be a little more than 21 blocks east of Broadway, just beyond Vine Street.

Main thoroughfares that parallel Broadway to the east include **Downing Street** (1200 block), **York Street** (2300 block; it becomes **University Blvd.** south of 6th), **Colorado Boulevard** (4000 block), **Monaco Street Parkway** (6500 block), and **Quebec Street** (7300 block). Colorado Boulevard (Colo. 2) is the most significant commercial artery, intersecting I-25 on the south and I-70 on the north. North–south streets that parallel Broadway to the west include **Santa Fe Drive** (U.S. 85; 1000 block); west of I-25 are **Federal Boulevard** (U.S. 287 North; 3000 block), and **Sheridan Boulevard** (Colo. 95; 5200 block), the boundary between Denver and Lakewood.

EAST–WEST ARTERIES   Denver streets are divided into north and south at **Ellsworth Avenue,** about 2 miles south of Colfax. Ellsworth is a relatively minor street, but it's a convenient dividing point because it's just a block south of **1st Avenue.** With building numbers increasing by 100 each block, that puts an address like 1710 Downing St. at the corner of East 17th Avenue. **First, 6th, Colfax** (1500 block), and **26th** avenues, and **Martin Luther King, Jr. Boulevard** (3200 block) are the principal east–west thoroughfares. There are no numbered avenues south of Ellsworth. Major east–west byways south of Ellsworth are **Alameda** (Colo. 26; 300 block), **Mississippi** (1100 block), **Louisiana** (1300 block), **Evans** (2100 block), **Yale** (2700 block), and **Hampden avenues** (U.S. 285; 3500 block).

NEIGHBORHOODS IN BRIEF

Lower Downtown (LoDo) A 25-block area surrounding Union Station, and encompassing **Wynkoop Street** southeast to **Market Street** and **20th Street** southwest to **Speer Boulevard,** this delightful and busy historic district was until recently a somewhat seedy neighborhood of deteriorating Victorian houses and redbrick warehouses. A major restoration effort has brought it back to life. Today it is home to chic shops, art galleries, nightclubs, and restaurants. Listed as both a city and county historic district, it boasts numerous National Historic Landmarks; skyscrapers are prohibited by law. Coors Field, the 50,000-seat home of the Rockies baseball team, opened here in 1995.

Central Business District This extends along **16th, 17th,** and **18th streets** between **Lawrence Street** and **Broadway.** The ban on skyscrapers certainly does not apply here. In this area you'll find the Brown Palace Hotel, the Westin Hotel at Tabor Center, and other upscale lodgings; numerous restaurants and bars; plus the popular 16th Street Mall.

Far East Center Denver's Asian community is concentrated along this strip of **Federal Boulevard,** between **West Alameda** and **West Mississippi avenues.** It burgeoned in the aftermath of the Vietnam War to accommodate throngs of Southeast Asian refugees, especially Thai and Vietnamese. Look for authentic restaurants, bakeries, groceries, gift shops, and clothing stores. The Far East Center Building at Federal and Alameda is built in Japanese pagoda style.

Five Points The "five points" actually meet at 23rd Street and Broadway, but the cultural and commercial hub of Denver's black community, from **23rd** to **38th streets,** northeast of downtown, covers a much larger area and incorporates four historic districts. Restaurants offer soul food, barbecued ribs, and Caribbean cuisine, while jazz and blues musicians and contemporary dance troupes perform in theaters and nightclubs. The Black American West Museum and Heritage Center is also in this area.

La Alma Lincoln Park/Auraria Hispanic culture, art, food, and entertainment predominate along this strip of **Santa Fe Drive,** between **West Colfax** and **West 6th avenues.** It's notable for its Southwestern character and architecture. This neighborhood is well worth a visit for its numerous restaurants, art galleries, and crafts shops. Denver's annual Cinco de Mayo celebration takes place here.

Uptown Denver's oldest residential neighborhood, from **Broadway** east to **York Street** (City Park) and **23rd Avenue** south to **Colfax Avenue,** is best known today for two things: It's bisected by 17th Avenue, home to many of the city's finest restaurants, and several of its classic Victorian and Queen Anne–style homes have been converted to captivating bed-and-breakfasts (see "Where to Stay," later in this chapter).

Washington Park A grand Victorian neighborhood centered on the lush park of its namesake, "Wash Park" is one of Denver's trendiest and most popular neighborhoods. Bounded by **Broadway** east to **University Boulevard,** and **Alameda Avenue** south to **Evans Avenue,** it features a good deal of dining and recreational opportunities, but little in the way of lodging. It's a great place, however, for architecture and history buffs to drive or walk past the grand rows of houses.

Capitol Hill One of Denver's most diverse and oldest neighborhoods lies just southeast of downtown. Capitol Hill centers on the gold-domed Capitol Building, encompassing **Broadway** east to **York,** and **Colfax Avenue** south to **6th Avenue.** The north edge is improving after years of neglect and criminal activity, and now features such attractions as the Fillmore Auditorium and a lively restaurant and bar scene. There are several commercial and retail districts in the area, nestled amidst Victorian houses and modern lofts and apartments. Also here are the Molly Brown House Museum (see chapter 6) and several lodging options, ranging from B&Bs to luxury hotels (see "Where to Stay," below). You'll notice that there are no old wooden buildings here. After a disastrous fire in 1863, the government forbade the construction of wooden structures, a ban that stood until after World War II.

Cherry Creek Home of the Cherry Creek Shopping Center and Denver Country Club, this area extends north from **East 1st Avenue** to **East 8th Avenue,** and from **Downing Street** east to **Steele Street.** You'll find huge, ostentatious stone mansions here, especially around Circle Drive (southwest of 6th and University), where many of Denver's wealthiest families have lived for generations.

Denver Neighborhoods

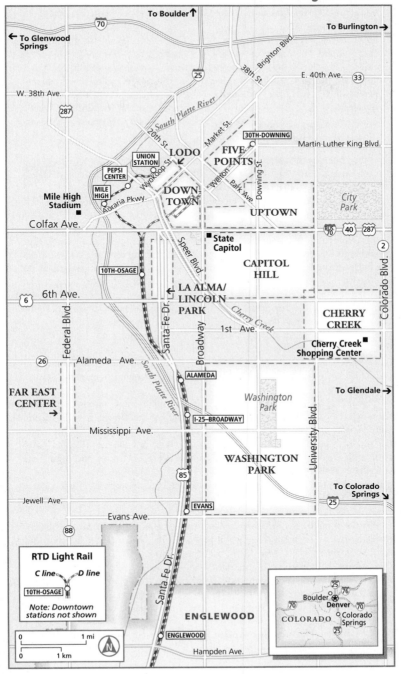

To Boulder ↑

To Burlington →

← To Glenwood
Springs

70

To Burlington →

25

33

E. 40th Ave.

W. 38th Ave.

287

South Platte River

Brighton Blvd.

38th St.

Market St.

30TH-DOWNING

Martin Luther King Blvd.

20th St.

UNION
STATION

LODO

FIVE
POINTS

Downing St.

PEPSI
CENTER

Wynkoop St.

Welton St.

Park Ave.

MILE
HIGH

DOWN-
TOWN

UPTOWN

City
Park

Mile High
Stadium

Auraria Pkwy.

Colfax Ave.

BUS
70

40

287

State
Capitol

2

10TH-OSAGE

Speer Blvd.

CAPITOL
HILL

Colorado Blvd.

6

6th Ave.

LA ALMA/
LINCOLN
PARK

Cherry Creek

CHERRY
CREEK

Federal Blvd.

Santa Fe Dr.

Broadway

1st Ave.

Cherry Creek
Shopping Center

26

Alameda Ave.

South Platte River

ALAMEDA

FAR EAST
CENTER
→

To Glendale →

Washington
Park

I-25–BROADWAY

University Blvd.

Mississippi Ave.

WASHINGTON
PARK

85

To Colorado
Springs ↘

Jewell Ave.

25

EVANS

88

Evans Ave.

RTD Light Rail

C line *D line*

10TH-OSAGE

*Note: Downtown
stations not shown*

Santa Fe Dr.

25

76

Boulder

COLORADO

70

Denver

70

Colorado
Springs

ENGLEWOOD

25

0   1 mi

0   1 km

ENGLEWOOD

Hampden Ave.

Glendale Denver surrounds Glendale, an incorporated city. The center of a lively entertainment district that is home to a slew of topless clubs, Glendale straddles Cherry Creek on **South Colorado Boulevard** south of **East Alameda Avenue.**

Tech Center At the southern end of the metropolitan area is the Denver Tech Center, along **I-25** between **Belleview Avenue** and **Arapahoe Road.** In this district, about a 25-minute drive from downtown, you will find the headquarters of several international and national companies, high-tech businesses, and a handful of upscale hotels heavily oriented toward business travelers.

2 Getting Around

BY PUBLIC TRANSPORTATION

The **Regional Transportation District,** or **RTD** (℡ **800/366-7433,** 303/299-6000, or TDD 303/299-6089 for route and schedule information; 303/299-6700 for other business; www.rtd-denver.com), calls itself "The Ride." It operates bus routes and a light-rail system, with free transfer tickets available. It provides good service within Denver and its suburbs and outlying communities (including Boulder, Longmont, and Evergreen), as well as free parking at 65 Park-n-Ride locations throughout the Denver-Boulder metropolitan area. The light-rail service is designed to get buses and cars out of congested downtown Denver; many of the bus routes from outlying areas deliver passengers to light-rail stations rather than downtown.

The local one-way fare is $1.25; seniors and passengers with disabilities pay 60¢, and children age 5 and under travel free. Regional bus fares vary (for example, Denver to Boulder costs $3.75). Exact change is required for buses, and train tickets can be purchased at vending machines beneath light-rail station awnings.

Depending on the route, the departure time of the last bus or train varies from 9pm to 2am. Maps for all routes are available at any time at the RTD **Civic Center Station** (16th St. and Broadway) and the **Market Street Station** (Market and 16th sts.). RTD also provides special service to Colorado Rockies (baseball) and Denver Broncos (football) games. All RTD buses and trains are completely wheelchair accessible.

Free buses run up and down the 16th Street Mall between the Civic Center and Market Street every 75 seconds during peak hours (less frequently at other times), daily from 6am to 1am.

Visitors should take particular note of the light-rail **C Line.** After diverting from the main north–south light-rail line at Colfax Avenue, it veers west and stops at Invesco Field at Mile High, the Pepsi Center, and Six Flags Elitch Gardens before chugging into Union Station at 17th and Wynkoop streets in lower downtown. The fare is the same as on any other local route, but the schedule is extended, with the last train leaving Union Station at about 2am. By the end of 2006, a new train along I-25 from Broadway to Mineral Avenue in the south suburbs will begin running.

The open-air **Platte Valley Trolley** (℡ **303/458-6255;** www.denvertrolley. org) operates year-round. From June through October between noon and 4pm

Thursday through Sunday, there's a half-hour "Denver Sightseeing Route" ride ($3 adults, $1 seniors and children), which operates from 15th Street at Confluence Park, south to Decatur Street along the west bank of the Platte River. Different routes are offered at other times.

BY TAXI

The main companies are **Yellow Cab** (© **303/777-7777**) and **Metro Taxi** (© **303/333-3333**). Taxis can be hailed on the street, though it's preferable to telephone for a taxi or wait for one at a taxi stand outside a major hotel. On weekends, however, hailing a taxi can be difficult when the bars close down for the night.

For the traveler seeking true luxury, Denver has several limousine services, including **Presidential Limousines** (© **800/828-8680** or 303/320-1101), and **Executive Transportation** (© **800/546-6120** or 303/755-5089), which covers the entire state, offering Suburbans, 15-passenger vans, town cars, and limos.

BY CAR

Because cars are not really necessary downtown, visitors can save the cost of renting and parking by arranging to stay downtown while in Denver, then renting a car to leave the area.

The Denver office of the **American Automobile Association (AAA)** is at 4100 E. Arkansas Ave., Denver, CO 80222-3405 (© **800/222-4357** or 303/753-8800); there are several other locations in the Denver area.

T-Rex, a major highway and light-rail project, began in 2001 and will slow traffic on I-25 until 2006. The area affected is south of downtown, so travelers to the Denver Technological Center and other environs south of Denver should expect delays and possible closures. For more information, call © **303/786-8739** for recorded information or visit **www.trexproject.com**.

CAR RENTALS   Most major car-rental agencies have outlets in or near downtown Denver, as well as at Denver International Airport. These include **Alamo,** 24530 E. 78th Ave. (© 800/462-5266 or 303/342-7373); **Avis,** 1900 Broadway (© 800/831-2847 or 303/839-1280; 303/342-5500 at DIA); **Dollar,** 10343 N. Federal Blvd., Westminster (© 800/800-4000 or 303/790-0970; 303/317-1142 at DIA); **Enterprise,** 5179 S. Broadway (© 800/736-8222 or 303/794-3333; 303/342-7350 at DIA); **Hertz,** 2001 Welton St. (© 800/654-3131 or 303/297-9400; 303/342-3800 at DIA); **National,** at Denver International Airport (© 800/227-7368 or 303/342-0717); and **Thrifty,** 8006 E. Arapahoe Ave. (© 800/847-4389 or 303/220-1020; 303/342-9400 at DIA). You can rent campers, travel trailers, motor homes, and motorcycles from **Cruise America,** 8950 N. Federal Blvd. (© 800/327-7799 or 303/426-6699; www.cruiseamerica.com).

Per-day rentals for midsize cars range from $30 to $60, although AAA and other discounts are often available, and weekend and multiday rates can also save money. Four-wheel-drive vehicles, trucks, and campers cost more.

PARKING   Downtown parking-lot rates vary from 75¢ per half-hour to $15 per full day. Rates are higher near the 16th Street Mall, in the central business district, and in hotel lots (some downtown hotels charge as much as $26 per night). Keep a handful of quarters if you plan to use on-street parking meters.

FAST FACTS: Denver

American Express The American Express travel agency, 555 17th St. (✆ **303/383-5050**), is open Monday through Friday from 8am to 5pm. It offers full member services and currency exchange. To report a lost card, call ✆ **800/528-4800**; to report lost traveler's checks, call ✆ **800/221-7282.**

Area Code Area codes are **303** and **720,** and local calls require 10-digit dialing. See the "Telephone, Telegraph, Telex & Fax" section under "Fast Facts," in chapter 3.

Babysitters Front desks at major hotels can often arrange for babysitters for their guests.

Business Hours Generally, business offices are open weekdays from 9am to 5pm and government offices are open from 8am until 4:30 or 5pm. Stores are open 6 days a week, with many also open on Sunday; department stores usually stay open until 9pm at least 1 day a week. Discount stores and supermarkets are often open later than other stores, and some supermarkets are open 24 hours a day.

Banks are usually open weekdays from 9am to 5pm, occasionally a bit later on Friday, and sometimes on Saturday. There's 24-hour access to automated teller machines (ATMs) at most banks, plus in many shopping centers and other outlets.

Car Rentals See "Getting Around," above.

Doctors/Dentists Doctor and dentist referrals are available by calling ✆ **800/DOCTORS. Centura Health Advisor** (✆ **800/327-6877** or 303/ 777-6877) provides free physician referrals and answers health questions; the **Parent Smart Health Line** (✆ **303/861-0123**) specializes in referrals to children's doctors and dentists, and also has staff on hand to provide advice.

Drugstores Throughout the metropolitan area, you will find Walgreens and other chain pharmacies, as well as Safeway and King Soopers grocery stores (which also have drugstores). The **Walgreens** at 2000 E. Colfax Ave. (✆ **303/331-0917**) is open 24 hours a day. For the locations of other Walgreens, call ✆ **800/WALGREENS.**

Emergencies Call ✆ **911.** For the **Rocky Mountain Poison Center,** call ✆ **800/323-3073** or 303/739-1123. For the **Rape Crisis and Domestic Violence Hotline,** call ✆ **303/318-9989.**

Eyeglasses One-hour replacements and repairs are usually available at **Pearle Vision,** 2720 S. Colorado Blvd. at Yale Avenue (✆ **303/758-1292**), and **LensCrafters,** in Cherry Creek Shopping Center (✆ **303/321-8331**).

Hospitals Among Denver-area hospitals are **St. Joseph's,** 1835 Franklin St. (✆ **303/837-7111**), just east of downtown, and **Children's Hospital,** 1056 E. 19th Ave. (✆ **303/861-8888**).

Maps Denver's largest map store, **Mapsco Map and Travel Center,** 800 Lincoln St., Denver, CO 80203 (✆ **800/456-8703** or 303/830-2373; www.mapsco. com), offers USGS and recreation maps, state maps and travel guides, raised relief maps, and globes.

Newspapers/Magazines The *Denver Post* (www.denverpost.com) is Colorado's largest daily newspaper. The *Rocky Mountain News* (www.rocky mountainnews.com) also covers the metropolitan area. Under a joint operating agreement, each publishes a separate weekday edition; only the *News* prints on Saturday, and only the *Post* appears on Sunday. A widely read free weekly, *Westword* (www.westword.com), is known as much for its controversial jibes at local politicians and celebrities as it is for its entertainment listings. National newspapers such as *USA Today* and the *Wall Street Journal* can be purchased at newsstands and at major hotels.

Photographic Needs For photographic supplies, equipment, 1-hour processing, and repairs, visit **Wolf Camera** at 1 of its 15 Denver locations; its downtown branch, at 1545 California St. (© **303/623-1155,** or **888/644-WOLF** for other locations; www.wolfcamera.com), claims to be the biggest single-floor camera store in the world. Check Sunday's *Denver Post* for discount coupons for Wolf Camera's services. Another good source for photo supplies and film processing is **Mike's Camera,** 759 S. Colorado Blvd. (© **303/733-2121;** www.mikescamera.com).

Post Office The main downtown post office, 951 20th St., is open Monday through Friday from 7am to 10:30pm, Saturday and Sunday from 8:30am to 10:30pm. For full 24-hour postal service, go to the General Mail Facility, 7500 E. 53rd Place. For other post office locations and hours, call the U.S. Postal Service (© **800/275-8777;** www.usps.com).

Safety Although Denver is a relatively safe city, it's not crime-free. Safety is seldom a problem on the 16th Street Mall, but even streetwise Denverites avoid late-night walks along certain sections of East Colfax Avenue, just a few blocks away. If you are unsure of the safety of a particular area you wish to visit, ask your hotel concierge or desk clerk.

Taxes State and local sales tax in Denver is about 7% (it varies slightly in neighboring counties and suburbs). The hotel tax is about 7%, bringing the total tax on accommodations to nearly 14%.

Useful Telephone Numbers For a weather report, time, and temperature, call © **303/337-2500.** Statewide road condition reports are available by calling © **303/639-1111.** For information on possible road construction delays in the Denver area and statewide, see **www.cotrip.org.** Information on the T-Rex (the highway-widening and rail-expansion project that's slowing Denver's traffic through 2006) is available by calling © **303/786-8739** or browsing **www.trexproject.com.**

3 Where to Stay

Although most hotels and motels in the Denver area do not have seasonal rates (as you'll find in many other parts of Colorado), hotels that cater to business travelers, such as the **Brown Palace** and the **Warwick** (see below), often offer substantial weekend discounts, sometimes as much as 50% off the regular rates. Rates listed below do not include the 13.6% accommodations tax.

The lodging industry is still trying to catch up with the construction of Denver International Airport several years ago, and you'll find that many of the major chains and franchises have built or are in the process of constructing facilities near the new airport. Among those now open are **Courtyard by Marriott at DIA,** 6901 Tower Rd., Denver, CO 80249 (© **800/321-2211** or 303/371-0300), with rates of $69 to $149 for a double; **Fairfield Inn–DIA,**

Denver Accommodations

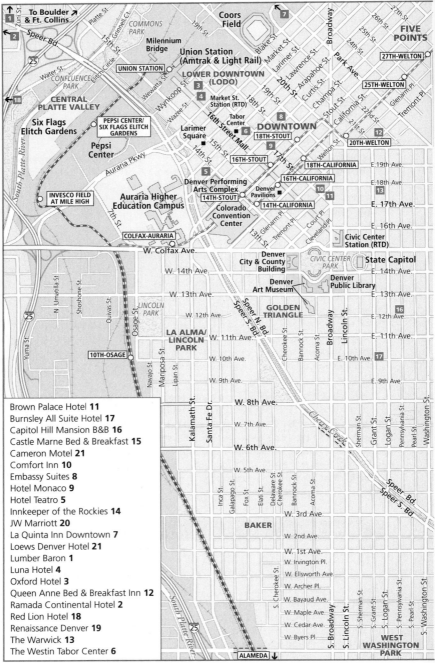

Brown Palace Hotel **11**
Burnsley All Suite Hotel **17**
Capitol Hill Mansion B&B **16**
Castle Marne Bed & Breakfast **15**
Cameron Motel **21**
Comfort Inn **10**
Embassy Suites **8**
Hotel Monaco **9**
Hotel Teatro **5**
Innkeeper of the Rockies **14**
JW Marriott **20**
La Quinta Inn Downtown **7**
Loews Denver Hotel **21**
Lumber Baron **1**
Luna Hotel **4**
Oxford Hotel **3**
Queen Anne Bed & Breakfast Inn **12**
Ramada Continental Hotel **2**
Red Lion Hotel **18**
Renaissance Denver **19**
The Warwick **13**
The Westin Tabor Center **6**

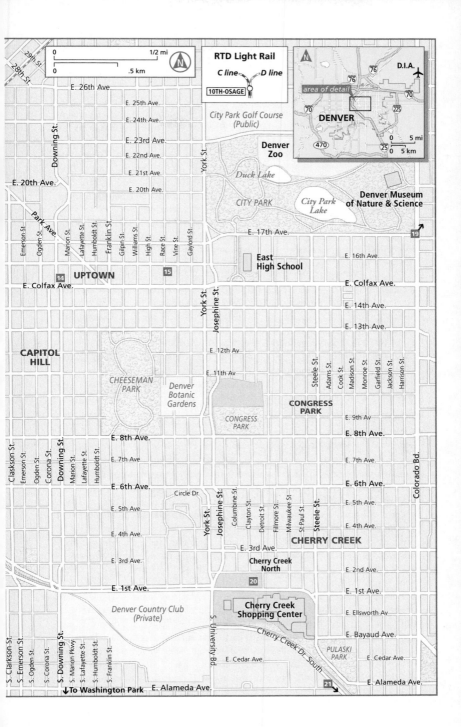

6851 Tower Rd., Denver, CO 80249 (☏ **800/228-2800** or 303/576-9640), which charges $79 to $109 for a double; and **Hampton Inn DIA,** 6290 Tower Rd., Denver CO 80249 (☏ **800/426-7866** or 303/371-0200), with a rate of $100 for a double.

Reliable chain hotels in the downtown area include: **Comfort Inn,** 401 17th St., Denver, CO 80202 (☏ **800/228-5150** or 303/296-0400), with a convenient location and rates of $149 double and $189 to $289 suite; **Embassy Suites,** 1881 Curtis St. (☏ **800/733-3366** or 303/297-8888), with suites for $129 to $159 on weekend nights and $175 to $250 during the week; **La Quinta Inn Downtown,** 3500 Park Ave. W. (at I-25 exit 213), Denver, CO 80216 (☏ **800/531-5900** or 303/458-1222), charging $90 to $100 for a double; and **Red Lion Hotel at Invesco Field,** 1975 Bryant St. (at I-25 exit 210B), Denver, CO 80204 (☏ **800/388-5381** or 303/433-8331), with rates of $79 to $129 double. A budget option is the **Ramada Continental Hotel,** 2601 Zuni St. (at I-25 exit 212B for Speer Blvd.), Denver, CO 80211 (☏ **800/2RAMADA** or 303/433-6677), which charges $79 for a double.

Outside downtown, chain lodgings include: **Hampton Inn,** 4685 Quebec St., Denver, CO 80216 (☏ **800/HAMPTON** or 303/388-8100), with a double rate of $59 to $84; and **Motel 6,** 480 Wadsworth Blvd., Lakewood, CO 80226 (☏ **800/466-8356** or 303/232-4924), charging $44 to $54 double. Among the four Best Westerns in the metro area is **Best Western Denver Stapleton,** 3535 Quebec St., Denver, CO 80207 (☏ **800/328-2268** or 303/333-7711), which has double rates from $69 to $89.

These official, or "rack," rates do not take into consideration any discounts, such as those offered to members of AAA or AARP. Be sure to ask if you qualify for a reduced rate. Because a chain hotel's national reservation service may not be able to offer discounts, your best bet may be to call the hotel directly.

DOWNTOWN
VERY EXPENSIVE
Brown Palace Hotel ✦✦✦ *Moments*   For more than 100 years, the city's finest hotel has been the place to stay for anyone who is anyone. It combines great rooms and amenities with the intangibles: interesting history, romantic atmosphere, regional personality, and impeccable service. A National Historic Landmark, the Brown Palace has operated continuously since it opened in 1892. Designed with an odd triangular shape by the renowned architect Frank Edbrooke, it was built of Colorado red granite and Arizona sandstone. The lobby's walls are paneled with Mexican onyx, and elaborate cast-iron grillwork surrounds six tiers of balconies up to the stained-glass ceiling. Every president since 1905 (except Calvin Coolidge) has visited the hotel, and Dwight Eisenhower made the Brown his home away from the White House. His former room, now known as the Eisenhower Suite, is a vision of stately elegance, with a preserved dent in the fireplace trim that is the alleged result of an errant golf swing. There are also lavish, unique suites named after Teddy Roosevelt, Ronald Reagan, and The Beatles, each recently redecorated.

Standard rooms are also lush and comfortable, either Victorian or Art Deco in style with reproduction furnishings and fixtures. Each has a desk, a duvet, and individual climate control. The staterooms on the ninth floor are especially enticing, with cordless phones, big-screen TVs, fridges, fax/printers, and safes. The water's great here: The Brown Palace has its own artesian wells!

321 17th St., Denver, CO 80202. (C) **800/321-2599** or 303/297-3111. Fax 303/312-5900. www.brownpalace. com. 241 units. $279–$339 double; $359–$1,159 suite. Weekend rates from $169 double. AE, DC, DISC, MC, V. Valet parking $22 overnight. Pets up to 20 lb. accepted. **Amenities:** 3 restaurants (all Continental; see "Where to Dine," later in this chapter); 2 lounges; exercise room; concierge; courtesy car; business center; 24-hr. room service; in-room massage (for an extra charge). *In room:* A/C, TV w/pay movies, 2-line phone (with dataport, voice mail, and complimentary high-speed Internet access), hair dryer, iron.

Hotel Monaco *(Kids)* Billing itself as "Denver's hippest high-style luxury hotel," the Hotel Monaco is a standout for the Kimpton Group chain. With eye-catching interiors inspired equally by Art Deco and French design, the hotel occupies a pair of renovated historic buildings in the heart of the central business district. This is one of the few downtown hotels that is 100% pet-friendly—the staff even delivers guests a named goldfish upon request. Rooms have a rich style, equal parts sinful red and snazzy yellow, with perks such as CD stereos, terry-cloth robes, and Starbucks coffee. With jetted tubs, wet bars, and VCRs, the generously sized suites are even more luxurious. You might bump into a celebrity here—the Monaco is a favorite of pro sports teams, rock bands, and Hollywood types, who often stay in the "music suites" named for and decorated after John Lennon, Janis Joplin, and Miles Davis. Another perk is the nightly "Altitude Adjustment Hour" in the lobby, where guests enjoy complimentary glasses of wine along with 5-minute massages from the employees of the on-site Aveda Spa. Panzano, the resident eatery, is a standout, one of the best Italian restaurants in Denver.

1717 Champa St. (at 17th St.), Denver, CO 80202. (C) **800/397-5380** or 303/296-1717. Fax 303/296-1818. www.monaco-denver.com. 189 units. $170–$205 double; $215–$970 suite; call for weekend rates. AE, DC, DISC, MC, V. Valet parking $19. Pets accepted. **Amenities:** Restaurant (Italian); lounge; exercise room; spa; concierge; 24-hr. room service; in-room massage (for an extra charge); laundry service. *In room:* A/C, TV w/pay movies, fax, dataport (high-speed Internet access), minibar, fridge, coffeemaker, hair dryer, iron, safe.

Hotel Teatro *(Finds)* Hotel Teatro is one of Denver's newest hotels. It's also the most dramatic: The Denver Center for the Performing Arts (across the street) inspired the decor, which features masks, playbills, and wardrobes from past productions of its resident theater company. The hotel caters to travelers with exquisitely furnished guest rooms that hold Indonesian marble, cherry-wood desks and fixtures, and frette linens and towels. The nine-story building is a historic landmark, constructed as the Denver Tramway Building in 1911. An $18-million restoration brought 21st-century perks, such as free high-speed Web access and a combination fax/scanner/copier/printer in each room. Each room also features Aveda amenities and a shower massager. Kevin Taylor, one of Denver's best-known chefs, runs both restaurants and the room service.

1100 14th St. (at Arapahoe St.), Denver, CO 80202. (C) **303/228-1100.** Fax 303/228-1101. www.hotel teatro.com. 111 units. $195–$325 double; $345–$1,400 suite. AE, DC, DISC, MC, V. Valet parking $24 overnight. Pets accepted. **Amenities:** 2 restaurants (American bistro, French); lounge; concierge; courtesy car; 24-hr. room service; massage; laundry service; dry cleaning. *In room:* A/C, TV w/pay movies, fax, dataport (with high-speed Internet access), minibar, fridge, coffeemaker, hair dryer, iron.

Fun Fact **On the Hoof**

If you're in town for the National Western Stock Show, make sure to visit the Brown Palace Hotel for a study in contrasts—the champion steer is traditionally corralled in the lobby during one of the event's final mornings.

The Westin Tabor Center 🟊🟊   The focal point of the 2-square-block Tabor Center shopping-and-office complex, the 19-story Westin bridges the gap between the central business district and lower downtown, and is conveniently located near Coors Field. Its contemporary design incorporates architectural elements of nearby Victorian-era structures. The elegant second-floor lobby features three-dimensional murals and modern fountains. The workout room is downtown Denver's best.

The spacious guest rooms, three-quarters of which contain king-size beds, were renovated with a contemporary flair from 2003 to 2004. Every room has Westin's trademark pillow-topped mattresses and deluxe showerheads. The Executive Club on the top three floors provides upgraded features and amenities, including an in-room wet bar, continental breakfast, afternoon cocktails, and a resident concierge.

1672 Lawrence St., Denver, CO 80202. 🕾 **800/228-3000** or 303/572-9100. Fax 303/572-7288. www.westin.com. 430 units. $219–$279 double; $400–$1,400 suite; call for weekend rates and packages. Children under 18 stay free in parent's room. AE, DC, DISC, MC, V. Valet parking $24; self-parking $12. **Amenities:** 2 restaurants (American, steakhouse); lounge; heated indoor/outdoor pool; health club (with weight room and racquetball courts); Jacuzzi; sauna; concierge; business center; shopping arcade; limited room service; massage; laundry service; dry cleaning; executive level. *In room:* A/C, TV w/pay movies, dataport, minibar, coffeemaker, hair dryer, iron, safe.

EXPENSIVE

Burnsley All Suite Hotel 🟊🟊   This small, elegant hotel offers suites with private balconies and separate living, bedroom, dining, and fully stocked kitchen areas. The units are handsomely furnished, featuring marble entrance floors and antiques. The suites are expansive (averaging 700 sq. ft.) and popular with travelers who prefer to be a bit away from the hubbub of downtown. The hotel sits on a relatively quiet one-way street a few blocks southeast of the State Capitol.

The restaurant serves breakfast, lunch, and dinner on weekdays, and breakfast and dinner on weekends. The menu features fresh salmon, tenderloin, Colorado game plate, and vegetarian dishes. The lounge is a local favorite, a swank space with live jazz on Thursdays and Fridays. The hotel is conveniently situated near the Cherry Creek shopping areas and is only 5 blocks from downtown.

1000 Grant St. (at E. 10th Ave.), Denver, CO 80203. 🕾 **800/231-3915** or 303/830-1000. Fax 303/830-7676. www.burnsley.com. 80 suites. $109–$209 double. Weekend rates available. AE, DC, MC, V. Free covered parking. **Amenities:** Restaurant (Continental); lounge; seasonal outdoor pool; access to nearby health club; business center; room service until 10pm; laundry service. *In room:* A/C, TV, dataport, kitchen, coffeemaker, hair dryer, iron.

Luna Hotel 🟊🟊   Formerly the LoDo Inn, this contemporary boutique hotel is one of the few lodging options in the lively LoDo neighborhood. It's sleek and smart, combining the personal service of a B&B with the conveniences of a full-service hotel. The guest rooms, featuring spare yet inviting decor, offer perks like CD and DVD players, unique art prints, and large armoires. Some rooms have private balconies and others have jetted tubs; the suite has a copper-topped table and a small kitchen. The property is also the first in downtown Denver to set up a Wi-Fi network, affording guests a high-speed Internet connection in their rooms, the lobby, the Manhattan-esque Flow Lounge, and the restaurants without any pesky cables. The hotel is entirely nonsmoking.

1612 Wazee St., Denver, CO 80202. 🕾 **303/572-3300.** Fax 303/623-0773. www.thelunahotel.com. 19 units. $169–$219 double; $249–$299 suite. AE, DC, DISC, MC, V. Parking $10. **Amenities:** 2 restaurants (cafe, eclectic); lounge; exercise room; concierge. *In room:* A/C, TV w/DVD player, dataport, kitchenette, coffeemaker, hair dryer, iron.

Oxford Hotel ★★ *Finds*   Designed by the architect Frank Edbrooke, this is one of Denver's few hotels that has survived from the 19th century (another being the Brown Palace, described above). The facade is simple red sandstone, but the interior boasts marble walls, stained-glass windows, frescoes, and silver chandeliers, all of which were restored between 1979 and 1983 using Edbrooke's original drawings. The hotel is listed on the National Register of Historic Places.

Antique pieces imported from England and France furnish the large rooms, which were created by combining smaller rooms during the restoration. No two units are alike (they're either Art Deco or Victorian in style), but all are equipped with one king or queen bed, individual thermostats, dressing tables, and large closets.

An Art Deco gem, the Cruise Room Bar boasts perhaps the swankest cocktail atmosphere in Denver, and McCormick's Fish House and Bar is the best seafood in town. The spa is the largest in the area.

1600 17th St. (at Wazee St.), Denver, CO 80202. ② **800/228-5838** or 303/628-5400. Fax 303/628-5413. www.theoxfordhotel.com. 80 units. $189–$229 double; $369 suite. Children under 18 stay free in parent's room. AE, DC, DISC, MC, V. Valet parking $21. **Amenities:** Restaurant (seafood); 2 lounges; exercise room; complimentary access to a nearby health club; spa (with Jacuzzi and sauna); concierge; courtesy car; salon; 24-hr. room service; massage; laundry service; dry cleaning. *In room:* A/C, TV, dataport, minibar, hair dryer, iron.

The Warwick ★★   This handsome midsize choice boasts an exterior and rooms reminiscent of hotels in Paris. In contrast, the earth-tone lobby stylishly reflects the region, with classic European design, contemporary Western furnishings, and slate-and-red-sandstone stonework. The hotel completed a $20-million renovation in 2000 that updated the property and cemented its status as one of the city's finest.

Every room features a full private balcony with a great city view, and most are equipped with a fridge and wet bar. Each has one king- or two queen-size beds, contemporary mahogany furniture, floral prints on the walls, cable TV (with pay-per-view movies), and two incoming phone lines—as well as wireless high-speed Internet access. There's also a phone in each bathroom. The standard rooms are very spacious, averaging 750 square feet each, and the 42 suites, which range from two-room parlor suites to grand luxury suites, are even more so.

1776 Grant St. (at E. 18th Ave.), Denver, CO 80203. ② **800/525-2888** or 303/861-2000. Fax 303/832-0320. www.warwickdenver.com. 220 units. Weekdays $139–$210 double, $129–$650 suite; weekends $79–$99 double, from $129 suite. Children under 18 stay free in parent's room. AE, DC, DISC, MC, V. Valet parking $16 per day; self-parking $10 per day, both underground. **Amenities:** Restaurant (contemporary); lounge; rooftop heated pool; exercise room; concierge; courtesy town car; business center; limited room service; laundry service. *In room:* A/C, cable TV w/pay movies, dataport, coffeemaker, hair dryer, iron, safe.

INEXPENSIVE

Innkeeper of the Rockies *Value*   A member of Hostelling International, this centrally located hostel is in a bustling urban area just off Colfax Avenue, within walking distance of more than 50 restaurants as well as all the major downtown attractions. Facilities include a community kitchen, lockers, laundry machines, Internet access, and a cafe. Each dorm room has no more than four beds; there are also five private bed-and-breakfast rooms in two adjacent houses. The front door is always locked and someone is on the premises all night. Under the same ownership are a nearby B&B and guesthouse, and a lodge in the Rockies.

1530 Downing St., Denver, CO 80218. ② **800/909-4776** or 303/861-7777. www.innkeeperrockies.com. 80 beds, 5 private units. $19 per person ($16 for Hostelling International members); $40 private unit. Rates include full breakfast. AE, DISC, MC, V. **Amenities:** Free pickup and delivery at bus and train stations; coin-op laundry. *In room:* No phone.

BED & BREAKFASTS

Capitol Hill Mansion Bed & Breakfast ★★   Located on Denver's "Mansion Row" just southeast of downtown and the State Capitol, this turreted B&B exemplifies Richardsonian Romanesque design with its ruby sandstone exterior and curving front porch. The mansion, built in 1891, is listed on the National Register of Historic Places and boasts the original woodwork and stained glass.

The inn is outfitted for the 21st century, with refrigerators, color TVs, and wireless high-speed Web access. Each individually decorated room is named after a Colorado wildflower; some feature two-person Jacuzzi tubs, fireplaces, and private balconies. The elegant Elk Thistle Suite on the third floor features a panoramic view of the Rockies, a claw-foot tub, and a kitchen. Honeymooners might enjoy the second-floor Shooting Star Balcony Room, which has a separate whirlpool tub and shower, and a private balcony with a city view.

Breakfasts include such items as crème brûlée French toast and pecan bread pudding. Smoking is not permitted inside the inn.

1207 Pennsylvania St., Denver, CO 80203. ℂ **800/839-9329** outside 303 and 720 area codes or 303/839-5221. Fax 303/839-8046. www.capitolhillmansion.com. 8 units. $95–$175 double; $145–$175 suite. Rates include full breakfast and evening wine and refreshments. AE, DC, DISC, MC, V. Free off-street parking. *In room:* A/C, cable TV, dataport, fridge, coffeemaker, hair dryer, iron.

Castle Marne Bed & Breakfast ★★   A National Historic Landmark, Castle Marne is an impressive stone fortress designed and built in 1889 by the renowned architect William Lang for a contemporary silver baron. It was so named because a subsequent owner's son fought in the Battle of the Marne during World War I.

The inn is furnished with antiques, fine reproductions, and family heirlooms. Several rooms have private balconies with hot tubs, and 2002 saw the addition of a second suite with an outdoor hot tub for two. Three rooms have old-fashioned bathrooms with pedestal sinks and cast-iron claw-foot tubs. A gourmet breakfast (two seatings) is served in the original formal dining room, and a proper afternoon tea is served daily in the parlor. Smoking is not permitted.

1572 Race St., Denver, CO 80206. ℂ **800/92-MARNE** or 303/331-0621 for reservations. Fax 303/331-0623. www.castlemarne.com. 9 units. $105–$170 double; $200–$255 suite. Rates include full breakfast and afternoon tea. AE, DC, DISC, MC, V. Free off-street parking. *In room:* A/C.

Lumber Baron ★★ *Finds*   After buying this turreted mansion in Denver's Highlands neighborhood on April Fool's Day 1991, Walt Keller began a 4-year, $1.5-million renovation. Built in 1890 by lumber baron John Mouat (hence the name), the 8,500-square-foot house held many surprises: a myriad of ornate wood fixtures (cherry, poplar, maple, and oak, to name a few) and a once-hidden third-story ballroom under a pyramidal dome. The rooms feature antique furnishings from around the world and unique themes: the Honeymoon Suite has a neoclassical bent, a four-poster mahogany queen bed, and a gargantuan mirror; and the Helen Keller Suite (named for Walt's distant relative) has a garden motif with historic photos and intricate Anglo-Japanese wallpapering. For those seeking entertainment, the Lumber Baron hosts 50 "murder mystery parties" annually for $37 (dinner included; two-for-one pricing for guests), comedic events with a handful of actors amongst the 50 to 100 partygoers. Candlelit dinners are available in-room for $45 to $65.

2555 W. 37th Ave., Denver, CO 80211. ℂ **303/477-8205.** Fax 303/477-0269. www.lumberbaron.com. 5 units. $145 double; $195–$235 suite. Rates include full breakfast. AE, DISC, MC, V. *In room:* A/C, hair dryer, iron.

Queen Anne Bed & Breakfast Inn ✸✸   The Queen Anne might be considered the perfect bed-and-breakfast in the perfect home. It consists of two Victorian houses: one built by the well-known architect Frank Edbrooke in 1879, and the other built in 1886. Innkeeper extraordinaire Tom King provides piped-in chamber music, fresh flowers, and fax services. Each of the 10 double rooms in the 1879 Pierce-Tabor House is decorated with period antiques. Three rooms boast original murals: All four walls of the Aspen Room are filled with (what else?) aspen trees; the third-floor Park Room overlooks a park and has a mural depicting the view that visitors would have seen in 1879. Each of the four two-room suites in the adjacent 1886 Roberts House is dedicated to a famous artist (Norman Rockwell, Frederic Remington, John Audubon, and Alexander Calder). The suites have deep soaking tubs, and the Remington suite has a hot tub. Half of the rooms have cable television.

Located in the Clements Historic District, the Queen Anne borders downtown Denver and is within easy walking distance of the major attractions. Smoking is not permitted.

2147–51 Tremont Place, Denver, CO 80205. ✆ **800/432-4667** or 303/296-6666. Fax 303/296-2151. www.queenannebnb.com. 14 units. $85–$165 double; $145–$175 suite. Rates include hot breakfast and Colorado wine each evening. AE, DC, DISC, MC, V. Free off-street parking. *In room:* A/C, dataport.

OUTSIDE DOWNTOWN
VERY EXPENSIVE

JW Marriott ✸✸ *Kids*   Opening in summer 2004, the high-end JW Marriott is the first hotel in the Cherry Creek neighborhood, and it was well worth the wait. Sumptuous interiors and bold primary colors make for a distinctive ambience, and the attention to detail is excellent. The little touches are what this hotel is all about: jumbo flatscreen TVs with DVD players, spectacular views, big bathrooms with granite aplenty, user-friendly thermostats, and excellent service. For shoppers, it's beyond ideal, a block from the Cherry Creek Mall and surrounded by chic retailers of all stripes. Standout amenities include Mirepoix, the sleek eatery; a huge exercise room; and an upscale shopping arcade. Conveniently, the hotel is next door to the Cherry Creek Bike Rack, where you can rent bikes and also park them for free, and very close to the Cherry Creek bike path.

150 Clayton Lane, Denver, CO 80206. ✆ **800/228-9290** or 303/316-2700. Fax 303/316-4697. www.jwmarriott denver.com. 196 units. $189–$229 double; $349–$1,099 suite; weekend rates from $159. AE, DC, DISC, MC, V. Free valet and self-parking. Pets accepted. **Amenities:** Restaurant (contemporary American; see "Where to Dine," below); lounge; exercise room; concierge; courtesy car; business center; shopping arcade; 24-hr. room service; massage; coin-op washers & dryers; dry cleaning; executive level. *In room:* A/C, TV w/pay movies and DVD player, dataport (with high-speed Internet access), minibar, coffeemaker, hair dryer, iron, safe.

EXPENSIVE

Loews Denver Hotel ✸ *Kids*   Located just east of Colorado Boulevard and south of Cherry Creek, the Loews Denver's sleek, towering exterior is black steel with a reflecting glass tower. Inside, it's bella Italia, with columns finished in imitation marble, and Renaissance-style murals and paintings that look 500 years old. The location, about a 15-minute drive from downtown, is good for those who want access to scattered attractions or the Denver Tech Center. Throughout the hotel, much use has been made of floral patterns, Italian silk wall coverings, and marble-top furnishings. All of the spacious rooms have elegant decor, along with all of the business perks any traveler could want: at least three phones, high-speed Internet access, and a fax machine. The resident eatery, The Tuscany, is also excellent.

4150 E. Mississippi Ave., Denver, CO 80246. ☎ **800/345-9172** or 303/782-9300. Fax 303/758-6542. www.loewshotels.com. 200 units. $109–$189 double; $209–$1,000 suite; weekend rates from $89. Children under 18 stay free in parent's room. AE, DC, DISC, MC, V. Free valet and self-parking. Pets accepted. **Amenities:** Restaurant (Mediterranean); lounge; exercise room; access to nearby health club; concierge; courtesy van; business center; secretarial services; 24-hr. room service; massage; laundry service; dry cleaning; business-traveler rooms. *In room:* A/C, TV w/pay movies, fax, dataport (with high-speed Internet access), minibar, coffeemaker, hair dryer, iron.

MODERATE

Renaissance Denver 🌟   About midway between downtown and Denver International Airport, the Renaissance is our pick for a comfortable but still somewhat elegant hotel that offers all the amenities we might want. Particularly impressive is the architecture—a white double pyramid 12 stories high. The 10-story atrium lobby has tropical palms and fig trees growing beneath the central skylight, fountains, lots of marble and brass, and plants draping down from the balconies. Each spacious room—among the largest you'll find in Denver—is decorated in a contemporary style and includes an easy chair and ottoman, two phones, and a private balcony. The hotel is adjacent to now-closed Stapleton Airport, and most of its patrons are businesspeople. It's also a good choice for budget-minded tourists looking for a convenient stopover between the mountains and DIA, with lower rates than comparable downtown properties.

3801 Quebec St., Denver, CO 80207. ☎ **800/HOTELS-1** or 303/399-7500. Fax 303/321-1966. www.renaissance hotels.com. 400 units. $99 double; $195–$650 suite; weekend rates from $64 double. AE, DC, DISC, MC, V. Free self-parking; valet parking $5. **Amenities:** Restaurant (American); lounge; indoor and outdoor pools; exercise room; 2 Jacuzzis; sauna; concierge; business center; 24-hr. room service; complimentary washers and dryers; dry cleaning; executive-level rooms. *In room:* A/C, cable TV w/pay movies, dataport, minibar, coffeemaker, hair dryer, iron.

INEXPENSIVE

Cameron Motel *Value*   A small mom-and-pop motel located about 10 minutes from downtown, the Cameron provides a quiet alternative to some of the more expensive chains. Built in the 1940s, the property has been completely renovated. The walls of the average-size rooms are glazed brick; remote-control cable TVs offer 60 channels. Three rooms are equipped with kitchenettes, and some also have dataports. The owners live on-site, and their pride of ownership shows.

4500 E. Evans Ave. (I-25 exit 203), Denver, CO 80222. ☎ **303/757-2100**. Fax 303/757-0974. 35 units (14 with shower only). $45–$58 double; $72 suite. AE, DISC, MC, V. Free off-street parking. Pets accepted with $5 nightly fee. *In room:* A/C, cable TV.

CAMPING

Chatfield State Park 🌟   On the south side of Denver, 1 mile south of the intersection of Colo. 121 (Wadsworth) and Colo. 470, Chatfield has a 1,550-acre reservoir with ample opportunities for boating, water-skiing, fishing, and swimming, plus around 20 miles of trails for horseback riding, mountain biking, and hiking. Facilities include hot showers, picnic areas, a dump station, boat ramps and rentals, and electric hookups. The campground is open from May to October.

11500 N. Roxborough Park Rd., Littleton, CO 80125. ☎ **303/791-7275**, or 800/678-2267 for state park reservation service. www.parks.state.co.us. 197 sites. $16–$22, plus $5–$6 day-use fee. MC, V only for advance reservations.

Chief Hosa Campground   Those seeking the amenities and easy accessibility of a commercial campground close to Denver will find a nice (but often quite busy) campground at this longstanding establishment 20 miles west of Denver. There are tent and RV sites, and most of the latter have electric and water hookups. When it opened in 1913, the south campground here was dubbed "America's First Motor-Camping Area." The campground is open year-round. The amenities include showers, grills, and a volleyball court.

27661 Genesee Dr., Golden, CO 80401. ℂ **800/244-3346** or 303/526-0242. www.campdenver.com. 87 sites. $22–$28. AE, DC, DISC, MC, V. Just off I-70 exit 253, 20 miles west of Denver.

Delux R.V. Park   The only RV campground actually in Denver city limits, this campground has shaded sites, hot showers, laundry, a dumpsite, and full hookups. It's convenient to buses (no. 31 RTD), shopping, and recreational facilities. Open year-round, the campground is 5 blocks north of I-70 exit 272, and 2 blocks south of I-76 exit 3, on the east side of Federal Boulevard.

5520 N. Federal Blvd., Denver, CO 80221. ℂ **303/433-0452**. www.deluxrvpark.com. 51 sites. $25–$31. MC, V.

4 Where to Dine

DOWNTOWN

VERY EXPENSIVE

Buckhorn Exchange ★★★ ROCKY MOUNTAIN   In the same rickety premises where it was established in 1893, this landmark restaurant displays its Colorado Liquor License No. 1 above the 140-year-old bar in the upstairs saloon. On the first level, the densely decorated dining room, dominated by a daunting menagerie of taxidermy, will alarm vegetarians, but meat lovers will not be disappointed one bit. The Buckhorn's game dishes (slow-roasted buffalo prime rib, lean and served medium rare; elk; pheasant; and quail) are the best in the city. The beefsteaks, ranging from 8-ounce tenderloins to 64-ounce table steaks for five, are also quite good. With fried alligator tail, Rocky Mountain oysters, and smoked buffalo sausage among the options, the appetizers will surely broaden one's palate. Our recommendation: rattlesnake, served in cream cheese–chipotle dip with tricolor tortilla chips. For dessert, try a slab of hot Dutch apple pie—if you have room. Lunch is lighter and more affordable, with an assortment of charbroiled meat entrees, sandwiches, and hearty homemade soups. A mile southwest of the State Capitol, the Buckhorn sits adjacent to the Osage light-rail stop, making it an easy trip from downtown.

1000 Osage St. (at W. 10th Ave.). ℂ **303/534-9505**. Reservations recommended. Main courses $8–$16 lunch, $18–$44 dinner. AE, DC, DISC, MC, V. Mon–Fri 11am–2pm; Mon–Thurs 5:30–9pm; Fri–Sat 5–10pm; Sun 5–9pm. Bar open all day.

Palace Arms ★★★ CONTINENTAL/REGIONAL   Despite the dramatic Napoleonic decor in this Brown Palace Hotel restaurant—antiques dating from 1670 include a dispatch case and a pair of dueling pistols that may have belonged to Napoleon—the Palace Arms' cuisine is a combination of traditional American, new American, and classical French. To begin, the sherry-braised rabbit loin is a special treat, or maybe you'd rather have the superb Caesar salad, prepared tableside for two. For an excellent main course, try the bison steak, horseradish-crusted veal loin, or roasted rack of Colorado lamb. There are a number of tasty "heart healthy" items on the menu, and the wine list has received *Wine Spectator*'s "Best of" award.

If you're short a coat, try the **Ship Tavern,** also in the hotel (ℂ **303/ 297-3111**), with a similar, less expensive menu. The lunch menu at the Brown's third restaurant, **Ellyngton's,** has some great gourmet sandwiches, and is also the site of the Brown's luxuriant Sunday brunch.

In the Brown Palace Hotel, 321 17th St. ℂ **303/297-3111**. Reservations recommended. Jacket and tie required at dinner. Main courses $29–$42 dinner. AE, DC, DISC, MC, V. Daily 6–10pm.

Denver Dining

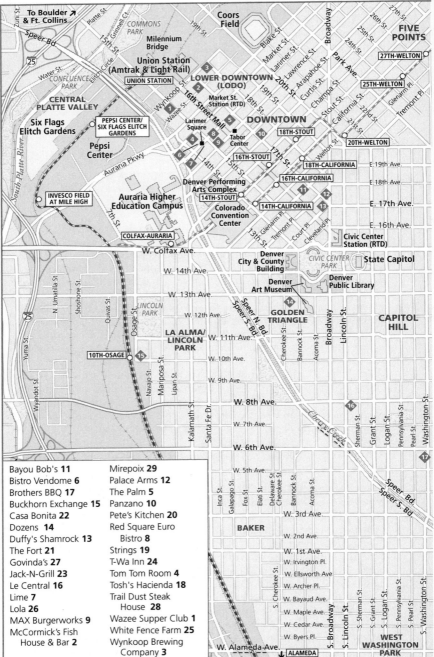

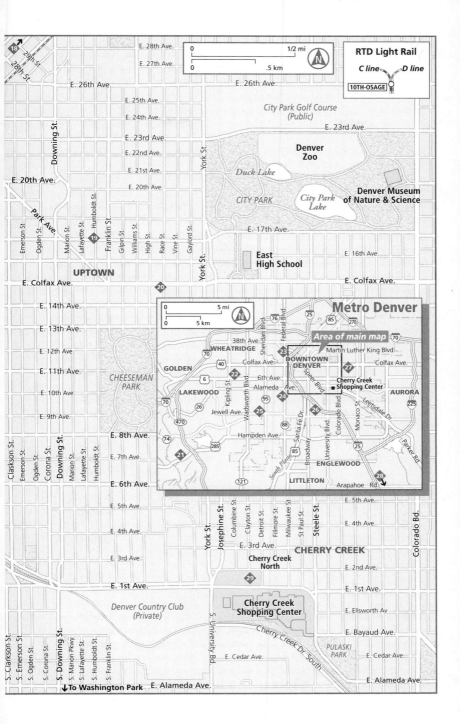

EXPENSIVE

Bistro Vendome ★★ FRENCH BISTRO   Chef-owner Eric Roeder serves up splendid interpretations of Gallic standbys (dubbing it "French soul food") at his intimate space on Larimer Square, which opened in 2003. The steak tartare, which we loved for its spicy kick and flavors of beef, onions, cumin, and sweet soy, is the perfect starting point. Bistro Vendome is also known for having some of Denver's best mussels, prepared three ways. The menu changes regularly, but you can expect excellent seafood—say, trout amandine with caviar or slow-roasted salmon with French lentils—as well as a succulent seared duck breast and some creative game dishes. The salty-sweet steak frites (aka french fries) are also beloved by locals, and the side dishes and desserts don't disappoint. The patio is one of the best in Denver.

1424-H Larimer Square. ✆ **303/825-3232.** Reservations accepted. Main courses $15–$23 dinner, $7–$14 brunch. AE, DC, DISC, MC, V. Sun and Tues–Thurs 5–10pm; Fri–Sat 5–11pm; brunch Fri–Sun 10am–2pm.

The Palm ★★ ITALIAN/STEAK/SEAFOOD   Pio Bozzi and John Ganzi opened the first Palm restaurant in New York City in 1926. It originally specialized in cuisine from their hometown of Parma, Italy, but whenever a customer requested steak, Ganzi ran to a nearby butcher shop, bought a steak, and cooked it to order. This eventually led to The Palm's having its own meat wholesale company to ensure the quality of its steaks. The current third-generation owners introduced seafood to the menu and expanded the business by opening a dozen more restaurants across the country. Most famous for its prime cuts of beef and live Nova Scotia lobsters, The Palm celebrates tradition, with some of Ganzi's original Italian dishes still popular (and cheaper) menu items. The dining room is plastered with caricatures of local celebrities; customers are seated at either booths or tables.

In the Westin at Tabor Center, 1672 Lawrence St. ✆ **303/825-7256.** www.thepalm.com. Reservations recommended. Main courses $8.50–$18 lunch, $17–$40 dinner. AE, DC, DISC, MC, V. Mon–Fri 11am–11pm; Sat 5–11pm; Sun 5–10pm.

Strings ★★ CONTEMPORARY   Modern and sleek in its decor, Strings attracts a hip crowd of loyal locals, as well as visiting celebrities who contribute to a wall of autographed photos. Popular and typically crowded, the restaurant welcomes guests in T-shirts as well as tuxedos; it's especially busy during the before- and after-theater hours. The menu focuses on fusion cuisine, creative noodle dishes, and fresh seafood, such as cashew-crusted sea bass. Another popular entree is Rocky Mountain lamb chops with a cool cucumber-mint sauce and lemon mashed potatoes. Lunch and dinner specials change weekly to match the season and the mood of the chef. Strings has an outdoor patio for summer dining and four private rooms.

1700 Humboldt St. (at E. 17th Ave.). ✆ **303/831-7310.** Reservations recommended. Main courses $11–$18 lunch, $14–$30 dinner. AE, DISC, MC, V. Mon–Thurs 11am–10pm; Fri–Sat 5–11pm; Sun 5–9pm.

Tom Tom Room ★★ JAPANESE   An über-trendy new spot in LoDo, the Tom Tom Room is one of just a handful of restaurants in the entire country that specializes in *robata:* skewers of meat, seafood, and veggies placed over charcoal, served in the center of the table to be shared. The Tom Tom Room also does some excellent sushi rolls as well as a spicy calamari that defies expectations, and offers kobe beef that you grill yourself as an appetizer. The decor and atmosphere are slick, sleek, and ultra contemporary; the bar features a video wall that resembles flowing water, beaded curtains, and a TV with constant marine wildlife videos playing. There are private rooms, canopied tables, and a sushi and *robata* bar to choose from, each distinct in personality.

1432 Market St. © **303/534-5050.** Reservations accepted. Robata items $1–$7; sushi rolls $1–$5.50. AE, DC, DISC, MC, V. Sun and Tues–Thurs 5–10pm; Fri–Sat 5pm–midnight. Lounge and sushi/*robata* bar open later.

MODERATE

Le Central ★★ *Value* FRENCH   Seven blocks south of the Colorado State Capitol, Le Central is a romantic restaurant that prides itself on creating French dishes that are both top quality and affordable. Housed in an aged urban structure with a distinctive European vibe, the restaurant changes its menus daily, but you can always expect to find a selection of fresh chicken, pork, beef, lamb, and seafood. They're available grilled, sautéed, or roasted and finished with some of the tastiest sauces this side of Provence. Bouillabaisse and paella are usually available, and every menu features a vegetarian dish. Shellfish fanatics, take note: Le Central's mussel-and-clam menu is legendary, and served with all the french fries you can eat.

112 E. 8th Ave. (at Lincoln St.). © **303/863-8094.** Reservations recommended. Main courses $7–$9 lunch, $14–$22 dinner. AE, DC, DISC, MC, V. Mon–Thurs 11:30am–2:15pm and 5:30–10pm; Fri 11:30am–2:15pm and 5–10pm; Sat 11am–2pm and 5–10pm; Sun 11am–2pm and 5–9pm.

MAX Burgerworks *Kids* BURGERS   Founders Greg Waldbaum and Gerard Rudofsky say they wanted to "take a standard food group and raise the bar," and they've accomplished that with this bright and modern burger joint. The menu lists no less than 20 varieties of burger, with veggie burgers, salmon burgers, bison burgers, Italian sausage burgers, and myriad beef options. (The beef is top-grade stuff from Niman Ranch, typically reserved for steaks.) We like the Southwestern Burger, with pepper jack, chipotle mayonnaise, and onion rings. Also of note are a nice selection of upscale salads, Big City Reds hot dogs, the shakes and malts, and the draft beers and martinis.

1512 Larimer St. at Writer Square. © **303/534-0944.** Reservations accepted. Main courses $7.50–$13. AE, MC, V. Mon–Wed 11am–9pm; Thurs–Sat 11am–10pm. Shorter winter hours.

Red Square Euro Bistro ★★ RUSSIAN/CONTEMPORARY   After the Little Russian Café closed in 2003, its all-Russian staff reunited under owner Steve Ryan and opened Red Square. They did their old place one better, with a rich red interior, contemporary Russian art, and a vodka bar stocked with infusions made in-house (ranging from raspberry to garlic) and about 100 brands from 17 countries, including Russia, Holland, Poland, Sweden, and even Mexico. Chef Maxim Ionikh's excellent entrees are not purely Russian: The steak stroganoff has a salmon counterpart, the menu has Asian and French influences, and the appetizers include pâté and goat-cheese ravioli. But there is cold borsht, a roasted Russian wild boar chop, *golubtsi* (a meat-filled cabbage roll), and, of course, the vodka. Lots and lots of vodka.

1512 Larimer St. at Writer Square. © **303/595-8600.** Main courses $7.50–$14 lunch, $13–$20 dinner. AE, DC, DISC, MC, V. Mon–Fri 11am–2pm; daily 5–10pm. Bar open later.

Tosh's Hacienda ★ *Finds* MEXICAN   In a city brimming with Mexican restaurants, the food here stands out. Open for more than half a century in the Five Points neighborhood, Tosh's has an easygoing atmosphere, and tile-and-red-brick decor. The reasonably priced combination plates feature one or two main dishes with rice and beans. You can't go wrong with enchiladas, burritos, or rellenos, and the margaritas are both tart and strong.

3090 Downing St. © **303/295-1861.** Main courses $7–$14. AE, DC, DISC, MC, V. Sun–Thurs 11am–9pm; Fri–Sat 11am–10pm.

Wynkoop Brewing Company ★ (Kids) REGIONAL AMERICAN/PUB
When the Wynkoop opened its doors in 1988 as Denver's first new brewery in
more than 50 years, it started a minirevolution: Since then, about 75 microbreweries have opened in Colorado. Wynkoop occupies a renovated warehouse across
from Union Station and close to Coors Field. The menu offers pub fare, sandwiches, soups, and salads, plus dinners of steak, Denver-cut elk medallions, and
honey-beer-mustard chicken breast. A hearty option is buffalo sirloin steak with
spicy, buffalo-wing-style shrimp. See also "Denver After Dark," in chapter 6.

1634 18th St. (at Wynkoop St.). © **303/297-2700.** Reservations recommended for large parties. Main
courses $8–$16. AE, DC, DISC, MC, V. Mon–Thurs 11am–11pm; Fri–Sat 11am–midnight; Sun 11am–10pm. Bar
open later.

INEXPENSIVE

In addition to the options listed below, there are a number of great breakfast
spots in the downtown area. **Dozens,** 236 W. 13th Ave. (© **303/572-0066**), is
a local favorite of everyone from plumbers to politicians with a beloved breakfast menu: One omelet is named after former Denver Broncos quarterback and
local legend John Elway. Established in 1942, **Pete's Kitchen,** 1962 E. Colfax
Ave. (© **303/321-3139**), is a prototypical urban diner, with checkerboard
floors, a breakfast bar, booths, plenty of local color, and killer breakfast burritos.
The menu has a nice selection of Greek, Mexican, and American standbys. Pete's
is open 24 hours on weekends, making it a favorite of the barhopping crowd.
For Denver's best barbecue, hit **Brothers BBQ,** 568 Washington St. (© **720/
570-4227**) for brisket, links, chicken, and other dishes coated with a thick,
sweet sauce that is seriously habit-forming.

Bayou Bob's CAJUN   Fishnets, street signs, and Southern-tinged bric-a-brac
cover the walls of Bayou Bob's, which serves Denverites reasonably priced Cajun
food in its bar and dining room. Gumbo, red beans and rice, fresh crawfish
étoufée, and jambalaya are all favorites, as are the huge Mardi Gras–style Hurricanes. The spicy fried alligator is a great starter, and the many combination
plates are a good bet for almost any taste. Catfish, po' boys, and hamburgers are
also available.

1635 Glenarm St. (in the Paramount Theatre Building). © **303/573-6828.** Main courses $6–$14. AE, DC,
DISC, MC, V. Mon–Sat 11am–10pm; Sun 4–9pm.

Duffy's Shamrock ★ (Finds) AMERICAN   This traditional Irish bar and
restaurant with fast, cheerful service has been thriving since the late 1950s.
Drink specialties include Irish coffees and imported Irish beers, but the food is
mostly American. Daily specials may include prime rib, fried Louisiana prawns,
low-carb plates, or grilled liver and onions. Sandwiches, on practically every
kind of bread imaginable, include corned beef, Reuben, roast beef with gravy,
and BLT.

1635 Court Place. © **303/534-4935.** Main courses $2–$6 breakfast, $5–$8 lunch, $5–$11 dinner. AE, DC,
DISC, MC, V. Mon–Fri 7am–1:30am; Sat 7:30am–1:30am; Sun 11am–1:30am.

Lime ★ MEXICAN   When you first take your seat at the Lime, your server
promptly delivers a basket of homemade chips and salsa along with halved limes
filled with tequila. This is a pretty good indication of what to expect: a festive
atmosphere, affordable and creative Mexican fare, and a serious emphasis on
tequila. The house specialties are "Scorpions": flash-fried jalapeño halves stuffed
with shrimp and cream cheese. These spicy little numbers are our favorites, but
the fare is uniformly good. The menu runs to creative updates on Mexican

standbys, including a zesty green chile, a fiery-sweet stew made of chile peppers, with shredded chicken instead of pork. In contrast to the sleek dining room, the bar is one of Denver's liveliest and loudest, and the wait for a table can seem an eternity if you're looking for an intimate evening. But the bar mixes seven types of margaritas to help while away the time; the potent Mi-T Marg is the one to watch out for—it's about 50% tequila.

1424 Larimer St. ⓒ **303/893-5463.** Main courses $7.50–$13. AE, MC, V. Mon–Tues 4–9pm; Wed–Thurs 4–10pm; Fri–Sat 4–11pm. Bar open later.

Wazee Supper Club ⓡ (Finds) PIZZA/SANDWICHES   A former plumbing-supply store in lower downtown, the Wazee is a Depression-era relic with a black-and-white tile floor and a bleached mahogany burl bar—a magnificent example of 1930s Art Deco. It's been popular for more than 20 years with artists, architects, theatergoers, entertainers, businesspeople, and just about everybody else. Pizza lovers throng the place (some believe the pizza here is the best in town, if not the world), but you'll also find an array of overstuffed sandwiches, from turkey and Swiss to Philly cheese steaks, plus buffalo burgers, and about a dozen draft beers. Don't miss the dumbwaiter used to shuttle food and drinks to the mezzanine floor—it's a converted 1937 garage-door opener.

1600 15th St. (at Wazee St.). ⓒ **303/623-9518.** Most menu items $3.50–$9; large pizzas $14 and up. AE, MC, V. Mon–Sat 11am–2am; Sun noon–midnight.

OUTSIDE DOWNTOWN
VERY EXPENSIVE

The Fort ⓡⓡⓡ (Moments) ROCKY MOUNTAIN   There are several reasons to drive 18 miles southwest (and 800 ft. up) from downtown to The Fort in Denver's foothills. First, the atmosphere: The building was hand-constructed of adobe bricks in 1962 as a full-scale reproduction of Bent's Fort, Colorado's first fur-trading post. The equally authentic interior boasts striking views of Denver's city lights. Second: owner Sam Arnold, a local celeb and master chef who has been known to open champagne bottles with a tomahawk. Third: The Fort's impeccable, gracious service might just be the best in town.

The fourth and best reason to go is the food. The Fort built its reputation on high-quality, low-cholesterol buffalo, of which it claims to serve the largest variety and greatest quantity of any restaurant in the world. There's steak, roast marrow, tongue, and even "bison eggs"—hard-boiled quail eggs wrapped in buffalo sausage. Our pick is the game plate, with elk chop, teriyaki-style quail, and buffalo filet, served with a salad (and extraordinary homemade dressings), rice, and vegetables. Other house specialties include Rocky Mountain oysters and elk medallions with wild-huckleberry sauce. Die-hards can get good ol' beefsteak.

19192 Colo. 8 (just north of the intersection of Colo. 8 and W. Hampden Ave./U.S. 285), Morrison. ⓒ **303/ 697-4771.** Reservations recommended. Main courses $20–$45. AE, DC, DISC, MC, V. Mon–Thurs 6–9:30pm; Fri 5:30–9:30pm; Sat 5–9:30pm; Sun 5–8:30pm. Call for special holiday hours.

Mirepoix ⓡⓡⓡ CONTEMPORARY AMERICAN   Located in the JW Marriott in Cherry Creek, Mirepoix is dark, intimate, and stunningly contemporary. The eye-catching back wall is adorned with purple neon and displays the restaurant's impressive wine racks. But the food is the real centerpiece: impeccable presentation, an obvious thirst for experimentation, and contrasting flavors that work unexpectedly well together. Locally lauded Chef Bryan Moscatello employs vegetable stocks as few other chefs can, although Mirepoix is far from vegetarian. A few examples of Moscatello's creativity: grilled beef rib-eye with sheep's milk ricotta ravioli and cauliflower poached in herb-infused cream with a sea scallop. The breakfast and lunch menus also contain quite a few quirky but wonderfully realized dishes (e.g., applewood-smoked bacon crisp and a crab-and-ham Monte Cristo sandwich). Most of the items on the menu are "small plates"; entrees are on the small side and they beg to be shared.

In JW Marriott Hotel, 150 Clayton Lane. © **303/253-3000.** Reservations recommended. Small plates $9–$15 breakfast, $7–$15 lunch, $9–$30 dinner. AE, DC, DISC, MC, V. Daily 6am–2pm and 5–10pm.

EXPENSIVE

Lola ★★ MEXICAN SEAFOOD   A new trend in Denver dining of late are upscale Mexican restaurants with hipper and pricier dishes than most of their older, simpler cousins—often too hip and too pricey to attract average burrito aficionados. Of them, we like the striking Lola, about 4 miles southeast of downtown. Start off with some guacamole, prepared fresh tableside, before moving onto a bowl of yellow-tomato gazpacho, served cold and nicely spiced. The entrees, such as albacore tuna fajitas and succulent grilled shrimp, come mainly from the sea. Sunday brunch means that the guacamole cart serves as a Bloody Mary cart. The brunch favorite is chicken-fried steak smothered in chorizo gravy, which can sweep away even the most twisted of Saturday night's cobwebs. On Saturday night, however, Lola's margaritas and caipirinhas, sweet Brazilian cocktails with entire quartered limes, are quite good at spinning them.

1469 S. Pearl St. © **720/570-8686.** Main courses $15–$23. AE, DC, MC, V. Mon–Sat 5–10pm; Sun 10am–2pm and 5–9pm.

MODERATE

Trail Dust Steak House STEAK   Country-music lovers flock to the Trail Dust, which serves up live dance music along with mesquite-grilled steaks and ribs. Steaks range from 7 to 30 ounces and come with salad, beans, and bread. Chicken, fish, pasta, and Mexican dishes are also available. The decor is made up of necktie tips and Western antiques interspersed with large photos of Hollywood western heroes. The necktie tips are the result of a Trail Dust tradition: Wear a tie and the staff will snip it off with scissors, then buy you a drink.

There's a second **Trail Dust** at the north end of Denver, at 9101 Benton St., Westminster (© **303/427-1446**), next to the Westminster Mall.

7101 S. Clinton St., Tech Center, Englewood. © **303/790-2420.** Reservations accepted. Main courses $5–$15 lunch, $10–$28 dinner. AE, DC, DISC, MC, V. Mon–Fri 11am–2pm; Sun–Thurs 11am–10pm; Fri–Sat 11am–11pm. Exit I-25 south at Dry Creek Rd., drive 1 block east, and turn left onto Clinton St.

White Fence Farm ★ *Kids* AMERICAN   Locals come to this seemingly rural spot in suburban Lakewood for family-style fried-chicken dinners—a delicately fried half chicken per person, plus heaping bowls of potatoes, corn fritters, homemade gravy, coleslaw, cottage cheese, pickled beets, and bean salad. Also available are T-bone steaks, pork chops, deep-fried shrimp, roast turkey, and liver and onions. For dessert, try the fresh pies. A children's menu is available, as are a children's playground, farm animals, carriage rides, and a unique gift shop, all in a beautiful country setting a 20-minute drive from downtown Denver.

6263 W. Jewell Ave., Lakewood. © **303/935-5945.** Reservations accepted for parties of 15 or more. Complete meals $12–$21. DISC, MC, V. Tues–Sat 4:30–8:30pm; Sun 11:30am–8pm. Closed Jan.

INEXPENSIVE

Casa Bonita *Kids* MEXICAN/AMERICAN   A west Denver landmark, Casa Bonita is more of a theme park than a restaurant. A pink Spanish cathedral–type bell tower greets visitors, who discover nonstop action inside: divers plummeting into a pool below a 30-foot waterfall, puppet shows, a video arcade, "Black Bart's Cave," and strolling mariachi bands. The cafeteria-style service is quite an undertaking for a restaurant that seats 1,100! There's standard Mexican fare—enchiladas, tacos, and fajitas—along with country-fried steak and fried chicken dinners. While the food is average at best, many plates are all-you-can eat, and patrons need only raise a miniature flag to get another round of tacos. Meals include hot *sopaipillas* (deep-fried sweet dough), served with honey.

In the JCRS Shopping Center, 6715 W. Colfax Ave., Lakewood. (C) **303/232-5115.** Reservations not accepted. Main courses $7–$13; children's meals around $3. DISC, MC, V. Mon–Thurs 11am–9:30pm; Fri–Sat 11am–10pm.

Govinda's Spiritual Food *(Finds* VEGETARIAN Attached to—and operated by—a Hare Krishna temple, Govinda's is a gem of a restaurant and a godsend to vegetarians and vegans. With a different all-you-can-eat buffet every day, patrons can select from one of the city's best salad bars, great soups, fresh-baked bread, and an array of meatless main dishes, from enchiladas to casseroles to stir-fry dishes, with a good deal of Indian and Middle Eastern fare. The seasonal patio is a pleasant, breezy spot for a meal. There are free Sunday dinners in the attached temple at 6pm, if you're on an extremely tight budget.

1400 N. Cherry St. (C) **303/333-5461.** Buffet $5–$8. MC, V. Mon–Fri 11:30am–2:30pm; Mon–Sat 5–8pm.

Jack-N-Grill *(Finds* NEW MEXICAN "We are not fast food," reads a sign at Jack-N-Grill, and it's spot on: This is clearly a restaurant that takes its time, and its food is worth the wait. Named for Jack Martinez and his ever-present grill, the food reflects Jack's father's motto: *"Comida sin chile, no es comida,"* or "A meal without chile is not a meal." Not surprisingly, just about everything at Jack-N-Grill has chile in it, which are roasted by the Martinez family on-site. Both the green and red chile are top notch, as are the Mexican dishes and the fresh homemade salsa. Also popular: frito pies and *calabasitas,* bowls with squash, zucchini, corn, green, chile, and onions.

2524 N. Federal Blvd. (C) **303/964-9544.** Plates $5–$10, a la carte dishes $2–$4.50. AE, MC, V. Tues–Thurs 11am–3pm and 5–8pm; Fri 11am–3pm and 5–9pm; Sat–Sun 9am–9pm.

T-Wa Inn *(Finds* VIETNAMESE Denver's oldest Vietnamese restaurant is still the best. With simple, pleasant decor and relics from the Far East on display, it looks the part, but the food is what makes it work. Everything is excellent, but we especially like the succulent shrimp, perfect pork tenderloin, and the attention to authentic Vietnamese flavors. T-Wa also serves several spicy Thai dishes, as well as Asian beers and specialty drinks.

555 S. Federal Blvd. (2 blocks south of Alameda Ave.). (C) **303/922-2378.** Most main courses $6–$13. AE, DISC, MC, V. Sun–Thurs 11am–9:30pm; Fri–Sat 11am–10pm.

What to See & Do in Denver

Denver, an intriguing combination of modern American city and sprawling Old West town, offers a wide variety of attractions, activities, and events. You'll discover art, history, sports, recreation, shopping, and, of course, dining. It is quite easy to spend a week in the city and never be bored. Denver also makes a convenient base for easy day trips to Boulder, to Colorado Springs, or up into the mountains.

1 Attractions

THE TOP ATTRACTIONS

Denver Art Museum ★★ Founded in 1893, this seven-story museum is wrapped by a thin 28-sided wall faced with one million sparkling tiles. Construction on a jagged, avant-garde addition, designed by renowned architect Daniel Libeskind, began in 2003. When finished in fall 2006, the unique structure will double the size of the museum and give Denver its most distinctive building by a long shot.

The museum's collection of Western and regional works include Frederic Remington's bronze *The Cheyenne,* Charles Russell's painting *In the Enemy's Country,* plus 19th-century photography, historical pieces, and works by Georgia O'Keeffe. In 2001, Dorothy and William Harmsen, longtime Colorado residents and founders of the Jolly Rancher Candy Company, donated their prestigious Western art collection to the museum. Assembled over 40 years, the collection immediately made the museum's inventory of Western art one of the most impressive in the nation.

The American-Indian collection is also excellent, consisting of more than 17,000 pieces from 150 tribes of North America, spanning nearly 2,000 years. Other collections include architecture and design; graphics; and Asian, African, Oceanic, modern and contemporary, pre-Columbian, and Spanish Colonial art.

Overview tours are available Tuesday through Sunday at 1:30pm, plus 11am on Saturday; an in-depth tour of a different area of the museum is offered each Wednesday and Friday at noon and 1pm; and child-oriented and family programs are scheduled regularly. There's also a gift shop. Allow 2 to 3 hours.

100 W. 14th Ave. (at Civic Center Park). © 720/865-5000. www.denverartmuseum.org. Admission $6 adults, $4.50 students and seniors, free for children under 12; free for Colorado residents Sat. Tues and Thurs–Sat 10am–5pm; Wed 10am–9pm; Sun noon–5pm. Bus: 5, 7, 8, 9, or 50.

Denver Museum of Nature & Science ★★ *Kids* The largest museum of its kind in the Rocky Mountain region, the Denver Museum of Nature & Science features scores of world-renowned dioramas, an extensive gems and minerals display, a pair of Egyptian mummies, a terrific fossil collection, and other award-winning exhibitions. The museum focuses on six areas of science: anthropology, health science, geology, paleontology, space science, and zoology.

Fun Fact **Robbery at the Mint**

A daring armed robbery took place at the Denver Mint in 1922, just 1 week before Christmas, and although police were certain they knew who the culprits were, no one ever served a day in jail for the crime. The most secure building in Denver, the Mint seemed an unlikely target for a robbery. In fact, the thieves did not rob the Mint itself—they simply waited for guards to carry the money out the front door.

A Federal Reserve Bank truck was parked outside the Mint on West Colfax Avenue at about 10:30am on December 18. It was being loaded with $200,000 worth of brand-new $5 bills, to be taken to a bank about 12 blocks away, when a black Buick touring car pulled up. Two men jumped out and began firing sawed-off shotguns, killing one guard and spraying the Mint and nearby buildings, while a third robber grabbed the bags of money. Guards inside the Mint quickly pulled their guns and returned fire, but within a minute and a half the robbers were gone—$200,000 richer.

Mint guards were certain they had hit one of the thieves, and 4 weeks later the Buick turned up in a dusty Denver garage. Lying in the front seat was the frozen, bloody body of Nick Trainor, a convicted criminal who had recently been released on parole from the Nebraska State Penitentiary. Trainor had been shot several times.

Secret Service agents recovered $80,000 of the missing loot the following year in St. Paul, Minnesota, but no arrests were made, and little more was mentioned until 1934, when Denver police announced that they knew the identities of the other men involved. Still, no charges were filed. Two of the suspects were already serving life sentences for other crimes.

At the time, police said a Midwest gang had pulled off the robbery and immediately fled to the Minneapolis–St. Paul area. The robbers gave the money to a prominent Minneapolis attorney, who also was never charged.

The newest permanent exhibition, "Space Odyssey," opened in 2003. Visitors experience a carefully crafted mix of exhibits, live programming, digital multimedia, and interactive modules that engage them in contemporary stories of space exploration. The Gates Planetarium, which also reopened in 2003 after renovations, has been transformed into a state-of-the-art digital planetarium. The new facility has an advanced computer graphics and video system, unlike any planetarium in the world.

The "Prehistoric Journey" exhibit traces the history of life on earth through 3.5 billion years. Dinosaur skeletons, fossils, interactive exhibits, and dioramas of ancient ecologies make this one of the museum's most popular attractions, especially with children.

Another popular exhibit is the "Hall of Life," which focuses on the science of the human body. Using a magnetic card, visitors gather information on themselves as they move through the interactive exhibits. When finished, they receive a printout about their own physical condition.

Denver Attractions

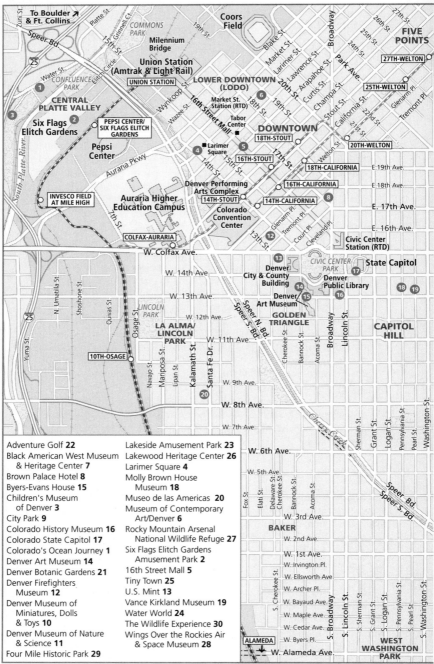

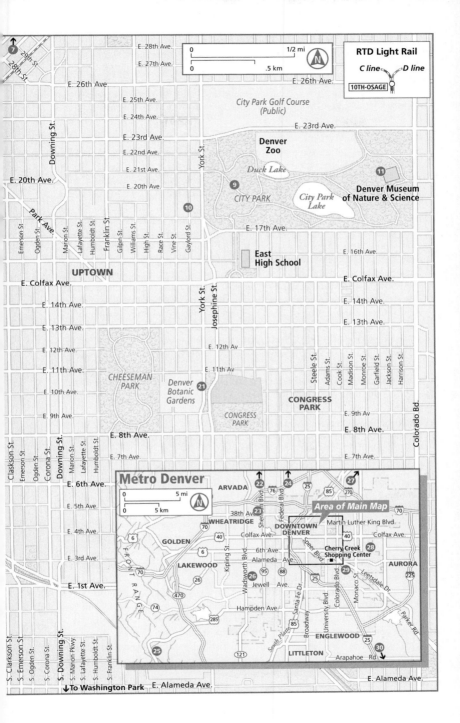

An **IMAX theater** (✆ **303/322-7009**) presents science, nature, or technology-oriented films with surround-sound on a screen that measures 4½ stories tall. Allow 2 to 4 hours.

City Park, 2001 Colorado Blvd. ✆ **800/925-2250** outside metro Denver, or 303/322-7009; 303/370-8257 for the hearing impaired. www.dmns.org. Admission to museum $9 adults, $6 children 3–18, seniors 65 and older; IMAX $8 adults, $5.50 children and seniors; planetarium additional $4 adults, additional $3 children and seniors. Daily 9am–5pm. Closed Dec 25. Bus: 24, 32, or 40.

U.S. Mint ★★   Whether we worship it or simply consider money a necessary commodity, we all have to admit a certain fascination with the coins and bills that seem to make the world turn. There are four mints in the United States, but the Denver Mint is one of only two (the other is the Philadelphia Mint) where we can actually see the process of turning lumps of metal into shiny coins.

Opened in 1863, the Mint originally melted gold dust and nuggets into bars. In 1904 the office moved to this site, and 2 years later began making gold and silver coins. Copper pennies were added a few years later. The last silver dollars (containing 90% silver) were coined in 1935. In 1970, all silver was eliminated from dollars and half dollars (today they're made of a copper-nickel alloy). The Denver Mint stamps billions of coins each year, and each has a small D on it.

Although visitors today don't get as close as they once did, a self-guided tour along the visitors' gallery provides a good look at the process, with a bird's-eye view from the mezzanine of the actual coin-minting process. A variety of displays help explain the minting process, and an adjacent **gift shop** on Cherokee Street (✆ **303/572-9500**) offers a variety of souvenirs. Allow 1 hour.

Note: Due to greatly increased security, individuals are now required to arrange tours at least 3 weeks in advance with their congressional representatives at www.senate.gov or www.house.gov, and there are quite a few requirements for entering the mint. It is uncertain that walk-in visitors will be allowed in the future.

320 W. Colfax Ave. (between Cherokee and Delaware sts.). ✆ **303/405-4757** or 303/405-4761. www.usmint.gov. Free admission. Tours Mon–Fri 8am–1pm; gift shop 8am–3:30pm. Closed 1–2 weeks in summer for audit; call for exact date. Bus: 7.

Colorado State Capitol ★★   Built to last 1,000 years, the capitol was constructed in 1886 of granite from a Colorado quarry. The dome, which rises 272 feet above the ground, was first sheathed in copper, then replaced with gold leaf after a public outcry: Copper was not a Colorado product.

Murals depicting the history of water in the state adorn the walls of the first-floor rotunda, which offers a splendid view upward to the underside of the dome. The rotunda resembles the layout of the U.S. Capitol in Washington, D.C. South of the rotunda is the governor's office, paneled in walnut and lit by a massive chandelier.

On the first floor, the west lobby hosts revolving temporary exhibits. To the right of the main lobby is the governor's reception room. The second floor has main entrances to the House, Senate, and old Supreme Court chambers. On the third floor are entrances to the public and visitor galleries for the House and Senate (open to the public during legislative session from Jan through early May).

Lincoln St. and Colfax Ave. ✆ **303/866-2604.** Free admission. 1-hr. tours offered year-round (more frequently in summer), Memorial Day to Labor Day Mon–Fri 9am–3:30pm; rest of year Mon–Fri 9:15am–2:30pm. Bus: 2, 7, 8, 12, or 15.

MORE ATTRACTIONS
HISTORIC BUILDINGS

Denver encompasses 17 recognized historic districts, including Capitol Hill, the Clements District (around 21st and Tremont sts., just east of downtown), and 9th Street Park in Auraria (off 9th St. and W. Colfax Ave.). **Historic Denver,** P.O. Box 480491, Denver, CO 80248-0491 (© **303/534-5288;** www.historic denver.org), offers walking-tour maps of many of these areas and organizes several annual events. The **Colorado Historical Society** (© **303/866-3682**) also arranges free tours of historic mansions in July and August. For additional information on some of Denver's historic areas, also see the "Neighborhoods in Brief" section in chapter 5.

Byers-Evans House   This elaborate Victorian home, built by *Rocky Mountain News* founding editor William Byers in 1883, has been restored to its appearance of 1912 to 1924, when it was owned by William Gray Evans, son of Colorado's second territorial governor. (The Evans family continued to reside here until 1981.) Guided tours describe the architecture and explain the fascinating lives of these prominent Denver families. There's also a gift shop. Allow 45 minutes.

1310 Bannock St. (in front of the Denver Art Museum). © **303/620-4933.** Admission $3 adults, $2.50 seniors, $1.50 children 6–16, free for children under 6. Tues–Sun 11am–3pm. Closed state holidays. Bus: 8.

Larimer Square ⊛   This is where Denver began. Larimer Street between 14th and 15th streets was the entire community of Denver City in 1858, with false-fronted stores, hotels, and saloons to serve gold-seekers and other pioneers. In the mid-1870s it was the main street of the city and the site of Denver's first post office, bank, theater, and streetcar line. By the 1930s, however, this part of Larimer Street had deteriorated so much that it had become a skid row of pawn-shops, gin mills, and flophouses. Plans had been made to tear these structures down, when a group of investors purchased the entire block in 1965.

The Larimer Square project became Denver's first major historic preservation effort. All 16 of the block's commercial buildings, constructed in the 1870s and 1880s, were renovated, providing space for street-level retail shops, restaurants, and nightclubs, as well as upper-story offices. A series of courtyards and open spaces was created, and in 1973 it was added to the National Register of Historic Places. Allow at least a half-hour.

Larimer Square hosts numerous special events, many tied to local sporting occasions (the National Western Stock Show, the Denver Grand Prix, and so forth). Oktoberfest (Sept) features German music, dancing, heritage booths, and authentic *bier;* June's La Piazza dell'Arte features 200 artists creating pastel masterpieces on the street.

1400 block of Larimer St. © **303/534-2367** or 303/685-8143 (events line). www.larimersquare.com. Bus: 2, 7, 12, 15, 16, 28, 31, 32, 38, or 44.

Molly Brown House Museum ⊛   Built in 1889 of Colorado rhyolite with sandstone trim, this was the residence of J. J. and Margaret (Molly) Brown from 1894 to 1932. The "unsinkable" Molly Brown became a national heroine in 1912 when the *Titanic* sank. She took charge of a group of immigrant women in a lifeboat and later raised money for their benefit.

Restored to its 1910 appearance, the Molly Brown House has a large collection of early-20th-century furnishings and art objects, many of which belonged to the Brown family. There are also temporary exhibits (recent ones detailed the lives of servants in Brown's day and trends in Victorian undergarments), and a carriage house with a museum store at the rear is open to visitors. The house can be seen on guided tours. Allow 1 hour.

1340 Pennsylvania St. ℂ 303/832-4092. www.mollybrown.org. Guided tour $6.50 adults, $5 seniors over 65, $3 children 6–12, free for children under 6. June–Aug Mon–Sat 10am–4pm, Sun noon–4pm; Sept–May Tues–Sat 10am–4pm, Sun noon–4pm. Guided tours every 30 min.; last tour of the day begins at 3:30pm. Closed major holidays. Bus: 2 on Logan St. to E. 13th, then 1 block east to Pennsylvania.

MUSEUMS & GALLERIES

Black American West Museum & Heritage Center ☆   Nearly one-third of the cowboys in the Old West were black, and this museum chronicles their little-known history, along with that of black doctors, teachers, miners, farmers, newspaper reporters, and state legislators. The extensive collection occupies the Victorian home of Dr. Justina Ford, the first black woman licensed to practice medicine in Denver. Known locally as the "Lady Doctor," Ford (1871–1951) delivered more than 7,000 babies—most of them at home because she was denied hospital privileges—and consistently served the disadvantaged and underprivileged of Denver.

The museum's founder and curator emeritus, Paul Stewart, loved to play cowboys and Indians as a boy, but his playmates always chose him to be an Indian because "there was no such thing as a black cowboy." He began researching the history of blacks in the West after meeting a black cowboy who had led cattle drives in the early 20th century. Stewart explored almost every corner of the American West, gathering artifacts, memorabilia, photographs, oral histories—anything to document the existence of black cowboys—and his collection served as the nucleus for this museum when it opened in 1971. Allow 1 hour.

3091 California St. (at 31st St.). ℂ 303/292-2566. Admission $6 adults, $5.50 seniors, $4 children 5–12, free for children under 5. June–Sept daily 10am–5pm; Oct–May Wed–Fri 10am–2pm, Sat–Sun 10am–5pm. Light rail: Stop no. 1.

Colorado History Museum ★   The Colorado Historical Society's permanent exhibits include "The Colorado Chronicle," an 1800-to-1949 timeline that uses biographical plaques and a remarkable collection of photographs, news clippings, and paraphernalia to illustrate Colorado's past. Dozens of dioramas portray episodes in state history, including an intricate re-creation of 19th-century Denver. There's also a life-size display on early transportation and industry.

The first major new permanent exhibit at the museum in some time, "Ancient Voices," is slated to open in early 2005, a $400,000 multimedia exhibit dedicated to Colorado's native tribes and their history. It will be followed by another new exhibit, "Confluence of Cultures," which will depict the pioneer era when it opens in 2006. The museum offers a series of lectures and statewide historical and archaeological tours. Its gift shop is also worth a visit. Allow 1 hour.

1300 Broadway. ℂ 303/866-3682. www.coloradohistory.org. Admission $5 adults, $4.50 seniors and students, $3.50 children 6–12, free for children under 6. Mon–Sat 10am–4:30pm; Sun noon–4:30pm. Bus: 8.

Denver Firefighters Museum *Kids*   The history of the Denver Fire Department is preserved and displayed here, in historic Fire Station No. 1. Built in 1909 for Engine Company No. 1, it was one of the largest firehouses in Denver, occupying 11,000 square feet on two floors. In its early years, it lodged men, fire engines, and horses. Motorized equipment replaced horse-drawn engines by 1923, and in 1932 the firehouse was "modernized." Concrete replaced the wooden floor, the stables and hayloft were removed, and the plumbing was improved. Visitors today see firefighting equipment dating to 1866, as well as historic photos and newspaper clippings. Allow 45 minutes.

1326 Tremont Place. (C) **303/892-1436.** www.denverfirefightersmuseum.org. Admission $4 adults, $3 seniors, $2 children under 15. Mon–Sat 10am–4pm. Closed major holidays. Located 2 blocks west of Civic Center Park on the north side of Colfax.

Denver Museum of Miniatures, Dolls & Toys *Finds*   This late-19th-century property is home to an intriguing collection of antique and collectible dolls, from rag and wood to exquisite German and French bisque. Also on display are dollhouses, from a Santa Fe adobe with hand-carved furniture to a replica of a 16-room home in Newport, Rhode Island. The museum also displays wonderful old toys, from teddy bears to model cars. Allow 45 to 60 minutes.

1880 Gaylord St. (just west of City Park). (C) **303/322-1053.** www.dmmdt.com. Admission $5 adults, $4 seniors and children 5–16, free for children under 5. Tues–Sat 10am–4pm; Sun 1–4pm.

Four Mile Historic Park *star*   Four miles southeast of downtown Denver—thus the name—the oldest log home (1859) still standing in Denver serves as the centerpiece for this 12-acre open-air museum. Everything is authentic to the period from 1859 to 1883, including the house (a former stagecoach stop), its furnishings, outbuildings, and farm equipment. There are draft horses and chickens in the barn, and crops in the garden. Weekend visitors can enjoy horse-drawn carriage rides ($2), weather permitting. Seasonal "Heritage Events" feature pioneer-era musicians and actors as well as many food and craft demonstrations. Big events include July 4th and an outdoor theater series. Allow 1 hour.

715 S. Forest St. (at Exposition Ave.). (C) **303/399-1859.** www.fourmilepark.org. Free admission; museum tours $3.50 adults, $2 seniors and children 6–15, free for children under 6. Apr–Sept Wed–Fri noon–4pm, Sat–Sun 10am–4pm; Oct–Mar Sat–Sun noon–4pm. 1 mile east of Colorado Blvd. via Cherry Creek Dr.

Lakewood's Heritage Center at Belmar Park   In Denver's early days, many wealthy residents maintained summer estates in the rural Lakewood area, and this historic village tells their story as well as that of others who lived and worked here. Your first stop should be the visitor center, for an introduction to the museum; you can begin a personalized guided or self-guided tour here. The village includes an 1870s farmhouse, a 1920s one-room school, a 1950s variety store, and the Barn Gallery. There's an exhibit on "Lakewood People and Places," antique and vintage farm machinery, self-guided history walks through the surrounding 127-acre park, changing art exhibits, and a picnic area. On-site are also an amphitheater and festival area, hosting a summer concert series and a slate of seasonal fairs and celebrations. Allow 1 to 2 hours.

801 S. Yarrow Blvd. (near Wadsworth and Ohio), Lakewood. (C) **303/987-7850.** Admission $3 adults, $2 children 4–18, free for children under 4. Mon–Fri 10am–4pm; Sat noon–4pm. Bus: 76.

Museo de las Americas *star Finds*   The only museum in the Rocky Mountains focusing exclusively on the art, culture, and history of Latinos, the Museo is worth a stop, as is a stroll through the surrounding gallery-laden neighborhood. The exhibits here change regularly, and a semipermanent exhibit tells the story of pre-Colombian Latin America, with a replica of an ornate sunstone and exhibits on Tenochtitlan, the Aztec metropolis (on the site of present-day Mexico City) destroyed by invading Spaniards in the 16th century . In 2005, a major exhibit on folk art is being displayed. Allow 1 to 2 hours.

861 Santa Fe Dr. (C) **303/571-4401.** www.museo.org. Admission $4 adults, seniors and students $3, free for children under 13. Tues–Sat 10am–5pm. Located one mile south of downtown.

Museum of Contemporary Art/Denver   Rotating avant-garde exhibitions by numerous local and national artists are the main attraction at this downtown museum. Temporary exhibits rotate every 5 months. The museum will likely moving to a new LoDo location in 2006 or 2007. Allow at least 1 hour.

1275 19th St. at Sakura Sq. (19th and Larimer sts.). *C* **303/298-7554.** www. mcartdenver.org. Admission $5 adults, $3 seniors and students, free for children under 12. Tues–Sat 11am–5:30pm; Sun noon–5pm.

Vance Kirkland Museum *Finds*   This relatively new museum covers Colorado's most illustrious artist, Vance Kirkland (1904–81), in grand fashion, while also presenting a world-class collection of decorative arts. Kirkland was a watercolor painter focused on Western landscapes when he started experimenting and combined oils and watercolors on one canvas. The traditional arts establishment dropped his modern ideas like a bad habit, but he later won accolades for creating his own artistic universe in his stunning paintings, about 60 of which are on display here. His preserved brick studio (first built in 1911) has an unusual harness he used for painting on flat canvases face down (dating from his "dot" period). The decorative arts collection includes about over 3,000 pieces ranging from teacups to armchairs, and there are also over 600 works by notable Colorado artists other than Kirkland.

1311 Pearl St. *C* **303/832-8576.** www.kirklandmuseum.org. Admission $6 adults, $5 students, teachers, and seniors. No one under 13 permitted due to the fragile nature of the collection. Children 13–17 must be accompanied by an adult. Mon–Fri 1–5pm. Guided tour Tues at 1:30pm. Closed major holidays. Located at 13th Ave. and Pearl St., about 1 mile southeast of Civic Center Park.

The Wildlife Experience   This impressive $40-million museum has three foci: natural history, nature films, and wildlife art, with nine galleries of paintings, sculptures, and photography. The museum's aim is to educate visitors about conservation and the delicate balance between people and the environment, and to do so in an aesthetically pleasing fashion. They accomplish the task, with such highlights as a National Geographic Channel screening room and an interactive Children's Gallery. Also here are a 315-seat Iwerks Extreme Screen Theater, a restaurant, and a gift shop. Allow 1 hour.

10035 S. Peoria St. *C* **720/488-3300.** www.thewildlifeexperience.org. Admission or theater tickets $6 adults, $5 seniors, $3 children; combination museum/theater tickets $10 adults, $8 seniors, $5 children. Tues–Sun 9am–5pm. Closed major holidays and non-holiday Mondays. Located 1 mile east of I-25 via Lincoln Ave.

Wings Over the Rockies Air & Space Museum *Kids*   More than 40 planes and spacecraft occupy cavernous Hangar No. 1, which became a museum when Lowry Air Force Base closed in 1995; now it's a burgeoning residential area about 6 miles southeast of downtown. On display are antique biplanes, a search-and-rescue helicopter, an F-14 Tomcat, a massive B-1A bomber—one of only two in existence—and most of the F-100 fighter series. You can also see a World War II uniform collection, a Norden bombsight, U3A Blue Canoe, and the Freedom space module, plus seasonal exhibits. On each month's second Saturday the museum hosts "Demo Cockpit Day," when visitors get to climb into the planes' cockpits. Sci-fi fans take note: A full-size X-Wing prop used in the filming of *Star Wars* is on permanent display. The store is filled with aviation- and space-oriented souvenirs. Allow 1½ hours.

7711 E. Academy Pkwy., Hangar No. 1. *C* **303/360-5360.** www.wingsmuseum.org. Admission $6 adults, $5 seniors, $4 children 6–17, free for children under 6. Mon–Sat 10am–5pm; Sun noon–5pm. Bus: 6.

PARKS, GARDENS & ZOOS

Butterfly Pavilion & Insect Center ★★ *Kids*   A walk through the butterfly conservatory introduces the visitor to a world of grace and beauty. The constant mist creates a hazy habitat to support the lush green plants that are both food and home to the inhabitants. If you stand still for a few minutes, a butterfly might land on you, but don't try to pick them up—the oils on your hands contaminate their senses, interfering with their ability to find food. One display describes the differences among butterflies, moths, and skippers, and color charts help with identification. (A butterfly guide is available for a nominal fee.)

In the insect room you'll discover that honeybees beat their wings some 200 times per second, and beetles comprise one-fifth of all living things on earth. A fascinating "touch cart" allows you to get up close to a cockroach or tarantula, assuming that you really want to.

A 31,000-square-foot expansion was completed in 2004, housing "Shrunk!"—giant robotic insects (it can be scary for little ones) and nifty interactive exhibits about the biomechanics of bugs. Also on the premises are a large gift shop and snack bar. Outside, a ½-mile nature trail meanders amidst cacti and other desert-friendly plants. Allow 2 to 3 hours.

6252 W. 104th Ave., Westminster. © 303/469-5441. www.butterflies.org. Admission $7.95 adults, $5.95 seniors, $4.95 children 4–12, free for children under 4. Memorial Day to Labor Day daily 9am–6pm; rest of year 9am–5pm. Take the Denver–Boulder Turnpike (U.S. 36) to W. 104th Ave. and go east for about a block. The pavilion is on your right.

City Park   Denver's largest urban park covers 330 acres (96 sq. blocks) on the east side of uptown. Established in 1881, it retains Victorian touches. The park encompasses two lakes (with boat rentals), athletic fields, jogging and walking trails, a free children's water feature, playgrounds, tennis courts, picnic areas, and an 18-hole municipal golf course. In summer, there are concerts. The park is also the site of the Denver Zoo and the Denver Museum of Nature and Science (including its IMAX theater), discussed elsewhere in this chapter.

E. 17th to E. 26th aves., between York St. and Colorado Blvd. Free admission to park. Separate admission to zoo, museum, golf course, and other sites. Daily 24 hrs. Bus: 24 or 32.

Colorado's Ocean Journey   A decade in the making, Denver's state-of-the-art aquarium—the largest between Chicago and Monterey, California—opened in 1999 as a nonprofit, and then nearly went bankrupt, and in 2003 was sold to the for-profit Landry's seafood restaurant chain, which plans to open a theme restaurant once permitting allows. Permanent exhibits include re-creations of two ecosystems that are on opposite sides of the planet: the Colorado River in North America and the Kampar River in Indonesia. The Colorado River path features the greenback cutthroat trout (the Colorado state fish) as well as river otters and other aquatic denizens. It culminates in a flash-flood simulation and the 187,000-gallon Sea of Cortez display, populated with exotic fish and moray eels. The Kampar River path features endangered Sumatran tigers. Allow 2 hours.

700 Water St., just east of I-25, via 23rd Ave. (exit 211). © 303/561-4450. www.oceanjourney.org. Admission $15 adults, $13 youths 13–17 and seniors, $6.95 children 4–12, free for children under 4. Memorial Day to Labor Day daily 10am–6pm; rest of year daily 10am–5pm. Closed Dec 25.

Denver Botanic Gardens ★★   Twenty-three acres of outstanding outdoor and indoor gardens display plants native to the desert, plains, mountain foothills, and alpine zones. There's also a traditional Japanese garden, herb garden, water garden, fragrance garden, and a garden inspired by the art of Monet.

Romantic Gardens feature a waterway, and the Gardens of the World holds plants from Asia, Europe, Africa, Australia, and the Tropics.

Even in the cold of winter, the dome-shaped, concrete-and-Plexiglas Tropical Conservatory houses thousands of species of tropical and subtropical plants. Huge, colorful orchids and bromeliads share space with a collection of plants used for food, fibers, dyes, building materials, and medicines. The Botanic Gardens also have a gift shop, library, and auditorium. Special events are scheduled throughout the year; offerings range from garden concerts in summer to a cornfield maze southwest of Denver in the fall. Allow 1 to 2 hours.

1005 York St. © 720/865-3500. www.botanicgardens.org. Admission May to mid-Sept $8.50 adults, $5.50 seniors, $5 children 4–15; mid-Sept to Apr $7.50 adults, $4.50 seniors, $4 children 4–15; free for children under 4 year-round. May to mid-Sept Sat–Tues 9am–8pm, Wed–Fri 9am–5pm; mid-Sept to Apr daily 9am–5pm. Bus: 2, 6, or 10.

Denver Mountain Parks ★★   Formally established in August 1913, the city's Mountain Parks system immediately began acquiring land in the mountains near Denver to be set aside for recreational use. Today it includes more than 14,000 acres, with 31 developed mountain parks and 16 unnamed wilderness areas that are wonderful places for hiking, picnicking, bird-watching, golfing, or lazing in the grass and sun.

The first and largest, **Genesee Park,** is 20 miles west of Denver off I-70 exit 254; its 2,341 acres contain the Chief Hosa Lodge and Campground (the only overnight camping available in the system), picnic areas with fireplaces, a softball field, a scenic overlook, and an elk-and-buffalo enclosure.

Among the system's other parks is **Echo Lake,** about 45 minutes from downtown Denver on Colo. 103. At 10,600 feet elevation on Mount Evans, the park has good fishing, hiking, and picnicking, plus a restaurant and curio shop. (*Note:* A fee program is being tested here; the charge is $10 per carload.) Other parks include 1,000-acre **Daniels Park** (23 miles south of Denver; take I-25 to Castle Pines Parkway, then go west to the park), which offers picnic areas, a bison enclosure, and a scenic overlook; and **Dedisse Park** (2 miles west of Evergreen on Colo. 74), which provides picnic facilities, a golf course, restaurant, clubhouse, and opportunities for ice-skating, fishing, and volleyball.

Dept. of Parks and Recreation. © 303/697-4545. www.denvergov.org. Free admission.

Denver Zoo ★★ *Kids*   More than 750 species of animals (more than 4,000 individuals) live in this spacious zoological park, home to the rare deerlike okapi as well as endangered cheetahs, Komodo dragons, and western lowland gorillas. The newest (and most ambitious) habitat here is Predator Ridge, a re-created African savannah with lions, hyenas, and other African predators, opening along with a new entrance and parking facility in 2004. The exhibit is modeled after a Kenyan preserve, complete with artificial termite mounds that disperse insects for the banded mongoose that live here.

The zoo is home to the nation's first natural gas–powered train zoo ($1). The electric Safari Shuttle ($2.50 adults, $1.50 children) tours all zoo paths from spring through fall. An especially kid-friendly attraction is the Conversation Carousel ($1), featuring wood-carved renditions of such endangered species as okapi, polar bears, Komodo dragons, and hippos. The Hungry Elephant, a cafeteria with an outdoor eating area, serves full meals, and picnicking is popular, too. Feeding times are posted near the zoo entrance so you can time your visit to see the animals at their most active. Allow from 2 hours to a whole day.

City Park, 23rd Ave. and Steele St. (main entrance between Colorado Blvd. and York St.). *C* **303/376-4800.** www.denverzoo.org. Admission summer $11 adults, $9 seniors 62 and over, $7 children 3–12 (accompanied by an adult); winter $9 adults, $7 seniors 62 and over, $5 children 3–12; free year-round children under 3. Apr–Sept daily 9am–5pm; Oct–Mar daily 10am–4pm. Bus: 24 or 32.

Rocky Mountain Arsenal National Wildlife Refuge   Once a site where the U.S. Army manufactured chemical weapons such as mustard gas and GB nerve agent, and later leased to a private enterprise to produce pesticides, the Rocky Mountain Arsenal has become an environmental success story. The 27-square-mile Superfund cleanup site, an area of open grasslands and wetlands just west of Denver International Airport, is home to more than 330 species, including deer, coyotes, prairie dogs, and birds of prey. An estimated 100 bald eagles make this one of the country's largest eagle-roosting locales during the winter.

The Rocky Mountain Arsenal Wildlife Society Bookstore is at the visitor center, and there are 10 miles of hiking trails and catch-and-release fishing. For a guided tour, it's best to call a day or two in advance. Allow at least an hour.

56th Ave. at Quebec St. *C* **303/289-0930.** Free admission. Sat–Sun 8am–4:30pm. Bus: 48.

ESPECIALLY FOR KIDS

Denver abounds in child-oriented activities, and the listings below will probably appeal to young travelers of any age. In addition, some sights listed in the previous sections may appeal to families. They include the Butterfly Pavilion and Insect Center; Colorado History Museum; Colorado's Ocean Journey; Denver Art Museum; Denver Museum of Miniatures, Dolls & Toys; Denver Museum of Nature and Science; Denver Zoo; Four Mile Historic Park; and the U.S. Mint.

Adventure Golf *(Kids*   Each of the 54 holes at this miniature golf course has a theme to challenge you, such as a haunted house, pirate battle, fairy castle, fire-breathing dragon, and fiery volcano. Or perhaps you'd prefer to visit the Lost Continent, with "deadly" piranha pools and quicksand pits. Allow 1 to 2 hours.

9650 N. Sheridan Blvd. (at 96th Ave.). *C* **303/650-7587.** 18 holes $5.95 adults, $5.75 seniors over 65, $4.95 children 4–12, free for children under 4. Mar–Nov (weather permitting) Sun–Thurs 10am–10pm, Fri–Sat 10am–11pm. Hours may be shorter in spring and fall; closed Dec–Feb. Bus: 51.

Children's Museum of Denver *(Kids*   Denver's best hands-on experience for children, this intriguing museum is both educational and just plain fun. Focusing on the zero-to-8 age bracket, the museum uses educational "playscapes" to entertain and activate young minds.

New playscapes for 2004 are "Fire Station No. 1," which teaches safety with such exhibits as a real fire engine, and "Community Market," a faux supermarket that allows kids to role-play as shoppers and clerks. There are several other playscapes with themes ranging from biology to engineering. There's also a resource center that provides parenting information to adults, and a cafe that serves sandwiches, snacks, and beverages. Allow at least 2 hours.

2121 Children's Museum Dr. *C* **303/433-7444.** www.mychildsmuseum.org. Admission $7 ages 1–59, $5 seniors 60 and over, free for children under 1. Mon–Fri 9am–4pm; Sat–Sun 10am–5pm. Take exit 211 (23rd Ave.) east off I-25; turn right on 7th St., and again on Children's Museum Dr.

Fat City *(Kids*   This 3.5-acre indoor entertainment mall, completely renovated in 2000, bills itself as "fun for everyone." It's not much of an exaggeration—inside are 40 lanes of bowling, minigolf, Laser Tag, roller-skating, and a large video arcade for the kids; for the more mature crowd, there's scads of TVs, billiards, a restaurant, and a 50-foot martini bar. Allow 1 to 4 hours.

9670 W. Coal Mine Ave. (at Kipling St.), Littleton. (© 303/972-4344. www.fatcityinfo.com. Free admission; activities $5–$7; multiactivity tickets available. Sun–Thurs 11am–midnight; Fri–Sat 11am–2am; call for activity availability. About 15 miles southwest of downtown Denver. Bus: 67 or 76.

Lakeside Amusement Park (Kids) Among the largest amusement parks in the Rocky Mountains, Lakeside has about 40 rides, including a Cyclone roller coaster, a midway with carnival and arcade games, and a rare steam-powered miniature train that circles the lake. There are also food stands and picnic facilities, plus a separate Kiddie's Playland with 15 rides. Allow 3 hours.

4601 Sheridan Blvd. (just south of I-70 exit 271). (© 303/477-1621. www.lakesideamusementpark.com. Admission $2 to Kiddie's Playland. Ride coupons 50¢ (rides require 1–4 coupons each); unlimited rides $13 Mon–Fri, $18 Sat–Sun and holidays. May Sat–Sun and holidays noon–11pm; June to Labor Day Mon–Fri 6–11pm, Sat–Sun and holidays noon–11pm. Kiddie's Playland Mon–Fri 1–10pm; Sat–Sun and holidays noon–10pm. Closed from the day after Labor Day to Apr.

Six Flags Elitch Gardens Theme Park ⭐ (Kids) A Denver tradition established in 1889, this amusement park moved to its present downtown site in 1995. The 45-plus rides include Twister II, an unbelievable 10-story roller coaster with a 90-foot drop and dark tunnel; the Flying Coaster, a one-of-a-kind "hang gliding" experience where passengers lie facedown; the Halfpipe, a snowboarding-themed thrill ride that involves 16 passengers on a 39-foot board; the 220-foot, free-fall Tower of Doom; and a fully restored 1925 carousel with 67 hand-carved horses and chariots. Patrons of all ages can enjoy the Island Kingdom Water Park while the little ones have fun on pint-sized rides in the Looney Tunes MovieTown. There are also musical revues and stunt shows, games, arcades, food, shopping, and beautiful flower gardens. Allow 3 hours.

Speer Blvd., at I-25 exit 212A. (© 303/595-4386. www.sixflags.com/elitchgardens. Gate admission with unlimited rides $37 for those taller than 4 ft., $20 for those 4 ft. and under and seniors 55–69, free for children under 4 and seniors over 69. Memorial Day to Labor Day daily 10am–10pm; call for hours Apr to late May and early Sept to Oct weekends.

Tiny Town and Railroad (Kids) (Finds) Originally built in 1915 at the site of a Denver-Leadville stagecoach stop, Tiny Town is exactly what its name implies—a one-sixth scale Western village. Nestled in a scenic mountain canyon about 20 miles southeast of downtown Denver, Tiny Town is made up of 100 colorful buildings and a steam-powered locomotive visitors can ride for an additional $1. Allow 1 hour.

6249 S. Turkey Creek Rd., Tiny Town, CO 80465. (© 303/697-6829. www.tinytownrailroad.com. Admission $3 adults, $2 children 2–12, free for children under 2. Memorial Day to Labor Day daily 10am–5pm; early to mid-May and early Sept to Oct Sat–Sun 10am–5pm. Closed Nov–Apr.

Water World ⭐ (Kids) This 64-acre complex, billed as America's largest family water park, has two oceanlike wave pools, river rapids for inner tubing, twisting water slides, a small children's play area, plus other attractions—more than 40 in all. Allow at least 3 hours.

88th Ave. and Pecos St., Federal Heights. (© 303/427-SURF. www.waterworldcolorado.com. Admission $28 adults, $24 children 4–12, free for seniors and children under 4. Memorial Day to Labor Day daily 10am–6pm; closed some school days in Aug and the rest of year. Take the Thornton exit (exit 219, 84th Ave.) off I-25 north.

WALKING TOUR   DOWNTOWN DENVER

Start: Denver Information Center, Civic Center Park.

Finish: State Capitol, Civic Center Park.

Time: 2 to 8 hours, depending on how much time you spend shopping, eating, and sightseeing.

Best Times: Any Tuesday through Friday in late spring.

Worst Times: Monday and holidays, when the museums are closed.

Start your tour of the downtown area at Civic Center Park, on West Colfax Avenue at 14th Street.

❶ Civic Center Park

This 2-square-block oasis features a Greek amphitheater, fountains, statues, flower gardens, and 30 different species of trees, 2 of which (it is said) were originally planted by Abraham Lincoln at his Illinois home.

Overlooking the park on its east side is the State Capitol. On its south side is the:

❷ Colorado History Museum

The staircaselike building houses exhibits that make the state's colorful history come to life.

Also on the south side of the park are the Denver Public Library and the:

❸ Denver Art Museum

Designed by Gio Ponti of Milan, Italy, the art museum is a 28-sided, 10-story structure that resembles a medieval fortress with a skin of more than a million tiny glass tiles. Inside are more than 35,000 works of art, including renowned Western- and American Indian-collections.

On the west side of Civic Center Park is the:

❹ City and County Building

During the Christmas season, a rainbow of colored lights decorates it in spectacular fashion.

A block farther west is the:

❺ U.S. Mint

Modeled in Italian Renaissance style, the building resembles the Palazzo Riccardi in Florence. More than 60,000 cubic feet of granite and 1,000 tons of steel went into its construction in 1904.

Cross over Colfax and go diagonally northwest up Court Place. Two blocks ahead is the:

❻ Denver Pavilions

The city's newest retail hot spot sits at the south end of the 16th Street Mall, featuring a Hard Rock Cafe, a 15-screen movie theater, and a Barnes & Noble superstore.

Three blocks up the 16th Street Mall, head southwest 2 blocks on California Street past the Colorado Convention Center and turn right on 14th Street. Walk 2 blocks to the:

❼ Denver Center for the Performing Arts

The complex covers 4 square blocks between 14th Street and Cherry Creek, Champa Street, and Arapahoe Street. The entrance is under a block-long, 80-foot-high glass archway. The center includes seven theaters, a symphony hall in the round, a voice research laboratory, and a smoking solar fountain. Free tours are offered.

Two more blocks up 14th past the arts center is:

❽ Larimer Square

This is Denver's oldest commercial district. Restored late-19th-century Victorian buildings accommodate more than 30 shops and a dozen restaurants and clubs. Colorful awnings, hanging flower baskets, and quiet open courtyards accent the square, once home to such notables as Buffalo Bill Cody and Bat Masterson. Horse-drawn carriage rides originate here for trips up the 16th Street Mall or through lower downtown.

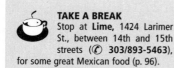

TAKE A BREAK
Stop at **Lime**, 1424 Larimer St., between 14th and 15th streets (© **303/893-5463**), for some great Mexican food (p. 96).

A walkway at the east corner of Larimer and 15th leads through:

❾ Writer Square

Quaint gas lamps, brick walkways, and outdoor cafes dot this shopping-and-dining complex.

At 16th Street, cross to the:

❿ Tabor Center

The glass-enclosed shopping complex spreads over three levels. In effect a 2-block-long greenhouse (with the Westin Hotel within), the Tabor Center was developed by the Rouse Company, the same firm that created Faneuil Hall Marketplace in Boston, South Street Seaport in New York, and Harborplace in Baltimore.

To the east, the Tabor Center is anchored by the:

⓫ D & F Tower

The city landmark was patterned after the campanile of St. Mark's Basilica in Venice, Italy, in 1910.

Here, with the State Capitol building to the southeast, begin a leisurely stroll down the:

⓬ 16th Street Mall

The $76-million pedestrian path affords the finest people-watching spot in the city. You'll see everyone from street entertainers to lunching office workers to travelers like yourself. Built of red and gray granite, it is lined with 200 red oak trees, a dozen fountains, and a lighting system straight out of *Star Wars*. You'll also see outdoor cafes, restored Victorian buildings, modern skyscrapers, and hundreds of shops—with an emphasis on sports—plus restaurants and department stores. Sleek European-built shuttle buses run through, offering free transportation up and down the mall as often as every 90 seconds.

You'll walk 7 blocks down 16th Street from the Tabor Center before reaching Tremont Place. Turn left, go 1 block farther, and across the street, on your right, you'll see the:

⓭ Brown Palace Hotel

One of the most beautiful grande-dame hotels in the United States, it was built in 1892 and features a nine-story atrium lobby topped by a Tiffany stained glass ceiling. Step into the lobby for a look, and if you're hungry . . .

TAKE A BREAK
The **Brown Palace Hotel**, 321 17th St. (© **303/297-3111**), serves lunch in several restaurants and also offers afternoon tea in its elegant lobby. Reservations are recommended for the English tea, which includes sandwiches and pastries from the Brown Palace bakery (p. 84).

Continue across Broadway on East 17th Avenue. Go 2 blocks to Sherman Street, turn right, and proceed 2 blocks south on Sherman to East Colfax Avenue. You're back overlooking Civic Center Park, but this time you're at the:

⓮ State Capitol

If you stand on the 18th step on the west side of the building, you're exactly 5,280 feet (1 mile) above sea level. Architects modeled the Colorado capitol after the U.S. Capitol in Washington, D.C., and used the world's entire known supply of rare rose onyx in its interior wainscoting. A winding 93-step staircase leads to an open-air viewing deck beneath the capitol dome; on a clear day, the view can extend from Pikes Peak near Colorado Springs to the Wyoming border.

Walking Tour: Downtown Denver

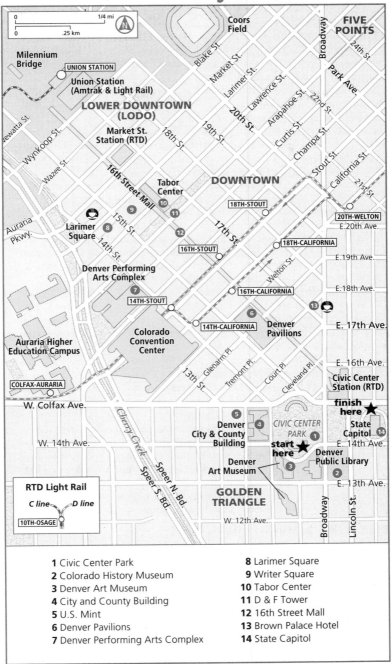

1 Civic Center Park
2 Colorado History Museum
3 Denver Art Museum
4 City and County Building
5 U.S. Mint
6 Denver Pavilions
7 Denver Performing Arts Complex

8 Larimer Square
9 Writer Square
10 Tabor Center
11 D & F Tower
12 16th Street Mall
13 Brown Palace Hotel
14 State Capitol

2 Organized Tours

Visitors who want to be personally guided to the attractions of Denver and the surrounding areas by those in the know have a variety of choices. In addition to the following, see "Packages for the Independent Traveler" and "Escorted General Interest Tours" in chapter 2.

Half- and full-day bus tours of Denver and the nearby Rockies are offered by the ubiquitous **Gray Line,** P.O. Box 17646, Denver, CO 80217 (© **800/ 348-6877** for information only; 303/289-2841 for reservations and information; www.coloradograyline.com). Fares for children 12 and under are half the adult prices listed below. Prices include entry fees but usually no food. Tours depart the Cherry Creek Shopping Center at 1st Avenue and Milwaukee Street, as well as local hotels and hostels on a reservation basis.

A 4-hour tour (no. 27), leaving at 1:30pm, takes in Denver's mountain parks: Red Rocks Park, Bergen Park, and Buffalo Bill's grave atop Lookout Mountain. It costs $30 for adults. The Denver city tour (no. 28), which departs daily at 8:30am and takes about 3½ hours, gives you a taste of both old Denver— through Larimer Square and other historic buildings—and the modern-day city. It's $25 for adults. The city tour combined with the mountain-parks tour costs $55. Gray Line also offers tours of Rocky Mountain National Park and the Colorado Springs area; call or check the website for information.

The Colorado Sightseer, 6780 W. 84th Circle, Suite 60, Arvada, CO 80003 (© **303/423-8200;** www.coloradosightseer.com), offers guided tours of Denver and environs. The Historic Denver tour includes a visit to LoDo and some of the city's earliest buildings, the State Capitol, the Molly Brown House, and Four Mile Historic Park. It lasts about 4 hours and costs $40 for adults, $30 for children 5 to 12. A Rocky Mountain National Park tour, lasting about 9½ hours, costs $75 for adults and $55 for children 5 to 12, including a box lunch. The 4½-hour Foothills Tour includes stops at Coors Brewery, the Buffalo Bill memorial, and scenic Red Rocks Park. The costs are $35 for adults, $25 for children 5 to 12, and free for children 4 and younger.

The **LoDo District** (© **303/628-5428;** www.lodo.org) leads guided walking tours of the storied area June to October. Tours depart from Union Station (17th and Wynkoop sts.) on Saturday at 10am; the cost is $7 per person. Take advantage of your cellphone with **Rocky Mountain Audio Guides** (© **303/ 898-7073;** www.rmaguides.com), which delivers 40- and 80-minute walking tours of downtown Denver. Call 24 hours before your tour to buy the tours; then you simply dial a number and walk around town, guided via satellite.

BICYCLING & MULTISPORT TOURS

A few companies operate bicycling and hiking tours out of the Denver area. In and around town, give **RMP&E Bike Tours** (© **720/641-3166;** www.mountain biketours.us) a holler. They offer 3-hour custom tours of Denver and the foothills west of town for $50 per person. They also lead annual guided trips to Telluride and Moab, Utah.

The World Outdoors (© **800/488-8483** or 303/413-0938; www.theworld outdoors.com) offers a 6-day, 5-night multisport hut-to-hut tour that begins and ends in Vail (100 miles west of Denver). The huts, described by *Mountain Bike Magazine* as "luxurious backcountry accommodations," act as recreational headquarters for guests, who have plenty of hiking, rafting, and sightseeing opportunities between mountain-biking treks.

The trips aren't cheap, running about $1,295 to $1,395 per person, but this might be the best way for the outdoors enthusiast to enjoy the Rockies west of Denver. The trip runs twice each summer, in June and August.

Another company that offers weeklong tours in the area is **Bicycle Tour of Colorado** (© **303/985-1180;** www.bicycletourcolorado.com). For about $300, a biker can join a tour involving more than 1,000 riders and 70 volunteers—including medical and bike-tech support as well as guiding services—on a 400-mile journey that hits six different cities each year, crossing the Continental Divide several times in the process. While accommodations can be prearranged at hotels, most riders elect to stay at facilities provided by the city (for example, the local high school). All meals are provided for about $300 for the week.

A good resource for bicyclists is the **Denver Bicycle Touring Club** (© **303/756-7240;** www.dbtc.org), which organizes local rides and publishes a monthly newsletter. See also "Bicycling & Skateboarding," below.

3 Outdoor Activities

Denver's proximity to the Rocky Mountains makes it possible to spend a day skiing, snowmobiling, horseback riding, hiking, river running, sailing, fishing, hunting, mountain climbing, or rock-hounding and return to the city by nightfall. Within the city limits and nearby, visitors will find more than 200 miles of jogging and bicycle paths, over 100 free tennis courts, and several dozen public golf courses.

The city has an excellent system of **mountain parks** (© **303/697-4545**), covering more than 14,000 acres, which are discussed earlier in this chapter in the "Parks, Gardens & Zoos" section.

Campsites are easy to reach from Denver, as are suitable sites for hang gliding and hot-air ballooning. Sailing is popular within the city at Sloan's Lake and in Washington Park (both Denver city parks), and the Platte River is clear for many miles of river running in rafts, kayaks, and canoes.

The Denver Metro Convention and Visitors Bureau (see "Visitor Information," in chapter 5) can supply detailed information about activities in the city. Information on nearby outdoor activities is available from: **Colorado State Parks,** 1313 Sherman St., Suite 618, Denver, CO 80203 (© **303/866-3437;** www.parks.state.co.us; the **U.S. Forest Service,** Rocky Mountain Region, 740 Sims St., Golden, CO 80401 (© **303/275-5350;** www.fs.fed.us/r2); the **U.S. Bureau of Land Management,** 2850 Youngfield St., Lakewood, CO 80215 (© **303/239-3600;** www.co.blm.gov); and the **National Park Service,** P.O. Box 25287, Denver, CO 80225 (© **303/969-2000;** www.nps.gov).

Visitors who don't bring the necessary equipment have several rental sources. **Sports Rent,** 8761 Wadsworth Blvd., Arvada (© **303/467-0200;** www.sportsrent.net), has just about everything imaginable, including bikes, in-line skates, canoes, camping equipment, skis, snowboards, snowshoes, ski racks, and clothing. The **REI** flagship store, 1416 Platte St. (© **303/756-3100**), also has a rental department stocked with tents, backpacks, stoves, mountaineering equipment, kayaks, and other gear.

BALLOONING   You can't beat a hot-air balloon ride for viewing the magnificent Rocky Mountain scenery. **Life Cycle Balloon Adventures, Ltd.** (© **800/980-9272** or 303/216-1990; www.lifecycleballoons.com), offers sunrise champagne flights daily and has over 30 years of experience. **Colorado Balloon Rides** (© **800/873-8927** or 303/978-1813; www.flywithpride.com) generally schedules daily flights year-round from all over Colorado's Front Range. **Looney Balloons** (© **303/979-9476**) offers daily 1-hour flights year-round, weather permitting. The cost at all three companies is usually $175 to $250 per person.

BICYCLING & SKATEBOARDING   The paved bicycle paths that crisscross Denver include a 12-mile scenic stretch along the bank of the South Platte River and along Cherry Creek beside Speer Boulevard. All told, the city has 85 miles of off-road trails for bikers and runners, and is *Bicycle Magazine*'s top city for bicyclists. Bike paths link the city's 205 parks, and many streets have bike lanes. In all, the city has more than 130 miles of designated bike paths and lanes. For more information, contact **Bike Denver** (© **303/322-3320;** www.bikedenver. org) or **Bicycle Colorado** (© **303/417-1544;** www.bicyclecolo.org). Bike tours are available from several companies and clubs (see "Organized Tours," above). The **Cherry Creek Bike Rack,** 171 Detroit St. (© **303/388-1630;** www.cherry creekbikerack.com), opened in 2004, offering rentals, service, and free parking for bikes.

Denver also has the largest free skateboarding park (3 acres) in the country, the **Denver Skatepark,** 19th and Little Raven sts. (© **720/913-0696**). It is quite popular and open between the hours of 6am and 11pm.

BOATING   A quiet way to view some of downtown Denver is from a punt on scenic Cherry Creek. **Venice on the Creek** (© **303/893-0750**) operates from May to August, Tuesday through Thursday by reservation, Friday and Saturday from 5 to 10pm and Sunday from 3 to 6:30pm. On weekdays it accommodates only groups of 12 or more; smaller groups are taken on weekends. Guides describe the history of the city while pointing out landmarks. Tickets are available at the kiosk at Creekfront Plaza, at the intersection of Speer Boulevard and Larimer Street. A 1-hour trip costs $15 for adults, $12 for seniors, and $7 for children. Half-hour trips are also available, for about two-thirds the cost.

Commercial rafting companies offer raft trips on the Platte River through Littleton and Englewood in Denver's south suburbs. Water level permitting, **Flexible Flyers Rafting** (© **970/247-4628**) offers 2½-hour trips; call for the current schedule. The cost is $40 for adults and $20 for children 12 and under.

You'll find powerboat marinas at **Cherry Creek State Park,** 4201 S. Parker Rd., Aurora, CO 80014 (© **303/699-3860**), 11 miles from downtown off I-225; and **Chatfield State Park,** 11500 N. Roxborough Park Rd., Littleton, CO 80125 (© **303/791-7275**), 16 miles south of downtown Denver off Colo. 470. Jet-skiing and sailboarding are also permitted at both parks. Sailboarding, canoeing, and other wakeless boating are popular at **Barr Lake State Park,** 13401 Picadilly Rd., Brighton, CO 80601 (© **303/659-6005**), 21 miles northeast of downtown on I-76.

For a different watersports experience, try riverboarding with **RipBoard** (© **866/311-2627** or 303/904-8367; www.ripboard.com), which entails going down Clear Creek face-first with flippers on your feet and a helmet on your head. It's exciting and exhausting, but can be a lot of fun in the right water. Lessons (including equipment) are $35 for 2 hours; rentals and sales are also available.

For information on other boating opportunities, contact Colorado State Parks, the National Park Service, or the U.S. Forest Service (see above).

FISHING   A couple of good bets in the metropolitan area are Chatfield State Park, with trout, bass, and panfish, and Cherry Creek State Park, which boasts trout, walleye pike, bass, and crappie (see "Boating," above). In all, there are more than 7,100 miles of streams and 2,000 reservoirs and lakes in Colorado. For information, contact Colorado State Parks, the Colorado Division of Wildlife (© **303/297-1192**), or the U.S. Fish and Wildlife Service (© **303/236-7917**). Within Denver city limits, the **Denver Department of Parks and Recreation** (© **720/913-0696**) stocks 24 lakes with fish.

A number of sporting-goods stores can provide more detailed information. The skilled and experienced staff at **The Flyfisher Ltd.,** 120 Madison St. (© **303/322-5014**), can help with equipment choices and recommendations for where to go. The Flyfisher also offers lessons, seminars, clinics, and guided wade and float trips ($395 a day for two people).

GOLF   Throughout the Front Range, it's often said that you can play golf at least 320 days a year, because the sun always seems to be shining, and even when it snows, the little snow that sticks melts quickly. There are more than 50 courses in the Denver area, including seven municipal golf courses, with nonresident greens fees up to $22 for 18 holes. City courses include: **City Park Golf Course,** East 25th Avenue and York Street (© **303/295-4420**); **Evergreen Golf Course,** 29614 Upper Bear Creek Rd., Evergreen (© **303/674-4128**); the par-3 **Harvard Gulch Golf Course,** East Iliff Avenue and South Clarkson Street (© **303/698-4078**); **Kennedy Golf Course,** 10500 E. Hampden Ave. (© **303/751-0311**); and **Overland Park Golf Course,** South Santa Fe Drive and West Jewell Avenue (© **303/698-4975**).

Other city courses are **Wellshire Golf Course,** 3333 S. Colorado Blvd. (© **303/692-5636**) and **Willis Case Golf Course,** 4999 Vrain St. near West 50th Avenue (© **303/458-4877**). Wellshire is the best overall course, but we prefer Willis Case for its spectacular mountain views. You can make same-day reservations by calling the course; otherwise, nonresident golfers must purchase a $10 card at any municipal course, then make reservations through the **automated phone system** (© **303/784-4000**). The one exception to this policy is Evergreen Golf Course, where you can call the starter for reservations 3 days in advance. For information on any course, you can also call the **Department of Parks and Recreation** (© **720/913-0696**).

For information on the state's major golf courses, contact the **Colorado Golf Resort Association,** 2110 S. Ash St., Denver, CO 80222 (© **303/680-9967;** www.coloradogolfresorts.com).

A new Frisbee golf course will open in mid-2005 at Lakewood Gulch, near Federal Boulevard and 12th Street. Call the **Department of Parks and Recreation** (© **720/913-0696**) for more information.

HIKING & BACKPACKING   The **Colorado Trail** ★★ is a hiking, horse, and mountain-biking route stretching 500 miles from Denver to Durango. The trail is also open to cross-country skiing, snowshoeing, and llama-pack hiking. For information, contact the **Colorado Trail Foundation,** 710 10th St., Room 210, Golden, CO 80401-1022 (© **303/384-3729;** www.coloradotrail.org).

For hikes in the Denver area, contact the city **Department of Parks and Recreation** (© **720/913-0696**) for information on Denver's park system. Or contact any of the following agencies: Colorado State Parks, Colorado Division of Wildlife, National Park Service, U.S. Bureau of Land Management, or U.S. Forest Service (see the introduction to this section and "Fishing," above). A good source for the many published area maps and hiking guides is **Mapsco Map and Travel Center,** 800 Lincoln St., Denver (© **800/456-8703** or 303/623-4299; www.mapsco.com).

Mount Falcon Park ⟨ offers excellent trails that range from easy to moderate in difficulty, making this a good place for families with children. There are also picnic areas, shelters, and ruins of an old castlelike home. From Denver, go west on U.S. 285 and north on Parmalee Gulch Road; the park is open daily from dawn to dusk, and admission is free. Mountain bikes and horseback riding are permitted, as are leashed dogs.

Other relatively easy trails near Denver are in **Roxborough State Park** (☎ **303/973-3959**), 10 miles south of Littleton—the 1-mile **Willow Creek Trail** and the 2.3-mile **Fountain Valley Trail** ⟨. To get to Roxborough Park, exit Colo. 470 south onto U.S. 85 and turn west onto Titan Road, then south again at Roxborough Park Road to the main entrance. Admission costs $5 per vehicle. The park is open daily from 8am to 8pm in summer, with shorter hours the rest of the year. Dogs, bikes, and horseback riding are not permitted.

HORSEBACK RIDING   Equestrians can find a mount year-round at **Stockton's Plum Creek Stables,** 7479 W. Titan Rd., Littleton (☎ **303/791-1966**), near Chatfield State Park, 15 miles south of downtown. Stockton's offers hayrides and barbecue picnics, as well as lessons ($50 an hr.). **Paint Horse Stables,** 4201 S. Parker Rd., Aurora (☎ **303/690-8235**), at Cherry Creek State Park, also rents horses, boards horses, and provides riding lessons, hayrides, and pony rides for kids.

SKIING   Several ski resorts are close to Denver. They include **Eldora Mountain Resort,** 45 miles west (☎ **303/440-8700; www.eldora.com**), which covers almost 700 acres and has 53 trails, with skiing rated 20% beginner, 50% intermediate, and 30% advanced. **Loveland Basin and Valley,** 56 miles west on I-70, exit 216 (☎ **800/736-3754** or 303/569-3203; fax 303/571-5580; www.skiloveland.com), covers 1,365 acres and has 70 trails, rated 17% beginner, 42% intermediate, and 41% advanced. **Winter Park Resort** ⟨, 73 miles west of Denver on I-70 and U.S. 40 (☎ **800/729-5813** or 970/726-5514; fax 970/726-1572; www.winterparkresort.com), boasts 2,762 skiable acres with 134 trails, rated 10% beginner, 36% intermediate, and 54% advanced.

Eldora and Winter Park offer Nordic as well as alpine terrain.

Full information on statewide skiing is available from **Colorado Ski Country USA,** 1507 Blake St., Denver, CO 80202 (☎ **303/837-0793;** www.coloradoski.com), and the **Colorado Cross Country Ski Association** (www.coloradoxc.org).

Some useful Denver telephone numbers for skiers include: **ski-area information and snow report** (☎ 303/825-7669), **weather report** (☎ 303/337-2500), and **road conditions** (☎ 303/639-1111).

SWIMMING   The Denver Department of Parks and Recreation (☎ **303/458-4795**) operates 17 outdoor swimming pools (open daily mid-June to mid-Aug) and 12 indoor pools (open Mon–Sat year-round). Nonresident fees are $3 for adults and $2 for children.

TENNIS   The Denver Department of Parks and Recreation (☎ **720/913-0696**) manages or owns close to 150 tennis courts, more than one-third of them lit for night play. Among the most popular courts are those in **City Park** (York St. and E. 17th Ave.), **Berkeley Park** (Tennyson St. and W. 17th Ave.), **Green Valley East Ranch Park** (Jebel St. and E. 45th Ave.), **Washington Park** (S. Downing St. and E. Louisiana Ave.), and **Sloan's Lake Park** (Sheridan Blvd. and W. 17th Ave.). The public courts are free. For more information, contact the **Colorado Tennis Association,** 1241 S. Parker Rd., Suite 100, Denver, CO 80231 (☎ **303/695-4116;** www.coloradotennis.com).

Travel Tip: He who finds the best hotel deal has more to spend on facials involving knobbly vegetables.

Hello, the Roaming Gnome here. I've been nabbed from the garden and taken round the world. The people who took me are so terribly clever. They find the best offerings on Travelocity. For very little cha-ching. And that means I get to be pampered and exfoliated till I'm pink as a bunny's doodah.

1-888-TRAVELOCITY / travelocity.com / America Online Keyword: Travel

GREAT NEARBY STATE PARKS

Colorado has a number of excellent state parks offering a wide range of activities and scenery. Information on the state's parks is available at **www.parks. state.co.us.**

BARR LAKE STATE PARK   About 25 miles northeast of Denver on I-76 in Brighton, this wildlife sanctuary of almost 2,800 acres comprises a prairie reservoir and surrounding wetlands and uplands. Boats with motors exceeding 10 horsepower are not allowed, but you can sail, paddle, row, and fish. A 9-mile hiking and biking trail circles the lake. A boardwalk from the nature center at the south parking lot leads to a good view of a heron rookery, and bird blinds along this trail allow wildlife observation and photography. Three picnic areas provide tables and grills; there's a commercial campground opposite the park on the west side. The entrance is at 13401 Picadilly Rd. Admission costs $5 per vehicle. Call ✆ **303/659-6005** for more information.

CASTLEWOOD CANYON STATE PARK ✿   Steep canyons, a meandering stream, a waterfall, lush vegetation, and considerable wildlife distinguish this 2,000-acre park. You can see the remains of Castlewood Canyon Dam, which was built for irrigation in 1890; it collapsed in 1933, killing two people and flooding the streets of Denver. The park, 30 miles south of Denver on Colo. 83, east of Castle Rock in Franktown, provides picnic facilities and hiking trails. The entrance is at 2989 S. State Hwy. 83; admission is $5 per vehicle. Call ✆ **303/688-5242** for more information.

CHATFIELD STATE PARK ✿   Sixteen miles south of downtown Denver on U.S. 85 in Littleton, this park occupies 5,600 acres of prairie against a backdrop of the steeply rising Rocky Mountains. Chatfield Reservoir, with a 26-mile shoreline, invites swimming, boating, fishing, and other watersports. The area also has 18 miles of paved bicycle trails, plus hiking and horseback-riding paths. In winter, there's ice fishing and cross-country skiing. The park also has a hot-air-balloon launch pad, a radio-controlled model aircraft field, and a 21-acre manmade wetlands area.

Facilities include 197 pull-through campsites, showers, laundry, and a dump station. Admission is $5 to $6 per vehicle; the camping fee is $16 to $22 daily. The entrance is 1 mile south of Colo. 470 on Wadsworth Boulevard (✆ **303/ 791-7275**).

CHERRY CREEK STATE PARK   The 880-acre Cherry Creek Reservoir, created for flood control by the construction of a dam in 1950, is the central attraction of this popular park, which draws 1.5 million visitors each year. Located at the southeast Denver city limits (off Parker Rd. and I-225) about 12 miles from downtown, the park encompasses 4,200 acres in all.

Watersports include swimming, water-skiing, boating, and fishing. There's a nature trail, dog-training area, model-airplane field with paved runways, jet-ski rental facility, rifle range, pistol range, and trap-shooting area. Twelve miles of paved bicycle paths and 12 miles of bridle trails circle the reservoir (horse rentals are available). Rangers offer guided walks by appointment, as well as evening campfire programs in an amphitheater. In winter, there's skating, ice fishing, and ice boating.

Each of the park's 102 campsites has access to showers, laundry, and a dump station. Most sites have full hookups with water and electric. Admission costs $6 to $7 per vehicle; the camping fee is $12 to $22 daily. Campgrounds are open year-round. The entrance is at 4201 S. Parker Rd. in Aurora. Call ✆ **800/678-2267** for camping reservations or ✆ 303/699-3860 for general information.

GOLDEN GATE STATE PARK ☆ One hour west of Denver, this 14,000-acre park ranges in elevation from 7,400 to 10,400 feet and offers camping, picnicking, hiking, biking, fishing, hunting, and horseback riding. A daily vehicle pass costs $5, and camping fees range from $10 to $18 in developed campgrounds, $7 for backcountry camping. There are around 160 developed campsites, with a limited number of electrical hookups. Reverend's Ridge, the park's largest campground, has coin-operated showers and laundry facilities.

To get to Golden Gate, take Colo. 93 north from Golden 1 mile to Golden Gate Canyon Road. Turn left and continue 13 miles to the park. For more information, call ✆ **303/582-3707.**

4 Spectator Sports

Tickets to many sporting events can be obtained from **Ticketville USA,** 101 W. 84th Ave., Denver, CO 80260 (✆ **303/430-1100;** www.ticketvilleusa.com), which delivers to hotels; or **Ticketmaster** (✆ **303/830-TIXS**), with several outlets in the Denver area.

AUTO RACING The **Grand Prix of Denver** (✆ **303/830-TIXS** for tickets or 720/873-5021 for information; www.denvergrandprix.com) is held over Labor Day weekend in the streets surrounding the Pepsi Center (Speer Blvd. and Chopper Circle). General-admission tickets run $20 to $40 per day for adults, less for children; grandstand seats are more expensive.

For drag racing, head to **Bandimere Speedway,** 3051 S. Rooney Rd., Morrison (✆ **303/697-6001,** or 303/697-4870 for a 24-hr. recording; www.bandimere.com), with races scheduled from April through October. There are motorcycles, pickup trucks, street cars, and sports cars, plus car shows, special events for high school students, and a junior drag-racing series for ages 8 to 17.

BASEBALL The **Colorado Rockies** (✆ **800/388-7625** or 303/762-5437; www.coloradorockies.com), who began as a National League expansion team in 1993, initially enjoyed record-breaking fan support, but attendance has fallen recently. The team plays at the attractive Coors Field, in historic lower downtown. The 50,000-seat stadium, with a redbrick exterior and on-site microbrewery, was designed in the style of baseball stadiums of old. Tickets are easy to come by, from either the box office or the gaggle of scalpers on the street.

BASKETBALL The traditionally floundering **Denver Nuggets** (✆ **303/405-1111** for ticket information; www.nuggets.com) of the National Basketball Association have skyrocketed in popularity thanks to new superstar Carmelo Anthony. The Nuggets play their home games at the handsome Pepsi Center (downtown at Speer Blvd. and Auraria Pkwy.). There are 41 home games a year between November and April, with playoffs continuing into June.

The **University of Denver** (✆ **303/871-2336** for ticket office) plays a competitive college basketball schedule from late November through March.

FOOTBALL The **Denver Broncos** (✆ **720/258-3333** for tickets; www.denverbroncos.com) of the National Football League make their home at the new Invesco Field at Mile High, after abandoning the legendary Mile High Stadium in 2001. Home games are sold out months in advance, so call early; your best bet may be to find someone hawking tickets outside the stadium entrance on game day. Pricing tickets above face value is technically illegal, but the law is rarely enforced.

The **University of Colorado Buffaloes** (✆ **303/492-8337;** www.cu-sports.com) of the Big Twelve Conference play in Boulder. Other top college football teams in the area are Colorado State University, in Fort Collins, and the Air Force Academy, in Colorado Springs.

GREYHOUND RACING Wembley Park, East 62nd Avenue and Dahlia Street, Commerce City (© **303/288-1591**), has parimutuel dog races from June to February, as well as simulcast horse racing year-round. Call for the current schedule.

HOCKEY Denver's National Hockey League team, the **Colorado Avalanche** (© **303/405-1111** for ticket information; www.coloradoavalanche.com), plays in front of sellout crowds at the Pepsi Center (Speer Blvd. and Auraria Pkwy.). The season runs from October through April. Tickets are typically expensive and hard to come by.

For a cheaper ticket (and a fun atmosphere), the **University of Denver** (© **303/871-2336** for ticket office) men's hockey team (the 2004 National Champions) plays a competitive schedule between October and mid-March.

HORSE RACING   Arapahoe Park, 26000 E. Quincy Ave., Aurora (© **303/ 690-2400**), offers horse racing each summer, with simulcast wagering the rest of the year.

LACROSSE   In sports-crazy Denver, even the pro lacrosse team, the **Colorado Mammoth** (© **303/405-1111**), sell out the 18,000-seat Pepsi Center. Tickets are inexpensive and the atmosphere is festive, to say the least.

RODEO   The **National Western Stock Show and Rodeo** (© **303/297-1166;** www.nationalwestern.com) is held the second and third weeks of January. The rodeo takes place at the Denver Coliseum, and other activities at the National Western Complex and the Event Center. With more than $500,000 available in prize money and 600,000 people in attendance, this is one of the world's richest and largest rodeos.

SOCCER   The **Colorado Rapids** (© **303/405-1111;** www.coloradorapids.com) of Major League Soccer play home games at Invesco Field at Mile High.

5 Shopping

If you're in Denver on foot, you'll find that most visitors do their shopping along the **16th Street Mall** (the mile-long pedestrian walkway between Market St. and Tremont Place), and adjacent areas, including **Larimer Square, The Shops at Tabor Center, Writer Square,** and the newest retail development downtown, **Denver Pavilions.**

Outside the downtown area there are more options, primarily the huge **Cherry Creek Shopping Center**—a shopper's dream—south of downtown. There are also numerous funky urban retail areas within city limits, as well as suburban shopping malls.

Business hours vary from store to store. Generally, stores are open 6 days a week, with many open on Sunday, too; department stores usually stay open until 9pm at least 1 evening a week. Discount stores and supermarkets are often open later than other stores, and some supermarkets are open 24 hours a day. You should always call in advance to double-check hours before heading out.

SHOPPING A TO Z
ANTIQUES
Denver's main antiques area is **Antique Row,** along **South Broadway** between Mississippi and Iowa streets, with some 400 dealers selling all sorts of fine antiques, collectibles, and junk. Wandering through the gigantic rooms, where

each dealer has his or her own little space, is great fun. Just remember that prices are often negotiable; unless you're quite knowledgeable about antiques, it wouldn't hurt to do some comparison shopping before making a major purchase.

Occupying a major part of Antique Row are the **Antique Guild** (© **303/722-3359**), a dealers' mall in the 1200 block of South Broadway, and the adjacent **Antique Market** (© **303/744-0281**). Together they have about 100 dealers selling every type of antique and collectible imaginable.

Serious antiques hunters will also want to explore the **Antique Mall of Lakewood,** 9635 W. Colfax Ave. (© **303/238-6940**), which has a 34,000-square-foot showroom where some 130 dealers display a wide variety of items from the 18th and 19th centuries, as well as more recent collectibles. A cafe serves breakfast and lunch.

ART & FINE CRAFTS

The renaissance of Denver's lower downtown (LoDo) has resulted in the creation of the **Lower Downtown Arts District,** where you can explore more than two dozen galleries. The district runs from Larimer to Wynkoop streets between 14th and 20th streets. Call © **303/628-5424** or browse **www.lodo.org** for additional information.

A mile to the southeast, the Golden Triangle neighborhood, bordered by Lincoln Street, Speer Boulevard, and Colfax Avenue, has over 50 galleries. The **Golden Triangle Arts District** (© **303/534-0771;** www.gtad.org) puts together an open gallery event the first Friday night of every month, complete with a free shuttle.

Andenken   Open weekends, this hip LoDo gallery shows the work of contemporary young artists working in every medium under the sun, usually outside the boundaries of tradition. 2110 Market St. © **303/292-3281.**

Camera Obscura *Finds*   This highly respected gallery exhibits vintage and contemporary photographs, including works by internationally renowned photographers. Closed Monday. 1309 Bannock St. © **303/623-4059.**

Native American Trading Company   Older weavings, pottery, baskets, jewelry, and other American-Indian works from the Rocky Mountain region are the focus at this fine gallery. Appropriately, it's across the street from the Denver Art Museum. 213 W. 13th Ave. © **303/534-0771.**

Pirate   Denver's oldest arts co-op, Pirate has showcased the work of cutting-edge contemporary artists of all kinds for more than 20 years. It's in a funky north Denver neighborhood with several dining options and a theater. 3659 Navajo St. © **303/458-6058.**

Pismo Contemporary Art Glass   Nationally renowned glass artists, as well as emerging stars, are represented in this gallery, located in Cherry Creek North. 235 Fillmore St. © **303/333-2879.**

Sandy Carson Gallery   Established regional artists are represented at this respected gallery in a burgeoning gallery area on Santa Fe Drive, which is known for showing contemporary works in traditional media. 760 Santa Fe Dr. © **303/573-8585.**

BOOKS

Barnes & Noble   Barnes & Noble has a large selection of all kinds of books and music, often at discounted prices. There's a particularly good travel section, where you'll find local and regional maps. The store also has a Starbucks Coffee attached. 500 16th St. (in the Denver Pavilions). © **303/825-9166.**

Mile High Comics Megastore *Kids*   One of five Mile High Comics locations in the Denver area, this is the largest comic-book store in the nation. Its 11,000 square feet are packed with comics of all descriptions, plus games, toys, posters, and other books. 9201 N. Washington St., Thornton (10 miles north of downtown Denver). © 303/457-2612.

Tattered Cover *★★*   This shop is so big it supplies maps to help you find your way through its maze of shelves. The store also provides a wide selection of newspapers and magazines, a bargain-book section, free gift wrapping, mail order, and out-of-print search services. An elevator serves all four floors. In addition, there's a full-service coffee bar, an excellent restaurant, and occasional storytelling in the children's section. Hours are Monday through Saturday from 9am to 11pm, Sunday from 10am to 6pm.

The **Tattered Cover** has a second location in Denver's LoDo at 16th and Wynkoop streets (© **303/436-1070**). 2955 E. 1st Ave. (opposite Cherry Creek Shopping Center). © **800/833-9327** or 303/322-7727. www.tatteredcover.com.

FASHION

Eddie Bauer   This is the place to come for good deals on the famous Eddie Bauer line of upscale outdoor clothing. This extra-large store features a wide variety of men's and women's fashions alongside outdoor-oriented gadgetry. 3000 E. Cherry Creek Ave. (in the Cherry Creek Mall). © 303/377-2100.

Lawrence Covell   This renowned upscale shop, established in 1967 by Lawrence and Cathy Covell, offers the finest men's and women's fashions, including designer clothing by Kiton, John Lobb, Etro, and Paul Smith. 225 Steele St. (in Cherry Creek North). © 303/320-1023.

Rockmount Ranch Wear *★★*   Founded in 1946 by Jack A. Weil, Rockmount is one of the last real Western landmarks in town. The three-generation family business—which was the first company to put a snap on a shirt!—recently turned its longtime warehouse into a retail store, and it's even got a museum of Western wear and memorabilia. The place sells dusters, shirts, scarves, and everything else anyone might need to dud up like a cowboy or cowgirl. 1626 Wazee St. © 303/629-7777.

FOOD & DRINK

King Soopers, Safeway, and **Albertson's** are the main grocery-store chains.

Applejack Liquors *Value*   This huge store, which covers some 40,000 square feet and claims to be America's largest beer, wine, and liquor supermarket, offers some of the best prices in the area. It also delivers. The store has a wide choice of single-malt scotches; an extensive wine section, which includes a number of Colorado wines; and a good selection of cigars. It's open Monday through Thursday until 10pm, and Friday and Saturday until 11pm. No credit cards. 3320 Youngfield St. (in the Applewood Shopping Center), Wheat Ridge (I-70 exit 264). © **800/879-5225** or 303/233-3331.

Argonaut Wine & Liquor Supermarket   You'll find an excellent selection of inexpensively priced wines, as well as beer and liquor, at this large store 4 blocks east of the State Capitol. It's open Monday through Thursday until 10pm and Friday and Saturday until 11:45pm. 718 E. Colfax Ave. (at Washington St.). © 303/831-7788.

Stephany's Chocolates   Colorado's largest manufacturer and wholesaler of gourmet confections is best known for its Denver Mint and Colorado Almond

Toffee. In business for more than 3 decades, it offers tours twice daily on week-days, by advance reservation only. Retail outlets are located in malls throughout the city. 6770 W. 52nd Ave., Arvada (north of I-70 via Wadsworth Blvd.). ✆ 800/888-1522 or 303/421-7229. www.stephanys-chocolates.com.

Whole Foods   This enormous store helps perpetuate Coloradans' healthy lifestyles. No food sold here contains artificial flavoring or preservatives, nor was any grown using pesticides, chemicals, or other additives. There's sushi, a salad bar, and many to-go lunch and dinner offerings as well. This Cherry Creek–area store opened in 2001; others are scattered throughout the metropolitan area. 2375 E. 1st Ave. (at University Blvd.). ✆ 720/941-4100.

GIFTS & SOUVENIRS

Colorado History Museum Store   This museum shop carries unique made-in-Colorado gifts and souvenirs, including American-Indian jewelry and sand paintings, plus an excellent selection of books on Colorado. 1300 Broadway. ✆ 303/866-4993.

Where the Buffalo Roam   Here you'll find the gamut of traditional Denver and Colorado souvenirs, from T-shirts to buttons to hats to mugs. 535 16th St. ✆ 303/260-7347.

JEWELRY

Atlantis Gems   This store features unique custom jewelry plus a large selec-tion of loose gemstones and exotic minerals. It also stocks fossils, estate jewelry, and vintage watches. 910 16th St. Mall. ✆ 303/825-3366.

Jeweler's Center at the University Building   Here you'll find 12 floors of retail and wholesale outlets in what is billed as Denver's largest concentration of jewelers, in business since 1924. 910 16th St. ✆ 303/534-6270.

John Atencio   John Atencio has received several awards for his unique jewelry designs. Located on historic Larimer Square, his store offers 14- and 18-karat gold jewelry accented with high-quality stones, plus special collections such as "Elements," which features unusual combinations of gold, sterling silver, and stones. 1440 Larimer St. (on Larimer Sq.). ✆ 303/534-4277.

MALLS & SHOPPING CENTERS

Cherry Creek Shopping Center   Saks Fifth Avenue, Neiman Marcus, Foley's, and Lord and Taylor anchor this deluxe million-square-foot mall, with more than 160 shops, restaurants, and services, including an eight-screen movie theater. Across the street is Cherry Creek North, an upscale retail neighborhood. The mall is open Monday through Friday from 10am to 9pm, Saturday from 10am to 8pm, and Sunday from 11am to 6pm. 3000 E. 1st Ave. (between University Blvd. and Steele St.). ✆ 303/388-3900.

Denver Pavilions   The Pavilions are several massive retail structures on the southern end of the 16th Street Mall. The three-level complex features Denver's only Hard Rock and Wolfgang Puck cafes, a movieplex, and Nike Town, Virgin Records, and Barnes & Noble megastores (see "Books," above). Store hours are Monday to Thursday from 10am to 9pm, Friday and Saturday from 10am to 10pm, and Sunday from 11am to 6pm; the restaurants and movie theaters are open later. 500 16th St. (between Welton and Tremont sts.). ✆ 303/260-6000.

Larimer Square   This restored quarter of old Denver (see "More Attractions," earlier in this chapter) includes numerous art galleries, boutiques, restaurants, and nightclubs. Most shops are open Monday through Thursday from 10am to 7pm, Friday and Saturday from 10am to 6pm, and Sunday from noon to 5pm. Restaurant and nightclub hours vary, and hours are slightly shorter during the winter. 1400 block of Larimer St. © 303/534-2367.

Mile High Flea Market   Just 10 minutes northeast of downtown Denver, this huge market attracts more than 1.5 million shoppers a year to its 80 paved acres. Besides close-outs, garage sales, and seasonal merchandise, it has more than a dozen places to eat and snack, plus family rides. It's open year-round on Wednesday, Saturday, and Sunday from 7am to 5pm. Admission is $2 Saturday, $3 Sunday, $1 Wednesday, and it's always free for children under 12. 7007 E. 88th Ave. (at I-76), Henderson. © 303/289-4656.

The Outlets at Castle Rock   This outlet mall between Denver and Colorado Springs, about 30 minutes south of Denver, has well over 100 stores, including Levi's, Van Heusen, Bass, Nike, Big Dog, Gap, and Toy Liquidators, plus a food court. Camp Coleman has practically every camping supply you can imagine, all manufactured by the reliable Coleman company. Wheelchair and stroller rentals are available. Open Monday through Saturday from 10am to 9pm and Sunday from 11am to 6pm. I-25 exit 184. © 303/688-4494.

Park Meadows Retail Resort   Located at the Colo. 470/I-25 interchange south of Denver, this is the largest shopping center in Colorado, and is now the heart of a mind-boggling retail area. Very posh and upscale, Park Meadows features Nordstrom, Dillard's, Foley's, and 160 specialty shops and restaurants. Stores are open Monday through Saturday from 10am to 9:30pm, Sunday from 11am to 6pm. 8401 Park Meadows Center Dr. (south of Colo. 470 on Yosemite St.), Littleton. © 303/792-2533.

SPORTING GOODS

Those in need of a bike should talk to the experts at **Campus Cycles,** 2102 S. Washington St. (© **303/698-2811**), which carries the Gary Fisher, Raleigh, and Giant brands. Sports fans looking for that Rockies cap or Broncos shirt will have no trouble finding it at the appropriately named **Sportsfan,** 1962 Blake St., across from Coors Field (© **303/295-3460;** www.sportsteams.com). There are several other locations in the Denver area, and mail orders are accepted.

For information on where to rent sporting-goods equipment, see the "Outdoor Activities" section earlier in this chapter.

Gart Sports Castle   Active travelers will be pleased to discover that Denver has the world's largest sporting-goods store—this five-story monster. With everything from footballs to golf clubs to tents, the selection is comprehensive. Extras include a driving cage for golfers, ball courts on the roof, and the annual Sniagrab (that's bargains spelled backwards), featuring rock-bottom prices on ski equipment every Labor Day weekend. There are also a number of Gart outlets in the Denver area. 1000 Broadway. © 303/861-1122. www.gartsports.com.

REI ✦✦   While the Seattle-based co-op has several stores in the metro area, its flagship store, a beautifully restored redbrick just west of downtown, is one of the country's best and biggest outdoor-oriented retailers. This is the place to go before heading for an excursion in the Rockies. The gargantuan store features a climbing wall, an outdoor bike-testing area, a kayaking area on adjacent Cherry Creek, and a "cold room" to try out outerwear and sleeping bags. 1416 Platte St. © 303/756-3100. www.rei.com.

TOYS & HOBBIES

Caboose Hobbies   Model-train buffs should plan to spend at least half a day here. Billed as the world's largest train store, it stocks electric trains, accessories, books, and so much train-related stuff that it's hard to know where to start. The knowledgeable employees seem just as happy to talk about trains as to sell them. Naturally, there are model trains of every scale winding through the store, as well as test tracks so that you can check out a locomotive before purchasing it. There are also mugs, patches, and decals from just about every railroad line that ever existed in North America. 500 S. Broadway. 𝄢 **303/777-6766**. www.caboosehobbies.com.

Wizard's Chest *(Kids)*   This store's magical design—a castle with drawbridge and moat—and legendary wizard out front are worth the trip alone, but be sure to go inside. The Wizard's Chest is paradise for kids of all ages, specializing in games, toys, and puzzles. The costume department is fully stocked with attire, wigs, masks, and professional makeup. 230 Fillmore St. in Cherry Creek North. 𝄢 **303/321-4304.**

6 Denver After Dark

The anchor of Denver's performing arts scene, an important part of this increasingly sophisticated city, is the 4-square-block **Denver Performing Arts Complex,** located downtown just a few blocks from major hotels. The complex houses nine theaters, a concert hall, and what may be the nation's first symphony hall in the round. It is home to the Colorado Symphony, Colorado Ballet, Opera Colorado, and the Denver Center for the Performing Arts (an umbrella organization for resident and touring theater companies).

Denver has some 30 theaters, more than 100 cinemas, and dozens of concert halls, nightclubs, discos, and bars. Clubs offer country-and-western music, jazz, rock, and comedy.

Current entertainment listings appear in special Friday-morning sections of the two daily newspapers, the *Denver Post* and *Rocky Mountain News. Westword,* a weekly newspaper distributed free throughout the city every Wednesday, has perhaps the best listings: It focuses on the arts, entertainment, and local politics.

You can get tickets for nearly all major entertainment and sporting events from **Ticketville USA,** 101 W. 84th Ave., Denver, CO 80260 (𝄢 **303/ 430-1100;** www.ticketvilleusa.com), which offers delivery to hotels. Also try **Ticketmaster** (𝄢 **303/830-TIXS**), which has several outlets in the Denver area.

Business hours vary. Generally, bars are open 6 or 7 days a week, and close around 2am. Clubs are open less frequently, but also close around 2am. You should always call in advance to double-check hours before heading out.

THE CLUB & MUSIC SCENE
ROCK, JAZZ & BLUES

Bluebird Theater   This historic theater, built in 1913 to show silent movies, has been restored and now offers a diverse selection of rock, alternative, and other live music, as well as films. The performers generally target teens and 20-somethings. Tickets usually run $7 to $20. 3317 E. Colfax Ave. (at Adams St.). 𝄢 303/322-2308. www.nipp.com.

The Church   Located just a few blocks southeast of downtown, this former church features three dance floors and several bars (including wine and sushi bars) scattered around a bizarre configuration—it's easy to get lost here. The semireligious decor and diverse crowd, in conjunction with the loud music, make for near sensory overload. 1160 Lincoln St. 𝄢 303/832-3528.

El Chapultepec   Denver's oldest jazz club, the "Pec" offers live jazz nightly in a noisy, friendly atmosphere. You'll often find standing-room only, not to mention a hearty helping of local color—young and old, poor and rich, in equal measure. A small burrito kitchen and poolroom adjoins the club. 1962 Market St. ℂ 303/295-9126. No cover.

Gothic Theatre   One of metro Denver's best-looking (and best-sounding) midsize venues, the Gothic is light years beyond the heavy-metal dive it was in the 1980s. Both local and national acts play the stage here. Tickets usually cost $7 to $30. 3263 S. Broadway, Englewood. ℂ 303/380-2333. www.nipp.com.

Larimer Lounge   This bar on old Larimer Street has been serving drinks since 1892 and serving loud punk rock and alternative music since 2003. The place is out of the hustle and bustle of LoDo, in an old neighborhood east of Broadway, and has seen such national acts as J Mascis and the Black Rebel Motorcycle Club take the stage The average patron is young and tattooed. 2721 Larimer St. ℂ 303/291-1007.

Mercury Cafe   It's hard to classify the Mercury as specializing in any genre of music, but there's always something exciting happening, even on poetry night. It attracts a casual, eclectic clientele. Offerings usually range from avant-garde jazz to classical violin and harp to big band to progressive rock. Also here is a healthful-oriented restaurant. 2199 California St. (at 22nd St.). ℂ 303/294-9258. www.mercurycafe.com. Cover free to $10.

COUNTRY MUSIC

Grizzly Rose ✪   Known to locals as "the Griz" or "the Rose," its 5,000-square-foot dance floor beneath a 1-acre roof draws such national acts as George Thorogood, Garth Brooks, Willie Nelson, Don Williams, LeAnn Rimes, Tanya Tucker, and Johnny Paycheck. There's live music Tuesday through Saturday; Sunday is family night. The cafe serves a full-service menu, and dance lessons are available. 5450 N. Valley Hwy., at I-25 exit 215. ℂ 303/295-1330 or 303/295-2353. www.grizzly rose.com.

Stampede   This colossal nightclub offers free country-western dance lessons on Friday and Saturday, a huge solid-oak dance floor, pool tables, a restaurant, and seven bars. It's off I-225 exit 4 (north on Parker Rd. about 2 miles to Havana St.). Closed Sunday through Tuesday. 2430 S. Havana St. (at Parker Rd.), Aurora. ℂ 303/337-6909.

THE BAR SCENE

The first permanent structure on the site of modern Denver was supposedly a saloon, and the city has built on that tradition ever since. Today, there are sports bars, dance bars, lots of brewpubs, outdoor cafe bars, English pubs, Old West saloons, city-overlook bars, Art Deco bars, gay bars, and a few bars we don't want to discuss here.

Appropriately, the newest Denver "in" spot for barhopping is also the oldest part of the city—LoDo—which has been renovated and upgraded, and now

---

Bottoms Up!

More beer is brewed in metropolitan Denver than in any other city in the United States.

---

attracts all the smart Generation-Xers and other young professionals. Its trendy nightspots are often noisy and crowded, but if you're looking for action, this is where it's at.

Glendale, an enclave surrounded by southeastern Denver where Colorado Boulevard crosses Cherry Creek, is another well-established hangout for Denver's party set. In recent years, however, as Glendale has become the Denver area's nexus for topless bars, the other bars have suffered.

Other popular "strips" are along North and South Broadway, and along East and West Colfax Avenue. For those who prefer caffeine to alcohol, there are also a number of good coffee bars throughout downtown Denver, as well as the Capitol Hill and uptown neighborhoods.

The following are among the popular bars and pubs, but there are plenty more, so be sure to check out the publications mentioned at the beginning of this section.

BJ's Carousel   Decorated with miniature and full-size carousel horses (but, alas, no carousel), this longstanding south Denver gay bar features drag entertainment on Fridays and Saturdays and free popcorn all the time. The restaurant serves dinner and Sunday brunch, and Wednesday is karaoke night. 1380 S. Broadway. ✆ 303/777-9880.

Bull & Bush Pub & Brewery   A neighborhood hangout in Cherry Creek, this re-creation of a famous London pub always has about 10 of its own award-winning beers on tap—its IPA won the silver medal at the 2003 Great American Beer Festival. On Sunday evening, there's traditional jazz by regional groups. A full brew-house menu is available. 4700 Cherry Creek Dr. S., Glendale. ✆ 303/759-0333.

Charlie Brown's Bar & Grill   Just south of downtown, Charlie Brown's is a popular piano bar, some version of which has been in existence since 1927. The atmosphere is casual, with Elvis decanters, a baby grand piano, and a large central bar that attracts a diverse array of Denverites. The grill serves breakfast, lunch, and dinner, inside and out on a great patio. 980 Grant St. (at 10th Ave.). ✆ 303/860-1655.

Churchill Bar   You'll find an excellent selection of fine cigars, single-malt Scotch, and after-dinner drinks at this refined cigar bar, which caters to older, well-to-do Establishment types. In the Brown Palace Hotel, 321 17th St. ✆ 303/297-3111.

Cruise Room Bar   Modeled after a 1930s-era bar aboard the *Queen Mary*, the Cruise Room opened in 1933 on the day Prohibition ended. Recently restored to its Art Deco best, it draws a sophisticated, fairly young crowd with a free jukebox and one of the best martinis in town. In the Oxford Hotel, 1600 17th St. (at Wazee St.). ✆ 303/825-1107.

Falling Rock Tap House   Comfy, woody, and just down the street from Coors Field, this LoDo pub has 69 beers on tap—the best selection of good beer in Denver. You'll also find darts and pool, happy hours, and occasional live music. 1919 Blake St. ✆ 303/293-8338.

Herb's Hideout   Herb's is a downtown bar with an atmosphere steeped in nostalgia. The checkerboard floors, dim lighting, lengthy bar, and intimate booths give the bar a retro aura, making Herb's a haven for the young and hip. There's live jazz, rock, and blues, as well as regular DJs spinning records. Closed Monday. 2057 Larimer St. ✆ 303/299-9555.

My Brother's Bar   A Platte Valley fixture since the Beat Generation, this is the locals' choice for big, juicy burgers, wrapped in wax paper and served with

Finds Brewery Tours

Whether or not you drink beer, it can be fun to look behind the scenes and see how beer is made. Denver's first modern microbrewery, the **Wynkoop Brewing Co.,** 1634 18th St., at Wynkoop Street (© **303/ 297-2700**), offers tours every Saturday between 1 and 5pm. Housed in the renovated 1898 J. S. Brown Mercantile Building across from Union Station, the Wynkoop is also a popular restaurant (see "Where to Dine," in chapter 5). At least 10 beers are always on tap, including a few exotic recipes—the spicy chile beer is our favorite. If you can't decide which one to try, the "taster set" provides a nice sampling: nine 4-ounce glasses of different brews. For non–beer drinkers, the Wynkoop offers some of the best root beer in town. On the second floor is a top-notch pool hall with billiards, snooker, and darts.

Since it opened in 1991, **Rock Bottom Brewery,** 1001 16th St. (© **303/534-7616**), has been one of the leading brewpubs in the area. Tours, which are given upon request, offer great views of the brewing process, plus a sampling of the product. The Rock Bottom also has eight billiard tables and a good menu, starting at $8.

Breckenridge Brewery, 471 Kalamath St. (© **303/623-BREW**), a mile south of downtown, also lets you see the brewing process. Free brewery tours are given by appointment. In addition to its award-winning ales, the brewery serves traditional pub fare. Breckenridge also has a downtown tasting room at 2220 Blake St., across from Coors Field (© **303/297-3644**).

In Cherry Creek, **Bull & Bush Pub & Brewery,** 4700 Cherry Creek Dr. S. (© **303/759-0333**), produces about 10 handcrafted ales and will give tours of its facilities upon request. Northwest of Denver, the **Cheshire Cat,** 7803 Ralston Rd., Arvada (© **303/431-9000**), is an authentic English pub in a historic building (1891) that offers tours on request.

Those who are really serious about visiting Colorado's microbreweries should consider an organized tour with **Actually Quite Nice Brew Tours** (© **303/431-1440**). Participants sample the beers at Denver- and Boulder-area microbreweries on lunch and dinner tours that last 4 to 5 hours. Full-day excursions visit breweries in Breckenridge and other mountain towns, or the Front Range cities of Colorado Springs and Fort Collins. Prices range from $50 to $75, and include beer samples and lunch or dinner. Custom tours are also available.

For a look at the other side of the coin, take a trip to nearby Golden for a look at **Coors,** the world's largest single-site brewery (see "A Side Trip to Colorado's Gold Circle Towns," below).

an array of condiments and a side helping of friendly, unpretentious vibes. 2376 15th St. © **303/455-9991.**

Samba Room   The atmosphere at the Samba Room—Cuban murals, booming Latin music, a fashionable young clientele—is right up there with Denver's flashiest nightclubs. The menu of Latin-Caribbean fusion, albeit a bit pricey and uneven, adds to the theme. 1460 Larimer St. © **720/956-1701.**

Sing Sing   A noisy, eclectic crowd dominates the scene at this LoDo hot spot, located beneath the Denver ChopHouse & Brewery. You'll often find low-priced beer specials, which encourage the hard-partying college types to sing along (loudly and badly) with the dueling pianos. A fun place, but hang on tight. Closed Sunday. 1735 19th St. ✆ **303/291-0880.**

Wynkoop Brewing Company   Many suds aficionados say this, Denver's first modern brewpub, is still the city's best. Among its most interesting offerings are India pale ale, chile beer, and Scotch ale, but you really can't go wrong with any of the selections. An added attraction is a large upstairs pool hall, which generally attracts a more party-hearty crowd than the restaurant and bar. 1634 18th St. (at Wynkoop St.). ✆ **303/297-2700.**

THE PERFORMING ARTS
CLASSICAL MUSIC & OPERA

Colorado Symphony Orchestra   This international-caliber orchestra performs more than 100 classical, pops, and family concerts each year at locations throughout the metropolitan area, mostly at the Denver Center for the Performing Arts. Tickets run $15 to $70. 821 17th St., #700. ✆ **303/893-4100.** www.denvercenter.org.

Opera Colorado   The company stages three operas (four performances each) with English supertitles each season at the Denver Performing Arts Complex. Internationally renowned singers and local favorites sing the lead roles. The typical schedule is three evening performances and one matinee each week from February through May. Tickets usually cost $30 to $120. 695 S. Colorado Blvd., #20. ✆ **303/893-4100** or 303/778-1500. www.operacolorado.org.

THEATER & COMEDY

Comedy Works   Considered one of the region's top comedy clubs for more than 20 years, this is your best bet for seeing America's hot comics at work—Dave Chappelle and Lewis Black recently took to the stage. Admission is $7 to $10 on weekdays, more on weekends and for marquee performers. Several shows a week are nonsmoking. 1226 15th St. ✆ **303/595-3637.** www.comedyworks.com.

Denver Center for the Performing Arts   An umbrella organization for resident and touring theater, youth outreach, and conservatory training, the DCPA includes the **Denver Center Theatre Company,** the largest professional resident theater company in the Rockies. With 40 artists on its payroll, the troupe performs about 10 plays in repertory from October through June, including classical and contemporary dramas, musicals, and premieres of new plays. Tickets cost roughly $30 to $50. **Denver Center Attractions** brings in over 10 touring Broadway productions annually. Tickets run $20 to $65. For both companies, many shows sell out well in advance. 14th and Curtis sts. ✆ **800/641-1222** or 303/893-4100, or 303/893-DCPA for recorded information. www.denvercenter.org.

Denver Civic Theatre   A recently restored 1921 gem, the Denver Civic Theatre is a burgeoning outlet for touring productions, typically a bit edgy. Tickets usually cost $30 to $40. 721 Santa Fe Dr. ✆ **303/309-3773.** www.denvercivic.com.

El Centro Su Teatro   A Hispanic theater and cultural center, El Centro presents bilingual productions on a regular basis. Tickets cost $10 to $15. 4725 High St. ✆ **303/296-0219.** www.suteatro.org.

Germinal Stage Denver   This 100-seat theater presents works by modern playwrights such as Brecht, Albee, and Pinter. Tickets generally cost $13 to $18. 2450 W. 44th Ave. ✆ **303/455-7108.** www2.privatei.com/~gsden.

Hunger Artists Ensemble Theatre   This award-winning theater group presents contemporary and children's works at the LIDA Project . Tickets run $16 or $17. 2180 Stout St. ℂ **303/893-5438**. www.hungerartists.org.

Rattlebrain Theater   A new—and quite hilarious—entry in Denver's comedy scene, the Rattlebrain players perform sketch and improv shows Thursday through Saturday on a stage in the landmark D & F Tower on the 16th Street Mall. Shows often sell out, so reservations are key; tickets cost $15 to $30. In the D & F Tower, 1601 Arapahoe St. ℂ **720/932-7384**. www.rattlebraintheater.com.

DANCE

Cleo Parker Robinson Dance   A highly acclaimed multicultural modern-dance ensemble and school, the Cleo Parker Robinson group performs a varied selection of programs each year, both on tour around the world and at several Denver locations. Tickets usually run $25 to $35. 119 Park Ave. W. ℂ **203/893-4100** or 303/295-1759. www.cleoparkerdance.org.

Colorado Ballet   The state's premier professional resident ballet company performs at various theatres downtown. The company presents four productions during its fall-through-spring season—a balance of classical and contemporary works that always includes *The Nutcracker* at Christmastime. Tickets range from $15 to $55. 1278 Lincoln St. ℂ **303/837-8888**. www.coloradoballet.org.

MAJOR CONCERT HALLS & AUDITORIUMS

Arvada Center for the Arts & Humanities   This multidisciplinary arts center is in use almost every day of the year for performances by internationally known artists and its own theater companies, its historical museum and art gallery exhibitions, and hands-on education programs for all ages. In addition, the children's theater program performs in front of an annual audience of 60,000. A new, fully handicapped-accessible playground features a 343-foot sea creature by the name of Squiggles. The 2003–04 theater season included *Pinocchio, Jekyll & Hyde, the Musical,* and *The Women.* Visiting musicians included Dave Brubeck, Michelle Shocked, and Brazilian jazz songbird Claudia Villela. The indoor theater seats 500 and the outdoor amphitheater seats 1,200. 6901 Wadsworth Blvd., Arvada (2½ miles north of I-70). ℂ **720/898-7200**. www.arvadacenter.org.

Coors Amphitheatre   Formerly Fiddler's Green, alfresco summer concerts here feature national and international stars of rock, jazz, classical, and country music. The amphitheater has about 6,500 reserved seats and room for 10,000 more on its spacious lawn. Located in the southwestern section of the metropolitan area, just west of I-25 between Arapahoe and Orchard roads, it's open from May through September. 6350 Greenwood Plaza Blvd., Englewood. ℂ **303/220-7000**.

Denver Performing Arts Complex   Covering 4 square downtown blocks, from Speer Boulevard to 14th Street and Champa to Arapahoe streets, the Center for the Performing Arts (called the "Plex" by locals) is impressive even to those not attending a performance. Its numerous theaters seat from 157 to 2,800, and there's also a restaurant and shopping promenade. 14th and Curtis sts. ℂ **800/641-1222** or 303/893-4100, or 303/893-DCPA for recorded information. www.denvercenter.org.

Fillmore Auditorium   The 3,600-seat Fillmore is the former Mammoth Gardens, which was recently renovated by proprietors of the legendary Fillmore in San Francisco. The slickly remodeled venue is now one of Denver's best, loaded with bars and countless vintage rock photos. It attracts national rock acts from Ween to Bob Dylan, as well as many jam bands. Tickets generally cost $20 to $50. 1510 Clarkson St. ℂ **303/860-7181**. www.fillmoreauditorium.com.

Paramount Theatre A performing-arts center since 1929, this restored 2,000-seat downtown theater is a wonderful place to enjoy jazz, pop, and folk performances, as well as comedy, lectures, and theater. Recent bookings have included Tom Waits and Diana Krall. 1621 Glenarm Place. © 303/825-4904.

Red Rocks Amphitheatre ★★★ Quite possibly the country's best and most beautiful venue for top-name outdoor summer concerts, Red Rocks is in the foothills of the Rocky Mountains, 15 miles southwest of the city. Four-hundred-foot-high red sandstone rocks flank the 9,000-seat amphitheater, a product of the Civilian Conservation Corps. At night, with the lights of Denver spread across the horizon, the atmosphere is magical.

The Beatles performed here, as have Jimi Hendrix, Paul Simon, the Grateful Dead, Sting, Bonnie Raitt, Lyle Lovett, and Willie Nelson and top symphony orchestras from around the world. Renovated in 2002–03, the venue now has a sparkling new **visitor center** at the amphitheater's apex, which affords amazing views and displays detailing the varied performances that have taken place here since it opened in 1941. There's also a restaurant. The **trading post** carries a good selection of American-Indian jewelry and pottery, plus a variety of other curios and souvenirs. I-70 exit 259 S., 16351 County Rd. 93, Morrison. © 303/295-4444. www.redrocksonline.com.

Universal Lending Pavilion This 5,000-seat outdoor amphitheater on the southwest side of the Pepsi Center is the largest outdoor venue in the downtown area. An eclectic range of performers (from Travis Tritt to comedian Dave Chappelle in 2004) takes the stage here. 1700 7th St. © 303/405-1111.

7 A Side Trip to Colorado's Gold Circle Towns

Golden, Idaho Springs, and **Georgetown** make up most of the fabled Gold Circle—those towns that boomed with the first strikes of the gold rush in 1859. Central City, once the richest of the four towns but now the least attractive, completes the circle. Central City is trying to relive its glory days with a return to gambling, largely supported by locals from Denver, and although the exteriors of its historic buildings remain appealing, the rows of electronic slot machines and other gambling devices inside are a turn-off. Visitors to the area might like to make a brief stop and then move on to Idaho Springs.

GOLDEN ★★

Golden, 15 miles west of downtown Denver by way of U.S. 6 or Colo. 58 off I-70, is better known for the Coors Brewery (founded in 1873) and the Colorado School of Mines (established in 1874) than for its years as territorial capital.

For tourist information, contact the **Greater Golden Area Chamber of Commerce,** 1010 Washington Ave. (P.O. Box 1035), Golden, CO 80402 (© **303/279-3113;** www.goldencochamber.org).

WHAT TO SEE & DO

Historic downtown Golden centers on the **Territorial Capitol** in the **Loveland Building,** 12th Street and Washington Avenue. Built in 1861, it housed the first state legislature from 1862 to 1867, when the capital was moved to Denver. Today it contains offices and a restaurant. The **Armory,** 13th and Arapahoe streets, is probably the largest cobblestone structure in the United States; 3,300 wagonloads of stone and quartz went into its construction. **The Rock Flour Mill Warehouse,** 8th and Cheyenne streets, dates from 1863; it was built with red granite from nearby Golden Gate Canyon and still has its original cedar beams and wooden floors.

Astor House Museum   This handsome native stone structure, believed to be the first stone hotel built west of the Mississippi River, was constructed in 1867 to house legislators when Golden was the territorial capital. Scheduled for demolition to make space for a parking lot, the Astor House was instead restored in the 1970s and is now listed on the National Register of Historic Places. Today the Western-style Victorian hotel offers glimpses into life in Golden during the town's heyday in the late 19th century. Allow 30 to 60 minutes.

While there, you can obtain a walking-tour guide for the 12th Street Historic District or visit the Victorian Gift Shop, whose proceeds benefit the museum.

822 12th St. ℂ 303/278-3557. www.astorhousemuseum.org. Admission $3 adults ($4.50 for combo ticket that also includes Clear Creek History Park), $2 children under 13 ($3 combo ticket). Tues–Sat 10am–4:30pm.

Boettcher Mansion   This historic Jefferson County estate was built by Charles Boettcher in 1917 as a summer home and hunting lodge. It contains displays of furnishings and other items from the American Arts and Crafts period of the late 1800s and early 1900s. Other exhibits explore the history of Golden and the Boettcher family. Allow 1 hour.

900 Colorow Rd. (on Lookout Mountain). ℂ 303/526-0855. http://mansion.co.jefferson.co.us. Free admission, donations accepted. Mon–Fri 8am–5pm, or by appointment.

Buffalo Bill Museum & Grave 🏇 *(Kids)*   William Frederick Cody, the famous Western scout, is buried atop Lookout Mountain, south of Golden. (Some folks claim that friends stole Cody's body and buried it in Wyoming, but we were assured that this was the real McCoy.) The museum contains memorabilia from the life and legend of Buffalo Bill, who rode for the Pony Express, organized buffalo hunts for foreign royalty, and toured the world with his Wild West Show. There are also displays of American-Indian artifacts, guns, and Western art; an observation deck provides a great view of Denver. The museum is in 66-acre **Lookout Mountain Park,** a Denver municipal park popular for picnicking. Allow 1 to 1½ hours.

987½ Lookout Mountain Rd. ℂ 303/526-0747. www.buffalobill.org. Admission $3 adults, $2 seniors, $1 children 6–15, free for children under 6. May–Oct daily 9am–5pm; Nov–Apr Tues–Sun 9am–4pm. Closed Dec 25. I-70 exit 256.

Clear Creek History Park   This 3-acre creek-side park illustrates the history of the area's ranching, with two log cabins, several animal barns, a blacksmith's shop, and a one-room schoolhouse from the 1870s. The buildings were moved to this site to save them from development in nearby Golden Gate Canyon, their original location. Allow about an hour.

11th and Arapahoe sts. in downtown Golden. ℂ 303/278-3557. www.clearcreekhistorypark.org. Admission $3 adults ($4.50 for combo ticket that also includes the Astor House Museum), $2 children under 13 ($3 combo ticket). June–Aug Tues–Sat 10am–4:30pm; May and Sept Sat 10am–4:30pm. Closed Oct–Apr.

Colorado Railroad Museum 🏇   Housed in a replica of an 1880 railroad depot, this museum 2 miles east of Golden is a must-see for railroad buffs. On display are more than four dozen narrow- and standard-gauge locomotives and cars, plus other historic equipment, artifacts, photos, documents, and model trains. The exhibits cover 12 acres, including the two-story depot and a working roundhouse. You can climb into many of the old locomotives and wander through the parlor cars. The excellent gift-and-souvenir shop sells hundreds of railroad-related items, from coffee mugs to posters to T-shirts. Allow 1 to 2 hours.

17155 W. 44th Ave. ℂ **800/365-6263** or 303/279-4591. www.crrm.org. Admission $7 adults, $6 seniors over 60, $4 children under 16, children under 2 free, $16 families. June–Aug daily 9am–6pm; Sept–May daily 9am–5pm. Closed Jan 1, Thanksgiving, and Dec 25. Follow signs from I-70 exit 265 westbound, exit 266 east-bound.

Colorado School of Mines Geology Museum ⭐ Exhibits here help explain the history of mining in Colorado with a replica of a uranium mine and other displays. On exhibit are some 50,000 minerals, gems, fossils, and artifacts from around the world, plus displays on geology, earth history, and paleontology. There's also a kids' corner. The Colorado School of Mines, founded in 1874, has an enrollment of about 3,000. Allow 1 hour.

13th and Maple sts. ℂ **303/273-3815**. Free admission. School year Mon–Sat 9am–4pm, Sun 1–4pm; summer Mon–Sat 9am–4pm. Closed Colorado School of Mines holidays.

Coors Brewing Company Reputedly the world's largest single-site brewery, this facility produces 1.5 million gallons of beer each day. Coors conducts free public tours, followed by free samples of the various beers produced. The entire presentation lasts about 1½ hours. Tours leave a central parking lot at 13th and Ford streets, where visitors board a bus for a short drive through historic Golden before arriving at the brewery. There, a 30-minute walking tour covers the history of the Coors family and company, the barley malting process, the 13,640-gallon gleaming copper kettles, and the entire production process all the way to packaging. Children are welcome, and arrangements can be made for visitors with disabilities and non-English speakers. There's also a gift shop and an interactive time line in the reception area. Allow about 2 hours. *Note:* Visitors 18 and under must be accompanied by an adult.

13th and Ford sts. ℂ **303/277-2337**. www.coors.com. Free admission. Tours Mon–Sat 10am–4pm; shop Mon–Sat 10am–5pm. Closed holidays.

Foothills Art Center Housed in an 1872 Gothic-style Presbyterian church (which is on the National Historic Register), this exhibition center evolved from the annual Golden Sidewalk Art Show and features changing national and regional exhibits. A gift shop next door—Foothills Two—sells crafts by local artisans. Allow 30 minutes.

809 15th St. ℂ **303/279-3922**. www.foothillsartcenter.org. Free admission. Mon–Sat 10am–5pm; Sun 1–5pm.

Golden Pioneer Museum This museum exhibits an impressive collection of furniture, household articles, photographs, and other items, including a re-created 19th-century parlor and boudoir. Especially impressive is its collection of 200 American-Indian dolls, representing 39 different groups from all around North America. There's also a genealogical and historic research library and a small gift shop. Allow 1 hour.

923 10th St. ℂ **303/278-7151**. www.goldenpioneermuseum.com. Free admission. Mon–Sat 10am–4:30pm; Memorial Day to Labor Day also Sun 11am–5pm. Closed major holidays.

Heritage Square *Kids* A family-oriented shopping, dining, and entertainment village with a Wild West theme, Heritage Square features some Victorian specialty shops, a Ferris wheel, a stocked fishing pond, and a dinner theater. Warm-weather activities include go-carts, bumper boats, and a 2,350-foot alpine slide with bobsled-style carts. Heritage Square Music Hall offers shows for adults and children, and there's a nostalgic ice-cream parlor. Allow 1 to 2 hours.

18301 Colfax Ave. (U.S. 40). (℃ **303/279-2789**. www.heritagesquare.info. Free admission; separate charges for individual activities. Memorial Day to Labor Day Mon–Sat 10am–8pm, Sun noon–8pm; rest of year Mon–Sat 10am–6pm, Sun noon–6pm. I-70 exit 259.

Lookout Mountain Nature Center *(Kids*   A 1.5-mile self-guided nature trail winds through this 110-acre preserve among ponderosa pines and pretty mountain meadows. A free trail guide is available at the Nature Center when it's open, and a map is on display at a kiosk for those walking the trail at other times. The nonprofit Nature Center has displays on the pine beetle, pollination, and Colorado wildlife, plus an interactive exhibit on the ponderosa pine forest. The building is also worth a look—it's constructed of used and recycled materials such as ground-up plastic soda containers and the pulp of aspen trees. The center schedules free naturalist-guided environmental education activities year-round. Topics vary, but could include the flowers, butterflies, or wildlife of the area, or a look at the night sky. Advance registration is required for most programs, and age restrictions may apply. Call for details. Allow at least 1 hour.

910 Colorow Rd. (on Lookout Mountain). (℃ **303/526-0594**. Free admission. Trail daily 8am–dusk; Nature Center Tues–Sun 10am–4pm.

Mother Cabrini Shrine   A 22-foot statue of Jesus stands at the top of a 373-step stairway adorned by carvings representing the Stations of the Cross and mysteries of the rosary. Terra-cotta benches provide rest stops along the way. The shrine is dedicated to the country's first citizen saint, St. Frances Xavier Cabrini, who founded the Order of the Missionary Sisters of the Sacred Heart. The order has a convent here with a gift shop that's open from 9am to 5pm daily. Allow 45 to 90 minutes.

20189 Cabrini Blvd. (I-70 exit 259), Lookout Mountain. (℃ **303/526-0758**. www.den-cabrini-shrine.org. Free admission, donations welcome. Summer daily 7am–7:30pm; winter daily 7am–5:30pm; masses daily 7:30am, Sun 11am.

National Earthquake Information Center   The U.S. Geological Survey operates this facility to collect rapid earthquake information, transmit warnings over the Earthquake Early Alerting Service, and publish and disseminate earthquake data. Tours of 30 to 45 minutes can be scheduled by appointment when a guide is available.

1711 Illinois St. (℃ **303/273-8500**. neic.usgs.gov. Free admission. Tues–Thurs 9–11am and 1–3pm, by appointment only.

Rocky Mountain Quilt Museum   This museum presents changing exhibits, including works from its permanent collection of some 250 quilts. Consigned works are for sale in the gift shop. Allow 30 minutes.

1111 Washington Ave. (℃ **303/277-0377**. www.rmqm.org. Admission $4 adults, $3 seniors, $1 children 6–12, free for children under 6. Mon–Sat 10am–4pm.

WHERE TO STAY & DINE

La Quinta Inn—Golden, just off I-70 exit 264, at 3301 Youngfield Service Rd. (℃ **800/531-5900** or 303/279-5565), is a dependable choice, with 129 units and rates of $89 for a double room. **Table Mountain Inn,** 1310 Washington Ave. (℃ **800/762-9898** or 303/277-9898; www.tablemountaininn.com), is a smaller, slightly more expensive alternative, with 65 standard rooms and 9 suites. Rates are $122 to $147 single or double, $167 to $207 suite. The place is loaded with Southwest charm, featuring beautiful views of the surrounding mesas and a good restaurant.

For a good meal in a historic setting, try the **Old Capitol Grill** in downtown Golden, 1122 Washington Ave. at 12th Street (© **303/279-6390**), offering steak and burgers plus a good selection of sandwiches. Located in the Territorial Capitol Building constructed in 1862, the restaurant is open daily for lunch and dinner, with dinner prices in the $8-to-$18 range. A more upscale dinner choice is **Coburn's,** in the Coburn Hotel, 800 11th St. (© **303/279-0100**). It serves creative regional fare in the $16-to-$23 range.

IDAHO SPRINGS ⚔

For visitor information, contact the **Idaho Springs Chamber of Commerce,** P.O. Box 97, Idaho Springs, CO 80452 (© **303/567-4382;** www.idahosprings chamber.com). Information on Idaho Springs and the nearby towns of Empire, Georgetown, and Silver Plume is available from the **Clear Creek County Tourism Board,** P.O. Box 100, Idaho Springs, CO 80452 (© **800/88-BLAST** or 303/567-4660; www.clearcreekcounty.org).

WHAT TO SEE & DO

The scenic "Oh My God" dirt road, a steep, winding thoroughfare, runs from Central City through Virginia Canyon to Idaho Springs, although most visitors prefer to take I-70 directly to this community 35 miles west of Denver. Site of a major gold strike in 1859, today Idaho Springs beckons visitors to try their luck at panning for any gold that may remain. The quaint Victorian downtown is worth a look; don't miss the Bridal Veil Falls tumbling through the largest waterwheel in Colorado, right across from City Hall.

The **Argo Gold Mine, Mill, and Museum,** 2350 Riverside Dr. (© **303/ 567-2421;** www.historicargotours.com), is listed on the National Register of Historic Places, and offers tours daily from mid-April into October from 9am to 6pm. Visitors can see the Double Eagle Gold Mine, relatively unchanged since the early miners first worked it more than 100 years ago, and the mill, where ore was processed into gold. Everyone is welcome to take part in gold- and gem-stone-panning. Admission is $13 for adults, $7.50 for children 7 to 12, and free for kids under 7. Allow at least 45 minutes.

At the **Phoenix Gold Mine** ⚔, on Trail Creek Road (© **303/567-0422**), you can don a hard hat and follow a working miner through narrow tunnels to see what mining 100 years ago was all about. You can also pan for gold on the prop-erty and relax in the picnic area. Weather permitting, the mine is open daily from 10am to 6pm in the summer (until 5pm in the winter); the tours are infor-mal and entertaining. Cost is $10 for adults, $9 for seniors, $5 for children 5 to 11, and free for children under 5. Allow about 1 hour.

Just outside Idaho Springs is **Indian Springs Resort,** 302 Soda Creek Rd. (© **303/567-2191** or 303/989-6666; www.indianspringsresort.com), a fine spot for a relaxing soak in the hot springs after a long day of skiing or hiking. The resort has a covered swimming pool, indoor and outdoor private baths, and a vapor cave with soaking pools. Rates are $16 to $23 per person for an hour in the private baths or all-day use of the vapor cave, $12 to $14 for all-day use of the pool, and $12 for a mud bath in "Club Mud." Lodging ($60–$125 for two), meals, and weekend entertainment are also offered. The resort is open daily from 7:30am to 10:30pm year-round.

Idaho Springs is the starting point for a 28-mile drive to the summit of 14,260-foot **Mount Evans** ⚔⚔. From I-70 exit 240, follow Colo. 103—also called Mt. Evans Highway—as it winds along Chicago Creek through Arapahoe

National Forest to **Echo Lake Park,** another Denver mountain park with fireplaces, hiking trails, and fishing. From here, Colo. 5—the highest paved auto road in North America—climbs to the Mount Evans summit. Views along this highway are of spectacular snowcapped peaks even in June, and you're likely to see mountain goats, bighorn sheep, marmots, eagles, and other wildlife. The road is generally open from Memorial Day to Labor Day. Allow at least 4 hours.

Another way to see this area's great scenery is by horseback. **A&A Historical Trails Stables,** 5 miles up Virginia Canyon from Idaho Springs (✆ **303/ 567-4808;** www.aastables.com), offers a variety of trail rides, including breakfast and moonlight rides. Rides are usually offered from May through November, weather permitting. A 1-hour ride costs $25 per person, and a 2-hour ride costs $45.

WHERE TO STAY & DINE

H&H Motor Lodge, 2445 Colorado Blvd. (P.O. Box 1359), Idaho Springs, CO 80452 (✆ **800/445-2893** or 303/567-2838; www.hhlodge.com), is a mom-and-pop motel on the east side of town. It offers bright and cheery rooms, TVs with HBO, a hot tub, and a sauna. The 34 rooms and suites include several larger family units. Rates are $59 double for a standard room, kitchenettes $10 to $20 extra; two-bedroom suites start at $69. Pets are accepted for a $5 nightly fee.

Beau Jo's Colorado Style Pizza, 1517 Miner St. (✆ **303/567-4376**), offers a wide variety of so-called mountain pizzas, including standard pepperoni; "Skier Mike's," with Canadian bacon, green peppers, and chicken breast; and a roasted-garlic-and-veggie combo. Sandwiches are also available, plus a salad bar set up in a pair of old claw-foot bathtubs. The bill usually comes out to $7 to $12 per person. Smoking is not permitted.

GEORGETOWN ✦

A pretty village of Victorian-era houses and stores, Georgetown, 45 miles west of Denver on I-70 at an elevation of 8,500 feet, is named for an 1860 gold camp. Among the best preserved of the foothill mining towns, Georgetown is one of the few that didn't suffer a major fire during its formative years. Perhaps to acknowledge their blessings, townspeople built eye-catching steeples on top of their firehouses, not their churches.

For information on attractions and travel services, drop by or contact the **Georgetown Visitors Center,** 613 6th St. (P.O. Box 444), Georgetown, CO 80444 (✆ **800/472-8230** or 303/569-2888), which runs a visitor information center at 6th and Argentine streets across from the Georgetown post office; or **Historic Georgetown, Inc.,** 15th and Argentine streets, P.O. Box 667, Georgetown, CO 80444-0667 (✆ **303/569-2840;** www.historicgeorgetown.org).

WHAT TO SEE & DO

The Georgetown–Silver Plume Mining Area was declared a National Historic Landmark District in 1966, and more than 200 of its buildings have been restored.

A convenient place to begin a **walking tour** is the Old County Courthouse, 6th and Argentine streets. Now the community center and tourist information office, it was built in 1867. Across Argentine Street is the Old Stone Jail (1868); 3 blocks south, at 3rd and Argentine, is the Hamill House (see below).

Sixth Street is Georgetown's main commercial strip. Walk east from the Old Courthouse. On your left are the Masonic Hall (1891), the Fish Block (1886), the Monti and Guanella Building (1868), and the Cushman Block (1874); on your right, the Hamill Block (1881) and the Kneisel & Anderson Building (1893). The Hotel de Paris (see below) is at the corner of 6th and Taos. Nearly opposite, at 6th and Griffith, is the Star Hook and Ladder Building (1886), along with the town hall and marshal's office.

If you turn south on Taos Street, you'll find Grace Episcopal Church (1869) at 5th Street, and the Maxwell House (1890) a couple of steps east on 4th. Glance west on 5th to see Alpine Hose Company No. 2 (1874) and the Courier Building (1875). North on Taos Street from the Hotel de Paris are the Old Georgetown School (1874) at 8th Street, First Presbyterian Church (1874) at 9th, Our Lady of Lourdes Catholic Church (1918) at 9th, and the Old Missouri Firehouse (1870) at 10th and Taos.

If you turn west on 9th at the Catholic church, you'll find two more historic structures: the Bowman-White House (1892) at Rose and 9th, and the Tucker-Rutherford House (ca. 1860), a miner's log cabin with four small rooms and a trapper's cabin in back, on 9th Street at Clear Creek.

Georgetown Energy Museum   This small museum is dedicated to educating people about the history of hydropower in Georgetown and Colorado. Located at Georgetown's power plant—built in 1900 and still operating—the museum allows visitors an up-close look at a pair of hydroelectric-generating units in action. The museum also features photographic and text displays detailing the history of similar plants in the region, as well as a collection of antiques: washing machines, stoves, and generator meters. Allow 30 minutes.

600 Griffith St. ℂ **303/569-3557.** www.georgetownenergymuseum.org. Free admission, donations accepted. June–Sept Mon–Sat 10am–4pm, Sun noon–4pm; open Oct–May by appointment only.

Hamill House   Built in Country Gothic Revival style, this house dates from 1867, when silver speculator William Hamill owned it. When Historic Georgetown, Inc., acquired it in 1971, the house had its original woodwork, fireplaces, and wallpaper. A delicately carved outhouse had two sections: one with walnut seats for the family; the other with pine seats for servants. Allow 30 to 60 minutes.

305 Argentine St. ℂ **303/569-2840.** Admission $5 adults, $4 seniors 60 and older, $4 students, free for children under 6. Memorial Day to Sept daily 10am–4pm; Oct–Dec Sat–Sun noon–4pm. Closed Jan to late May except for prearranged tours.

Hotel de Paris ⭐   The builder of the hotel, Louis Dupuy, once explained his desire to build a French inn so far away from his homeland: "I love these mountains and I love America, but you will pardon me if I bring into this community a remembrance of my youth and my country." The hotel opened in 1875 and soon became famous for its French provincial luxury.

Today it's a historic museum run by the National Society of Colonial Dames of America, embellished with many of its original furnishings, including Haviland china, a big pendulum clock, paintings and etchings, photographs by William Henry Jackson, and carved walnut furniture. The kitchen contains an antique stove and other cooking equipment, and the wine cellar houses early wine barrels, with their labels still in place. Allow 45 to 60 minutes.

409 6th St. (at Taos St.). ℂ **303/569-2311.** www.hoteldeparismuseum.org. Admission $4 adults, $3 seniors 60 and older, $2 children 6–16, free for children under 6. Memorial Day to Labor Day daily 10am–4:30pm; early Sept to Dec and Apr Sat–Sun noon–4pm, weather permitting. Closed Jan–Apr and major holidays.

WHERE TO STAY & DINE

Colorado's oldest continuously operating hotel, about 5 minutes from George-town, is the **Peck House Hotel and Restaurant,** 83 Sunny Ave. (P.O. Box 428), on U.S. 40 off I-70 exit 232, Empire, CO 80438 (© **303/569-9870;** fax 303/569-2743; www.thepeckhouse.com). Established in 1862 as a stagecoach stop for travelers and immigrants from the East Coast, the hotel has an antique-filled parlor lined with photos of the Peck family and their late-19th- and early-20th-century guests. The rooms are comfortable and quaint (claw-foot tubs grace many bathrooms). One of the best parts of a stay here is the fine panoramic view of the Empire Valley afforded by the wide veranda. There are 11 rooms (9 with private bathroom), and rates for two are in the $65-to-$100 range. The hotel's excellent **restaurant** serves fish and steak entrees and seriously delicious hot-fudge cake and raspberries Romanoff. The restaurant serves dinner daily year-round; prices for entrees are $20 to $30.

Back in Georgetown, **The Happy Cooker,** 412 6th St. (© **303/569-3166**), serves unusual soups, sandwiches on homemade breads, crepes, quiches, and more substantial fare such as frittatas and eggs Benedict, in a converted home in Georgetown's historic business district. It's open Monday through Friday from 7am to 4pm, Saturday and Sunday from 7am to 5pm. Prices are in the $4-to-$8 range, and breakfast is served all day. For a beer, a burger, and a dose of local color, head to the **Red Ram Restaurant & Saloon,** 606 6th St. (© **303/569-2300**). The menu also has Mexican plates and slow-cooked baby back ribs; prices run from $6 to $15 for a main course.

Colorado Springs

Magnificent scenic beauty, a favorable climate, and dreams of gold have lured visitors to Colorado Springs and neighboring Pikes Peak Country for well over 100 years.

Nearly 2 centuries ago, in 1806, army Lt. Zebulon Pike led a company of soldiers on a trek around the base of an enormous mountain. He called it "Grand Peak," declared it unconquerable, and moved on. Today, the 14,110-foot mountain we know as Pikes Peak has been conquered so often that an auto highway and a cog railway take visitors to the top.

Unlike many Colorado towns, neither mineral wealth nor ranching was the cornerstone of Colorado Springs' economy during the 19th century—tourism was. In fact, Colorado Springs, founded in 1871, was the first genuine resort community west of Chicago. Gen. William J. Palmer, builder of the Denver & Rio Grande Railroad, established the resort on his rail line, at an elevation of 6,035 feet. The state's growing reputation as a health center, with its high mountains and mineral springs, convinced him to build at the foot of Pikes Peak. In an attempt to lure affluent Easterners, he named the resort Colorado Springs, because most fashionable Eastern resorts were called "springs." The mineral waters at Manitou Springs were only 5 miles away, and soon Palmer exploited them by installing a resident physician, Dr. Samuel Solly, who exuberantly trumpeted the benefits of Manitou's springs both in print and in person.

The 1890s gold strikes at Cripple Creek, on the southwestern slope of Pikes Peak, added a new dimension to life in Colorado Springs. Among those who cashed in on the boom was Spencer Penrose, a middle-aged Philadelphian and Harvard graduate who arrived in 1892, made some astute investments, and became quite rich. Penrose, who believed that the automobile would revolutionize life in the United States, promoted the creation of new highways. To show the effectiveness of motorcars in the mountains, he built (1913–15) the Pikes Peak Highway, using more than $250,000 of his own money. Then, during World War I, at a cost of more than $2 million, he built the luxurious Broadmoor hotel at the foot of Cheyenne Mountain. World War II brought the military and defense industry to this area, and in 1958 the $200-million U.S. Air Force Academy opened.

Modern Colorado Springs is a growing city of 358,000, with over half a million people in the metropolitan area. The majority of its residents are conservative (one-third are active or retired military personnel), and in recent years it has developed a reputation for right-wing political activism. The city is also home to some of the country's largest nondenominational churches and conservative groups, such as Focus on the Family.

To many visitors, the city retains the feel and mood of a small Western town. Most tourists come to see the Air Force Academy, marvel at the scenery at Garden of the Gods and Pikes Peak, and explore the history of America's West. We're pleased to report that Colorado Springs also has some of the best lodging and dining in the state.

1 Orientation

ARRIVING

BY PLANE

Major airlines offer nearly 100 flights a day to **Colorado Springs Airport,** located north of Drennan Road and east of Powers Boulevard in the southeastern part of the city (✆ **719/550-1972;** www.flycos.com).

Airlines serving Colorado Springs include **Allegiant** (✆ 888/594-6937), **American** (✆ 800/433-7300; www.aa.com), **America West** (✆ 800/235-9292; www.americawest.com), **Continental** (✆ 800/525-0280; www.flycontinental.com), **Delta** (✆ 800/221-1212; www.delta.com), **Mesa** (✆ 800/637-2247; www.mesa-air.com), **Northwest** (✆ 800/225-2525; www.nwa.com), and **United** (✆ 800/241-6522; www.ual.com).

GETTING TO & FROM THE AIRPORT   Several companies provide airport shuttle services; call ✆ **719/550-1930** for information.

BY CAR

The principal artery to and from the north and south, I-25, bisects Colorado Springs. Denver is 70 miles north; Pueblo, 42 miles south. U.S. 24 is the principal east–west route through the city.

Visitors arriving on I-70 from the east can take exit 359 at Limon and follow U.S. 24 into the Springs. Arriving on I-70 from the west, the most direct route is exit 201 at Frisco, then Colo. 9 through Breckenridge 53 miles to U.S. 24 (at Hartsel), and then east 66 miles to the Springs. This route is mountainous, so check road conditions before setting out in winter.

VISITOR INFORMATION

The **Colorado Springs Convention and Visitors Bureau** is at 515 S. Cascade Ave., Colorado Springs, CO 80903 (✆ **800/888-4748** or 719/635-7506; fax 719/635-4968; www.coloradosprings-travel.com). Ask for the free *Official Visitor Guide to Colorado Springs and the Pikes Peak Region,* a colorful booklet with a comprehensive listing of accommodations, restaurants, and other area visitor services, as well as a basic but efficient map. Inquire at the Visitor Information Center or local bookstores for more detailed maps. An excellent one is the Pierson Graphics Corporation's *Colorado Springs and Monument Valley Street Map.*

The **Visitor Information Center,** at the southeast corner of Cascade Avenue and Cimarron Street, is open from 8:30am to 5pm daily in summer, Monday through Friday in winter. From I-25, take the Cimarron Street exit (exit 141), and head east about 4 blocks. The center also operates a weekly events line with a 24-hour recording (✆ **719/635-1723**).

Visitors to Manitou Springs—every Colorado Springs visitor should also get to Manitou Springs—can get information from the **Manitou Springs Chamber of Commerce & Visitors Bureau,** 354 Manitou Ave., Manitou Springs, CO 80829 (✆ **800/642-2567** or 719/685-5089; www.manitousprings.org). You can also contact the **Pikes Peak Country Attractions Association** at the same address (✆ **800/525-2250** or 719/685-5894; www.pikes-peak.com).

Heads Up

At an elevation of 6,035 feet, Colorado Springs has two-thirds the oxygen found at sea level; Pikes Peak, at 14,110 feet, has only one-half the oxygen.

CITY LAYOUT

It's easy to get around central Colorado Springs, which is laid out on a classic grid pattern.

If you focus on the intersection of I-25 and U.S. 24, downtown Colorado Springs lies in the northeast quadrant, bounded on the west by I-25 and on the south by U.S. 24 (Cimarron St.). Boulder Street to the north and Wahsatch Avenue to the east complete the downtown frame. Nevada Avenue (Bus. 25 and U.S. 85) parallels the freeway for 15 miles through the city, intersecting it twice; Tejon Street and Cascade Avenue also run north–south through downtown between Nevada Avenue and the freeway. **Colorado Avenue** and **Platte Avenue** are the busiest east–west downtown cross streets.

West of downtown, Colorado Avenue extends through the historic Old Colorado City district and the quaint foothill community of **Manitou Springs,** rejoining U.S. 24—a busy but less interesting artery—as it enters Pike National Forest.

South of downtown, **Nevada Avenue** intersects **Lake Avenue,** the principal boulevard into the Broadmoor hotel, and proceeds south as Colo. 115 past Fort Carson.

North and east of downtown, **Academy Boulevard** (Colo. 83) is the street name to remember. From the south gate of the Air Force Academy north of the Springs, it winds through residential hills, crosses Austin Bluff Parkway, then runs without a curve 8 miles due south, finally bending west to intersect I-25 and Colo. 115 at Fort Carson. U.S. 24, which exits downtown east as Platte Avenue, and Fountain Boulevard, which leads to the airport, are among its cross streets. Austin Bluffs Parkway extends west of I-25 as **Garden of the Gods Road,** leading to that natural wonder.

City street addresses are divided by Pikes Peak Avenue into north and south; by Nevada Avenue into east and west.

2 Getting Around

Although Colorado Springs has public transportation, most visitors prefer to drive. Parking and roads are good, and some of the best attractions, such as the Garden of the Gods, are accessible only by car (or foot or bike for the truly ambitious).

BY CAR

For regulations and advice on driving in Colorado, see "Getting Around" in chapter 2. The **American Automobile Association (AAA)** maintains an office in Colorado Springs at 3525 N. Carefree Circle (© **800/283-5222** or 719/591-2222; www.aaa.com), open Monday through Friday from 8:30am to 5:30pm and Saturday from 9am to 1pm.

CAR RENTALS   Car-rental agencies in Colorado Springs, some of which have offices in or near downtown as well as at the airport, include **Advantage** (© 800/777-5500 or 719/574-1144), **Alamo** (© 800/462-5366 or 719/574-8579), **Avis** (© 800/831-2847 or 719/596-2751), **Budget** (© 800/527-7000 or 719/473-6535), **Enterprise** (© 800/736-8222 or 719/636-3900),

Hertz (© 800/654-3131 or 719/596-1863), **National** (© 866/342-0717 or 719/596-1519), and **Thrifty** (© 800/367-2277 or 719/390-9800).

PARKING   Most downtown streets have parking meters; the rate is 25¢ for a half-hour. Look for city-run parking lots, which charge 25¢ per half-hour and also offer day rates. Outside of downtown, free parking is generally available on side streets.

BY BUS

Colorado Springs Transit (© **719/385-7433;** www.springsgov.com) provides city bus service. Buses operate Monday through Friday from 5:20am to 10:40pm and Saturday from 7am to 6pm, except holidays. Fares on in-city routes are $1.25 for adults; 95¢ students; 60¢ for children 6 to 11, seniors, and passengers with disabilities; and free for children under 6. Fares for routes outside the city limits are 35¢ higher, except for free trolley service in Manitou Springs. Bus schedules can be obtained at terminals, city libraries, and the Colorado Springs Convention and Visitors Bureau.

BY TAXI

Call **Yellow Cab** (© **719/634-5000**) for taxi service.

ON FOOT

Each of the main sections of town can easily be explored without a vehicle. It's fun, for instance, to wander the winding streets of Manitou Springs or explore the Old Colorado City "strip." Between neighborhoods, however, distances are considerable. Unless you're particularly fit, it's wise to drive or take a bus or taxi.

FAST FACTS: Colorado Springs

American Express To report a lost card, call © **800/528-4800;** to report lost traveler's checks, call © **800/221-7282.**

Area Code The telephone area code is **719.**

Babysitters Front desks at major hotels often can make arrangements.

Business Hours Most banks are open Monday through Friday from 9am to 5pm, and some have Saturday hours. Major stores are open Monday through Saturday from 9 or 10am until 5 or 6pm (sometimes until 9pm Fri), and often Sunday from noon until 5pm. Stores that cater to tourists are usually open longer in the summer, with shorter hours in winter.

Car Rentals See "Getting Around," above.

Dentists For referrals for dentists who accept emergency patients, contact the **Colorado Springs Dental Society** (© **719/598-5161**).

Doctors For referrals and other health information, call **Healthlink** (© **719/444-2273**).

Drugstores **Walgreens,** 920 N. Circle Dr. (© **719/473-9090**), has a 24-hour prescription service.

Emergencies For police, fire, or medical emergencies, dial © **911.** To reach **Poison Control,** call © **800/332-3073.**

Eyeglasses You can get 1-hour replacement of lost or broken glasses at **Pearle Vision Express** in Citadel Mall (© **719/597-0757**) and **LensCrafters,** in Erindale Centre on North Academy Boulevard (© **719/548-8650**).

Hospitals **Memorial Hospital,** 1400 E. Boulder St. (© **719/365-5000**), offers full medical services, including 24-hour emergency treatment, as does **Penrose Hospital,** 2215 N. Cascade Ave. (© **719/776-5000**).

Newspapers/Magazines The *Gazette* (www.gazette.com), published daily in Colorado Springs, is the city's most widely read newspaper. The *Denver Post* is also available at newsstands throughout the city. The glossy *Springs* magazine and the politically oriented *Independent* are other free local periodicals. *USA Today* and the *Wall Street Journal* can be purchased on the street and at major hotels.

Photographic Needs There are dozens of photo-finishing outlets throughout the city, including **Walgreens** and **Shewmaker's Camera Shop,** in the Woodmen Valley Shopping Center, 6902 N. Academy Blvd. (© **719/ 598-6412**). For camera and video supplies and repairs as well as photo finishing, go to the central location of **Shewmaker's Camera Shop,** 30 N. Tejon St., downtown (© **719/636-1696**; www.shewmakers.com).

Post Office The main post office is downtown at 201 E. Pikes Peak Ave. Contact the U.S. Postal Service (© **800/275-8777**; www.usps.com) for hours and locations of other post offices.

Safety Although Colorado Springs is generally a safe city, it is not crime-free. Try to be aware of your surroundings at all times, and ask at your hotel or the visitor center about the safety of neighborhoods you plan to explore, especially after dark.

Taxes Total taxes on retail sales in Colorado Springs amount to about 6.4%; room taxes total about 9%. Rates in Manitou Springs are a bit higher.

Useful Telephone Numbers For **weather and road conditions,** including road construction, throughout the state, call © **303/639-1111** or visit www.cotrip.org.

3 Where to Stay

You'll find a wide range of lodging possibilities here, from Colorado's ritziest resort—The Broadmoor—to basic budget motels. There are also several particularly nice bed-and-breakfasts. The rates listed here are the officially quoted prices ("rack rates") and don't take into account individual or group discounts. Generally, rates are highest from Memorial Day to Labor Day, and lowest in the spring. During graduation and other special events at the Air Force Academy, rates can be absolutely ridiculous, and you may have trouble finding a room at any price. Rates listed below do not include the lodging tax (about 9% in Colorado Springs, almost 10% in Manitou Springs).

In addition to the accommodations described below, a number of moderately priced chain and franchise motels offer reliable lodging. These include the economical **Best Western Pikes Peak Inn,** 3010 N. Chestnut St., Colorado Springs, CO 80907 (© **800/223-9127** or 719/636-5201), which charges $49 to $99 double; **Econo Lodge Downtown,** 714 N. Nevada Ave., Colorado Springs, CO 80903 (© **800/553-2666** or 719/636-3385), with rates from $35 to $85 double; and **Super 8,** 4604 Rusina Rd., Colorado Springs, CO 80907 (© **800/800-8000** or 719/594-0964), which charges $45 to $70 double.

Those looking for a more upscale chain won't go wrong with the **Doubletree Hotel World Arena,** 1775 E. Cheyenne Mountain Blvd. (I-25 exit 138), Colorado Springs, CO 80906 (© **800/222-TREE** or 719/576-8900); or the **Sheraton Colorado Springs Hotel,** 2886 S. Circle Dr. (I-25 exit 138), Colorado Springs, CO 80906 (© **800/981-4012** or 719/576-5900).

VERY EXPENSIVE

The Broadmoor ★★★ (Kids   We thought The Broadmoor couldn't get much better, but it's amazing what a mere $75 million can do. A massive renovation and restoration project, completed in spring 2002, has taken it to new heights of luxury, and also restored much of the historic building's grandeur. The Broadmoor is a sprawling resort complex of historic pink Mediterranean-style buildings with modern additions, set at the foot of Cheyenne Mountain on magnificently landscaped 3,000-acre grounds about 3½ miles southwest of downtown Colorado Springs. The Italian Renaissance–style Broadmoor opened in 1918. Its marble staircase, chandeliers, Italian tile, hand-painted beams and ceilings, and carved-marble fountain remain spectacles today. The priceless art collection features original work by Toulouse-Lautrec and Ming dynasty ceramicists. The first names entered on the guest register were those of John D. Rockefeller, Jr. and his party.

Behind the main building is lovely Cheyenne Lake; a swimming pool almost seamlessly attached to the west end looks like a part of the lake. This swimming complex will make you think you're at an oceanside beach resort, with water slides, two outdoor hot tubs, 13 cabanas, and an outdoor cafe.

The guest rooms occupy a series of separate buildings centered on the lake and pool area. The spacious, luxurious rooms are beautifully decorated in European style, with chandeliers, Italian fabrics, rich wood, and limited-edition works of art. Most units hold two double beds or one king-size bed, desks and tables, plush seating, and two-line portable phones, dataports, and Internet access through Web TV. Many rooms contain large soaking tubs and separate marble showers. The service is impeccable: The hotel averages two employees for every guest.

Lake Circle, at Lake Ave. (P.O. Box 1439), Colorado Springs, CO 80901. © **800/634-7711** or 719/634-7711. Fax 719/577-5700. www.broadmoor.com. 700 units. May–Oct $325–$470 double, $800 standard suite; Nov–Apr $225–$345 double, $295–$635 standard suite; year-round up to $3,100 large suite. AE, DC, DISC, MC, V. Free parking. **Amenities:** 11 restaurants (all Continental, American, or both); 4 lounges; outdoor pool cafe; 3 swimming pools (indoor, outdoor with water slide, outdoor lap pool); 2 18-hole golf courses (3 in spring 2006); 9 all-weather tennis courts; state-of-the-art fitness center and full-service spa with aerobics classes, saunas, and whirlpool tubs; 2 outdoor hot tubs; bicycle rentals; children's programs (summer); concierge; car-rental agency; shopping arcade; 24-hr. room service; in-room massage; valet laundry; riding stables; fly-fishing school; movie theater; shuttle bus between buildings; service station. *In room:* A/C, cable TV, dataport, minibar, coffeemaker, hair dryer, iron, safe.

EXPENSIVE

Antlers Hilton Hotel ★★   The Antlers has been a Colorado Springs landmark for more than a century, and remains a most impressive facility that is a cut above other high-end chain properties. Although the Antlers is in many ways geared to business travelers, for vacationers it offers first-rate accommodations within a short walking distance of many of Colorado Springs' major attractions and restaurants. There have been three different Antlers on this site. The first, a turreted Victorian showcase built in 1883, was named for General William Palmer's collection of deer and elk trophies. After it was destroyed by fire in 1898, Palmer built an extravagant Italian Renaissance–style building that

Colorado Springs Accommodations & Dining

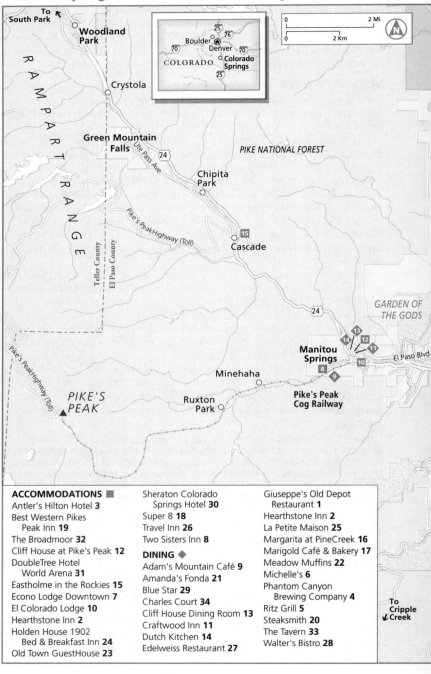

ACCOMMODATIONS ■
Antler's Hilton Hotel **3**
Best Western Pikes
Peak Inn **19**
The Broadmoor **32**
Cliff House at Pike's Peak **12**
DoubleTree Hotel
World Arena **31**
Eastholme in the Rockies **15**
Econo Lodge Downtown **7**
El Colorado Lodge **10**
Hearthstone Inn **2**
Holden House 1902
Bed & Breakfast Inn **24**
Old Town GuestHouse **23**

Sheraton Colorado
Springs Hotel **30**
Super 8 **18**
Travel Inn **26**
Two Sisters Inn **8**

DINING ◆
Adam's Mountain Café **9**
Amanda's Fonda **21**
Blue Star **29**
Charles Court **34**
Cliff House Dining Room **13**
Craftwood Inn **11**
Dutch Kitchen **14**
Edelweiss Restaurant **27**

Giuseppe's Old Depot
Restaurant **1**
Hearthstone Inn **2**
La Petite Maison **25**
Margarita at PineCreek **16**
Marigold Café & Bakery **17**
Meadow Muffins **22**
Michelle's **6**
Phantom Canyon
Brewing Company **4**
Ritz Grill **5**
Steaksmith **20**
The Tavern **33**
Walter's Bistro **28**

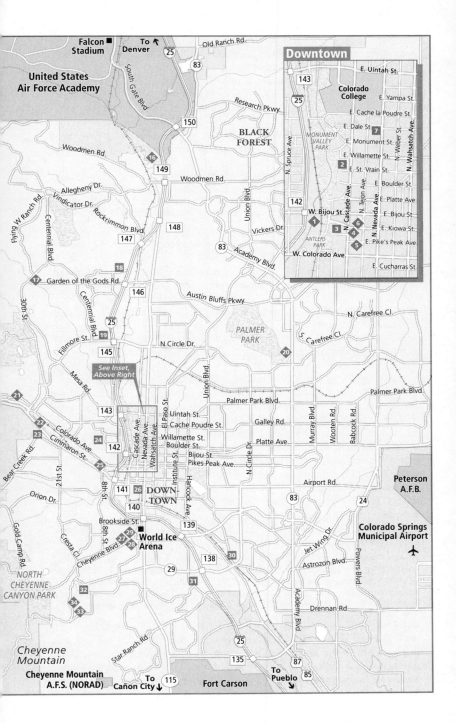

survived until 1964, when it was leveled to make room for the more contemporary Antlers Plaza, set off from the street and featuring a modern, 13-story hotel with a rich marble- and woodwork-laden lobby.

Antique black-walnut nightstands from the previous incarnation provide a touch of historic continuity to the spacious guest rooms, which are handsomely decorated in earth tones with rich wood furnishings. Each room has two telephones, dataports, voice mail, a large working desk, and ample closet space. The corner rooms are larger, and we prefer the west-side rooms, which provide great views of Pikes Peak. On-site is Colorado Springs' first microbrewery, Judge Baldwin's Brewing Company.

4 S. Cascade Ave., Colorado Springs, CO 80903. ℂ **877/754-9940** or 719/473-5600. Fax 719/389-0259. www.antlers.com. 292 units. Summer $129–$240 double; $250–$750 suite. Off-season discounts (10%–30%) available. AE, DC, DISC, MC, V. Self-parking $8, valet $12. **Amenities:** 2 restaurants (American); indoor pool; fitness center; whirlpool; salon; room service (6:30am–11pm); laundry. *In room:* A/C, cable TV, coffeemaker, hair dryer, iron.

Cliff House at Pikes Peak ★★ *Finds*   Striving to compete with the best that Colorado has to offer (and doing a pretty good job), the Cliff House is an old yet new facility. Built in 1874, it was designated a National Historic Landmark in 1980, and has hosted such eminent guests as Theodore Roosevelt, Clark Gable, and Thomas Edison. A major fire forced the Cliff House to close in 1982, and it remained closed until a massive reconstruction in 1997. The project incorporated several pieces of the hotel's original decor, including ornate woodwork and a tile fireplace, and what the fire destroyed was replicated with an emphasis on attention to detail. Once again a grand and luxurious hotel, the Cliff House reopened in July 1999.

Today, the lovely, uniquely decorated accommodations vary in size and personality, although the overall decor is Queen Anne–Victorian. Units range from average-size, relatively simple studios to large, luxurious celebrity suites named for former guests. Some units have gas fireplaces, two-person spas, steam showers, and terrific views of the mountains. All have live flowering plants, robes, heated toilet seats, working desks, and high-speed Internet access. We wouldn't turn down any room at the Cliff House, but our favorite is definitely the Clark Gable Suite ($475 double in summer), which is decorated in subdued Hollywood style—if you can call leopard-print wallpaper subdued—and contains a shower for two, a jetted tub, a wet bar and refrigerator, two TVs, a gas fireplace, and photos of Clark, who stayed at the hotel in the early 1940s.

There's a fine dining restaurant (see "Where to Dine," below), and the entire property is nonsmoking.

306 Cañon Ave., Manitou Springs, CO 80829. ℂ **888/212-7000** or 719/685-3000. Fax 719/685-3913. www.thecliffhouse.com. 55 units. $145–$200 double; $189–$475 suite. Children under 13 stay free in parent's room. Rates include breakfast buffet. AE, DC, DISC, MC, V. **Amenities:** Restaurant (American); bar; small fitness center; concierge; activities desk; airport pickup; room service (7am–11pm); on-call massage; valet laundry service. *In room:* A/C, cable TV, VCR, CD player, dataport, coffeemaker, hair dryer, iron, safe.

Old Town GuestHouse ★★   Just a half block south of the main street of Colorado Springs' historic Old Colorado City stands this three-story redbrick inn. It may appear to be from the 19th century, but innkeepers Kaye and David Caster designed and built it in 1997 to provide all the modern amenities in a warm and inviting atmosphere. The spacious rooms and modern conveniences make it an especially good choice for vacationers who will be doing a little work during their R and R.

All eight of the individually decorated rooms are named for flowers: for example, Colorado Columbine, with an attractive red, white, and blue quilt on the king bed; Moroccan Jasmine, with a Sahara desert theme; Oriental Poppy, decorated with collectibles from the Orient; and romantic Victorian Rose. Each room has individual climate control, robes, and a queen- or king-size bed. Several have gas-log fireplaces, seven have a private porch or balcony, and some have steam showers for two or private outdoor hot tubs. There's an elevator, and one room is Americans with Disabilities Act compliant.

The attractive library has a fireplace, music, and overstuffed chairs. Downstairs is a game room with pool table and exercise equipment, plus wireless Web access throughout the inn. On many weekends, Dave parks his 1936 Cadillac in front to add a festive historic touch.

115 S. 26th St., Colorado Springs, CO 80904. © **888/375-4210** or 719/632-9194. Fax 719/632-9026. www.oldtown-guesthouse.com. 8 units. $99–$205 double. AE, DISC, MC, V. Off-road parking. Children under 12 not accepted. *In room:* A/C, cable TV, VCR, CD player, fridge, coffeemaker, hair dryer, iron.

MODERATE

Eastholme in the Rockies *☆*   Nestled in the quaint Pikes Peak mountain village of Cascade, 10 miles west of downtown Colorado Springs, this Victorian B&B gives guests an opportunity to see the city and get away from it all in the same day. Originally built in 1885 as a resort hotel, this property has a storied history that includes a stint as a boarding house before becoming a guest inn in 1988. Today it is a favorite of vacationers who want to be within striking distance of city attractions, but whose main interests lay in the Rockies.

The parlor holds a bay window, fireplace, and antiques. Most of the inn's large rooms feature 10-foot ceilings, and all provide plush quilts and remarkable views. The Marriott and Eisenhower suites feature original furnishings and a plethora of antiques, and the cottages offer VCRs, fireplaces, and spacious bathrooms with whirlpool tubs.

Breakfasts include freshly baked breads, pastries, and entrees such as soufflés or frittatas. The mountainous pine scenery of the Pike National Forest surrounds Eastholme, and stargazers love the views from the second-floor balcony, free of the light pollution of Colorado Springs. Guest amenities include a pleasant gazebo, shared kitchen, and library. Smoking is not permitted.

4445 Hagerman Ave. (P.O. Box 98), Cascade, CO 80809. © **800/672-9901** or 719/684-9901. www.eastholme. com. 8 units (6 with bathroom), including 2 cottages. $75–$120 double; $120 suite; $150 cottage. Rates include full breakfast. AE, DISC, MC, V. Free parking. 10 miles west of I-25, about 1 mile off U.S. 24. **Amenities:** Hot tub. *In-room:* Cable TV w/VCR, fridge, coffeemaker, hair dryer.

Hearthstone Inn *☆☆*   Among our top choices in Colorado Springs is this comfortably elegant small downtown lodging, a true old world–style inn that combines the allure of a grand, historic hotel with the intimacy of a small B&B. Actually two connected historic homes, built in 1885 and 1900, the Hearthstone is listed on the National Register of Historic Places and has won numerous preservation awards. Old photographs, numerous antiques, and reproductions decorate the inn. Some of the rooms can accommodate three or four people, and each unit has its own personality. The Study, for instance, is a parlor-style room with built-in bookcases and a fireplace. The Solarium features an open-air latticed porch, and the third-floor Loft has three dormer windows, a queen-size brass bed, and a tiny child's bed with a child-size rocking chair. Three rooms have fireplaces, and five have telephones with dataports. Breakfasts are wonderful, offering a choice of a half-dozen or so items such as breakfast burritos and eggs Benedict. The restaurant, which is open to the public (see "Where to Dine," below), also serves lunch and dinner. A common parlor has games, a piano, and fresh coffee. Children of all ages are welcome. Smoking is not permitted.

506 N. Cascade Ave., Colorado Springs, CO 80903. (C) **800/521-1885** or 719/473-4413. Fax 719/473-1322. www.hearthstoneinn.com. 25 units (2 with shared bathroom). $99–$159 double with private bathroom, $69 double with shared bathroom; $199 suite. Rates include full breakfast. AE, DISC, MC, V. Free off-street lighted parking. Small, well-behaved pets accepted. **Amenities:** Restaurant (American). *In room:* A/C.

Holden House 1902 Bed & Breakfast Inn Innkeepers Sallie and Welling Clark restored this storybook 1902 Colonial Revival–style Victorian house and its adjacent carriage house, and filled the rooms with antiques and family heirlooms. Located near Old Colorado City, the inn has a living room with a tile fireplace, a front parlor with a TV, verandas, and a gazebo out back in a lovely garden. Guests enjoy 24-hour coffee-and-tea service with a bottomless cookie jar, plus a gourmet breakfast in the formal dining room. Smoking is not allowed and pets are not permitted, but there are two resident cats, Ming-toy and Muffin.

Two rooms are in the main house and two are in the adjacent carriage house. Each guest room bears the name of a Colorado mining area and contains memorabilia of that district. All have sitting areas, queen-size beds, fireplaces, CD players, and tubs for two. The Cripple Creek suite features Victorian fretwork in the sitting area, a mahogany fireplace, and a magnificent Roman marble tub. The Independence Suite, in the adjacent building, is accessible to guests with disabilities and is cat-free for those with allergies.

1102 W. Pikes Peak Ave., Colorado Springs, CO 80904. (C) **888/565-3980** or 719/471-3980. Fax 719/471-4740. www.holdenhouse.com. 5 suites. $125–$150 double. Rates include full breakfast. AE, DC, DISC, MC, V. Children not accepted. *In room:* A/C, TV w/DVD player, fridge, iron, hair dryer.

Two Sisters Inn Built by two sisters in 1919 as a boardinghouse, this splendid bed-and-breakfast has been owned and operated by two women—sisters in spirit if not in blood—since 1990. Wendy Goldstein and Sharon Smith have furnished the four bedrooms and separate honeymoon cottage with family heirlooms and photographs, in a style best described as informal elegance. The rooms in the main house feature Victorian frills and furnishings, such as quilts and claw-foot bathtubs. The two rooms that share a bathroom are only rented together ($69 for the second bedroom), which is a great choice for two couples or for parents traveling with teenagers. Across a splendid garden area, the small cottage, with a separate bedroom and living room, has a feather bed, gas-log fireplace, refrigerator, and shower with skylight. Fresh flowers adorn each room, and homemade chocolates and baked goods are served upon arrival. The rooms are great, but we especially like the breakfasts, which the proprietors describe as "healthy decadence." They often cook with herbs and vegetables from their garden, and do some marvelous things with fruit. In the summer, Wendy and Sharon's lemonade, made fresh with naturally sparkling Manitou Springs water, is the perfect refreshment. Smoking is not permitted.

10 Otoe Place, Manitou Springs, CO 80829. (C) **800/2SISINN** or 719/685-9684. www.twosisinn.com. 5 units. $105 double; $125 cottage. Rates include full breakfast. DISC, MC, V. Children under 11 not accepted. Located 1 block south of the town clock on Manitou Ave. *In room:* No phone.

INEXPENSIVE

El Colorado Lodge While not particularly ritzy, El Colorado is an economical lodging and more interesting than a standard motel. The Southwestern-style cabins are a tad dated, but all of them have fireplaces and beamed ceilings, and nine have kitchens. Each holds one to three rooms and can accommodate two to six people. The lodge boasts the largest outdoor swimming pool in Manitou Springs and an outdoor pavilion for groups. Complimentary coffee is served during the summer.

23 Manitou Ave., Manitou Springs, CO 80829. ℂ 800/782-2246 or 719/685-5485. Fax 719/685-4699. www.pikes-peak.com/elcolorado. 26 cabins (6 with shower only). Summer $69–$125 cabin. Winter discounts available. AE, DC, DISC, MC, V. Free parking. **Amenities:** Large outdoor pool. *In room:* A/C, cable TV, kitchens, fridge, microwave.

Travel Inn *Value* Popular with both business travelers and vacationers on a budget, the Travel Inn offers a comfortable place to sleep at very reasonable rates. The two-story motel with bright turquoise trim is conveniently located near downtown Colorado Springs, with easy access to all the area attractions on I-25 and U.S. 24. The recently remodeled rooms are simple and comfortable, with white stucco walls and dark-wood furnishings. There is one apartment with a kitchenette that is designed for longer stays.

512 S. Nevada Ave., Colorado Springs, CO 80903. ℂ 719/636-3986. Fax 719/636-3980. 34 units (most with shower only). Summer $45–$52 double; winter $32–$37 double. Rates include continental breakfast. AE, DC, DISC, MC, V. Free parking. **Amenities:** Coin-op laundry. *In room:* A/C, cable TV, kitchenette.

CAMPING

Also see the section on **Mueller State Park** under "Parks & Zoos," later in this chapter.

Garden of the Gods Campground Located near Garden of the Gods (see "Attractions," later in this chapter), this large, tree-shaded campground offers 250 full RV hookups (30- and 50-amp service, some with modems and phones) and additional tent sites. Facilities include tables, barbecue grills, bathhouses, a grocery store, Internet cafe, laundry, heated swimming pool, whirlpool tub, playground, and clubhouse with pool tables and game room. The 12 camping cabins, which share the campground's bathhouse, rent for $40 double. Tours are also offered (see "Organized Tours," later in this chapter).

3704 W. Colorado Ave., Colorado Springs, CO 80904. ℂ 800/248-9451 or 719/475-9450. www.colorado campground.com. $28–$38 for 2 people. Extra person $3. DISC, MC, V. Take I-25 exit 141, head west on U.S. 24, then north (right) on 31st St., then left on Colorado Ave. for 6 blocks (keep right), and turn right to gate.

4 Where to Dine

Colorado Springs has an excellent variety of above-average restaurants, with a good sampling of Continental cuisine, Mexican restaurants, and steak joints. See also the section on dinner theaters in "Colorado Springs After Dark," later in this chapter. A good online resource for information on area restaurants and nightlife is www.sceneinthesprings.com.

VERY EXPENSIVE

Charles Court ★★ PROGRESSIVE AMERICAN The English country-manor atmosphere of this outstanding restaurant at The Broadmoor resort, with picture windows looking across Cheyenne Lake to the renowned hotel, lends itself to a fine dining experience. The creative American menu, which changes seasonally, has a decidedly Rocky Mountain emphasis. You'll usually find such delicacies as Colorado rack of lamb, beef tenderloin, salmon filet, grilled ahi tuna, and a wild-game selection such as Colorado elk. The wine list includes more than 600 selections, service is superlative, and the desserts are extraordinary. A seasonal outdoor patio provides splendid views of the mountains across the lake.

Broadmoor W., in The Broadmoor, Lake Circle. © **719/634-7711.** Reservations recommended. Breakfast $7.75–$16; dinner main courses $18–$36. AE, DC, DISC, MC, V. Daily 7–11am and 6–10pm.

Cliff House Dining Room ★★ AMERICAN   The Cliff House Dining Room is an excellent choice for a romantic occasion. The Villeroy & Boch china, damask linen, crystal glassware, and 19th-century tiled fireplace evoke the charm of the Victorian era. Dinners are the main event; old favorites expertly prepared in new ways. We recommend the filet mignon, charbroiled with roasted garlic pepper, and the seafood (trout to scallops and prawns), but everything is quite good. As would be expected, service is impeccable. The breakfast menu offers traditional American selections, plus a nifty wild-mushroom Florentine with smoked bacon, and lunches are upscale sandwiches and entrees like quiche du jour and blackened ruby-red trout. The excellent wine list includes some 600 selections.

Cliff House Inn, 306 Cañon Ave., Manitou Springs. © **719/785-2415.** Reservations recommended. Lunch main courses $7–$24; fixed-price lunch $18; dinner main courses $24–$32. AE, DC, DISC, MC, V. Daily 6:30–10:30am, 11:30am–2:30pm, and 5:30–9:30pm.

Craftwood Inn ★★★ *Finds* COLORADO CUISINE   Ensconced in an English Tudor building with beamed ceilings, stained-glass windows, and a copper-hooded fireplace, the casually elegant Craftwood Inn, built in 1912, was originally a coppersmith's shop. Today this excellent restaurant specializes in regional game and also offers steak, seafood, and vegetarian dishes. The extensive selection of game—elk, venison, pheasant, quail, caribou, antelope, wild boar, ostrich, and buffalo—attracts the most acclaim. We especially recommend grilled Rocky Mountain elk steak (when available), marinated in herb-and-smoke-infused oil, and served with wild-mushroom ragout, cabernet sauvignon glace, and cheddar-sage whipped potatoes. The adventurous might opt for the wild grill: grilled North American elk, seared loin of antelope, and braised venison sausage, served with pear potato. Be sure to save room for one of the superb—and somewhat unusual—desserts, such as jalapeño white-chocolate mousse with raspberry sauce, or prickly pear sorbet. The outdoor patio provides wonderful views of Pikes Peak.

404 El Paso Blvd., Manitou Springs. © **719/685-9000.** Reservations recommended. Main courses $18–$38. AE, DC, DISC, MC, V. Daily 5:30–8:30pm. Turn north off Manitou Ave. onto Mayfair Ave., go uphill 1 block, and turn left onto El Paso Blvd.; the Craftwood is on your right.

Walter's Bistro ★★★ CONTINENTAL   Slick but not stuffy, Walter's manages to be classy, casual, and classic, all at once. Proprietor Walter Iser, a native of Salzburg, Austria, has long worked the front of the house in various upscale properties in the Springs and environs, but he's truly hit his stride with Walter's, which opened in 1999 and relocated to a handsome new location in 2004. Watching over four dining areas—including a richly decorated "red room" and a chef's table beneath windows into the kitchen—Iser's gracious style and steady direction leads right into an expertly prepared menu of continental staples that manage to simultaneously taste traditional and completely original. The menu changes regularly, but our visit included a terrific rack of lamb, herb-roasted and served with a creamy English pea risotto, pan-roasted Chilean sea bass, and a truly phenomenal bone-in filet mignon with an equally superlative bread pudding with wild mushrooms and andouille sausage. Desserts are decadent, including a chocolate "bag" filled with tiramisu, and the wine list is long and varied.

136 E. Cheyenne Mountain Blvd. © **719/630-0201.** Reservations recommended. Lunch main courses $7–$24; fixed-price lunch $18; dinner main courses $24–$32. AE, DC, DISC, MC, V. Mon–Fri 11am–2pm; Sun–Thurs 5:30–9pm; Fri–Sat 5:30–10pm; Sun brunch 10:30am–2pm.

EXPENSIVE

Blue Star MEDITERRANEAN   In a quiet area just south of downtown, Blue Star is one of the most popular eateries in Colorado Springs, and deservedly so. The menu changes weekly, but it always includes filet mignon, fresh fish (flown in daily), pasta, pork, and chicken, prepared with a nose for invention. The culinary inspiration from both Mediterranean and Pacific Rim cultures; the restaurant might serve Thai beef tips one week and beef bourguignon the next. Standing room only on weekends, the bar features sleek wood-and-metal decor and well-lighted artwork on the walls, while the dining room's atmosphere is milder with an open kitchen. Each serves its own menu: The bar one is "eating" (i.e. lunch, dinner, tapas, live jazz Mondays, dancing on weekends) and the main room is serious "dining," dinner only, as the proprietors say. Blue Star won *Wine Spectator's* "Best of" award with its 6,000-bottle cellar in 2003.

1645 S. Tejon St. © **719/632-1086.** Reservations recommended. Main courses $7–$13 lunch, $15–$24 dinner. AE, MC, V. Dining room Sun–Thurs 5:30–9pm; Fri–Sat 5:30–10pm. Bar open during restaurant hours; bar food service Mon–Fri 11:30am–midnight.

Hearthstone Inn AMERICAN   Located in one of our favorite Colorado Springs inns, this restaurant offers a splendid atmosphere and equally splendid food. The dining room, like the rest of the historic Hearthstone Inn, is decorated in elegant yet comfortable Victorian style. The cuisine is innovative American—you'll always recognize what you're eating, but you've likely never seen or tasted it quite this way before. The breakfast menu includes well-prepared standards and more exotic dishes such as blue-crab fritters with jalapeño hollandaise and sweet-potato scallion cakes. At lunch, try cayenne-dusted rainbow trout, served with simmered black beans and green chile polenta. Dinners include mostly beef and seafood. Grilled New York strip steak with bourbon sauce is quite good, and we also recommend pan-roasted North Atlantic salmon with cranberry-tarragon aioli and goat-cheese polenta.

506 N. Cascade Ave. © **800/521-1885** or 719/473-4413. Main courses $7–$12 lunch, $12–$25 dinner. AE, DISC, MC, V. Mon–Tues 7am–2pm; Wed–Thurs and Sun 7am–7pm; Fri–Sat 7am–9pm.

La Petite Maison FRENCH/CONTEMPORARY   This delightful 1894 Victorian cottage houses a gem of a restaurant. It serves a blend of classic French and eclectic modern cuisine in a friendly, intimate setting with jazz playing in the background. The food is innovative, interesting, and well presented; service is impeccable. This is where locals go to celebrate special occasions. An attractive patio is open in warm weather, and the luncheon/patio menu is available anytime the patio is open (until 11pm in summer). The menus change monthly; if they're available, we suggest curried chicken salad with cashews and grapes, and crab cakes with corn pico de gallo. Being beefeaters, we especially like a dinner of grilled Black Angus filet with fresh horseradish-and-peppercorn crust and shallot jus. Another good dinner item is nut-crusted duck breast with brandy-infused cherries. There's also usually a handmade vegetarian pasta of the day. Desserts, all made in-house, might include white-chocolate mousse with fresh berries, fresh fruit tart with almond paste, or crème brûlée.

1015 W. Colorado Ave. © **719/632-4887.** Reservations recommended. Main courses $8–$15 patio/lunch, $17–$28 dinner. AE, DC, DISC, MC, V. Mon–Fri 11am–2pm; Mon–Sat 5–10pm.

Margarita at PineCreek ☆☆ ECLECTIC   A delightful spot to sit and watch the sun setting over Pikes Peak, the Margarita is tucked away above two creeks on the north side of the city. The decor is attractively simple, with tile floors and stucco walls; a tree-shaded outdoor patio is open in summer. Saturday evenings bring live harpsichord music in the dining room, and Friday nights often feature live acoustic music—bluegrass to Celtic.

Although the style of cooking may vary, depending on the chef's whim, the emphasis is on fresh ingredients, and everything is prepared from scratch, including breads and stocks. Lunches feature a choice of soup (usually a broth and a bisque), salad, and fresh bread; there's also a Southwestern special. Six-course dinners offer three entree choices, usually fresh fish, veal, steak, pasta, lamb, or duckling.

7350 Pine Creek Rd. ℂ 719/598-8667. Reservations recommended. Fixed-price lunch $9.50; fixed-price dinner $30–$35; brunch $10–$15. AE, DISC, MC, V. Tues–Fri 11:30am–2pm; Tues–Sat 5:30–9pm; Sun 10:30am–2pm.

Steaksmith ☆☆ STEAK/SEAFOOD   The Steaksmith serves some of the best steaks and seafood in the region, and is our choice for an evening of serious beefeating. Lots of wood and hanging plants give the dining room a comfortable, relaxing atmosphere, and a big fireplace is the centerpiece of the lounge. This is the place to come for top-quality choice-aged, house-cut beef. We especially recommend cracked-peppercorn top sirloin, served on a bed of demi-glace with cognac cream sauce. Not keen on sauces on your steak? You won't be sorry trying rib-eye, broiled under high heat. The Steaksmith also offers excellent fresh fish and seafood; if it's on the menu, you can't miss with wild-caught Alaskan king salmon. The Mexican jumbo shrimp plate, either broiled or deep-fried, is also something special. Be warned that some items often sell out early in the evening—a sure sign of success. The menu, much of which changes daily, also may include Colorado lamb chops, vegetarian entrees, homemade soups, and delicious homemade desserts. There's a full-service bar and an extensive wine list. Smoking is allowed only in the fireside cocktail lounge.

3802 Maizeland Rd. (at Academy Blvd.). ℂ 800/201-2736 or 719/596-9300. Reservations recommended. Main courses $14–$35. AE, DISC, MC, V. Daily 5–10pm. Bar opens at 4:30pm.

The Tavern ☆☆ STEAK/SEAFOOD   Authentic Toulouse-Lautrec lithographs on the walls and knotty pine furniture and paneling mark the Tavern as a restaurant with unusual ambience. In the front dining room, a four-piece ensemble follows piano music nightly—guests are welcome to take a turn around the dance floor between courses. The quieter garden room, with luxuriant tropical foliage, gives the feeling of outdoor dining without being outdoors. Service in both rooms is impeccable.

Many selections are prepared in the restaurant's stone grill, and the emphasis is on fresh ingredients and classic cuisine. The lunch menu changes seasonally, but typically includes steaks, gourmet burgers, crab cakes, and a variety of sandwiches and salads. Dinners are more elaborate: Choose from slow-roasted prime rib, filet mignon, blackened or broiled salmon, or half a roast duck or chicken. All entrees come with a selection of homemade breads.

Broadmoor Main, at The Broadmoor, Lake Circle. ℂ 719/634-7711. Reservations recommended. Main courses $7.50–$17 lunch, $17–$35 dinner. AE, DC, DISC, MC, V. Daily 11am–11pm.

MODERATE

Edelweiss Restaurant ☆ *Kids* GERMAN   The Edelweiss occupies an impressive stone building with a trio of fireplaces and an outdoor patio. Strolling folk musicians on weekends underscore its Bavarian atmosphere, which gives it a party feel that makes this a fun place for kids. It offers a hearty menu of Jäger-schnitzel, Wiener schnitzel, sauerbraten, bratwurst, and other old-country spe-cials, as well as New York strip steak, fresh fish, and chicken. The fruit strudels are excellent, and there are some great German beers.

34 E. Ramona Ave. (southwest of I-25, 1 block west of Nevada Ave.). © 719/633-2220. Reservations rec-ommended. Main courses $6–$8.25 lunch, $9.75–$20 dinner. AE, DC, DISC, MC, V. Tues–Fri 11:30am–9pm; Sat 5–9pm; Sun noon–9pm.

Giuseppe's Old Depot Restaurant ✦ Kids ITALIAN/AMERICAN

Located in a restored Denver & Rio Grande train station with glass ticket win-dows lining the walls, Giuseppe's is a fun place with a lot of historic ambience. You can see freight trains going by just outside the windows. The same extensive menu is served all day. Spaghetti, lasagna (vegetarian spinach or spicy sausage and ground beef), and stone-baked pizza are house specialties. American dishes include our favorite—baby back pork ribs, smothered in Giuseppe's secret sauce—plus prime rib, grilled salmon filet, and fried chicken.

10 S. Sierra Madre St. © 719/635-3111. Menu items $5–$23; pizzas $10–$15. AE, DC, DISC, MC, V. Sun–Thurs 11am–9pm; Fri–Sat 11am–10pm.

Marigold Café and Bakery ✦ INTERNATIONAL

This bustling restau-rant and bakery is known for its fresh ingredients and homemade breads and pastries. A low wall separates the bakery counter from the cafelike dining area. Breakfast and lunch are casual, featuring traditional menus and gourmet-savvy items such as Greek pizzas and innovative sandwiches served on fresh breads. The restaurant takes on a more refined atmosphere at dinner, when the menu reflects a wide range of international influences. Favorites include *culotte* of beef (grilled sirloin steak with shallot red-wine sauce) and papillotte salmon, baked with sun-dried-tomato pesto, fresh lemon, dill, and leeks. The bakery counter bustles through the early afternoon, offering splendid breads, pastries, and sand-wiches. Box lunches, coffee, lattes, and cappuccinos are also available.

4605 Centennial Blvd. (at Garden of the Gods Rd.). © 719/599-4776. Main courses $5.50–$10 lunch, $9.25–$23 dinner. AE, DC, DISC, MC, V. Restaurant Mon–Sat 7–10:30am, 11am–2:30pm, and 5–9pm; coffee bar and bakery Mon–Fri 6am–9pm, Sat 7am–9pm.

Phantom Canyon Brewing Co. ✦ CONTEMPORARY AMERICAN

This popular, busy, noisy brewpub is in the Cheyenne Building, home to the Chicago Rock Island & Pacific Railroad in the early 1900s. On any given day, 8 to 10 of Phantom Canyon's specialty beers are on tap, including homemade root beer. The signature beer is the Phantom, a traditional India pale ale; others include an amber ale, a light ale called Queen's Blonde, and Zebulon's Peated Porter.

The dining room is large and wide open, with ceiling fans, hardwood floors, and sizeable brewing vats, visible in the corner. Lunch is typical but well-pre-pared brewpub fare: wood-fired pizzas, hearty salads, half-pound beef or buffalo burgers, fish and chips, and the like. The dinner menu is varied and more inno-vative, with choices such as sesame chicken stir-fry with sticky rice, or brie-stuffed top sirloin, or even macaroni and smoked gouda cheese tossed with bacon, spinach, and shiitake mushrooms. The menu changes periodically. On the second floor is a billiard hall with its own menu of pizza, calzones, salad, and appetizers. See also "Colorado Springs After Dark," later in this chapter.

2 E. Pikes Peak Ave. © 719/635-2800. Main courses $7.25–$11 lunch, $9.95–$19 dinner. AE, DC, DISC, MC, V. Mon–Thurs 11am–10pm; Fri–Sat 11am–midnight; Sun 9am–10pm.

(Kids) **Family-Friendly Restaurants**

Edelweiss Restaurant (p. 156)   Kids will enjoy the strolling musicians who play German folk music on weekends, and they'll love the apple and cherry strudels.

Giuseppe's Old Depot Restaurant (p. 157)   An original locomotive stands outside this old Denver & Rio Grande Railroad station. Most kids will adore the spaghetti and pizza.

Meadow Muffins (p. 159)   The junk-store appearance and kid-friendly food (like a burger with peanut butter) make this place a hit with the younger set.

Ritz Grill ⋆ NEW AMERICAN   This lively restaurant-lounge with a large central bar is where it's at for many of the city's young professionals. The decor is Art Deco, the service fast and friendly. The varied, trendy menu offers such specialties as Garden Ritz veggie pizza, with fresh spinach, sun-dried tomatoes, bell peppers, onions, mushrooms, fresh pesto, and three cheeses; and Chinese chicken salad—served with rice noodles, tomatoes, water chestnuts, and other veggies. For beefeaters, we recommend the mesquite-grilled 8-ounce center-cut filet mignon, served on a bed of raspberry-chipotle demi-glace, or the semolina-crusted salmon with shrimp and spinach nantua sauce. See also "Colorado Springs After Dark," later in this chapter.

15 S. Tejon St. ⓒ 719/635-8484. Main courses $6–$12 brunch and lunch, $10–$25 dinner. AE, MC, V. Mon–Thurs 11am–midnight; Fri–Sat 11am–1am; Sun 9:30am–midnight. Bar open later with a limited menu.

INEXPENSIVE

Adam's Mountain Cafe ⋆⋆ (Finds) AMERICAN/VEGETARIAN   Not strictly vegetarian, Adam's Mountain Cafe is one of the best restaurants in the area for those seeking vegetarian or what we might call health food. Exposed brick and stone, antique tables and chairs, fresh flowers, and original works by a local artist create a country French–Victorian appearance. The menu includes grilled items, fresh fish, and many Mediterranean-style entrees. Breakfast specialties include orange-almond French toast, our top choice, and the P. W. Busboy Special, consisting of two whole-grain pancakes, two scrambled eggs, and slices of fresh fruit. Lunch offerings include sandwiches, soups, salads, fresh pasta, and Southwestern plates. We recommend the harvest crepes, packed with roasted butternut squash and finished with a vegetarian red chile, and the Caribbean jerked chicken.

110 Cañon Ave., Manitou Springs. ⓒ 719/685-1430. Main courses $4.50–$7.50 breakfast and lunch, $7–$16 dinner. AE, DISC, MC, V. Daily 8am–3pm; Tues–Sat 5–9pm.

Amanda's Fonda ⋆ (Finds) AMERICAN   Our pick for Mexican food in Colorado Springs, Amanda's Fonda is the handiwork of a family that has owned Mexican restaurants for five generations. Clearly they've honed the art of making remarkable chili in that time: Both the chili Colorado and the green chili are excellent; the former is red with big hunks of steak, the latter spicier with pork. The burritos, spinach-and-mushroom enchiladas, and seafood are also quite tasty, and the menu includes both menudo and *pozole,* a Mexican soup, on weekends. The interior of the place is a funky maze, one part log cabin, one part suburban family restaurant, and one part Mexican bar and grill.

3625 W. Colorado Ave. ✆ **719/227-1975.** Main courses $6–$12. AE, DISC, MC, V. Mon–Sat 11:30–9pm; Sun noon–9pm.

Dutch Kitchen ✮ *Value* AMERICAN   Good homemade food served in a casual, friendly atmosphere is the draw at this relatively small restaurant, which the Flynn family has owned and operated since 1959. We especially like the corned beef, pastrami, and ham sandwiches, and if you're there in summer, be sure to try the fresh rhubarb pie. Other house specialties include buttermilk pie and homemade soups.

1025 Manitou Ave., Manitou Springs. ✆ **719/685-9962.** Main courses $4.25–$6.45 lunch, $5.60–$12 dinner. Sat–Thurs 11:30am–3:30pm and 4:30–8pm. Closed Thurs in spring and fall. Closed Dec–Feb.

Meadow Muffins ✮ *Value* *Kids* AMERICAN   A fun spot for a good, inexpensive meal in a lively atmosphere, Meadow Muffins is a boisterous bar packed with movie memorabilia and assorted oddities. The decorations range from two buckboard wagons (hung from the ceiling near the front door) that were supposedly used in *Gone with the Wind* to a 5-ton cannon used in a number of war movies. The menu includes chicken wings, onion rings, sandwiches, salads, and the like. The burgers are especially good—just ask anyone in the Springs—but we have to admit that we couldn't bring ourselves to try the Jiffy Burger: a large ground-beef burger topped with bacon, provolone cheese, and—believe it or not—peanut butter. On most days, there are great food and drink specials. See also "Colorado Springs After Dark," later in this chapter.

2432 W. Colorado Ave., in Old Colorado City. ✆ **719/633-0583.** Most menu items $4.25–$6.75. AE, DISC, MC, V. Daily 11am–2am (or earlier, depending on business).

Michelle's ✮ *Value* AMERICAN/GREEK/SOUTHWESTERN   The menu is eclectic, but it's amazing how many different dishes Michelle's prepares well— and at such reasonable prices. Since it opened in 1952, this charming little diner and candy store hasn't changed much: It's long been known for its excellent handmade chocolates, fresh-churned ice cream, and Greek specialties such as gyros and spanakopita. It also serves good burgers, croissant sandwiches, a half-dozen salads, numerous omelets, and a delicious breakfast burrito. A three-page ice-cream menu includes everything from a single scoop of vanilla to the "Believe It or Not Sundae" featured in *Life* magazine in November 1959: It weighs 42 pounds and includes every flavor of ice cream Michelle's makes!

122 N. Tejon St. ✆ **719/633-5089.** Reservations not accepted. Lunch and dinner $5–$8.50. AE, DC, DISC, MC, V. Mon–Thurs 9am–11pm; Fri–Sat 9am–midnight; Sun 10am–11pm.

5 Attractions

Most of the attractions of the Pikes Peak region fit in two general categories: natural, such as Pikes Peak, Garden of the Gods, and Cave of the Winds, and historic/educational, including the Air Force Academy, Olympic Complex training center, museums, historic homes, and art galleries. There are also gambling houses in Cripple Creek.

If you visit Colorado from a sea-level area, you might want to schedule mountain excursions, such as the cog railway to the top of Pikes Peak, at the end of your stay. This will give your body time to adapt to the lower oxygen level at these higher elevations. See also "Health & Safety," in chapter 2.

Colorado Springs Attractions

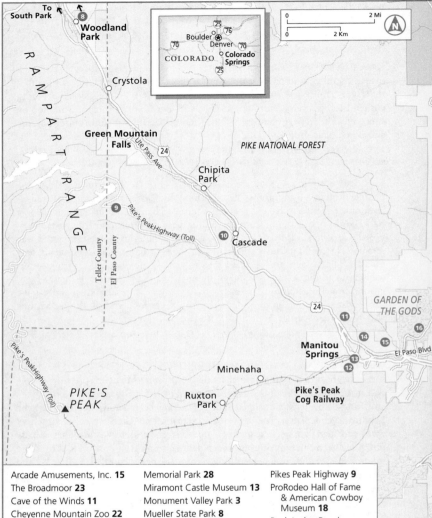

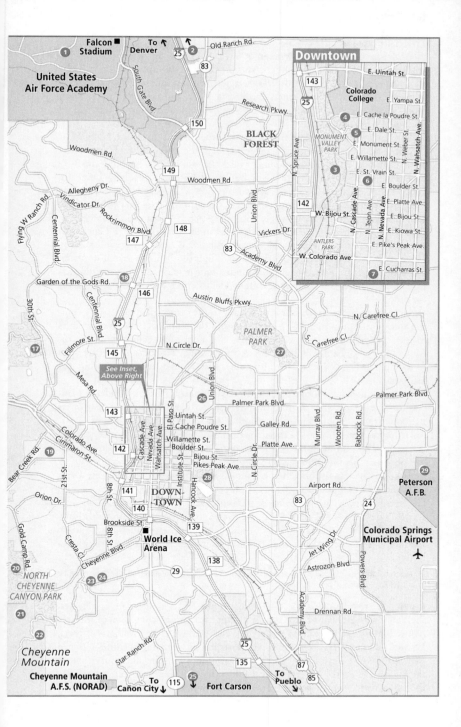

Falcon ■ Stadium
1
To ↑ Denver
2 ↑ Old Ranch Rd.
25
83

United States
Air Force Academy

South Gate Blvd.

Research Pkwy.

150

BLACK
FOREST

Woodmen Rd.

149

Woodmen Rd.

Allegheny Dr.
Vindicator Dr.
Rockrimmon Blvd.

147
148

Vickers Dr.

83
Academy Blvd.

Union Blvd.

Downtown

143
25
Colorado
College
E. Uintah St.
E. Yampa St.
4 E. Cache la Poudre St.
5 E. Dale St.
MONUMENT
VALLEY
PARK
E. Monument St.
3 E. Willamette St.
E. St. Vrain St.
6 E. Boulder St.
142 W. Bijou St.
E. Platte Ave.
E. Bijou St.
E. Kiowa St.
ANTLERS
PARK
E. Pike's Peak Ave.
W. Colorado Ave.
7 E. Cucharras St.

N. Spruce Ave.
N. Cascade Ave.
N. Tejon St.
N. Nevada Ave.
N. Wahsatch Ave.
N. Weber St.

Garden of the Gods Rd.
18
146

Austin Bluffs Pkwy.

PALMER
PARK

N. Carefree Cl.
S. Carefree Cl.

Flying W Ranch Rd.
Centennial Blvd.

30th St.

Centennial Blvd.

25

145

Fillmore St.

17

Mesa Rd.

N Circle Dr.

27

Union Blvd.

Palmer Park Blvd.

See Inset,
Above Right

143

26

Palmer Park Blvd.

Galley Rd.

Platte Ave.

Murray Blvd.
Wooten Rd.
Babcock Rd.

Colorado Ave.
Cimmaron St.

Bear Creek Rd.
19
21st St.

142

Cascade Ave.
Nevada Ave.
Wahsatch Ave.
El Paso St.
Uintah St.
Cache Poudre St.
Willamette St.
Boulder St.
Bijou St.
Pikes Peak Ave.

Institute St.

N. Circle Dr.

Airport Rd.

29
Peterson
A.F.B.

Orion Dr.

8th St.

141

DOWN-
TOWN

Hancock Ave.

28

83

24

Colorado Springs
Municipal Airport
✈

140
Brookside St.
■ World Ice
Arena

8th St. Blvd.
Cheyenne Blvd.
Cresta Cl.

139

Jet Wing Dr.

Gold Camp Rd.
20
NORTH
CHEYENNE
CANYON PARK

23 24
29

138

Astrozon Blvd.

Powers Blvd.

21

22

Cheyenne
Mountain

Cheyenne Mountain
A.F.S. (NORAD)

Star Ranch Rd.

To
Cañon City ↓
115
25 ↓
Fort Carson

25

135

To
Pueblo ↓

87
85

Academy Blvd.

Drennan Rd.

THE TOP ATTRACTIONS

United States Air Force Academy ★★ Colorado Springs' pride and joy got its start in 1954 when Congress authorized the establishment of a U.S. Air Force Academy and chose this 18,000-acre site from among 400 prospective locations. The first class of cadets enrolled in 1959, and each year since, about 4,000 cadets have enrolled for the 4 years of rigorous training required to become Air Force officers.

The academy is 12 miles north of downtown; enter at the North Gate, off I-25 exit 156B. Soon after entering the grounds, at the intersection of North Gate Boulevard and Stadium Boulevard, you'll see an impressive outdoor B-52 bomber display. Where North Gate Boulevard becomes Academy Drive (in another mile or so), look to your left to see the Cadet Field House, where the basketball and ice hockey teams play (see "Spectator Sports," later in this chapter), and the Parade Ground, where you can sometimes spot cadets marching.

Academy Drive soon curves to the left. Six miles from the North Gate, signs mark the turnoff to the Barry Goldwater Air Force Academy Visitor Center. Open daily, it offers a variety of exhibits and films on the academy's history and cadet life, extensive literature and self-guided tour maps, and the latest information and schedules on academy activities. There's also a large gift shop and coffee shop.

A short trail from the visitor center leads to the Cadet Chapel. Its 17 gleaming aluminum spires soar 150 feet, and within the building are separate chapels for the major Western faiths as well as an "all-faiths" room. The public can visit Monday through Saturday from 9am to 5pm; Sunday services at 10am are open to the public. The chapel is closed for 5 days around graduation and during special events.

Also within easy walking distance of the visitor center are the Academy Planetarium, a classroom for astronomy, physics, and navigation classes that offers periodic free public programs; Arnold Hall, the social center that houses historical exhibits, a cafeteria, and a theater featuring a variety of public shows and lectures; and Harmon Hall, the administration building, where prospective cadets can obtain admission information.

After leaving the visitor center, continue south, then east, on Academy Drive to Stadium Boulevard; you will see Falcon Stadium on your right. Turn right on Stadium Boulevard and follow it out to South Gate Boulevard, which leaves the academy grounds at I-25 exit 150B. En route, you'll pass the Thunderbird Airmanship Overlook, where you might be lucky enough to see cadets parachuting, soaring, and practicing their takeoffs and landings in U.S. Air Force Thunderbirds.

Off I-25 exit 156B. ✆ 719/333-8723. www.usafa.af.mil. Free admission. Summer daily 9am–6pm; winter daily 9am–5pm; additional hours for special events.

Garden of the Gods ★★★ *Value* One of the West's unique geological sites, the 1,300-acre Garden of the Gods is a giant rock garden composed of spectacular red sandstone formations sculpted by rain and wind over millions of years. Located where several life zones and ecosystems converge, the beautiful city-run park harbors a variety of plant and animal communities. The oldest survivors are the ancient, twisted junipers, some 1,000 years old. The strangest animals are the honey ants, which gorge themselves on honey in the summer and fall, becoming living honey pots to feed their colonies during winter hibernation.

The park has a number of hiking trails—mostly easy to moderate—that offer great scenery and an opportunity to get away from the crowds. Leashed dogs are

---

Fun Fact Fit for the Gods

In 1859 large numbers of pioneers were arriving in Colorado hoping to find gold (their motto: "Pikes Peak or Bust"). Many of them established communities along what is now called the Front Range, including Colorado City, which was later incorporated within Colorado Springs.

Legend has it that certain pioneers who explored the remarkable sandstone formations in the area wanted to establish a beer garden there. However, one Rufus Cable objected: "Beer Garden! Why, this is a fit place for a Garden of the Gods!"

Fortunately for posterity, Charles Elliott Perkins (head of the Burlington Railroad) bought the area some 20 years later and kept it in its natural state. Upon Perkins's death in 1907, his heirs gave the remarkable area to Colorado Springs on the condition that it be preserved as a park and open to the public. The park was dedicated in 1909 and is now a Registered National Landmark.

---

permitted on trails (owners should clean up after their pets). Many trails are also open to horseback riding and mountain biking. You can get trail maps for the park at the **Visitor Center,** which also offers exhibits on the history, geology, plants, and wildlife of the area; a cafeteria; and other conveniences.

A 12-minute multimedia theater presentation, *How Did Those Red Rocks Get There?* ($2 adults, $1 children 5–12, free for children under 5), is a fast-paced exploration of the geologic history of the area. In summer, park naturalists lead free 45-minute walks through the park and conduct free afternoon interpretive programs. You can also take a 20-minute bus tour of the park ($3.75 adults, $2.50 children under 13). You may spot technical rock climbers on some of the park spires; they are required to register at the visitor center.

Also in the park is the **Rock Ledge Ranch Historic Site** (see "More Attractions," below).

1805 N. 30th St. © 719/634-6666. www.gardenofgods.com or www.springsgov.com (follow links). Free admission. Park May–Oct daily 5am–11pm, Nov–Apr daily 5am–9pm; Visitor Center June–Aug daily 8am–8pm, Sept–May daily 9am–5pm. Take Garden of the Gods Rd. west from I-25 exit 146 and turn south on 30th St.

Pikes Peak Cog Railway ★★ For those who enjoy rail travel, spectacular scenery, and the thrill of mountain climbing without all the work, this is the trip to take. The first passenger train climbed Pikes Peak on June 30, 1891, and diesel slowly replaced steam power between 1939 and 1955. Four custom-built Swiss twin-unit rail cars, each seating 216 passengers, went into service in 1989. The 9-mile route, with grades up to 25%, takes 75 minutes to reach the top of 14,110-foot Pikes Peak; the round-trip requires 3 hours and 10 minutes (including a 40-min. stopover at the top). Runs depart between 8am and 5pm in midsummer, with shorter hours at other times.

The journey is exciting from the start, but passengers really begin to ooh and aah when the track leaves the forest, creeping above timberline at about 11,500 feet. The view from the summit takes in Denver, 75 miles north; New Mexico's Sangre de Cristo range, 100 miles south; the Cripple Creek mining district, on the mountain's western flank; wave after wave of Rocky Mountain subranges to the west; and the seemingly endless sea of Great Plains to the east. This is also where you'll want to watch for Rocky Mountain bighorn

---

Fun Fact **Top of the Charts**

Teacher Katharine Lee Bates (1859–1929) wrote the patriotic song "America the Beautiful" after an 1895 wagon trip to the top of Pikes Peak.

---

sheep and yellow-bellied marmots. The Summit House at the top of Pikes Peak has a restaurant (sandwiches, snacks, beverages, and box lunches) and a gift shop.

Take a jacket or sweater—it can be cold and windy on top, even on warm summer days. This trip is not recommended if you have cardiac or respiratory problems. Even those in good health may feel faint or light-headed.

515 Ruxton Ave., Manitou Springs. (✆) **719/685-5401.** www.cograilway.com. $26–$27 adults, $14–$15 children under 12, free for children under 3 held on an adult's lap. Mid-Apr to early Jan, with 2 to 8 departures daily; call or check schedules online. Closed Jan to mid-Apr. Reservations required (available online). Take I-25 exit 141 west on U.S. 24 for 4 miles, turn onto Manitou Ave. west and go 1½ miles to Ruxton Ave., turn left and go about ½ mile.

Pikes Peak Highway   Perhaps no view in Colorado equals the 360-degree panorama from the 14,110-foot summit of Pikes Peak. Whether you go by cog railway (see above) or private vehicle, the ascent is a spectacular, exciting experience—although not for those with heart or breathing problems or a fear of heights. The 19-mile toll highway (paved for 7 miles, all-weather gravel thereafter) starts at 7,400 feet, some 4 miles west of Manitou Springs. There are numerous photo stops as you head up the mountain, and deer, mountain sheep, marmots, and other animals often appear on the slopes, especially above timberline (around 11,500 ft.). This 156-curve road is the site of the annual Pikes Peak International Hill Climb (see "Spectator Sports," later in this chapter). Allow 3 hours minimum.

Off U.S. 24 at Cascade Ave. (✆) **800/318-9505** or 719/385-7325. www.pikespeakcolorado.com. Admission $10 adults, free for children under 16, or $35 per car. Memorial Day to Labor Day daily 7am–7pm; Labor Day to late Sept daily 7am–5pm; Oct to Memorial Day daily 9am–3pm, weather permitting. Take I-25 exit 141 west on U.S. 24 about 10 miles.

Colorado Springs Pioneers Museum ★★ *Value*   Housed in the former El Paso County Courthouse (1903), which is on the National Register of Historic Places, this museum is an excellent place to begin your visit to Colorado Springs. Exhibits depict the community's rich history, including its beginning as a fashionable resort, the railroad and mining eras, and its growth and development in the 20th century. Also here are the Victorian home of writer Helen Hunt Jackson; an exhibit on the city's dental, medical, and pharmaceutical industry; and early-20th-century toys, quilts, and clothing.

You can ride an Otis birdcage elevator, which dates to the early 1900s, to the restored original courtroom, where several *Perry Mason* episodes were filmed. A recent renovation uncovered intriguing gold and silver images of goddesses painted on the courtroom walls in part to represent the two key resources of the state's economy at the time. However, it's believed that they were also painted as a subtle protest when the country was changing from a gold and silver standard to a gold-only monetary standard. Another series of murals depict over 400 years of Pikes Peak region history.

Changing exhibit areas house traveling shows such as quilts, historic photographs, aviation, American-Indian culture, and art pottery. The museum has hosted a wide range of events, including lectures on the American cowboy, antique-auto shows, jazz concerts, and Hispanic celebrations. The historic reference library and archives are available by appointment. Allow 1 to 3 hours.

215 S. Tejon St. ℂ 719/385-5990. www.cspm.org. Free admission, donations accepted. Year-round Tues–Sat 10am–5pm; Jun–Aug Sun 1–5pm. Take I-25 exit 141 east to Tejon St., turn right and go 4 blocks.

United States Olympic Complex   So you think your local fitness center is state of the art? Check out the 37-acre United States Olympic Complex, a sophisticated center where thousands of athletes train each year in a variety of Olympic sports. Free guided tours, available daily, take about an hour, and include a film depicting the U.S. Olympic effort. Visitors may also see athletes in training. The visitor center includes the U.S. Olympic Hall of Fame, interactive kiosks on Olympics subjects, various other displays, and a gift shop that sells Olympic-logo merchandise.

The complex includes the **Olympic Sports Center I,** with five gymnasiums and a weight-training room; **Sports Center II,** which accommodates 14 sports; the **Indoor Shooting Center,** the largest facility of its kind in the Western Hemisphere, with areas for rifle and pistol shooting, rapid-fire and women's sport pistol bays, running-target rifle ranges, and air-rifle and pistol-fire points; and the **Aquatics Center,** which contains a 50m-by-25m pool with two movable bulkheads, 10 50m and 20 25m lanes, and more than 800,000 gallons of water. The U.S. Olympic Committee also operates the **7-Eleven Velodrome,** with a banked track for bicycle and roller speed skating, about 1 mile south of the Olympic Complex, in Memorial Park (see "Parks & Zoos," later in this chapter) off Union Boulevard. Olympic figure skaters train at the **World Arena,** southwest of downtown. Allow 1 to 2 hours.

1 Olympic Plaza, corner of Boulder St. (entrance) and Union Blvd. ℂ 888/659-8687 or 719/866-4618. www.usolympicteam.com. Free admission. Complex daily 9am–6pm. Guided tours begin every half-hour 9am–5pm; reservations required for groups of 10 or more (ℂ 719/866-4656). From I-25, take exit 143.

MORE ATTRACTIONS
ARCHITECTURAL HIGHLIGHTS

The Broadmoor   This famous Italian Renaissance–style resort hotel has been a Colorado Springs landmark since Spencer Penrose built it in 1918. (See "Where to Stay," earlier in this chapter.)

Lake Circle, at Lake Ave. ℂ 719/634-7711. www.broadmoor.com. Free admission. Daily year-round. Located at the foot of Cheyenne Mountain, 1 mile west of I-25, exit 140.

Miramont Castle Museum   Architecture buffs will love this place. Built into a hillside by a wealthy French priest as a private home in 1895 and converted by the Sisters of Mercy into a sanatorium in 1907, this unique Victorian mansion has always aroused curiosity. The structure incorporates at least nine identifiable architectural styles in its four stories, 46 rooms, 14,000 square feet of floor space, and 2-foot-thick stone walls. If you like tiny stuff, don't miss the room housing the miniatures museum. In summer, light meals and tea are served Tuesday through Saturday from 11am to 4pm in the Queen's Parlour. The museum lies on the route from Manitou Avenue to the Pikes Peak Cog Railway. Allow at least 1 hour.

9 Capitol Hill Ave. (off Ruxton Ave.), Manitou Springs. ℂ 888/685-1011 or 719/685-1011. www.pikespeak.com. Admission $5 adults, $4.50 seniors 60 and over, $1 children 6–11, free for children under 6. Memorial Day to Labor Day Tues–Sun 10am–5pm; Apr to late May and early Sept to mid-Dec Tues–Sun 11am–4pm; mid-Dec to Mar Tues–Sun noon–3pm. Located 1 block west of the intersection of Manitou and Ruxton aves.

HISTORIC BUILDINGS

McAllister House   This Gothic cottage, listed on the National Register of Historic Place, is a good place for a quick look at the Colorado of the late 19th century. It was built in 1873, and the builder, an army major named Henry McAllister, decided to construct the house with brick when he learned that the local wind was so strong it had blown a train off the tracks nearby. The house has many original furnishings, including three marble fireplaces. It is now owned by the Colonial Dames of America, whose knowledgeable volunteers lead guided tours. Allow about 1 hour.

423 N. Cascade Ave. (at St. Vrain St.). ℂ 719/635-7925. www.oldcolo.com/~mcallister. Admission $5 adults, $4 seniors 62 and older, $3 children 6–12, free for children under 6. Summer Wed–Sat 10am–4pm, Sun noon–4pm; winter Thurs–Sat 10am–4pm. Take I-25 exit 141 east to Cascade Ave., go left and continue for about 6 blocks.

Rock Ledge Ranch Historic Site   Visitors can explore the history of three pioneer eras at this living-history farm at the east entrance to Garden of the Gods park. Listed on the National Register of Historic Places, the ranch presents the rigors of the homestead era at the 1860s Galloway Homestead, the agricultural difficulties of the working-ranch era at the 1880s Chambers Farm and Blacksmith Shop, and the more sophisticated estate period at the 1907 Orchard House. Special events, which take place frequently, include an old-fashioned Fourth of July celebration, an 1860s vintage baseball game in late summer, a Victorian Halloween party, and holiday celebrations from Thanksgiving through Christmas. The General Store stocks a wide selection of historic reproductions, books, and gift items, and the proceeds help with preservation and restoration of the ranch. Allow 1 to 2 hours.

Gateway Rd., Garden of the Gods. ℂ 719/578-6777. www.springsgov.com (follow links). Admission $5 adults, $3 seniors 55 and older and students 13–18, $1 children 6–12, free for children under 6. June to Labor Day Wed–Sun 10am–5pm; early Sept to Dec Sat 10am–4pm, Sun noon–4pm. Closed Jan–May. Take I-25 exit 146, then follow signs west to Garden of the Gods.

HISTORIC NEIGHBORHOODS

Manitou Springs, which centers on Manitou Avenue off U.S. 24 West, is a separate town with its own government. It is one of the country's largest National Historic Districts. Legend has it that Utes named the springs Manitou, their word for "Great Spirit," because they believed that the Great Spirit had breathed into the waters to create the natural effervescence of the springs. Pikes Peak soars above the town nestled at its base.

Today, the community offers visitors a chance to step back to a slower and quieter time. It boasts numerous elegant Victorian buildings, many of which house delightful shops, galleries, restaurants, and lodgings. Manitou Springs is also home to many fine artists and artisans, whom you might spot painting or sketching about town. A small group of sculptors began the Manitou Art Project in 1992; it installed over 20 sculptures in various locations downtown and in the parks, creating a large sculpture garden for all to enjoy. The works, which stay on display for a year, are for sale, with 25% of the proceeds used to purchase permanent sculpture for the city. Five pieces have been purchased to date.

Visitors are encouraged to take the self-guided tour of the nine restored mineral springs of Manitou. Pick up the *Manitou Springs Visitor's Guide,* which contains a map and descriptions to help you find each spring. It's available at the Manitou Springs Chamber of Commerce & Visitors Bureau, 354 Manitou Ave. (ℂ **800/642-2567** or 719/685-5089; www.manitousprings.org), which is open daily.

Old Colorado City, Colorado Avenue between 21st and 31st streets, was founded in 1859, 12 years before Colorado Springs. The town boomed in the 1880s after General Palmer's railroad came through. Tunnels led from the respectable side of town to this saloon and red-light district so that the city fathers could carouse without being seen coming or going—or so the legend goes. Today this historic district has an interesting assortment of shops, galleries, and restaurants.

MUSEUMS & GALLERIES

Colorado Springs Fine Arts Center 🎨   The center's permanent collection includes works by Georgia O'Keeffe, John James Audubon, John Singer Sargent, Charles Russell, Albert Bierstadt, Nicolai Fechin, and other famed painters and sculptors, as well as a world-class collection of American-Indian and Hispanic works. Opened in 1936, the center also houses a 450-seat performing-arts theater, a 32,000-volume art-research library, the Bemis Art School, a tactile gallery for those who are visually impaired, and a delightful sculpture garden. Changing exhibits showcase local collections as well as touring international exhibits. Designed by renowned Santa Fe architect John Gaw Meem, the Art Deco–style building reflects Southwestern mission and Pueblo influences. Allow 1 to 3 hours.

30 W. Dale St. (west of N. Cascade Ave.). ✆ **719/634-5581.** www.csfineartscenter.org. Admission to galleries and museum $5 adults, $3 seniors and children 6–16, free for children under 6. Free to all Sat 9am–5pm. Separate admission for performing-arts events. Galleries and museum Mon–Sat 9am–5pm, Sun 1–5pm. Open the 1st Thurs of every month until 8pm; closed federal holidays. Take I-25 exit 143 east to Cascade St., turn right to Dale St., and then turn right again.

Ghost Town *Kids*   A fun place to take the family, Ghost Town is part historic attraction but more theme park. Made up of authentic 19th-century buildings relocated from other parts of Colorado, this "town" is sheltered from the elements in Old Colorado City. There's a sheriff's office, jail, saloon, general store, livery stable, blacksmith shop, rooming house, and assay office. Animated frontier characters tell stories of the Old West, while a shooting gallery, antique arcade machines, and nickelodeons provide additional entertainment. During the summer you can even pan for real gold. Allow about 2 hours.

400 S. 21st St. (on U.S. 24). ✆ **719/634-0696.** www.ghosttownmuseum.com. Admission $6 adults, $3 children 6–16, free for children under 6. June–Aug Mon–Sat 9am–6pm, Sun 11am–6pm; Sept–May Mon–Sat 10am–5pm, Sun 11am–5pm. Take I-25 exit 141; town is just west of exit.

Manitou Cliff Dwellings Preserve & Museums 🎨 *Kids*   The cliff dwelling ruins here are real, although originally they were located elsewhere. This put us off at first—they would be more authentic if they were in their original location—but the move here may have saved them. In the early 1900s, archaeologists, who saw such dwellings being plundered by treasure hunters, dismantled some of the ancient buildings, gathered artifacts found there, and hauled them away. Some of these ruins, constructed from 1100 to 1300 A.D., can be seen here, in a village reconstructed by archaeologists. There are also two museums with exhibits on prehistoric American-Indian life, and several gift shops that sell Indian-made jewelry, pottery, and other crafts, plus Colorado souvenirs. American-Indian dancers perform during the summer. Allow 2 hours.

U.S. 24, Manitou Springs. ✆ **800/354-9971** or 719/685-5242. www.cliffdwellingsmuseum.com. Admission $8 adults, $7 seniors 60 and over, $6 children 7–11, free for children under 7. May–Sept daily 9am–6pm; Oct–Apr daily 9am–5pm. Closed Thanksgiving and Dec 25. Take I-25 exit 141, go west on U.S. 24 about 5 miles.

May Natural History Museum of the Tropics *(Kids)*   Here you'll find one of the world's best public collections of giant insects and other tropical invertebrates. James F. W. May (1884–1956) spent more than half a century exploring the world's jungles while compiling his illustrious collection, which has grown to more than 100,000 invertebrates, about 8,000 of which are on display at any given time. The specimens are irreplaceable, because many came from areas that are now so politically unstable that no one is willing or able to explore the backcountry to collect them again. Exhibits change periodically.

Also on the grounds is the **Museum of Space Exploration,** where you can take a pictorial trip through the history of space exploration, beginning with man's first attempts to fly and continuing through the most recent photos from NASA. Also on display are numerous models of early aircraft, World War II planes, and spacecraft. Take time to view one or more of the NASA space films, which include the first moon landing. Allow 2 to 3 hours for both museums. There's also a 500-site campground ($20–$22 for campsites) with hiking trails, fishing, and a playground area.

710 Rock Creek Canyon Rd. *(C)* **719/576-0450.** Admission (includes Museum of Space Exploration) $4.50 adults, $3.50 seniors 60 and older, $2.50 children 6–12, free for children under 6. May–Sept daily 9am–6pm. Closed Oct–Apr except for groups of 10 or more. Take Colo. 115 and drive southwest out of Colorado Springs for 9 miles; watch for signs and the Hercules Beetle of the West Indies that mark the turnoff to the museum.

Museum of the American Numismatic Association *★ (Finds)*   The largest collection of its kind west of the Smithsonian Institution, this museum consists of four galleries of coins, tokens, medals, and paper money from around the world. Of special note is the earliest *reale* (Spanish coin) struck in the New World, in Mexico in 1536. There's also an 1804 dollar, a 1913 "V" nickel, and a nice collectors' library. Allow 1 hour.

818 N. Cascade Ave., on the campus of Colorado College. *(C)* **719/632-2646.** www.money.org. Free admission, donations welcome. Tues–Fri 9am–4pm; Sat 10am–4pm. Take I-25 exit 143 east to Cascade Ave., then turn right and go about 6 blocks.

Peterson Air & Space Museum   Through its exhibits, this museum traces the history of Peterson Air Force Base, NORAD, the Air Defense Command, and Air Force Space Command. Of special interest are 17 historic aircraft, including P-47 Thunderbolt and P-40 Warhawk fighters from World War II, plus four missiles and jets from the Korean War to the present. To mark the 50th anniversary of the U.S. Air Force, a memorial grove of 58 conifer trees honoring the USAF Medal of Honor recipients was planted. There's also a small gift shop. Allow 1 to 2 hours. *Note:* Visitors must have a military ID or give administration at least 3 days' advance notice to get on the base.

Peterson Air Force Base main gate, off U.S. 24. *(C)* **719/556-4915.** www.petemuseum.org. Free admission. Tues–Sat 8:30am–4:30pm. Closed holidays and occasionally during military exercises; call ahead. Take I-25 exit 141, then follow U.S. 24 east about 7½ miles.

ProRodeo Hall of Fame & American Cowboy Museum *★★ (Kids)*   No rhinestone cowboys here. This is the real thing, with exhibits on the development of rodeo, from its origins in early ranch work to major professional sport. You'll learn about historic and modern cowboys, including those brave (or crazy) enough to climb onto bucking broncos and wild bulls, in Heritage Hall. The Hall of Champions displays photos, gear, personal memorabilia, and trophies honoring rodeo greats. There are two multimedia presentations, and the museum features changing exhibits of Western art. Outside you'll find a replica rodeo arena, live rodeo animals, and a sculpture garden. Allow 2 hours.

101 ProRodeo Dr. (off Rockrimmon Blvd.). 📞 **719/528-4764**. www.prorodeo.com. Admission $6 adults, $5 seniors 55 and older, $3 children 6–12, free for children under 6. Daily 9am–5pm. Closed Jan 1, Easter, Thanksgiving, and Dec 25. Take I-25 to exit 147.

Western Museum of Mining & Industry 🛝🛝   Machines are fun, and the bigger the better. Historic hard-rock mining machinery and other equipment from Cripple Creek and other late-19th-century Colorado gold camps form the basis of this museum's 4,000-plus-item collection. Visitors can see an operating Corliss steam engine with a 17-ton flywheel (now that's big!), a life-size underground mine reconstruction, and an exhibit on mining-town life showing how early Western miners and their families lived. You can also pan for gold—there's a wheelchair-accessible trough—and view a 23-minute video presentation on life in the early mining camps. Various hands-on family activities focus on themes such as life in a mining town, minerals in everyday products, and recycled art. Free guided tours are available; call for information and times. Allow at least 2 hours.

1025 North Gate Rd., at I-25 exit 156A (off Gleneagle Dr. just east of the north gate of the U.S. Air Force Academy). 📞 **719/488-0880**. www.wmmi.org. Admission $7 adults, $5 seniors 60 and older and students 13–17, $3 children 3–12, free for children under 3. Mon–Sat 9am–4pm. Guided tours begin at 10am and 1pm. Located just east of I-25 via Gleneagle Dr. (exit 156A).

World Figure Skating Museum & Hall of Fame   This is the only museum of its kind in the world, exhibiting 1,200 years of ice skates—from early versions of carved bone to highly decorated cast-iron examples and finally the steel blades of today. There are also skating costumes, medals, and other memorabilia, changing exhibits, films, a library, and a gift shop. A gallery displays skating-related paintings, including works by the 17th-century Dutch artist Pieter Brueghel and Americans Winslow Homer and Andy Warhol. The museum is recognized by the International Skating Union, the international governing body, as the repository for the history and official records of figure skating and the sport's official hall of fame. Here also are the U.S. national, regional, sectional, and international trophies. Allow 1 to 2 hours.

20 1st St. 📞 **719/635-5200**. www.worldskatingmuseum.org. Admission $3 adults, $2 seniors 60 and over and children 6–12, free for children under 6. Mon–Sat 10am–4pm. Closed major holidays. Take I-25 exit 138, west on Lake Ave.; just before The Broadmoor, turn right onto 1st St.

NATURAL ATTRACTIONS

Cave of the Winds 🛝   Discovered by two boys on a church outing in the 1880s, this impressive underground cavern has offered public tours for well over a century. It provides a good opportunity to see the beauty of the underworld. The 45-minute Discovery Tour takes visitors along a well-lit ¾-mile passageway through 20 subterranean chambers, complete with classic stalagmites, stalactites, crystal flowers, and limestone canopies. In the Adventure Room, modern lighting techniques return visitors to an era when spelunking was done by candle and lantern. The 1½-hour Lantern Tour follows unpaved and unlighted passageways and corridors. This tour is rather strenuous, with some stooping required in areas with low ceilings; it might muddy your shoes, but not your clothes.

Impressions

The air is so refined that you can live without much lungs.
—Shane Leslie, *American Wonderland* (1936)

Kids especially like the outdoor laser shows (with stereophonic sound) presented nightly during the summer at 9pm ($10 adults, $5 children 6–15, free for children under 6).

U.S. 24, Manitou Springs. ℂ **719/685-5444**. www.caveofthewinds.com. Discovery Tour $15 adults, $8 children 6–15, free for children under 6. Tours depart every 15–30 min. Memorial Day to Labor Day daily 9am–9pm; early Sept to Apr daily 10am–5pm. Lantern Tours (3 times daily in summer and on weekends; other times by reservation) $18 adults, $9 children 6–15, not recommended for children under 6. Visitors with heart conditions, visual impairment, or other physical limitations are advised not to take Lantern Tour and may not take Explorer Tour. Take I-25 exit 141, go 6 miles west on U.S. 24.

Seven Falls   This is a good choice for those who have not yet gotten their fill of Colorado's spectacular mountain scenery. A picturesque 1-mile drive through a box canyon takes you between the Pillars of Hercules, where the canyon narrows to just 42 feet, ending at these cascading falls. Seven separate waterfalls dance down a granite cliff, cascading some 181 feet. A free elevator takes visitors to the Eagle Nest viewing platform. A mile-long trail atop the plateau passes the grave of 19th-century novelist Helen Hunt Jackson, the author of *Ramona,* and ends at a panoramic view of Colorado Springs. Watch for birds and other wildlife along the way. Allow 2 hours.

At the end of S. Cheyenne Canyon Rd. ℂ **719/632-0765**. www.sevenfalls.com. Day admission $8.25 adults, $7.25 seniors, $5.25 children 6–15, free for children under 6; night admission $9.75 adults, $8.75 seniors, $6.25 children 6–15, free for children under 6; lower rates in winter. Mid-May to early June and mid-Aug to early Sept daily 8:30am–9:30pm; early June to mid-Aug daily 8:30am–10:30pm; early Sept to mid-May daily 9am–5:15pm. Christmas lighting Dec 16–26 5–9:30pm. Closed major holidays. Take I-25 exit 141, head west on U.S. 24, turn south on 21st St. for about 3 miles, turn west on Cheyenne Blvd., and then left onto S. Cheyenne Canyon Rd.

PARKS & ZOOS

Cheyenne Mountain Zoo 🐾🐾 *(Kids)*   On the lower slopes of Cheyenne Mountain at 6,800 feet above sea level, this medium-size zoological park is our top choice for a family outing. The zoo's 650-plus animals, many in "natural" environments, include wolves, lions, leopards, red pandas, elephants, hippos, monkeys, giraffes, reptiles, snakes, and lots of birds. Rocky cliffs have been created for the mountain goats; there's a pebbled beach for penguins and a new animal-contact area for children. The zoo is home to more than 30 endangered species, including the Siberian tiger, Amur leopard, and black-footed ferret. The zoo's giraffes are the most prolific captive herd in the world; there have been 180 live births since the 1950s. Visitors can actually feed the long-necked beasts.

There's also a colorful antique carousel, built in 1926, the year the zoo was founded. A stroller- and wheelchair-accessible tram makes a full loop of the zoo in about 15 minutes; it operates from Memorial Day to Labor Day, and you can ride all day for $1. Admission to the zoo includes road access to the nearby **Will Rogers Shrine of the Sun,** a granite tower built in 1937, with photos and information on the American humorist. The tower also affords great views of the city and surrounding countryside. Strollers, double strollers, wheelchairs, and wagons are available for rent at Thundergod Gift and Snack Shop. Allow 2 to 4 hours for the zoo and an extra 45 minutes for the shrine.

4250 Cheyenne Mountain Zoo Rd. ℂ **719/633-9925**. www.cmzoo.org. Admission $12 adults, $10 seniors 65 and over, $6 children 3–11, free for children under 3. Summer daily 9am–6pm; off season daily 9am–5pm. Take I-25 exit 138, drive west to The Broadmoor hotel and follow signs.

Memorial Park   One of the largest parks in the city, Memorial is home to the Mark "Pa" Sertich Ice Center and the Aquatics and Fitness Center, as well as the famed 7-Eleven Velodrome, which is used for world-class bicycling events. Other facilities include baseball and softball fields, volleyball courts, tennis courts, a bicycle criterium, and jogging trails. The park also stages a terrific fireworks display on Independence Day. See the sections on ice skating, swimming, and tennis under "Outdoor Activities," below.

1605 E. Pikes Peak Ave. (between Hancock Ave. and Union Blvd.). ✆ 719/385-5940. www.springsgov.com (follow links). Free admission. Daily year-round. Located 1 mile east of downtown.

Monument Valley Park   This long, slender park follows Monument Creek through downtown Colorado Springs. At its south end are formal zinnia, begonia, and rose gardens, and in the middle are demonstration gardens of the Horticultural Art Society. Facilities include softball and baseball fields, a swimming pool (open daily in summer; $4 adults, $2.50 children), volleyball and tennis courts, children's playgrounds, and picnic shelters. Also in the park are the 4.2-mile Monument Creek Trail for walkers, runners, and cyclists, and the 1-mile Monument Valley Fitness Trail at the north end, beside Bodington Field.

170 W. Cache La Poudre Blvd. ✆ 719/385-5940. www.springsgov.com (follow links). Free admission. Daily year-round.

Mueller State Park ★★★ *Finds*   Somewhat like a junior version of Rocky Mountain National Park, Mueller contains over 5,000 acres of prime scenic beauty along the western slope of Pikes Peak. The 55 miles of trails, designated for hikers, horseback riders, and mountain bikers, afford opportunities to observe elk, bighorn sheep, black bear, and the park's other wildlife. The best times to spot wildlife are spring and fall, just after sunrise and just before sunset. In the summer, rangers lead hikes and offer campfire programs in a 100-seat amphitheater. The park has 132 campsites (✆ **800/678-2267** for reservations), with fees ranging from $12 for walk-in sites to $16 for drive-in sites with electricity; coin-operated pay showers are available from mid-May to mid-October.

P.O. Box 39, Divide, CO 80814. ✆ 719/687-2366. www.parks.state.co.us. Admission $4 per vehicle. Take U.S. 24 west from Colorado Springs to Divide (25 miles), then go 3½ miles south on Colo. 67.

North Cheyenne Cañon Park and Starsmore Discovery Center ★★   A delightful escape on a hot summer day, this 1,600-acre park includes North Cheyenne Creek, which drops 1,800 feet over the course of 5 miles in a series of cascades and waterfalls. The heavily wooded park contains picnic areas and hiking/biking/horseback riding trails. The small visitor center at the foot of scenic Helen Hunt Falls has exhibits on history, geology, flora, and fauna. The **Starsmore Discovery Center,** at the entrance to the park, holds maps, information, and interactive exhibits for both kids and adults, including audiovisual programs and a climbing wall where you can learn about rock climbing. Call for current climbing-wall hours. During the summer, the center schedules a series of free programs on subjects such as rock climbing, butterflies, and hummingbirds, and guided walks and hikes (call for the current schedule). The park also has excellent rock-climbing areas for experienced climbers; pick up information at the Starsmore Discovery Center or Helen Hunt Falls visitor center.

2120 S. Cheyenne Cañon Rd. (west of 21st St.). ✆ 719/578-6146. www.springsgov.com (follow links). Free admission. Park May–Oct daily 5am–11pm; Nov–Apr daily 5am–9pm. Starsmore Discovery Center summer daily 9am–5pm; call for hours at other times. Helen Hunt Falls Visitor Center Memorial Day to Labor Day daily 9am–5pm; closed rest of year. Located just west of the Broadmoor Gold Club via Cheyenne Blvd.

Palmer Park   Deeded to the city in 1899 by Colorado Springs founder Gen. William Jackson Palmer, this 737-acre preserve offers hiking, biking, and horseback riding across a mesa overlooking the city. It boasts a variety of minerals (including quartz, topaz, jasper, and tourmaline), rich vegetation (including a yucca preservation area), and considerable wildlife. The Edna Mae Bennet Nature Trail is a self-guided excursion, and there are numerous other trails. Other facilities include 12 separate picnic areas, softball and baseball fields, and volleyball courts.

3650 Maizeland Rd. off Academy Blvd. ℂ 719/385-5940. www.springsgov.com (follow links). Free admission. Daily year-round. Located 3 miles east of I-25 via Austin Bluffs Pkwy (exit 146).

ESPECIALLY FOR KIDS

In addition to the listings below, children will probably enjoy the **Cheyenne Mountain Zoo, May Natural History Museum,** and **Ghost Town,** described above.

Arcade Amusements, Inc. ⚐ *Kids* Among the West's oldest and largest amusement arcades, this game complex just might be considered a hands-on arcade museum as well as a fun place for kids of all ages. Some 250 machines range from original working penny pinball machines to modern video games, Skee-Ball, and 12-player horse racing.

930 Block Manitou Ave., Manitou Springs. ℂ 719/685-9815. Free admission; arcade games from 1¢. Early May to Labor Day daily 10am–10pm. Call for winter hours. Located in downtown Manitou Springs.

North Pole/Santa's Workshop *Kids* A good spot for young kids, Santa's workshop is busy from mid-May right up until Christmas Eve. Not only can kids visit shops where elves have some early Christmas gifts for sale, but they can also see Santa and whisper their requests in his ear. This 26-acre village features numerous rides, including a miniature train, a 60-foot Ferris wheel, and a space shuttle replica that swings to and fro, as well as magic shows and musical entertainment, snack shops, and an ice-cream parlor.

At the foot of Pikes Peak Hwy. off U.S. 24, 5 miles west of Manitou Springs. ℂ 719/684-9432. www.santas-colo.com. Admission (includes all rides, shows, and attractions) $15 ages 2–59, $5.95 seniors 60 and over, free for children under 2. June to mid-Aug daily 9:30am–6pm; mid-May to May 31 and mid-Aug to Dec 24 (weather permitting) Fri–Tues 10am–5pm. Closed Dec 25 to mid-May. Take I-25 exit 141, go west on U.S. 24 about 10 miles.

ORGANIZED TOURS

Half- and full-day bus tours of Colorado Springs, Pikes Peak, the Air Force Academy, and other nearby attractions are offered by **Gray Line of Colorado Springs,** 3704 W. Colorado Ave. (ℂ 800/348-6877; www.coloradograyline.com). From May through October, it offers a variety of other tours, including an excursion to Royal Gorge and white-water rafting trips. Prices range from $30 to $75 per person.

A free downtown **walking tour** brochure, with a map and descriptions of more than 30 historic buildings, is available at the Colorado Springs Convention and Visitors Bureau, as well as at local businesses.

Another free brochure, *Old Colorado City,* shows the location of more than a dozen historic buildings and lists shops, galleries, and other businesses.

The **Manitou Springs Chamber of Commerce & Visitors Bureau** (see "Visitor Information," earlier in this chapter) distributes the free *Manitou Springs Visitor's Guide,* which includes a self-guided walking-tour map of Mineral Springs, as well as information on where to find a variety of outdoor sculptures. See "Historic Neighborhoods," earlier in this chapter.

6 Outdoor Activities

For information on the city's parks and programs, contact the **Colorado Springs Parks and Recreation Department** (© 719/385-5940; www.springs gov.com). Most of the state and federal agencies concerned with outdoor recreation are headquartered in Denver. There are branch offices in Colorado Springs for **Colorado State Parks,** 2128 N. Weber St. (© 719/471-0900; www.parks.state.co.us); the **Colorado Division of Wildlife,** 2126 N. Weber St. (© 719/227-5200, or 719/227-5201 for 24-hr. recorded information; www.wildlife.state.co.us); and the **U.S. Forest Service,** Pikes Peak Ranger District of the Pike National Forest, 601 S. Weber St. (© 719/636-1602; www.fs.fed.us/r2/psicc/pp).

You can get hunting and fishing licenses at many sporting-goods stores, as well as at the Colorado Division of Wildlife office listed above.

AERIAL SPORTS   The **Black Forest Soaring Society,** 24566 David C. Johnson Loop, Elbert, CO 80106 (© 303/648-3623; http://soarBFSS.org), some 50 miles northeast of Colorado Springs, offers glider rides, rentals, and instruction. Rides cost about $100, with rentals (to those with gliding licenses) running $15 per hour and instruction $24 an hour. Advance reservations are required.

The area's commercial ballooning companies include **High But Dry Balloons,** 4164 Austin Bluffs Pkwy., #146, Colorado Springs, CO 80918 (© 800/897-3066 or 719/260-0011; www.highbutdryballoons.com), for tours, champagne flights, and weddings. Sunrise flights are scheduled daily year-round, weather permitting. Cost depends on the number of passengers, locations, and type of flight, but averages about $150 per person. Generally, flights last 2 or 3 hours, with a minimum of 1 hour. On Labor Day weekend, the **Colorado Springs Balloon Classic** ✿✿ (© 719/471-4833; www.balloonclassic. com) sees more than 100 hot-air balloons launched from the city's Memorial Park. Admission is free.

BICYCLING   Aside from the 4.3-mile loop trail around Monument Valley Park (see "Parks & Zoos" under "Attractions," above), there are numerous other urban trails for bikers. You can get information at the city's Visitor Information Center (see "Visitor Information," earlier in this chapter). For guided tours and rentals ($25/day), contact **Challenge Unlimited** (see "Mountain Biking," below).

FISHING   Most serious Colorado Springs anglers drive south 40 miles to the Arkansas River or west to the Rocky Mountain streams and lakes, such as those found in Eleven Mile State Park and Spinney Mountain State Park on the South Platte River west of Florissant. Bass, catfish, walleye pike, and panfish are found in the streams of eastern Colorado; trout is the preferred sport fish of the mountain regions.

Angler's Covey, 917 W. Colorado Ave. (© 800/753-4746 or 719/471-2984; www.anglerscovey.com), is a specialty fly-fishing shop and a good source of general fishing information for southern Colorado. It offers guided half- and full-day trips ($195–$345 for one to three persons), as well as state fishing licenses, rentals, flies, tackle, and so forth.

GOLF   Public courses include the **Patty Jewett Golf Course,** 900 E. Española St. (© 719/385-6950); **Pine Creek Golf Club,** 9850 Divot Trail (© 719/594-9999); and **Valley Hi Golf Course,** 610 S. Chelton Rd. (© 719/385-6917). Nonresident greens fees range from $29 to $35 for 18 holes (not including a cart).

The finest golf courses in the Colorado Springs area are private. Guests of The Broadmoor hotel can play the 45-hole **Broadmoor Golf Club** (© **719/ 577-5790**).

HIKING Opportunities abound in municipal parks (see "Parks & Zoos" under "Attractions," above) and Pike National Forest, which borders Colorado Springs to the west. The U.S. Forest Service district office can provide maps and general information (see address and phone number in the introduction to this section).

Especially popular are the 7.5-mile **Waldo Canyon Trail,** with its trail head just east of Cascade Avenue off U.S. 24; the 6-mile **Mount Manitou Trail,** starting in Ruxton Canyon above the hydroelectric plant; and the 12-mile **Barr Trail** to the summit of Pikes Peak. **Mueller State Park** (© **719/687-2366**), 3½ miles south of Divide en route to Cripple Creek, has 55 miles of trails. See "Parks & Zoos" under "Attractions," above.

HORSEBACK RIDING You'll find good opportunities at city parks, including Garden of the Gods, North Cheyenne Cañon Park, and Palmer Park, plus Mueller State Park (see "Attractions," earlier in this chapter). The **Academy Riding Stables,** 4 El Paso Blvd., near the Garden of the Gods (© **888/700-0410** or 719/633-5667; www.academyridingstables.com), offers guided trail rides for children and adults by reservation ($33 for 1 hour, $50 for 2).

ICE SKATING The **Mark "Pa" Sertich Ice Center** at Memorial Park (© **719/385-5983**) is open daily, offering prearranged instruction and rentals. The U.S. Olympic Complex operates the **Colorado Springs World Arena Ice Hall,** 3185 Venetucci Blvd. (© **719/477-2100;** www.worldarena.com), with public sessions daily. Admission is $1 to $2, skate rentals $2. If you have hockey equipment, you can join a pickup game ($5); call for times. To get there, take I-25 exit 138, go west on Circle Drive to Venetucci Boulevard, and south to the arena.

MOUNTAIN BIKING There are abundant mountain-biking opportunities in the Colorado Springs area; contact the U.S. Forest Service for details (see address and phone number, in the introduction to the section). From May through early October, **Challenge Unlimited,** 204 S. 24th St. (© **800/798-5954** or 719/633-6399; www.bikithikit.com), hosts fully equipped, guided rides for every level of experience. Your guide on the 19-mile ride down the Pikes Peak Highway, from the summit at 14,110 feet to the tollgate at 7,000 feet, presents an interpretation of the nature, history, and beauty of the mountain. Participants must be at least 10 years old; advance reservations are advised. Rates are $55 to $100 per person. Challenge Unlimited also rents bikes and guides multiday excursions.

RIVER RAFTING Colorado Springs is 40 miles from the Arkansas River near Cañon City. Several licensed white-water outfitters tackle the Royal Gorge. **Echo Canyon River Expeditions,** 45000 U.S. 50 West, Cañon City, CO 81212 (© **800/755-3246** or 719/275-3154; www.raftecho.com), offers half-day to

---

Impressions

Could one live in constant view of these grand mountains without being elevated by them into a lofty plane of thought and purpose?
—General William J. Palmer, founder of Colorado Springs (1871)

3-day trips on "mild to wild" stretches of river. The company uses state-of-the-art equipment, including self-bailing rafts. Costs range from $41 (half-day, adult) to $95 for a daylong rental of an inflatable kayak. **Arkansas River Tours,** P.O. Box 337, Cotopaxi, CO 81223 (© **800/321-4352** or 719/942-4362; www.arkansas rivertours.com), offers white-water trips of lengths from a quarter of a day to all day for $32 to $100, and 2-day trips for about $240.

SWIMMING & TENNIS   Many city parks have pool or lake swimming, for which they charge a small fee, and free tennis courts. Contact the Colorado Springs Parks and Recreation Department (© **719/385-5940**) for locations and hours.

7 Spectator Sports

The **Air Force Academy Falcons** football team dominates the sports scene, and there are also competitive baseball, basketball, hockey, and soccer teams. Call for schedules and ticket information (© **800/666-USAF** or 719/472-1895; www.airforcesports.com).

AUTO RACING   The **Pikes Peak International Hill Climb** (© **719/ 685-4400;** www.ppihc.com), known as the "Race to the Clouds," takes place annually in late June or early July. An international field of drivers negotiates the hairpin turns of the final 12⅓ miles of the Pikes Peak Highway to the top of the 14,110-foot mountain.

NASCAR and Indy Racing make annual stops at **Pikes Peak International Raceway,** 16650 Midway Ranch Rd., Fountain, CO 80817 (© **888/306-7223;** www.ppir.com), 15 miles south of Colorado Springs, exit 123 off I-25. The track held its inaugural season in 1997, with a capacity crowd of 40,000. Event tickets usually range from $50 to $100 for a weekend pass, to $15 to $60 for a single day. Advance tickets cost less than those bought on race day. The facility also schedules motorcycle races, driving schools, and occasional concerts.

BASEBALL   The **Colorado Springs Sky Sox** of the Pacific Coast League, the AAA farm team for the Colorado Rockies of Denver, play a full 144-game season, with 72 home games at Sky Sox Stadium, 4385 Tutt Blvd., off Barnes Road east of Powers Boulevard (© **719/591-7699;** www.skysox.com). The season runs from April through Labor Day. Tickets cost $8.50 for adults, $7.50 for children 2 to 12 and seniors 60 and over for reserved box seating; $7.50 and $5, respectively, for upper reserved seats; and $4.25 for general admission.

HOCKEY   In addition to Air Force Academy Hockey (see above), the **World Arena,** 3185 Venetucci Blvd. (© **719/477-2100;** www.worldarena.com), is home to the Colorado College Tigers (© **719/389-6100**) and the Colorado Gold Kings (© **719/579-9000**) of the West Coast Hockey League.

RODEO   The **Pikes Peak or Bust Rodeo,** held annually (since 1941) in early August, is a major stop on the Professional Rodeo Cowboys Association circuit. Its purse of more than $150,000 makes it the second-largest rodeo in Colorado, after Denver's National Western Stock Show. Events are at the **World Arena,** 3185 Venetucci Blvd. (© **719/477-2100;** www.worldarena.com). Various events around the city, including a parade and a street breakfast, mark rodeo week. In late July the national finals for the **National Little Britches Rodeo** (© **719/389-0333**) take place at the Penrose Equestrian Center, 1045 W. Rio Grande Ave., off Fountain Creek Boulevard (© **719/635-3547;** www.colorado springsrodeo.com).

8 Shopping

Five principal areas attract shoppers in Colorado Springs. The Manitou Springs and Old Colorado City neighborhoods are excellent places to browse for art, jewelry, arts and crafts, books, antiques, and other specialty items. The Chapel Hills and Citadel malls combine major department stores with a variety of national chain outlets. Downtown Colorado Springs also has numerous fine shops.

SHOPPING A TO Z

ANTIQUES

Antique Emporium at Manitou Springs   The shop's 4,000 square feet of floor space provides ample room for displaying its collection of antique furniture, china, glassware, books, collectibles, and primitives. 719 Manitou Ave., Manitou Springs. ✆ 719/685-9195.

Nevada Avenue Antiques   This well-established multidealer mall, covering some 7,000 square feet, is filled with a wide variety of antiques and collectibles, including a good selection of lower-priced items. 405 S. Nevada Ave. ✆ 719/473-3351.

The Villagers   Here you will find a diverse array of quality antiques and collectibles. Volunteers run the shop, and all proceeds go to Cheyenne Village, a community of adults with developmental disabilities. 2514 W. Colorado Ave., Old Colorado City. ✆ 719/632-1400.

ART GALLERIES

Business of Art Center   Primarily an educational facility to help artists learn the business end of their profession, the center also has workshops, classes, and lectures, plus numerous artists' studios (open for viewing), six exhibition galleries, and a gift shop. Features include renowned Colorado artists and juried exhibits of regional art. The shop offers a varied selection of regional artwork, including prints, photographs, jewelry, sculpture, ceramics, wearable art, handblown glass, and carved-wood objects. Theater, music, and dance performances are occasionally staged. 513 Manitou Ave., Manitou Springs. ✆ 719/685-1861.

Commonwheel Artists Co-op   Original art and fine crafts by area artists fill this excellent gallery, where you'll find a good selection of paintings, photography, sculpture, jewelry, textiles, and other items. 102 Cañon Ave., Manitou Springs. ✆ 719/685-1008. www.commonwheel.com.

Flute Player Gallery   This gallery offers contemporary and traditional American-Indian silver and turquoise jewelry, Pueblo pottery, Navajo weavings, and Hopi kachina dolls. 2511 W. Colorado Ave., Old Colorado City. ✆ 719/632-7702.

Michael Garman's Gallery *Kids*   A showcase for Garman's sculptures and casts depicting urban and Western life, this gallery also holds "Magic Town," a large model of an old-time inner city, with sculptures and holographic actors. Admission to Magic Town is $3 for adults, $1.50 for children 6 to 13, and free for children under 6. 2418 W. Colorado Ave., Old Colorado City. ✆ 800/731-3908 or 719/471-9391. www.michaelgarman.com.

BOOKS

Book Sleuth *Finds*   For all your mystery needs, visit this bookstore. In addition to a wide selection of mystery novels (including a good stock of out-of-print books), the shop offers numerous puzzles and games. 2501 W. Colorado Ave. #105, Old Colorado City. ✆ 719/632-2727.

CRAFTS

Simpich Character Dolls *Kids*   These exquisite handmade dolls are the creation of Bob and Jan Simpich, who made their first dolls in 1952 as Christmas gifts for their parents. Friends would see the dolls and ask about buying them—and the business grew from there. Today, numerous dolls represent characters from literature, the Victorian era, and early American life. Other creations range from the whimsical—such as leprechauns and elves—to the historical (an Abraham Lincoln bust). Visitors to this gallery and studio can wander through the display and work areas, and watch the process as the dolls are created. 2413 W. Colorado Ave., Old Colorado City. ℂ 719/636-3272. www.simpich.com.

Van Briggle Art Pottery   Founded in 1900 by Artus Van Briggle, who applied Chinese matte glaze to Rocky Mountain clays molded into imaginative Art Nouveau shapes, this is one of the oldest active art potteries in the United States. Artisans demonstrate their craft, from throwing on the wheel to glazing and firing. Free tours are available, and finished works are sold in the showroom. 600 S. 21st St., Old Colorado City. ℂ 800/847-6341 or 719/633-7729. www.vanbriggle.com.

JEWELRY

Manitou Jack's Jewelry & Gifts   Black Hills gold, 10- and 14-karat, is the specialty here. There's also an extensive collection of American-Indian jewelry, pottery, sand paintings, and other art. The shop will create custom jewelry and make repairs. 814 Manitou Ave., Manitou Springs. ℂ 719/685-5004.

Zerbe Jewelers   This well-established downtown Colorado Springs jeweler is known for beautiful custom work and one-of-a-kind designer jewelry. 26 N. Tejon St. ℂ 719/635-3521.

MALLS & SHOPPING CENTERS

Chapel Hills Mall   Foley's, Sears, Mervyn's, JCPenney, and Dillard's are among the 150 stores at this mall, which also houses an ice-skating arena, 40-foot climbing wall, children's play area, 15-screen movie theater, and about two dozen food outlets. 1710 Briargate Blvd. (N. Academy Blvd., at I-25 exit 150A). ℂ 719/594-0111.

The Citadel   This is southern Colorado's largest regional shopping mall, with Dillard's, Foley's, JCPenney, Mervyn's, and more than 170 specialty shops and restaurants. 750 Citadel Dr. E. (N. Academy Blvd. at E. Platte Ave.). ℂ 719/591-5516.

SPORTING GOODS

In business since 1968, the independent **Mountain Chalet,** 226 N. Tejon St. (ℂ 719/633-0732), sells camping gear, outdoor clothing, hiking and climbing gear, and winter-sports equipment. Another good source for all sorts of outdoor clothing and equipment is **Gart Sports,** with stores at 7730 N. Academy Blvd. (ℂ 719/532-1020) and 1409 N. Academy Blvd. (ℂ 719/574-1400).

WESTERN WEAR

Lorig's Western Wear *🐎*   This Colorado Springs institution is where real cowboys get their hats, boots, jeans, and those fancy belts with the big buckles. 15 N. Union Blvd. ℂ 719/633-4695.

WINE & LIQUOR

Cheers Liquor Mart   This liquor supermarket has a huge selection of beer and wine, including Colorado wines, at good prices. 1105 N. Circle Dr. ℂ 719/574-2244.

The Wines of Colorado This tasting room and sales outlet offers the greatest number of Colorado wines available for tasting under one roof. There are also gift items, and the restaurant offers a grill menu. 8045 W. U.S. 24, Cascade (about 10 miles west of Colorado Springs). © **719/684-0900.**

9 Colorado Springs After Dark

The Colorado Springs entertainment scene spreads throughout the metropolitan area. Pikes Peak Center, the Colorado Springs Fine Arts Center, City Auditorium, Colorado College, and various facilities at the U.S. Air Force Academy are all outstanding venues for the performing arts. The city also supports dozens of cinemas, nightclubs, bars, and other after-dark attractions. Downtown is the major nightlife hub, but Old Colorado City and Manitou Springs also have their fair share of interesting establishments.

Weekly entertainment schedules appear in the Friday *Gazette Telegraph.* Also look at the listings in *Springs* magazine and *The Independent,* free entertainment tabloids. Or call the city's weekly **events line** (© **719/635-1723**). A good online resource for information on events and nightlife, as well as restaurants, is www.sceneinthesprings.com.

Tickets for many major entertainment and sporting events can be obtained from **Ticketmaster** (© 719/520-9090; www.ticketmaster.com) and **TicketsWest** (© 866/464-2626; www.ticketswest.com).

THE CLUB & MUSIC SCENE

Cowboys Two-steppers and country-and-western music lovers flock to this east-side club, which boasts the largest dance floor in the area. It's open Wednesday to Sunday, and dance lessons are available. 3910 Palmer Park Blvd. © **719/596-1212.**

Poor Richard's Restaurant An eclectic variety of performers appears at this bohemian landmark 1 or 2 nights a week, presenting everything from acoustic folk to Celtic melodies to jazz to bluegrass. The menu includes pizza, sandwiches, and the best nachos in the Springs (blue corn chips and mozzarella) as well as beer and wine. Adjacent are Poor Richard's Bookstore and Little Richard's Toy Store, all owned by local politico Richard Skorman. 324½ N. Tejon St. © **719/632-7721.**

Rum Bay Located in the renovated Woolworth Building downtown, the lively Rum Bay is a massive nightclub sporting a wall full of rum bottles and a tropical theme. Disc jockeys spin records for two dance floors; there's also a piano bar featuring dueling players. The entire block contains six additional bars under the same management, ranging from "the world's smallest bar" to Rum Bay–like clubs focusing on tequila and bourbon. 20 N. Tejon St. © **719/634-3522.**

32 Bleu This hip downtown nightspot actually has two spaces: a bistro/bar downstairs and the Springs' best midsize live music venue upstairs. Performers are local and national, with steady streams of hip-hop, indie rock, and reggae. 32 S. Tejon St. © **719/955-5664.**

Underground Pub This popular hangout attracts a diverse crowd, from college students and other young people to baby boomers and retirees. Patrons come to dance or just listen to the equally eclectic music (live or recorded), which ranges from rock to jazz to reggae, with some occasional folk. 110 N. Nevada Ave. © **719/633-0590.**

THE BAR SCENE

Golden Bee *(Moments)*   An opulent 19th-century English pub was disassembled, shipped from Great Britain, and reassembled piece by piece to create this delightful drinking establishment. You can have imported English ale by the yard or half-yard while enjoying steak-and-potato pie, Devonshire cheddar-cheese soup, sandwiches, or other British specialties. Evenings bring a ragtime pianist to enliven the atmosphere; interested guests are given songbooks for sing-along. Lower level entrance of The Broadmoor International Center, Lake Circle. © 719/634-7711.

Hide 'n' Seek   The Hide 'n' Seek, which opened in 1972, is one of the oldest and largest gay bars in the West, covering some 12,500 square feet. It has five bars with country-western and other themes, four dance floors with DJs most nights and live music on weekends, and a restaurant. 512 W. Colorado Ave. © 719/634-9303.

Meadow Muffins   A boisterous barroom packed to the gills with movie memorabilia and assorted knickknacks, Meadow Muffins certainly doesn't lack personality. It features DJs or live music several nights a week. The food is standard bar fare, but the burgers are great. On most days, there are several specials, with happy hour from 4 to 7pm daily and 4pm until closing on Friday. There are also pool tables, a pair of big-screen TVs, and arcade games. Also see the restaurant listing on p. 159. 2432 W. Colorado Ave., in Old Colorado City. © 719/633-0583.

Oscar's   Featuring aquariums above the bar, this downtown hangout shucks more oysters than anyplace in the Springs, including The Broadmoor's eateries. The menu here is Cajun, the crowd eclectic, the music tending towards jazz and blues. 333 S. Tejon St. © 719/471-8070.

Phantom Canyon Brewing Co.   This popular brewpub generally offers 8 to 10 of its specialty beers, including homemade root beer. The beers are unfiltered and unpasteurized, served at the traditional temperature for the style. We recommend Railyard Ale, a light amber ale with a smooth, malty taste; Hefeweizen, a traditional German wheat beer; and a very hoppy India pale ale. A billiard hall is on the second floor. See also the restaurant listing on p. 157. 2 E. Pikes Peak Ave. © 719/635-2800.

Ritz Grill   Especially popular with young professionals after work and the chic clique later in the evening, this noisy restaurant-lounge, known for its martinis and large central bar, brings an Art Deco feel to downtown Colorado Springs. There's live music (usually rock) starting at 9pm Thursday through Saturday. See also the restaurant listing on p. 158. 15 S. Tejon St. © 719/635-8484.

THE PERFORMING ARTS

Among the major venues for performing arts is the 8,000-seat **Colorado Springs World Arena,** 3185 Venetucci Blvd., at I-25 exit 138 (© 719/477-2100; www.worldarena.com). The area's newest entertainment center, it presents big-name country and rock concerts and a wide variety of sporting events. Other major facilities include the handsome **Pikes Peak Center,** 190 S. Cascade Ave. (© 719/520-7453 for general information, or 719/520-7469 for the ticket office; www.pikespeakcenter.org), a 2,000-seat concert hall in the heart of downtown that has been acclaimed for its outstanding acoustics. The city's symphony orchestra and dance theater call the Pikes Peak Center home, and top-flight touring entertainers, Broadway musicals, and symphony orchestras appear here as well. The **Colorado Springs Fine Arts Center,** 30 W. Dale St. (© **719/634-5581** for general information, or 719/634-5583 for the box office; www.csfineartscenter. org), is a historic facility (see "Museums & Galleries" under "Attractions," earlier in this chapter) that includes a children's theater program, a repertory theater company, dance programs and concerts, and classic films. Recent productions have included *Annie* and *Oklahoma.* At the historic **City Auditorium,** 221 E. Kiowa St. (© **719/578-6652;** www.springsgov.com, follow links), you can often attend a trade show or big-name concert—Willie Nelson performed recently—or drop in at the Lon Chaney Theatre, with its resident Star Bar Players (see below) and Pikes Peak Youth Theatre.

THEATER & DANCE

BlueBards   The Air Force Academy's cadet theater group performs Broadway and other productions; it recently staged *Jesus Christ Superstar.* Arnold Hall Theater, U.S. Air Force Academy. © **719/333-4497.** www.usafa.af.mil/wing/clubs/bluebards.

Colorado Springs Dance Theatre   This nonprofit organization presents international dance companies from September to May at Pikes Peak Center, Colorado College's Armstrong Hall, and other venues. Notable productions have included Mikhail Baryshnikov, Alvin Ailey Repertory Ensemble, Ballet Folklorico of Mexico, and other traditional, modern, ethnic, and jazz dance programs. Each year, three to five performances are scheduled, and master classes, lectures, and other programs often coincide with the performances. Tickets are $20 to $30; senior and student discounts are available. 7 E. Bijou St., Suite 209. © **719/630-7434.** www.csdance.org.

Star Bar Players   This resident theater company presents several full-length plays each year, ranging from Greek comedies to modern murder mysteries. Recent productions have included *Arsenic and Old Lace* and Neil Simon's *Lost in Yonkers.* Tickets are typically $10 to $20. Lon Chaney Theatre, City Auditorium, 221 E. Kiowa St. © **719/573-7411.** www.starbarplayers.org.

DINNER THEATERS

Flying W Ranch 🏵   This working cattle and horse ranch just north of the Garden of the Gods encompasses a Western village of more than a dozen restored buildings and a mine train. There are also demonstrations of Navajo weaving and horse shoeing. A Western stage show features bunkhouse comedy, cowboy balladry, and foot-stompin' fiddle, mandolin, and guitar music. From mid-May through September the town opens each afternoon at 4:30pm; a chuck-wagon dinner (barbecued beef or chicken, potatoes, beans, biscuits, and cake) is served ranch-style at 7:15pm, and the show begins at 8:30pm. The winter steakhouse is open October to December and March to May on Friday and Saturday, with seatings at 5 and 8pm and a Western stage show at each seating. 3330 Chuckwagon Rd. © **800/232-FLYW** or 719/598-4000. www.flyingw.com. Reservations recommended. Chuck-wagon dinners $19 adults, $8 children under 9; winter steakhouse $21–$22 adults, $7.50 children under 9. MC, V.

Iron Springs Chateau Melodrama 🏵   Located near the foot of the Pikes Peak Cog Railway, this popular comedy and drama dinner theater urges patrons to boo the villain and cheer the hero. Past productions have included *Farther North to Laughter or Buck of the Yukon, Part Two,* and *When the Halibut Start Running or Don't Slam the Door on Davy Jones' Locker.* A family-style dinner, with free seconds, includes oven-baked chicken and barbecued beef brisket, mashed potatoes, green beans almandine, pineapple coleslaw, and buttermilk biscuits. A sing-along and a vaudeville-style olio show follow the performance. Iron Springs Chateau is open from April through September and from late November through December. Dinner is served on Tuesday, Wednesday, Friday, and Saturday between 6 and 6:45pm; the show follows at 8pm.

444 Ruxton Ave., Manitou Springs. ℂ 719/685-5104 or 719/685-5572. www.pikes-peak.com. Reservations required. Dinner and show $24 adults, $23 seniors, $15 children; show only $13 adults and seniors, $8.50 children. MC, V.

10 A Side Trip to Florissant Fossil Beds National Monument

Approximately 35 miles west of Colorado Springs on U.S. 24 is the small village of Florissant, which means "flowering" in French. It couldn't be more aptly named—every spring its hillsides virtually blaze with wildflowers. Just 2 miles south is one of the most spectacular, yet relatively unknown, fossil deposits in the world, **Florissant Fossil Beds National Monument** 🐾🐾. From Florissant, follow the signs along Teller C.R. 1.

The fossils in this 6,000-acre National Park Service property are preserved in the rocks of ancient Lake Florissant, which existed 34 million years ago. Volcanic eruptions spanning half a million years trapped plants and animals under layers of ash and dust; the creatures were fossilized as the sediment settled and became shale.

The detailed impressions, first discovered in 1873, offer the most extensive record of its kind in the world. Scientists have removed thousands of specimens, including 1,100 separate species of insects. Dragonflies, beetles, and ants; more fossil butterflies than anywhere else in the world; plus spiders, fish, some mammals, and birds are all perfectly preserved from 34 to 35 million years ago. Leaves from willows, maples, and hickories; extinct relatives of birches, elms, and beeches; and needles of pines and sequoias are also plentiful. These fossil plants, very different from those living in the area today, show how the climate has changed over the centuries.

Mudflows also buried forests during this long period, petrifying the trees where they stood. Nature trails pass petrified tree stumps; one sequoia stump is 10 feet in diameter and 11 feet high. There's a display of carbonized fossils at the visitor center, which also offers interpretive programs. An added attraction within the monument is the homestead of Adeline Hornbek, who pioneered the area with her children in 1878. The national monument also has some 14 miles of hiking trails. Nearby, about ½ mile north of the monument, there's superb fishing for German browns and cutthroats at Spinney Mountain Reservoir.

Admission to the monument is $3 per adult and free for children under 17, making a visit here an incredibly affordable outing. It's open from 9am to 5:30pm daily from May to September; 8am to 4:30pm daily October to April. It's closed January 1, Thanksgiving, and December 25. Contact Florissant Fossil Beds National Monument, P.O. Box 185, Florissant, CO 80816-0185 (ℂ **719/748-3253;** www.nps.gov/flfo).

8

Boulder

Although Boulder is known primarily as a college town (the University of Colorado is here), it would be inaccurate to begin and end the description there. Sophisticated and artsy, Boulder is home to numerous high-tech companies and research concerns; it also attracts countless outdoor sports enthusiasts with its delightful climate, vast open spaces, and proximity to Rocky Mountain National Park.

Set at the foot of the Flatirons of the Rocky Mountains, just 30 miles northwest of downtown Denver and only 74 feet higher than the Mile High City, Boulder was settled by hopeful miners in 1858 and named for the large rocks in the area. Welcomed by Chief Niwot and the resident southern Arapaho, the miners struck gold in the nearby hills the following year. By the 1870s, Boulder had become a regional rail and trade center for mining and farming. The university, founded in 1877, became the economic mainstay of the community after mining collapsed around the beginning of the 20th century.

In the 1950s, Boulder emerged as a center for scientific and environmental research. The National Center for Atmospheric Research and the National Institute of Standards and Technology are located here, as are dozens of high-tech and aerospace companies. Alongside the ongoing high-tech boom, the university and attendant vibrant culture have attracted a diverse mix of intellectuals, individualists, and eccentrics. Writers William S. Burroughs, Jr., Stephen King, and Allen Ginsberg, founder of the city's Naropa Institute, all called Boulder home at one time or another.

Today's residents are a mix of students attending the University of Colorado (called CU by locals); employees of the many computer, biotech, and research firms; and others attracted by the casual, bohemian, environmentally aware, and otherwise hip lifestyles that prevail here. Whatever differences exist among the residents, they are united by a common love of the outdoors. Boulder has 30,000 acres of open space within its city limits, 56 parks, and 200 miles of trails. On any given day, seemingly three-quarters of the population is outside making great use of this land, generally from the vantage point of a bicycle seat, the preferred mode of transport—there are about 100,000 bicycles in Boulder, which has a human population of roughly 95,000.

1 Orientation

ARRIVING

BY PLANE

Boulder doesn't have a commercial airport. Air travelers must fly into Denver International Airport, then make ground connections to Boulder, a trip of about an hour.

GETTING TO & FROM THE AIRPORT The **SuperShuttle Boulder** (© 800/525-3177 or 303/444-0808; www.supershuttle.com) leaves Denver hourly from 7am to 11pm, and Boulder hourly between 4am and 10pm, with fewer departures on holidays. Scheduled pickups in Boulder are at the University of Colorado campus and area hotels; pickups from other locations are made on call. The one-way fare from a scheduled pickup point to the airport is $20 per person, or $26 for residential pickup service from other points; children 8 and under ride free. **Boulder Express** (© 303/457-4646) offers airport shuttle service to and from the Boulder area for $18 to $25 one-way, $32 to $40 round-trip.

Boulder Yellow Cab (© 303/777-7777) charges $70 one-way to the airport for up to five passengers.

Buses operated by the **Regional Transportation District,** known locally as **RTD** (© 800/366-7433 or 303/299-6000, TDD 303/299-6089; www.rtd-denver.com), charge $10 for a one-way trip to the airport (exact change required). Buses leave from, and return to, the main terminal at 14th and Walnut streets daily every hour from 6am to 11pm.

Boulder Limousine Service (© 800/910-7433 or 303/449-5466; www.whitedovelimo.com) charges $100 to $250 to take up to three people from Boulder to Denver International Airport in a limousine or minibus. Charter services are also available.

BY CAR
The Boulder Turnpike (U.S. 36) branches off I-25 north of Denver and passes through the suburbs of Westminster, Broomfield, and Louisville before reaching Boulder. The trip takes about 30 minutes. If you are coming from Denver International Airport, E-470 west to I-25 south is the best route to U.S. 36.

If you're arriving from the north, take the Longmont exit from I-25 and follow Colo. 119 all the way. Longmont is 7 miles due west of the freeway; Boulder is another 15 miles southwest on the Longmont Diagonal Highway.

VISITOR INFORMATION
The **Boulder Convention and Visitors Bureau,** 2440 Pearl St. (at Folsom St.), Boulder, CO 80302 (© 800/444-0447 or 303/442-2911; www.bouldercoloradousa.com), is open Monday through Thursday from 8:30am to 5pm, Friday from 8:30am to 4pm, and can provide excellent maps, brochures, and general information on the city.

There are also visitor information kiosks on **Pearl Street Mall** and at the **Davidson Mesa overlook,** several miles southeast of Boulder on U.S. 36. Brochures are available at both sites year-round.

CITY LAYOUT
The north–south streets increase in number going from west to east, beginning with 3rd Street. (The eastern city limit is at 61st St., although the numbers continue to the Boulder County line at 124th St. in Broomfield.) Where U.S. 36 enters Boulder (and does a 45-degree turn to the north), it becomes 28th Street, a major commercial artery. The Longmont Diagonal Highway (Colo. 119) enters Boulder from the northeast and intersects 28th Street at the north end of the city.

To reach downtown Boulder from U.S. 36, turn west on Canyon Boulevard (Colo. 119 west) and north on Broadway, which would be 12th Street if it had a number. It's 2 blocks to the Pearl Street Mall, a 4-block, east–west pedestrian-only strip from 11th to 15th streets that constitutes the historic downtown

Fun Fact **A Job Well Done**

The National Trust for Historic Preservation has named Boulder one of the nation's "dozen distinctive destinations" for preserving historic sites, managing growth, and maintaining a vibrant downtown.

district. Boulder's few one-way streets circle the mall: 13th and 15th streets are one-way north, 11th and 14th one-way south, Walnut Street (a block south of the mall) one-way east, and Spruce Street (a block north) one-way west.

Broadway continues across the mall, eventually joining U.S. 36 north of the city. South of Arapahoe Avenue, Broadway turns southeast, skirting the University of Colorado campus and becoming Colo. 93 (the Foothills Hwy. to Golden) after crossing Baseline Road. Baseline follows a straight line from east Boulder, across U.S. 36 and Broadway, past Chautauqua Park and up the mountain slopes. To the south, Table Mesa Drive takes a similar course.

The Foothills Parkway (not to be confused with the Foothills Hwy.) is the principal north–south route on the east side of Boulder, extending from U.S. 36 at Table Mesa Drive to the Longmont Diagonal; Arapahoe Avenue, a block south of Canyon Boulevard, continues east across 28th Street as Arapahoe Road.

2 Getting Around

BY PUBLIC TRANSPORTATION

The **Regional Transportation District,** known as the **RTD** (*©* **800/366-7433** or 303/299-6000; www.rtd-denver.com), provides bus service throughout Boulder as well as the Denver greater metropolitan area. The Boulder Transit Center, 14th and Walnut streets, is open Monday through Friday from 5am to midnight and Saturday and Sunday from 6am to midnight. Fares within the city are $1.25 for adults and children (65¢ for seniors and passengers with disabilities; children under 6 ride free). Schedules are available at the Transit Center, the Chamber of Commerce, and other locations. Buses are wheelchair accessible.

The city of Boulder runs a shuttle bus service called the **HOP** (*©* **303/447-8282**), connecting downtown, University Hill, the University of Colorado, and 30th and Pearl. The HOP operates Monday through Thursday from 7am to 10pm, Friday and Saturday from 9am to 10pm, and Sunday from 10am to 6pm. While the University of Colorado is in session, the night HOP runs Friday through Saturday from 10pm to 3am. Buses run about every 8 to 15 minutes during the day, every 15 to 20 minutes at night; the fare is $1.25 (65¢ for seniors).

The RTD runs a complementary local shuttle, the **SKIP,** Monday through Friday from 5:12am to 12:30am, Saturday from 7am to 12:30am, and Sunday from 7am to 11pm. Buses run north and south along Broadway, with a loop through the west Table Mesa neighborhood, every 6 to 10 minutes during peak weekday times and less frequently in the evenings and on weekends.

BY CAR

The **American Automobile Association (AAA)** has an office at 1933 28th St., #200 (*©* **303/753-8800**). It's open Monday through Friday from 8:30am to 5:30pm, Saturday from 9am to 1pm.

CAR RENTALS   Most people who fly to Colorado land at Denver International Airport and rent a car there. To rent a car in Boulder, contact **Avis**

(© 800/331-1212), **Budget** (© 800/527-0700), **Dollar** (© 800/800-4000), **Enterprise** (© 800/736-8222), **Hertz** (© 800/654-3131), or **National** (© 888/227-7368).

PARKING   Most downtown streets have parking meters, with rates of about 25¢ per 20 minutes. Downtown parking lots cost $1 to $3 for 3 hours. Parking can be hard to find around the Pearl Street Mall, but new lots have eased the pain. Outside downtown, free parking is generally available on side streets.

BY BICYCLE

Boulder is a wonderful place for bicycling; there are bike paths throughout the city and an extensive trail system leading for miles beyond Boulder's borders (see "Bicycling" under "Outdoor Activities," later in this chapter).

You can rent and repair mountain bikes and buy trail and city maps at **University Bikes,** 839 Pearl St., about 2 blocks west of the Pearl Street Mall (© **303/444-4196;** www.ubikes.com), and **Full Cycle,** 1211 13th St., near the campus (© **303/440-7771**). Bike rentals cost $20 to $30 daily. Maps and other information are also available at the **Boulder Convention and Visitors Bureau,** 2440 Pearl St. (© **800/444-0447** or 303/442-2911).

BY TAXI

Boulder Yellow Cab (© 303/777-7777) operates 24 hours, but you need to call for service—there are no taxi stands, and taxis won't stop for you on the street. Another company that serves Boulder is **Metro Taxi** (© **303/333-3333**).

ON FOOT

You can walk to most of what's worth seeing in downtown Boulder, especially around the Pearl Street Mall and University of Colorado campus. **Historic Boulder, Inc.** (© **303/444-5192;** www.historicboulder.org), can provide advice about exploring the city's historic neighborhoods on foot. It prints a brochure, *Walking Tours of Boulder,* that's available for $3 at the Convention and Visitors Bureau, 2440 Pearl St.

FAST FACTS: Boulder

Area Code   Area codes are **303** and **720,** and local calls require 10-digit dialing. See the "Telephone, Telegraph, Telex & Fax" section under "Fast Facts," in chapter 3.

Babysitters   The front desk at a major hotel often can make arrangements on your behalf. Boulder's **Child Care Referral Service** (© **303/441-3180**) can also help if you call in advance.

Business Hours   Most banks are open Monday through Friday from 9am to 5pm, and some have Saturday hours, too. Major stores are open Monday through Saturday from 9 or 10am until 5 or 6pm, and often Sunday from noon until 5pm. Department and discount stores often have later closing times.

Car Rentals   See "Getting Around," above.

Drugstores   Reliable prescription services are available at the Medical Center Pharmacy in the **Boulder Medical Center,** 2750 N. Broadway (© **303/440-3111**). The pharmacy at **King Soopers Supermarket,** 1650 30th St., in

Sunrise Plaza (☎ **303/444-0164**), is open from 8am to 9pm weekdays, 9am to 6pm Saturdays, and 10am to 6pm Sundays.

Emergencies For police, fire, or medical emergencies, call ☎ **911**. For the **Poison Control Center,** call ☎ **800/332-3073** or 303/739-1123. For the **Rape Crisis Hotline,** call ☎ **303/443-7300**.

Eyeglasses You can get fast repair or replacement of your glasses at **Boulder Optical,** 1928 14th St. (☎ **303/442-4521**), or **Aspen Eyewear,** 2525 Arapahoe Ave. (☎ **303/447-0210**).

Hospitals Full medical services, including 24-hour emergency treatment, are available at **Boulder Community Hospital,** 1100 Balsam Ave., at North Broadway (☎ **303/440-2273**).

Newspapers/Magazines Newspaper options include Boulder's award-winning *Daily Camera* and the new *Boulder Weekly.* Many townspeople also read the campus paper, the *Colorado Daily,* available all over town. Both Denver dailies—the *Denver Post* and *Rocky Mountain News*—are available at newsstands throughout the city. You can also find the *New York Times, Wall Street Journal,* and *Christian Science Monitor* at many newsstands. The free *Boulder* magazine, published three times a year, lists seasonal events and other information on restaurants and the arts.

Photographic Needs For standard processing requirements (including 2-hr. slide processing), as well as custom lab work, contact **Photo Craft,** 3550 Arapahoe Ave. (☎ **303/442-6410**). For equipment, supplies, and repairs, visit **Mike's Camera,** 2500 Pearl St. (☎ **303/443-1715;** www.mikescamera. com).

Post Office The main downtown post office is at 15th and Walnut streets. Contact the U.S. Postal Service (☎ **800/275-8777;** www.usps.com) for hours and other locations.

Safety Although Boulder is generally a safe city—safer than Denver, for instance—it is not crime-free. Many locals avoid walking alone late at night along the Boulder Creek Path because of the transients who tend to hang out there.

Taxes State and city sales taxes total almost 7%.

Useful Telephone Numbers Call ☎ **303/639-1111** for **road conditions;** ☎ **303/825-7669** for **ski reports;** and ☎ **303/494-4221** for **weather reports.**

3 Where to Stay

You'll find a good selection of comfortable lodgings in Boulder, with a wide range of rates to suit almost every budget. Be aware, though, that the town literally fills up during the popular summer season, making advance reservations essential. It's also almost impossible to find a place to sleep during any major event at the University of Colorado, particularly graduation. Those who do find themselves in Boulder without lodging can check with the Boulder Convention and Visitors Bureau (see "Visitor Information" under "Orientation," above), which keeps track of availability. You can usually find a room in Denver, a half hour or so away. Rates listed below do not include the 9.7% accommodations tax. Parking is free unless otherwise specified.

Major chains and franchises that provide reasonably priced lodging in Boulder include **Best Western Golden Buff Lodge,** 1725 28th St., Boulder, CO 80301 (© **800/528-1234** or 303/442-7450), with 112 units, charging $94 to $114 double; **Best Western Boulder Inn,** 770 28th St., Boulder, CO 80303 (© **800/233-8469** or 303/449-3800), with 98 units and rates of $66 to $104 double; **Boulder Creek Quality Inn and Suites,** 2020 Arapahoe Ave., Boulder, CO 80302 (© **888/449-7550** or 303/449-7550), with 46 units and rates of $99 to $160 double; **Super 8,** 970 28th St., Boulder, CO 80303 (© **800/ 525-2149** or 303/443-7800), with 71 units and rates of $70 to $90 double; and **Days Inn,** 5397 S. Boulder Rd., Boulder, CO 80303 (© **800/329-7466** or 303/499-4422), with 78 units and rates of $69 to $109 double.

VERY EXPENSIVE

St. Julien ★★ The first new hotel in downtown Boulder since the Boulderado opened in 1909, the $24-million St. Julien began welcoming guests in early 2005. The flagstone-and-Norman brick exterior (accented by patina copper and red roof tiles) sheaths 200 exquisite guest rooms, averaging a healthy 400 square feet each. Everything from the frette linens to the premium bath amenities to the in-room artwork is first rate. Honeyed tones and French doors accent the guest rooms, which feature either one California king or two queens. The bathrooms are the best in town; there are separate tubs and showers in every granite-laden one. The facilities include a restaurant, a bar (T-Zero, named for a local climbing route), a two-lane lap pool, and a spa that offers "indigenous therapies" using local minerals and plants. Expect to be wowed.

900 Walnut St., Boulder, CO 80302. © **877/303-0900** or 720/406-9696. Fax 720/406-9668. www.stjulien. com. 200 units, including 15 suites. $245 double; $285–$300 suite. Lower weekend rates. AE, DC, DISC, MC, V. **Amenities:** Restaurant (American); lounge; indoor and outdoor heated pools; fitness center; spa; bike rentals; concierge; business center; dry cleaning. In room: A/C, cable TV w/pay movies, high-speed wireless Internet, coffeemaker, hair dryer, iron, safe.

EXPENSIVE

The Alps ★★ *(Finds)* A stage stop in the late 1800s, this historic log lodge sits on a mountainside about 7 minutes west of downtown Boulder. Converted into a beautiful bed-and-breakfast decorated with Arts and Crafts and Mission furnishings by owners Jeannine and John Vanderhart, the Alps is ideal for travelers planning to split time between Boulder and its outlying wilderness and scenery. Each room here is different and named after a Colorado mining town, including Magnolia, Solina, and Wall Street. All have functional fireplaces with Victorian mantels, queen beds with down comforters, and individual thermostats. Most are spacious, with a claw-foot or double whirlpool tub plus a double shower, and many have private porches. Shared spaces include a beautiful lounge with a huge rock fireplace and VCR, plus delightful gardens and patio areas. The entrance is the original log cabin built in the 1870s. Smoking is not permitted.

38619 Boulder Canyon Dr., Boulder, CO 80302. © **800/414-2577** or 303/444-5445. Fax 303/444-5522. www.alpsinn.com. 12 units. $139–$225 double. Rates include full breakfast. AE, DC, DISC, MC, V. **Amenities:** Jacuzzi; concierge; activities desk; in-room massage. In room: A/C, TV, dataport, hair dryer, iron.

Boulder Marriott ★ Until the St. Julien came along, the Marriott was the newest full-service hotel in the city. It's conveniently located just a block off 28th Street (U.S. 36), providing great access to everything in town. Furnished with Southwestern touches, the rooms are geared to the business traveler, with multiline phones, large work desks, and ergonomic chairs. Local and toll-free calls cost $1. Half of the rooms are on two concierge levels, which have a private

Boulder Accommodations & Dining

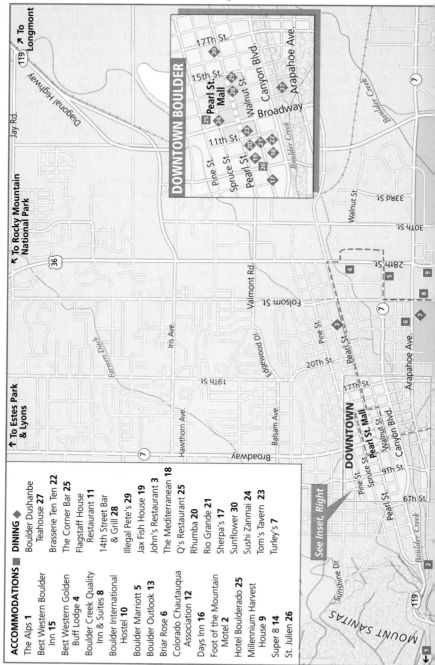

ACCOMMODATIONS

The Alps **1**
Best Western Boulder Inn **15**
Best Western Golden Buff Lodge **4**
Boulder Creek Quality Inn & Suites **8**
Boulder International Hostel **10**
Boulder Marriott **5**
Boulder Outlook **13**
Briar Rose **6**
Colorado Chautauqua Association **12**
Days Inn **16**
Foot of the Mountain Motel **2**
Hotel Boulderado **25**
Millennium Harvest House **9**
Super 8 **14**
St. Julien **26**

DINING

Boulder Dushanbe Teahouse **27**
Brasserie Ten Ten **22**
The Corner Bar **25**
Flagstaff House Restaurant **11**
14th Street Bar & Grill **28**
Illegal Pete's **29**
Jax Fish House **19**
John's Restaurant **3**
The Mediterranean **18**
Q's Restaurant **25**
Rhumba **20**
Rio Grande **21**
Sherpa's **17**
Sunflower **30**
Sushi Zanmai **24**
Tom's Tavern **23**
Turley's **7**

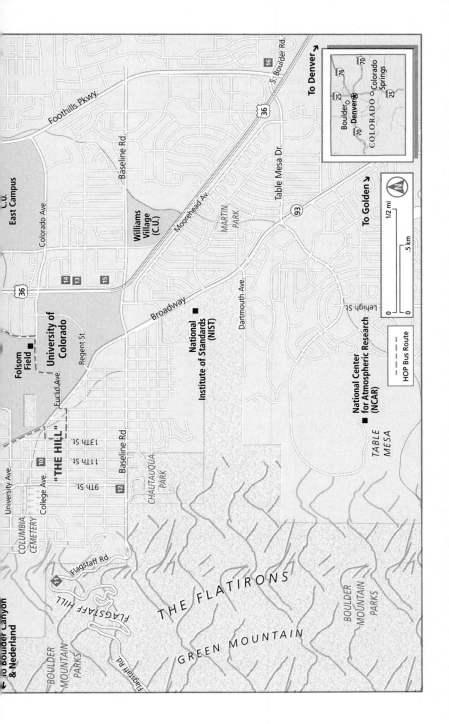

lounge; rates include continental breakfast, happy hour, and hors d'oeuvres. Three-quarters of the rooms feature mountain views.

2660 Canyon Blvd., Boulder, CO 80302 (1 block west of Canyon and 28th St.). © **303/440-8877**. Fax 303/440-3377. www.marriott.com/DENBO. 155 units. $109–$209 double; $139–$239 suite. AE, DC, DISC, MC, V. Free valet and self-parking. **Amenities:** Restaurant (steakhouse); lounge; indoor heated pool; exercise room; spa; Jacuzzi; 24-hr. business center; shopping arcade; limited room service; massage; laundry service; dry cleaning; executive level. *In room:* A/C, cable TV w/pay movies, dataport, coffeemaker, hair dryer, iron, safe.

Briar Rose 🏵🏵 A country-style brick home built in the 1890s, this midcity bed-and-breakfast might remind you of Grandma's place. Every room is furnished with antiques, from the bedrooms to the parlor to the sunny back porch, and the lovely gardens offer a quiet escape. Several rooms have business amenities, such as modem hookups, large worktables, and super lighting. A fax/copy machine is also available.

Two of the six units in the main house have fireplaces; four in a separate cottage come with either a patio or a balcony. All are furnished with feather comforters. The suite, designed for extended executive stays, is also popular with families. It can sleep four, and features a full kitchen and dining room. Weekly and monthly rates are available.

The continental breakfast is gourmet quality: yogurt, homemade granola, fresh nut breads, yogurt with fruit, and much more. Refreshments are available in the lobby from 8am to 9pm. Smoking is permitted only in the outside garden areas.

2151 Arapahoe Ave., Boulder, CO 80302. © **303/442-3007**. Fax 303/786-8440. www.briarrosebb.com. 10 units (6 with shower only). May–Oct $134–$164 double, $199 suite; Nov–Apr $149–$164 double, $129–$199 suite. Rates include continental breakfast. AE, DC, MC, V. *In room:* A/C, dataport.

Hotel Boulderado 🏵🏵 Opened on January 1, 1909, this elegant and historic hotel still has the same Otis elevator that wowed visiting dignitaries that day. The colorful leaded-glass ceiling and cantilevered cherrywood staircase are other reminders of days past, along with the rich woodwork of the balusters around the mezzanine and the handsome armchairs and settees in the main-floor lobby. The hotel's Christmas tree, a 35-footer with 1,000 white lights, is a Boulder tradition, and the setting for afternoon tea on the mezzanine in December.

Five stories tall and just a block off the Pearl Street Mall, this welcome contemporary of Denver's Brown Palace has 42 original guest rooms, all bright and cozy, and each a little bit different. Although the rooms are continuously renovated and refurbished, they retain a Victorian flavor, with lush floral wallpapering, candlewick-knit spreads, and furnishings alternately stately and plush. The construction of a spacious North Wing in 1989 almost quadrupled the number of rooms; while these are larger and more typical of a modern hotel, they also embody the early-20th-century theme. All units have a few high-tech touches: electronic locks and two-line phones with voice mail; some rooms have refrigerators, and a few have jetted tubs.

2115 13th St. (at Spruce St.), Boulder, CO 80302. © **800/433-4344** or 303/442-4344. Fax 303/442-4378. www.boulderado.com. 160 units. $185–$215 double; $275–$325 suite. AE, DC, DISC, MC, V. **Amenities:** 2 restaurants (contemporary American, see "Where to Dine," below); 2 lounges; access to nearby health club; business center; laundry service. *In room:* A/C, cable TV, dataport, high-speed Internet access, coffeemaker, hair dryer, iron.

Millennium Harvest House 🇰🇮🇩🇸 The Harvest House is exceptional: a full-service hotel with spacious and lovely grounds. Located on the west side of U.S. 36 on the south side of Boulder, the former Regal Harvest House looks like almost any other four-story hotel from the front—but its backyard melts into a park that surrounds the east end of the 10-mile Boulder Creek Path (see "Attractions," later in this chapter), where bike rentals are available.

All rooms hold one king-size or two double beds, a lounge chair and ottoman, remote-control cable TV, and direct-dial phone. Spacious VIP Tower accommodations provide upgraded amenities such as hair dryers and bathrobes, and some rooms have high-speed Internet access. Rates for these units include continental breakfast and evening hors d'oeuvres in the Millennium Club Lounge. Our favorite rooms here are the two dozen that look out on the Boulder Creek Path.

1345 28th St., Boulder, CO 80302. ℂ 800/545-6285 or 303/443-3850. Fax 303/443-1480. www.millennium hotels.com. 268 units. $129–$145 double; $175–$395 suite. AE, DC, DISC, MC, V. **Amenities:** Restaurant (American); 2 lounges; indoor lap pool; outdoor heated swimming pool; 15 tennis courts (5 indoor); fitness center; 2 Jacuzzis (indoor and outdoor); bike rental; game room; airport shuttle; business center; limited room service; on-call masseur; valet and self-service laundry, executive level. *In room:* A/C, cable TV w/pay movies, coffeemaker, hair dryer, iron.

MODERATE

Boulder Outlook ★★ *Kids* *Value* The proprietors of this former Ramada and Holidome have outdone every chain motel in town. The Outlook is fun, fresh, and definitively Boulder, with such unique perks as two bouldering rocks (one is 11 feet high, the other a 4-footer), a fenced, 4,000-square-foot dog run, and discounts on bike rentals and other activities. The brightly painted motel has 40 rooms which have an outdoor entrance; the rest are accessed indoors. Overall, the rooms are larger than average and contemporary; the baths nicely tiled. In-room recycling containers and all-natural bath amenities are two more distinctly Boulder touches. The indoor pool is superb, complete with a waterfall and a mural of a cloud-speckled sky, and the bar and grill here features bluegrass on Fridays.

800 28th St., Boulder, CO 80303. ℂ 800/542-0304 or 303/443-3322. Fax 303/449-5130. www.boulder outlook.com. 162 units. $89–99 double; lower rates off season. Rates include continental breakfast. AE, DC, DISC, MC, V. Pets accepted, $10/night. **Amenities:** Restaurant (American); lounge; indoor heated pool; exercise room; Jacuzzi; men's and women's saunas; game room; activities desk; 24-hr. business center; limited room service; massage; coin-op washers and dryers; dry cleaning; executive level. *In room:* A/C, cable TV, dataport, coffeemaker, hair dryer, iron, safe.

Colorado Chautauqua Association ★ *Finds* During the late 19th and early 20th centuries, more than 400 Chautauquas—adult education and cultural entertainment centers—sprang up around the United States. This 26-acre park, at the foot of the Flatiron Mountains, is one of the few remaining. In summer, it hosts a wide-ranging arts program, including the Colorado Music Festival (see "Boulder After Dark," later in this chapter).

Lodging is in attractive cottages and in rooms and apartments in two historic lodges. All units were outfitted with new furnishings in 2003 and come with linens and towels. They have balconies or porches, and either private or shared kitchens. Cottages range from efficiencies to three-bedroom, two-bathroom units. Larger groups might take the newly restored Mission House, which has eight bedrooms, a kitchen, and a screened-in porch and rents for $967 a night. From September to May, many cottages and apartments are rented by the month or longer, but nightly accommodations are generally available.

Guests have access to the park's playgrounds, picnic grounds, and hiking trail heads. The historic Chautauqua Dining Hall, which opened on July 4th, 1898, serves three moderately priced meals a day year-round.

900 Baseline Rd. (at 9th St.), Boulder, CO 80302. ✆ **303/442-3282**, ext. 11 for lodging, 303/440-3776 for restaurant. Fax 303/449-0790. www.chautauqua.com. 87 units. $69–$114 lodge room; $89–$104 efficiency cottage; $114–$124 1-bedroom cottage; $129–$169 2- or 3-bedroom cottage. MC, V. Bus: 203. Pets accepted in cottages for a nonrefundable $100 fee. Pets not accepted in lodges. **Amenities:** Restaurant (creative American); 4 tennis courts; children's programs during summer; self-service laundry. *In room:* Kitchens, coffeemakers, no phone.

Foot of the Mountain Motel *(Kids) (Value)*   This motel, a series of connected, cabin-style units with bright red trim near the east gate of Boulder Canyon, dates from 1930 but has been fully modernized. The location is inspiring, on the west edge of town where city meets mountains, and right across the street is the top end of the Boulder Creek Path and the trail head that leads to the summit of Flagstaff Mountain. The pleasant pine-walled cabins are furnished with queen or double beds and individual water heaters; two suites (converted manager's quarters) are big enough for families and outfitted with full kitchens.

200 Arapahoe Ave., Boulder, CO 80302. ✆ **866/773-5489** 303/442-5688. www.footofthemountainmotel. com. 20 units (2 with shower only), including 2 suites. $85 double; $165–$175 suite. AE, DISC, MC, V. Pets accepted for $5 nightly fee and a $50 refundable deposit. *In room:* Cable TV, kitchens, fridge.

INEXPENSIVE

Boulder International Hostel *(Value)*   As at most hostels, guests come here expecting to share—and they do. The toilets, showers, kitchen, laundry, and TV room are communal. Individual phones can be arranged for private rooms (with a deposit), but others share a phone. Just 2 blocks from the University of Colorado campus, the hostel is open for registration daily from 8am to 11pm. To stay in a bunk, you must present identification proving you are not a resident of Colorado.

1107 12th St., Boulder, CO 80302-7029. ✆ **888/442-0522** or 303/442-0522. Fax 303/442-0523. 50 units. $17 dorm bed; $35–$45 private unit. AE, DISC, MC, V. *In room:* No phone.

4 Where to Dine

Partly because Boulder is a young, hip community, it has attracted a variety of small, with-it restaurants. At these chef-owned and -operated establishments, innovative and often-changing cuisine is the rule. You'll find a lot of California influences here, as well as a number of top-notch chefs doing their own thing.

A Boulder city ordinance prohibits smoking inside restaurants.

VERY EXPENSIVE

Flagstaff House Restaurant *★★★ (Moments)* NEW AMERICAN/ REGIONAL   Named for its perch on Flagstaff Mountain, this restaurant attracts patrons from across the state and nation with excellent cuisine and service, and the spectacular nighttime view of the lights of Boulder spread out 1,000 feet below. A local institution since 1951, this family-owned and -operated restaurant has an elegant, candlelit dining room with glass walls that maximize the view. The prices aren't for the budget-minded, but those seeking a romantic setting and superlative food can't miss with the Flagstaff House.

The menu, which changes daily, offers an excellent selection of seafood and Rocky Mountain game, all prepared with a creative flair. Typical appetizers include smoked rabbit or duck, oysters, wild mushrooms, and cheeses. Entrees, many of which are seasonal, might include Colorado buffalo, ahi tuna, Canadian halibut, and soft-shell crabs. The restaurant also boasts dessert soufflés, a world-renowned wine cellar (at, 20,000 bottles, undoubtedly the best in Colorado), and an impressive selection of after-dinner drinks.

1138 Flagstaff Rd. (west up Baseline Rd.). © **303/442-4640.** Reservations recommended. Main courses $25–$60. AE, DC, MC, V. Sun–Fri 6–10pm; Sat 5–10pm.

EXPENSIVE

John's Restaurant ★★★ *Finds* CONTINENTAL/MEDITERRANEAN
This funky but elegant converted house has set the pace for the Boulder dining scene for nearly 30 years. The emphasis here is squarely on the food. Chef-owner Corey Buck (who bought the place from founder John Bizzarro in 2004) starts with the classic cuisine of southern Europe, but adds his own creative signature spin to each dish; compared with Bizzarro, Buck prepares bigger plates and is fonder of game dishes. For starters, apple Stilton pecan salad and ricotta-and-spinach gnocchi verde set the stage for the continually changing main-course offerings. Menu mainstays include filet mignon with Stilton ale sauce, surrounded by grilled Bermuda onions; chile-crusted pork tenderloin with cranberry-orange sauce; and a variety of fresh seafood dishes—chowder and several succulent plates featuring plump Gulf shrimp are always available. The menu also includes vegetarian items, and the homemade desserts (still by John's daughter Stella) include caramel cheesecake that verges on transcendental. There's a full bar as well.

2328 Pearl St. © **303/444-5232.** www.johnsrestaurantboulder.com. Reservations recommended. Main courses $19–$35. AE, DISC, MC, V. Tues–Sat 5:30pm–closing (call ahead for hours).

Q's Restaurant ★★ CONTEMPORARY AMERICAN   The historic ambience that makes the Hotel Boulderado such a delightful place to stay also makes its way into Q's, the hotel's main restaurant. The dining room combines the old—rich polished wood and stained glass—with the comfortable, casually elegant feel of today. Of course, the important thing is the food, and chef-owner John Platt does an excellent job, using locally grown organic vegetables whenever possible.

Platt, who claims seafood as his specialty after years on Cape Cod, always includes several fresh fish selections on the menu, such as grilled ahi tuna served with potato-leek purée with roasted cauliflower, apple-smoked bacon, and a sweet-pepper salad. Rotisseried meats often include allspice-cured pork loin served with shoestring onions, whipped potatoes, and barbecue jus. You'll also likely find several pasta dishes, roasted chicken and quail, venison, and beef.

In the Hotel Boulderado, 2115 13th St. (at Spruce St.). © **303/442-4880.** Reservations recommended. Main courses $5–$10 breakfast, $8–$16 lunch, $16–$27 dinner. AE, DC, DISC, MC, V. Mon–Fri 6:30–11am and 11:30am–2pm; Sat–Sun 7am–2pm; daily 5–10pm.

Sushi Zanmai ★ *Kids* SUSHI/JAPANESE   Boulder is a hot spot for great sushi: Zanmai is a go-to stalwart but faces stiff competition from a number of like-minded upstarts. We still prefer the place for its festive atmosphere, impeccable service, and traditional sushi. Prepared while you watch—at the sushi bar or tableside—the options include everything from tuna and trout to sea urchin and octopus, with such exotic rolls as Colorado (raw filet mignon), Z-No. 9 (shrimp tempura, avocado, salmon, and eel sauce), and LSD (lettuce shrimp deluxe). There are lunch specials as well as sushi happy-hour specials during lunch and dinner. Karaoke sing-along takes place every Saturday from 10pm to midnight.

1221 Spruce St. (at Broadway). © **303/440-0733.** Reservations recommended for groups of 4 or more. Main courses $7.50–$13 lunch, $15–$26 dinner; sushi rolls $2–$12. AE, DC, MC, V. Mon–Fri 11:30am–2pm; Sun–Fri 5–10pm; Sat 5pm–midnight.

MODERATE

Boulder Dushanbe Teahouse ★★ *Finds* ETHNIC WORLD CUISINE   In 1990, 200 crates were shipped to Colorado as a gift from Dushanbe, Tajikistan, Boulder's sister city. From the ornately hand-carved and painted pieces of a Persian teahouse in the crates, the building was assembled at its present site with help from four Tajik artisans. It's the only teahouse of its kind in the Western Hemisphere. Lavishly and authentically decorated, the teahouse holds 14 pillars carved from Siberian cedar, and a grand central fountain. The cuisine includes traditional ethnic dishes from the Middle East, Asia, and elsewhere, including several noodle and vegetarian options. There are even a few Tajik specialties, often a lamb dish. Pastries, coffees, and more than 70 teas are also available. There is a full bar on-site as well.

1770 13th St. ⓒ **303/442-4993.** Main courses $6–$13 lunch, $8–$18 dinner. AE, DISC, MC, V. Mon–Fri 8–10:30am and 11am–3pm; Sat–Sun 8am–3pm; daily 5–10pm. Tea and coffee bar daily 8am–10pm.

Brasserie Ten Ten ★★ FRENCH BISTRO   From the same folks who brought you The Med across the street, Brasserie Ten Ten is a more than respectable sequel. The breezy bistro, done up with frosted glass, brick walls, and a handsome marble bar, serves delectable oysters (both raw and Rockefeller are quite good) for starters, and some well-thought-out variations on French stand-bys, such as a scrumptious lamb shank braised with burgundy and poblano pepper and a nice skirt steak with *pommes frites* (yep, french fries). We recommend the *brique de poulet*, a salt-and-rosemary-crusted chicken cooked with the help of a perfectly shaped stone. The duck-breast salad is excellent, as are the baked goods and the desserts, both made in-house at a bakery that also supplies The Med.

1011 Walnut St. ⓒ **303/998-1010.** Reservations accepted. Main courses $5–$11 brunch, $5–$11 lunch, $9–$27 dinner. AE, DC, DISC, MC, V. Mon–Wed 11am–10pm; Thurs–Fri 11am–11pm; Sat 9am–11pm; Sun brunch 9am–3pm.

14th Street Bar & Grill ★ CONTEMPORARY AMERICAN   An open restaurant with large windows facing the street, this is a great spot for people-watching as well as dining. The open wood grill and pizza oven, the long, crowded full-service bar, and a changing display of abstract art let you know that this is a fun place. The menu centers around what chef-owner Kathy Andrade calls "American grill" cuisine, which includes grilled sandwiches, Southwestern chicken salads, and unusual homemade pizzas, such as a pie topped with chorizo sausage, garlic, and roasted green chiles. A variety of pasta dishes are also offered, plus changing dinner specials such as beef tenderloin stuffed with cheese and cilantro.

1400 Pearl St. (at 14th St.). ⓒ **303/444-5854.** Main courses $9–$22. AE, MC, V. Daily 11:30am–10pm.

Jax Fish House ★ SEAFOOD   Fresh seafood is flown in daily from the East and West coasts to supply this restaurant, a lively space with colored chalk graffiti and oceanic art on its brick walls, social patrons, and a booming stereo system. At patio, bar, and table seating, you can order one of the house specialties—the Mississippi catfish skillet is a good bet—or simply slurp down raw oysters and martinis to your heart's content. Entrees usually include shrimp, New Zealand bluenose, Rocky Mountain trout, and ahi tuna, along with lobster and soft-shell crab when available. Or try a smoked salmon carpaccio or clam, rock shrimp, catfish, or calamari po' boy, with slaw and your choice of a side. Those who prefer beef can choose from New York strip steak and all-natural burgers.

928 Pearl St. (1 block west of the mall). © 303/444-1811. Main courses $8–$24. AE, DC, MC, V. Mon–Thurs 4–10pm; Fri–Sat 4–11pm; Sun 4–9pm.

The Mediterranean ⋆ (Value) MEDITERRANEAN/TAPAS   Known as "The Med," this local favorite is designed as an homage to the casual eateries of Spain and Italy. With a multihued tile interior and an enjoyable breezy patio, the Med draws a bustling after-work drinking crowd for its weekday tapas hour (3–6:30pm), which includes such delicacies as fried artichoke hearts, risotto-and-crab fritters, and hummus for very reasonable prices. (A few shared tapas can prove a fairly satisfying meal for two or three people.) For a full dinner, the selection is extensive, ranging from pasta to poultry, steaks to gourmet wood-fired pizzas, with several vegetarian dishes to please the health-conscious Boulder crowd. Our favorite: the delectable *paellas,* traditional Spanish rice dishes that come in five varieties. The lunch menu is similar, with a nice selection of panini sandwiches (including lamb, salmon, and vegetarian). There are also several daily specials.

1002 Walnut St. © 303/444-5335. Main courses $7–$13 lunch, $9–$19 dinner; most tapas $3–$5. AE, DC, DISC, MC, V. Mon–Wed 11am–10pm; Thurs–Sat 11am–11pm; Sun 4–10pm.

Rhumba ⋆ SEAFOOD   A loud and lively Caribbean cafe, Rhumba has earned a loyal following since it opened in 1999. With a curved bar that abuts a popular patio and plenty of plants, sun, and original art, this hip eatery dishes out plates of jerked pork and chicken, noodle bowls, and curried dishes, served with such sides as black beans, sweet-potato hash browns, and grilled flatbread. More exotic offerings include the seviche of the day, conch chowder, and seared calamari. Even the cheeseburgers have an island flavor when doused with Rhumba's banana-guava ketchup. There is spice aplenty for fiery-foods fanatics, but there are also plenty of dishes that won't set meeker mouths afire. The cocktail of choice is the mojito: silver rum, fresh mint and lime, sugar, and soda water. There is live music (reggae, Latin, jazz, and funk) on a regular basis.

950 Pearl St. © 303/442-7771. Main courses $10–$19. AE, DC, MC, V. Mon–Thurs 4–10pm; Fri 11:30am–10pm; Sat–Sun 1–10pm.

Sunflower ⋆⋆ (Finds) CONTEMPORARY/ORGANIC   This pleasant contemporary eatery, eclectically decorated with murals, rotating local art, and a flagstone floor, touts itself as "Boulder's most unique restaurant," based on its dedication to healthy cuisine. The ingredients include certified organic produce and free-range, hormone-free poultry and game. Owner-chef Jon Pell takes a multicultural approach: Sunflower features a diverse selection of dinner entrees, including grilled ahi tuna served with a coconut–lemon grass infusion; seared elk tenderloin with raspberry-vermouth coulis; and tempeh scallopini with wine, lemon, and fresh herbs. Lunch includes fresh variations on sandwiches—such as a blackened salmon burger—as well as specialties like pad Thai and penne pomodoro. An all-you-can-eat organic salad buffet is served daily until 4pm, and there's a popular weekend brunch.

1701 Pearl St. (2 blocks east of the mall). © 303/440-0220. Main courses $7–$12 lunch, $13–$26 dinner. AE, MC, V. Tues–Fri 11am–2:30pm; Sat–Sun brunch 10am–3pm; dinner Tues–Sun 5–10pm.

INEXPENSIVE

Corner Bar ⋆ CONTEMPORARY AMERICAN   With the same chef as the highly rated Q's Restaurant (see above), the Corner Bar is far above your average sandwich shop, although sandwiches and burgers are on the menu, too. Here you can savor a grilled-salmon sandwich, served with red-onion marmalade, spinach, and horseradish aioli. Or you might try a roast turkey BLT with herbed mayo, or pan-roasted halibut with avocado, tomato, orange, and a black-bean cake.

In the Hotel Boulderado, 2115 13th St. (at Spruce St.). © **303/442-4560.** Main courses $7–$14. AE, DC, DISC, MC, V. Daily 11am–midnight.

Illegal Pete's *Value* MEXICAN   Located at the far east end of the Pearl Street Mall, Illegal Pete's is renowned locally for its creative, healthy burritos, packed with chicken, steak, veggies, or fish. The menu also includes a similar range of tacos, as well as salads, quesadillas, and chili. Margaritas and domestic and Mexican beers are available, as are takeout and delivery.

1447 Pearl St. © **303/440-3955.** Menu items $4–$6. AE, DISC, MC, V. Sun–Thurs 11am–10pm; Fri–Sat 11am–2:30am.

Rio Grande MEXICAN   This popular neighborhood restaurant and bar, just south of the Pearl Street Mall, is probably best known for its huge, award-winning margaritas—so potent that the staff enforces a strict limit of three. Frequented by college students and Boulder's under-30 crowd, the Rio is bustling for reasons beyond its alcoholic concoctions—the loud, social atmosphere and the food, a good variety of oversize Mexican entrees and combos. Our favorites are hearty fajitas (steak or veggie, with handmade tortillas), zesty Yucatan shrimp, and creative chiles rellenos.

1101 Walnut St. © **303/444-3690.** Meals $6–$14. AE, MC, V. Mon–Thurs 11am–2pm; Mon–Wed 5–10pm; Thurs 5–10:30pm; Fri–Sun 11am–10:30pm.

Sherpa's *Finds* TIBETAN/NEPALI   Owned by Pemba Sherpa—a native of Nepal who in fact is a sherpa, or Himalayan mountain guide—Sherpa's is located in a converted Victorian house just southwest of the Pearl Street Mall. Decorated with Himalayan relics and photography of the peaks of Nepal and Tibet, the restaurant serves up food to match: Tibetan dishes like *thupka* (noodle bowls) and sherpa stew as well as spicier Nepali and Indian cuisine, including *saag* (creamed spinach with garlic, cumin, ginger, and your choice of veggie or meat) and curry dishes. There are lunch specials daily, as well as a comfortable bar with a library full of climbing tomes.

825 Walnut St. © **303/440-7151.** Reservations accepted. Main courses $5–$9 lunch, $6–$13 dinner. AE, DISC, MC, V. Daily 11am–3pm; Sun–Thurs 5–9:30pm; Fri–Sat 5–10pm.

Tom's Tavern *Finds* AMERICAN   Boulder's most popular place for a good hamburger, Tom's has been a neighborhood institution owned by local politician Tom Eldridge for almost 40 years. Located in an early-20th-century building that once housed an undertaker, the tavern has vinyl-upholstered booths and patio seating. Besides the ⅓-pound burgers (made from all-organic Coleman beef) and other sandwiches, you can get a 10-ounce steak, fried chicken, or a veggie burger, not to mention a variety of barbecue plates. Tom's serves dinner anytime.

1047 Pearl St. © **303/443-3893.** Menu items $6–$12. AE, DC, DISC, MC, V. Mon–Thurs 10am–10pm; Fri–Sat 10am–11pm; Sun 12:30–8:30pm.

Turley's *Kids* AMERICAN   A feel-good family restaurant with a healthier menu than the norm, Turley's is a Boulder landmark. Its sunny atmosphere and friendly staff provide a pleasant, homey backdrop for any meal, and breakfast is served all day. The bars serve everything from wheat-grass juice to martinis. A menu featuring omelets, burgers, sandwiches, fresh fish, and dinner entrees ranging from buffalo meatloaf to tofu scramble ensures that everyone's tastes will be satisfied. Turley's moved from its longtime Arapahoe Avenue location to Pearl Street in March 2004.

2805 Pearl St. (at 28th St.) ℂ 303/442-2800. Most menu items $4–$15. AE, DC, DISC, MC, V. Mon–Sat 6:30am–10pm; Sun 7am–9pm.

ESPRESSO BARS, COFFEEHOUSES & RELATED ESTABLISHMENTS

Espresso fans will have no problem finding a decent espresso, cappuccino, or latte: Boulder has a number of **Starbucks** establishments, as well as many more interesting independent coffeehouses. Many of the independents, located near the Pearl Street Mall, provide outdoor seating in nice weather. Attached to the Boulder Book Store, the **Bookend Cafe,** 1115 Pearl St. (ℂ **303/440-6699**), offers a variety of coffee drinks and a delightful array of baked goods, soups, and pies. At the east end of the mall (at 18th St.) is the somewhat bohemian **Penny Lane** (ℂ **303/443-9516**), a gathering place for talking, playing chess, or reading while you sip regular coffee, espresso, cappuccino, or a latte, and munch on a bagel or muffin. There's a wide variety of newspapers and nightly live entertainment, including poetry, an open stage, and a diverse range of music by local and regional performers. See also "Boulder After Dark," later in this chapter. **Trident Booksellers & Café,** 940 Pearl St. (ℂ **404/443-3133**), features indoor and outdoor seating as well as a comprehensive selection of used books. The **Boulder Dushanbe Teahouse,** 1770 13th St. (ℂ **303/442-4993;** p. 194), offers an authentic Persian setting for quaffing more than 70 varieties of tea and a good selection of coffees from 8am to 10pm daily. Homemade baked goods are also available.

5 Attractions

THE TOP ATTRACTIONS

Boulder Creek Path ★★ *Kids*   Following Boulder Creek, this nature corridor provides about a 16-mile-long oasis and recreation area through the city and west into the mountains. With no street crossings (there are bridges and underpasses instead), the path is popular with Boulder residents, especially on weekends, when you'll see numerous walkers, runners, bicyclists, and in-line skaters. (Walkers should stay to the right; the left lane is for faster traffic.) The path links the CU campus, several city parks, and office buildings. Near the east end, watch for deer, prairie-dog colonies, and wetlands, where some 150 species of birds have been spotted. You might see Canada geese, mallard ducks, spotted sandpipers, owls, and woodpeckers.

At 30th Street, south of Arapahoe Road, the path cuts through **Scott Carpenter Park** (named for the astronaut and Colorado native), where you can swim in summer and sled in winter. Just west of Scott Carpenter Park, you'll find **Boulder Creek Stream Observatory,** which is adjacent to and maintained by the Millennium Harvest House (see "Where to Stay," earlier in this chapter). In addition to observing trout and other aquatic wildlife, you're invited to feed the fish with trout food purchased from a vending machine (25¢). **Central Park,** at Broadway and Canyon Boulevard, preserves some of Boulder's history with a restored steam locomotive. The **Boulder Public Library** is also in this area.

Traveling west, watch for the **Charles A. Heartling Sculpture Garden** (with the stone image of local Indian chief Niwot) and the **Kids' Fishing Ponds;** the

Boulder Attractions

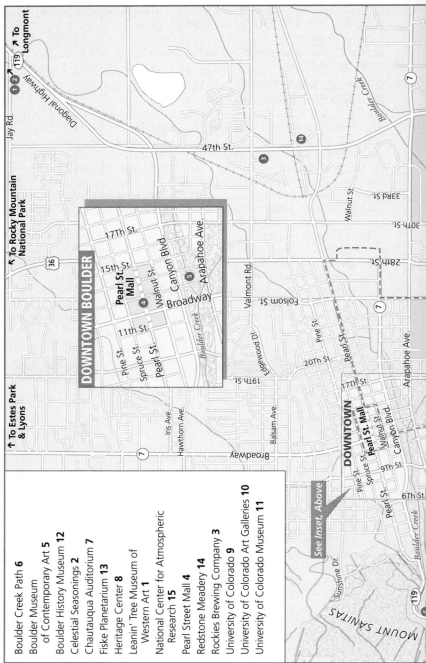

DOWNTOWN BOULDER

See Inset, Above

DOWNTOWN

Boulder Creek Path **6**
Boulder Museum
 of Contemporary Art **5**
Boulder History Museum **12**
Celestial Seasonings **2**
Chautauqua Auditorium **7**
Fiske Planetarium **13**
Heritage Center **8**
Leanin' Tree Museum of
 Western Art **1**
National Center for Atmospheric
 Research **15**
Pearl Street Mall **4**
Redstone Meadery **14**
Rockies Brewing Company **3**
University of Colorado **9**
University of Colorado Art Galleries **10**
University of Colorado Museum **11**

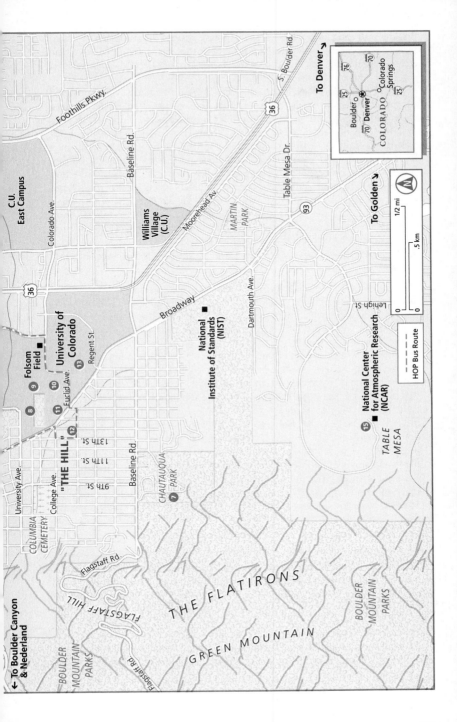

To Boulder Canyon & Nederland

COLUMBIA CEMETERY

University Ave.

College Ave.

9TH ST.

11TH ST.

13TH ST.

"THE HILL"

Baseline Rd.

Flagstaff Rd.

FLAGSTAFF HILL

BOULDER MOUNTAIN PARKS

Flagstaff Rd.

THE FLATIRONS

GREEN MOUNTAIN

BOULDER MOUNTAIN PARKS

CHAUTAUQUA PARK
7

National Center for Atmospheric Research (NCAR)
15

TABLE MESA

Lehigh St.

National Institute of Standards (NIST)

Dartmouth Ave.

Broadway

MARTIN PARK

Moorehead Av.

Table Mesa Dr.

93

To Golden →

Baseline Rd.

36

Williams Village (C.U.)

S. Boulder Rd.

36

To Denver →

Foothills Pkwy.

Colorado Ave.

C.U. East Campus

University of Colorado
13

Folsom Field
9
10
11
8
12

Regent St.
Euclid Ave.

HOP Bus Route

0   1/2 mi
0   .5 km

Boulder
Denver
Colorado Springs
70
76
25
25
70
COLORADO

Boulder Fish and Game Club stocks the ponds, which are open only to children under 12, who can fish for free and keep what they catch. Near 3rd Street and Canyon Boulevard, you'll find the **Xeriscape Garden,** where drought-tolerant plants are tested for reduced water intake.

The **Eben G. Fine Park** is named for the Boulder pharmacist who discovered Arapaho Glacier on nearby Arapaho Peak. To the west, **Red Rocks Settlers' Park** marks the beginning of the **Boulder Canyon Pioneer Trail,** which leads to a continuation of Boulder Creek Path. The park is named for Missouri gold-seekers who camped at this spot in 1858 and later found gold about 12 miles farther west. Watch for explanatory signs along the 1.3-mile path. The **White-water Kayak Course** has 20 slalom gates for kayakers and canoeists to use free; to the west, **Elephant Buttresses** is one of Boulder's more popular rock-climbing areas. The path ends at **Four Mile Canyon,** the old town site of Orodell.

Note: Although the path is generally well populated and quite safe, Boulderites warn against using it late at night if you are alone; one of the problems is the number of transients who take refuge there.

55th St. and Pearl Pkwy., to the mouth of Boulder Canyon. © 303/413-7200. Free admission. Daily 24 hours. Bus: HOP.

National Center for Atmospheric Research ✿ (Finds)
Inspired by the cliff dwellings at Mesa Verde National Park, I. M. Pei designed this striking pink-sandstone building, which overlooks Boulder from high atop Table Mesa in the southwestern foothills. (You might recognize the center from Woody Allen's *Sleeper;* scenes were shot here.) Scientists study such phenomena as the greenhouse effect, wind shear, and ozone depletion to gain a better understanding of the earth's atmosphere. Among the technological tools on display are satellites, weather balloons, interactive computer monitors, robots, and supercomputers that can simulate the world's climate. There are also hands-on, weather-oriented exhibits from the San Francisco Exploratorium Museum, now on permanent display. The **Walter Orr Roberts Weather Trail** outside the building's west doors takes visitors on a 0.4-mile, wheelchair-accessible loop along a path with interpretive signs describing various aspects of weather and climate plus the plants and animals of the area. The center also houses a changing art exhibit and a science-oriented gift shop. Allow 1 to 2 hours.

1850 Table Mesa Dr. © 303/497-1174. www.ncar.ucar.edu. Free admission. Self-guided tours daily 8am–5pm; holidays 9am–4pm; there is also a self-guided audio tour. 1-hr. guided tours daily at noon. Take Broadway heading southwest out of town to Table Mesa Dr., and follow it west to the center.

Pearl Street Mall ✿✿ (Kids)
This 4-block-long tree-lined pedestrian mall marks Boulder's downtown core and its center for dining, shopping, strolling, and people-watching. Musicians, mimes, and other street entertainers hold court on the landscaped mall day and night, year-round. Buy your lunch from one of the many vendors and sprawl on the grass in front of the courthouse to relax and eat. Locally owned businesses and galleries share the mall with trendy boutiques, sidewalk cafes, and major chains including Banana Republic and Abercrombie & Fitch. There's a wonderful play area for youngsters, with climbable boulders set in gravel. Don't miss the bronze bust of Chief Niwot (of the southern Arapaho) in front of the Boulder County Courthouse between 13th and 14th streets.

Pearl St. from 11th to 15th sts. Bus: HOP.

University of Colorado ✿
The largest university in the state, with nearly 29,000 students (including about 4,600 graduate students), CU dominates the

city. Its student population, cultural and sports events, and intellectual atmosphere have helped shape Boulder into the city it is today. The school boasts 16 alumni astronauts who have flown in space and three Nobel laureates on the faculty.

Old Main, on the Norlin Quadrangle, was the first building erected after the university was established in 1876; at that time, it housed the entire school. Later, pink-sandstone Italian Renaissance–style buildings came to dominate the campus. Visitors may want to take in the university's **Heritage Center,** on the third floor of Old Main; the **University of Colorado Museum** (see "More Attractions," below), a natural-history museum in the Henderson Building on Broadway; the **Mary Rippon Outdoor Theatre,** behind the Henderson Building, site of the annual Colorado Shakespeare Festival; **Fiske Planetarium,** between Kittredge Loop Drive and Regent Drive on the south side of campus; and the **Norlin Library,** on the Norlin Quadrangle, the largest research library in the state, with extensive holdings of American and English literature. Other attractions include the CU Art Museum, University Memorial Center (the student center), and the Integrated Teaching and Learning Laboratory in the College of Engineering. Prospective students and their parents can arrange campus tours by contacting the admissions office (© **303/492-6301**).

Tours are available weekdays at the **Laboratory for Atmospheric and Space Physics** (© **303/492-6412**), on the east campus, with at least 1 week's advance notice. The **Sommers-Bausch Observatory** (© **303/492-6732** during the day, 303/492-2020 at night) offers tours and Friday-evening open houses. Among the telescopes there are 16-, 18-, and 24-inch Cassegrain reflectors and a 10-inch aperture heliostat.

East side of Broadway, between Arapahoe Ave. and Baseline Rd. © 303/492-1411. www.colorado.edu. Bus: HOP, SKIP, STAMPEDE, and Denver buses.

MORE ATTRACTIONS
INDUSTRIAL TOURS
Beyond the attractions listed below, the **Boulder Creek Winery,** 6440 Odell Place (© **303/516-9031;** www.bouldercreekwine.com) offers a complimentary tasting on Fridays through Sundays from noon to 5pm.

Celestial Seasonings ⭐ (Value)   The nation's leading producer of herbal teas, housed in a modern building in northeastern Boulder, offers tours that are an experience for the senses. The company, which began in a Boulder garage in the 1970s, now produces more than 50 varieties of tea from more than 75 different herbs and spices imported from 35 foreign countries. You'll understand why the company invites you to "see, taste, and smell the world of Celestial Seasonings" as you move from a consumer taste test in the lobby to marketing displays, and finally into the production plant where 9 million tea bags roll off the line daily. The overpowering "mint room" is a highlight. The tour lasts about 45 minutes, and there is a cafe on-site.

4600 Sleepytime Dr. © 303/581-1202. www.celestialseasonings.com. Free admission. Mon–Sat 10am–3pm; Sun 11am–3pm; tours on the hour. Reservations required for groups of 8 or more. Exit Colo. 119, Longmont Diagonal, at Jay Rd. and go east to Spine, then north on Spine. Bus: J.

Redstone Meadery ⭐ (Finds)   Drunk by Beowulf and Shakespeare, mead is the original fermented beverage. There are about 60 active meaderies in the United States, including this standout in Boulder. Founded by David Myers in 2000, the meadery crafts several beverages (ranging from sparkling to portlike) that quickly demonstrate why this amateur mead maker turned pro. The meadery offers free 30-minute tours and tasting, and sells its wares ($15–$25 for a liter) and other regional foods and gifts. The meadery is the host of the International Mead Festival, held annually in the fall.

4700 Old Pearl St., #2A. ℂ 720/406-1125. www.redstonemeadery.com. Free admission. Tours Mon–Fri 3pm, Sat 12:30pm; tasting room Mon–Fri 3:30–6:30pm, Sat 1–5pm. Located 1 block northeast of the Pearl St. exit off Foothills Pkwy.

Rockies Brewing Company   From the grinding of the grain to the bottling of the beer, the 25-minute tour of this attractive "designer" microbrewery ends as all brewery tours should: in the pub. Tours pass by glistening copper vats that turn out hundreds of kegs of Boulder Beer a day. The pub is a restaurant that overlooks the bottling area, so even if you visit without taking a tour, you still get a good view of the brewing process. The menu includes burgers, burritos, salads, and appetizers; entrees run $6 to $8.

2880 Wilderness Place. ℂ 303/444-8448. www.boulderbeer.com. Free admission. Tours Mon–Sat at 2pm; pub Mon–Fri 11am–9pm. Take U.S. 36 north to Valmont Rd., then head east to Wilderness Place.

MUSEUMS & GALLERIES

There are three art galleries on the University of Colorado campus, all with free admission. The **CU Art Museum,** in the Sibell Wolle Fine Arts Building near Euclid Avenue and Broadway (ℂ **303/492-8300**), displays the work of CU students and faculty as well as pieces from the Colorado Collection, about 5,000 works by international artists including Warhol, Dürer, Rembrandt, Tiepolo, Hogarth, Hiroshige, Matisse, and Picasso. There are also rotating exhibits. The gallery is open Monday to Friday from 10am to 5pm, Tuesday to 7pm, and Saturday from noon to 4pm. Bus: HOP, SKIP.

At the University Memorial Center, the **UMC Art Gallery** (ℂ **303/492-7465**) organizes and hosts a variety of exhibitions featuring regional and national artists. In the music-listening rooms, visitors can peruse current periodicals while listening to modern and classical music. The gallery is on the second floor of the center, just left of the information desk; it's open Monday to Friday from 9am to 6pm. Bus: HOP, SKIP, STAMPEDE.

The **Andrew J. Macky Gallery** (ℂ **303/492-8423**), at the main entrance of Macky Auditorium, shows touring exhibits and works by local artists. It's open Wednesday from 9am to 4pm. Bus: HOP, SKIP, STAMPEDE.

There are also studios and a gallery at the **Dairy Center for the Arts,** 2590 Walnut St. (ℂ **303/440-7826;** www.thedairy.org), which also houses two theaters, classrooms, and several dance, theater, and arts organizations. See "Theater & Dance," later in this chapter.

Boulder History Museum ⭑   Ensconced on University Hill in the 1899–1900 Harbeck-Bergheim House, a Victorian mansion with a Dutch-style front door and Italian tile fireplaces, the museum houses one of the most comprehensive local-history collections in the region. There are more than 30,000 artifacts (from snake oil to sidesaddles), plus hundreds of thousands of photographs and historical documents from Colorado's early days to the present.

Semipermanent exhibits include "Storymakers: A Boulder History," featuring a rich collection of oral histories and late-19th- to early-20th-century photographs. There are also rotating exhibits that stay up for 6 to 10 months. The museum also hosts numerous lectures, programs, tours, and community events, including the Great Boulder Pie Festival and Quilt Raffle in July, Northern Arapaho Pow Wow in June, and Boulder History Day in May. Allow 1 to 2 hours.

1206 Euclid Ave. ℂ 303/449-3464. www.boulderhistorymuseum.org. Admission $5 adults, $3 seniors, $2 children and students, free for children under 5. Tues–Fri 10am–4pm; Sat noon–4pm. Guided tours by appointment. Closed Sun–Mon and major holidays. Bus: HOP.

Boulder Museum of Contemporary Art   This multidisciplinary art center, created in 1972 to exhibit the work of local artists, has evolved into an exciting venue where one can expect to see almost anything art-related, from the light-hearted to the elegant, political to religious, by local, regional, and international contemporary artists. There are special programs for young children and a variety of other events throughout the year. Performing arts—from poetry and dance to music and drama—are presented in the museum's award-winning "black box" performance venue, featuring local, national, and international performers. Allow 30 to 45 minutes. In addition, on Saturday evenings in summer, classic movies such as *Citizen Kane* and cult classics are shown outside ($5 per person). Take a lawn chair or blanket.

1750 13th St. ℂ 303/443-2122. www.bmoca.org. Admission $4 adults, $3 students and seniors, free for children under 12. Wed–Fri noon–6pm; Sat 9am–4pm; Sun noon–4pm. Hours change seasonally; call ahead for current information. Closed major holidays. Bus: HOP, SKIP.

Heritage Center   Located in the oldest building on campus, this museum reflects the history of the university. Its seven galleries hold exhibits on early student life (together with a complete set of yearbooks), CU's contributions to space exploration, campus architecture, distinguished alumni, and an overview of the university's history. Allow 30 minutes; a lot more if you're an alum.

3rd floor of Old Main, University of Colorado. ℂ 303/492-6329. Free admission. Mon–Fri 10am–4pm; Sat 10am–2pm. Bus: HOP, SKIP, STAMPEDE.

Leanin' Tree Museum of Western Art   You may know Leanin' Tree as the world's largest publisher of Western-art greeting cards. What's not so well known is that the company's headquarters houses an outstanding 400-piece collection of original paintings and bronze sculptures by contemporary artists. All depict scenes from the Old or New West, including a collection of humorous cowboy art. Some of the works have been reproduced on the company's greeting cards, which are for sale in the gift shop. Free guided tours are available. Allow 1 hour.

6055 Longbow Dr. (exit Jay Rd. and Longmont Diagonal). ℂ 800/777-8716 or 303/530-1442, ext. 299. www.leanintree.com. Free admission. Mon–Fri 8am–4:30pm; Sat–Sun 10am–4pm. Bus: 205.

University of Colorado Museum (Kids)   The natural history and anthropology of the Rocky Mountains and Southwest are the focus of this campus museum, founded in 1902. Featured exhibits include Ancestral Puebloan pottery and collections pertaining to dinosaurs, geology, paleontology, botany, entomology, and zoology. A children's area has interactive exhibits. Allow 1 to 3 hours.

University of Colorado, Henderson Bldg., Broadway at 15th St. ℂ 303/492-6892. Free admission, donations accepted. Mon–Fri 9am–5pm; Sat 9am–4pm; Sun 10am–4pm. Bus: HOP.

ESPECIALLY FOR KIDS

City parks (see "Outdoor Activities," below) offer the best diversions for children.

On the **Boulder Creek Path** (see "The Top Attractions," earlier in this chapter), the underwater fish observatory behind the Millennium Harvest House fascinates youngsters. They can feed the huge trout swimming behind a glass barrier on the creek (machines cough up handfuls of fish food for 25¢). Farther up the path, on the south bank around 6th Street, Kids' Fishing Ponds, stocked by the Boulder Fish and Game Club, are open to children under 12. There's no charge for either activity.

The **Fiske Planetarium** (© **303/492-5001**) offers visitors a walk through the solar system. Dedicated to the memory of CU alumnus Ellison Onizuka and the six other astronauts who died in the space shuttle *Challenger* explosion, the outdoor scale model begins at the entrance to the planetarium with the sun and inner planets, and continues across Regent Drive to the outer planets, located along the walkway to the Engineering Center. Admission is free; allow at least a half-hour. The planetarium offers after-school and summer discovery programs for kids, star shows, and other programs where you get a chance to look at the sky through the planetarium's telescopes. Admission for these events is usually $2 to $4; call for the latest schedule. Bus: HOP.

6 Outdoor Activities

Boulder is one of the leading spots for outdoor sports in North America. The city manages over 38,000 acres of parklands, including more than 200 miles of hiking trails and bicycle paths. Several canyons lead down from the Rockies directly into Boulder, attracting mountaineers and rock climbers. Families enjoy picnicking and camping. It seems that everywhere you look, people of all ages are running, walking, biking, skiing, or engaged in other active sports.

The **Boulder Parks and Recreation Department** (© **303/413-7200**; www. ci.boulder.co.us/parks-recreation) manages many of the outdoor facilities and schedules a variety of year-round activities for children as well as adults. Seasonal booklets on activities and city parks are available free from the Chamber of Commerce office and through the parks and recreation department's website (see above). Although many of the programs last for several weeks or months, some are half- or full-day activities that visiting children can join, usually at a slightly higher price than that for city residents. The department sponsors hikes, fitness programs, ski trips, watersports, special holiday events, performances in local parks, and even operates a skate park and a pottery lab.

One destination where you can enjoy several kinds of outdoor activities is **Eldorado Canyon State Park** ✦. This mountain park, just 5 miles southwest of Boulder in Eldorado Springs, is a favorite of technical rock climbers, but the 850-foot-high canyon's beauty makes it just as popular with hikers, picnickers, and others who want to get away from it all. The 1,448-acre park features 9 miles of hiking and horseback-riding trails, plus 7½ miles of trails suitable for mountain bikes; fishing is permitted, but camping is not. An exhibit at the visitor center describes the history of the park; there's also a bookstore and rotating displays covering topics from wildflowers to climbing. Admission is $5 to $6 per vehicle and $2 to $3 per pedestrian; the park is open daily from dawn to dusk. For further information, contact Eldorado Canyon State Park, Box B, Eldorado Springs, CO 80025 (© **303/494-3943**; www.parks.state.co.us).

BALLOONING   Float above the majestic Rocky Mountains in a hot-air balloon, watching as the early morning light gradually brightens to full day. Flights often include champagne and an elaborate continental breakfast or brunch. **Fair Winds Hot Air Balloon Flights** (© **303/939-9323**; www.fairwindsinc.com) flies 7 days a week year-round, weather permitting. Prices are $175 to $200 per person, and include a certificate, T-shirt, and photograph.

BICYCLING   On some days, you can see more bikes than cars in Boulder. Paths run along many of the city's major arteries, and local racing and touring events are scheduled year-round. Bicyclists riding at night are required to have lights; perhaps because of the large number of bicyclists in Boulder, the local police actively enforce traffic regulations that apply to them. Generally, bicyclists must obey the same laws that apply to operators of motor vehicles.

For current information on biking events, tips on the best places to ride, and equipment sales and repairs, check with **University Bicycles,** 839 Pearl St., about 2 blocks west of the Pearl Street Mall (© **303/444-4196;** www.ubikes. com), and **Full Cycle,** 1211 13th St., near the campus (© **303/440-7771;** www.fullcycleboulder.com). University Bikes rents bikes for $15 to $20 per day, and has maps of the city's 90 miles of bike lanes, paths, and routes. See also "By Bicycle" under "Getting Around," earlier in this chapter.

CLIMBING & BOULDERING   If you would like to tackle the nearby mountains and cliffs with ropes and pitons, contact the **Colorado Athletic Training School,** 2800 30th St. (© **303/939-9699**), and the **Boulder Rock Club,** 2829 Mapleton Ave. (© **303/447-2804;** www.boulderrock.com). The latter houses 10,000 square feet of indoor climbing surfaces and offers guide services.

Boulderers (those who climb without ropes) should check out **The Spot,** the country's largest bouldering gym at 3240 Prairie Ave. (© **303/379-8806;** www.thespotgym.com). Lessons and guiding service are available, and there's a cafe and a yoga studio on-site.

The Flatiron Range (easily visible from downtown Boulder) and nearby Eldorado Canyon are two favorite destinations for expert rock scalers. The "amphitheater" in the Flatirons is among the most revered of the nearby climbing areas. For bouldering, Carter Lake (30 miles north on U.S. 36) and Boulder Canyon (west of the city on Canyon Blvd.) are two of the top spots.

FISHING   Favored fishing areas near Boulder include **Boulder Reservoir,** North 51st Street, northeast of the city off the Longmont Diagonal, where you can try your luck at walleye, catfish, largemouth bass, bluegill, crappie, and carp. The Boulder Parks and Recreation Department (© **303/441-3461**) manages the reservoir. Other favorite fishing holes include **Lagerman Reservoir,** west of North 73rd Street off Pike Road, about 15 miles northeast of the city, where only nonmotorized boats can be used; **Barker Reservoir,** just east of Nederland on the Boulder Canyon Drive (Colo. 119), for bank fishing; and **Walden Ponds Wildlife Habitat,** about 6 miles east of downtown on North 75th Street. Fly-fishing is also popular in the area; guide service is available through **Kinsley Outfitters,** 1155 13th St. (© **800/442-7420** or 303/442-6204), for $225 for one person for a full day or $295 for two. Kinsley's fly shop offers a good selection of supplies.

GLIDER FLYING & SOARING   The atmospheric conditions generated by the peaks of the Front Range are ideal for year-round soaring and gliding. **Mile High Gliding,** 5534 Independence Rd. (© **303/527-1122**), offers rides and lessons on the north side of Boulder Municipal Airport, 2 miles northeast of downtown. Rides for one person range from $60 to $200 and last from 15 minutes to an hour or more; a 25-minute ride for two costs $160.

GOLF   Local courses include the 18-hole **Flatirons Golf Course** (run by Boulder Parks and Recreation), 5706 E. Arapahoe Ave. (© **303/442-7851**), and the 9-hole **Haystack Mountain Golf Course,** 5877 Niwot Rd. in Niwot, 5 miles north of Boulder (© **303/530-1400**). Nonresident greens fees range from $15 to $32.

HIKING & BACKPACKING   The Boulder Mountain Parks system includes 4,625 acres bordering the city limits, including the Flatirons and Flagstaff Mountain. You can obtain a map with descriptions of more than 60 trails from the **Boulder Convention and Visitors Bureau,** 2440 Pearl St. (© **800/444-0447** or 303/442-2911).

Numerous Roosevelt National Forest trail heads leave the Peak-to-Peak Scenic Byway (Colo. 72) west of Boulder. Check with the **U.S. Forest Service,** Boulder Ranger District, 2140 Yarmouth Ave. (© **303/541-2500**), for hiking and backpacking information. During dry weather, check on possible fire and smoking restrictions before heading into the forest. The trail heads leading to Long, Mitchell, and Brainard lakes are among the most popular, as is the 2-mile hike to Isabel Glacier.

About 70 miles west of Boulder, on the Continental Divide, is the **Indian Peaks Wilderness Area** (© **303/541-2500**). More than half of the area is fragile alpine tundra; a $5 permit is required for camping from June 1 to September 15. North of Boulder, via Estes Park, is **Rocky Mountain National Park** (© **970/586-1206**), one of the state's prime destinations for hikers and those seeking beautiful mountain scenery. The 2.5-mile **Mills Lake Trail** ☆, one of our favorites, is here. Another good hike is the 6-mile Mesa Trail, which departs from the Bluebell Shelter in Chautauqua Park.

RUNNING   The Boulder Creek Path (see "The Top Attractions," earlier in this chapter) is one of the most popular routes for runners in Boulder. A good resource for the traveling runner is **Boulder Road Runners** (© **303/499-2061;** www.boulderroadrunners.org). They organize group runs in the area and can provide information. The **Bolder Boulder** (© **303/444-RACE;** www.bolderboulder.com), held every Memorial Day, attracts about 50,000 runners who circle its 6¼-mile course. The **Boulder Running Company,** 2775 Pearl St. (© **303/786-9255**), sells a wide variety of running shoes and gear, going as far as analyzing customers' strides on a treadmill to find the perfect shoe.

SKIING   Friendly **Eldora Mountain Resort,** P.O. Box 1697, Nederland, CO 80466 (© **888/235-3672** or 303/440-8700; fax 303/440/8797; www.eldora.com), is just 21 miles west of downtown Boulder. It's about a 40-minute drive on Colo. 119 through Nederland. RTD buses leave Boulder for Eldora four times daily during ski season. For downhill skiers and snowboarders, Eldora has 53 trails, rated 30% novice, 50% intermediate, and 20% expert terrain on 680 acres. It has snow making on 320 acres and a terrain park with a 600-foot super-pipe. The area has two quad lifts, two triple and four double chairlifts, four surface lifts, and a vertical rise of 1,500 feet. Lift tickets (2004–05 rates) are roughly $49 for adults, $20 for children 6 to 12 and seniors 65 to 69, and just $5 for those under 6 and over 69. There are also discount packages that include lessons and rental equipment for both skiers and snowboarders. The season runs from mid-November to mid-April, snow permitting.

For cross-country skiers, Eldora has 28 miles of groomed and backcountry trails, and an overnight hut available by reservation. About 15% of the trails are rated easy, 50% intermediate, and 35% difficult. The trail fee is $14, or $8 for children 6 to 12 and seniors 65 to 69.

You can rent all your ski, snowboard, and snowshoeing equipment at the ski-rental center, and Nordic equipment at the Eldora Nordic Center. A free base-area shuttle runs throughout the day from the lodge to the Little Hawk area and the Nordic Center.

In Boulder, you can rent or buy telemark and alpine touring equipment from **Mountain Sports,** 2835 Pearl St. (© **303/442-8355**) or **Eldora Mountain Sports,** 2775 Canyon Blvd. (© **303/447-2017**).

SWIMMING   Five public pools are located within the city. Indoor pools, all open daily year-round, are at the newly renovated **North Boulder Recreation Center,** 3170 N. Broadway (© **303/413-7260**); the **East Boulder Community Center,** 5660 Sioux Dr. (© **303/441-4400**); and the **South Boulder Recreation Center,** 1360 Gillaspie Dr. (© **303/441-3448**). The two outdoor pools (both open daily from Memorial Day to Labor Day) are **Scott Carpenter Pool,** 30th Street and Arapahoe Avenue (© **303/441-3427**), and **Spruce Pool,** 2102 Spruce St. (© **303/441-3426**). Swimming fees for all municipal pools are $5.50 adults, $3.50 seniors, $3 teens, and $2.75 children 4 to 12.

TENNIS   There are more than 30 public courts in the city. The North and South Boulder Recreation centers (see "Swimming," above) each have four lighted courts and accept reservations ($8 an hr.). The North Boulder Recreation Center also has two platform tennis courts. Play is free if you arrive and there's no one using the courts or with a reservation. For locations of other public tennis courts, contact the Boulder Parks and Recreation Department (© **303/413-7200**).

WATERSPORTS   For both motorboating and human-powered boating, sailboard instruction, or swimming at a sandy beach, head for the square-mile **Boulder Reservoir** (© **303/441-3461**), on North 51st Street off the Longmont Diagonal northeast of the city. Human-powered boats and canoes (no personal watercraft) can be rented at the **boathouse** (© **303/441-3456**). Rates start at $35 per full day, with sailboards at $65 per full day. There's also a boat ramp.

SPECTATOR SPORTS

The major attractions are **University of Colorado football, women's volleyball,** and **men's and women's basketball.** For tickets, contact the Ticket Office, Campus Box 372, Boulder, CO 80309 (© **303/49-BUFFS;** www.cubuffs.com). Football tickets sometimes sell out early, particularly for homecoming and games with Nebraska and Oklahoma, so it would be wise to make reservations in advance.

7 Shopping

For the best shopping in Boulder, head to the **Pearl Street Mall** (see "The Top Attractions," earlier in this chapter), where you'll find not only shops and galleries galore but also street entertainers.

The indoor-outdoor, 1½-million-square-foot **FlatIron Crossing** (© **720/887-9900;** www.flatironcrossing.com), an upscale mall featuring Nordstrom, Dillard's, and Lord & Taylor among its 200 shops, is a more comprehensive option for the devout shopper. It's 9 miles southeast of Boulder off U.S. 36 in Broomfield. Hours are 10am to 9pm Monday through Saturday and 11am to 6pm on Sunday.

SHOPPING A TO Z
ARTS & CRAFTS

Art Source International   Natural-history prints, maps, and other items relevant to Western Americana, mainly from the 18th and 19th centuries, are the specialty here, along with collections of hundred-year-old Colorado photographs, maps, and prints. The store also features a great selection of new globes, as well as a few reproductions. 1237 Pearl St. ℂ 303/444-4080.

Boulder Arts & Crafts Cooperative   This is a good place to find a unique gift or souvenir. The shop, owned and operated by its artist members since 1971, features a wide variety of original handcrafted works. Pieces range from watercolors, serigraphs, and other fine art to top-quality crafts, including blown glass, stained glass, handmade jewelry, and functional pottery. Many of the items are made locally. 1421 Pearl St. ℂ 303/443-3683.

Niwot Antiques *(Finds)*   With dozens of dealers (including New England antiques specialist Elysian Fields), this antiques mall, in business since the 1950s, is the area's best, and a good excuse to make a trip to Niwot, 5 miles north of Boulder on the Longmont Diagonal. 136 2nd Ave., Niwot. ℂ **303/652-2587.**

BOOKS

Being a college town, Boulder is one of the best cities in the world for a browsing bookworm. It reportedly has more used-book stores per capita than any other U.S. city. Chain outlets include **Barnes & Noble,** 2915 Pearl St. (ℂ **303/442-1665**), and **Borders,** 1600 Pearl St. (ℂ **720/565-8266**). The independents run the gamut from the Kerouac and Burroughs specialists at **Beat Bookshop,** 1713 Pearl St. (ℂ **303/444-7111**), to the lesbian/feminist/gay selection at **Word Is Out,** 2015 10th St. (ℂ **303/449-1415**). **Trident Booksellers,** 940 Pearl St. (ℂ **303/443-3133**), is a good used-book shop with a coffeehouse attached.

Boulder Book Store   This meandering, four-story, 20,000-square-foot bookstore has been locally owned and operated since the 1970s. It attracts students, bohemians, and businesspeople alike with its homey vibe, and features great selections of Buddhism tomes and travel guides. It is attached to a coffeehouse with patio seating on the Pearl Street Mall, The Bookend Cafe (see "Espresso Bars, Coffeehouses & Related Establishments," earlier in this chapter.) 1107 Pearl St. ℂ 303/447-2074. www.boulderbookstore.com.

FASHION

Alpaca Connection   Come here for natural-fiber clothing from around the world, including alpaca-and-wool sweaters from South America. 1326 Pearl St. ℂ 303/447-2047.

Rocky Mountain Kids *(Kids)*   Offering clothing for newborns to 12-year-olds, this bright store specializes in quality brands and is known for its kid-friendliness: complimentary animal crackers and plenty of toys in the box. 2525 Arapahoe Ave. ℂ 303/447-2267.

Weekends   The selection of men's and women's fashions is somewhat pricey but chosen for comfort and style—and it shows. 1101 Pearl St. ℂ 303/444-4231.

FOOD & DRINK

Boulder Wine Merchant   This store has a solid selection of wines from around the world, plus knowledgeable salespeople who can help you make the right choice. 2690 Broadway. ℂ 303/443-6761.

Liquor Mart   Here you'll find a huge choice of discounted wine and liquor, with more than 5,000 wines and 900 beers, including a wide selection of imported and microbrewed beers. 1750 15th St. (at Canyon Blvd.). ℂ 303/449-3374.

Whole Foods   The latest and greatest of Boulder's organic supermarkets, this huge store—part of the national chain—has a wide-ranging, fresh inventory, and is a favorite lunch spot of locals. Offerings include a deli, soup and salad bar, sushi, and more free samples than you could possibly eat. It's also 100% wind-powered. 2905 Pearl St. (C) **303/545-6611.**

GIFTS & SOUVENIRS

The best stops for T-shirts, University of Colorado paraphernalia, and other Boulder souvenirs are **Jackalope and Company,** 1126 Pearl St. ((C) **303/ 939-8434**); **Where the Buffalo Roam,** 1320 Pearl St. ((C) **303/938-1424**); and the **CU Bookstore,** 1111 Broadway ((C) **303/442-5051**).

HARDWARE

McGuckin Hardware   McGuckin's claims to have the world's largest hardware selection, with more than 200,000 items in stock. In addition to the nuts, bolts, brackets, paints, tools, and assorted whatchamacallits that most hardware stores carry, you'll also find sporting goods, kitchen gizmos, automotive supplies, stationery, some clothing, electronics, outdoor furniture, fresh flowers, and a whole lot of other stuff. 2525 Arapahoe Ave. (C) **303/443-1822** or 86-MCGUCKIN. www. mcguckin.com.

JEWELRY

El Loro   Distinctively Boulder, this bohemian jewelry shop has been a Pearl Street Mall resident for more then 25 years. Aside from a nice selection of sterling silver items with semiprecious stones, El Loro also sells clogs and incense. 1416 Pearl St. (C) **303/449-3162.**

KITCHENWARE

Peppercorn   From cookbooks to pasta makers, you can find anything and everything for the kitchen here at "the Smithsonian of cookstores." In business since 1977, this vast store (12,000 sq. ft.!) has hundreds of kitchen gadgets and appliances—everything you might need to prepare, serve, and consume the simplest or most exotic meal. 1235 Pearl St. (C) **800/447-6905** or 303/449-5847.

SPORTING GOODS

Gart Sports, 3320 N. 28th St. ((C) **303/449-9021**), is a good all-purpose source, while the following are more specialized—and interesting—retail outlets.

Boulder Army Store   Just east of the Pearl Street Mall, this shop has the best inventory of camping gear in the city, along with a limited amount of fishing equipment. There is also a good supply of outdoor clothing and military surplus items such as fatigues, helmets, and that disarmed hand grenade you've always wanted. 1545 Pearl St. (C) **303/442-7616.**

Mountain Sports   This shop, which opened in 1958, boasts of being Boulder's oldest mountaineering shop. It specializes in equipment, clothing, and accessories for backpacking, camping, rock and ice climbing, mountaineering, backcountry skiing, and snowshoeing. Equipment rentals include sleeping bags, tents, backpacks, and snowshoes; backcountry and telemark ski packages are available. Mountain Sports also sells maps and guidebooks, and the knowledgeable staff—which includes several trained guides—can help you plan your trip. 2835 Pearl St. (C) **303/442-8355.**

8 Boulder After Dark

As a cultured and well-educated community (59% of adult residents have at least one college degree), Boulder is especially noted for its summer music, dance, and Shakespeare festivals. Major entertainment events take place year-round, both downtown and on the University of Colorado campus. There's also a wide choice of nightclubs and bars, but it hasn't always been so: Boulder was dry for 60 years, from 1907 (13 years before national Prohibition) to 1967. The first new bar in the city opened in 1969, in the Hotel Boulderado. The notoriously healthy city banned smoking in 1995; only a few establishments allow patrons to ignore the policy.

Entertainment schedules can be found in the *Daily Camera*'s weekly *Friday Magazine;* in either of the Denver dailies, the *Denver Post* or the *Rocky Mountain News;* in *Westword,* the Denver weekly; or in the free *Boulder Weekly.*

THE CLUB & MUSIC SCENE

Boulder Theater *Finds*   Rock, folk, bluegrass, jazz, hip-hop, comedy, and who knows what else—performed by musicians such as Lou Reed, Bill Maher, Herbie Hancock, and Norah Jones—takes the stage here. During the week, you'll also find independent and otherwise alternative film. 14th and Pearl sts. ℂ **303/786-7030.** www.bouldertheater.com.

The Catacombs   This popular bar books live blues and jazz by local and regional performers. The loud, somewhat raucous atmosphere (and smoking room) draws a crowd of CU students and an eclectic mix of locals and traveling businesspeople. A limited pub menu is served. In the basement of the Hotel Boulderado, 13th and Spruce sts. ℂ **303/443-0486.**

Fox Theatre and Cafe *Finds*   A variety of live music (including, but not limited to, bluegrass, funk, blues, hip-hop, reggae, and punk) is presented here 5 or 6 nights a week, featuring a mix of local, regional, and national talent. You'll find three bars at this converted movie theater, which is revered for its great acoustics. 1135 13th St. ℂ **303/443-3399** or 303/447-0095. www.foxtheatre.com.

Penny Lane Coffee House   By day a bohemian gathering place for talking, playing chess, or reading while sipping espresso, this Greenwich Village–style coffeehouse comes alive at night. There's usually a poetry reading on Monday, 1 night of live jazz each week, several open-stage evenings, and a diverse mixture of live music by local and regional artists on Friday and Saturday. See also "Espresso Bars, Coffeehouses & Related Establishments," earlier in this chapter. Pearl and 18th sts. ℂ **303/443-9516.**

'Round Midnight   A hip basement joint on the Pearl Street Mall, 'Round Midnight specializes in malt scotch, good beer, and dancing. An eclectic array of performers (hip-hop, techno, jazz, rock) take the stage here on weekends and DJs during the week. 1005 Pearl St. ℂ **303/442-2176.**

Trilogy Wine Bar   This hip venue is tucked in the back of a stylish restaurant with a diverse international menu and a great wine list. Performers include reggae bands, acid and Latin jazz acts, DJs, and hip-hop acts. 2017 13th St. ℂ **303/473-WINE.** www.trilogywinebar.com.

THE BAR SCENE

Barrel House   Consistently voted the number-one sports bar in Boulder by local newspaper readers, the Barrel House offers a choice of 25 beers on tap, mostly Colorado microbrews. There are close to 40 TVs, including four big-screen sets, and a huge menu of burgers, pizza, sandwiches, and Mexican dishes. The bar is a traditional pregame meeting place for University of Colorado football fans. 2860 Arapahoe Ave. ℂ **303/444-9464.**

Conor O'Neill's *(Finds*   Everything in this pub—from the bar to the art to the timber floors—was designed and built in Ireland. The atmosphere is rich, with a "shop pub" upfront and two back rooms centered on a pair of fireplaces that were constructed by visiting Irish stonemasons. There are over a dozen beers on tap, primarily from (where else?) Ireland, and the pub menu features fish and chips, burgers, and a mean shepherd's pie. There's live music (surf to Celtic) every night of the week except Mondays, which feature a popular trivia game, and Irish music Sunday afternoons. 1922 13th St. (C) **303/449-1922.**

Mountain Sun Pub & Brewery   An English-style neighborhood pub and microbrewery, Mountain Sun produces dozens of barrels of beer each week and provides tours on request during the day. The mostly made-from-scratch menu features soups, salads, burgers, sandwiches, and a few Mexican dishes. There's live folk, acoustic, and bluegrass music on Sunday night. 1535 Pearl St. (east of the mall). (C) **303/546-0886.**

The Republic of Boulder   Subtitled "The People's Pub," the former Oasis has been rethought to reflect the passions and quirks of its home city—in the form of hemp fan blades, a large dance floor, and creative but affordable eats. The cavernous pub also produces its own beer and has a full array of bar games: pool, darts, and retro video games like Ms. Pac-Man. 1095 Canyon Blvd. (C) **303/ 443-1460.**

The Sink *(Finds*   This off-campus establishment opened in 1923 (CU dropout Robert Redford was once the janitor) but has been updated with new spacey wall murals that help make it one of Boulder's funniest—and most fun— nightspots. There's a full bar with more than a dozen regional microbrews, live music, and fare such as Sinkburgers and "ugly crust" pizza. 1165 13th St. (C) **303/ 444-SINK.** www.thesink.com.

Sundown Saloon   This raucous dive is a CU institution. In a spacious basement on the west end of the Pearl Street Mall, pool is the pastime of choice and the drinks are reasonably priced. The Sundown Saloon has the largest and most popular smoking room in town (legal under Boulder's smoking ban), resulting in one of the smokiest rooms known to humankind. 1136 Pearl St. **303/449-4987.**

Walnut Brewery   In a historic brick warehouse a block from the Pearl Street Mall, this large restaurant/bar/microbrewery is popular with the after-work crowd, both young and old. 1123 Walnut St. (near Broadway). (C) **303/447-1345.**

West End Tavern   A 2004 makeover of this popular neighborhood bar left the brick walls and the classic bar intact, but gave the rest of the joint a contemporary shot in the arm and a slick look. Beyond the 48 bourbons stocked by the bar, fare includes a different specialty burger every day, barbecue, and more upscale items. The tavern's roof garden is an ideal spot to unwind and enjoy some of the best views in town and outdoor cinema on certain summer nights. 926 Pearl St. (C) **303/444-3535.**

THE PERFORMING ARTS

Music, dance, and theater are important aspects of life for Boulder residents. Many of these activities take place at **Macky Auditorium** at the University of Colorado ((C) **303/492-8008;** www.colorado.edu/music) and other campus venues, as well as the **Chautauqua Auditorium,** 900 Baseline Rd. ((C) **303/442- 3282**), and the **Dairy Center for the Arts,** 2590 Walnut St. ((C) **303/440- 7826;** www.thedairy.org).

CLASSICAL MUSIC & OPERA

Boulder Bach Festival   First presented in 1981, this celebration of the music of Johann Sebastian Bach includes not only a late-January festival but also concerts and other events year-round. Tickets run $10 to $30. Series tickets are also available. P.O. Box 1896, Boulder, CO 80306. ℂ **303/652-9101.** www.boulderbachfest.org.

Boulder Philharmonic Orchestra   This acclaimed community orchestra performs an annual fall-to-spring season, primarily at Macky Auditorium, with world-class artists who have included singer Marilyn Horne, guitarist Carlos Montoya, cellist Yo-Yo Ma, and violinist Itzhak Perlman. Tickets cost $10 to $65, more for concerts that feature premier performers. P.O. Box 4626, Boulder, CO 80306. ℂ **303/449-1343.** www.peakarts.org.

Colorado MahlerFest   Begun in 1988, this international festival is the only one of its kind in the world. For a week each January it celebrates the work of Gustav Mahler with a performance of one of his symphonies as well as chamber concerts, films, discussions, seminars, and other musical programs. Most events are free; admission to symphony concerts ranges from $8 to $25. P.O. Box 1314, Boulder, CO 80306. ℂ **303/447-0513** for information, 303/449-1343 for box office. www.mahler fest.org.

Colorado Music Festival *Finds*   Begun in 1976, this series is the single biggest annual arts event in Boulder, with visiting musicians from around the world performing in the acoustically revered Chautauqua Auditorium. The festival presents works of the classical through modern eras, such as Bach, Beethoven, Mozart, Dvorak, and Gershwin, plus living composers. It usually runs from mid-June to mid-August, with symphony orchestra performances Thursday and Friday, chamber-orchestra concerts Sunday, and a chamber-music series Tuesday; all shows start at 7:30pm. There's also a children's concert in late June and a free Independence Day concert at CU's Folsom Field. Adult ticket prices range from $10 to $37. 900 Baseline Rd., cottage 100, Boulder, CO 80302. ℂ **303/449-1397** for general information, 303/440-7666 or visit website for tickets. www.coloradomusicfest.org.

CU Concerts   The university's College of Music presents music, theatre, a summer opera, the Artist Series, the Takács String Quartet Series, and a Holiday Festival at Macky Auditorium and Grusin Music Hall. General-admission tickets usually cost $10 to $38. The Artist Series features an outstanding lineup of classical soloists, jazz artists, dance companies, and multidisciplinary events. Call early for tickets for performances of the renowned Takács String Quartet. The annual Holiday Festival includes the University Symphony Orchestra, university choirs, several smaller ensembles, and soloists from the College of Music's student body and faculty. University of Colorado. ℂ **303/492-8008.** www.cuconcerts.org.

THEATER & DANCE

Colorado Shakespeare Festival *Moments*   Considered one of the top three Shakespearean festivals in the United States, this 2-month annual event attracts more than 40,000 theatergoers between late June and late August. Held since 1958 in the University of Colorado's Mary Rippon Outdoor Theatre, and indoors at the University Theatre Main Stage, it offers more than a dozen performances of each of four plays. Actors, directors, designers, and everyone associated with the productions are fully schooled Shakespearean professionals. Tickets run from $10 to $50 for single performances, with series packages also available. Campus Box 277, University of Colorado, Boulder, CO 80309. ℂ **303/492-0554** for information and the box office. www.coloradoshakes.org.

Nomad Theatre   Boulder's only resident professional theater, the Nomad has presented a mix of classic and contemporary dramas, comedies, and musicals since the curtains first opened in 1951. Recent productions have included *Wit, Alarms & Excursions,* and *Darwin in the Dreamtime.* Tickets cost $18 to $22. 1410 Quince Ave. (C) **303/443-7510** or 303/774-4037 (box office). www.nomadstage.com.

Upstart Crow Theatre Company   Specializing in Shakespeare and more contemporary classics, the Upstart Crow is the resident theater company at the Dairy Center for the Arts. They perform on two stages: a 99-seat theater (where no seat is more than three rows from the stage) and an 86-seat proscenium theater. Dairy Center for the Arts, 2590 Walnut St. (C) **303/258-7939** or 303/449-5151. www. theupstartcrow.org.

9

Northeastern Colorado

Here are the spacious skies, stretch-ing without interruption hundreds of miles eastward from the foot of the Rocky Mountains. Here also are the golden, rolling, irrigated fields of wheat and corn, spreading along the valleys of the South Platte and Repub-lican rivers and their tributaries.

A different Colorado exists on the sparsely populated plains, one that inspired James Michener's novel *Centennial.* Alive are stories of the pre-historic buffalo hunters who first inhabited the region; trailblazers and railroad crews who opened up the area

to Anglo settlement; hardy pioneer farmers who endured drought, eco-nomic ruin, and so many other hard-ships; and ranchers such as John W. Iliff, who carved a feudal empire built on longhorn cattle. Pioneer museums, frontier forts, old battlefields, and pre-served downtown districts won't let history die. Vast open stretches—wet-lands swollen with migrating water-fowl, the starkly beautiful Pawnee National Grassland—remind us that Colorado is not only the Rocky Mountains.

1 Fort Collins

65 miles N of Denver, 34 miles S of Cheyenne, Wyoming

A bustling college town, Fort Collins was founded in 1864 as a military post on the Cache la Poudre (pronounced *Poo*-der) River, named for a powder cache left by French fur traders. The fort, named for Lieutenant Colonel William O. Collins, was abandoned in 1867, but the settlement prospered, first as a center for quarrying and farming, and by 1910 with sugar-beet processing.

Today Fort Collins is among the fastest-growing cities in the United States, with an average annual growth rate of about 3%. Population leaped from 43,000 in 1970 to 65,000 in 1980 to more than 125,000 today, not including the many Colorado State University students. CSU was established in 1870; today it is nationally known for its forestry and veterinary medicine schools, as well as its research advances in space engineering and bone cancer.

Fort Collins, at just under 5,000 feet elevation, makes a good base for fish-ing, boating, rafting, or exploring Rocky Mountain National Park (see chap-ter 10). It also has several historic sites and offers a treat for beer lovers, with tours of breweries ranging from micro to the huge facilities operated by Anheuser-Busch.

ESSENTIALS

GETTING THERE **By Car** Coming from south or north, take I-25 to exit 269 (Mulberry St., for downtown Fort Collins), exit 268 (Prospect Rd., for Colorado State University), or exit 265 (Harmony Rd., for south Fort Collins). From Rocky Mountain National Park's Estes Park entrances, follow U.S. 34 to Loveland, then turn north on U.S. 287. The drive takes about 1¼ hours from Denver or Estes Park and about 40 minutes from Cheyenne, Wyoming.

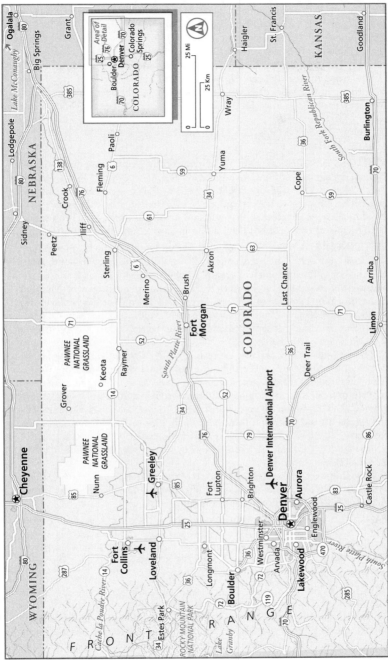

By Plane   Many visitors to Fort Collins fly into **Denver International Airport** (see chapter 5). The **Fort Collins/Loveland Municipal Airport** (© **970/962-2852;** www.fcgov.com/airport), off I-25 exit 259, 7 miles northeast of downtown Loveland, offers regularly scheduled commercial service with Frontier Airlines (© **800/432-1359** or 303/371-7300); call for the current schedule.

Shamrock Airport Express (© **866/482-0505** or 970/482-0505; www.ride shamrock.com) provides daily shuttle services between Denver and Fort Collins (one-way rates: $24 adults, $8 children 11 and younger, free for children who sit on a parent's lap). Car rentals in Fort Collins are provided by **Advantage** (© **800/777-5500** or 970/224-2211) and **Enterprise** (© **800/325-8007** or 970/224-2592).

VISITOR INFORMATION   The **Fort Collins Convention and Visitors Bureau** operates a visitor information center at 3745 E. Prospect Rd., Suite 200, Fort Collins, CO 80525 (© **800/274-3678** or 970/491-3388; www.ftcollins. com). That's just east of I-25 at Prospect Road (exit 268); the angular, two-story building's unique architecture makes it hard to miss. It's open daily from 8am to 6pm Memorial Day to Labor Day, and from 8am to 5pm the rest of the year.

GETTING AROUND   Fort Collins is located on the Cache la Poudre River, 4 miles west of I-25. College Avenue (U.S. 287) is the main north–south artery and the city's primary commercial strip; Mulberry Street (Colo. 14) is the main east–west thoroughfare. Downtown Fort Collins extends north of Mulberry Street on College Avenue to Jefferson Street; Old Town is a triangle east of and bounded by College Avenue, 4 blocks north of Mulberry. The main Colorado State University campus covers a square mile on the west side of College Avenue 2 blocks south of Mulberry.

The city bus system, known as **Transfort** (© **970/221-6620;** www.fcgov. com/transfort), operates more than a dozen routes throughout Fort Collins Monday through Saturday, except major holidays. Most routes run from about 5:30am to 6:30pm, and additional runs are made, including some on Sundays, when CSU is in session. All buses have bike racks. Fares are $1.25 for adults, 60¢ for seniors 60 and older and those with disabilities; youths 17 and under ride free. Exact change is required. A 10-ride ticket costs $9.

Taxi service is provided 24 hours a day by **Shamrock Yellow Cab** (© **970/ 224-2222**).

Bicycling is a popular and viable means of transportation in Fort Collins. Just about the only place you can't ride is College Avenue. See "Sports & Outdoor Activities," below, for information about bike rentals.

FAST FACTS   The **Poudre Valley Hospital** is at 1024 S. Lemay Ave. (© **800/ 252-5784** or 970/495-7000), between Prospect Road and Riverside Avenue just east of downtown. The main **post office** is located at 301 E. Boardwalk Dr. Contact the U.S. Postal Service (© **800/275-8777;** www.usps.com) for hours and other post office locations.

SPECIAL EVENTS   Gem & Mineral Show, late March; Cinco de Mayo in Old Town, first weekend in May; Colorado Brewers' Festival on Old Town Square, last full weekend in June; Fabric of Legacies Quilt Show, mid-June; New WestFest in Old Town and Library Park, mid-August; Museum of Contemporary Art Studio Tour; and Oktoberfest in Old Town, late September.

WHAT TO SEE & DO

Anheuser-Busch Brewery ✯✯   One of Fort Collins's leading employers— and its top tourist attraction—this Anheuser-Busch brewery produces some

6 million barrels of beer each year, distributed to 10 Western states. The 1¼-hour tours leave from the visitor center and gift shop, and include exhibits on the history of the Anheuser-Busch company, nostalgic displays of ads from the 1950s and other periods, and a complete look at the brewing process, from the huge brew kettles to the high-speed packaging plant that fills 2,000 cans per minute. The tours end at the tasting room for a free sample. You can also visit the barn and see the giant Clydesdale draft horses used to promote Budweiser and other Anheuser-Busch beers since 1933; the first Saturday of each month (year-round) from 1 to 3pm is Clydesdale Camera Day, when the horses are brought out to pose with visitors.

2351 Busch Dr. (I-25 exit 271). ℭ **970/490-4691.** www.budweisertours.com. Free admission. June–Aug daily 9:30am–4:30pm; Sept daily 10am–4pm; Oct–May Thurs–Mon 10am–4pm. Closed some major holidays.

Avery House   Custom-built in 1879 for banker-surveyor Franklin Avery and his wife, Sara, this Victorian home at the corner of Mountain Avenue and Meldrum Street was constructed of red-and-buff sandstone from the quarries west of Fort Collins. The Poudre Landmarks Foundation and the city of Fort Collins purchased the house in 1974, restoring it to its original Victorian splendor—from furniture to wallpaper to wallpapered ceilings. The grounds, with a gazebo, carriage house, and fountain, are popular for weddings and receptions. Allow 30 minutes to 1 hour.

328 W. Mountain Ave. ℭ **970/221-0533.** Free admission (donations welcome). Wed and Sun 1–3pm except Easter, Christmas, and New Year's Day.

Colorado State University   Fort Collins revolves around this university, with its 25,000 students, from every state and close to 100 foreign countries. Founded in 1870 as Colorado Agricultural College, it was renamed Colorado A&M in 1935 and became Colorado State University in 1957. The "A" constructed on the hillside behind Hughes Stadium by students and faculty in 1923 stands for "Aggies" and remains a cherished tradition, even though the school's athletic teams have been called the Rams for decades.

Those wanting to see the campus should stop first at the **visitor center,** at the southwest corner of College Avenue and Pitkin Street (ℭ **970/491-4636**), for information, maps, and parking passes. It's open year-round Monday through Friday from 8am to 5pm. Among suggested stops are the **Administration Building,** on the Oval where the school began, and the **Lory Student Center,** at University and Center avenues, which houses a food court, bookstore, art gallery, floral shop, activities center, ballroom, and other facilities. Allow about an hour for a stroll around campus.

Appointments can be made to visit the renowned **Veterinary Teaching Hospital** and the **Equine Teaching Center**. The **Art Department** has five different galleries with revolving exhibits, and the **University Theatre** in Johnson Hall, on East Drive (ℭ **970/491-5562,** or 970/491-5116 for tickets), presents student productions year-round. The university's **Environmental Learning Center** covers some 200 acres, and has 2½ miles of trails, with opportunities to see wildlife such as golden eagles, muskrats, and white-tail deer, and a variety of plants. Dogs, horses, and bikes are not permitted on the trails.

CSU has all the usual sports teams. For information on who's playing during your visit, check with the Athletic Department (ℭ **970/491-RAMS**; www.csurams.com).

University and College aves. ℭ **970/491-1101.** www.colostate.edu.

Fun Fact **Horsing Around**

Firecracker, the world's first test-tube horse, was born July 2, 1996, at Colorado State University's Animal Reproduction and Biotechnology Laboratory.

The Farm at Lee Martinez Park *(Kids)*   Early-20th-century farm machinery is on display, crafts are sold in the Silo Store, and oats are available to feed the animals. The Farm Museum has exhibits depicting farming techniques from the late 19th and early 20th centuries. Special programs are scheduled year-round, and kids can take advantage of the weekend pony rides ($4) from mid-March through October. Forty-five-minute trail rides ($15) along the Poudre River are offered to adults and children ages 8 and older June through September; group hayrides and tours can be booked in advance. A gift shop is open from mid-March through October. Allow 1 to 2 hours.

600 N. Sherwood St. ✆ **970/221-6665.** Free admission, donations accepted. June to mid-Aug Tues–Sat 10am–5pm, Sun noon–5pm; mid-Aug to May Wed–Sat 10am–5pm, Sun noon–5pm.

Fort Collins Municipal Railway   One of the few remaining original trolley systems in the nation, this restored 1919 Birney streetcar runs on its original route, along Mountain Avenue for 1½ miles from City Park to Howes Street. It's certainly more for fun than practical urban transport. Allow 20 to 30 minutes.

Oak and Roosevelt, at City Park. ✆ **970/482-8246.** Admission $1 adults, 75¢ seniors, 50¢ children 12 and under. May–Sept weekends and holidays only, noon–5pm.

Fort Collins Museum   Located in the 1903 Carnegie Library Building just a block south of Old Town, this museum boasts the largest collection of Folsom points of any western museum, plus historical artifacts from Fort Collins as well as pioneer and Victorian objects. You can see an 1850s cabin that is among the oldest surviving pioneer buildings in Colorado, an 1864 log officers' mess hall known locally as "Auntie Stone's cabin," and a log one-room schoolhouse built in 1905. Annual events include Rendezvous and Skookum Day in July, a living-history day with blacksmithing, quilting, weaving, branding, and milking demonstrations. Allow 2 hours.

200 Mathews St. ✆ **970/221-6738.** www.fcgov.com/museum. Free admission, donations accepted. Tues–Sat 10am–5pm; Sun noon–5pm.

Old Town   A redbrick pedestrian walkway, flanked by street lamps and surrounding a bubbling fountain, is the focus of this restored historic district, which offers a look at the earliest roots of the city, and has plenty of good shopping opportunities. The main plaza, which covers several square blocks, extends diagonally to the northeast from the intersection of College and Mountain avenues; on either side are shops and galleries, restaurants, and nightspots. Outdoor concerts and a string of special events keep the plaza lively, especially from mid-spring to mid-fall. Self-guided walking-tour maps are available from the Convention and Visitors Bureau, individual merchants, and city offices; and the Fort Collins Museum (see above) conducts guided tours of Old Town during the summer on Saturdays at 11am, 1pm, and 3pm (call the museum for additional information). You'll find public restrooms just east of the intersection of South

College Avenue and Oak Street, open daily from 8am to 9pm. Allow about an hour, more if you want to do a lot of shopping.

Between College and Mountain aves. and Jefferson St.

Swetsville Zoo ⭑⭑ *Kids*   Don't come to Bill Swets's zoo expecting to find animals—not live ones, that is. The Sculpture Park is a constantly growing menagerie of more than 150 dinosaurs and other real and imaginary animals, flowers, and windmills—all constructed from car parts, farm machinery, and other scrap metal. The whimsical nature of the sculptures is a delight for kids as well as adults. Several galleries offer works by other local artists, ranging from pottery to paintings to sculptures. Allow at least 1 hour.

4801 E. Harmony Rd. ℂ **970/484-9509.** Free admission, donations appreciated. Daily, dawn to dusk. The zoo is ¼ mile east of I-25 exit 265.

Brewery Tours

There's no denying that Fort Collins is a beer town. Not only is it home to the giant **Anheuser-Busch Brewery,** with its famous Clydesdale horses (see above), but the city also boasts several excellent microbreweries.

Coopersmith's Pub & Brewing Co. (see "Where to Dine," later in this chapter) provides patrons a view of the brewing process from inside the restaurant, and offers guided tours on Saturdays from 1 to 4pm (by appointment only). Using English malted barley and hops from the Pacific Northwest, Coopersmith's brews from 6 to 10 ales. For those averse to beer, the brewery also makes its own root beer, ginger ale, and cream soda.

Just northeast of Old Town, across the railroad tracks, **New Belgium Brewing Company,** 500 Linden St. (ℂ **888/622-4044** or 970/221-0524; www.newbelgium.com), concentrates on beer making only, producing top-quality Belgian-style ales including the very popular Fat Tire. The brewery is open Monday through Saturday from 10am to 6pm. Tours are offered weekdays at 2pm and 4pm, and Saturdays on the hour from 11am to 4pm, with self-guided tours anytime. Beer can be purchased, along with glasses, caps, T-shirts, and other souvenirs.

You'll find **Odell Brewing Company** at 800 E. Lincoln Ave. (ℂ **970/ 498-9070;** www.odellbrewing.com). Specializing in English-style ales, Odell produces draft and bottled beers, which are available in restaurants and bars throughout the Rocky Mountains and the Southwest. Tours are given Monday through Friday anytime between 10am and 3pm and at 2pm on Saturdays. The tasting room is open Monday through Friday from 10am to 6pm, Saturday from noon to 5pm. Beer, which you can sample before making your choice, plus beer glasses, shirts, ball caps, and other souvenirs, are all available.

Also brewing beer in Fort Collins are **Fort Collins Brewery,** 1900 E. Lincoln Ave. (ℂ **970/472-1499;** www.fortcollinsbrewery.com), which specializes in lagers; and **Big Horn Brewery,** 1415 W. Elizabeth St. (ℂ **970/ 221-5954**), which brews a variety of beer styles. Contact these two breweries for tour information.

SPORTS & OUTDOOR ACTIVITIES

With its prime location, nestled in the foothills of the Rockies, Fort Collins is ideally situated for those who want to get out under Colorado's clear blue sky and experience the delights of nature. There are several convenient multiuse trails. The **Poudre River Trail** is an 8.3-mile paved trail that follows the Poudre River from North Taft Hill Road to East Drake Road and the CSU Environmental Learning Center, passing Lee Martinez Park along the way. The paved **Spring Creek Trail** runs 6.5 miles along Spring Creek, passing through several city parks, from West Drake Road to East Prospect Road at the Poudre River, where you can pick up the Poudre River Trail. Both trails are popular with hikers, cyclers, and skaters during warm weather, and cross-country skiers when the snow flies. Contact the Fort Collins Convention and Visitors Bureau (see "Visitor Information," above) for additional information.

There is a vast amount of public land under the jurisdiction of the U.S. Forest Service within easy access of Fort Collins, offering opportunities for hiking, mountain biking, horseback riding, fishing, camping, snowshoeing, and cross-country skiing. For details, check with the information center of the **Arapaho-Roosevelt National Forest and Pawnee Grasslands,** 1311 S. College Ave., Fort Collins, CO 80524 (© 970/498-2770; www.fs.fed.us/r2/arnf).

Major Fort Collins city parks include: **City Park,** 1500 W. Mulberry St., with a lake, picnic shelters, playgrounds, playing fields, tennis courts, a fitness course, a pottery studio, miniature train rides, a 9-hole golf course, and an outdoor swimming pool; **Edora Park,** 1420 E. Stuart St., with the excellent Edora Pool Ice Center (combination indoor swimming pools and ice rink), plus playgrounds, ball fields, tennis courts, a disc golf course, a fitness course, and horseshoe pits; and **Rolland Moore Park,** which features an outdoor complex for racquetball and handball players, plus tennis courts, picnic grounds, softball fields, and basketball courts. For information on these and other city recreation facilities contact the Fort Collins Parks Department (© **970/221-6600;** www.fcgov.com/parks).

Among the most popular areas for outdoor recreation is **Horsetooth Reservoir** (© **970/679-4554;** www.larimer.org/parks/horsetooth.htm), about 15 minutes west of downtown, just over the first ridge of the Rocky Mountain foothills. The 6½-mile-long, man-made lake is named for a distinctive tooth-shaped rock that has long been an area landmark. It's reached via C.R. 44E or 42C, both off Overland Trail, or C.R. 38E off Taft Hill Road. At the reservoir and nearby **Horsetooth Mountain Park,** located several miles west via C.R. 38E (same phone as above), you'll find a wide array of outdoor activities from fly-fishing to rock climbing to swimming and water-skiing.

Lory State Park, just west of Fort Collins along the northwest edge of Horsetooth Reservoir (© **970/493-1623**), is known for its scenic beauty and extensive trail system. To get to the park, take U.S. 287 north out of Fort Collins, leaving it to take 54G Road through Laporte, then head west on C.R. 52E for 1 mile, turn left (south) onto C.R. 23N for about 1½ miles to C.R. 25G, where you turn right and drive about 1½ miles to the park entrance. **State Forest State Park,** about 75 miles west of Fort Collins via Colo. 14 (© **970/723-8366**), covers 70,000 acres with spectacular mountain scenery, alpine lakes, an abundance of wildlife, camping, and numerous trails. See below for details on activities at these areas, and check out the comprehensive **www.parks.state.co.us** on the Web.

Tips City Parks Going to the Dogs

Our hats are off to the people and elected officials of Fort Collins for having the foresight to create two **dog parks,** with more in the planning stages. These totally fenced areas are safe havens for dogs, where our canine friends can legally shed their leashes and run to their hearts' content. The parks have water fountains for both humans and dogs, and small fenced-off areas for small or shy dogs. One dog park is located at the west end of Horsetooth Road, in the undeveloped Spring Canyon Community Park; the other is at 5821 S. Lemay Ave., at the entrance to Fossil Creek Community Park. For information contact the Fort Collins Parks Department (© **970/221-6600;** www.fcgov.com/parks).

BICYCLING There are more than 75 miles of designated bikeways in Fort Collins, including the Spring Creek and Poudre River Trails, both paved (see above). There's also a dirt trail, the 5.8-mile Foothills Trail, parallel to Horsetooth Reservoir from Dixon Reservoir north to Campeau Open Space and Michaud Lane. For rentals of road and mountain bikes (from $25 per day), check with **Recycled Cycles,** 4031 S. Mason St., (© **970/223-1969**); and if you need repairs for your own bike visit **Lee's Cyclery,** 202 W. Laurel St. (© **800/748-2453** or 970/482-6006), or its second location at 931 E. Harmony Rd. (© **970/226-6006**). Also see "Mountain Biking," below.

FLY-FISHING Guided fly-fishing trips and clinics are available from **Rocky Mountain Adventures,** 1117 N. U.S. 287 (P.O. Box 1989), Fort Collins, CO 80522 (© **800/858-6808** or 970/493-4005; www.shoprma.com). They access the Big Thompson, Cache la Poudre, and North Platte rivers, plus waters on two private ranches and in Rocky Mountain National Park. Half-day guided walk and wade trips cost $125 for one person or $180 for two people, and full-day trips cost $210 and $265, respectively. Those who'd like to strike out on their own might try nearby **Roosevelt National Forest.** For further information, contact the information center of the Arapaho-Roosevelt National Forest and Pawnee Grasslands (see above) and the Colorado Division of Wildlife, 317 W. Prospect Rd. (© **970/472-4300;** http://wildlife.state.co.us). Anglers heading out to State Forest State Park have a good chance of catching a variety of trout species; only artificial flies and lures are permitted in some lakes there.

GOLF Fort Collins has three municipal courses: **Collindale Golf Course,** 1441 E. Horsetooth Rd. (© **970/221-6651**); **City Park Nine,** 411 S. Bryan Ave. (© **970/221-6650**); and **SouthRidge Golf Club,** 5750 S. Lemay Ave. (© **970/226-2828**). Tee times should be reserved 3 days in advance. Two privately owned courses that are open to the public are **Link-N-Greens Golf Course,** 777 E. Lincoln Ave. (© **970/221-4818**), and **Mountain Vista Greens Golf Course,** 2808 NE Frontage Rd. (© **970/482-4847**). Courses are open year-round, weather permitting, and greens fees for all of the above are in the $22 to $24 range for 18 holes.

HIKING The **Comanche Peak Wilderness area,** 67,500 acres of pine and spruce-fir forests below expanses of alpine tundra, offers scenic hiking trails along the north and east sides of Rocky Mountain National Park. Contact the information center of the **Arapaho-Roosevelt National Forest and Pawnee Grasslands** (see above).

State Forest State Park has miles of hiking trails and even gives overnight visitors the opportunity to stay in a yurt (see "Skiing & Other Winter Sports," below). There are 26 miles of trails at **Horsetooth Mountain Park** that are shared by hikers, mountain bikers, and horseback riders. Finally, **Lory State Park** has about 25 miles of hiking trails, where the top of Arthur's Rock—a hike of 2 miles—offers a marvelous view across Fort Collins and the northeastern Colorado plains. For more information on these parks, see the introduction to the "Sports & Outdoor Activities" section, above.

HORSEBACK RIDING   For the most part, riding is permitted anywhere in the Estes-Poudre District of the Roosevelt National Forest without special permit or license. Horsetooth Mountain Park, State Forest State Park, and Lory State Park have horse trails as well. Lory State Park has the added advantage of the **Double Diamond Stable** (© **970/224-4200**), which offers guided trail rides and hayrides. Prices for trail rides start at about $15 per hour, and hayrides are about $5 per person; these charges are in addition to park entrance fees.

KAYAKING   **Rocky Mountain Adventures** (see "Fly-Fishing," above) offers kayaking classes covering the Eskimo roll, paddling techniques, and white-water skills. Tuition prices are $60 for the roll, $40 for paddling, and $195 for a 2-day white-water class. Private instruction is also available.

Classes for all levels are also available from **Poudre River Kayaks, Inc.,** a part of the Mountain Shop, 632 S. Mason St., Fort Collins, CO 80524 (© **800/ 403-5720** or 970/493-5720; www.poudreriverkayaks.com), which also offers kayak rentals ($25 for 2 days, including needed gear).

LLAMA PACKING   Using llamas as pack animals is relatively new in the United States, but they are rapidly becoming the pack animal of choice in the Rocky Mountains. Guided llama trips, overnight pack trips, and llama leasing are the specialty of **Buckhorn Llama Co.** (© **970/667-7411**; www.llamapack. com). Guided pack trips for one to three people cost $300 per person per day.

MOUNTAIN BIKING   A good choice for mountain bikers is the **Foothills Trail,** which runs along the east side of Horsetooth Reservoir from Dixon Dam north to Michaud Lane. Horsetooth Mountain Park, Lory State Park, and State Forest State Park have excellent trails appropriate for mountain biking as well. In addition, there are yurts for overnighting at State Forest State Park (see "Skiing & Other Winter Sports," below). Also see "Bicycling," above.

RIVER RAFTING   River-rafting enthusiasts have ample opportunities for boating the Cache la Poudre, a nationally designated wild-and-scenic river. **Rocky Mountain Adventures** (see "Fly-Fishing," above), offers half-day and full-day trips on the Cache la Poudre and four other regional rivers. Costs range from $42 to $60 for a half-day and $72 to $95 for a full day. **A Wanderlust Adventure,** 3500 Bingham Hill Rd., Fort Collins, CO 80521 (© **800/745- 7238** or 970/484-1219; www.awanderlustadventure.com), offers half-day trips on the Cache la Poudre River for $43 to $59, and full-day trips for $89.

SKIING & OTHER WINTER SPORTS   Cross-country skiers will find plenty of trails and rolling hills at Lory State Park, surrounding national forests (© **970/498-2770**), and in State Forest State Park, where they can stay overnight in a backcountry yurt system owned by **Never Summer Nordic, Inc.,** P.O. Box 1983, Fort Collins, CO 80522 (© **970/482-9411;** www.neversummer nordic.com). The yurts, which are circular, tentlike canvas-and-wood structures on a high wood deck, have wood-burning stoves, padded bunks, and complete, albeit nonelectrified, kitchens. Most sleep up to six, and one sleeps at least 10.

Winter rates for the entire yurt are $85 to $105. In summer, rates are $55 to $65. Seven yurts (one near Lake Agnes and the other six at North Michigan Reservoir) can be rented by reservation by calling the number above. State Forest State Park also has an extensive system of snowmobile trails, either groomed or packed, that is separate from its cross-country ski trail system.

There's year-round **ice skating** at Edora Pool Ice Center (see "Swimming," below); it costs $4 for adults to age 59, $3 for youths 2 to 17, $3.50 for seniors 60 to 84, and free for infants under 2 and seniors 85 and older. Call for current hours.

SWIMMING   Edora Pool Ice Center (EPIC), at 1801 Riverside Dr. in Edora Park (© 970/221-6683), offers swimming, water exercise programs, and diving. The indoor **Mulberry Pool,** 424 W. Mulberry St. (© 970/221-6659), has lap lanes, a diving area, and "Elrog the Frog," a poolside slide. Both have recreational swimming and lap swimming; call for the current schedule or check out **www.fcgov.com/recreation**. The **City Park Outdoor Pool,** 1599 City Park Ave. (© **970/484-7665**), is open afternoons during warm weather (closed in inclement weather). Admission at each of the three above pools costs $3.75 for adults to age 59, $2.75 for youths 2 to 17, $3.25 for seniors 60 to 84, and is free for infants under 2 and seniors 85 and older. There's also swimming at Horsetooth Reservoir (see the "Sports & Outdoor Activities," above).

WILDLIFE WATCHING   Although you'll see some wildlife and water birds at Lory State Park and Horsetooth Reservoir, go to State Forest State Park to try to catch a glimpse of the state's largest moose population, along with elk, mule deer, mountain lions, big horn sheep, and black bears. State Forest Park's Moose Visitor Center has wonderful displays and wildlife-viewing information.

SHOPPING

Visitors enjoy shopping in **Old Town Square,** at Mountain and College avenues, with numerous shops, galleries, and restaurants. Old Town is also the site of various events; contact the Downtown Business Association (© **970/484-6500;** www.downtownfortcollins.com). Northern Colorado's largest enclosed shopping mall is the **Foothills Mall,** just north of the intersection of South College Avenue and Horsetooth Road (© **970/226-5555;** www.shopfoothills.com). Anchored by four department stores—Foley's, JCPenney, Sears, and Mervyn's—it has more than 120 specialty stores and a food court, and is open Monday through Saturday from 10am to 9pm and on Sunday from 11am to 6pm.

WHERE TO STAY

Lodging rates in Fort Collins are usually higher in summer, and rooms can be especially expensive and hard to find during college graduation and other major college events. The city has numerous chain motels, including the **Best Western Kiva Inn,** 1638 E. Mulberry St., Fort Collins, CO 80524 (© **888/299-5482** or 970/484-2444), with rates of $87 to $109 double; **Best Western University Inn,** 914 S. College Ave., Fort Collins, CO 80524 (© **800/937-8376** or 970/484-1984), with rates of $74 to $125 double; **Hampton Inn,** 1620 Oakridge Dr., Fort Collins, CO 80525 (© **800/426-7866** or 970/229-5927), with rates of $99 to $119 double; **Quality Inn & Suites,** 4001 S. Mason St., Fort Collins, CO 80525 (© **800/424-6423** or 970/282-9047), with rates of $89 to $139 double; and **Super 8 Motel,** 409 Centro Way, Fort Collins, CO 80524 (© **800/800-8000** or 970/493-7701), with rates of $45 to $70 double.

Rates may be higher during special events, like college graduation. Room taxes add almost 10% to hotel bills.

Mulberry Inn   Those seeking a pleasant standard motel with reasonable rates will like the Mulberry Inn. Each of the average-size rooms has a quality queen or king bed, a desk, and other usual furnishings. VCRs and movies are available for rent. There are hot tubs in 35 rooms and one suite has a wet bar.

4333 E. Mulberry St., Fort Collins, CO 80524. (℃ 800/234-5548 or 970/493-9000. Fax 970/224-9636. www.mulberry-inn.com. 120 units. $55–$100 double; $95–$140 suite; $75–$140 hot tub unit. Rates include morning coffee and muffins. AE, DC, DISC, MC, V. Pets accepted, $5 nightly. **Amenities:** Restaurant (steakhouse); seasonal outdoor pool. *In room:* A/C, TV.

Sheldon House Bed & Breakfast ★★   Step back into the early 20th century at this foursquare Victorian home, with golden oak floors and woodwork, leaded windows, and all the ornate furnishings you would expect from the prominent Fort Collins banker who had the home built in 1905. The attractive three-story inn has spacious rooms and an abundance of historic charm. It's an ideal choice for couples intent on exploring downtown Fort Collins or visiting the university (it's just 2 blocks away). Each room is unique—two have four-poster beds—but all have down comforters and attractively appointed private bathrooms with bathrobes (several have showers only). The smallest and least expensive room—Bob's Hideaway—is decorated in Old West style and has one twin bed. Other rooms have queen-size beds, and Miss Olive's Room has a queen and an additional single bed, plus a delightful outdoor balcony. There is also a suite available for long-term stays; call for availability and rates.

616 W. Mulberry St., Fort Collins, CO 80521. (℃ 877/221-1918 or 970/221-1917. Fax 970/495-6954. www.bbonline.com/co/sheldonhouse. 5 units. $90–$125 double. Rates include full breakfast. AE, MC, V. Children 10 and older welcome. *In room:* A/C.

CAMPING
There are several full-service campgrounds in the Fort Collins area. The **Fort Collins KOA** is about 10 miles northwest of downtown on Colo. 14 (℃ **800/ 562-2648** for reservations, or 970/493-9758), open mid-April through mid-October, with rates from $24 for both tent and RV. A second **KOA,** open year-round, is just off I-25 exit 281, north of Fort Collins at Wellington (℃ **800/ 562-8142** for reservations, or 970/568-7486), with rates from $22 per site. Campers looking for a lakeside RV resort might consider **Heron Lake RV Park,** northwest of Fort Collins at 1910 N. Taft Rd. (℃ **877/254-4063** or 970/484-9880; www.heronlakerv.com), which is open year-round and has rates of $30 to $45 for RV sites and $22 for tent sites.

Nearby Arapahoe and Roosevelt national forests have a number of established campgrounds, many with restrooms, water, and picnic tables. For rates and other information, contact the **Arapaho-Roosevelt National Forest and Pawnee Grasslands** office (see "Sports & Outdoor Activities," above).

WHERE TO DINE
EXPENSIVE
Nico's Catacombs CONTINENTAL   A classic, dimly lit cellar restaurant, with a richly decorated lounge separated from the main dining room by a stained-glass partition, Nico's is a good choice for celebrating a special occasion. Daily specials (including fresh seafood) are announced on blackboards. Start with a shellfish dish such as mussels Marseilles, or perhaps the Galantine de foie gras, then move on to steak Diane flambé, shrimp Parmesan, or one of the house specialties, such chateaubriand *bouquetière* (filet mignon with Burgundy sauce)

for two. The lounge, which opens at 4pm, offers a bar menu including baked brie and oysters Rockefeller, plus desserts and cappuccinos.

115 S. College Ave. ⓒ **970/484-6029.** Reservations recommended. Main courses $20–$35. AE, DC, DISC, MC, V. Mon–Sat 5–10pm.

MODERATE

Bisetti's ⓚⓚ ITALIAN A delightful atmosphere and good food make Bisetti's one of our favorite dining stops in northeast Colorado. The remodeled dining rooms glow with a Tuscan atmosphere and the new mahogany bar offers casual dining at lunch. The menu features a variety of homemade pastas, from spaghetti and lasagna to fettuccine and manicotti. Our favorite main course is the basil fettuccine with chicken. If it's a romantic dinner you're looking for, ask about the private cubby for two, which is available by reservation. There's also a private dining room for parties of 8 to 12.

120 S. College Ave. ⓒ **970/493-0086.** Reservations accepted for parties of 6 or more only. Main courses $6–$10 lunch, $8–$19 dinner. AE, DC, DISC, MC, V. Sun–Thurs 11am–9pm; Fri–Sat 11am–10pm.

Coopersmith's Pub & Brewing Co. MICROBREWPUB One of the oldest brewpubs in Colorado, Coopersmith's has been pleasing its customers since 1989. Located in historic Old Town Square, this American brewpub isn't just a place for knocking back a few. Within its brick walls is an open kitchen that prepares such traditional pub specialties as fish and chips, as well as less typical bangers and mash and Highland cottage pie, plus fresh fish and steak. You can also get hamburgers, sandwiches, salads, and soups, plus pizzas baked in a wood-fired oven. Portions are generous, and the two outdoor patios are popular in good weather. There's also a short children's menu and a great little pool hall with a half-dozen tables, especially popular with university students.

5 Old Town Sq. ⓒ **970/498-0483.** www.coopersmithspub.com. Main courses $6–$20. AE, MC, V. Fri–Sat 11am–2am; Sun–Thurs 11am–midnight.

INEXPENSIVE

Cozzola's Pizza North ⓚ PIZZA This is the place to come for the best pizza in Fort Collins. And you don't need to take our word for it: That's been the consensus of the Coloradoan Readers Poll for 12 years running. You serve yourself during the day, as waiters don't appear until evening. The wooden booths and tables, rough wood walls, and hanging plants give the small dining room a homey feel. In addition to offering the traditional chewy white pizza crust, the restaurant offers a whole-wheat poppy-seed or herb crust, in three sizes—10, 12, and 14 inch. Next choose your sauce: sweet basil, fresh garlic, *salsa del drago* (sauce of the dragon), pesto, or Spanish ricotta. As if that's not enough, there are more than two-dozen toppings, including artichoke hearts, feta cheese, sundried tomatoes, pineapple, and almonds. If you're not in the mood for pizza, you might try the spinach calzone or stromboli. Takeout and delivery are available.

Cozzola's Pizza South (takeout and delivery only) is located at 1112 Oakridge Dr. (ⓒ **970/229-5771**).

241 Linden St. ⓒ **970/482-3557.** Pizza $6–$15; lunch main courses $4.50–$6. AE, MC, V. Tues–Fri 11am–9pm; Sat 11:30am–9pm; Sun 4–8pm.

The Egg & I AMERICAN Consistently voted by locals as offering the best breakfast in town, The Egg & I creates a number of imaginative egg dishes, such as scrambled eggs with shrimp, an especially tasty Wisconsin scramble with four types of cheese, and several variations on eggs Benedict. There are also numerous omelets, frittatas, skillet breakfasts (our favorite), huevos rancheros, and other Mexican dishes. Pancakes, French toast, sandwiches, and salads round out the menu. Service is prompt and friendly.

2809 S. College Ave. ⓒ **970/223-5271**. Reservations not accepted on weekends. Main courses $3.35–$6.50. AE, DISC, MC, V. Mon–Sat 6am–2pm; Sun 7am–2pm.

El Burrito *Finds* MEXICAN   The Godinez family has been concocting authentic Mexican specialties at this cozy north-of-downtown restaurant since 1960, and year-in, year-out, Fort Collins residents have been filling up on the restaurant's popular burritos. It also serves good tacos, enchiladas, and chiles rellenos, and you can eat in or order your food to go.

404 Linden St. ⓒ **970/484-1102**. Main courses $3.50–$10. AE, MC, V. Daily 11am–2pm and 5–9pm (open until 10pm Fri–Sat).

Silver Grill Cafe ★★ *Finds* AMERICAN   In operation since 1933, this working-man's cafe attracts blue- and white-collar types, as well as seniors, students, and families for tasty, home-style food at very reasonable prices. When there's a line outside, as there often is on weekends, coffee is served to those waiting. You can't go wrong with one of the giant cinnamon rolls, but the rest of the menu is good, too. It's standard American fare: eggs, pancakes, and biscuits 'n' gravy for breakfast (served all day); burgers, other sandwiches, or the excellent homemade soups for lunch; and "noontime dinners" such as chicken-fried steak and beef pot roast.

218 Walnut St., Old Town. ⓒ **970/484-4656**. www.silvergrill.com. Main courses $3.50–$9. DISC, MC, V. Mon–Sat 6am–2pm; Sun 7am–2pm.

PERFORMING ARTS & NIGHTLIFE

The college crowd does much of its drinking and partying at **Washington's,** a large, bustling, multilevel dance and drink emporium at 132 Laporte Ave. (ⓒ **970/493-1603**), with a variety of recorded music and drink specials. You might try the somewhat bohemian **Avogadro's Number,** 605 S. Mason St. (ⓒ **970/493-5555**), which attracts a mixed crowd for live bluegrass and acoustic music. Country-and-western fans head to the big dance floor at the **Sundance Steak House and Country Club,** 2716 E. Mulberry St. (ⓒ **970/ 484-1600**), for live country music and free dance lessons. Sports freaks like the **SportsCaster Bar & Grill,** 165 E. Boardwalk (ⓒ **970/223-3553**), which has 50 TV screens and 20 beers on tap; smoking is not permitted. When you just want to quaff a cool beer at the end of the day, **Coopersmith's Pub & Brewing Co.,** 5 Old Town Sq. (ⓒ **970/498-0483**), may be the best place in town.

Many Fort Collins folk drive 14 miles up the Poudre River to the **Mishawaka Amphitheatre & Restaurant,** 13714 Poudre Canyon (ⓒ **970/482-4420;** www.mishawakaconcerts.com), where top regional bands—and occasional national acts—perform during the summer in an outdoor amphitheater on the banks of the Poudre River. Concert tickets range from $5 to $35, and you can dine on an outside deck over the river or inside, with a view of the water.

The principal venue for the performing arts in Fort Collins is **Lincoln Center,** 417 W. Magnolia St., at Meldrum Street (ⓒ **970/221-6730** box office, or 970/221-6735 administration; www.fcgov.com/lctix). Built in 1978, the center includes the 1,180-seat Performance Hall and the 220-seat Mini-Theatre, as well as three art galleries and an outdoor sculpture and performance garden. It's home to the Fort Collins Symphony, Opera Fort Collins, Canyon Concert Ballet, Larimer Chorale, OpenStage Theatre, and the Children's Theater. Concert, dance, children's, and travel film series are presented annually. The center is wheelchair accessible and has an infrared sound system for the hearing impaired.

Ticket prices vary considerably, but children's programs are often free or less than $10, and big name acts and Broadway shows are $18 to $36.

The **Fort Collins Symphony** (© **970/482-4823;** www.fcsymphony.org), established in 1948, performs both classical and pops music plus special events with guest performers. For those who enjoy a casual atmosphere with their classical music, the informal **Cranberry Pops** concert is performed the week after Thanksgiving by the symphony and a sizeable cast of singers and actors.

The **OpenStage Theatre Company** (© **970/484-5237;** www.openstage. com) is the area's leading professional stage group. It offers six productions annually, as well as various popular, classical, and operatic performances. Recent productions have included Shakespeare's *The Tempest,* Molnar's *The Play's the Thing,* and Agatha Christie's *The Mousetrap.*

Those who enjoy an intimate theater experience head to the 49-seat **Bas Bleu Theatre Company,** 216 Pine St., in Old Town (© **970/498-8949;** www.bas bleu.org), which presents a variety of plays, concerts, poetry readings, and other events.

Broadway musicals are presented year-round at **Carousel Dinner Theatre,** 3509 S. Mason St. (© **970/225-2555**; www.adinnertheatre.com), Thursday through Saturday at 6pm and Sunday at noon. A choice of three entrees is offered, and prices are $34 to $38, which includes dinner, show, and tax, but not beverages or dessert. Recent productions have included *Hello Dolly, Phantom of the Opera, Father of the Bride, Miss Saigon,* and *Forever Plaid.*

The **Colorado State University Department of Music, Theater, and Dance** (© **970/491-5529;** call 970/491-7978 for recorded information during the school year; www.colostate.edu/Depts/Music) presents a variety of dramas and musicals, plus concerts by music faculty ranging from jazz to classical during the school year. Many of these events are free or very inexpensive.

2 Loveland

13 miles S of Fort Collins, 52 miles N of Denver

Named for Colorado Central Railroad President W. A. H. Loveland in the 1870s, this former trading post now calls itself the "Sweetheart City" because every February some 300,000 Valentine's Day cards are remailed from here with a Loveland postmark. Established as a trading post in the late 1850s, this community at the foot of the Rockies grew around a flour mill in the late 1860s, before being platted on a wheat field near the railroad tracks in 1877. Today the city is a shipping and agriculture center with a population of just over 50,000. It also has a growing arts community and several foundries, and, like Fort Collins, its proximity to Rocky Mountain National Park and other outdoor recreation opportunities make this small city a good home base for those exploring the region. Elevation is just under 5,000 feet.

ESSENTIALS

GETTING THERE   By Car   Downtown Loveland is near the junction of U.S. 287 and U.S. 34. Coming from south or north, take I-25 exit 257B. From the west (Rocky Mountain National Park) or east (Greeley), follow U.S. 34 directly to Loveland. The drive takes about 1 hour from Denver.

By Plane   Many visitors to Loveland fly into **Denver International Airport** (see chapter 5). The **Fort Collins/Loveland Municipal Airport** (© **970/ 962-2852;** www.fcgov.com/airport), off I-25 exit 259, 7 miles northeast of

---

⌒Tips   Valentines from Loveland

To get your Valentine's Day cards remailed with a four-line Valentine cachet from Loveland, address and stamp each one, making sure to leave room in the lower-left-hand corner of the envelopes for the special Loveland stamp, and mail them in a large envelope to the Postmaster, Attn.: Valentines, Loveland, CO 80538-9998. To ensure delivery by February 14, mail for the United States must be received in Loveland by February 9, and foreign mail should be received by February 3.

---

downtown Loveland, offers regularly scheduled commercial service with Frontier Airlines (© **800/432-1359** or 303/371-7300); call for the current schedule.

Shamrock Airport Express (© **866/482-0505** or 970/482-0505; www.ride shamrock.com) provides daily shuttle services between Denver and Fort Collins (one-way rates: $24 adults, $8 children 11 and younger, free for children who sit on a parent's lap).

VISITOR INFORMATION   The **Loveland Chamber of Commerce** operates a visitor center at 5400 Stone Creek Circle, Loveland CO 80538, just northwest of the junction of I-25 and U.S. 34 (© **800/258-1278** or 970/667-5728; www.loveland.org). In summer it's open daily from 8am to 6pm; winter hours are Monday through Saturday from 8am to 5:30pm.

GETTING AROUND   U.S. 34, Eisenhower Boulevard, is the main east–west thoroughfare and does a slight jog around Lake Loveland, just west of city center. Lincoln Avenue (one-way northbound) and Cleveland Avenue (one-way southbound) make up U.S. 287 through the city. The downtown district is along Lincoln and Cleveland south of Seventh Street, 7 blocks south of Eisenhower.

For a taxi, call **Shamrock Yellow Cab** (© **970/224-2222**).

FAST FACTS   The hospital, with a 24-hour emergency room, is **McKee Medical Center,** 2000 N. Boise Ave. (© **970/669-4640;** www.bannerhealth.com), in the northeastern part of the city. The **post office** is at 446 E. 29th St., just off Lincoln Avenue. Contact the U.S. Postal Service (© **800/275-8777;** www.usps.com) for hours and locations of other nearby post offices.

SPECIAL EVENTS   Larimer County Fair and Rodeo, early August; Loveland Invitational Sculpture Show and Sale and Sculpture in the Park, early August; Corn Roast Festival, mid- to late August.

SPORTS & OUTDOOR ACTIVITIES

Loveland has more than two dozen city parks, a mountain park, three golf courses, and hiking trails, some of which are discussed below. Information on the city-run recreation sites is available from **Loveland Parks and Recreation Department,** 500 E. Third St. (© **970/962-2727;** www.ci.loveland.co.us/parks rec/prmain.htm).

Boyd Lake State Park (© **970/669-1739;** www.parks.state.co.us) is located a mile east of downtown Loveland via Madison Avenue and C.R. 24E. One of the largest lakes in the northern Front Range, with 1,700 surface acres when full, Boyd Lake is geared to watersports, including water-skiing (on the south end of the lake only), sailing, and windsurfing. There are sandy beaches for swimming, 148 campsites ($12–$18), including some with electric hookups, plus showers, a dump station, picnic areas, a children's playground, a paved walking/biking trail that connects to the city's path system, two paved boat ramps, and excellent fishing (especially for walleyes). Visitors often see foxes, beavers, coyotes, great-horned owls, hawks, eagles, and other wildlife. The daily park entrance fee is $6 per vehicle Memorial Day to Labor Day, $5 the rest of the year. A commercially run **marina** (✆ **970/663-2662**) is open in summer, with boat slips and moorings, a full-service gas dock, boat rentals, bait, groceries, and other supplies. A **restaurant** is also open daily in summer.

BICYCLING & JOGGING   A combination biking/jogging/walking path that will eventually circle the city, joining with a 3-mile path at Boyd Lake State Park, is gradually being constructed. For a map showing completed sections, stop at the Loveland Chamber of Commerce (see above).

GOLF   Golfers can enjoy two 18-hole municipal golf courses: **Olde Course at Loveland,** 2115 W. 29th St., which charges $20 to $25 for 18 holes; and **Marianna Butte,** 701 Clubhouse Dr., with greens fees of $28 to $36 for 18 holes. The 9-hole **Cattail Creek Golf Course,** 2116 W. 29th St. (across the street from Olde Course), charges $7 to $10 for 9 holes. For tee times and other information for all three courses, contact the city (✆ **970/669-5800;** www.ci.loveland. co.us/golf/golfmain.htm).

HIKING   The city-run **Viestenz-Smith Mountain Park,** in Big Thompson Canyon 12 miles west of Loveland along U.S. 34, is one of your best bets for hiking, with two trails. The **Summit Adventure Trail,** a moderately difficult 4.8-mile (one-way) hike, climbs 2,750 feet to offer scenic views of the mountains to the west and plains to the east. Those not interested in that much exercise will enjoy the easy 1-mile (one-way) **Foothills Nature Trail.** The park also has picnic tables, a playground, and a fishing stream, and is open year-round.

SWIMMING   The city-run **Loveland Swim Beach,** at 29th Street and Taft Avenue, has a free swimming beach, fishing, tennis and racquetball courts, a playground, and a miniature narrow-gauge train. There's also swimming at Boyd Lake State Park (see above).

IN-TOWN ATTRACTIONS

Benson Sculpture Garden   More than 60 sculptures are permanently displayed among the trees, plants, and ponds at this city park, and three or four more are added each year. This is also the site of Sculpture in the Park, the largest juried outdoor sculpture show in the United States, which takes place each year over the second weekend in August. The show, with all submissions available for purchase, features some 1,600 works by about 200 different sculptors from across the United States and Canada. Allow 1 hour.

29th St. between Aspen and Beech sts. ✆ **970/663-2940.** www.sculptureinthepark.org. Free admission.

Loveland Museum/Gallery   Changing exhibits of local historical subjects and the work of regional, national, and international artists fill this fine, small museum. A "Life on Main Street" exhibit area depicts Loveland at the turn of the 20th century, and there's an exhibit on the city's Great Western Sugar Factory. The museum also sponsors programs on art and history, workshops, concerts, and poetry readings. Allow an hour.

503 N. Lincoln Ave., at E. Fifth St. ✆ **970/962-2410.** www.ci.loveland.co.us/museum/museum.htm. Free admission. Tues–Wed and Fri 10am–5pm; Thurs 10am–9pm; Sat 10am–4pm; Sun noon–4pm.

A FOUNDRY TOUR

For a behind the scenes look at an art foundry, make an appointment to tour **Art Castings of Colorado,** 511 Eighth St. SE (© **970/667-1114,** ext. 15; www.artcastings.com), which gives foundry tours Tuesday and Thursday mornings. Cost is $5 per adult, $4 for seniors, free for children 16 and under; children under 10 must have adult supervision. Tours take about an hour, and those taking the tours are asked to wear closed shoes; safety glasses are provided.

WHERE TO STAY & DINE

Affordable chain motels in Loveland include the **Best Western Coach House Resort,** 5542 E. U.S. 34 (at I-25 exit 257B), Loveland, CO 80537 (© **888/ 818-6223** or 970/667-7810), with rates of $65 to $95 double; the **Budget Host Exit 254 Inn,** 2716 S. E. Frontage Rd. (at I-25 exit 254), Loveland, CO 80537 (© **800/283-4678** or 970/667-5202), charging $49 to $76 double; and **Super 8,** 1655 E. Eisenhower Blvd., Loveland, CO 80537 (© **800/800-8000** or 970/663-7000), with rates of $51 to $86 double. State and county taxes add about 7% to hotel bills.

There are numerous chain restaurants in Loveland, with plentiful choices on Lincoln Avenue and Eisenhower Boulevard. For breakfast and lunch we suggest **The Egg & I,** 2525 N. Lincoln Ave. (© **970/635-0050**), which is open from 6am to 2pm daily (from 7am Sun), offering numerous egg dishes (isn't that surprising!), plus sandwiches, salads, and Mexican dishes, mostly in the $3.35 to $6.50 range.

Sylvan Dale Guest Ranch ★★ (Kids)   Owners of a 3,200-acre working cattle and horse ranch on the banks of the Big Thompson River, the Jessup family invites guests to join in with daily ranch chores, horseback riding, and cattle drives, or just kick back, relax, and enjoy the many other available activities. Accommodations here are delightful, quiet, and comfortable; the homey rooms and cabins have a touch of Western charm, and are carpeted and furnished with antiques. Some cabins have fireplaces. A lodge, the Heritage, provides a gathering room with a large stone fireplace, library, gift shop, and exhibits on the history of the ranch, which dates to 1946.

Ranch facilities and activities include horseshoe pits, basketball and volleyball courts, lakes stocked with rainbow trout, trophy trout fly-fishing, hayrides, and an indoor recreation room. Summer entertainment includes live Western music, country-western dancing, nature walks, bird banding, gymkhana, American-Indian programs, and a children's program. Horseback-riding lessons, overnight pack trips, breakfast rides, and adventure rides are included in the summer adult riding package. White-water rafting is available for an extra charge. Summer guests must schedule 6-night full-board stays; the rest of the year, overnight guests are welcome for "bunk and breakfast." The ranch is also open year-round for retreat packages (including all meals) for groups from 6 to 60. Smoking is not permitted inside buildings.

2939 N. C.R. 31D, Loveland, CO 80538. © 877/667-3999 or 970/667-3915. Fax 970/635-9336. www. sylvandale.com. 26 units, including 11 cabins. Mid-June to late Aug, 6-night packages only, $1,495 per adult, nonriding adult package $1,250, $995 per youth (ages 5–12), $595 per child (ages 2–4); packages include all meals. Sept to mid-June, $85–$119 double, $95–$119 cabin, $15 extra person; includes full breakfast. Guest houses with kitchen also available (call for rates). MC, V. 7 miles west of Loveland via U.S. 34. **Amenities:** Restaurant; outdoor heated pool; 2 tennis courts; children's program (summer); game room. *In room:* No phone.

3 Greeley

30 miles SE of Fort Collins, 54 miles N of Denver

Greeley is a good spot to see the "other Colorado," the flatlands to the east of the state's famous mountains, as well as to delve into the area's history at several museums. One of the few cities in the world that owes its existence to a newspaper, Greeley was founded in 1870 as a sort of prairie Utopia by Nathan C. Meeker, a farm columnist for the *New York Tribune*. Meeker named the settlement—first known as Union Colony—in honor of his patron, *Tribune* publisher Horace Greeley. Through his widely read column, Meeker recruited more than 100 pioneers from all walks of life and purchased a tract on the Cache la Poudre from the Denver Pacific Railroad. Within a year, the colony's population was 1,000, and it's been growing steadily ever since, to around 77,000 today.

Greeley's economy is supported in large part by agriculture, with about 75% of Weld County's 1.9 million acres devoted to either farming or the raising of livestock. A combination of irrigated and dry-land farms produce grains, including oats, corn, and wheat, and root vegetables such as sugar beets, onions, potatoes, and carrots. In recent years, the community has been attracting major corporations such as Eastman Kodak and ConAgra food products. The University of Northern Colorado (UNC), with about 12,000 students, offers undergraduate and graduate degree programs. Elevation is 4,658 feet.

ESSENTIALS

GETTING THERE   By Car   Greeley is located at the crossroads of U.S. 34 (east–west) and U.S. 85 (north–south), midway between Denver and Cheyenne, Wyoming—both of which are more directly reached by U.S. 85 than by I-25. U.S. 34 heads west 17 miles to I-25, beyond which are Loveland and Rocky Mountain National Park. To the east, U.S. 34 connects Greeley to Fort Morgan via I-76, 37 miles away.

By Airport Shuttle   Visitors who fly into Denver International Airport can travel on to Greeley with **Rocky Mountain Shuttle** (✆ **888/444-3580** or 970/ 356-3366).

VISITOR INFORMATION   Contact the **Greeley Convention & Visitors Bureau,** 902 Seventh Ave., Greeley, CO 80631 (✆ **800/449-3866** or 970/352-3567; www.greeleycvb.com).

GETTING AROUND   Greeley is laid out on a standard grid, and is an easy city to navigate—provided you don't get confused by the numbered streets (which run east–west) and numbered avenues (which run north–south). It helps to know which is which when you're standing at the corner of 10th Street and 10th Avenue. Eighth Avenue (U.S. 85) is the main north–south street through downtown. Ninth Street is U.S. 34 Business, jogging into 10th Street west of 23rd Avenue. The U.S. 34 Bypass joins U.S. 85 in a cloverleaf just south of town.

The city bus system, called simply **The Bus** (✆ **970/350-9287;** www.ci. greeley.co.us) provides in-town transportation. For a taxi call **Shamrock Yellow Cab** (✆ **970/686-5555**).

FAST FACTS   The hospital, **North Colorado Medical Center,** is at 1801 16th St. (✆ **970/352-4121;** www.bannerhealth.com), just west of downtown. The **post office** is at 925 11th Ave. Contact the U.S. Postal Service (✆ **800/ 275-8777;** www.usps.com) for hours and locations of other area post offices.

SPECIAL EVENTS   Colorado Farm Show, late January; the UNC Jazz Festival, April; Semana Latina and Cinco de Mayo, late April and early May; Greeley's Rocky Mountain Stampede, late June and early July; Weld County Fair (second largest county fair in the state), early August; Potato Day celebrates Greeley's heritage, early September; Festival of Trees, early December.

SPORTS & OUTDOOR ACTIVITIES

Beginning about 25 miles northeast of Greeley and extending 60 miles east, the 200,000-acre **Pawnee National Grassland** is a popular destination for hiking, mountain biking, birding, wildlife viewing, and horseback riding. Nomadic tribes lived in this desertlike area until the late 19th century, and farmers subsequently had little success in cultivating the grasslands. Although primarily grassland, the dramatic **Pawnee Buttes, located** in the eastern section, are a pair of sandstone formations that rise some 250 feet. A dirt road leads to an overlook that offers good views of the buttes, and from the overlook a 1.5-mile trail leads to the base of the west butte. The most popular springtime activity is birdwatching, when you're apt to see white-crowned sparrows, lark buntings, meadowlarks, thrushes, orioles, and burrowing owls among the 300-plus species known to frequent the area. Pronghorn, coyotes, mule deer, fox, badger, prairie dogs, and short-horned lizards are among the prolific wildlife.

There are many routes to the grassland; one is to follow U.S. 85 north 11 miles to Ault, then east on Colo. 14 toward Briggsdale, 23 miles away. As much of the grassland is interspersed with private land, those planning to explore the area are advised to pick up a map ($6) and some free advice before setting out by stopping at the U.S. Forest Service office, 660 O St., Greeley (© **970/346-5000;** www.fs.fed.us/r2/arnf).

In Greeley itself, the 10-mile **Poudre River Trail** is popular with in-line skaters, bikers, walkers, and runners. While it remains under construction in some areas, it will eventually connect with the trail system in Fort Collins. For more information, call © **970/350-9783** or visit **www.poudretrail.org**.

SPECTATOR SPORTS

RODEO   Greeley's **Rocky Mountain Stampede** ★★ comes to town for 2 weeks, starting in late June, and boasts the world's largest Fourth of July Rodeo. Hundreds of professional cowboys and cowgirls compete for over $300,000 in prize money at Greeley's Island Grove Regional Park, with bareback bronc riding, calf roping, saddle bronc riding, team roping, steer racing, barrel racing, and bull riding. Festivities include country and classic rock concerts, art shows, a carnival, a children's rodeo, fun-runs, a demolition derby, barbecues, and a parade and fireworks display. For information, call © **800/982-2855** or 970/356-2855 or see **www.rockymountainstampede.com**.

ATTRACTIONS

Centennial Village Museum ★   A fun step back to times long gone, this collection of more than 30 structures—more are added each year—on 5½ acres depicts life on the High Plains of Colorado from the 1860s to the 1940s. Visit the blacksmith shop, print shop, and fire station of the commercial district, and stroll through Hanna Square, surrounded by elegant Victorian homes, a school, depot, and church. Watch for the exhibit of Rattlesnake Kate's dress, a flapper dress made of rattlesnake skins. Frequent living-history demonstrations and special events bring the past alive. In addition, the gardens here—ranging from an elegant Victorian-style garden to a kitchen herb garden—are beautiful, with the most colorful displays from July through September. Allow 2 to 3 hours.

1475 A St. at N. 14th Ave., adjacent to Island Grove Regional Park. 🕿 970/350-9220. www.greeley museums.com. Admission $5 adults, $4 seniors 60 and older, $3 children 6–11, free for children under 6. MC, V. Tues–Sat 10am–4pm. Closed mid-Oct to mid-Apr.

Meeker Home Museum   A good place to step back into the 19th century, this impressive two-story adobe home was built in 1870 for Greeley founder Nathan Cook Meeker. Now on the National Register of Historic Places, it is furnished with original Meeker family belongings and 19th-century antiques, including a 10-foot-tall diamond dust mirror. Interpretive panels discuss the history of Greeley and northeastern Colorado, with an emphasis on the Meeker family and their struggle for survival after Nathan's death in the 1879 Meeker Massacre. Allow 30 minutes to 1 hour.

1324 Ninth Ave. 🕿 970/350-9220. www.greeleymuseums.com. Free admission. Wed–Fri 1–4pm. Closed Oct–Apr.

WHERE TO STAY

A building boom of chain motels in the past few years has greatly increased lodging choices. Highest rates are during the summer. Options include the **Best Western Regency Hotel,** 701 Eighth St., Greeley, CO 80631 (🕿 **800/937-8376** or 970/353-8444), with double rates of $65 to $105; the handsome **Country Inn & Suites by Carlson,** 2501 W. 29th St., Greeley, CO 80631 (🕿 **800/456-4000** or 970/330-3404), with rates of $72 to $99 double; **Fairfield Inn,** 2401 W. 29th St., Greeley, CO 80631 (🕿 **800/228-2800** or 970/ 339-5030), with rates of $59 to $90 double; the **Microtel Inn & Suites,** 5630 W. 10th St., Greeley, CO 80634 (🕿 **888/771-7171** or 970/392-1530), which charges $57 to $77 double; and the **Super 8,** 2423 W. 29th St., Greeley, CO 80631 (🕿 **800/800-8000** or 970/330-8880), with double rates of $49 to $79. Lodging taxes add about 9% to hotel bills.

Greeley Guest House 🔿   A modern inn—it was built from the ground up and opened in 1996—the Greeley Guest House balances country charm with modern convenience. Centered around a shady courtyard, the brick-and-wood, ranch-style structure houses two levels of spacious, distinctively furnished rooms, all with gas fireplaces, microwaves, and high-speed Internet access. VCRs and videos are available. The beds are king- and queen-size, and the wooden furnishings and country-style decor are subtly pleasant.

5401 W. Ninth St., Greeley, CO 80634. 🕿 **800/314-3684** or 970/353-9373. Fax 970/353-9297. www. greeleyguesthouse.com. 19 units. $109 double; $129–$159 double for units with whirlpool tubs. Rates include continental breakfast. AE, MC, V. Located 1 block north of 10th St. (U.S. 34) in west Greeley. **Amenities:** Access to nearby fitness center; business center; laundry service; dry cleaning. *In room:* A/C, TV, fridge, microwave.

Sod Buster Inn Bed & Breakfast 🔿🔿   This is a great choice for those who love the ambience of a historic lodging but aren't ready to give up modern conveniences. This attractive three-story inn, which immediately stands out for its octagonal shape and wraparound veranda, is located in a historic district and is surrounded by 100-year-old structures. But the Sod Buster was actually built in 1997, designed to blend in with its older neighbors. Innkeepers LeeAnn and Bill Sterling have created what may be the best of both worlds—an exceedingly comfortable and attractive modern inn with the look and feel of an historic property, but without the steep staircases, noisy pipes, creaks, groans, and other "charms" you often find in old buildings.

Each guest room is individually decorated with a blend of antiques and country-style furnishings, and all include a king or queen bed, desk, dataport, good reading lamps, CD player (CDs available), comfortable seating, and individual climate control. Six rooms have TV/VCR combinations, with videos available. Several rooms have jetted tubs, while others offer soaker tubs or old-fashioned claw-foot tubs, and all have separate showers. The inn's common area has comfortable overstuffed furniture, a fireplace, big-screen TV with VCR, chess, and other games. A refreshment bar is stocked with a variety of home-baked items, coffee, tea, and soft drinks. The inn's country-style breakfasts might include an egg entree, pancakes, a meat dish, fruit, fresh-baked breads, juices, and hot beverages. Smoking is permitted on the veranda only.

1221 Ninth Ave., Greeley, CO 80631. © **888/300-1221** or 970/392-1221. Fax 970/392-1222. www.sod busterinn.com. 10 units. $99–$129 double. Rates include full breakfast. AE, DC, MC, V. Well-behaved children accepted with advance notification. *In room:* A/C.

WHERE TO DINE

The Armadillo *Finds* *Kids* MEXICAN   There's a fiesta atmosphere at this downtown Mexican restaurant, which is part of a small regional chain started in 1970 by the Lucio family. The Armadillo serves a variety of Mexican-food standards, and many of the recipes come from the Lucio family. Especially recommended are the Mexican Turnover (a deep-fried meat pie) and the Burrito Supreme. Fajitas are also popular.

819 Ninth St. © **970/304-9024.** $5–$12. AE, DISC, MC, V. Daily 11am–9pm.

Fat Albert's Food & Drink AMERICAN   A casual and homey family restaurant, this establishment owned by Roger and Susan Albert has been in business since 1982. Diners can sit at the bar, tables, or booths bedecked in brick and stained glass, and choose from a lunch menu that includes a good variety of salads, burgers, and sandwiches—ranging from a veggie melt to a perennially popular Monte Cristo. At 5pm, the menu expands to include trout, steak, and several chicken dishes. The award-winning homemade pies and cakes are extra special, and include traditional favorites such as apple crumb pie and carrot cake, as well as more exotic recipes such as chocolate zucchini cake and peanut butter pie. Smoking is not permitted.

1717 23rd Ave., in Cottonwood Square shopping center. © **970/356-1999.** Lunch $6–$9; dinner $9–$18. AE, DC, DISC, MC, V. Sun–Thurs 10:30am–9:30pm; Fri–Sat 10:30am–10:30pm.

Potato Brumbaugh's Restaurant & Saloon ⋆ AMERICAN   Named for a character in James Michener's *Centennial,* this casually elegant restaurant follows the novel's theme in its Western decor and is a solid if not spectacular choice. Our choice here is the excellent slow-roasted prime rib, and you won't go wrong with the daily fresh fish selection. The menu also features filet mignon, chicken, Colorado lamb and roast duck, plus pastas, such as pasta primavera, which is available with chicken or shrimp and in a marinara or Alfredo sauce.

2400 17th St., in Cottonwood Square shopping center. © **970/356-6340.** Reservations recommended. Lunch $8–$10; dinner $12–$45 (most $16–$22). AE, DC, DISC, MC, V. Mon–Fri 11:15am–2pm; Mon–Sat 5–10pm; Sun 5–9pm.

4 Fort Morgan

51 miles E of Greeley, 81 miles NE of Denver

A pleasant, laid-back city of just over 11,000 people, Fort Morgan may be best known as the childhood home of famed big-band leader Glenn Miller, who graduated from Fort Morgan High School in 1921 and formed his first band, the Mick-Miller Five, in the city. Established as a military outpost in 1864, the original Fort Morgan housed about 200 troops who protected stagecoaches and pioneers traveling the Overland Trail from marauding Cheyenne and Arapaho warriors. The threat had passed by 1870, and the fort was dismantled, but the name stuck when the city was founded in 1884. Nothing of the fort remains, but a monument on Riverview Avenue marks the fort's site.

The town grew in the 20th century with the establishment of the Great Western Sugar Company for sugar-beet processing, and with a pair of oil discoveries in the 1920s and 1950s. Cattle and sheep ranching remain important today, as well as dairy farming. In addition to sugar beets, the area grows alfalfa, onions, beans, corn, potatoes, sorghum, and wheat. Visitors enjoy the community's historic district and the fine Fort Morgan Museum, and use the town as home base while boating and fishing at Jackson Lake State Park.

About 10 miles east of Fort Morgan is the community of **Brush,** with a population of about 5,000. Also a farming and ranching center, Brush offers food and lodging, easy access to a popular pheasant-hunting area, and a variety of special events. Elevation in the Fort Morgan–Brush area is about 4,300 feet.

ESSENTIALS

GETTING THERE   By Car   Fort Morgan is located on U.S. 34 at I-76, the main east–west route between Denver and Omaha, Nebraska. U.S. 34 proceeds west to Greeley and Estes Park, and east to Wray and southern Nebraska. Colo. 52 is the principal north–south route through Fort Morgan.

By Plane   Denver International Airport is less than 90 minutes away (p. 72).

By Train   Amtrak (© 800/872-7245; www.amtrak.com) trains make daily stops on the Denver-to-Chicago route.

VISITOR INFORMATION   Contact the **Fort Morgan Area Chamber of Commerce,** 100 Ensign St. (P.O. Box 971), Fort Morgan, CO 80701 (© 800/ 354-8660 or 970/867-6702; www.fortmorganchamber.org). The chamber is located in the historic railroad depot, built in the 1920s, and is open Monday through Friday from 8am to 5pm. For information on events and activities in the nearby community of Brush, contact the **Brush Chamber of Commerce,** 1215 Edison St., Brush, CO 80723 (© 800/354-8659 or 970/842-2666; www. brushchamber.org).

GETTING AROUND   Platte Avenue (U.S. 34) is Fort Morgan's principal east–west thoroughfare. The north–south artery, Main Street, divides it and other streets into east and west designations. I-76 exits onto Main Street north of downtown.

FAST FACTS   The **Colorado Plains Medical Center,** with a 24-hour emergency room, is located at 1000 Lincoln St. (© 970/867-3391). The **Fort Morgan Post Office** is at 300 State St. Contact the U.S. Postal Service (© 800/275-8777; www.usps.com) for hours and the addresses of other post offices.

SPECIAL EVENTS   Morgan County Home and Garden Show in Fort Morgan, early March; Windmill Century Classic Bike Ride in Fort Morgan, early June; the Glenn Miller Festival in Fort Morgan, fourth weekend in June; the Brush Rodeo, early July; Festival in the Park in Fort Morgan, mid-July; Morgan County Junior Fair in Brush, August; Pedal the Prairie in Fort Morgan, September; Fall Harvest Car Show in Fort Morgan, September.

WHAT TO SEE & DO

In addition to the attractions discussed below, visitors interested in U.S. military history will want to call ahead to arrange a tour of the **U.S. Military Historical Museum,** 404 State St. (© **970/867-5520** or 970/867-8875), where there are more than three dozen life-size mannequins dressed in authentic military uniforms from the Revolutionary War to the present, plus numerous artifacts from all the wars in which the United States has fought. The museum has no scheduled hours, so appointments are necessary; admission is by donation.

Fort Morgan Museum ★★ *Finds*   Among our favorite small-town museums in Colorado, the Fort Morgan Museum completed a major expansion and renovation project in 2003 that has given it more space for exhibits, a gift shop, and educational programs. The museum contains an impressive collection of northeastern Colorado American-Indian artifacts, beginning with 13,000-year-old tools. Other permanent exhibits focus on farming, ranching, and the military and railroad history of Morgan County, plus our favorites—a display on the life of native son Glenn Miller and a fully restored 1920s soda fountain. The museum also hosts traveling exhibits and stages temporary shows from its collection, and is a good source for genealogical information in the area. There's a gift shop, and you'll find picnic areas and a playground in the surrounding City Park. Allow about 2 hours.

City Park, 414 Main St. © **970/867-6331.** www.ftmorganmus.org. Free admission. Mon–Fri 10am–5pm; Tues–Thurs 6–8pm; Sat 11am–5pm.

Rainbow Bridge   Also called the James Marsh Arch Bridge, this 11-arch concrete bridge was built over the South Platte River in 1923, at a construction cost of $69,290. Listed on the National Register of Historic Landmarks and the National Register of Engineering Landmarks, the 1,110-foot bridge is the only rainbow-arch design in Colorado. For information, contact the Fort Morgan Museum (see above), and allow 15 to 30 minutes.

At the northwest corner of Riverside Park (I-76 and Colo. 52).

Sherman Street National Historic District   Fort Morgan Museum (see above) publishes a walking-tour brochure both for Sherman Street and for the 9-block downtown district, the latter noting 44 buildings that made up the early town. These are available at the chamber of commerce (see "Visitor Information," above) and the museum.

Four Victorian mansions in the Sherman Street District are of special interest. Located around the intersection of Sherman Street and East Platte Avenue, they include the Warner House, an 1886 Queen Anne home; the Curry House, an 1898 Queen Anne with decorative spindle work porches, a barn, carriage house, and water tower; the Graham House, a 1914 American foursquare home; and the Bloedorn House, a 1926 brick Georgian revival–style building. Each is associated with a prominent city pioneer. They are private homes, not open to the public, but it's worth the walk to see the architecture from the sidewalk. For additional information contact the Fort Morgan Museum (see above). Allow at least 2 hours.

400 block of Sherman St.

SPORTS & OUTDOOR ACTIVITIES

The main recreation spot in this area is **Jackson Lake State Park,** located about 25 miles northwest of Fort Morgan (© **970/645-2551;** www.parks.state.co.us). The park offers swimming, boating, fishing, and picnicking in summer; and ice fishing, ice skating, and cross-country skiing in winter ($5 day-use fee).

Water-skiing, sailboarding, and boating are the most popular activities on the park's 2,700-acre reservoir, which has sandy beaches and boat ramps. The **Shoreline Marina** (© **970/645-2628**) has fuel, fishing and boating supplies, propane tank exchange, an ATM, a snack bar, and boat rentals May through September (depending on lake water levels). Fishing boats start at $25 for 2 hours, personal watercraft are $45 per hour, and 18-foot pontoon boats are $75 for 2 hours. The lake is closed to motorized boats from November until all the ice is gone in spring.

Anglers try for walleye, bass, and catfish, except when fishing is prohibited during the migratory waterfowl season. There's also a .5-mile nature trail, plus 260 campsites (some with electric hookups), showers, and a dump station ($12–$18). To get to Jackson Lake, follow Colo. 144 northwest for about 22 miles; the park is about 2½ miles north of the community of Goodrich via paved C.R. 3.

One of the nicest city parks in the region is **Riverside Park** 🎯🎯 (© **970/867-3808;** www.cityoffortmorgan.com), located off Main Street between I-76 and the South Platte River. Admission is free, and it has a large children's playground, more than 4 miles of nature trails along the river, tennis courts, basketball courts, playing fields, horseshoe pits, an in-line hockey rink, a picnic area, a duck pond (open to fishing by children 16 and younger and accompanying adults), and an attractive swimming pool open in summer ($1.50 adults, $1 children 6–18, free for children under 6). There are no sports equipment rentals. The park offers free overnight RV camping with electrical hookups, as well as free tent camping.

SPECTATOR SPORTS

RODEO   The **Brush Rodeo,** billed as the world's largest open rodeo (both amateurs and professionals compete), is held in Brush on the first 4 days of July, with all the usual rodeo events (including the popular wild-cow milking contest), plus a parade, kids' games, a dance, and fireworks. Contact the Brush Chamber of Commerce (see above) or check the Web at **www.brushcolo.com/rodeo.htm**.

STOCK-CAR RACING   Fans head to Fort Morgan's I-76 Speedway (© **970/867-2101;** www.i76speedway.com), where they can see late-model, street stocks, mini-stocks, midgets, minisprints, microsprints, dwarf cars, and IMCA modifieds race on a quarter-mile, high-banked dirt oval track from late March through October.

WHERE TO STAY & DINE

Lodging possibilities in Fort Morgan (zip 80701) include the well-maintained **Best Western Park Terrace Inn,** 725 Main St. (© **888/593-5793** or 970/867-8256), which charges $59 to $88 double and has an excellent restaurant on-site (see below); and the **Super 8,** 1220 N. Main St. (© **800/800-8000** or 970/867-9443), charging $52 to $64 double. State and county taxes add just under 8% to hotel bills.

Restaurants in Fort Morgan include **Memories,** at the Best Western Park Terrace Inn (© **970/867-8205;** www.memoriesrestaurant.com), which offers a good selection of well-prepared American standards daily from 6am to 9pm, with prices for lunch $4.75 to $9.75, and for dinner $6.50 to $17.

Another good dining choice in Fort Morgan is **Country Steak Out,** 19592 E. Eighth Ave. (© **970/867-7887**), which serves steak and seafood (and has an extensive salad bar), with prices from $5 to $12 at lunch and $7 to $20 at dinner. It's open Tuesday through Saturday from 11am to 9pm and Sunday from 11am to 2pm.

5 Burlington

163 miles E of Denver, 385 miles W of Topeka, Kansas

As the first major Colorado community to greet motorists traveling I-70 from the east, Burlington is an excellent place to overnight and spend some time at the beginning or end of a Colorado vacation. It's the largest town in east-central Colorado, with a population of about 3,200, and sits at an elevation of 4,165 feet. Those passing through might want to take a break and see how the community has preserved its turn-of-the-20th-century heritage with an impressive Old Town and famous carousel. Dry-land farmers established Burlington and other "outback" communities along the Kansas City–Denver rail line in the 1880s, and while wheat is very much the dominant crop today, you'll also find corn, dry beans, and sunflowers.

ESSENTIALS

GETTING THERE   By Car   Burlington is located on east–west I-70, 13 miles from the Kansas border. U.S. 385, which runs the length of Colorado's eastern frontier, makes a north-to-south pass through the town.

VISITOR INFORMATION   The **Colorado Welcome Center** is along I-70 beside Burlington Old Town (© **800/288-1334** or 719/346-8404), and is open daily from 9am to 5pm Monday through Saturday, noon to 5pm Sundays. For information specifically on Burlington, contact the **Burlington Chamber of Commerce,** 415 15th St., Burlington, CO 80807 (© **719/346-8070;** www.burlingtoncolo.com).

GETTING AROUND   The town lies on the north side of I-70. Rose Avenue (U.S. 24) runs east–west through the center of Burlington. Main north–south streets are Eighth Street (U.S. 385 north) on the east side of town, 14th Street (which locals call Main St.), and Lincoln Street (U.S. 385 south) on the west side of town.

FAST FACTS   The **Kit Carson County Memorial Hospital** is at 286 16th St. (© **719/346-5311**). The **post office** is at 259 14th St. Contact the U.S. Postal Service (© **800/275-8777;** www.usps.com) for hours and other information. During inclement weather (but not at other times), you can get a **road condition report** by calling © **719/346-8778.**

SPECIAL EVENTS   Kit Carson County Fair, August; Old Town Ghost Town, last Saturday in October; Country Christmas Jubilee at Old Town, first Sunday in December; and Storybook Christmas and Parade of Lights, December.

WHAT TO SEE & DO

Kit Carson County Carousel ★★★ *(Kids)*   This is the town's pride and joy, the only National Historic Landmark in eastern Colorado, and a must-see for everyone who stops in Burlington. Carved in 1905 by the Philadelphia Toboggan Company and one of the few wooden carousels left in America that still wears its original coat of paint, it's fully restored and operational. The 46 stationary animals—mostly horses, but also giraffes, zebras, camels, a hippocampus (sea horse), lion, tiger, and others—march counterclockwise around three tiers of oil paintings, representing the lifestyles and interests of the American Victorian middle class. A Wurlitzer Monster Military Band Organ, one of only two of its size and vintage in operation today, provides the music. Allow 1 hour.

County Fairgrounds, 15th St. at Colorado Ave. ⓒ **719/346-8070.** Admission 25¢ per ride. Memorial Day to Labor Day daily 1–8pm. Private tours given at other times with 2 weeks' advance notice; write P.O. Box 28, Stratton, CO 80836.

Old Town ⚐ *Kids*   For a look at the real Old West, take a trip to Old Town. Close to 20 turn-of-the-20th-century-style Old West buildings make up this living-history museum, where you're likely to see a gunfight, or, in the summer months, a cancan show in the Longhorn Saloon. Nine of the buildings are original historic structures, moved to Old Town, and the rest are reproductions, all furnished with genuine Old West artifacts to show what it was like here 100 years ago.

Visit the blacksmith shop, bank, law office, newspaper office and operating print shop, general store, schoolhouse, and barn. The railroad depot, built in 1889 in Bethune, Colorado, is the oldest structure in Old Town. Of course there's the saloon, where you're likely to find the piano player tinkling the ivories, or perhaps you'd prefer to stop at the church, built in 1921 and still used for weddings.

The dollhouse is home to a number of unique dolls, and in the wood shop you'll see tools more than 100 years old. The original Burlington town jail cells are also here; and the two-story, six-bedroom Manor house, built in the early 1900s, is magnificent, furnished with splendid antiques of the period. Heritage Hall contains a large collection of 45 wagons, guns, and other exhibits. There's also a 2,000-square-foot gift shop, with handcrafted items and other souvenirs. On summer weekends the horse-drawn "Old Town Express" gives rides from Old Town to the Kit Carson County Carousel (see above). Allow 1 to 3 hours.

420 S. 14th St. ⓒ **800/288-1334** or 719/346-7382. Admission $6 adults 19–59, $4 youths 12–18, $2 children 3–11, $5 seniors 60 and older. Memorial Day to Labor Day daily 9am–5pm; rest of the year Mon–Sat 9am–5pm, Sun noon–5pm. Last admission at 4pm.

SPORTS & OUTDOOR ACTIVITIES

As soon as the winter snows are gone, the folks in Burlington and other eastern Colorado communities head to the beach, and that means **Bonny Lake State Park,** 23 miles north of Burlington on U.S. 385, then east on county roads 2 or 3 for about 1½ miles (ⓒ **970/354-7306;** www.parks.state.co.us). Built as a flood control project in 1951, the reservoir contains 1,900 surface acres of relatively warm water, perfect for swimming, water-skiing, windsurfing, and fishing. The daily entrance fee is $5 per vehicle.

The lake has two swimming areas (no lifeguards) and four campgrounds with a total of 190 campsites ($12–$22). Some sites have electric hookups, and several are handicapped accessible. Facilities include restrooms, pay showers, picnic areas, a self-guided nature trail (not handicapped accessible), and a fish-cleaning station. Fishing is good for walleye, northern pike, and a variety of bass.

Boat launching ramps are available, and the **Bonny Dam Marina** (ⓒ **970/354-7339**) sells fuel, groceries, and boating and fishing supplies. The marina also rents fishing boats, 20- to 24-foot pontoon boats, and personal watercraft between May and September. Call for current rates. The 5,000-acre park provides opportunities to see wildlife, with some 250 species of birds, mule and whitetail deer, coyotes, badgers, muskrats, bobcats, beavers, and rabbits.

If you're traveling this way in winter, stop by for an afternoon of cross-country skiing, ice skating, or ice fishing, but don't forget your long underwear—winter winds are bone-chilling out here on the plains. During winter, electric and water are available in the campgrounds, and there are vault toilets, but the showers and flush toilets are shut down.

If you're passing through town and looking for some quick R & R, a good place to take the kids is the **Burlington Swimming Pool,** located at the south end of Mike Lounge Drive. Open afternoons and evenings during the summer, the city-run pool has a new 175-foot flume slide. There's also a wading pool with a sloping entrance and a special slide just for younger kids. Admission costs $2.50 for adults and $1.50 for children 2 to 17. Another good family stop in Burlington is **Outback Territory Park Playground,** which covers a full block between 15th and 16th streets and Railroad and Martin avenues. It's got a marvelous playground (designed by Burlington Elementary School children) and delightful picnic areas with lots of shade. Admission is free. For additional information, contact the Colorado Welcome Center in Burlington or the Burlington Chamber of Commerce (see "Visitor Information," above).

WHERE TO STAY

Because Burlington (zip 80807) is simply an overnight stop for many travelers along the interstate highway, you won't have any trouble finding a room here, with all the motels easily accessible from I-70 exits 437 and 438. In addition to the motels discussed below, there's a **Comfort Inn,** 282 S. Lincoln St. (℗ **800/ 228-5150** or 719/346-7676), with double rates of $59 to $120; and a **Super 8,** 2100 Fay St. (℗ **800/800-8000** or 719/346-5627), charging double rates of $49 to $69. Tax adds about 7% to lodging bills.

Chaparral Motor Inn ⭐ *(Value*   This conveniently located modern motel is an excellent choice for those seeking an exceptionally clean and well-maintained place to spend the night at a reasonable price. The rooms are set back a bit from the road so they're fairly quiet. Rooms and bathrooms are of average size, simply but attractively decorated in a contemporary Southwestern style. All rooms have a small working desk, and a table with two chairs; refrigerators and hair dryers are available on request. An adjacent restaurant serves three meals daily.

405 S. Lincoln St., Burlington, CO 80807. ℗ **800/456-6206** or 719/346-5361. Fax 719/346-8502. 39 units. $45–$60 double; rates include continental breakfast. AE, DISC, MC, V. Small pets accepted ($7 per dog per night; $10 per cat per night). **Amenities:** Outdoor heated pool (seasonal); indoor hot tub. *In room:* A/C, TV, coffeemaker.

Claremont Inn ⭐⭐   One of the few bed-and-breakfasts on Colorado's eastern plains, the striking Claremont Inn is a good choice for those who want more than a clean place to sleep for the night. The three-story inn blends an intimate atmosphere with modern conveniences, and features uniquely decorated rooms such as the flower- and birdhouse–bedecked Waverly Room and the romantic Secret Garden Room, with its own whirlpool for two. The public rooms, which include the domed-ceiling Hearth Room and a theater, are similarly impressive. Innkeeper Dave Dischner, a seasoned professional chef, prepares the meals, which might include bananas Foster or French toast for breakfast. The restaurant here also serves eclectic dinners (call for details), and the inn also regularly hosts cooking weekends, often with French and Italian themes. Smoking is not permitted.

800 Claremont Dr., Stratton, CO 80836. ℗ **888/291-8910** or 719/348-5125. Fax 719/348-5948. www.claremont inn.com. 7 units. $169–$219 double; rates include full breakfast. AE, DC, DISC, MC, V. Located 18 miles west of Burlington, off I-70, exit 419. *In room:* A/C, TV.

Sloan's Motel   A well-kept, comfortable establishment, this Best Value Inn affiliate offers clean, basic lodging at reasonable rates. All rooms have firm queen or long-boy beds, and cable TV. Two family units have two rooms, and the American with Disabilities Act (ADA)-compliant room has a roll-in shower. Eighteen rooms have shower/tub combos, and the remaining 11 have shower only. There's a nice little children's playground, and a heated pool in season.

1901 Rose Ave., Burlington, CO 80807. ℂ **888/315-2378** or 719/346-5333. Fax 719/346-9536. 29 units. $35–$47 double. Family units from $55. Rates include continental breakfast. AE, DC, DISC, MC, V. Pets accepted with management approval. **Amenities:** Enclosed heated pool (seasonal). *In room:* A/C, TV, data-port, coffeemaker.

WHERE TO DINE

Interstate House AMERICAN   A longtime favorite of locals, this family restaurant is popular because of its good home-cooked food, quick service, and low prices. House specialties include the aged, charbroiled steaks that are cut in-house, plus the waffles, which, like many of the other breakfast entrees, are served all day. Tasty burgers, sandwiches, seafood selections, pork chops, tacos, burritos, chili, and a steak-and-eggs special round out the menu.

415 S. Lincoln St., at I-70 exit 437. ℂ **719/346-7041**. Breakfast $1.95–$6.95; lunch and dinner $3.95–$17. DISC, MC, V. Daily 6am–9pm.

The Route Steakhouse AMERICAN   This family restaurant boasts an especially good salad bar, and a large selection of well-prepared American staples. The large dining room is what we might call contemporary Western, with solid wood tables and booth seating. There are various half-pound burgers and sandwiches for lunch—try the Trail Boss sandwich, piled high with brisket, turkey, and ham, and topped with melted Swiss and cheddar. From the dinner menu, we like the 14-ounce rib-eye steak (all steaks are hand-cut on the premises) and the house specialty, chicken-fried steak. Salads here are also very good, especially the Cobb salad, with chicken, bacon, chopped eggs, diced tomatoes, shredded cheddar, and fresh mushrooms on a bed of salad greens.

218 S. Lincoln St. ℂ **719/346-8790**. Lunch items $5–$8; dinner entrees $6–$17. AE, DISC, MC, V. June–Aug daily 11am–10pm; Sep–May 11am–9pm.

10

The Northern Rockies

Literally and figuratively, this is the mother lode. It's where scrappy silver and gold miners struck it rich time and time again in the late 19th century, yet it's also where Colorado's rugged beauty is shown off to fullest effect.

The northern Rockies begin just outside of Denver and extend on either side of the meandering Continental Divide down sawtooth ridgelines, through precipitous river canyons, and across broad alpine plains. Here, snowfall is measured in feet, not inches; it's where you'll find Colorado's hottest ski resorts—Aspen, Vail, and Steamboat—as well as a few smaller areas that are making headlines, such as Winter Park. And then there's Summit County, with possibly more major ski areas within a half-hour's drive than anywhere else in the country. If you're easily bored, rent a condo or take a room in Breckenridge and spend your days skiing a different mountain every day. With Copper, Keystone, Arapahoe Basin, and even tiny Loveland all within a few miles' drive, you've got plenty of choices.

When spring's sun finally melts away the walls of white, a whole new world opens up amid the brilliantly colored alpine wildflowers. You can head to any of the area's ski resorts to shop their stores and hike or cycle their trails. Perhaps best of all, though, is a trip to the West's premier mountain vacation spot, and our very favorite mountain destination in Colorado—Rocky Mountain National Park. Here you can enjoy some of the most spectacular scenery in America as well as a broad range of outdoor activities, from hiking to wildlife viewing to cross-country skiing.

1 Estes Park & Grand Lake: Gateways to Rocky Mountain National Park

71 miles NW of Denver, 42 miles SW of Fort Collins, 34 miles NW of Boulder

Estes Park is the eastern gateway to Rocky Mountain National Park, and Grand Lake is the closest town to the park's western entrance. Of the two, Estes Park is more developed. It has more lodging and dining choices, as well as a few noteworthy sights that are worth a visit. If you're driving to Rocky Mountain National Park via Boulder or Denver, you'll want to make Estes Park your base camp.

Grand Lake is a more rustic spot, with plenty of places to camp, a number of motels, and a few guest ranches. If you're coming from Steamboat Springs or Glenwood Springs, Grand Lake is a more convenient base. At any time of year, you can get there via U.S. 34. In summer, you can also get to Grand Lake by taking the Trail Ridge Road through Rocky Mountain National Park from Estes Park. Both routes are scenic, although the national park route (closed in winter) is definitely prettier.

Columbine

Cowdrey

To Laramie

0   20 mi
0   20 km

ROUTT NATIONAL FOREST

Glendevey

Red Feather Lakes

Steamboat Lake

Clark

Walden

Mount Zirkel Wilderness Area

Beaver Creek

NORTH PARK

14

ROOSEVELT NATIONAL FOREST

Rustic

GORE RANGE

125

14

Steamboat Springs

Coalmont

Gould

14

Estes Park

Milner

Rand

34

131

Rabbit Ears Pass

Continental Divide

Rocky Mountain National Park

Oak Creek

ROUTT NAT'L FOREST

ARAPAHO NAT'L FOREST

40

Allens-park

Phippsburg

ARAPAHO NAT'L FOREST

Lake Granby

Grand Lake

Yampa

Granby

ROOSEVELT NATIONAL FOREST

Toponas

Kremmling

40

Arapaho Nat'l Recreation Area

72

Flat Tops Wilderness Area

134

MIDDLE PARK

ARAPAHO NAT'L FOREST

McCoy

Radium

9

WHITE RIVER NAT'L FOREST

Winter Park

Nederland

Burns

State Bridge

40

Blackhawk

131

Berthoud Pass

Central City

Wolcott

70

Georgetown

70

6

Eagle

Edwards

Vail

Silverthorne

Dillon

Idaho Springs

Avon

Minturn

Vail Pass

To Denver

To Glenwood Springs

WHITE RIVER NAT'L FOREST

Red Cliff

Frisco

Dillon Res.

Copper Mountain

Breckenridge

Basalt

Divide

24

Grant

FRONT RANGE

Snowmass

Turquoise Lake

91

9

PIKE NAT'L FOREST

Woody Creek

Continenta

Alma

SOUTH PARK

Aspen

Leadville

Fairplay

82

Independence Pass

9

SAWATCH RANGE

24

285

Ski area

Continental Divide

Area of Detail

Boulder

25

76

70

Denver

70

COLORADO

Colorado Springs

25

ESTES PARK

Unlike most Colorado mountain communities, which got their starts in mining, Estes Park (elevation 7,522 ft.) has always been a resort town. Long known by Utes and Arapahos, it was "discovered" in 1859 by rancher Joel Estes. He soon sold his homestead to Griff Evans, who built it into a dude ranch. One of Evans' guests, the Welsh Earl of Dunraven, was so taken by the region that he purchased most of the valley and operated it as his private game reserve, until thwarted by such settlers as W. E. James, who built Elkhorn Lodge as a "fish ranch" to supply Denver restaurants.

The growth of Estes Park, however, is inextricably linked with two individuals: Freelan Stanley and Enos Mills. Stanley, who, together with his brother Francis, invented the kerosene-powered Stanley Steamer automobile in 1899, settled in Estes Park in 1907, launched a Stanley Steamer shuttle service from Denver, and in 1909 built the landmark Stanley Hotel. Mills was one of the prime advocates for the establishment of Rocky Mountain National Park. Although less well known than John Muir, Mills is an equally important figure in the history of the U.S. conservation movement. His efforts increased sentiment nationwide for preserving our wild lands, and resulted in President Woodrow Wilson signing a bill to set aside 400 square miles for Rocky Mountain National Park in 1915. Today the park attracts some 3 million visitors annually. Estes Park, meanwhile, has a year-round population of some 5,400.

ESSENTIALS

GETTING THERE   By Car   The most direct route is U.S. 36 from Denver and Boulder. At Estes Park, U.S. 36 joins U.S. 34, which runs up the Big Thompson Canyon from I-25 and Loveland, and continues through Rocky Mountain National Park to Grand Lake and Granby. An alternative scenic route to Estes Park is Colo. 7, the "Peak-to-Peak Scenic Byway" that traverses Central City (Colo. 119), Nederland (Colo. 72), and Allenspark (Colo. 7) under different designations.

By Plane   The closest airport is Denver International Airport, 80 miles away. The **Estes Park Shuttle** (© **970/586-5151;** www.estesparkshuttle.com) connects DIA with Estes Park. Rates are $39 one-way and $75 round-trip.

VISITOR INFORMATION   The **Estes Park Chamber Resort Association,** 500 Big Thompson Ave., Estes Park, CO 80517 (© **800/44-ESTES** or 970/586-4431; www.estesparkresort.com), has a visitor center on U.S. 34, just east of its junction with U.S. 36. In summer, it's open Monday through Saturday from 8am to 9pm and Sunday from 9am to 5pm; winter hours are Monday through Saturday from 8am to 6pm and Sunday from 9am to 5pm.

GETTING AROUND   There's year-round taxi service with **Estes Park Shuttle** (see "Getting There," above), which also provides tours into Rocky Mountain National Park during the summer.

FAST FACTS   The hospital, **Estes Park Medical Center,** with a 24-hour emergency room, is at 555 Prospect Ave. (© **970/586-2317**). The **post office** is at 215 W. Riverside Dr. Call the U.S. Postal Service (© **800/275-8777;** www.usps.com) for hours and locations of other post offices. For statewide **road conditions,** call © **303/639-1111** or check **www.cotrip.org**. For a **current weather report,** call © **970/586-5555.**

SPECIAL EVENTS   Jazz Fest and Art Walk, mid-May; the Wool Market, mid-June; the Scandinavian Mid-Summer Festival, on a weekend close to the summer solstice; the Rooftop Rodeo, mid-July; Longs Peak Scottish Irish Festival, the weekend after Labor Day in September; and Autumn Gold—A Festival of Brats and Bands, late September.

WHAT TO SEE & DO

In addition to the attractions discussed here, be sure to check out the art galleries and other visual arts venues discussed under "Shopping," below.

Enos Mills Homestead Cabin   This 1885 cabin and homestead belonged to the late-19th- and early-20th-century conservationist, Enos A. Mills, a major force behind the establishment of Rocky Mountain National Park. A short walk down a nature trail brings you to the cabin, with displays of his life and work. Also on the premises are a bookshop and gallery. Allow 30 minutes to 1 hour.

6760 Colo. 7 (opposite Longs Peak Inn). ℭ **970/586-4706.** $5 adults, $3 children 6–12. Memorial Day to Labor Day usually Tues–Fri 11am–4pm, but call to confirm. Usually Sat 11am–4pm and by appointment in other seasons.

Estes Park Aerial Tramway 🐾   Going up! This tram, which climbs 1,100 vertical feet in less than 5 minutes, offers a great ride up the side of Prospect Mountains and provides spectacular panoramic views of Longs Peak, the Continental Divide, and Estes Park village itself. Its lower terminal is a block south of the post office. You'll find a gift shop, snack bar, and observation deck at the upper terminal, and numerous trails converge atop the mountain. Allow at least 1 hour.

420 E. Riverside Dr. ℭ **970/586-3675.** www.estestram.com. Admission $8 adults, $7 seniors 60 and older, $4 children 6–11, free for children 5 and under. Memorial Day to Labor Day daily 9am–6:30pm.

Estes Park Museum 🐾🐾   The lives of early homesteaders in Estes Park are depicted in this excellent museum, which includes a completely furnished turn-of-the-20th-century log cabin, an original Stanley Steamer car, and a changing exhibit gallery. The museum also features a permanent "Tracks in Time" exhibit that helps visitors see the impact that ordinary people, from the region's American Indians and women pioneers to today's area residents and travelers, have had on Estes Park. You can also see Rocky Mountain National Park's original headquarters building, which has been moved here. In addition, the museum sponsors a variety of programs and distributes a historical walking-tour brochure on downtown Estes Park. Allow 1½ hours.

Included in the admission fee is a visit to the award-winning 1909 Fall River Hydroplant museum at 1754 Fish Hatchery Rd. (ℭ **970/577-7683**). It's open Memorial Day through Labor Day, Tuesday through Sunday from 1 to 4pm.

200 Fourth St. at U.S. 36. ℭ **970/586-6256.** www.estesnet.com/museum. Admission $2.50 adults, $2 seniors 60 and older, $1 children 12 and under, $10 maximum for families. May–Nov Mon–Sat 10am–5pm, Sun 1–5pm; Dec–Apr Fri–Sat 10am–5pm, Sun 1–5pm.

Michael Ricker Pewter Gallery & Museum   Ricker is an internationally recognized artist and sculptor, whose works have been displayed in the Great Hall of Commerce in Washington, D.C., and at both Disneyland and Disney World. This museum and gallery has more than 1,000 pewter sculptures, including Ricker's masterpiece, Park City, claimed to be the world's largest miniature pewter sculpture. Free guided tours are available daily. Allow 1 hour.

107 N. College Ave. ℭ **800/588-3070** or 970/221-1004. www.ricker.com. Free admission. Summer Mon–Wed 10am–7pm, Thurs–Sat 10am–8pm, Sun 11am–5pm; winter daily 9am–5pm.

SHOPPING

Elkhorn Avenue is the main shopping area in Estes Park, and this is also where you'll find public restrooms and free parking lots (watch for the signs). Among the notable galleries and gift shops are those in the **Old Church Shops,** 157 W. Elkhorn Ave. (✆ **970/586-5860;** www.churchshops.com). Also worth looking for are **The Glassworks,** 323 W. Elkhorn Ave. (✆ **800/490-6695** or 970/586-8619; www.garthsglassworks.com), a gallery and studio with hand-glass-blowing demonstrations; and **Serendipity Trading Company,** 117 E. Elkhorn Ave. (✆ **800/832-8980** or 970/586-8410; www.serendipitytrading.com), traders in American-Indian arts and crafts.

The **Cultural Arts Council of Estes Park,** 304 E. Elkhorn Ave. (P.O. Box 4135), Estes Park, CO 80517 (✆ **970/586-9203;** www.estesarts.com), has a fine art gallery featuring changing exhibits of works by nationally recognized artists as well as exhibits on loan from private collections and museums. The council sponsors an Art in Public Places series (call for details), and hosts Art Walks—self-guided tours of galleries, artists' studios, special exhibits, and events throughout the area. The Art Walks take place in mid-May, June through Labor Day, late September, and early December; and maps are available. The council also sponsors an outdoor performance series, Thursday nights at 7pm from June through August at Estes Park's Performance Park (west side of downtown). Events, which are free or have a nominal admission fee, start at 7pm and offer classical, jazz, folk or contemporary music, plus theater and dance.

The **Art Center of Estes Park** in the Stanley Village Shopping Center, 517 Big Thompson Ave. (✆ **970/586-5882;** www.artcenterofestes.com), is a community visual arts center that features changing exhibits of a wide variety of local and regional art, including paintings, sculpture, photography, textiles, glass work, and wood carvings. Works are for sale, and the center also presents workshops and classes, lasting from several hours to a full day, on subjects such as oil painting, sketching, stained glass, and jewelry-making. Cost is usually in the $50 to $100 range, including materials. The Art Center is a bit hard to find; once you get to the shopping center, go up the stairs behind the fountain.

WHERE TO STAY

The highest rates here, sometimes dramatically higher, are in summer. For help in finding accommodations, call the **Estes Park Chamber of Commerce Lodging Referral Service** (✆ **800/379-3708;** www.estesparkresort.com). National chains here include **Best Western Silver Saddle,** 1260 Big Thompson Hwy. (U.S. 34), Estes Park, CO 80517 (✆ **800/WESTERN** or 970/586-4476), with rates of $99 to $199 double from June to mid-September, $79 to $149 double off season; **Super 8,** 1040 Big Thompson Ave., Estes Park, CO 80517 (✆ **800/800-8000** or 970/586-5338), charging $72 to $90 double in summer, $52 to $64 double off season; and **Travelodge,** 1220 Big Thompson Ave., Estes Park, CO 80517 (✆ **800/578-7878** or 970/586-4421), charging $85 to $189 double in summer, $59 to $149 double off season.

Although many lodging facilities in the Estes Park area do not have air-conditioning, it is seldom needed at this elevation. Unless otherwise noted, pets are not permitted. Taxes add about 8% to hotel bills.

Expensive

Aspen Lodge at Estes Park ★★★   Among Colorado's top dude ranches (and touted as the largest log lodge on the continent), Aspen Lodge is a full-service Western-style resort, offering horseback riding, hiking, mountain biking, fishing, cross-country skiing, ice skating, snowshoeing, and a myriad of other activities. Guests stay in the handsome log lodge, which has a commanding stone fireplace in the lobby, or in cozy one-, two-, or three-room cabins nestled among the aspens. All lodge rooms have balconies, and most rooms and cabins have splendid views of Longs Peak, the tallest mountain in Rocky Mountain National Park. Trails on the lodge's 82 acres of grounds lead directly into the national park. Guests can also enjoy a sports center, which has racquetball and a weight room. Meals are great—varied and well prepared, and the lodge restaurant is also open to the general public (see "Where to Dine," below). The lodge also schedules numerous activities to entertain both children and teens.

6120 Colo. 7, Longs Peak Route, Estes Park, CO 80517. ℭ **800/332-6867** or 970/586-8133. Fax 970/586-8133. www.aspenlodge.net. 59 units. June–Aug 3-day minimum, packages include 3 meals, children's program, entertainment, van tours, and recreation (horseback riding extra; call for rates): 3 days shared room $549 each adult, $359 each child 3–12 years, free for children under 3; 6 nights shared room $999 each adult, $699 each child 3–12 years, free for children under 3. Sept–May $89–$179 double per night for lodge rooms or 1-room cabins, including full breakfast. Holiday rates higher. Call for 2- and 3-room cabin rates. AE, DISC, DC, MC, V. **Amenities:** Restaurant; bar; outdoor heated pool; health club; hot tub; sauna; activities desk; coin-op laundry.

Fawn Valley Inn   Located only a half mile from the Fall River entrance to Rocky Mountain National Park, Fawn Valley offers an attractive range of accommodations at reasonable prices. Spread across a steep bank between U.S. 34 and Fall River, each unit has a private outdoor area: deck, balcony, or patio, overlooking the river and surrounding forest-skirted mountains. The inn is often frequented by elk, deer, bighorn sheep, raccoons, and other local wildlife. Some units have a tub-shower combo, some have a shower only, nine have their own hot tub, and there are six Jacuzzi suites. Most units have microwaves, and all except motel units have gas or wood-burning fireplaces. All units are spacious—even the smallest motel rooms—and have modern American decor with homey touches. The various units can accommodate from 2 to 10 people, with king and queen beds plus sofa beds. The largest condos are usually booked months in advance for summer, so call early.

2760 Fall River Rd. (P.O. Box 4020), Estes Park, CO 80517. ℭ **800/525-2961** or 970/586-2388. Fax 970/586-0394. www.fawnvalleyinn.com. 35 units. Summer $135–$245 double; winter $115–$155 double. Minimum stay may be required at certain times. AE, DISC, MC, V. **Amenities:** Outdoor heated pool (Memorial Day to Labor Day); outdoor hot tub. *In room:* TV, fridge, coffeemaker.

Lake Shore Lodge ★★   This handsome and modern lodge offers guests a difficult choice: Do you want a room looking out on the lake or one with a view of the mountains? Although most rooms in the area have some kind of view, not many offer such a choice. For a standard room, we think the best views are in the third-floor rooms facing the lake, but, if you can afford them, the third-floor corner suites offer views of both the lake and the mountains. Of course, we expect nice interiors, too, and the Lake Shore Lodge comes through in that category as well. Decorated in Western Victorian style, with oak furnishings and rich colors of burgundy and forest green, the rooms are slightly larger than average, and third-floor units with vaulted ceilings feel especially spacious. All units have either two queen-size beds or a king and sofa sleeper. Second- and third-floor units have decks. The six suites have fireplaces, and two also have whirlpool tubs. All rooms are nonsmoking.

Owing to its role as a conference center, the lodge has an abundance of public areas, from outdoor decks to inside seating areas with comfortable couches, fireplaces, and, of course, great views out large windows. There's a small indoor swimming pool, and a game room with video games and a pool table. The adjacent Lake Estes Marina offers boat rentals, and fishing is available from a boat or the lakeshore. The lodge's Silverado restaurant boasts wonderful views and dinner entrees prepared just the way we like them—top-quality meat and fish, with only limited use of sauces.

1700 Big Thompson Ave., Estes Park, CO 80517. ☎ **800/332-6867** or 970/577-6400. Fax 970/577-6420. www.lakeshorelodge.com. 54 units. June–Sept $149–$219 double, $259–$329 suite; Oct–Nov 3 $119–$159 double, $259–$299 suite; Nov 4–May $109–$149 double, $199–$299 suite. Rates include full breakfast. AE, DISC, MC, V. **Amenities:** Restaurant (steak and seafood); bar; indoor pool; health club; indoor hot tub; sauna; game room; coin-op laundry. *In room:* TV, dataport, fridge, coffeemaker, hair dryer, iron/ironing board, safe.

Romantic RiverSong Inn ★

A 1920 Craftsman mansion on the Big Thompson River, this elegant bed-and-breakfast has 27 forested acres with hiking trails and a trout pond, as well as prolific wildlife and beautiful wildflowers. Very quiet, the inn is at the end of a country lane, the first right off Mary's Lake Road after it branches off U.S. 36 south. The comfortable bedrooms are decorated with a blend of antique and modern country furniture. All have large tubs, separate showers, and fireplaces; six units offer jetted tubs for two. Smoking is not permitted. Gourmet candlelight dinners are available by advance arrangement ($101 per couple), but you must supply your own alcoholic beverages.

1765 Lower Broadview Rd. (P.O. Box 1910), Estes Park, CO 80517. ☎ **970/586-4666.** Fax 970/577-0699. www.romanticriversong.com. 10 units. $150–$295 double. Rates include full breakfast. DISC, MC, V. Not suitable for small children. *In room:* Fridge (some).

Stanley Hotel ★★

F. O. Stanley, inventor of the Stanley Steam Car (the Stanley Steamer), built this elegant hotel in 1909, and a flurry of recent projects have restored it to its Victorian grandeur. (New for 2004: a spa and a series of unattached one- to three-bedroom condo units that are the most lavish in town.) The equal of European resorts the day it opened, the Stanley was constructed in solid rock at an elevation of 7,800 feet on the eastern slope of the Colorado Rockies. Today the hotel and its grounds are listed on the National Register of Historic Places as the Stanley Historic District. Each room differs in size and shape, offering a variety of views of Longs Peak, Lake Estes, and surrounding hillsides. We prefer the deluxe rooms in the front of the building, which provide views of Rocky Mountain National Park.

333 Wonderview Ave. (P.O. Box 1767), Estes Park, CO 80517. ☎ **800/976-1377** or 970/586-3371. Fax 970/586-4964. www.stanleyhotel.com. 140 units. $149–$249 double; $269–$329 suite; $349–$799 condominium; $1,500 presidential cottage. AE, DISC, MC, V. **Amenities:** Restaurant (American); pool (heated outdoor); tennis court (outdoor, unlit); exercise room; spa. *In room:* Cable TV w/pay movies, dataport.

Streamside of Estes Park

These cabin suites, on 17 acres along the Fall River, about a mile west of Estes Park on U.S. 34, are surrounded by woods and meadows of wildflowers. Deer, elk, and bighorn sheep are such regular visitors that many have been given names. Everything is top drawer inside these cabins: All have king- or queen-size beds, fireplaces, and decks or patios with gas grills. Many have beamed cathedral ceilings, skylights, and whirlpool tubs or steam showers. Guests can wander the nature trails on the property. A variety of special-occasion packages are offered.

1260 Fall River Rd. (P.O. Box 2930), Estes Park, CO 80517. ☎ **800/321-3303** or 970/586-6464. Fax 970/586-6272. 19 units. Early May to late Oct $95–$225 double; late Oct to early May $75–$145 double; extra person $15. AE, DISC, MC, V. **Amenities:** Indoor hot tub. *In room:* Cable TV/VCR, kitchen (most), in-room hot tubs.

Moderate & Inexpensive

In addition to the properties discussed here, there are also cabins and cottages available at the **Estes Park KOA,** listed under "Camping," below.

All Budget Inn *Value* This pleasant motel, smack up against Rocky Mountain National Park, offers simple rooms with homey touches such as fresh flowers, and nature prints adorning the white walls. The units, which sleep from two to six people each, have firm queen- or king-size beds and shower-tub combos. Some have kitchenettes and private balconies. There's also a picnic area with barbecue grills.

945 Moraine Ave., Estes Park, CO 80517. ℂ **800/628-3438** or 970/586-3485. www.allbudgetinn.com. 22 units. Summer $89–$130 double, $130–$250 suite or condominium; off season $69–$98 double, $110–$175 suite or condominium. MC, V. Pets accepted. **Amenities:** Outdoor hot tub. *In room:* A/C, cable TV, fridge, coffeemaker, hair dryer, microwave.

Allenspark Lodge Bed & Breakfast *★★* *Finds* We love historic properties, and this one has just the right ambience for a visit to Rocky Mountain National Park. The three-story lodge was built in 1933 of hand-hewn ponderosa pine logs, and includes a large native stone fireplace. Located 16 miles south of Estes Park, in a tiny village at the southeast corner of the national park, all lodge rooms offer mountain views and original handmade 1930s pine furniture. At the top end is the Hideaway Room, with a queen-size brass bed, bear-claw-foot tub, fine linens, and a gas-log stove. Guests share the large sunroom, the stone fireplace in the Great Room, videos in the recreation room, and books in the library. A hot family-style breakfast, afternoon and evening coffee, tea, and cookies are complimentary. There is also a hot tub, espresso coffee shop, and wine and beer bar; horseback riding is available across the street in the summer.

184 Main St., Colo. 7 Business Loop (P.O. Box 247), Allenspark, CO 80510. ℂ **303/747-2552.** www. allensparklodge.com. 13 units (7 with bathroom). $75–$145 double. Rates include full breakfast. DISC, MC, V. Children under 14 not accepted. **Amenities:** Bar; hot tub. *In room:* No phone.

Baldpate Inn *★* *Finds* Built in 1917, the Baldpate was named for the novel *Seven Keys to Baldpate,* a murder mystery in which seven visitors believe each possesses the only key to the hotel. In 1996, the Baldpate was added to the National Register of Historic Places. Guests today can watch several movie versions of the story, read the book, and contribute to the hotel's collection of more than 20,000 keys.

Baldpate is located 7 miles south of Estes Park, adjacent to Rocky Mountain National Park. Guests can enjoy complimentary refreshments by the handsome stone fireplace in the lobby, relax on the large sun deck, or view free videos on the library VCR. But it might be difficult to stay inside once you experience the spectacular views from the inn's spacious porch and see the nature trails beckoning. Each of the early-20th-century-style rooms is unique, with handmade quilts on the beds. Several of the rooms are a bit small, and although most of the lodge rooms share bathrooms (five bathrooms for nine units), each room does have its own sink. Among our favorites are the Mae West Room (yes, she was a guest here), with a red claw-foot tub and wonderful views of the valley; and the Pinetop Cabin, which has a whirlpool tub, canopy bed, and gas fireplace. In summer, an excellent soup-and-salad buffet is served for lunch and dinner daily (see "Where to Dine," later in this chapter). Smoking is not permitted.

4900 S. Colo. 7 (P.O. Box 700), Estes Park, CO 80517. ℂ **866/577-5397** or 970/586-6151. www.baldpate inn.com. 14 units (5 with bathroom), 4 cabins. $100 double with shared bathroom, $115 double with private bathroom; $175 cabin. Rates include full breakfast. DISC, MC, V. Closed Nov–Apr. **Amenities:** Restaurant (seasonal). *In room:* No phone.

Boulder Brook ★★   It'd be hard to find a more beautiful setting for lodging than this. Surrounded by tall pines and cradled in a ruggedly majestic valley 2 miles from the park entrance, all suites face the Fall River and have private river-front decks and full or partial kitchens. The spa suites are the epitome of comfort and luxury, with two-person spas, fireplaces, sitting areas with cathedral ceilings, and king-size beds. The nicely appointed one-bedroom suites hold king-size beds, window seats, two TVs, and bathrooms with whirlpool tub–and-shower combinations. The grounds, a serene jumble of forest, rock, and running water, include an outdoor hot tub and barbecue area. Smoking is not permitted.

1900 Fall River Rd., Estes Park, CO 80517. © **800/238-0910** or 970/586-0910. Fax 970/586-8067. www.boulderbrook.com. 19 units. $109–$225 double. AE, DISC, MC, V. **Amenities:** Year-round outdoor hot tub; large free video library. *In room:* Cable TV, DVD/VCR, kitchens.

Estes Park Center/YMCA of the Rockies ★   This extremely popular family resort is an ideal place to get away from it all, and serves as a great home base while exploring the Estes Park area. Lodge units are simply decorated and perfectly adequate, but we prefer the spacious mountain cabins. These have two to four bedrooms (accommodating up to 10), complete kitchens, and some have fireplaces. The center, which occupies 860 wooded acres, offers hiking, horseback riding, miniature golf, fishing, a skate park, and winter activities.

2515 Tunnel Rd., Estes Park, CO 80511-2550. © **970/586-3341**, or 303/448-1616 direct from Denver. Fax 970/586-6088. www.ymcarockies.org. 510 lodge rooms (450 with bathroom), 205 cabins. Lodge rooms summer $69–$127, winter $52–$98; cabins year-round $71–$266. YMCA membership required (available at a nominal charge). No credit cards. Pets are permitted in the cabins, but not the lodge rooms. **Amenities:** Indoor heated pool; tennis courts (3 outdoor); bike rentals. *In room:* Kitchen (cabins).

Glacier Lodge *Kids*   Deer and elk frequently visit these lovely cottages, which spread across 19 acres of woodland along the Big Thompson River. There are poolside chalets; cozy, homey river duplexes with outside decks overlooking the stream; and river triplexes range from earthy to country quaint in decor. All have a porch or patio, and almost all feature kitchens and fireplaces, with a bundle of wood delivered daily. Facilities include a sports court, playground, fishing, gift shop, ice-cream shop, and stables. Breakfast cookouts, barbecues, and special kids' activities take place in summer, at an extra charge. There are also four large lodges available for groups that sleep from 12 to 30 (call for rates).

Colo. 66 (P.O. Box 2656), Estes Park, CO 80517. © **800/523-3920** or 970/586-4401. www.glacierlodge.com. 26 units. Early June to late Aug $80–$218; mid-May to early June and late Aug to late Sept $60–$150; late Sept to mid-Oct $50–$130. Rates are per unit (2–5 people). Minimum stays of 2–4 nights may be required. DISC, MC, V. Closed mid-Oct to mid-May. **Amenities:** Outdoor pool. *In room:* TV, no phone.

Lake Estes Inn & Suites *Kids*   This unique property has a wide variety of room and bed choices, making it an excellent choice for families and even for several families traveling together. The standard rooms are simply but attractively furnished, with upholstered seating areas and good lighting. They have either one king or two queen-size beds, and some also have hide-a-beds and/or gas fireplaces. Family units are similar to the standard rooms, but have two separate bedrooms to accommodate six to eight people. As would be expected, the suites are more luxurious, with handsome fireplaces, large whirlpool tubs, and hide-a-beds; some also have kitchenettes and private patios. The cottage, with sleeping for eight, has two bedrooms, a full-size kitchen, a gas fireplace, and a large deck with a gas barbecue grill and a seasonal hot tub. Most units have great views of the mountains and Lake Estes. There's a playground and a shuffleboard court; and guests have access to the recreational activities at Aspen Lodge at Estes Park (see above), under the same ownership.

1650 Big Thompson Ave., Estes Park, CO 80517. ℂ **800/332-6867** or 970/586-3386. Fax 970/586-9000. www.lakeestes.com. 58 units. Late May to early Sept $70–$130 double, $120–$270 suite, family unit, and cottage; early Sept to late May $60–$80 double, $90–$220 suite, family unit, and cottage. Rates include continental breakfast May–Sept. AE, DC, DISC, MC, V. **Amenities:** Large outdoor heated pool; wading pool; large enclosed hot tub; sauna. *In room:* TV, fridge, hair dryer, iron, safe.

CAMPING

Estes Park KOA   This member of the reliable national KOA campground chain, with mostly open, sunny sites, is located across the street from Lake Estes and within walking distance of the Big Thompson River, about 1 mile east of Estes Park on U.S. 34. Although it lacks a swimming pool, it does offer a scenic location, cable TV hookups, fishing, a basketball court, a game room, and bike rentals. It also sells LP gas. There are fire pits in the tent and cabin areas, but not at RV sites. Cabins have bedrooms only (you share the campground bathhouses); cottages also have a full kitchen and private bathroom.

2051 Big Thompson Ave., Estes Park, CO 80517. ℂ **800/562-1887** for reservations, or 970/586-2888. www. estes-park.com/koa. 62 sites, 16 cabins. $30–$35 per RV campsite for 2 people, extra person $3; $20–$23 for tent sites for 2 people, extra person $3; cabins $40–$56 double; cottage $95–$120 double. Open May to mid-Oct. *In room:* Kitchen (cottages only).

Mary's Lake Campground   Here you'll find mostly open campsites that can accommodate everything from tents to 40-foot RVs, with full hookups that include cable TV. Facilities include bathhouses, a laundry, a dump station, a playground, a basketball court, a small store, a heated swimming pool, horseshoe pits, and a game room. Fishing licenses, bait, and tackle for shore fishing at the lake and stream fishing in the national park are available.

2120 Mary's Lake Rd. (P.O. Box 2514), Estes Park, CO 80517. ℂ **800/445-6279** or 970/586-4411. Fax 970/ 586-4493. www.maryslakecampground.com. 150 sites. $36–$39 per RV hookup campsite for 2 people; $25 for non-hookup sites for 2. Extra person (over age 5) $3. Extra fee for phone and A/C or electric heater use. Open May–Sept. DISC, MC, V. **Amenities:** Pool; coin-op laundry.

Spruce Lake R.V. Park   This meticulously well-maintained campground offers large sites, a heated pool, free miniature golf, a large playground, a stocked private fishing lake, and spotless bathhouses. Ground tents are not permitted. Cabins sleep up to 5, with refrigerators and microwaves, TV, and a bathroom with shower. There are also Sunday pancake breakfasts and weekly ice-cream socials. Reservations are strongly recommended, especially in the summer.

1050 Mary's Lake Rd., Estes Park, CO 80517. ℂ **800/536-1050** or 970/586-2889. www.sprucelakerv.com. 110 sites. $35–$37 for sites with full hookups for 2 people, cabins $89 double. Extra person (over age 3) is $4; $1 per pet per night. MC, V. Open mid-Apr to mid-Oct. **Amenities:** Pool.

WHERE TO DINE

In addition to the restaurants described here, see the Lazy B Ranch under "Arts & Entertainment," below.

Expensive

Aspen Lodge Dining Room WESTERN/CONTINENTAL   Enjoy casually elegant dining in one of two large rooms, both of which feature cathedral ceilings, wagon-wheel chandeliers, and Western artwork. Broad windows (as well as the large redwood deck) provide unfettered views of the grand outdoors: a small lake in front, evergreen and aspen trees on the sloping grounds, and the Rocky Mountains. For lunch there are burgers (including excellent low-fat buffalo burgers), the popular Rocky Mountain trout, chicken-fried steak, salads, sandwiches, and vegetarian selections. Dinners include a salad bar, fresh rolls, the vegetable of the day, and potato or rice. We suggest the steaks or prime rib, and you can also get various game entrees, pasta, and seafood. A variety of decadent desserts are available.

At the Aspen Lodge, 6120 Colo. 7, Longs Peak Route, about 8 miles south of Estes Park. ✆ **970/586-8133.** Reservations recommended. Lunch main courses $7–$10; dinner main courses $14–$22. AE, DC, DISC, MC, V. Daily 7–10am, 11am–2pm, and 5–8pm. Shorter hours Nov–May; call for current schedule.

Dunraven Inn ★★ ITALIAN   This is a great spot to celebrate a special occasion in an intimate setting, but it's not so fancy that you wouldn't want to take the (well-behaved) kids. The decor is eclectic, to say the least: Images of the Mona Lisa are scattered about, ranging from a mustachioed lady to opera posters, and autographed dollar bills are posted in the lounge area. House specialties include shrimp scampi, lasagna, and our favorite, the Dunraven Italiano (an 11-oz. charbroiled sirloin steak in a sauce of peppers, onions, and tomatoes). There's a wide choice of pastas, fresh seafood, vegetarian plates, and desserts, plus a children's menu. Another Dunraven (same owner, but smaller and more casual) is located downtown at 101 W. Elkhorn Ave. (✆ **970/586-3818**).

2470 Colo. 66. ✆ **970/586-6409.** Reservations highly recommended. Main courses $8–$34. AE, DISC, MC, V. Sun–Thurs 5–10pm; Fri–Sat 5–10pm; closes slightly earlier in winter.

Moderate

Baldpate Inn SOUP/SALAD   Don't be misled by the simple cuisine—the buffet is deliciously filling and plentiful. Everything is freshly prepared on the premises, with the cooks barely staying one muffin ahead of the guests. Soups— a choice of two is offered each day—include hearty stews, chili, chicken rice, garden vegetable, and classic French onion. The salad bar provides fresh greens and an array of toppings, chunks of cheese, and fruit and vegetable salads. Honey-wheat bread is a staple, plus wonderful rolls, muffins, and corn bread. Topping off the meal are fresh homemade pies and cappuccino. Smoking is not permitted.

4900 S. Colo. 7. ✆ **970/586-6151.** www.baldpateinn.com. Reservations recommended. Buffet $11 adults, $8.75 children under 10. DISC, MC, V. Memorial Day to Aug. daily 11:30am–8pm. Shorter hours Sept to mid-Oct; call for current schedule.

Estes Park Brewery AMERICAN   Pizzas, burgers, sandwiches—including meatball and grilled turkey—and bratwurst made with the brewery's own beer are the fare here. Our choice is generally a pepperoni pizza or a juicy burger. Vegetarians can order a veggie burger and a variety of salads; kids have their own menu. In addition, a number of full dinners are also offered, ranging from barbecued chicken and ribs to steak. The brewery offers about 10 fresh beers at any given time, specializing in Belgian-style ales. It also produces an excellent India pale ale and an especially pleasant stout.

470 Prospect Village Dr. ✆ **970/586-5421.** www.epbrewery.net. Sandwiches and salads $5.45–$8.95; dinner main courses (after 4pm) $9.95–$17. AE, DC, DISC, MC, V. Summer daily 11am–midnight; closes earlier in winter.

Grumpy Gringo ★ *Kids* MEXICAN   Dine in style at this classy Mexican restaurant without breaking the bank. The private booths, whitewashed plaster walls, green plants, bright poppies, and a few choice sculptures provide a posh atmosphere. And although the food is excellent and portions are large, the prices are surprisingly low. Our first choice here is the burrito, but which one to choose? We also recommend the huge enchilada *olé*—it's actually three enchiladas: one each of cheese, beef, and chicken—and the chicken or beef fajitas. There are six sauces from which to choose, each homemade, and rated mild, semihot, or hot. The house specialty drink is the Gringo Margarita, made with Sauza Gold tequila from an original (and secret) recipe.

1560 Big Thompson Ave. (U.S. 34). © **970/586-7705.** Main courses $4.95–$15. AE, DISC, MC, V. Daily 11am–10pm summer, 11am–8pm off season. Closed last week of Jan, 1st week of Feb. On U.S. 34, 1 mile east of the junction of U.S. highways 34 and 36.

Molly B ★ *Finds* AMERICAN   It's hard not to feel right at home at this busy restaurant, where the atmosphere is casual and the staff treats you like an old friend. Located in an older downtown building, the dining room has light-colored pine walls and tables that add to the down-home atmosphere. Molly B is especially popular at breakfast, with specialties such as our favorite, the sunrise stuffer—a large tortilla filled with scrambled eggs, potatoes, cheese, and spicy chorizo. Lunch and dinner selections include vegetarian entrees, fresh seafood (we suggest the grilled Rocky Mountain trout), pasta, and steak. Desserts are made in-house—try the mud pie: chocolate and mocha ice cream in an Oreo cookie crust, topped with fudge. Patio seating, providing good people-watching along the noisy street, is available in warm weather.

200 Moraine Ave. © **970/586-2766.** Reservations recommended for dinner. Main courses $3–$7 breakfast, $5–$8 lunch, $8–$17 dinner. AE, MC, V. Year-round Thurs–Tues 6:30am–3pm; May–Oct Thurs–Tues 6:30am–3pm and 4–9pm.

Inexpensive

Bob and Tony's Pizza *Kids* PIZZA   This busy and somewhat noisy locally owned and operated pizza joint is what we think a pizza place should be—red-brick walls covered with chalk signatures, a large stone fireplace with chairs for those waiting for their to-go pies, and utilitarian tables. The pizza dough, sauce, and Italian sausage are made fresh in-house from family recipes. A variety of pizzas are offered, or you can "build your own" from a wide choice of toppings, although why anyone would want to put sauerkraut on a pizza is beyond our comprehension! Sandwiches range from Italian sausage to French dip to grilled chicken, and there are also "build your own" subs, and meals such as fish, fries, and slaw; spaghetti with meatballs; and even Rocky Mountain oysters with fries. There's also a soup-and-salad bar.

124 W. Elkhorn Ave. © **970/586-2044.** Sandwiches and main courses $6.25–$7.50; whole pizzas $9–$24. AE, DISC, MC, V. Daily 11am–10pm summer; closed Tues and shorter hours the rest of the year.

ARTS & ENTERTAINMENT

It's impossible to get bored in Estes Park, where you'll find a wide variety of performing arts events—many of them free—presented year-round. You'll hear classical music—from small ensembles to symphony orchestras—plus jazz, country, and Christian; and see dance and theater. The community boasts a new (opened in 2003) outdoor entertainment venue—Estes Park Performance Park—on West Elkhorn Avenue on the west side of town. For details on what's going on when you plan to be in town, contact the **Cultural Arts Council of Estes Park,** 304 E. Elkhorn Ave. (P.O. Box 4135), Estes Park, CO 80517 (© **970/586-9203;** www.EstesArts.com), which represents a number of arts groups and individual artists, and helps coordinate many of the community's arts events. These include a free outdoor concert series (including music, theater, and dance) Thursdays at 7pm June through August at the Estes Park Performance Park; a dance festival in November; and Imagine This, a family-oriented festival of performing and visual arts, each February.

   Among individual organizations presenting live productions is the **Fine Arts Guild of the Rockies,** which sponsors musicals and plays; the **Estes Park Music Festival,** which presents a series of classical music concerts each summer; and the **Chamber Music Society of Estes Park,** offering three concerts in early October.

The **Lazy B Ranch,** 1915 Dry Gulch Rd. (© **800/228-2116** or 970/586-5371; www.lazybranchinestespark.homestead.com), serves a chuck-wagon supper—chicken or beef, beans, potatoes, and biscuits, as well as spice cake and peach halves for dessert—with a show of live cowboy music and comedy. There's also a program on the history of Western music. Cost is $17 for people over 12, $15 for those 10 to 12 years old, $10 for children 3 to 9, and free for kids under 3. To get there, take U.S. 34 east from Estes Park about 1½ miles, turn left at Sombrero Stables, and follow the signs. The ranch is open from late May through September, but the schedule varies, so call for specific times and days.

For live rock music and dancing on weekends, check out **Lonigan's Saloon,** 110 W. Elkhorn Ave. (© **970/586-4346;** www.lonigans.com).

GRAND LAKE

The western entrance to Rocky Mountain National Park is at the picturesque little town of Grand Lake, in the shade of Shadow Mountain at the park's southwestern corner.

Here, in the crisp mountain air at 8,370 feet above sea level, you can stroll down an old-fashioned boardwalk as one of the locals rides by on horseback. In fact, take away the automobiles and electric lights, and this town looks and feels like the late 1800s. Located within the Arapaho National Recreation Area, Grand Lake is surrounded by three lakes—Grand Lake, Shadow Mountain Reservoir, and Lake Granby—each with a marina that offers boating (with rentals), fishing, and other watersports. Throughout the recreation area you'll also find miles of trails for hiking, horseback riding, four-wheeling, and mountain biking that become cross-country skiing and snowmobiling trails in winter.

The Grand Lake Yacht Club hosts the **Grand Lake Regatta** and **Lipton Cup Races** in late July or early August. The club was organized in 1902, and the regatta began 10 years later. Sailboats from around the world compete to win the prestigious Lipton Cup, given to the club by Thomas Lipton in 1912. Other summer events include an enormous **Fourth of July fireworks display** over Grand Lake, and **Western Weekend,** with a buffalo barbecue, 5K run, and a pancake breakfast, in mid-July. The **Rocky Mountain Repertory Theatre** (© **970/627-3421** or 970/627-5087; www.rockymountainrep.com) offers a summer program of Broadway shows and other theater, plus programs for children and teens.

Usually open daily from 11am to 5pm in summer, the **Kauffman House,** 407 Pitkin Ave. (© **970/627-9644;** www.kauffmanhouse.org), is a log structure that was built as a hotel in 1892. It has been restored and now serves as the museum of the Grand Lake Historical Society, with many of its original furnishings and exhibits on what life was like here back when everyone arrived on horseback or by stagecoach. Admission is free, although donations are welcome.

Golfers may want to test their skills at the 18-hole championship **Grand Lake Golf Course** (© **970/627-8008**), altitude 8,420 feet. Greens fees are $60 for 18 holes.

For further information on what to do in this area, stop at the **Visitor Information Center** on U.S. 34 at the turnoff into town (open daily 9am–5pm in summer, with shorter hours the rest of the year), or contact the **Grand Lake Area Chamber of Commerce,** P.O. Box 57, Grand Lake, CO 80447-0057 (© **800/531-1019,** or 970/627-3402 visitor center; www.grandlakechamber. com). Information is also available from the Forest Service's **Sulphur Ranger District office** (P.O. Box 10, Granby, CO 80446), 9 Ten Mile Dr., off U.S. 40 about a half-mile south of Granby (© **970/887-4100;** www.fs.fed.us/r2), open in summer Monday through Saturday from 8am to 4:30pm (until 6pm Fri), with shorter hours in winter.

WHERE TO STAY

There are plenty of lodging possibilities in Grand Lake. A good source for information is the **Grand Lake Area Chamber of Commerce** (see address above). In addition to the properties discussed below, lodging possibilities here include the **Black Bear Lodge,** 12255 U.S. 34 (P.O. Box 609), Grand Lake, CO 80447 (✆ **970/627-3654;** www.blackbeargrandlake.com), which offers well-maintained basic motel rooms, some with kitchenettes, that cost $75 to $175 for two. Those seeking the intimacy of a bed-and-breakfast should consider **EG's Country Inn,** 1000 Grand Ave. (P.O. Box 1618), Grand Lake, CO 80447 (✆ **970/627-8404;** www.egscountryinn.com), which has three luxury rooms, each with a gas fireplace, phone, and combination TV/VCR. Two are spacious, with a king-size bed and whirlpool tub, and the smaller room has a queen bed and hand-painted claw-foot tub. Rates run from $125 to $165 double, and only children 8 and older are accepted.

Daven Haven Lodge ✿   Set among pine trees about a quarter-mile from the lake, this group of cabins is a good choice for those seeking peace and quiet in a secluded mountain resort–type setting. There's a welcoming stone fireplace in the lobby plus old Coke machines and several antique jukeboxes—they actually play 78 rpm records! The cabins vary in size, sleeping from two to eight people; each has its own picnic table and six have stone fireplaces. Decor and furnishings vary, but most have attractive light wood walls and solid wood and upholstered furniture. You'll also find a lovely patio, volleyball court, horseshoes, and a bonfire pit. The Back-Street Steakhouse (see "Where to Dine," below) serves dinner nightly in summer and 4 nights a week in winter. All cabins are nonsmoking.

604 Marina Dr. (P.O. Box 1528), Grand Lake, CO 80447. ✆ **970/627-8144.** Fax 970/627-5098. www.daven havenlodge.com. 16 cabins. $85–$135 for units for 2–4, $135–$195 for units for 5–8. DISC, MC, V. 3-night minimum required on reservations during holidays. **Amenities:** Restaurant (steakhouse). *In room:* TV, kitchen (no microwaves).

Grand Lake Lodge ★   At an elevation of 8,769 feet, Grand Lake Lodge claims to have Colorado's "favorite front porch," affording panoramic views of Grand Lake—both the town and the lake—and the surrounding mountains. Established in 1921, the Lodge has been owned and operated by three generations of the Ted L. James family since 1953. It offers excellent service and food in a delightful rustic setting, with sleeping quarters in cabins scattered among the pines beyond the Main Lodge.

Units range from single rooms (that sleep two) in a duplex cabin, to two rooms with fully equipped kitchenettes and either gas heat or a Franklin stove (these units sleep four to six). There is also one cabin that sleeps 10 ($350–$375 per night) and a two-story building that sleeps 25 ($625–$700 per night). There are no TVs, but why would you come here to watch television? There are decks, a playground, a picnic area with grills, riding stables, volleyball, horseshoes, hiking trails, a recreation room, Ping-Pong, and a pool table. All cabins are nonsmoking. For a review of the lodge's restaurant, see p. 256.

15500 U.S. 34 (P.O. Box 569), Grand Lake, CO 80447. ✆ **970/627-3967.** Fax 970/627-9495. www.grand lakelodge.com. 56 units. $80–$105 for units for 2, $155–$185 for units for 4–6 double. Minimum stays apply to most units, and all units on weekends and holidays. AE, DISC, MC, V. Closed mid-Sept to early June. Take U.S. 34 north ½ mile from Grand Lake (or ½ mile south of the park entrance) and turn east (watch for their sign) onto the entrance road. **Amenities:** Restaurant (American); bar; large outdoor heated pool; hot tub; game room; coin-op laundry. *In room:* No phone.

WHERE TO DINE

In addition to the restaurants discussed more fully below, a favorite of locals is the **Chuck Hole Cafe,** 1131 Grand Ave. (© **970/627-3509**), open daily from 7am to 2pm, serving basic American breakfasts (especially good omelets) and a variety of sandwiches, burgers, and salads for lunch ($4–$8).

Back-Street Steakhouse ⭐ STEAK   This cozy, country inn–style restaurant in the Daven Haven lodge (see above) offers fine dining in a down-home atmosphere. Steaks—from the 8-ounce filet mignon to the 12-ounce New York strip—are all USDA choice beef, cooked to perfection. The house specialty, Jack Daniel's pork chops (breaded, baked, and served with a creamy Jack Daniel's mushroom sauce), has been featured in *Bon Appétit* magazine. Also on the menu are pasta, chicken, and fish dishes, plus slow-roasted prime rib, and children's items. Sandwiches and light entrees, such as the smoked salmon and Creole fried oyster plate, are served in the lounge.

In the Daven Haven Lodge, 604 Marina Dr. © **970/627-8144**. www.davenhavenlodge.com. Reservations recommended in summer and on winter weekends. Main courses in the dining room $13–$29, lounge menu $6–$13. DISC, MC, V. Summer and Christmas holidays Sun–Fri 5–9pm, Sat 5–10pm; winter Wed–Sat 5–9pm. Closed Nov and Apr.

EG's Garden Grill NEW AMERICAN/SOUTHWESTERN   The large stone fireplace, trellised ceiling, and spacious outdoor beer garden give this restaurant a warm atmosphere. The menu offers innovative variations on traditional American dishes, often with a southwestern flair. Although the menu changes seasonally, house specialties usually include fish and seafood dishes, such as mustard catfish with jalapeño tartar sauce and jicama slaw, live Maine lobster, and tortilla-crusted ruby red trout. We particularly like the baby back ribs with EG's homemade barbecue sauce. There are also pizza, sandwiches, soups and salads, and a children's menu, plus a fairly extensive wine list.

1000 Grand Ave. © **970/627-8404**. www.egscountryinn.com. Main courses $6–$10 at lunch, $7–$28 at dinner. AE, DISC, MC, V. Summer daily 11am–9pm; winter closed Sun evening (call for exact hours) and Mon.

Grand Lake Lodge Restaurant AMERICAN   Come here to enjoy a lunch on the sunny front porch (see "Where to Stay" above) overlooking Grand Lake and Shadow Mountain Reservoir. The lunch menu includes soups and salads and favorites such as buffalo or Angus beef burgers, a buffalo Reuben, or the lobster-and-asparagus quiche. For dinner you might try one of the signature dishes, such as roasted pork loin with crabmeat and a wild-mushroom cream sauce, grilled duck breast with roasted plum-lavender sauce and toasted cashews, or the slow-roasted prime rib of beef with horseradish sauce. All desserts are baked in-house. Afternoon appetizers are available in the bar from 2:30 to 4:30pm daily.

15500 U.S. 34. © **970/627-3185**. www.grandlakelodge.com. Reservations required for dinner and Sun brunch. Main courses lunch $7.25–$8.95, dinner $16–$24. AE, DISC, MC, V. Mon–Sat 7:30–10am and 11:30am–2:30pm; Sun brunch 9am–1pm; dinner daily 5:30–9pm. Closed mid-Sept to early June. Take U.S. 34 north ½ mile from Grand Lake (or ½ mile south of the park entrance) and turn east (watch for their sign) onto the entrance road.

2 Rocky Mountain National Park ⭐⭐⭐

Snow-covered peaks—17 mountains above 13,000 feet—stand over lush valleys and shimmering alpine lakes in the 415 square miles (265,727 acres) that comprise Rocky Mountain National Park. The highest, at 14,259 feet, is Longs Peak.

Rocky Mountain National Park

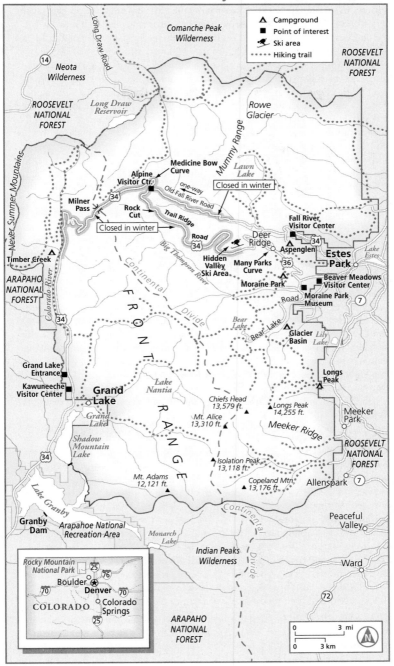

Legend:
- ▲ Campground
- ■ Point of interest
- 🎿 Ski area
- ⋯ Hiking trail

Comanche Peak Wilderness

ROOSEVELT NATIONAL FOREST

14 Neota Wilderness

ROOSEVELT NATIONAL FOREST

Long Draw Road

Long Draw Reservoir

Rowe Glacier

Mummy Range

Lawn Lake

Medicine Bow Curve

Alpine Visitor Ctr.

one-way
Old Fall River Road

Closed in winter

Milner Pass

Rock Cut

34

Trail Ridge

Closed in winter

Trail Ridge Road
34

Big Thompson River

Deer Ridge

Fall River Visitor Center

34

Aspenglen

Estes Park

Lake Estes

Hidden Valley Ski Area

Many Parks Curve

36

Moraine Park

Beaver Meadows Visitor Center

7

Timber Creek

ARAPAHO NATIONAL FOREST

Colorado River

Continental

Divide

Moraine Park Museum

Road

Bear Lake

Bear Lake

Glacier Basin

Lily Lake

34

FRONT

Grand Lake Entrance

Kawuneeche Visitor Center

Grand Lake

Grand Lake

Lake Nantia

Longs Peak

Chiefs Head 13,579 ft.

Longs Peak 14,255 ft.

Meeker Park

Mt. Alice 13,310 ft.

Meeker Ridge

ROOSEVELT NATIONAL FOREST

Shadow Mountain Lake

RANGE

34

Isolation Peak 13,118 ft.

Allenspark

7

Mt. Adams 12,121 ft.

Copeland Mtn. 13,176 ft.

Lake Granby

Granby Dam

Arapahoe National Recreation Area

Monarch Lake

Indian Peaks Wilderness

Continental

Divide

Peaceful Valley

Ward

72

ARAPAHO NATIONAL FOREST

0   3 mi
0   3 km

Rocky Mountain National Park

25

76

Boulder

70

Denver

70

Colorado Springs

COLORADO

25

But what really sets the park apart (after all, this sort of eye-popping beauty is not unusual in the Rockies) is its variety of distinct ecological zones. As you rise and descend in altitude, the landscape of the park changes dramatically. In relatively low areas, from about 7,500 to 9,000 feet, a lush forest of ponderosa pine and juniper cloaks the sunny southern slopes, with Douglas fir on the cooler northern slopes. Thirstier blue spruce and lodgepole pine cling to streamsides, with occasional groves of aspen. Elk and mule deer thrive. On higher slopes, a subalpine ecosystem exists, dominated by forests of Engelmann spruce and subalpine fir, but it's interspersed with wide meadows covered with wildflowers during spring and summer. The park is also home to bighorn sheep, which have become unofficial mascots of the park. Above 11,500 feet, the trees become increasingly gnarled and stunted, until they disappear altogether and alpine tundra predominates. Fully one-third of the park is at this altitude, and in this bleak, rocky world, many of the plants are identical to those found in the Arctic.

Trail Ridge Road ★★, the park's primary east–west roadway, is one of America's great alpine highways. It cuts west through the middle of the park from Estes Park, then south down its western boundary to Grand Lake. Climbing to 12,183 feet near Fall River Pass, it's the highest continuous paved highway in the United States. The road is usually open from Memorial Day into October, depending on snowfall. The 48-mile scenic drive from Estes Park to Grand Lake takes about 3 hours, allowing for stops at numerous scenic outlooks.

Fall River Road, the original park road, leads to Fall River Pass from Estes Park via Horseshoe Park. West of the Endovalley picnic area, the road is one-way uphill, and is closed to trailers and motor homes. As you negotiate its gravelly switchbacks, you get a clear idea of what early auto travel was like in the West. This road, too, is closed in winter. One of the few paved roads in the Rockies that leads into a high mountain basin is **Bear Lake Road;** it is kept open year-round, with occasional half-day closings to clear snow. Numerous trails converge at Bear Lake, southwest of the Park Headquarters/Visitor Center, via Moraine Park.

JUST THE FACTS

ENTRY POINTS   Entry into the park is from either the east (through the town of Estes Park) or the west (through the town of Grand Lake). The east and west sides of the park are connected by Trail Ridge Road, open during summer and early fall, but closed to all motor vehicle traffic by snow the rest of the year. Most visitors enter the park from the Estes Park side. The **Beaver Meadows Entrance,** west of Estes Park via U.S. 36, leads to the Beaver Meadows Visitor Center and park headquarters, and is the most direct route to Trail Ridge Road. U.S. 34 west from Estes Park takes you to the Fall River Visitor Center, just outside the park, and into the park via the **Fall River Entrance,** which is north of the Beaver Meadows Entrance. From there you can access Old Fall River Road or Trail Ridge Road. Those entering the park from the west side should take U.S. 40 to Granby and then follow U.S. 34 north to the **Grand Lake Entrance.**

GETTING AROUND   June through Labor Day, a free national-park **shuttle bus** runs from the Glacier Basin parking area to Bear Lake, with departures every 15 to 30 minutes.

FEES & REGULATIONS   Park admission for up to a week costs $20 per vehicle or $5 per person for motorcyclists, bicyclists, and pedestrians.

As is true for most of the national parks, wilderness permits are required for all overnight backpacking trips, and camping is allowed only in specified camp-sites. Pets must be leashed, and aren't permitted on trails or into the backcoun-try. Both motor vehicles and bicycles must remain on roads or in parking areas. Do not feed or touch any park animals, and do not pick any wildflowers.

VISITOR CENTERS & INFORMATION   Entering the park on U.S. 36 from Estes Park, the **Beaver Meadows Visitor Center** (℗ **970/586-1206**) has knowledgeable people to answer questions and give advice, a wide choice of books and maps for sale, and interpretive exhibits, including a relief model of the park and an audiovisual program. This center is open daily from 8am to 6pm, year-round.

Just outside the park, on U.S. 34 and just east of the Fall River entrance, is the **Fall River Visitor Center** (℗ **970/586-1206**). Located in a beautiful mountain lodge–style building, it is staffed by park rangers and volunteers from the Rocky Mountain Nature Association. It contains exhibits on park wildlife, including some spectacular full-size bronzes of elk and other animals, plus information and a bookstore. Next door is a large (but somewhat pricey) sou-venir and clothing shop plus a cafeteria-style restaurant with snacks and sand-wiches. Hours are from 9am to 6pm daily.

Near the park's west side entrance is the **Kawuneeche Visitor Center** (℗ **970/586-1513**), open daily from 8am to 6pm year-round. Located high in the mountains (11,796 ft. above sea level) is the **Alpine Visitor Center** (℗ **970/586-1206**), at Fall River Pass, open from late June to early October, daily from 9am to 5pm, with shorter hours toward the end of the season; exhibits here explain life on the alpine tundra. Visitor facilities are also available at the **Moraine Park Museum** (℗ **970/586-1206**) on Bear Lake Road on the east side of the park, open from mid-April to mid-October, daily from 9am to 5pm.

For more specifics on planning a trip, contact Rocky Mountain National Park, 1000 U.S. 36, Estes Park, CO 80517-8397 (℗ **970/586-1206;** www.nps.gov/romo). You can also get detailed information from the **Rocky Mountain Nature Association,** Rocky Mountain National Park, Estes Park, CO 80517 (℗ **800/816-7662** or 970/586-0108; www.rmna.org), which sells a variety of maps, guides, books, and videos. Those who would like to help this nonprofit association, and receive a 15% discount on purchases at this and most other national parks and monuments, can become members. Memberships cost $25 for individuals and $35 for families.

SEASONS   Even though the park is technically open daily year-round, Trail Ridge Road, the main east–west thoroughfare through the park, is almost always closed in winter, by about mid- to late October. The road is usually open by late May (after the snow has been cleared), but it is not uncommon for snowstorms to close the road for several hours or even a full day at any time, especially in early June and October. The high country is open during the summer and as snow conditions permit in winter.

AVOIDING THE CROWDS   Because large portions of the park are closed in winter, most people visit the park from late spring through early fall. The busiest period, though, is from mid-June to mid-August. In order to avoid the largest crowds, try to visit just before or just after that period. For those who don't mind chilly evenings, late September and early October are less crowded and can be beautiful, although there's always the chance of an early winter storm. Regard-less of when you visit, the absolute best way to avoid crowds is by putting on a

---

Tips   **Trail Ridge Road Construction**

The higher portions of Trail Ridge Road (U.S. 36 between Estes Park and Grand Lake), will be undergoing repairs throughout the summer and fall seasons of 2005 and 2006. This will cause delays on weekdays plus night closures, most probably Sunday through Thursday nights. It is anticipated that there will be no delays on weekends or federal holidays. Because Trail Ridge Road crests at 12,183 feet, the road repair season is very short and coincides with the same months (late May into Oct) that the road is free of snow but full of visitor vehicles. Upon arrival, check the park newspaper and ask at a visitor center for specifics during your visit. Before arrival you can check the park website (see "Visitor Centers & Information," above).

---

backpack or climbing onto a horse. Rocky Mountain has 346 miles of trails leading into all corners of the park (see "Sports & Outdoor Activities," below).

RANGER PROGRAMS   Evening programs take place at campground amphitheaters, and additional talks and other programs are offered at visitor centers between June and September. Consult the park's free *High Country Headlines* newspaper for scheduled activities, which vary from photo walks to fly-fishing and orienteering.

SEEING THE HIGHLIGHTS

Although Rocky Mountain National Park is generally considered the domain of hikers and climbers, it's surprisingly easy to thoroughly enjoy this park without working up a sweat. For that we can thank **Trail Ridge Road.** Built in 1932 and undoubtedly one of America's most scenic highways, it provides expansive and sometimes dizzying views in all directions. The drive from Estes Park to Grand Lake covers some 48 miles through the park, rising above 12,000 feet in elevation and crossing the Continental Divide. It offers spectacular vistas of snow-capped peaks, deep forests, and meadows of wildflowers, where bighorn sheep, elk, and deer browse. Allow at least 3 hours for the drive, and possibly more if you'd like to take a short hike from one of the many vista points.

To get a close look at the tundra, pull off Trail Ridge Road into the **Rock Cut** parking area (elevation 12,110 ft.), about halfway along the scenic drive. The views of glacially carved peaks along the Continental Divide are spectacular, and signs on the half-mile Tundra Nature Trail identify the hardy plants and animals that inhabit the region and explain how they have adapted to the harsh environment.

SPORTS & OUTDOOR ACTIVITIES

Rocky Mountain National Park is a fantastic area for a variety of outdoor activities, and many activities also take place just outside the park in the 1,240-square-mile Roosevelt National Forest. Obtain information on hiking, horseback riding, fishing, and other activities in advance from the **Canyon Lakes Ranger District Office,** 1311 S. College Ave., Fort Collins, CO 80524 (© **970/498-2770;** www.fs.fed.us/r2). In Estes Park, a **Forest Service Information Center** is located at 161 Second St. (© **970/586-3440**); it's usually open daily from 9am to 5pm in summer.

BICYCLING   Bicyclists share the park roadways with motor vehicles along narrow roads with 5% to 7% grades, and, like most national parks, bikes are not permitted off established roads. However, bicyclists still enjoy the challenge and scenery. One popular 16-mile ride is the **Horseshoe Park/Estes Park Loop,** which goes from Estes Park west on U.S. 34 past Aspenglen Campground and the park's Fall River entrance and visitor center, circles around Horseshoe Park, and then heads east again at the Deer Ridge Junction, following U.S. 36 out through the Beaver Meadows park entrance. There are plenty of beautiful mountain views; allow from 1 to 3 hours. A free park brochure provides information on safety, regulations, and other suggested routes. Tours, rentals, and repairs are available at **Colorado Bicycling Adventures,** 184 E. Elkhorn Ave., Estes Park (© **970/586-4241;** www.coloradobicycling.com). Bike rentals are about $15 to $40 for a half-day and $23 to $60 for a full day, depending on the type of bike. The company also offers guided downhill trips in the park for about $65 per person, and leads a variety of free group bike rides in the Estes Park area from May through September (call or check the website for the current schedule).

CLIMBING & MOUNTAINEERING   **Colorado Mountain School,** 341 Moraine Ave. (P.O. Box 1846), Estes Park, CO 80517 (© **888/267-7783** or 970/586-5758; www.cmschool.com), is an AMGA-accredited year-round guide service, and the sole concessionaire for technical climbing and instruction in Rocky Mountain National Park. The school has programs for all ages; cost for a 2-day excursion is about $350. The school also offers lodging in a hostel-type setting, at about $25 per night per person. (See also "Hiking & Backpacking," below.) Be sure to stop at the ranger station at the Longs Peak trailhead for current trail and weather information before attempting to ascend Longs Peak.

EDUCATIONAL PROGRAMS   The **Rocky Mountain Nature Association** (see contact information under "Visitor Centers & Information," above), offers a wide variety of seminars and workshops, ranging from 1 full day to several days. Subjects vary but might include songbirds, flower identification, edible and medicinal herbs, painting, wildlife photography, tracking park animals, and edible mushrooms. Rates are about $35 for a half-day program, $65 for a full-day program, $135 for 2-day programs, and $165 for 3-day programs. There are also kids' programs; prices start at $15.

FISHING   Four species of trout are fished in national park and national forest streams and lakes: brown, rainbow, brook, and cutthroat. A state fishing license is required, and only artificial lures or flies are permitted in the park. A number of lakes and streams in the national park are closed to fishing, including Bear Lake; free park brochures listing open and closed bodies of water plus regulations and other information are available at visitor centers. A good source for fishing equipment sales and rentals, licenses, and tips on where they're biting is **Scot's Sporting Goods,** 870 Moraine Ave., Estes Park (© **970/586-2877**), open daily, May through September only.

HIKING & BACKPACKING   The park visitor centers offer topographic maps and hiking guides for sale, and rangers can direct you to lesser-used trails. You can also get maps and information, plus clothing and gear, at **Scot's Sporting Goods** (see "Fishing," above).

One particularly easy park hike is the **Alberta Falls Trail** from the Glacier Gorge Parking Area (a half-mile one-way), which rises in elevation only 160 feet as it follows Glacier Creek to pretty Alberta Falls.

A slightly more difficult option is the **Bierstadt Lake Trail,** accessible from the north side of Bear Lake Road about 6½ miles from Beaver Meadows. This 1.5-mile (one-way) trail climbs 566 feet through an aspen forest to Bierstadt Lake, where you'll find excellent views of Longs Peak.

Starting at Bear Lake, the trail up to **Emerald Lake** ⚒ offers spectacular scenery en route, past Nymph and Dream lakes. The half-mile hike to Nymph Lake is easy, climbing 225 feet; from there the trail is rated as moderate to Dream Lake (another half-mile) and then on to Emerald Lake (another .8 mile), which is 605 feet higher than the starting point at Bear Lake. Another moderate hike is the relatively uncrowded **Ouzel Falls Trail,** which leaves from Wild Basin Ranger Station and climbs about 950 feet to a picture-perfect waterfall. The distance one-way is 2.8 miles.

Among our favorite moderate hikes here is the **Mills Lake Trail** ⚒⚒, a 2.5-mile (one-way) hike, with a rise in elevation of about 700 feet. Starting from Glacier Gorge Junction, the trail goes up to a picturesque mountain lake nestled in a valley among towering mountain peaks. This lake is an excellent spot for photographing dramatic Longs Peak, especially in late afternoon or early evening, and it's the perfect place for a picnic.

If you prefer a more strenuous adventure, you'll work hard but be amply rewarded with views of timberline lakes and alpine tundra on the **Timber Lake Trail,** in the western part of the park. It's 4.8 miles one-way, with an elevation gain of 2,060 feet. Another strenuous trail, only for experienced mountain hikers and climbers in top physical condition, is the 8-mile (one-way) **East Longs Peak Trail,** which climbs some 4,855 feet along steep ledges and through narrows to the top of Longs Peak.

Backcountry permits (required for all overnight hikes) can be obtained ($20 May–Oct, free Nov–Apr) at Park Headquarters and ranger stations (in summer); for information call ✆ **970/586-1242.** There is a 7-night backcountry camping limit from June to September, with no more than 3 nights at any one spot. Tents are not permitted in the backcountry in the summer.

HORSEBACK RIDING   Many of the national park's trails are open to horseback riders. Several outfitters provide guided rides inside and outside the park, ranging from 1 hour (about $25) to all day (about $100), plus breakfast and dinner rides and multiday pack trips. Recommended companies include S.K. Horses (www.cowpokecornercorral.com), which operates **National Park Gateway Stables,** at the Fall River entrance of the national park on U.S. 34 (✆ **970/586-5269**), and the **Cowpoke Corner Corral,** at Glacier Lodge, 3 miles west of town, 2166 Colo. 66 (✆ **970/586-9272**). **Hi Country Stables** (www.colorado-horses.com/hicountrystables) operates two stables inside the park: **Glacier Creek Stables** (✆ **970/586-3244**) and **Moraine Park Stables** (✆ **970/586-2327**).

SKIING & SNOWSHOEING   During the winter, when deep snow covers roads and trails, much of the park is closed to vehicular travel (including snowmobiles). But this produces ideal conditions for those with cross-country skis or snowshoes to experience the park without the crowds. Snow conditions are usually best January through March. A popular spot for cross-country skiing and snowshoeing in the park is Bear Lake, south of the Beaver Meadows entrance. A lesser-known area of the park is **Wild Basin,** south of the park's east entrances off Colo. 7, about a mile north of the community of Allenspark. A 2-mile road, closed to motor vehicles for the last mile in winter, winds through a subalpine forest to the Wild Basin Trail, from which you follow a picturesque creek to a waterfall, a rustic bridge, and eventually another waterfall. Total distance to the second falls is 2.8 miles. Along the trail, your chances are good for spotting birds such as Clark's nutcrackers, Steller's jays, and the American dipper. On winter weekends, the Colorado Mountain Club often opens a warming hut at the Wild Basin Ranger Station. Before you set forth, stop by park headquarters for maps, information on where the snow is best, and a permit if you plan to stay out overnight. Ski rentals, instruction, and guide service are available from **Colorado Mountain School** (see contact information under "Climbing & Mountaineering," above). Rangers often lead guided snowshoe walks on winter weekends.

WILDLIFE VIEWING & BIRD-WATCHING   Rocky Mountain National Park is a premier wildlife viewing area. Fall, winter, and spring are the best times, although we saw plenty of elk and squirrels, plus a few deer, a marmot, and a coyote during a recent mid-July visit. Large herds of elk and bighorn sheep can often be seen in the meadows and on mountainsides. In addition, you may spot mule deer, beavers, coyotes, and river otters. Watch for moose among the willows on the west side of the park. In the forests are lots of songbirds and small mammals; particularly plentiful are gray and Steller's jays, Clark's nutcrackers, chipmunks, and golden-mantled ground squirrels. There's a good chance of seeing bighorn sheep, marmots, pikas, and ptarmigan along Trail Ridge Road. For detailed and current wildlife viewing information, stop by one of the park's visitor centers, and check on the many interpretive programs, including bird walks. Rangers stress that it is both illegal and foolish to feed any wildlife. Not only do you risk personal injury or disease, but you also harm the animals by giving them food that is not good for them and making them dependent on humans.

CAMPING

The best place to camp for those visiting the national park is in the park itself. Although you won't have the modern conveniences of commercial campgrounds (see "Camping," in the "Estes Park & Grand Lake: Gateways to Rocky Mountain National Park" section, earlier in this chapter), you will have plenty of trees, an abundance of wildlife scurrying by your tent or RV, and a true national park experience. The park has five campgrounds with a total of 575 sites. Nearly half (247 sites) are at **Moraine Park;** another 150 are at **Glacier Basin.** Moraine Park, **Timber Creek** (98 sites), and **Longs Peak** (26 tent sites) are open year-round; Glacier Basin and **Aspenglen** (54 sites) are seasonal. Summer camping is limited to 3 days at Longs Peak and 7 days at other campgrounds; winter camping is limited to 14 days. Arrive early in summer if you hope to snare one of these first-come, first-served campsites.

Reservations for Moraine Park and Glacier Basin are accepted from Memorial Day through early September, and these campgrounds are usually completely booked well in advance. However, any sites not reserved (possibly because of cancellations) are available on a first-come, first-served basis. Contact the **National Park Reservation Service** (✆ **800/365-2267** or 301/722-1257; http://reservations.nps.gov). The other campgrounds are available on a first-come, first-served basis only. Campsites cost $20 per night during the summer, and $12 in the off season when water is turned off. No showers or RV hookups are available.

3 Steamboat Springs ⭐⭐

158 miles NW of Denver, 194 miles E of Grand Junction, 335 miles E of Salt Lake City, Utah

One of our favorite Colorado resort towns, in part because it's a real town in addition to being a resort, Steamboat Springs fuses two very different worlds— a state-of-the-art ski village with a genuine Western ranching center. This historic town, with a population of just under 10,000, is a pleasant laid-back community where ranchers still go about their business in cowboy boots and Stetsons, seemingly unaware of the fashion statement they are making to city-slicker visitors.

At an elevation of 6,695 feet, Steamboat Springs's numerous mineral springs and abundant wild game made this a summer retreat for Utes centuries before the arrival of white settlers. Mid-19th-century trappers swore they heard the chugging sound of "a steamboat comin' round the bend" until investigation revealed a bubbling mineral spring. Prospectors never thrived here as they did elsewhere in the Rockies, though coal mining has proven profitable. Ranching and farming were the economic mainstays until tourism arrived, and agriculture remains of key importance today.

But this area is perhaps best known as the birthplace of organized skiing in Colorado. Although miners, ranchers, and mail carriers used primitive skis as a means of transportation as early as the late 1880s, it wasn't until Norwegian ski-jumping and cross-country champion Carl Howelsen built Howelsen Hill ski jump here in 1914 that skiing began to be considered a recreational sport in Colorado. In 1963, Storm Mountain was developed for skiing, and Steamboat's future as a modern ski resort was ensured. The mountain was renamed Mount Werner after the 1964 avalanche death in Europe of Olympic skier Buddy Werner, a Steamboat Springs native. Today the mountain is managed by the Steamboat Ski & Resort Corporation and, more often than not, is simply called Steamboat. Howelsen Hill, owned by the city of Steamboat Springs, continues to operate as a facility for ski jumpers, as well as a fun little downtown ski area.

ESSENTIALS

GETTING THERE   By Car   The most direct route to Steamboat Springs from Denver is via I-70 west 68 miles to Silverthorne, Colo. 9 north 38 miles to Kremmling, and U.S. 40 west 52 miles to Steamboat. (*Note:* Rabbit Ears Pass, 25 miles east of Steamboat, can be treacherous in winter.) If you're traveling east on I-70, exit at Rifle, proceed 88 miles north on Colo. 13 to Craig, then take U.S. 40 east 42 miles to Steamboat. For statewide **road-condition reports,** call ✆ **303/639-1111.**

By Plane   The **Yampa Valley Regional Airport,** 22 miles west of Steamboat Springs near Hayden (✆ **970/276-3669;** www.co.routt.co.us and follow links), is served by **United Airlines** (✆ **800/241-6522**) with year-round commuter service from Denver and **Continental Airlines** (✆ **800/525-0280**) with summer service to Houston. During the winter, direct flights to major U.S. cities are available from **United** and **Continental** (see above), plus **American Airlines** (✆ **800/433-7300**), **Delta Airlines** (✆ **800/221-1212**), and **Northwest Airlines** (✆ **800/225-2525**).

Ground transportation from Yampa Valley Regional Airport is provided by **Alpine Taxi** (✆ **800/343-7433** or 970/879-2800; www.alpinetaxi.com); the cost is $44 per adult, $22 per child round-trip. The company also offers shuttle service between Steamboat and Denver International Airport. Car-rental

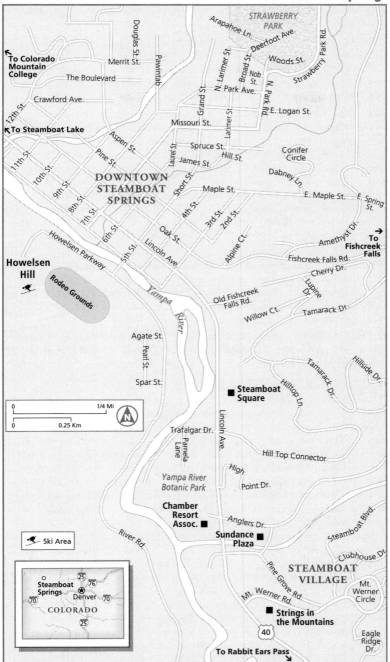

STRAWBERRY PARK

Arapahoe Ln.

Deerfoot Ave.

Woods St.

Strawberry Park Rd.

Douglas St.

Merrit St.

To Colorado
Mountain
College

Pawintab

The Boulevard

N. Larimer St.

Broad St.

Nob St.

N. Park Rd.

Park Ave.

E. Logan St.

Crawford Ave.

Grand St.

To Steamboat Lake

Missouri St.

Aspen St.

Larimer St.

Conifer Circle

Pine St.

Spruce St.

Hill St.

Dabney Ln.

11th St.

Laurel St.

James St.

10th St.

9th St.

DOWNTOWN
STEAMBOAT
SPRINGS

Short St.

Maple St.

E. Maple St.

E. Spring St.

8th St.

7th St.

4th St.

3rd St.

2nd St.

6th St.

Oak St.

Alpine Ct.

Amethyst Dr.

To
Fishcreek
Falls

5th St.

Lincoln Ave.

Fishcreek Falls Rd.

Howelsen Parkway

Cherry Dr.

Howelsen
Hill

Rodeo Grounds

Yampa River

Old Fishcreek
Falls Rd.

Lupine Dr.

Willow Ct.

Tamarack Dr.

Agate St.

Tamarack Dr.

Hillside Dr.

Pearl St.

Spar St.

■ Steamboat
Square

Hilltop Ln.

0   1/4 Mi

0   0.25 Km

N

Trafalgar Dr.

Pamela Lane

Lincoln Ave.

Hill Top Connector

Yampa River
Botanic Park

High

Point Dr.

Steamboat Blvd.

■ Chamber
Resort
Assoc. ■

Anglers Dr.

Sundance ■
Plaza

Ski Area

River Rd.

STEAMBOAT
VILLAGE

Clubhouse Dr.

Steamboat
Springs

25

76

Denver

70

COLORADO

25

70

Pine Grove Rd.

Mt. Werner Rd.

Mt.
Werner
Circle

■ Strings in
the Mountains

40

Eagle
Ridge
Dr.

To Rabbit Ears Pass

agencies at the airport include **Avis** (© 970/276-4377) and **Hertz** (© 800/654-3131).

VISITOR INFORMATION The **Steamboat Springs Chamber Resort Association,** 1255 S. Lincoln Ave. (P.O. Box 774408), Steamboat Springs, CO 80477 (© **970/879-0880;** www.steamboatchamber.com and www.steamboat summer.com), operates a visitor center, open in summer from 8am to 5pm Monday through Friday and from 10am to 4pm Saturday.

GETTING AROUND There are really two Steamboats. The ski resort, known as Steamboat Village, is about 2 miles southeast of the historic Steamboat Springs. If you're coming from Denver, U.S. 40 approaches Steamboat from the south and parallels the Yampa River through town. Mount Werner Road, which turns east off U.S. 40, leads directly to the ski resort, centered around Mount Werner Circle and Ski Time Square. U.S. 40 is known as Lincoln Avenue through the town of Steamboat, where it is crossed by 3rd through 13th streets. **Steamboat Springs Transit** (© 970/879-3717) provides free rides throughout the area. Buses run approximately every 20 to 30 minutes during peak hours; less frequently at other times. **Alpine Taxi** (see above) provides local taxi service.

FAST FACTS The **Yampa Valley Medical Center,** 1024 Central Park Dr. (© **970/879-1322;** www.yvmc.org), provides 24-hour medical service, a child care center, and a sports medicine center. The **post office** is at 200 Lincoln Ave. For hours and other information contact the U.S. Postal Service (© **800/275-8777;** www.usps.com).

SPECIAL EVENTS Winter Carnival, early February; Steamboat Marathon, early June; Cowboy Roundup Days, Fourth of July weekend; Fall Foliage and Brew Festival, mid-September.

SKIING & OTHER WINTER ACTIVITIES

STEAMBOAT ★★ When devoted skiers talk about Steamboat, they practically invent adjectives to describe its incredibly light powder.

Six peaks comprise the ski area: Mount Werner, Christie, Storm, Sunshine, Pioneer Ridge, and Thunderhead. Christie Peak, the lower mountain area, is ideal for beginners. Thunderhead Peak, served by a high-speed detachable quad chairlift called the Thunderhead Express and the gondola, is great for intermediate and advanced skiers and riders. Arrowhead Glade provides an advanced playground for everybody. The Morningside Park lift accesses the extreme double black diamond terrain—chutes, advanced mogul runs, powder bowls, and one-of-a-kind tree skiing, all from the top of Mount Werner. Buddy's Run, one of the Rockies' great intermediate cruisers, is located on Storm Peak. The most famous tree runs—Shadows, Closet, and Twilight—are on Sunshine Peak, along with more bump runs and cruising slopes. Morningside Park includes 179 acres on the back of Storm Peak, with intermediate to advanced terrain served by a triple chair.

The vertical drop here is one of the highest in Colorado: 3,668 feet from the 10,568-foot summit. Skiable terrain of 2,939 acres (61% groomable) includes 142 named runs, served by 20 lifts—an eight-passenger high-speed gondola, four high-speed quad chairs, one conventional quad, six triple chairs, six double chairs, and two surface lifts. Trails are rated 13% beginner, 56% intermediate, and 31% advanced; the longest run is Why Not, at over 3 miles.

Daily lift tickets cost $68 to $74 for adults, $54 to $65 for teenagers, $38 to $46 for children 6 to 12, $41 to $46 for seniors 65 to 69, $25 for seniors 70 and over, and free for children 5 and younger. The rates are lowest at the beginning of the season, highest during the Christmas–New Years holidays, and a bit lower the rest of the season. Lessons and rentals are available.

Steamboat is a great mountain for snowboarders, who especially love Mavericks Superpipe, which is 50 feet wide and 650 feet long, with 15-foot walls and a 17-foot transition!

Steamboat is usually open from the third week in November through mid-April, daily from 8:30am to 4pm. For further information, contact **Steamboat Ski & Resort Corporation,** 2305 Mt. Werner Circle, Steamboat Springs, CO 80487 (© **877/237-2658** or 970/879-6111; www.steamboat.com). For daily **ski reports,** check the resort's website (listed above) or dial © **970/879-7300.**

HOWELSEN HILL 🐾   In addition to Steamboat, there's Howelsen Hill (© **970/879-8499** or 970/879-4300), which has remained open every winter since its first day in 1915, making it the oldest ski area in continuous use in Colorado. The first accredited public-school ski classes in North America were taught on this slope, which is operated by the city of Steamboat Springs. It offers both day and night skiing and snowboarding on its 30 acres of terrain served by a double chair, a Poma lift, and a pony tow. There are 15 trails (the longest is 1 mile) and one half-pipe, and Howelsen Hill rises 440 feet to a 7,136-foot summit elevation.

Tickets are $15 for adults and $8 for children 18 and under and seniors 60 and older, and $5 for everyone for night skiing (5–8pm Tues–Thurs). It's usually open from late November through late March: Monday and Friday noon to 6pm, Tuesday and Thursday noon to 8pm, Wednesday 9am to 8pm, Saturday and Sunday 9am to 4pm.

Howelsen Hill has bred more North American skiers for international competition than any other ski resort—primarily because of its ski-jumping complex. The U.S. ski-jumping team trains each year on the 20m, 30m, 50m, 70m, and 90m jumps. Training and a variety of special events, including a Thursday night race series for adults and a Wednesday youth jumping series, are organized by the **Steamboat Springs Winter Sports Club** (© **970/879-0695;** www.sswsc.org), which was founded in 1914 and claims to be the oldest U.S. ski club west of the Mississippi River.

CROSS-COUNTRY SKIING, TELEMARK SKIING, SNOWSHOEING & ICE CLIMBING   Seasoned cross-country skiers swear by the **Steamboat Ski Touring Center** at the Sheraton Steamboat Resort (© **970/879-8180;** www.nordicski.net). Some 30km of groomed cross-country trails are set across the fairways beside Fish Creek, near the foot of the mountain; there are also 10 km of snowshoe trails. A full-day adult trail pass costs $14 a day; full-day passes for children 12 and under and seniors 65 and older are $8. Equipment rentals and lessons are available. Trails are open daily during the ski season from 9am to 4pm. To get to the center follow the signs off Mt. Werner Road.

There are also cross-country trails at **Howelsen Hill** (see above). Popular cross-country ski trails in nearby national forest land include **Rabbit Ears Pass,** 25 miles east of Steamboat on U.S. 40, and **Dunkley Pass,** 25 miles south on Colo. 131. For trail maps and information, contact **Medicine Bow–Routt National Forest,** Hahns Peak/Bears Ears Ranger Station, 925 Weiss Dr., Steamboat Springs, CO 80487-9315 (© **970/879-1870;** www.fs.fed.us/r2).

Snowshoeing is gaining in popularity. There are numerous spots ideal for snowshoeing in the surrounding national forests, as well as at Steamboat Ski

Touring Center (see above). Snowshoe and cross country ski rentals are available at several outlets, including **Straightline Sports** (see "Fishing," below).

ICE DRIVING ⭐ Okay all you NASCAR fans, you think you're great drivers? (Almost) any wimp can drive on dry pavement, but how good are you when your car's sliding down a sheet of ice? This is the place to find out. America's first (and only) school of ice driving is based at the foot of Mount Werner. Bridgestone Winter Driving School teaches safe winter driving the smartest way possible—hands-on, on a 1-mile circuit packed with frozen water and snow, and guarded by high snow banks. Classes combine instruction with on-track practice, and are available for average drivers as well as professionals. Classes include a half-day introductory course ($155) and the most popular—a full-day course for $285. There's also a 2-day performance course for $1,550. The school is open daily from mid-December to early March, and reservations are recommended. Contact **Bridgestone Winter Driving School,** 1850 Ski Time Square Dr. (P.O. Box 774167), Steamboat Springs, CO 80477 (✆ **800/949-7543** or 970/879-6105; www.winterdrive.com).

ICE SKATING   The Howelsen Ice Arena, 243 Howelsen Pkwy. (✆ **970/879-0341** or 970/871-1152; www.ci.steamboat.co.us/recreation/icerink/howelice.htm), is an enclosed Olympic-size ice arena open year-round that has open skating hours; rents skates; offers lessons in hockey and figure skating; organizes figure-skating, ice-hockey and broom-ball competitions; and hosts birthday parties. Admission is $5.50 adults, $5 youths 6 to 18, $3 for seniors 50 and older, and free for children 5 and younger. Skate rentals are $3 ($2 for seniors 50 and older), and skate sharpening costs $5. Call for the rink schedule.

SNOWMOBILING   Snowmobilers consider the **Continental Divide Trail,** running over 50 miles from Buffalo Pass north of Steamboat to Gore Pass, west of Kremmling, to be one of the finest maintained trails in the Rockies, with some of the most spectacular scenery you'll see anywhere. For information, check with **Medicine Bow–Routt National Forest** (see "**Cross-Country Skiing, Telemark Skiing, Snowshoeing, & Ice Climbing**" above).

Among those offering guided snowmobile tours is **Steamboat Lake Outfitters,** P.O. Box 749, Clark, CO 80428 (✆ **800/342-1889** or 970/879-4404; www.steamboatoutfitters.com), which boasts that it has the largest snowmobile trail system in Colorado. The cost is $90 for one person plus $50 for a passenger for a 2-hour ride, $140 for one person and $60 for a passenger for a half-day ride with lunch, $200 for one person (no passenger allowed) for a full-day tour with lunch. Dinner rides and overnight trips are also offered. Other companies offering snowmobile tours include **High Mountain Snowmobile Tours** (✆ **970/879-9073**) and **Steamboat Snowmobile Tours** (✆ **970/879-6500**), at similar rates.

WARM-WEATHER & YEAR-ROUND ACTIVITIES

Most outdoor recreation pursuits are enjoyed in 1.1-million-acre **Routt National Forest,** which virtually surrounds Steamboat Springs and offers opportunities for camping, hiking, backpacking, mountain biking, horseback riding, fishing, and hunting. For trail maps and information, contact **Medicine Bow–Routt National Forest,** Hahns Peak/Bears Ears Ranger Station, 925 Weiss Dr., Steamboat Springs, CO 80477 (✆ **970/879-1870;** www.fs.fed.us/r2).

Two wilderness areas in the forest are easily reached from Steamboat. Immediately north of town is the **Mount Zirkel Wilderness Area,** a region of rugged peaks approached through 10,800-foot Buffalo Pass, on Forest Road 60 off

Strawberry Park Road via Seventh Street. Southwest of Stillwater Reservoir, some 40 miles south of Steamboat via Colo. 131 through Yampa, is the **Flat Tops Wilderness Area,** with picturesque alpine meadows and sheer volcanic cliffs. No motorized vehicles or mountain bikes are allowed in wilderness areas, although horses and dogs are permitted (dogs must be leashed in some areas).

Howelsen Hill (© **970/879-8499** or 970/879-4300; www.ci.steamboat. co.us/recreation/howelsen.htm) offers several warm-weather activities. You'll find a BMX and skateboard park, tennis, softball, volleyball, horseback riding, and mountain biking, plus the rodeo grounds (see below). In addition, an alpine slide, which operates daily from 10am until dusk during the summer, has a 2,400-foot dual track down the face of Howelsen Hill. For current rates and other information, contact the **Steamboat Springs Winter Sports Club** (© **970/879-0695;** www.sswsc.org).

The **Steamboat Ski Resort** doesn't go into hibernation after the snow melts, it just changes its focus, offering hiking, mountain biking, gondola rides, disc golf, and a multitude of other activities, including many that are great for kids. For information check with **Steamboat Ski & Resort Corporation** (see "Skiing & Other Winter Activities," above).

Some 28 miles north of Steamboat Springs on Routt C.R. 129 is **Steamboat Lake State Park** (© **970/879-3922;** www.parks.state.co.us), encompassing 1,053-acre Steamboat Lake. At an elevation of 8,000 feet, activities include summer camping (198 campsites with fees of $12–$18 plus the $5 park entrance fee; camping reservations are available for an extra charge of $7 by calling © **800/ 678-2267** or through the state park website), picnicking, fishing, hunting, boating, swimming, canoeing, horseback riding, and nature walks. There's an attractive sandy beach (the sand was trucked in) and three boat-launching ramps. In winter, the park offers ice fishing, cross-country skiing, snowmobiling, and snowshoeing. Day-use fee is $5 per vehicle.

Steamboat Lake Marina (© **970/879-7019;** www.steamboatlakemarina. com), open year-round, has a small store with a deli—be sure to sample the especially good homemade fudge—plus groceries, fishing supplies, equipment rentals, boat fuel, and boat rentals. Canoes, kayaks, and paddleboats rent for $15 per hour, small fishing boats are $40 for 2 hours; 20-foot pontoon boats cost $100 for 2 hours; and 24-foot pontoon boats cost $140 for 2 hours. Pontoon boats are either outfitted for fishing or have barbecue grills (yes, you can fish from a boat with a grill—then you've got a grill for cooking your catch!) Rates for powerboats include fuel. Boat reservations are strongly recommended.

The marina also has 10 camper cabins that have coffeemakers, small refrigerators, and a shared bathhouse. The nightly rate is $60 for two, and $5 for each additional person or pet.

Stagecoach State Park (© **970/736-2436;** www.parks.state.co.us), south of Steamboat Springs, offers camping, picnicking, fishing, boating, and other watersports. From Steamboat Springs, head 3 miles south on U.S. 40 to Colo. 131, turn southwest (right) and go about 6 miles to Routt C.R. 14, turn south (left) about 5 miles to the park entrance. The main attraction here is a 780-acre reservoir, which is set among rolling hills, interspersed with forests and grasslands. The reservoir is fairly evenly divided for water-skiing and wakeless boating. The park has 92 campsites in four campgrounds, and two campgrounds have electric hookups. Camping fees are $12 to $18, plus the day-use fee of $5 per vehicle that everyone going to the park must pay. Camping reservations are available for an extra charge of $7 by calling (© **800/678-2267** or through the state park website above). The elevation at the park is 7,250 feet.

Stagecoach Marina (© 970/736-8342), usually open from mid-May through mid-September, has a store with fishing and camping supplies, plus boat fuel and boat rentals. Rates are highest Friday through Sunday, when canoes rent for $15 per hour, kayaks and paddleboats cost $13 an hour, small fishing boats are $35 for 2 hours, 20-foot pontoon boats are $83 for 2 hours, and 24-foot pontoon boats cost $100 for 2 hours. There are 30% discounts Monday through Thursday, and also discounts for longer time periods. Reservations are recommended.

The Steamboat Springs Chamber Resort Association produces a **trails map,** available at the information center on Lincoln Avenue, showing which trails are open to what sport: biking, horseback riding, hiking, 4WD, or ATVs. On the reverse side of the map are descriptions of several trails in the area.

ATV TOURS   For a quick, fun, and relatively easy way to see this area's beautiful backcountry, consider a guided trip on an all-terrain vehicle. **Steamboat Lake Outfitters,** P.O. Box 749, Clark, CO 80428 (© **800/342-1889** or 970/879-4404; www.steamboatoutfitters.com), leads rides along old mining roads into the mountains, offering splendid views of the Continental Divide and Mount Zirkel Wilderness Area. Rates for a 2-hour ride are $65 for a one-person ATV or $90 for a two-person machine, and half-day, full-day, and overnight rides are also offered.

BIKING & MOUNTAIN BIKING   The 5-mile, dual-surface **Yampa River Trail** connects downtown Steamboat Springs with Steamboat Village, and links area parks and national forest trails. The **Mount Werner Trail** links the river to the ski area, which has numerous slopes open to mountain bikers in summer. **Spring Creek Trail** climbs from Yampa River Park into Routt National Forest. Touring enthusiasts can try their road bikes on the 110-mile loop over Rabbit Ears and Gore passes, rated one of the 10 most scenic rides in America by *Bicycling* magazine. Another option, especially for those of us who don't believe that sweating our way up the side of a mountain is fun, is to take the Silver Bullet Gondola (see "Gondola Rides," below) into the mountains and then ride the more than 40 upper mountain trails. Mountain bike rentals are available at the top of the gondola (© **970/871-5252**), with $55 rates for 3 hours for an adult bike and slightly less for kids' bikes.

Stop at **Sore Saddle Cyclery** ✦✦, 1136 S. Yampa St. (© **970/879-1675;** www.soresaddle.com), for information on the best local trails (maps are on display), accessories, repairs, and rentals. Rentals are also available from **Sport-Stalker,** in Gondola Square at 2305 Mt. Werner Rd. (© **800/525-5520** or 970/879-0371). Rentals of basic mountain bikes cost $12 to $15 for a half-day and $17 to $20 for a full day, with hourly rates and multiday reductions generally available, and higher rates for fancier bikes.

CATTLE DRIVES ✦✦   The **Saddleback Ranch** ✦, on C.R. 179 about 14 miles southwest of Steamboat Springs (© **970/871-4697;** www.rockymountain fun.com/saddlehome.html), is a working cattle ranch—not some Hollywood-style dude ranch—that offers a genuine Old West experience. The ranch has some 1,500 head of cattle on its 7,200 acres, and participants join working cowboys in moving cattle from pasture to pasture and performing other ranching tasks that are still done the old-fashioned way. Horses, tack, slickers, and snacks are provided, and cost for a half-day on the trail is $65 for adults and $60 for youths from 8 to 16. Children under 8 are not permitted on the rides. The cattle drives are held from June through mid-September.

FISHING   The Steamboat Springs area and particularly the Yampa River has some of the best trout fishing in the state. All told, there are nearly 150 lakes and reservoirs and almost 600 miles of streams in Routt County, which surrounds Steamboat Springs. Trout—rainbow, brown, brook, and cutthroat—are prolific, and the Yampa River and Stagecoach Reservoir are known for northern pike as well. Especially popular is the 5-mile stretch of the Yampa in downtown Steamboat Springs that is designated a catch-and-release trout stream; the Yampa's northern pike, whitefish, and small mouth black crappy do not fall under the catch-and-release limitations.

Contact **Straightline Outdoor Sports,** 744 Lincoln Ave. (© **800/354-5463** or 970/879-7568; www.straightlinesports.com), for information, licenses, and either rental or purchase of equipment. Straightline also offers guide services (call for details).

GOLF   The golf season here usually runs May through October, or as long as the snow isn't falling. The 18-hole municipal **Haymaker Golf Course,** at the intersection of U.S. 40 and Colo. 131, east of Steamboat Springs (© **970/870-1846**), is a challenging links-style course with only 110 of its 233 acres used for fairways and greens. It conforms to the open-space philosophy of the Steamboat community, with native grasses, wetlands, and contours mimicking the surrounding valley and mountains. The greens fee during summer is $83 for 18 holes, and $54 at the beginning and end of the golfing season. Preferred tee times are available with lodging reservations at participating properties through Steamboat Central Reservations (© **800/922-2722**).

The course at the **Sheraton Steamboat Resort,** 2000 Clubhouse Dr. (© **970/879-1391**), designed by Robert Trent Jones, Jr. in 1972, is considered one of the Rockies' finest. The 18-hole, 6,906-yard course offers spectacular scenery and challenging fairways. Greens fees, including carts, are $75 to $100 for Sheraton guests, $75 to $135 for the public. The **Steamboat Golf Club,** 6 miles west of downtown Steamboat Springs along U.S. 40 (© **970/879-4295**), is a picturesque 9-hole course along the Yampa River, with greens fees of $36 for 9 holes and $54 for 18 holes.

GONDOLA RIDES   Summer visitors don't have to work hard to get up into the mountains above Steamboat—simply hop on the Silver Bullet Gondola (© **877/237-2628** or 970/879-0740; www.steamboat.com), which operates weekends in mid-June and mid-September, and daily from late June through early September. Prices for all-day passes are as follows: adults $17, seniors 65 and older $10, children 6 to 12 $7 (or $21 for one adult and one child 6–12), teens 13 to 17 $12, free for children 5 and younger. From the top of the gondola, hiking and mountain-biking trails can be accessed (see "Biking & Mountain Biking," above).

HIKING, BACKPACKING & MOUNTAINEERING   There are numerous trails in the **Mount Zirkel Wilderness Area,** immediately north of Steamboat, and the **Flat Tops Wilderness Area,** 48 miles southwest. An especially scenic 4-hour hike in the Flat Tops area takes you from Stillwater Reservoir to the Devil's Causeway, with unforgettable views. Contact the U.S. Forest Service (p. 267) for information. There are also hiking trails at Steamboat Ski Area, which are easily reached on the Silver Bullet Gondola (see "Gondola Rides," above).

HORSEBACK RIDING   Located behind the rodeo grounds in town (follow Fifth St. south from Lincoln Ave.) is **Sombrero Ranches** (© **970/879-2306;** www.sombrero.com), which offers 1- and 2-hour rides, breakfast rides, and special supervised rides for young children. Prices are $25 for an hour, $40 for the 2-hour and breakfast rides, and $20 for a half-hour lead-horse ride for kids.

Steamboat Lake Outfitters (see "ATV Tours," above) leads guided horseback tours at Steamboat Lake State Park, ranging from 1- and 2-hour rides ($35 and $40 per person, respectively) to half- and full-day rides, with lunch, for $95 and $160 per person, respectively. This company also offers breakfast and dinner rides plus pack trips and horseback fishing trips into nearby wilderness areas (call for details), and rents rooms and cabins (see "Where to Stay," below).

Dinner rides are offered during the summer by **Saddleback Ranch** (see "Cattle Drives," above), with a choice of New York strip steak, grilled chicken breast, or fresh-caught rainbow trout, plus all the extras. There's a 35-minute ride to the dinner site (transportation by hay wagon is also available), and the cost is $49 for adults and $39 for kids 6 to 16.

HOT SPRINGS   More than 150 mineral springs are located in and around the Steamboat Springs area. Several are located in city parks. Their healing and restorative qualities were recognized for centuries by Utes, and James Crawford, the area's first white settler, regularly bathed in Heart Spring and helped build the first log bathhouse over it in 1884.

Today, Heart Spring is part of the **Steamboat Springs Health & Recreation complex,** 136 Lincoln Ave. (✆ **970/879-1828;** www.sshra.org), in downtown Steamboat Springs. In addition to the man-made pools into which the spring's waters flow, there's a lap pool, water slide, spa, whirlpool, fitness center, tennis courts, and massage therapy. Pool admission is $7.50 for adults, $5 for youths 13 to 17, and $3.50 for children under 13 and seniors 62 and over. Suit and towel rentals are available. The complex is open year-round, Monday through Friday from 5:30am to 10pm, and Saturdays and Sundays from 8am to 9pm. The slide is open from noon to 6pm in summer and from 4 to 8pm in winter, and, in addition to the pool admission, costs $3 for five rides or $5 for 10 rides.

The **Hot Springs at Strawberry Park,** 44200 C.R. 36 (✆ **970/879-0342**), are 7 miles north of downtown (from Seventh St., follow the signs) up a rugged, rocky road navigable by regular cars in summer, but requiring four-wheel-drive in winter, and it's strongly recommended to ride the shuttle. The trip may be difficult, but it's a wonderful experience to spend a moonlit evening in a sandy-bottomed, rock-lined soaking pool, kept between 101° and 106°F (38°C–41°C), with snow piled high around you. The hot springs are open Sunday through Thursday from 10am to 10:30pm (no entry after 9:30pm except to shuttles); Friday and Saturday 10am to midnight (no entry after 10:30pm except to shuttles). Admission costs $10 adults, $5 youths 13 to 17, and $3 children 3 to 12. After dark, children under 18 are not permitted and clothing is optional. Massages are available, and rustic cabins and tent sites can be rented year-round (call for rates). There's a picnic area but no restaurant. Pets are not permitted.

RODEO   The **Steamboat Springs PRCA Summer ProRodeo Series** (✆ **970/879-0880;** www.steamboatrodeo.com) takes place each year from mid-June through late August at the Romick Rodeo Arena in Howelsen Park, at the corner of Fifth Street and Howelsen Parkway. Professional rodeo cowboys and cowgirls (or should that be cowpersons?) compete in bull riding, bareback and saddle bronc riding, steer wrestling, calf roping, team roping, and barrel racing. In the Calf Scramble, children are invited to try to pluck a ribbon from the tail of a calf. The rodeo takes place Friday and Saturday nights starting at 7:30pm. Admission costs $12 for adults, $6 for youths 7 to 15, and is free for children 6 and younger.

SOME GREAT OUTDOOR AREAS

Fish Creek Falls   Just 4 miles from downtown Steamboat in Routt National Forest, a footpath leads to a historic bridge at the base of this breathtaking 283-foot waterfall. There's also an overlook with a short .1-mile trail and ramp designed for those with disabilities, as well as a picnic area and hiking trails. Allow 1 to 2 hours.

Fish Creek Falls Rd. Information: Hahns Peak/Bears Ears Ranger Station, 925 Weiss Dr., Steamboat Springs, CO 80477. (C) **970/879-1870.** www.fs.fed.us/r2. Free admission. Turn right off Lincoln Ave. onto 3rd St., go 1 block, and turn right again onto Fish Creek Falls Rd. Daily 24 hr.

Yampa River Botanic Park ★★ *Finds*   For a pleasant and relaxing stroll among lovely gardens, stop at this botanic park along the Yampa River, between the ski mountain and downtown. Several picturesque ponds are set among low rolling hills, surrounded by a wide variety of flowering and nonflowering plants and trees of the Yampa River Basin plus many non-native plants from many areas. A brochure describes the planted areas, with a map to help you navigate the many paths. There are wetlands on each side of the park, and the Yampa River Core trail connects to the park on its west side. The park is not wheelchair accessible, but tours for people with disabilities are offered by appointment. Allow at least an hour.

From late June through August, the Strings in the Mountains Music Festival (see "Musical Mountains," below) presents free 1-hour concerts at the park each Thursday at noon. Dogs and bikes are not permitted in the park; bike racks and hitching posts for dogs are located at the park entrances.

1000 Pamela Lane (P.O. Box 776269, Steamboat Springs, CO 80477). (C) **970/879-4300.** Fax 970/870-0173. www.ci.steamboat.co.us/recreation/howelsen.htm. Free admission (donations welcome). Dawn–dusk spring–Oct (or the first heavy snow). From U.S. 40, turn west toward the river on Trafalger Dr. (the traffic light north of the Chamber Resort office light), then left on Pamela Lane, and go to the parking lot at the far end.

MORE TO SEE & DO

Amaze'n Steamboat Maze   This intriguing puzzle lets you test your skills, or perhaps luck, in finding your way through a confusing maze. A free observation deck gives a bird's-eye view of the maze, allowing your quicker companions to point and laugh as you stumble into one dead-end after another. In addition to the human maze, there is an 18-hole miniature golf course that uses items from Colorado's history, from a mine shaft to a Conestoga wagon. In 2004 they added bumper cars. Allow at least 1 hour.

1255 U.S. 40 (behind the chamber office.) (C) **970/870-8682.** www.amazenmazes.com. Admission to the maze $6 adults, $5 children 5–12; golf $6 adults, $5 children; for both maze and golf $8 adults, $7 children; free for children under 5. Additional maze runs $2; additional rounds of golf $3. Memorial Day weekend to mid-September daily; weekends only thereafter; call for hours.

Tread of Pioneers Museum ★   This excellent museum combines two beautifully restored Victorian homes and a separate gallery. Exhibits focus on the area's pioneer ranch life, including an extensive firearm collection and a Southwest American Indian collection. A special feature is the 1908 Queen Anne–style Victorian home, furnished with pioneer and turn-of-the-20-century artifacts. Two permanent displays are particularly interesting: "History of Skiing" (tracing the evolution of skiing from its roots as essential winter transportation to the multimillion-dollar recreational sport of today) and "History of Steamboat Springs" (showing the growth and changes in the county from the time of the Ute Indians through the agricultural and tourism growth of the last few decades). The museum also offers guided tours, kids' activities, and an excellent gift shop. Allow about 1½ hours.

Moments   Musical Mountains

Summer is a musically magical time in Steamboat Springs. **Strings in the Mountains Music Festival** ★★★ offers an incredible array of musical programs, from classical to jazz, lectures to cabarets, with performances indoors and out. The music directors—husband-and-wife team Katherine Collier, pianist, and Yizhak Schotten, violist—are adept at bringing together fine musicians and crafting superb programs, in addition to being excellent musicians themselves.

If **chamber music** is your choice—as it is ours—don't miss the Wednesday and Saturday evening concerts. The night we were there, the evening began with a gentle Chopin nocturne, progressed to a moving Schumann piano quartet, and finished off with a stupendous performance of Brahms' rich and soaring "String Sextet in G, Op. 36." Instead of extensive program notes, nuggets of information about the music and/or composer are presented before each piece by Dr. Ken Greene, professor and chair of the Department of Music at Trinity University in San Antonio, Texas. Dr. Greene and Strings' musicians present free **Tent Talks** each Wednesday at noon in the Strings Tent, located in Music Festival Park at the corner of Mt. Werner and Pine Grove roads.

Should **jazz, country, bluegrass, or pops** be the music that thrills your soul, check the schedule for Friday and Tuesday nights. The 2004 season included performances by singer-songwriter and film composer Randy Newman, jazz singer/songwriter Kermit Ruffins, Eileen Ivers offering Celtic and world music, the folk/pop singing group Trout Fishing in America, Grammy-award-winning artist Mark Cohn, and the Alpen Brass ensemble tossing out a wow of a patriotic concert for the Fourth of July.

Don't forget to pack your lunch for Strings' **"Music on the Green"** at the Yampa River Botanic Park each Thursday at 12:15pm. The

---

800 Oak St. ⓒ **970/879-2214.** Fax 970/879-6109. topmuseum@springsips.com. Admission $5 adults, $4 seniors 62 and older, $1 children under 12. Tues–Sat 11am–5pm.

SHOPPING

Lincoln Avenue, between Fifth and Ninth streets, is where most of the more interesting shops and galleries are located. Art lovers will enjoy **Artisans' Market of Steamboat,** 626 Lincoln Ave. (ⓒ **970/879-7512;** www.rockymountainfun.com/artisans.html), a nonprofit cooperative of local artists; and **Steamboat Art Company,** 903 Lincoln Ave. (ⓒ **800/553-7853** or 970/879-3383; www.steamboat-art.com), which offers an eclectic selection of limited-edition prints and other art, plus jewelry and crafts in wood, glass, and pottery. **The Homesteader** ★★, 821 Lincoln Ave. (ⓒ **800/321-4702** or 970/879-5880; www.thehomesteader.net), is a delightful kitchen shop with all manner of kitchen gadgets; salsa, chutney, and other Colorado-made food items; plus gourmet coffee beans and an espresso bar. The Homesteader also has an especially good website.

Hyperion Quartet delighted us with a fascinating comparison of two movements from Debussy's "Quartet in G minor, Op. 10" to two from Ravel's "Quartet in F major." You needn't worry about the sound dissipating in the great outdoors: It simply shimmered and filled the clear mountain air. It's a lovely way to spend your lunchtime—and many locals agree, so get there early to snag one of the free umbrellas to keep the scorching sun off your head.

When we attended, Strings' home was still the Performing Arts Tent at Torian Plum Plaza, but in 2004 they moved it to their new location on 7 acres at the base of Mount Werner, adjacent to the Village at Steamboat—an inspiring location, with the mountains a stirring backdrop.

What does all this cost, you ask? Surprisingly little for the quality and choices offered, including several free programs. Family concerts Tuesday or Thursday evenings, and youth concerts Tuesday morning, cost $5 to $12 for adults and $1 for those 18 and under; the Wednesday noon Tent Talks are free, as are the Thursday Music on the Green lunchtime programs. Chamber music performances, Wednesday and Saturday evenings, cost $16 to $30 for adults and $5 for kids; the Tuesday and Friday evening programs, which offer a variety of music, have widely varying prices; and there are several special events scattered throughout the summer and during the Christmas season (call for details). Strings also presents musical events at other times of the year, including a series of Christmas holiday concerts and a Winter Concert Series.

For additional information and a complete schedule, contact **Strings in the Mountains,** P.O. Box 774627, Steamboat Springs, CO 80477 (© **970/879-5056;** www.stringsinthemountains.com).

If you forgot to pack your cowboy hat, there's a tremendous selection of Stetsons, plus just about everything else a Westerner wears, at **F. M. Light & Sons,** 830 Lincoln Ave. (© **970/879-1822;** www.fmlight.com). A good choice for liquor, beer, and wine (including the locally produced wines from Steamboat Springs Cellars—its merlot is very good), is **The Bottleneck,** 734 Lincoln Ave. (© **970/879-1255**).

Lyon's Corner Drug & Soda Fountain ☞, at the corner of Ninth and Lincoln (© **970/879-1114**), isn't just a drugstore and card shop (although it does have an excellent selection of greeting cards); it also has a great old Wurlitzer jukebox spinning golden oldies (no charge!), and an old-time soda fountain where you can get real malts, ice-cream sodas, egg creams, phosphates, sundaes, a variety of gelato flavors, and fresh-squeezed lemonade.

WHERE TO STAY

As at all Colorado ski resorts, rates get progressively higher the closer you get to the slopes. You'll pay the highest rates during the Christmas holiday season (mid-Dec to New Year's Day). Next highest are the rates charged during

February and March. Value season is usually January, and the low season runs from Thanksgiving to mid-December and from April until the ski areas close. Rates are normally much lower during the summer, from Memorial Day to mid-October. *Note:* Because vacancy rates are so high during shoulder seasons—April to May and October to November—many accommodations close at these times.

Steamboat Central Reservations (© **877/237-2628** or 970/879-0740; www.steamboat.com) can book your lodging and make virtually all of your travel arrangements. Be sure to ask about special packages and programs. If you're staying in a condo or other unit with kitchen facilities, Steamboat Central Reservations can arrange for **Fridge Fillers** to stock your kitchen the day of your arrival. But it's certainly not a free service: Cost is $40 plus 10% of the total grocery bill.

Resort Quest Steamboat, 1855 Ski Time Square Dr., Steamboat Springs, CO 80487 (© **866/634-9618** or 970/879-8811; www.resortquest.com), manages 280 rental units spread among 11 properties. There are both condos and town homes, with accommodations for 4 to 12 persons; several of the properties are described below.

Steamboat Resorts, 1847 Ski Time Square Dr., P.O. Box 772995, Steamboat Springs, CO 80477 (© **800/525-5502** or 970/879-8000; www.steamboat resorts.com), manages 14 properties, offering a variety of possibilities, from small lodge rooms for 2 to condos that will accommodate up to 10. Several of the properties are described below.

Room tax adds about 9½% to lodging bills.

In addition to the properties discussed below, **Steamboat Lake Outfitters,** P.O. Box 749, Clark, CO 80428 (© **800/342-1889** or 970/879-4404; www. steamboatoutfitters.com), rents bunkhouse rooms and cabins in the mountains above Steamboat Lake State Park. Although rustic in decor, they have comfortable beds, kitchenettes, and indoor bathrooms, with rates for two starting at $75 per night in the bunkhouse rooms and $100 per night in the cabins. Call for details.

If you don't mind a walk to the bathroom, you'll certainly enjoy the beautiful scenery you'll see from the camper cabins at **Steamboat Lake Marina.** See "Warm-Weather & Year-Round Activities," above.

VERY EXPENSIVE

Château Chamonix 🐾 Made up of three condominium buildings just a few steps from the base of the Silver Bullet Gondola, this is one of the most convenient accommodations at Steamboat Village. Most units have two or three bedrooms—often with two king beds and two twins, with private decks, fireplaces, a whirlpool tub in the master bathroom, wet bars, and attractive wood furnishings. Each unit includes a washer and dryer plus free high-speed Internet connection. During ski season a free shuttle service into town is offered.

2340 Apres Ski Way, Steamboat Springs, CO 80487. © **800/833-9877** or 970/879-7511. Fax 970/879-9321. www.chateau-chamonix.com. 48 units. 2-bedroom $170–$210 summer, $255–$1,100 winter; 3-bedroom $210–$275 summer, $340–$1,500 winter; 4-bedroom $275–$375 summer, $500–$1,500 winter. Holiday rates higher; discounts possible between seasons. AE, MC, V. Covered parking. **Amenities:** Outdoor heated pool; exercise room; whirlpool; 2 hot tubs; sauna. *In room:* TV/VCR, kitchen.

Torian Plum at Steamboat 🐾🐾 These slope-side ski-in/ski-out condominiums have handsome light-wood furnishings, a tile kitchen complete with microwave and dishwasher, washer/dryer, gas fireplace, private balcony, ski locker, and two phone lines with voice mail and high-speed Internet connection. The Creekside Tower offers especially opulent master suites and handsome stone fireplaces. The property is scrupulously well maintained and attractive. Numerous free videos and a computer station are available.

1855 Ski Time Square Dr. (Resort Quest Steamboat, see above). ℂ 866/634-9618 or 970/879-8811. Fax 970/879-8485. 81 units. 1- to 3-bedroom units $150–$245 summer, $150–$380 early and late ski season, $460–$955 regular ski season, $570–$1,195 holiday season. AE, DISC, MC, V. Underground parking. **Amenities:** Outdoor heated pool; exercise room; hot tubs (4 outdoor, 2 indoor); sauna; concierge; ski shuttle. *In room:* TV, kitchen.

EXPENSIVE

Sheraton Steamboat Resort ★★   Steamboat Springs's premier hotel is located in the heart of Ski Time Square, at the foot of the Silver Bullet Gondola. The Sheraton opens directly onto the ski slopes, and every room has a view of the mountain, valley, or slopes. There's a great cross-country ski course (p. 267); and in summer, avid golfers enjoy its golf club (p. 271), one of the finest in the Rockies.

Most units have one king or two queen beds, humidifiers, and a private balcony. You'll find outdoor hot tubs on a rooftop spa deck, retail shopping space, plus a 23-unit luxury suite tower. Sevens Fine Dining offers magnificent views of the mountain and the Headwall chairlift, along with great meals three times a day. Dinner features steak, seafood, and poultry dishes ($12–$19). The hotel also offers après ski at the casual Western 3 Saddles Bar & Grill.

2200 Village Inn Court, Steamboat Springs, CO 80477. ℂ 800/848-8878 or 970/879-2220. Fax 970/879-7686. www.sheraton.com/steamboat. 315 units. Late May to mid-Oct $89–$169; winter low-season $129–$149; value season $199–$269; regular season $239–$289; Christmas $339–$379. Children under 17 stay free in parent's room in summer. AE, DC, MC, V. Underground parking. Closed 1 month in spring and fall. **Amenities:** 3 restaurants; bar; outdoor heated pool; golf club (18-hole); health club; spa; 7 hot tubs; steam room; children's programs; game room; concierge (8am–8pm); shopping arcade; room service (7am–10pm); massage; valet and coin-op laundry service. *In room:* A/C, TV/VCR, fridge, coffeemaker.

MODERATE

Hotel Bristol ★★   Among our top choices in Steamboat Springs, the Hotel Bristol offers lodging with character. Rooms are small (150 sq. ft.), in keeping with the heritage of this historic hotel, built in the 1940s. In fact, the reason we like this place so much is the historic ambience—Zane Grey may not have stayed here, but if he had he would have felt right at home. The standard rooms are what we consider sophisticated Old West, refined but not fancy, with solid dark-wood furnishings, lots of brass, Pendleton wool blankets, and reproduction 1940s-style phones. Rooms have one queen-size bed or two twins, and a bathroom with shower only (no tub). The former caretaker's unit has been converted into two suites with sleeper sofas in the living rooms and TVs with DVD players. The family units, which accommodate four people, are two standard rooms, each with its own toilet and sink, and a shared tub/shower combo. This is an especially quiet downtown lodging choice, in large part because it was built of concrete for fire prevention, a major concern in the 1940s. An on-site restaurant serves lunch and dinner daily. High-speed Internet access is available in the guest lounge.

719 Lincoln Ave. (P.O. Box 774927), Steamboat Springs, CO 80477. ℂ 800/851-0872 or 970/879-3083. Fax 970/879-8645. 18 units. Mid-May to mid-Sept $79–$99 double, $119–$149 family unit; mid-Sept to mid-Nov $69 double, $99 family unit; mid-Nov to mid-Apr $89–$129 double, $148–$218 family unit; rates higher Christmas through New Year's. AE, DC, DISC, MC, V. Closed mid-Apr to mid-May. **Amenities:** Restaurant (Italian); 6-person indoor whirlpool. *In room:* A/C, TV.

The Lodge at Steamboat ⭐ These well-maintained condominiums are just 200 yards from the Silver Bullet Gondola, and there's a free shuttle to take you to the mountain village, downtown, or shopping. The individually owned and decorated units have balconies; and upper-floor units have a cathedral ceiling with clerestory windows. A typical average-size unit is simply but pleasantly decorated in what might be termed mountain Western style, and includes an attractive brick fireplace, a sunny dining area, a counter island with high-stool seating between the kitchen and living area, a queen bed in the master bedroom, and twin beds in the second bedroom. Each unit boasts a fireplace and one bathroom per bedroom.

2700 Village Dr. (Steamboat Resorts, see above). (© 800/525-5502 or 970/879-8000. Fax 970/870-8061. 120 units. 1–3 bedrooms winter $105–$650; summer $175–$270. AE, MC, V. **Amenities:** Outdoor heated pool; 2 tennis courts; hot tubs (1 indoor, 4 outdoor); sauna; massage; babysitting; coin-op laundry; free shuttle. *In room:* TV/VCR (video rentals available), kitchen.

Sky Valley Lodge Located below Rabbit Ears Pass with a spectacular view of the upper Yampa River Valley, this lodge—8½ miles east of Steamboat Springs—offers country-manor charm in a woodsy setting, where guests can relax around a big fireplace in the lobby. Each room is a bit different, but all have an old-fashioned ski-lodge atmosphere. Most units have showers only (no tubs), and sinks are in the bedroom. Features include king and queen brass and feather beds, and there's a sun deck for all guests to enjoy. Snowshoe rentals are available. No smoking is permitted in the lodge.

31490 E. U.S. 40 (P.O. Box 3132), Steamboat Springs, CO 80477. (© 800/538-7519 or 970/879-7749. Fax 970/879-7752. www.steamboat-lodging.com. 12 units. Late May to Thanksgiving $69–$109 double; late Nov to mid-Apr $109–$149 double. Children 12 and under stay free. Rates include continental breakfast. AE, DC, MC, V. Closed mid-Apr to late May. **Amenities:** Outdoor hot tub; sauna; game room. *In room:* TV.

Thunderhead Lodge & Condominiums This ski-in/ski-out property offers a variety of accommodations, from lodge and hotel rooms to one- and two-bedroom condos. Condo units have either full kitchens or kitchenettes, and most have gas fireplaces, but lodge and hotel rooms have neither. Some units have a sleeping loft, all except lodge rooms have balconies, and most boast great views of the ski mountain or valley. Hotel rooms have louvered doors separating the bedroom from the sitting area. The lodge rooms are somewhat small, with a queen bed, a love seat, and no desk. The condos are generally spacious—even the studios, which have a queen bed and queen sofa sleeper. The Thunderhead is located in the heart of the mountain village, close to shopping and dining, and there's a sun deck, free coffee in the lobby, and a complimentary shuttle to grocery stores and downtown.

1965 Ski Time Square (Steamboat Resorts, see above). (© 800/525-5502 or 970/879-8000. Fax 970/870-8061. 125 units. Summer $85–$105 double, $130–$235 condo; winter $85–$240 double, $105–$715 condo. AE, MC, V. **Amenities:** Restaurant; lounge; outdoor heated pool; 3 indoor hot tubs; sauna; concierge; massage; babysitting; coin-op laundry; free shuttle. *In room:* TV, kitchen (condos only).

Trappeur's Crossing Resort *Value* This is the least expensive of the Resort Quest Steamboat properties, and given its location relatively close to the slopes and its neat, well-maintained condo units, we consider Trappeur's Crossing an especially good value. There are actually three separate properties here, and as with most condominiums, these are individually owned and decorated; all have gas fireplaces, private balconies, washers and dryers, and kitchens. Many units also have whirlpool tubs.

2900 Village Dr. and Medicine Springs Rd. (Resort Quest Steamboat, see above). © **866/634-9618** or 970/879-8811. Fax 970/879-8485. 102 units. 1- to 4-bedroom units $145–$280 summer; $160–$300 early and late ski season; $315–$565 regular ski season; $315–$925 holiday season. AE, DISC, MC, V. **Amenities:** Indoor-outdoor pool; tennis courts (2, summer only); fitness center; hot tubs (indoor, outdoor); concierge; ski shuttle. *In room:* TV, kitchen; iron/ironing board.

INEXPENSIVE

The Inn at Steamboat ⭐ *Value*   A large ranch-style lodging property, this well-maintained facility is one of the least expensive accommodations in the Steamboat Village area. Etched-pine decor and a large stone fireplace add flair to the lobby. Rooms are spacious, with one king-size bed, two queen beds, or a king and a queen sofa sleeper, and most have sliding glass doors that lead to private decks or terraces. Several upgraded rooms have log wall accents and pine furnishings. Microwaves and refrigerators are available for a fee, and there is free ski and bike storage. There are also several two-bedroom units, including one condo with a full kitchen. On premises are a sun deck and nature trail; ski-tuning is available, too, along with a private ski shuttle. Smoking is not permitted.

3070 Columbine Dr., Steamboat Springs, CO 80487. © **800/872-2601** or 970/879-2600. Fax 970/879-9270. www.inn-at-steamboat.com. 34 units. Summer $69–$109 double, 2-room units $89–$189; winter $59–$139 double, 2-room units $89–$269; Christmas holidays and special events higher; children under 13 stay free. Rates include continental breakfast. AE, DISC, MC, V. **Amenities:** Outdoor pool; hot tub; sauna; game room; coin-op laundry. *In room:* A/C (most), TV, dataport, coffeemaker, hair dryer.

Rabbit Ears Motel ⭐   Nothing fancy here, but we like this comfortable, homey place. The motel's original 10 rooms were built in 1952, with additional units added through 1991, some of which overlook the Yampa River. Completely remodeled in the mid-1990s, all rooms are clean and comfortable. Even the smallest rooms (which, at 216 sq. ft., are definitely tiny) have a desk and two upholstered chairs. The larger rooms are a more-than-comfortable 425 square feet. The motel is conveniently located on the east end of the downtown shopping district, with the river behind, Yampa River Park next door and the hot springs pool across the street (discount passes are available), and on the local free shuttle bus route. All rooms have 27-inch TVs and on-demand movies; most have a microwave and refrigerator combination, and some have private balconies. The continental breakfast is above average.

201 Lincoln Ave. (P.O. Box 770573), Steamboat Springs, CO 80477. © **800/828-7702** or 970/879-1150. Fax 970/870-0483. www.rabbitearsmotel.com. 65 units. Late Mar to mid-Dec $79–$119 double; early Jan to late Mar $95–$135 double; Christmas holiday $125–$165 double. Children under 12 stay free. Rates include continental breakfast. DC, DISC, MC, V. Pets accepted. **Amenities:** Coin-op laundry. *In room:* A/C, TV, dataport, fridge, coffeemaker, hair dryer, iron/ironing board, microwave.

Steamboat Bed & Breakfast ⭐⭐   Steamboat Springs's first house of worship, an 1891 Congregational Church that lost its steeple and top floor to lightning, is now a fine bed-and-breakfast with many stained-glass windows. There are beautiful European and American Victorian antiques in every room, reproduction antique beds, hardwood floors in the common areas and bathrooms, and carpeting in the bedrooms. Guests share a huge living/dining room with stone fireplace, where they can enjoy complimentary fresh fruit and baked goods. There's also a 24-hour nonalcoholic-beverage bar and a homemade cookie–and-biscotti bar. Other facilities include an upstairs library, sun deck, and a music conservatory with piano, TV, and VCR (videos are available). In summer, guests can enjoy an attractive deck, set in a lovely flower garden and lush lawn, or nap in a hammock under shady trees. Smoking is not permitted.

442 Pine St. (P.O. Box 775888), Steamboat Springs, CO 80477. © **877/335-4321** or 970/879-5724. Fax 970/870-8787. www.steamboatb-b.com. 7 units. $99–$189 double. Rates include full breakfast. AE, DISC, MC, V. **Amenities:** Hot tub, sauna.

WHERE TO DINE

Those on a budget can save quite a bit by stopping at local supermarkets. **City Market,** 1825 Central Park Plaza (© **970/879-3290**), is not only a good grocery store; it also has a great salad bar (salads to go by the pound), bakery, deli, bank, and pharmacy. **Safeway,** 37500 E. U.S. 40 (© **970/879-3766**), has a bakery, deli, ATM, and pharmacy, but no salad bar. Also see the information on **Fridge Fillers** in the introduction of "Where to Stay," above.

Many of the restaurants in Steamboat Springs cut back their hours or close completely in the slow seasons—primarily spring and fall—so if you're visiting at those times it's best to call first to confirm hours.

EXPENSIVE

Hazie's ★★ CREATIVE AMERICAN One of Steamboat Springs's most exciting dining experiences can be found at the top of the gondola, midway up Mount Werner. The views of the upper Yampa River valley are spectacular by day and romantic by night, as the lights of Steamboat Springs spread out at the foot of the mountain. Lunch features a variety of salads and sandwiches, plus a daily chef's special. But it's at dinner that Hazie's really excels. Start with an appetizer such as escargot *au fromage*, then try the soup du jour or Hazie's house salad with caramelized pear vinaigrette. Finally, choose from entrees like grilled mahimahi with roasted pineapple salsa; grilled rack of lamb marinated with roasted shallot and thyme oil; or lobster tail and scallops pasta, sautéed in wine and served over angel-hair pasta in a tarragon-brandy cream sauce. In summer you can enjoy lunch Wednesday through Saturday, overlooking the lush greenery of the Yampa Valley. Sunday brunch is popular with locals and visitors alike.

Steamboat Ski Area, 2305 Mt. Werner Circle, Thunderbird Terminal, top of the Silver Bullet Gondola. © **970/879-6111** or 970/871-5150. www.steamboat.com. Reservations recommended for lunch, required for dinner. Lunch main courses $8.75–$18; dinner 3-course meal $59 winter, $49 summer. AE, DISC, MC, V. Mid-Dec to early Apr daily 11:30am–2:30pm, Fri–Sun 6:00–10pm; mid-June to Labor Day, Wed–Sat 11:30am–2:30pm, Sat 6:30–10pm; Sun brunch 9am–1:30pm. Closed spring and fall.

La Montaña ★ SOUTHWESTERN/MEXICAN This isn't your everyday Mexican restaurant; it's a gourmet experience. The festive decor sets the mood, with greenhouse dining and handsome photos by owner Tom Garrett on the stuccoed walls. Southwestern dishes include unusual combinations such as grilled elk loin with a cilantro pesto crust and ancho chile demi-glace; the chef's award-winning dish of braided sausage, a mesquite-grilled combination of elk, lamb, and chorizo sausage; and enchiladas (which have been featured in *Gourmet* magazine) composed of blue corn tortillas, goat and Monterey Jack cheeses, roasted peppers, and onions.

2500 Village Dr. at Apres Ski Way. © **970/879-5800**. Fax 970/879-5373. www.la-montana.com. Reservations recommended. Main courses $12–$29. AE, DISC, MC, V. Daily 5–10pm (bar daily 4:30–10pm). Hours vary in spring, summer, and fall; call in advance.

MODERATE

Harwigs/L'Apogée at 911 Lincoln Avenue ★ *Moments* CONTEMPORARY FRENCH Located in downtown Steamboat Springs in an 1886 building that originally housed a saddle shop, this fine dining establishment serves French cuisine with an Asian flair in an elegant candlelit atmosphere enhanced by live piano music. The menu changes often, but main courses might include selections such as New Orleans jambalaya with chicken, shrimp, duck, and house sausage simmered in a fiery Creole sauce; or two-mushroom veal, medallions of veal sautéed with shallots and shitake and button mushrooms in a white-wine cream sauce. Our favorite item here is one of the cheapest—the half-pound chargrilled lamb burger with strawberry–green apple chutney and provolone cheese. Service is superb, there's an award-winning wine cellar, and outdoor seating is available. Smoking is not permitted.

911 Lincoln Ave. ℂ 970/879-1919. www.lapogee.com. Reservations recommended. Main courses $9–$20; steaks $3.50–$4.30 per ounce. AE, MC, V. Daily 5–11pm.

Mahogany Ridge Brewery & Grill INTERNATIONAL   This modern restaurant is more than a simple brewpub—it boasts a full bar with an extensive wine list in addition to its own microbrews, and the chef draws from all corners of the globe to offer a unique combination of flavors. First, choose your entree—maybe Thai baby back ribs or maple-glazed chicken, seared blackened salmon or tandoori-spiced yellowfin tuna. Next, choose two sauces ranging from a traditional salsa, spicy black-bean sauce, or apple chutney to creole remoulade, wasabi cream, or siracha-miso glaze (there are more than a dozen sauces). Then finally, let the dipping begin! The more the tastier, as sharing and double dipping are encouraged. For the less adventuresome, Mahogany Ridge also offers several soups, salads, sandwiches and burgers; plus fish and chips, fried chicken, and an unusual and delicious chipotle chicken pot pie. There's even a kid's menu and live music (see "Performing Arts & Nightlife," below)—ensuring that there's truly something for everybody here.

435 Lincoln Ave. (at Fifth St.). ℂ 970/879-3773. Main courses $6–$19. DISC, MC, V. Daily 4–11pm.

Slopeside Grill ⭐ AMERICAN/ITALIAN   This restaurant draws diners with large portions—bring a big appetite—and its views of the slopes. A large U-shaped light-colored wooden bar dominates the dining room, where diners face the ski slopes through large windows, and the walls are decorated with Western and early skiing memorabilia. When the weather cooperates, alfresco dining is popular on the patio under large umbrellas. Grill options (available after 6pm) include the deservedly popular slow-roasted rack of ribs, and we recommend the fresh Gulf mahi blackened and served with raspberry–beurre blanc sauce). We especially like the pizza here, from an Italian-style brick oven, with choices such as "The Chutes" (sweet and hot Italian sausage, fresh tomatoes, red onions, and mushrooms) and the "Vagabond," which combines garlic, feta cheese, sun-dried tomatoes, olive oil, and spinach, and tops it all with mozzarella. Stop in for the late-night happy hour from 10pm to midnight, when you can get pints for $2 and pizzas for $6.

Ski Time Square in Torian Plum Plaza. ℂ 970/879-2916. www.slopesidegrill.com. Reservations suggested. Pizza $8.95–$12; main courses $6.95–$19. AE, DISC, MC, V. Daily 11am–10pm; pizza oven open until midnight; bar open until 2am.

INEXPENSIVE

Cugino's Pizzeria ⭐ *Value* ITALIAN   Local families pack this restaurant in downtown Steamboat Springs, and with good reason—it offers great food, generous portions, and low prices. The simple decor consists of posters of Italian operas. The extensive menu includes pizza, of course, plus hoagies and steak sandwiches, pasta, and calzones. Those with healthy appetites might want to try one of the strombolis—fresh-baked pizza dough stuffed with various ingredients such as mushrooms, onions, peppers, mozzarella and provolone cheeses, plus ham, Genoa salami, and capacola or meatballs, pepperoni, and spicy sausage. A vegetarian version is also served. Beer and wine are available at any time, and liquor is served after 5pm.

825 Oak St. ✆ **970/879-5805**. Reservations not accepted. Pizzas $6.75–$9.50; sandwiches $5–$6; main courses $7.50–$17. No credit cards. Daily 11am–10pm. Delivery available 5–9:30pm.

The Tugboat Grill & Pub AMERICAN   Oak floors and rough barn-wood walls cloaked with game and fishing trophies, sports memorabilia, and celebrity photographs are the trademark of this foot-of-the-slopes establishment, which also boasts a sun deck for great people-watching. The hand-carved cherrywood bar, circa 1850, came from the Log Cabin Saloon in Baggs, Wyoming, a Butch Cassidy hangout; look for the bullet hole in one of the columns. The fare includes a variety of burgers, burritos, deli sandwiches, fish, soups, and huge salads throughout the day, and dinner entrees such as basil chicken, a lightly herbed chicken breast in a creamy vegetable sauce, with black olives, green onions, and tomatoes. Many folks sup on nachos, teriyaki wings, and other generous appetizer plates. There's also live music (see below).

1860 Ski Time Square. ✆ **970/879-7070**. Reservations not accepted. Main courses $4.75–$20. AE, DC, MC, V. Daily 11:30am–2am.

PERFORMING ARTS & NIGHTLIFE

The music scene in Steamboat Springs is dominated by the **Strings in the Mountains Music Festival,** which offers a wide variety of musical events almost daily throughout the summer, and with lesser frequency at other times of the year. See the sidebar "Musical Mountains," earlier in this chapter.

The **bar scene** in Steamboat, while never dull, comes especially alive in winter. In fact, like Steamboat's restaurants, its nightlife ranges from quiet to nonexistent in spring. One of the hottest new hangouts is **Level'z Nightclub,** at 1860 Ski Time Square (✆ **970/870-9090;** www.levelzonline.com), with live entertainment nightly, 20 beers on tap, pool tables, and video games, and some good happy hour specials. Other popular venues include the rustic **Tugboat Grill & Pub,** 1860 Ski Time Square (✆ **970/879-7070**), which attracts a noisy local crowd for a variety of live music and dancing, starting about 9:30pm.

In downtown Steamboat, **The Tap House,** 729 Lincoln Ave. (✆ **970/ 879-2431;** www.thetaphouse.com), has dozens of TVs (including a couple of huge ones) showing just about any sporting event you'd want to see. There are 21 beers on tap, good fajitas and chicken wings, pool tables, and a video arcade.

Looking for a good spot to sample the local brews? Head to **Mahogany Ridge Brewery & Grill,** 435 Lincoln Ave. (✆ **970/879-3773**), where you'll find a nice selection of handcrafted ales and a wide variety of live music.

4 Winter Park

67 miles NW of Denver

Originally an Arapaho and Ute hunting ground, today most of the hunting in Winter Park is for the best ski runs. First settled by whites in the 1850s, the laying of a rail track over Rollins Pass in 1905 and the completion of the 6¼-mile Moffat Tunnel in 1928 opened forests here to logging, which long supported the economy while providing Denver with raw materials for its growth.

The birth of the Winter Park ski area in January 1940, at the west portal of the Moffat Tunnel, helped give impetus to the Colorado ski boom. Although it hasn't yet achieved the notoriety of Vail or Aspen, the tiny town of Winter Park—population less than 700—still manages to attract more than a million skier visits per season. One of its draws is the Winter Park Ski Train, the last of its kind in the West. Elevation here is about 9,400 feet.

ESSENTIALS

GETTING THERE   By Car   From Denver or other points east or west, take I-70 exit 232, at Empire, and climb 24 miles north on U.S. 40 over Berthoud Pass to Winter Park. U.S. 40 links Winter Park directly to Steamboat Springs, 101 miles northwest, and, via U.S. 34 (at Granby) through Rocky Mountain National Park, to Estes Park, 84 miles north.

By Plane   Visitors fly into Denver International Airport and can continue to Winter Park with **Home James Transportation Services** (© **800/359-7503** or 970/726-5060; www.homejamestransportation.com); a one-way trip runs about $43.

By Train   Winter Park Resort is the only ski area in the western United States with rail service directly to the slopes. The dramatically scenic **Winter Park Ski Train** (© **303/296-4754;** www.skitrain.com) has been making regular runs between Denver and Winter Park since 1940, stopping just 50 yards from the foot of the lifts. On its 2-hour run, the train climbs almost 4,000 feet and passes through 29 tunnels (including the 6¼-mile Moffat Tunnel). The train operates Saturdays and Sundays from late December to early April, plus Fridays from late January through the ski season and on Saturdays in August. Fees for coach seating are $44 adults, $34 for seniors 62 and up and kids 3 to 13 (with an adult), and seats are free for infants 2 and younger. Rates for the upgraded club cars cost $69 per person, and include a continental breakfast, après-ski snacks, and non-alcoholic beverages.

The **Amtrak California Zephyr** (© **800/USA-RAIL;** www.amtrak.com) stops twice daily (once in each direction) in Fraser, 2 miles north of Winter Park, on its Chicago–West Coast run.

VISITOR INFORMATION   Main sources of visitor information are the **Winter Park–Fraser Valley Chamber of Commerce,** P.O. Box 3236, Winter Park, CO 80482 (© **800/903-7275** or 970/726-4118 for general information, 800/722-4118 for lodging; www.winterpark-info.com), and the **Winter Park Resort,** P.O. Box 36, Winter Park, CO 80482 (© **970/726-5514;** www.winter parkresort.com). The chamber of commerce's visitor center, on the east side of U.S. 40 in the center of town, is open year-round, daily from 8am to 5pm.

GETTING AROUND   U.S. 40 (Winter Park Dr.) runs almost directly north–south through the community. Vasquez Road, one of the few side roads with accommodations, is the first major left turn as you arrive from the south. Two miles north on U.S. 40 is Fraser, site of the Amtrak terminal and several condominium developments. **The Lift** (© **970/726-4163**), a free local shuttle service, runs between most accommodations and the ski area during the ski season, and from July 4th through Labor Day operates a free "Fun Bus" between Fraser and Winter Park. **Car rentals** are available from **Hertz** (© **800/654-3131** or 970/726-8993).

FAST FACTS   The hospital, **Seven Mile Medical Clinic,** at 145 Parsenn Road in the Winter Park Resort (© **970/726-8066**), can handle most medical emergencies (call for hours). The **post office** is in the heart of Winter Park at 78490 U.S. 40. For hours and other information contact the U.S. Postal Service (© **800/275-8777;** www.usps.com).

SPECIAL EVENTS   Women's Ski and Snowboard Weekend, late January or early February; Jazz Festival, mid-July; High Country Stampede Rodeo, Saturday nights from early July through August; Rocky Mountain Wine, Beer, and Food Festival, early August; Torchlight Parade, Christmas Eve.

SKIING & OTHER WINTER ACTIVITIES

Winter Park is one of those rare resorts that seem to have something for everyone. Experts rave about the chutes and steep mogul runs on Mary Jane Mountain and the extreme skiing in the Vasquez Cirque, but intermediates and beginners are well served on other slopes. Moreover, Winter Park is noted for wide-ranging programs for children and those with disabilities.

The resort includes three interconnected mountain areas totaling 134 designated trails on 2,762 acres of skiable terrain. There are 21 lifts, including eight high-speed express quads, three triples, seven double chairs, two Magic Carpet rolling conveyors, and a rope tow. It rates its trails as 9% beginner, 21% intermediate, 13% advanced, 54% most difficult, and 3% expert only.

Winter Park Resort comprises several distinct areas. **Winter Park Mountain** has mostly beginner and intermediate terrain. **Discovery Park** encompasses more than 20 acres of prime beginner terrain.

Mary Jane Mountain mainly offers intermediate, most difficult, and expert terrain. **Vasquez Ridge,** the resort's third mountain area, has primarily intermediate and most difficult terrain. Fans of tree-line skiing will like **Parsenn Bowl,** more than 200 acres of open-bowl and gladed-tree skiing that fan out from the summit at North Cone and merge with Mary Jane's Backside.

Vasquez Cirque is no place for beginners. It contains steep chutes and gladed pockets for advanced and expert skiers and snowboarders. Accessed by a short hike from the top of the Timberline chair in Parsenn Bowl, skiers and snowboarders can choose from numerous entrances along a groomed "ski-way" that runs from the top of Parsenn Bowl along the perimeter of the Cirque. The most difficult areas are at the farthest end of the traverse. The upper area boasts above-tree-line skiing in steep chutes or wide-open snowfields. Lower down, the glades gradually tighten, ending on a trail that brings skiers and snowboarders to the base of the Pioneer Express chair.

Annual snowfall at Winter Park averages over 359 inches (almost 30 ft.). The vertical drop is 3,060 feet, from the 12,060-foot summit off North Cone. There are about a dozen restaurants and several bars, including a mountaintop restaurant.

Winter Park's impressive **Children's Center** 𝄢 includes a play area, rental shop, restrooms, and a children's instruction hill. The **National Sports Center for the Disabled** 𝄢𝄢, founded in 1970, is one of the largest programs of its kind in the world.

Daily lift tickets cost $49 to $68 for adults ages 14–69, $29 to $35 for children 6 to 13, $35 to $57 for seniors 62 to 69 and seniors 70 and older Friday through Sunday, and are free for those under 6 and, on Monday through Thursday, for those over 69. Full-rental packages are available, as are alpine, telemark, and snowboard lessons, as well as snowshoe tours.

Winter Park is usually open for skiing from mid-November to mid-April. It's open for summer operations daily from early June until early September. For more information, contact **Winter Park Resort,** P.O. Box 36, Winter Park, CO 80482 (𝄞 **970/726-5514,** or 303/892-0961 in Denver; www.winterparkresort. com). For daily ski reports, call 𝄞 **970/726-7669** or 303/572-7669 in Denver.

> ### *Moments* Totally Tubular
>
> The **Fraser Valley Tubing Hill** (behind Kentucky Fried Chicken), Fraser (© **970/726-5954**), offers a return to childhood for many adults, as well as a lot of fun for kids (who must be 7 or older to ride alone). A lift pulls you and your big inner tube to the top of a steep hill, and then you slide down, sometimes reaching speeds of 45 mph. Hours Friday through Sunday are from 10am to 10pm, with slightly shorter hours Monday through Thursday, and the tubing hill is open November to April, snow permitting. Rides run about $12 an hour.

OTHER SKIING NEARBY   Just 78 miles from Denver, **SolVista Basin,** 1000 Village Rd. (P.O. Box 1110), Granby, CO 80446 (© **888/283-7458** or 970/887-3384; www.solvista.com), has long been a favorite with parents and kids for its easy access, affordable prices, and family-friendly atmosphere.

The ski area comprises two separate but interconnected mountains. The resort contains 433 acres of skiable terrain, with 33 trails rated 30% beginner, 50% intermediate, and 20% advanced. The longest run is 1½ miles and the vertical drop is 1,000 feet from the top elevation of 9,202 feet. It's served by one high-speed quad, one fixed-grip quad, one triple, one double, and a surface lift. Average annual snowfall is 220 inches, and 60% of the terrain has snow making, with top-to-bottom coverage on both mountains. Full-day lift tickets are $41 to $43 for adults, $19 to $22 for children 6 to 12, $27 to $29 for seniors 61 to 69, and are free for those under 6 and over 69.

CROSS-COUNTRY SKIING & SNOWSHOEING   The outstanding cross-country skiing in the Winter Park area is highlighted by what the *Denver Post* calls "the best touring center in Colorado." The **Devil's Thumb Cross-Country Center** at Devil's Thumb Ranch Resort (© **970/726-8231;** www.devils thumbranch.com) has more than 100km of groomed trails. Full rentals and instruction are available. Day passes are about $15, with discounts for those staying at the ranch.

There's also cross-country skiing at **SolVista Basin** (see "Other Skiing Nearby," above), with 40km of groomed trails. Use of the trails is free, with access at the base of the ski mountain. Those who want to avoid the work of skiing uphill can also access the cross-country trails from the top via a ski lift ($5 per trip).

Snow Mountain Ranch–YMCA Nordic Center, on U.S. 40 between Winter Park and Grand Lake (© **970/887-2152;** www.ymcarockies.org/smrnordic), features 100km of groomed trails for all abilities, including a short section of lighted track for night skiing. Trail passes cost $12 for adults and $5 for kids 6 to 12 and under and seniors 61 to 69. Children under 6 and seniors 70 and older ski free, and adults with YMCA membership receive $2 discounts. A 5-day adult trail pass costs $40.

All of the above provide **snowshoeing** opportunities, with rental equipment and guided tours. You can also rent snowshoes ($10 per day) and get tips on where to go at **Winter Park Sports Shop** in Kings Crossing Shopping Center, at the intersection of Winter Park Drive and Kings Crossing Road (© **800/ 222-7547** or 970/726-5554; www.winterparkski.com).

WARM-WEATHER & YEAR-ROUND ACTIVITIES

There are plenty of recreational opportunities in the **Arapaho National Forest** and **Arapaho National Recreation Area.** Maps and brochures on hiking, mountain biking, and other activities are available at the Sulphur Ranger District office, P.O. Box 10, 9 Ten Mile Dr., off U.S. 40 about half a mile south of Granby, CO 80446 (© **970/887-4100;** www.fs.fed.us/r2). The **Devil's Thumb Ranch** (see "Where to Stay," below) is famous for its numerous recreation packages, including rafting, hiking, and fly-fishing.

ALPINE SLIDE   Colorado's longest alpine slide, at 3,030 feet long and with 26 turns, cools summer visitors. Rates are $10 for adults, $8 for children 6 to 13 and for seniors 70 and older on Friday through Sunday. Kids under 6 get in free at all times and seniors 70 and older are admitted free Monday through Thursday. For information, contact the Winter Park Resort (see "Skiing & Other Winter Activities," above).

FISHING   Fraser Valley and surrounding Grand County are renowned among anglers. Head to Williams Fork Reservoir and the Three Lakes District for kokanee salmon, lake trout, brookies, and browns. Fishing ponds stocked with various species are in Fraser, across from the Fraser Valley Center on U.S. 40. The upper pond is reserved for children and people in wheelchairs; the lower pond is open to everyone. Ponds are generally open and stocked by mid-May.

Devil's Thumb Ranch (see "Where to Stay," below) offers guided fly-fishing trips starting at about $100 for a half-day.

GOLF   Local golf courses include **Pole Creek Golf Club,** 10 miles northwest of Winter Park on U.S. 40 (© **970/726-8847**); it's considered among the finest mountain courses in the state, with greens fees of $80 to $85 for 18 holes; and the new **Headwaters Golf Course,** formerly SolVista Golf Club (see "Other Skiing Nearby," above), with fees of $50 to $75.

HIKING & BACKPACKING   The nearby Arapaho National Forest and Arapaho National Recreation Area (see above) offer miles of hiking trails and plenty of backpacking opportunities. Beautiful Rocky Mountain National Park is less than an hour's drive north (see "Rocky Mountain National Park," earlier in this chapter).

MOUNTAIN BIKING   Winter Park and the Fraser Valley have won national recognition for their expansive trail system and established race program. Many off-road bike trails connect to the 600 miles of backcountry roads and trails in the adjacent national forest. The King of the Rockies Off-Road Stage Race and Festival, held each year in August, is one of the top professional mountain-bike races in America; part of it is run on the 30-mile **Tipperary Creek Trail** ⭑, among Colorado's best mountain-bike trails.

For advice, information, and maps, talk to the knowledgeable folks at **Winter Park Sports Shop** in Kings Crossing Shopping Center, at the intersection of Winter Park Drive and Kings Crossing Road (© **800/222-7547** or 970/726-5554; www.winterparkbike.com). In business since 1946, the shop is open daily year-round, providing mountain sales, repairs, and rentals (starting at $15 per half-day, $20 per day). Ask for a copy of the free trail map, also available from the **Winter Park–Fraser Valley Chamber of Commerce** (see "Visitor Information," above).

MORE TO SEE & DO

Amaze'n Winter Park   A human maze by Amaze'n Colorado, this two-level labyrinth of twists and turns offers prizes to participants who can "beat the clock." The maze is constructed in such a way that it can be easily changed, which is done weekly to maintain interest for repeat customers. A free observation deck gives a bird's-eye view of the maze, as well as the surrounding scenery. Allow about 1 hour.

At the base of Winter Park Resort. ✆ **970/726-0214.** www.amazenmazes.com. Admission $8 adults, $6 children 5–12, free for children under 5. Additional maze runs $2. Memorial Day weekend to Sept. Call for hours.

Cozens Ranch House Museum   This 1870s homestead is a National Historic Registry site and presents a glimpse into Colorado's pioneer past, with a restored and furnished family residence, small hotel, stagecoach stop, and the original Fraser Valley post office. There's also a replica of a stagecoach that traveled roads near here between 1875 and 1905, plus a small gift shop. Allow 30 minutes to an hour.

U.S. 40 between Winter Park and Fraser. ✆ **970/726-5488.** www.grandcountymuseum.com/Cozens Ranch.htm. Admission $4 adults, $3 seniors 62 and over, $2 students 6–18, free for children under 6. Memorial Day to Sept Tues–Sat 10am–5pm, Sun 1–5pm; rest of year Wed–Sat 11am–4pm.

WHERE TO STAY

There are more than 60 accommodations in the Fraser Valley, including hotels, condominiums, family-style mountain inns (serving breakfast and dinner daily), bed-and-breakfasts, lodges, and motels. Bookings can be made through **Winter Park Central Reservations** (✆ **800/979-0332** or 970/726-5587; www.winter parkresort.com). The agency can also book air and rail tickets, rental cars, airport transfers, lift tickets, ski-school lessons, ski rentals, and other activities.

Another option, for those interested in renting a private, upscale home, townhouse, or condo, is to contact **Destinations West** (✆ **800/545-9378;** www. mtnlodging.com).

In addition to the properties listed below, Winter Park has a very nice **Super 8,** downtown on U.S. 40 (✆ **800/800-8000** or 970/726-8088), with double rates of $62 to $162 during the ski season, and $62 to $132 the rest of the year.

Snow Mountain Ranch–YMCA of the Rockies, on U.S. 40 between Winter Park and Grand Lake, 1101 C.R. 53, Granby, CO 80446 (✆ **800/777-9622** or 970/887-2152; www.ymcarockies.org), offers a wide range of lodging possibilities, from economical lodge rooms to delightful Western-style cabins with up to five bedrooms. Rates start at $52 double; up to two pets are accepted in cabins, with a $5 per pet fee. Taxes add about 10% to lodging bills.

Devil's Thumb Ranch 👍👍   This is a wonderful place to escape the modern world, so it's not surprising that it attracts outdoor enthusiasts in droves. Established in 1937, the ranch—8 miles north of Winter Park—is as famous today for its cross-country skiing in winter (see "Skiing & Other Winter Activities," above) as for its horseback riding, fly-fishing, rafting, and inflatable-kayaking in summer. Winter also offers sleigh rides and, new in 2004, an ice-skating rink with a special program for kids and skate rentals. Summer 2004 saw the addition of a fly shop where anglers can get licenses and advice, rent gear, or sign up for lessons or a guided fishing trip.

Accommodations are available for all pocketbooks, from affordable lodge rooms to luxurious cabins. Both rooms and cabins offer a rustic elegance with down pillows, comforters, and warm bathrobes. The Ridgetop Cabins were completed in 2003, and boast cozy luxury amid crafted and antique furniture. Guests can enjoy board games, a library, or satellite TV in the common areas; and a complimentary wine-and-cheese tasting takes place each afternoon. The Ranch House Restaurant & Saloon lures Winter Park residents eager for creative country cuisine and seasonal specialties; it's open for dinner nightly and for lunch on weekends.

Grand County Rd. 83 (P.O. Box 750), Tabernash, CO 80478. © **800/933-4339** or 970/726-5632. Fax 970/726-9038. www.devilsthumbranch.com. 14 units (about half with private bathroom) plus 24 cabins. $69–$168 double; $139–$779 cabin. Rates include continental breakfast. Minimum stay required for some accommodations. MC, V. **Amenities:** Restaurant (American); bar; indoor/outdoor pool; spa; whirlpool; sauna.

Gästhaus Eichler ⚐ The charm of this small inn is exactly what you'd expect to find at a European resort. Lace curtains and down comforters grace the rooms—renovated in 2003—and each has its own whirlpool. Guests can also relax in the hot tub outside, and listen to the soothing sound of Vasquez Creek. The restaurant, open for two or three meals daily (depending on the time of year), offers innovative specials, fresh fish, and lighter fare. A sports shop in the building focuses on skiing in the winter and biking in the summer, and offers a discount to guests.

78786 U.S. 40 at Vasquez Creek (P.O. Box 3700), Winter Park, CO 80482. © **800/543-3899** or 970/726-5133. Fax 970/726-5175. 15 units. Summer $69–$89 double; winter $120–$170 double. Rates include buffet breakfast, winter rates also include dinner for 2. AE, MC, V. **Amenities:** Restaurant (European Continental); lounge; hot tub. *In room:* TV.

The Vintage Resort Hotel and Conference Center ⚐ The châteaulike Vintage rises five stories above the foot of Winter Park's ski slopes, not far from the Mary Jane base facilities. A full-service resort hotel, it offers convenient access to skiing, excellent dining and atmosphere, and luxury accommodations. The units range from average-size rooms with two queen beds to spacious two-bedroom suites with whirlpool tubs. Every room has a view of either the ski slopes or the Continental Divide, and many have kitchenettes and fireplaces. Some rooms also have high-speed Internet available. There are ski lockers and on-site ski rentals, mountain bike storage and work rooms, and a library with a pool table. The hotel's restaurant, Tipper's Tavern, offers good sandwiches and pizzas in a casual atmosphere. The entire property is nonsmoking.

100 Winter Park Dr. (P.O. Box 1369), Winter Park, CO 80482. © **800/472-7017** or 970/726-8801. Fax 970/726-9230. www.vintagehotel.com. 118 units. Summer (includes continental breakfast) $60–$105 double, $150–$230 suite; winter $75–$205 double, $180–$550 suite. Fri-Sat rates about 10% higher than weekday rates; rates higher during holidays and special events. AE, DC, DISC, MC, V. Pets accepted (one-time fee of $25). **Amenities:** Restaurant (American); bar; large outdoor heated pool; exercise room; access to a nearby health club; hot tub; sauna; video arcade; concierge; shuttle service; full-service business center; coin-op laundry. *In room:* TV w/pay movies, dataport, fridge (some), coffeemaker, hair dryer, iron.

WHERE TO DINE

In addition to the restaurants discussed here, other good choices are the restaurants at **Gästhaus Eichler** and **The Vintage Resort Hotel and Conference Center**, discussed above under "Where to Stay."

Deno's Mountain Bistro ⚐ CONTEMPORARY AMERICAN A favorite of locals and visitors alike, this bistro on Winter Park's main street has a casual atmosphere and impressive bar, with an extensive selection of national and international beers and an excellent wine list of more than 300 selections. The restaurant takes up two levels—the upstairs sports pub features copper-topped tables, while downstairs is casually elegant fine dining. Lunch here means excellent sandwiches, burgers, and salads. The gourmet cuisine at dinner includes such dishes as penne pomodoro, with fresh basil, garlic, tomatoes, and sautéed rock shrimp; broiled tenderloin of pork brochette, with mangos, plums, and roasted vegetables; and the absolute favorite of carnivores like us, the grilled aged New York strip steak, served with zesty Tabasco onion strings, roasted vegetables, and potatoes.

78911 U.S. 40 (downtown, across from Copper Creek Square). ℂ **970/726-5332.** www.denosmountain bistro.com. Salads and most sandwiches $4.95–$7.95; main courses $11–$28. AE, DC, DISC, MC, V. Daily 11:30am–11pm.

Untamed Steakhouse at Wildcreek ⚜ NEW AMERICAN/STEAK   This large Western restaurant, with 30-foot vaulted ceilings, exposed pine beams, and a handsome stone fireplace, offers well-prepared and innovative cuisine. For lunch there are sandwiches and light entrees, and for dinner we suggest the house specialty—wood-fired Angus beef prime rib, slowly roasted with a spicy rub, fresh herbs, and roasted garlic, then lightly grilled and served with crispy horseradish coleslaw and frizzled onions. Other dinner choices include the beef tournedos, roasted with bacon, brie cheese, artichoke bottoms, and a cognac sauce; eggplant lasagna with black olives, mushrooms, and spinach; and roasted salmon, coated in a brown sugar and ancho-chile rub, and presented on apricot-fig preserves. There's a very good wine list, plus a nice selection of draft beers and specialty martinis. There are also pool tables and frequent live entertainment.

78491 U.S. 40 (downtown). ℂ **970/726-1111.** Main courses $8–$24. AE, DISC, MC, V. Daily 11am–10pm.

5 Breckenridge & Summit County

67 miles W of Denver, 114 miles NW of Colorado Springs, 23 miles E of Vail

Breckenridge, and its neighbors throughout Summit County, comprise a major outdoor recreation center, with skiing in winter, and fishing, hiking, and mountain biking in summer. But the area actually offers much more, with a number of historical attractions, good shopping opportunities, a number of fine restaurants, and some interesting places to stay. The town of Breckenridge (elevation 9,603 feet) is a good place to base yourself, as the entire Victorian core of this 19th-century mining town has been carefully preserved, with colorfully painted shops and restaurants occupying the old buildings, most dating from the 1880s and 1890s.

Most of the mountain towns that surround the area's excellent ski resorts—Arapahoe Basin, Breckenridge, Copper, Keystone, and Loveland—were barely on the map in the 1880s, when the rest of the state was laying claim to its stake of history. Breckenridge, however, was a prosperous mining town in 1887 when the largest gold nugget ever found in Colorado, "Tom's Baby," was unearthed there. It weighed 13 pounds, 7 ounces, and is now in the Colorado History Museum in Denver. Today these communities are strictly in the tourism business, and fill to capacity during peak seasons. Breckenridge, for example, has a year-round population of only 2,800 people, but swells to almost 34,000 during its top tourism times.

ESSENTIALS
GETTING THERE   By Car   I-70 runs through the middle of Summit County. For Keystone, exit on U.S. 6 at Dillon; the resort is 6 miles east of the interchange. For Breckenridge, exit on Colo. 9 at Frisco and head south 9 miles to the resort. Copper Mountain is right on I-70 at the Colo. 91 interchange.

By Airport Shuttle Most visitors fly into Denver International or Colorado Springs and continue to Breckenridge, Frisco, Keystone, and/or Copper Mountain via shuttle. **Colorado Mountain Express** (📞 800/525-6363 or 970/926-9800; www.cmex.com) offers shuttles; the cost from Denver starts at about $40 per person, one-way. (For listings of airlines servicing Denver and Colorado Springs, see chapters 5 and 7, respectively.)

VISITOR INFORMATION For additional information on Breckenridge and other parts of Summit County, contact the **Breckenridge Resort Chamber,** with a visitor center at 309 N. Main St. (open daily 9am–5pm), and administrative offices at P.O. Box 1909, Breckenridge, CO 80424 (📞 800/221-1091 or 970/453-2913; www.gobreck.com).

A source of visitor information for the entire region is the **Summit County Chamber of Commerce,** P.O. Box 2010, Frisco, CO 80443 (📞 888/786-6482 or 970/668-2051; www.experiencethesummit.com). The chamber has an information center in Frisco (I-70 exit 203), and another in Silverthorne just off Colo. 9 N. Both are open daily from 9am to 5pm.

GETTING AROUND Dillon Reservoir is at the heart of Summit County, and I-70 lies along its northwestern shore, with Frisco at its west end, and Dillon and Silverthorne toward the east. From Dillon take U.S. 6 about 5 miles east to Keystone and another 15 miles to Arapahoe. Breckenridge is about 10 miles south of Frisco on Colo. 9, and Copper Mountain is just south of I-70 exit 195 (Colo. 91). Loveland is just across the county line at exit 216 on the east side of the Eisenhower Tunnel.

Summit Stage (📞 970/668-0999; www.summitstage.com) provides free year-round service between Frisco, Dillon, Silverthorne, Keystone, Breckenridge, and Copper Mountain, daily from 6am to midnight, from late November to mid-April and shorter hours the rest of the year.

You can get around Breckenridge on the **Breckenridge Free Ride** bus system (📞 970/547-3140), and there's also free shuttle service at the Keystone Resort (📞 970/496-4200).

FAST FACTS Medical facilities here include the **Breckenridge Medical Center,** located in The Village at Breckenridge, 555 S. Park Ave., Plaza II, Breckenridge (📞 970/453-1010). **Post offices** are at 305 S. Ridge Rd., Breckenridge, and 35 W. Main St., Frisco. For hours and other information contact the U.S. Postal Service (📞 800/275-8777; www.usps.com). For **weather and road conditions,** call 📞 970/668-1090.

SPECIAL EVENTS Ullr Fest, early January, in Breckenridge; International Snow Sculpture Championships, fourth week in January, in Breckenridge; Sunsation and Eenie Weenie Bikini Contest, early April, in Copper Mountain; Memorial Day Weekend Beach Party and Festival of the Brewpubs, Memorial Day weekend, in Arapahoe Basin; the Celtic Festival, late June, Keystone; Oktoberfest, mid-October, in Breckenridge. See also "The Festival Scene," later in this chapter.

SKIING & OTHER WINTER ACTIVITIES

Breckenridge and Keystone ski areas are now part of Vail Resorts, and any lift ticket purchased at Vail or Beaver Creek is valid without restriction at Breckenridge and Keystone. However, only multiday lift tickets for 3 or more days purchased at Breckenridge or Keystone are also valid at Vail and Beaver Creek.

Snowboarding is permitted at all local resorts.

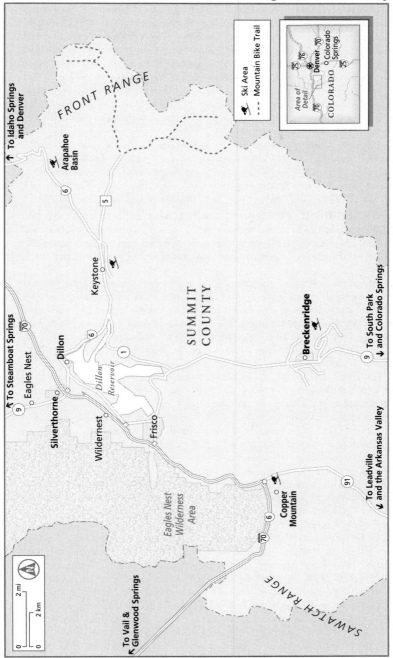

Ski Area
--- Mountain Bike Trail

FRONT RANGE

To Idaho Springs and Denver

Arapahoe Basin

6

5

Keystone

SUMMIT COUNTY

Breckenridge

To South Park and Colorado Springs

9

To Steamboat Springs

70

6

Dillon

1

Eagles Nest

9

Silverthorne

Dillon Reservoir

Wildernest

Frisco

To Leadville & the Arkansas Valley

91

Eagles Nest Wilderness Area

Copper Mountain

6

70

To Vail & Glenwood Springs

SAWATCH RANGE

2 mi

2 km

0

0

Area of Detail

Denver

Colorado Springs

COLORADO

25

76

70

70

25

ARAPAHOE BASIN Arapahoe Basin, 28194 U.S. 6, between Keystone and Loveland Pass, is one of Colorado's oldest ski areas, having opened in 1946. Several features make Arapahoe exceptional. Most of its 490 skiable acres are intermediate and expert terrain, much of it above timberline. It rates its 69 trails 15% beginner, 45% intermediate, 20% advanced, and 20% expert. Its longest run is 1½ miles. Arapahoe Basin receives an average of 367 inches of snow a year, and is frequently one of the last Colorado ski areas to close for the season—often not until mid-June. It usually opens in early November. Arapahoe offers a 2,270-foot vertical drop from its summit at 13,050 feet. It is served by two triple and three double chairs plus a conveyor.

Lift tickets during peak season cost $49 for adults, $38 for youths 15 to 19, $19 for children 6 to 14, $38 for seniors 60 to 69, $10 per day for seniors 70 and older, and they're free for children 5 and younger. For information, including a snow report, contact Arapahoe Basin, P.O. Box 8787, Keystone, CO 80435 (© **888/272-7246** or 970/496-0718; www.arapahoebasin.com).

BRECKENRIDGE ☆☆ Spread across four large mountains on the west side of the town of Breckenridge, this area ranks third in size among Colorado's ski resorts. Once known for its wealth of open, groomed beginner and intermediate slopes, Breckenridge in recent years has expanded its acreage for expert skiers as well.

Peak 8, the original ski mountain, is the highest of the four at 12,998 feet and has the greatest variety. Peak 9, heavily geared to novices and intermediates, rises above the principal base area. Peak 10, served by a single high-speed quad chair, is predominantly expert territory. The vast bowls of Peak 8 and the North Face of Peak 9 are likewise advanced terrain. There are restaurants high on Peaks 8, 9, and 10 and three cafeterias at the base of the slopes. Peak 7 is a double black-diamond challenge on over 1,200 feet of vertical.

All told, the resort has 2,208 skiable acres, with 146 trails, including Four O'Clock, the longest at 3½ miles! The resort rates its trails as 15% beginner, 33% intermediate, and 52% expert and advanced. There are 27 lifts—two high-speed six passenger chairs, six high-speed quads, one triple chair, six double chairs, five surface lifts, and seven carpet lifts. Vertical drop is 3,398 feet from a summit of 12,998 feet; average annual snowfall is 300 inches (25 ft.).

Lift tickets during peak season cost $71 for adults, $35 for children 5 to 12, $61 for seniors 65 to 69, and are free for children 4 and younger and seniors 70 and older. Tickets purchased at Breckenridge are also valid at Keystone and Arapahoe Basin, and multiday tickets for 3 or more days are also valid at Vail and Beaver Creek.

Among Breckenridge's programs are its women's ski seminars, taught exclusively by women for women skiers of all abilities. Three- and four-day seminars are offered in January, February, March, and April. Women-only ski-school classes are available throughout the ski season. For more information, call © **888/576-2754.** For snowboarders, the Breckenridge SuperPipe is a delight. This half-pipe has a 15-degree slope, 15-foot-high walls, and 17-foot transitions.

Breckenridge is usually open from mid-November to mid-May, daily from 8:30am to 4pm. For further information, contact **Breckenridge Ski Resort,** P.O. Box 1058, Breckenridge, CO 80424 (© **800/789-7669** or 970/453-5000; 970/453-6118 for snow conditions; www.breckenridge.snow.com). From Memorial Day weekend to Labor Day, the alpine slide is in operation, and the trails are open to mountain bikers; minigolf is also available. Call for off-season hours and chairlift schedule.

COPPER MOUNTAIN From Copper Mountain village, the avalanche chutes on the west face of Ten Mile Mountain seem to spell out the word SKI. Though this is a natural coincidence, locals like to say the mountain has terrain created for skiing.

Terrain is about half beginner and intermediate, with the rest ranging from advanced to "you better be really good." The area has a vertical drop of 2,601 feet from a peak elevation of 12,313 feet. There are 2,433 skiable acres and 125 trails served by 22 lifts—one high-speed six-person chair, four high-speed quads, five triple chairs, five double chairs, two surface lifts, four conveyors, and one tubing zone lift. Average annual snowfall is 280 inches. Copper Mountain has two terrain parks. Big floater jumps are spread out across an entire run, with proper takeoff and landing ramps; there's a regulation half-pipe, and several drainage and gladed runs have been thinned to provide challenging tree riding for more advanced snowboarders.

There are three restaurants on the mountain and several more in the base village. Also at the base are 25km of cross-country track, a tubing hill, and a full-service racquet and athletic club.

Lift tickets during the peak season cost $64 for adults, $32 for children 6 to 13, and $54 for seniors 65 to 69. Tickets are free for seniors 70 and older and children 5 and under.

Copper Mountain is usually open from early November to mid-April, Monday through Friday from 9am to 4pm, Saturday and Sunday from 8:30am to 4pm. For information, contact **Copper Mountain Resort,** P.O. Box 3001, Copper Mountain, CO 80443 (© **866/841-2481;** www.coppercolorado.com). For reservations, call © **888/219-2441;** for a snow report, call © **800/789-7609.**

KEYSTONE Keystone is actually three separate mountains, offering a variety of terrain. And the resort is one of the best spots for night skiing in America, open daily from 8:30am until 8pm.

From its peak elevation of 12,200 feet, Keystone's vertical drop is 3,128 feet. It's three interconnected mountains offer 2,870 acres of skiing, 117 trails (17 open for night skiing), and 20 lifts—including two connecting high-speed gondolas, a high-speed six-person chair, five high-speed quads, one quad, one triple, four doubles, two surface lifts, and four carpets. Average annual snowfall is 230 inches (about 19 ft.). Its trails are rated 12% beginner, 34% intermediate, and 54% expert and advanced.

For snowboarders, Keystone has 66 acres of terrain parks, including two half-pipes, which are lit for night riding.

Lift tickets during the peak season cost $65 for adults, $33 for children 5 to 12, $55 for seniors 65 and older, and are free for children 4 and younger. Tickets purchased at Keystone are also valid at Breckenridge and Arapahoe Basin, and multiday tickets for 3 or more days are also valid at Vail and Beaver Creek.

Excellent on-mountain dining is available at the Alpenglow Stube, located in The Outpost, a log-and-stone lodge atop North Peak (elevation 11,444 ft.). Access is via two scenic gondola rides.

Keystone is usually open from early November through mid-April. For further information, contact **Keystone Resort,** P.O. Box 38, Keystone, CO 80435 (© **800/468-5004** or 970/496-4386; www.keystone.snow.com). For snow reports call © **800/404-3535** or 970/496-4111.

LOVELAND Just across the county line, on the east side of I-70's Eisenhower Memorial Tunnel, is **Loveland Ski Area,** P.O. Box 899, Georgetown, CO

80444 (© **800/736-3754** or 303/571-5580; www.skiloveland.com). Comprising Loveland Basin and Loveland Valley, it was created in the late 1930s by a Denver ski club wanting to take advantage of the area's heavy snowfall (400 in., more than 33 ft., annually). You can still see the original rope-tow cabins from 1942, when all-day tickets cost $2. Inflation (and the cost of many improvements) has taken a toll. Today, tickets during the peak skiing season cost $46 for adults, $36 for seniors 60 to 69, and $19 for children 6 to 14; children under 6 ski free, and seniors 70 and older are offered a season pass for $30.

There's good beginner-intermediate terrain on the 1,365 lift-served acres—17% and 42% respectively, leaving 41% advanced. The vertical drop is 2,410 feet from a top elevation of 13,010 feet, and the longest run is 2 miles. Lifts include three quad chairs, two triples, four doubles, one surface lift, and one tow. Loveland's terrain parks offer natural half-pipes and big powder-filled bowls.

The resort usually opens in mid-October and remains open daily through May.

CROSS-COUNTRY SKIING & SNOWSHOEING The **Frisco Nordic Center,** at 18454 Colo. 9, south of Frisco (© **970/668-0866**), sits on the shores of Dillon Reservoir. Its trail network includes 43km of groomed cross-country ski trails. The lodge has a snack bar and a shop with rentals and retail sales; instruction and backcountry and snowshoe tours are also offered. From the Frisco Nordic Center you can ski to the **Breckenridge Nordic Center,** on Willow Lane near the foot of Peak 8 (© **970/453-6855**), with its own series of 30km of groomed trails. The two operations share 20km of snowshoe trails and 5km of snowshoe trails where leashed dogs are welcome. One trail pass ($12 for adults, $8 for seniors and children) covers both Nordic centers, and rental equipment is available. The **Gold Run Nordic Center** at the Breckenridge Golf Club, 200 Club House Dr. (© **970/547-7889**), charges similar rates and features more than 20km of groomed trails, from beginner to advanced, in addition to backcountry and snowshoe trails, and also offers rental equipment.

For additional information on these and other cross-country skiing centers check out **www.colorado-xc.org** on the Web. There are also numerous cross-country skiing possibilities in the area's national forests; contact the **Dillon Ranger District** (see below).

WARM-WEATHER & YEAR-ROUND ACTIVITIES

The **White River National Forest** encompasses the boundaries of Summit County. This recreational playground offers opportunities not only for downhill and cross-country skiing and snowmobiling in winter, but also for hiking and backpacking, horseback riding, boating, fishing, hunting, and bicycling in summer. White River National Forest includes the **Eagles Nest Wilderness Area** and **Green Mountain Reservoir,** both in the northern part of the county.

The **U.S. Forest Service's Dillon Ranger District,** located in the town of Silverthorne at 680 River Pkwy. (Colo. 9), Silverthorne, CO 80498, about half a mile north of I-70 exit 205 (© **970/468-5400;** www.fs.fed.us/r2), has an unusually good selection of information on outdoor recreation possibilities, including maps and guides to hiking and mountain-biking trails, jeep roads, cross-country skiing, snowmobiling, fishing, and camping. You can also get information on a wide variety of outdoor activities from the **Breckenridge Resort Chamber Activity Center,** 309 N. Main St. (© **877/864-0868**).

BICYCLING There are more than 40 miles of paved bicycle paths in the county, including a path from Breckenridge (with a spur from Keystone) to

Frisco and Copper Mountain, continuing across Vail Pass to Vail. This spectacularly beautiful two-lane path is off-limits to motorized vehicles of any kind. Also see "Mountain Biking," below.

BOATING   Dillon Reservoir, a beautiful mountain lake along I-70 between Dillon and Frisco, is the place to go. Also called Lake Dillon, the 3,300-acre reservoir, which provides drinking water to Denver, is more than 200 feet deep in spots. At 9,017 feet elevation, it claims to have America's highest altitude yacht club and holds colorful regattas most summer weekends. The popular Dillon Open, a huge sailboat race, occurs the first weekend in August. Swimming is not permitted.

The full-service **Dillon Marina,** 150 Marina Dr. (© **970/468-5100;** www.dillonmarina.com), is open from the last weekend of May through the last weekend of October, offering boats for 2-hour, half-day, or full-day rentals; sailing instruction; and charter cruises. Half-day boat-rental fees run $75 for fishing boats, $120 for runabouts, $160 for 22-foot pontoon boats, and $300 for 25-foot pontoons. Fuel is extra. The half-day rate for 18- and 20-foot sailboats is $110, and more upscale 22-foot sailboats rent for $145 to $165 for a half-day. An 8-hour sailing class costs $250 per person, and the "sailing experience" 2-hour sailboat tour for novice sailors costs $45 per person. There's also a small store, repair shop, restaurant, and bar.

FISHING   Major fishing rivers within an hour of Breckenridge include the South Platte, Arkansas, Eagle, Colorado, and Blue rivers, and for lake fishing, try Dillon Reservoir and Spinney Mountain Reservoir. The Blue River, from Lake Dillon Dam to its confluence with the Colorado River at Kremmling, is rated a gold-medal fishing stream. For tips on where they're biting, as well as supplies, fishing licenses, and all the rest, stop at **Mountain Angler** ✿, 311 S. Main St., Breckenridge, in the Main Street Mall (© **800/453-4669** or 970/453-4665; www.mountainangler.com), which also offers year-round guide service. Guided fly-fishing wading trips, for two anglers, start at $195 for a half-day; $275 for a full day, including lunch. A full-day float-fishing guided trip for two anglers costs $395. Guided fly-fishing trips are also offered by **The Adventure Company** (© **800/497-7238;** www.theadventurecompany.com) at similar rates.

GOLF   Among area golf courses, which all boast wonderful scenery, are the 18-hole **Breckenridge Golf Club,** 200 Clubhouse Dr., Breckenridge (© **970/453-9104**), designed by Jack Nicklaus, with the greens fee for 18 holes of $95; **Copper Creek Golf Club,** 104 Wheeler Place, Copper Mountain Resort (© **970/968-3333**), among the highest 18-hole courses in North America at 9,752 feet, with fees of $69 to $79, including cart, for 18 holes; **Keystone Ranch Golf Course,** 1239 Keystone Ranch Rd., Keystone (© **970/496-4250**), charging $125 to $140, including a cart, for 18 holes; and the **River Course at Keystone,** 155 River Course Dr., Keystone (© **970/496-4444**), which also charges $125 to $140, including cart, for 18 holes.

HIKING & BACKPACKING   The **Colorado Trail** ✿✿ cuts a swath through Summit County. It enters from the east across Kenosha Pass, follows the Swan River to its confluence with the Blue River, then climbs over Ten Mile Mountain to Copper Mountain. The trail then turns south toward Tennessee Pass, north of Leadville. Contact the **Colorado Trail Foundation,** American Mountaineering Center, 710 10th St. #210, Golden, CO 80401-5843 (© **303/384-3729;** www.coloradotrail.org).

In addition, there are myriad hiking opportunities in the national forests. Consult the U.S. Forest Service, the Breckenridge Resort Chamber Activity Center, or a visitor information center for maps and details.

HORSEBACK RIDING   For some spectacular views of this area from atop a horse, take a ride with **Kingdom of Breckenridge Stables,** located just above the Beaver Run ski lift on Village Road (© **970/453-4438;** www.colorado-horses.com/kingdom). The company offers rides of about 90 minutes, plus breakfast rides, for about $40 per person (half-price for children 6 and under). Reservations should be made at least 1 day in advance.

MOUNTAIN BIKING   Numerous trails are available for mountain bikers. Energetic fat-tire fans can try the Devil's Triangle, a difficult 80-mile loop that begins and ends in Frisco after climbing four mountain passes (including 11,318-ft. Fremont Pass). Check with the U.S. Forest Service or Breckenridge Resort Chamber Activity Center for directions and tips on other trails; for mountain bikers who prefer to not work so hard, check with the Breckenridge Resort Chamber Activity Center on times and costs for taking your bike up the mountain on the Breckenridge chairlift.

Among the companies providing bike rentals and information is **Lone Star Sports,** at 200 W. Washington St., Breckenridge (© **800/621-9733** or 970/453-2003; www.skilonestar.com), which charges full-day rates of $18 for a basic bike, $22 for a front-suspension bike, $31 for a full-suspension bike, and $25 for a tandem bike. Rates are about 30% less for a half-day and there are discounts for multiday rentals.

RIVER RAFTING   Trips through the white water of the Blue River—which runs through Breckenridge to Frisco—as well as longer journeys on the Colorado and Arkansas rivers, are offered by various companies, including **Good Times Rafting Company** (© **800/808-0357** or 970/453-5559; www.goodtimesrafting.com/goodtimes-whois.htm), **Performance Tours Rafting** (© **800/328-7238** or 970/453-0661; www.performancetours.com), and **The Adventure Company** (© **800/497-7238;** www.theadventurecompany.com), all based in Breckenridge. Rates for half-day trips on the Blue River cost about $42 to $45 for adults and $33 to $40 for children. Full-day trips on other area rivers are about $75 to $85 for adults and $65 to $75 for kids.

THE FESTIVAL SCENE

The **Breckenridge Music Festival** presents dozens of classical and nonclassical music performances, with concerts in the Riverwalk Center from mid-June through mid-August. Tickets cost from $15 to $25; they're only $5 for students under 18. Contact the Breckenridge Music Festival, P.O. Box 1254, Breckenridge, CO 80424 (© **970/453-9142** or 970/547-3100 for the box office; www.breckenridgemusicfestival.com).

Genuine Jazz in Breckenridge, on the last weekend of June, showcases Colorado jazz ensembles with styles ranging from Dixieland to bebop to New Age. Local bars and nightclubs host Friday- and Saturday-night performances, and there are also free outdoor concerts. Contact Peak Performances, Box 57, Breckenridge, CO 80424 (© **866/464-2626** for tickets; www.genuinejazz.com).

The **Breckenridge Festival of Film,** held in early September, attracts Hollywood directors and actors to town to discuss some two dozen films in all genres. Films that have premiered here include *American Beauty, The Shawshank Redemption, The Joy Luck Club,* and *L.A. Confidential.* Contact the Breckenridge

Festival of Film, P.O. Box 718, Breckenridge, CO 80424 (© **970/453-6200;** www.breckfilmfest.com).

MORE TO SEE & DO

Amaze'n Breckenridge Quite possibly Colorado's largest human maze, this is Amaze'n Colorado's original creation. The two-level labyrinth of twists and turns offers prizes to participants who can "beat the clock." Like the Amaze'n Winter Park (p. 287), the maze is changed weekly to maintain interest for repeat customers. A free observation deck provides a bird's-eye view of the maze, as well as the surrounding scenery. Allow 1 to 1½ hours.

1579 Ski Hill Rd. at the base of Peak 8, Breckenridge. © 970/453-7262. www.amazenmazes.com. Admission $6 adults, $5 children 5–12, free for children under 5. Additional maze runs $2. Mid-June to Labor Day. Call for hours.

Breckenridge National Historic District The entire Victorian core of this 19th-century mining town has been carefully preserved, and you can see it on your own (pick up a free walking tour brochure at the Visitor Information Cabin), or during the summer on guided 1½-hour walking tours conducted by the Summit Historical Society. Colorfully painted shops and restaurants occupy the old buildings, most dating from the 1880s and 1890s. Most of the historic district focuses on Main Street, and extends east on either side of Lincoln Avenue. The historical society also maintains the **Historical Museum,** 111 S. Main St., open daily from 10am to 8pm, with free admission. Among the 254 historic buildings in the district are the **1875 Edwin Carter Museum,** 111 N. Ridge St., and the **1896 William Harrison Briggle House,** 104 N. Harris St., in Milne Park. The society also leads tours during the summer to the outskirts of town to visit the underground shaft of the hard-rock **Washington Gold Mine** and the gold-panning operation at **Lomax Placer Gulch.** In winter, the historical society offers tours of the Edwin Carter Museum once each week—funding permitting—and slide shows on the historic district, at the Edwin Carter Museum, twice a week (call for times). Allow 2 to 4 hours.

Breckenridge. © 970/453-9022. www.summithistorical.org. Guided tours $6 per person. Tour tickets available at the Breckenridge Resort Chamber Activity Center, 309 N. Main St. Historic district tours mid-June to Sept; Edwin Carter Museum tours mid-June to Sept; museum open year-round, with free admission (call for times).

Country Boy Mine At this 100-year-old mine you can take a guided tour 1,000 feet underground, pan for gold in Eureka Creek, explore the mining exhibit and the five-story 75-year-old mill, and listen to the legends. Or take a hay ride up the mountain on old mining trails and enjoy hot chocolate and roasted marshmallows around a campfire. The mine is a constant 45°F (7°C) year-round, so take a jacket even in August. There's also a restored blacksmith shop, indoor gold panning in winter, and sleigh rides are available in the snowy months (www.brecksleighrides.com). Every summer sees the addition of a baby burro. Tours start on the hour. Allow at least an hour.

0542 French Gulch Rd., P.O. Box 8569, Breckenridge. © 970/453-4405. www.countryboymine.com. Mine tour $16 adults, $11 children 4–12, free for kids under 4; hay ride $22 adults, $17 children 4–12, free for kids under 4. Special rates and hours are available for families and groups. MC, V. Summer daily 10am–4pm; winter by reservation. The hours have some other seasonal fluctuations—call for details.

Dillon Schoolhouse Museum A one-room country school—built in 1883 and filled with such artifacts of early Colorado education as desks with inkwells, McGuffey readers, and scientific teaching apparatus—is the highlight of this historic park. Also on the site are the 1885 Lula Myers ranch house and the

Depression-era Honeymoon Cabin. All buildings were moved from Old Dillon (now beneath the waters of the reservoir) or Keystone. Tours are also conducted (by appointment) of the 1884 Montezuma Schoolhouse, located at 10,400 feet elevation in the 1860s silver-mining camp of Montezuma. Allow about an hour.

403 LaBonte St., Dillon. (© 970/453-9022. www.summithistorical.org. Admission/guided tour $6 adults, $3 children 12 and younger. Mid-June to Labor Day Tues–Sat 1–4pm; or by appointment.

Frisco Historic Park ★ Ten historic buildings—including the town's original 1881 jail, a one-room schoolhouse, log chapel, and homes dating from the 1880s—make up this beautifully maintained historic park. The schoolhouse contains displays and artifacts from Frisco's early days, and a trapper's cabin has a hands-on exhibit of animal pelts. Artisans sell their wares in several buildings, and a variety of events are scheduled during the summer. A self-guided walking tour of historic Frisco can be obtained at the park. Allow 1 hour.

120 Main St. (at Second St.), Frisco. (© 970/668-3428. www.townoffrisco.com. Free admission. Summer Tues–Sun 11am–4pm; winter Tues–Sat 11am–4pm.

SHOPPING

Breckenridge is the place to shop in Summit County, with a variety of shops and galleries in the historic buildings along Main Street.

For contemporary art, from realism to Impressionism, check out **Breckenridge Gallery,** 124 S. Main St. (© **970/453-2592;** www.breckenridge-gallery. com). Original Western paintings and bronzes, plus historic Navajo weavings and cowboy and Indian collectibles can be found at **Paint Horse Gallery,** 226 S. Main St. (© **970/453-6813;** www.painthorsegallery.com). Over 250 artists, working in a variety of styles and media, are represented at **Skilled Hands Gallery,** 110 S. Main St. (© **970/453-7818**). For beautiful photos of Colorado, either as individual prints or in coffee-table books, stop at **Colorado Scenics,** 124 S. Main St. (© **800/861-3261** or 970/453-4922; www.coloradoscenics. com); London native Steve Tohari has been photographing his adopted state since 1983.

If you're in the market for a unique hat—including some really hilarious ones—try the **Breckenridge Hat Company,** 411 S. Main St. (© **800/809-4287** or 970/453-2737; www.breckenridgehatcompany.com). Authentic traditional and contemporary American-Indian jewelry, pottery, and other crafts can be found at **Southwest Designs,** 101 S. Main St. (© **970/453-6008**). The **Silverthorne Factory Stores** (© **866/746-7686** or 970/468-9440; www.silver thornefactorystores.com) has about 80 outlet shops—from fashion and athletic wear to home accessories; take I-70 to exit 205.

WHERE TO STAY

Thousands of rooms are available here at any given time. Even so, during peak seasons, finding accommodations may be difficult. In many cases it will be best to simply call one of the reservation services, tell them when you plan to visit and how much you want to spend, and ask for their suggestions. Throughout the county, condominiums prevail. While they often offer the best value, they're sometimes short on charm. If you're planning to spend much time in one, it pays to ask about views and fireplaces before booking. Local reservation services include **Summit County Central Reservations** (© **800/365-6365;** www.skier lodging.com), **Breckenridge Central Reservations** (© **877/791-3968;** www. gobreck.com), and in Keystone, **Key to the Rockies** (© **800/248-1942;** www. keytotherockies.com).

In addition to the properties discussed below, there's the **Best Western Lake Dillon Lodge,** 1202 Summit Blvd., Frisco (© **800/727-0607** or 970/668-5094), charging $79 to $149 double; **Comfort Suites** in Dillon at I-70 exit 205 (© **800/424-6423** or 970/513-0300), with rates of $69 to $199 double; and **Super 8,** also at I-70 exit 205 (© **800/800-8000** or 970/468-8888), with double rates of $60 to $106. Rates are dramatically higher from Christmas to New Years.

Room taxes add about 9.5% to hotel bills.

Allaire Timbers Inn Bed & Breakfast ★★   This romantic mountain hideaway is a lovely contemporary log lodge, with a stone wood-burning fireplace in the living room and magnificent views of the mountains and town. All rooms are named for and decorated around the motif of a Colorado mountain pass. There are hand-painted tiled showers—no tubs—in standard rooms, but the two suites have hot tubs and river-rock gas-burning fireplaces. All units come with private decks, CD players, robes, and fuzzy fleece socks. The homemade gourmet breakfast includes a choice of a meat or vegetarian entree, plus fruit and muffins. In the afternoon, guests can enjoy hot citrus cider (an old family recipe), beer, or wine; and the beverage bar is available 24 hours. Located just outside the town limits, an easy path takes you right into town. The inn is also conveniently located on the free ski shuttle route; children 13 years and older are welcome. Neither smoking nor pets are allowed—the resident dog has prior claim.

9511 Colo. 9 (P.O. Box 4653), Breckenridge, CO 80424. © **800/624-4904** or 970/453-7530. Fax 970/453-8699. www.allairetimbers.com. 10 units. $145–$275 double; $250–$400 suite. Rates include full breakfast. AE, DISC, MC, V. **Amenities:** Outdoor hot tub. *In room:* TV; dataport.

East West Resorts at Breckenridge   There are several condominium complexes to choose from here, offering everything from simple studios to luxurious and spacious three-bedroom units. Most have mountain views or are nestled among tall pines, have a fireplace, and are within easy strolling distance of historic Victorian Main Street Breckenridge. Many units are ski-in and -out and there's a ski storage facility.

505 S. Main St. (P.O. Box 1748), Breckenridge, CO 80424. © **800/506-7632** or 970/453-4000. Fax 970/453-0463. www.eastwestbreckenridge.com. 220 units. Summer $83–$324; winter $115–$1,238. Weekly and monthly rates in summer. AE, DISC, MC, V. Underground parking. **Amenities:** Outdoor heated pool; state-of-the-art fitness center; 7 outdoor hot tubs. *In room:* TV, kitchen, hair dryer, iron.

Little Mountain Lodge Bed & Breakfast ★★   This handsome, whitewashed log lodge is among our top choices in Breckenridge. Nestled among the trees, the lodge offers breathtaking views of the mountains from the front rooms and the aspen forest from the back. All the rooms are open and airy, and boast a balcony or deck, handmade log furnishings, and ceiling fans. Some rooms have whirlpool tubs, one has a steam shower, and most of them feature vaulted ceilings. All units have Internet access; some have DSL. Two suites have fireplaces. There's an elevator and one handicapped-accessible room with a roll-in shower.

The living room has a huge river-rock fireplace, with overstuffed sofa and chairs comfortably arranged around it. A downstairs family room contains a stone fireplace, TV, and VCR and DVD player. There's also a ski and bike storage room and a ski boot dryer. Children of all ages are welcome (rare in B&Bs); smoking is not permitted.

98 Sunbeam Dr. (P.O. Box 2479), Breckenridge, CO 80424. © **800/468-7707** (outside Colorado) or 970/453-1969. Fax 970/453-1919. www.littlemountainlodge.com. 10 units. $140–$225 double; $170–$270 suite. Lower rates often available in spring and fall. Rates include full breakfast and evening appetizers. AE,

DISC, MC, V. **Amenities:** Large hot tub; business center (copier and fax service); common refrigerator and microwave. *In room:* TV/VCR (video library available), dataport.

The Lodge & Spa at Breckenridge Nestled on a forested cliff 5 minutes from the town of Breckenridge, this European-style spa features gas stone fireplaces and wrought-iron chandeliers—upscale, but with a Rocky Mountain atmosphere. The unique rooms have American-Indian or Southwestern decor and artwork and balconies (or views). Many also have fireplaces, feather duvets, and poster beds, contrasting rustic touches with a contemporary flair. Several suites have kitchenettes, and there's a luxury three-bedroom house with private hot tub, built in 2004.

The Top of the World Restaurant & Bar, named the community's best in recent "Taste of Breckenridge" competitions, serves American dinners with a regional influence ($15–$29) and has a dramatic mountain view. A 24-hour front desk, ski and boot storage, and a winter complimentary shuttle (7:30am–11pm) to anywhere in Breckenridge are available.

112 Overlook Dr. (P.O. Box 1078), Breckenridge, CO 80424. © **800/736-1607** or 970/453-9300. Fax 970/453-0625. www.thelodgeatbreck.com. 46 units. $77–$375 double; $375–$750 house. Rates include continental breakfast. AE, DC, DISC, MC, V. Pets accepted. **Amenities:** Restaurant (American); lounge; indoor pool; 24-hour health club and full-service spa; 2 hot tubs; sauna; limited room service. *In room:* TV, kitchen (some), coffeemaker; hair dryer.

Ridge Street Inn Bed & Breakfast This 1890 Victorian-style inn, located in the heart of the Breckenridge Historic District, is close to restaurants, shops, the town trolley, and shuttle services. The star of the inn is the Governor's Parlor, furnished with Eastlake antiques. It has bay windows, a queen bed, large private bathroom, TV, and private entrance. Rooms with private bathrooms also have TVs; the two rooms that share a bathroom also share a sitting room. Home-cooked breakfasts might include waffles, fresh strawberry crepes, or omelets, sausage, or bacon. Children are welcome but smoking is not permitted.

212 N. Ridge St. (P.O. Box 2854), Breckenridge, CO 80424. © **800/452-4680** or 970/453-4680. www.ridgestreetinn.com. 5 units (3 with bathroom). Summer $80–$90 double with private bathroom, $70 double with shared bathroom; winter $120–$140 double with private bathroom, $100 double with shared bathroom; holidays $150–$180 with private bathroom, $120 with shared bathroom. Higher rates between Christmas and New Year's. Rates include full breakfast. MC, V. *In room:* TV (some), no phone.

CAMPING

Tiger Run R.V. & Chalet Resort ★★ Named for a historic mine in the area, Tiger Run is both conveniently and beautifully located. Activities in winter include skiing, snowmobiling, cross-country skiing, and snowboarding; in summer there are wine-and-cheese parties, kids' s'mores night, and live music on Saturday. The clubhouse lodge, in the center of the park, is open year-round, with an indoor swimming pool, hot tubs, game room, TV room, laundry facilities, restrooms with showers, telephones, and two dataports for checking e-mail. There's a small no-food convenience store; tennis, volleyball, and basketball courts; a children's playground; and sports equipment available at the office. Pets are welcome in RV sites only. There are also 30 chalet-style cabins on the property, with rates of $70 to $135 for doubles ($10 per extra person); children 3 and under stay free. Smoking and pets are not permitted in the chalets.

85 Tiger Run Rd. (3 miles north of Breckenridge off Colo. 9), Breckenridge, CO 80424. © **800/895-9594** or 970/453-9690. Fax 970/453-6782. www.tigerrunresort.com. 250 sites. $29–$54. 10% discount for cash on stays less than a week. Rates include water, sewer, electric, and cable TV hookups. Weekly rates available. AE, DISC, MC, V.

WHERE TO DINE

You certainly won't go hungry in Breckenridge. Following are some of our favorite eateries, and for additional choices check out the very useful website **www.breckenridgedining.com**.

EXPENSIVE

Briar Rose Restaurant REGIONAL   Located uphill from the Main Street traffic light, the Briar Rose is among the town's most elegant (but still casual) restaurants. Classical paintings, fine music, and linen service underscore Briar Rose's sophisticated atmosphere. The adjoining trophy bar and lounge has big-game heads, sports memorabilia, and a 100-year-old back bar. In fine weather you can dine alfresco while gazing at the surrounding mountains from the new deck outside the lounge. You can start with escargot, crab-stuffed mushrooms, coconut shrimp, wild game sausage, or homemade soup. Dinners feature game—usually elk, ostrich, and caribou. Other popular choices include slow-roasted prime rib, veal, steak, duck, lamb, frog legs, seafood, and vegetarian and pasta entrees. A children's menu is available, and the extensive wine list offers domestic and imported wines.

109 E. Lincoln St. ✆ **970/453-9948.** Reservations recommended. Main courses $15–$30. AE, DISC, MC, V. Ski season daily 5–10pm; rest of year Mon–Sat 6–10pm.

Hearthstone Casual Dining REGIONAL   A favorite of locals because of its creative cuisine, the Hearthstone is in a historic home built in 1886. It has a rustic yet elegant interior, with fine mountain views from the upstairs lounge. Start with the house special, jalapeño-stuffed shrimp, or smoked trout with herbed Chevre cheese, capers, red onion, and lemon. Then choose from fresh seafood such as ginger-crusted scallops (pan-seared sea scallops coated in ginger) or ahi tuna medallions, spice-rubbed and served with a sweet soy reduction. Other choices include the granola-crusted elk chop, strawberry-pepper duck breast, slow-roasted prime rib, and a local favorite: filet au poivre—an 8-ounce black pepper–encrusted tenderloin with a brandy-Dijon-cream reduction. Come to the smoke-free Victorian Lounge during happy hour (4–6pm) for specials on drinks and appetizers.

130 S. Ridge St. ✆ **970/453-1148.** www.stormrestaurants.com/hearthstone. Reservations recommended. Main courses $12–$28. AE, DC, MC, V. Daily 5–10pm.

Keystone Ranch ⭐⭐ CREATIVE REGIONAL   A working cattle ranch for more than 3 decades until 1972, the Keystone Ranch now boasts riding stables, a golf course, and this outstanding gourmet restaurant, located in a 1940s ranch house with a mountain-lodge decor. Among the area's best restaurants, the Keystone Ranch offers a six-course menu with a choice of appetizer, followed by soup, salad, and fruit sorbet. Main dishes, which vary seasonally, might include roasted rack of Colorado lamb, grilled duck breast, elk or other game, or fresh seafood. An extensive array of desserts is served in the living room in front of a handsome stone fireplace. There's valet parking and a full bar.

Keystone Ranch Rd., Keystone. ✆ **970/496-4386.** Reservations strongly recommended. 6-course dinner $72 adults, $40 children. AE, DC, DISC, MC, V. Summer and winter daily 5:30–9pm, 2 seatings; call for spring and fall hours.

MODERATE & INEXPENSIVE

Breckenridge Brewery and Pub ⭐ AMERICAN/BREWPUB   This brew-pub was designed around its brewery, giving diners a first-hand view of the brewing process. Of the award-winning beers, try the Trademark Pale or the

Avalanche, a local favorite. Like many good brewpubs, lunch choices here include fish and chips, half-pound burgers, and soups and salads (try the mango spinach salad). But the menu also strives to be somewhat more interesting, offering items such as pan-fried walleye and grilled portobello mushroom sandwiches. The dinner menu adds tender tasty baby back ribs, New York sirloin, lemon-sesame salmon, and charbroiled fajitas for those who like it spicy, and desserts are homemade. Also see "Summit County After Dark," below.

600 S. Main St. © 970/453-1550. www.breckenridgebrewery.com. Reservations not accepted. Main courses lunch $4.95–$9.95, dinner $7.95–$17. AE, DC, DISC, MC, V. Daily 11am–10pm; bar open later.

Horseshoe II AMERICAN   A family-style restaurant in a historic 19th-century building, the Horseshoe II (yes, there was once a I) is set in the heart of downtown Breckenridge. It has a sunny split-level patio, ornate walls and ceilings, lace curtains, and, of course, mounted horseshoes. The popular bar has over 15 varieties of draft beer, including microbrewed choices.

Lunch offers salads, burgers, and sandwiches. Dinners are more elaborate. We particularly recommend the chicken-fried steak (breaded beefsteak topped with country-sausage cream gravy) and the fresh grilled Colorado trout. Other menu items include various types of pasta and a selection of light and vegetarian dishes. On weekends, start your day with the HAB (high-altitude breakfast), consisting of two eggs, two pancakes, breakfast meat, and juice. Smoking is not permitted anywhere in the establishment, including the bar.

115 S. Main St. © 970/453-7463. Breakfast items $2.95–$6.95; main courses lunch $4.95–$7.50, dinner $9.95–$18. AE, MC, V. Mon–Fri 11am–10pm; Sat–Sun 8am–10pm.

Mi Casa MEXICAN   Mi Casa is Breckenridge's best Mexican restaurant. Its newly remodeled cantina is the locals' favorite spot for happy hour, and the margaritas are consistently voted the best in Summit County. In addition to the standard burritos, tostadas, fajitas, and enchiladas, the restaurant is known for its seafood dishes—fish tacos, chile-encrusted trout, and tuna and swordfish burritos. There is also a good selection of beef, seafood, chicken, Southwestern, and vegetarian dishes.

600 Park Ave. © 970/453-2071. www.stormrestaurants.com. Reservations not accepted. Main courses $5–$15. AE, MC, V. Daily 11:30am–3pm and 5–9pm.

SUMMIT COUNTY AFTER DARK

Though every community has its watering holes, Breckenridge has the best nightlife in the area.

The **Backstage Theatre,** 121 S. Ridge St., Breckenridge (© 970/453-0199; www.backstagetheatre.org), has been presenting a variety of live theater since 1974. Recent productions have included *Me and Jezebel* by Elizabeth Fuller, Shakespeare's *A Midsummer Night's Dream,* Stuart Ross's *Forever Plaid,* and *Travels with My Aunt* by Giles Havergal. Ticket prices vary but most are $15 for adults and $8 for children under 12; reservations are strongly recommended.

Popular bars in Breckenridge include the **Breckenridge Brewery and Pub,** 600 S. Main St. (© 970/453-1550; www.breckenridgebrewery.com), where the microbrews include Avalanche Ale, a full-bodied amber ale, and our favorite, Trademark Pale, an American-style pale ale loaded with hops. Also see "Where to Dine," above.

The **Salt Creek Restaurant and Saloon,** 1101 E. Lincoln Ave. (© 970/453-4949), is a popular live-music dance club where you'll hear practically everything but country. For everything from live blues to reggae, try **Sherpa & Yeti's,** 318 S. Main St. (© 970/547-9299; sherpaandyetis.com), and the young, hip

Downstairs at Eric's, a bar and restaurant at 111 S. Main St. (© **970/453-1401;** www.downstairsaterics.com) that is popular with locals and the après-ski crowd alike and boasts 120 types of beer, including 22 on tap.

6 Vail & Beaver Creek

109 miles W of Denver, 150 miles E of Grand Junction

Consistently ranked the country's most popular ski resort by skiers and ski magazines almost since its inception, Vail is the big one. It's hard to imagine a more celebrated spot to schuss. Off the slopes, Vail is an incredibly compact Tyrolean village, frequented by almost as many Europeans as Americans, a situation that lends its restaurants, lodgings, and trendy shops a more transatlantic feel than other Colorado resorts. But the size of the mountain and the difficulty and excitement of many of its trails are still what draw the faithful.

Historically speaking, there was very little in the town's past to indicate that Vail would become the megadestination it has. Until U.S. 6 was built through Vail Pass in 1939, the only inhabitants were a handful of sheep ranchers. Dropping farther back into history, it's worth noting that the resort could never have been possible if it weren't for severe droughts in the 1850s and 1860s that resulted in numerous forest fires. The burnings created the wide-open ridges and back bowls that make skiers and snowboarders the world over quiver in their boots.

It was only when veterans of the 10th Mountain Division, who trained during World War II at Camp Hale, 23 miles south of the valley, returned in the 1950s that the reality of skiing was realized. One of them, Peter Siebert (1924–2002), urged development of this mountain land in the White River National Forest, and through his vision, Vail opened to skiers in December 1962, immediately becoming one of the largest ski areas in the United States. Additional ski-lift capacity made Vail America's largest ski resort by 1964.

Beaver Creek, built in 1980, has quickly garnered a reputation as an elegant (and pricey) vacation spot. Like Vail, it is a four-season resort that offers golf (the course was designed by Robert Trent Jones, Jr.), hot-air ballooning, mountain biking, fishing, and horseback riding, in addition to skiing. Its atmosphere is a bit more formal than the surrounding area, and its nightlife tends more toward refined piano bars than rowdy saloons, but the exclusivity of its après-ski spots isn't reflected on the slopes. At Beaver Creek, there's a trail for everyone. Experts are challenged but beginners aren't left out—they too can head straight to the top and then ski all the way down on a trail that matches their skill level.

ESSENTIALS

GETTING THERE   By Car   Vail is right on the I-70 corridor, so it's exceedingly easy to find. Just take exit 176, whether you're coming from the east (Denver) or the west (Grand Junction). A more direct route from the south is U.S. 24 through Leadville; this Tennessee Pass road joins I-70 5 miles west of Vail. Beaver Creek is located 12 miles west of Vail, off I-70 exit 167.

By Plane   From mid-December to early April visitors can fly directly into **Eagle County Regional Airport,** 35 miles west of Vail between I-70 exits 140 and 147 (© 970/524-9490; www.eagle-county.com/airport), which is served by **American** (© 800/433-7300), **Continental** (© 800/525-0280), **Delta** (© 800/221-1212), **Northwest** (© 800/225-2525), **United** (© 800/241-6522), and **US Airways** (© 800/428-4322). Call for possible availability of flights at other times.

By Airport Shuttle Many visitors fly into Denver International Airport and continue to Vail and Beaver Creek aboard a shuttle service such as **Colorado Mountain Express** (② 800/525-6363 or 970/926-9800; www.cmex.com), with one-way rates starting at about $50 per person. There are also shuttle services from the Eagle County Regional Airport to Vail and Beaver Creek; contact **High Mountain Taxi** (② 970/524-5555; www.hmtaxi.com), which charges $95 to $145 for up to six passengers, and also provides shuttle services between Vail and Aspen. Both of the above shuttle services offer online reservations. You can also get to the Vail/Beaver Creek area from the regional airport with **Vail Valley Taxi** (② 877/829-8294; www.vailtaxi.com) at similar rates to High Mountain Taxi, but to save a bundle of money, take the **bus** (see "Getting Around," below). Also, see **car rentals** under "Getting Around," below.

VISITOR INFORMATION For information or reservations in the Vail Valley, contact the **Vail Valley Chamber and Tourism Bureau,** 100 E. Meadow Dr., Suite 34, Vail, CO 81657 (② 800/525-3875 or 970/476-1000; www.visit vailvalley.com), or **Vail Mountain Resort,** P.O. Box 7, Vail, CO 81658 (② 800/ 525-2257 or 970/476-5601; www.vail.com or www.beavercreek.com). You can also get information on year-round activities and events by calling the **Vail Activities Desk** (② 970/476-9090).

Information centers are located at the parking structures in Vail and the Lionshead area on South Frontage Road.

GETTING AROUND Vail is one of only a few Colorado communities where you really don't need a car. The Town of Vail runs a **free shuttle-bus service** between 6am and 2am daily, although hours may be shorter in shoulder seasons. Shuttles in the Vail Village–Lionshead area run every 3 to 5 minutes, and there are regularly scheduled trips to West Vail and East Vail (② 970/328-8143). The **Eagle County Regional Transportation Authority,** known locally at ECO Transit ② 970/328-3520; www.eagle-county.com/eco_transit), runs shuttles between Vail and Beaver Creek, a 12-mile trip, plus regional bus service to Avon, Edwards, Minturn, Leadville, and the Edwards County Regional Airport daily ($2–$3 each way). Both **High Mountain Taxi** (② 970/524-5555; www. hmtaxi.com) and **Vail Valley Taxi** (② 877/829-8294; www.vailtaxi.com) operate throughout the area, around the clock.

Car rentals available at the Eagle County Regional Airport, including four-wheel-drive vehicles, include **Avis** (② 800/331-1212 or 970/524-7571), **Budget** (② 800/527-0700 or 970/524-8260), **Dollar** (② 800/800-4000 or 970/ 524-9429), **Hertz** (② 800/654-3131 or 970/524-7177), and **National** (② 800/227-7368 or 970/524-2277).

FAST FACTS The hospital, **Vail Valley Medical Center,** with 24-hour emergency care, is at 181 West Meadow Dr. between Vail Road and East Lionshead Circle (② 970/476-2451). The **post office** is at 1300 N. Frontage Rd.; for hours and other information contact the U.S. Postal Service (② 800/275-8777; www.usps.com). For **road conditions,** call ② 970/479-2226.

SPECIAL EVENTS Taste of Vail, early April; Big Wheel, Brews & Chili, last weekend in June in Vail; Vail America Days, July 4th; Beaver Creek Arts Festival, early August in Beaver Creek; Oktoberfest, mid-September in Vail; and New Year's Eve Celebration, December 31 in Beaver Creek. Also see "The Festival Scene," below.

Vail

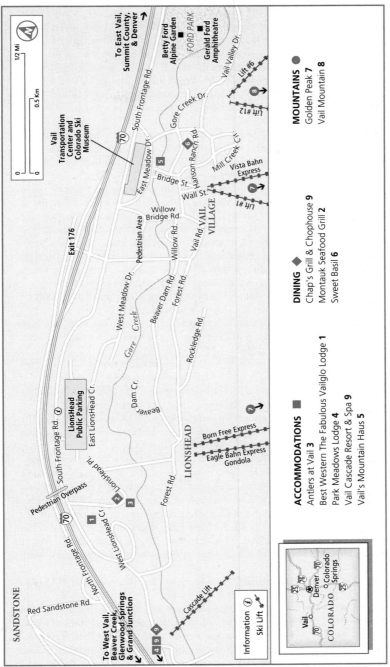

1/2 Mi
0.5 Km

SANDSTONE

To West Vail, Beaver Creek, Glenwood Springs & Grand Junction

Red Sandstone Rd.

North Frontage Rd.

South Frontage Rd.

Pedestrian Overpass

West LionsHead Cr.

LionsHead Public Parking

East LionsHead Cr.

LionsHead Pl.

LIONSHEAD

Forest Rd.

Forest Rd.

Rockledge Rd.

Dam Cr.

Gore Creek

Beaver Creek

Beaver Dam Rd.

West Meadow Dr.

Cascade Lift

Born Free Express

Eagle Bahn Express Gondola

Pedestrian Area

Willow Bridge Rd.

Willow Rd.

Vail Rd.

Bridge St.

Wall St.

VAIL VILLAGE

East Meadow Dr.

Gore Creek Dr.

Hanson Ranch Rd.

Mill Creek Cir.

Mill Creek Rd.

Vista Bahn Express

Lift #1

Lift #7

Lift #12

Lift #6

Lift #8

Vail Valley Dr.

FORD PARK

Betty Ford Alpine Garden

Gerald Ford Amphitheatre

To East Vail, Summit County, & Denver

South Frontage Rd.

Exit 176

70

Vail Transportation Center and Colorado Ski Museum

To Vail, West Vail

Information ℹ
Ski Lift

Vail
COLORADO
Denver
Colorado Springs
70
76
25
25

ACCOMMODATIONS ■

Antlers at Vail **3**
Best Western The Fabulous Vailglo Lodge **1**
Park Meadows Lodge **4**
Vail Cascade Resort & Spa **9**
Vail's Mountain Haus **5**

DINING ◆

Chap's Grill & Chophouse **9**
Montauk Seafood Grill **2**
Sweet Basil **6**

MOUNTAINS ●

Golden Peak **7**
Vail Mountain **8**

305

SKIING & OTHER WINTER ACTIVITIES

VAIL ★★★   America's top ski resort by practically any standard, Vail is something that all serious skiers must experience at least once. It has fantastic snow, great runs, and everything is so convenient that skiers can concentrate solely on skiing (and related enjoyments, if they so choose). You can arrive at the base village, unload and park your car, and not have to drive again until it's time to go. Your lodging choices offer as much pampering as you want, or can afford. You'll find all the shops, restaurants, and nightlife you could want within a short walk of your hotel or condominium.

In fact, our only real complaint about Vail (aside from the expense) is that it didn't exist before it became a ski resort, and so it lacks the historic ambience and Old West downtown area that you'll find in Aspen, Steamboat Springs, Telluride, Crested Butte, and a number of other Western ski centers.

Ski area boundaries stretch 7 miles from east to west along the ridge top, from Outer Mongolia to Game Creek Bowl, and the skiable terrain is measured at 5,289 acres. Virtually every lift on the front side of the mountain has runs for every level of skier, with a predominance of novice and intermediate terrain. The seven world-famous Back Bowls are strictly for advanced and expert skiers; snow and weather conditions determine just how expert you ought to be. They are served by four lifts, one of them a short surface lift to access the Inner and Outer Mongolia bowls. One trip down the Slot or Rasputin's Revenge will give you a fair idea of just how good you are. Blue Sky Basin, which opened in 2000 on the next mountain south of Vail, has two bowls accessed by three high-speed quad chairlifts, and intermediate to advanced terrain offering a wilderness-like experience. There is a warming hut at the top of the basin with water, restroom facilities, and a pair of gas grills.

Vail has a vertical drop of 3,450 feet; average annual snowfall is 346 inches (nearly 29 ft.). All told, there are 193 conventional trails served by 34 lifts—a gondola, 14 high-speed quad chairs, 1 fixed-grip quad, 3 triple chairs, 5 double chairs, and 10 surface lifts. Snowboarders have three terrain parks.

There are more than 18 **mountain restaurants** at Vail. **Game Creek** (© **970/ 479-4275**), in a handsome European-style chalet, offers creative regional cuisine and splendid views from its perch overlooking Game Creek Bowl at the top of Vail Mountain. **Two Elk Restaurant** on the top of China Bowl offers Southwestern cuisine, pizza, and pasta, plus baked potato and salad bars. At **Buffalo's** you'll find deli sandwiches, pizza, chili, soup, and a good variety of specialty coffees. **Wildwood** touts an eclectic selection of American dishes; **The Marketplace** serves various ethnic dishes in a cafeteria setting; and a variety of dishes are available at the full-service **Blue Moon Restaurant and Bar.** Mid-Vail has two levels of food courts that serve breakfast, lunch, and après-ski drinks, including **Sarge's Shelter,** which offers great barbecue and burgers and a wonderful outdoor deck.

Vail has a highly respected children's program, and there are daily NASTAR races.

Daily lift tickets during the peak season cost about $75 for adults, $45 for children 5 to 12, $65 for seniors 65 and older, and are free for children 4 and younger. Any lift ticket purchased at Vail is also valid at Beaver Creek, Keystone, and Breckenridge ski areas. Vail is usually open from mid-November to late April, daily from 9am to 3:30pm. For further information, contact **Vail Mountain,** P.O. Box 7, Vail, CO 81658 (© **800/404-3535** or 970/476-5601, 970/ 476-4888 for snow report; www.vail.com).

BEAVER CREEK 🐾🐾 Also owned by Vail Resorts, Beaver Creek is an outstanding resort in its own right, one with a more secluded atmosphere and maybe even more luxury than its better-known neighbor. Located in a valley 1½ miles off the I-70 corridor, Beaver Creek combines European château-style elegance in its base village with expansive slopes for novice and intermediate skiers. The Grouse Mountain Express and Westfall lifts reach expert terrain.

The big news here is the opening in 2004 of two new high-speed quad chairlifts, and the creation of a new entry point for Beaver Creek Mountain called Beaver Creek Landing. The additions are designed to improve access for skiers and riders, and also to reduce traffic congestion on the main road to Beaver Creek Village. From Beaver Creek Landing in Avon, skiers and riders can now take two lifts to the top of Strawberry Park.

From Beaver Creek Village, the Centennial Express lift to Spruce Saddle and Birds of Prey Express lift reach northwest-facing midmountain slopes and the Flattops beginners' area atop the mountain, offering a unique beginner's experience. Opposite, the Strawberry Park Express lift accesses Larkspur Bowl and the McCoy Park cross-country ski and snowshoe area at 9,840 feet. Three other lifts—Larkspur, Grouse Mountain, and Westfall (serving the expert Birds of Prey area, one of the steepest downhill slopes in the world) leave from Red-Tail Camp at midmountain. Arrowhead Mountain is also part of Beaver Creek. The two are connected through Bachelor Gulch, offering village-to-village skiing.

Beaver Creek's vertical drop is 4,040 feet from the 11,440-foot summit. There are 1,625 developed acres, though Vail Associates are licensed to develop up to 5,600. There are 16 lifts (nine high-speed quad chairs, three triple chairs, three doubles, and a surface lift) that serve 146 trails, and the average annual snowfall is 310 inches. There are three terrain parks and a half-pipe.

There are seven **mountain restaurants,** including the highly praised **Beano's Cabin** (see "Where to Dine," later in this chapter). Among other on-mountain eateries are the **Spruce Saddle Lodge,** a dining court offering burgers, wraps, pizza, and salads; the upscale **Zach's Cabin,** which is reached for dinner via sleigh; the **Red Tail Camp** barbecue fast-food stop; and the **Broken Arrow Café,** serving burgers, sandwiches, pizzas, and soups.

Peak season daily lift tickets are $75 for adults, $45 for children 5 to 12, $65 for seniors 65 and older, and free for children 4 and younger. Any lift ticket purchased at Beaver Creek is also valid at Vail, Keystone, and Breckenridge ski areas.

Beaver Creek is usually open from mid-November to late April, daily from 9am to 4pm. For more information, contact **Beaver Creek Resort,** P.O. Box 7, Vail, CO 81658 (② **800/404-3535** or 970/845-9090, 800/427-8308 for snow reports; www.beavercreek.com).

BACKCOUNTRY SKI TOURS Paragon Guides, P.O. Box 130, Vail, CO 81658 (② **877/926-5299** or 970/926-5299; www.paragonguides.com), is one of the country's premier winter guide services, offering backcountry ski trips on the 10th Mountain Trail and Hut System between Vail and Aspen (see "Cross-Country Skiing," below). A variety of trips are available, lasting from 3 to 6 days and designed for all ability levels. Costs start at $990 per person for the 3-day trip, and $1,860 for the 6-day trip (for experienced backcountry skiers only).

CROSS-COUNTRY SKIING Cross-country skiers won't feel left out here, with trails at both resorts as well as a system of trails through the surrounding mountains. **Vail's Nordic Center** (② **970/476-8366**) has 33km of trails, part of them on the Vail Golf Course, and offers guided tours, lessons, and snowshoeing. The **Beaver Creek Nordic Center** (② **970/845-5313**), at Beaver

Creek Resort, has a 32km mountaintop track system with a skating lane in 9,840-foot McCoy Park. Most of the high-altitude terrain here is intermediate, though there's some space for both beginner and advanced cross-country skiers; telemarking lessons are available.

For general information on the network of backcountry trails in the Vail area, contact the **Holy Cross Ranger District Office,** White River National Forest, at 24747 U.S. 24, 2 miles north of Minturn, off I-70 exit 171, Minturn, CO 81645 (© **970/827-5715;** www.fs.fed.us/r2).

Of particular note is the system of trails known as the **10th Mountain Division Hut System,** 1280 Ute Ave., Suite 21, Aspen, CO 81611 (© **970/925-5775;** www.huts.org). Generally following the World War II training network of the Camp Hale militia, the trails cover 300 miles and link Vail with Leadville and Aspen, with huts along the way where cross-country skiers and hikers can find shelter for the night. Huts are basic, with bunk beds, but do have wood stoves, propane burners, photovoltaic lighting, kitchen equipment, mattresses, and pillows. A one-person bed in one of the huts owned by the 10th Mountain Division Hut Association costs $26 per night for adults; huts owned by others but booked through the association cost $20 to $39 per adult. Children under 13 are charged half price.

WARM-WEATHER & OTHER YEAR-ROUND ACTIVITIES

Vail doesn't shut down once the skiers go home. Instead, visitors and locals alike trade their skis for mountain bikes and hiking boots, and hit the trails again. The resort closes parts of the mountain to access from early May to late June to protect elk-calving habitats, but other than that, warm-weather activities cover the mountains.

The **Piney River Ranch,** about 12 miles north of Vail on Piney Lake (© **866/447-4639** or 970/477-1171; www.pineyriverranch.com), offers a variety of outdoor activities, including horseback rides, wagon rides, and a canoeing and fishing lake. **Nova Guides,** P.O. Box 2018, Vail, CO 81658 (© **888/949-6682** or 970/827-4232; www.novaguides.com), offers guided fishing, mountain-bike, and off-road tours, plus white-water rafting. The **10th Mountain Division Hut System,** which runs for 300 miles, is open to hikers and mountain bikers (see "Cross-Country Skiing," above).

You'll find many of the companies listed below on the Internet at **www.visit vailvalley.com**, and **www.vailalways.com** also is a good source for information on summer activities. For maps and information on the numerous activities in the White River National Forest, consult the **Holy Cross Ranger District Office** (see "Cross-Country Skiing," above).

FISHING The streams and mountain lakes surrounding Vail are rich with rainbow, brook, brown, and cutthroat trout, plus mountain whitefish. Gore Creek, which runs through the town of Vail, is a popular anglers' venue, especially toward evening from its banks along the Vail Golf Course. Other prime spots are the Eagle River, joined by Gore Creek 5 miles downstream near Minturn; the Black Lakes near the summit of Vail Pass; and 60-acre Piney Lake (see directions under "Mountain Biking," below). The **Piney River Ranch** (see above) rents canoes ($20 for 2 hours) and paddle boats ($25 for 1 hour), plus fishing poles ($15 for 3 hours).

For a guided fishing trip call **Nova Guides** or **Piney River Ranch** (see above), or **Fly Fishing Outfitters, Inc.** (© **800/595-8090** or 970/476-3474; www.flyfishingoutfitters.net), which also has a retail store with fishing supplies and outdoor clothing in Avon, across from the entrance to Beaver Creek.

GOLF   Courses here are usually open from mid-May to mid-October. Both the **Vail Golf Club,** 1778 Vail Valley Dr., Vail (© **970/479-2260**), and the **Eagle-Vail Golf Course,** 6 miles west of Vail at 431 Eagle Dr., Avon (© **970/949-5267**), charge $90 to $100 for 18 holes.

HIKING & BACKPACKING   The surrounding White River National Forest has a plethora of trails leading to pristine lakes and spectacular panoramic views. The Holy Cross Wilderness Area, southwest of Vail, encompasses 14,005-foot Mount of the Holy Cross and is an awesome region with over 100 miles of trails. Eagle's Nest Wilderness Area lies to the north, in the impressive Gore Range. For information and maps for these and other hiking areas, consult the **Holy Cross Ranger District Office** (see "Cross-Country Skiing," above).

HORSEBACK RIDING & CATTLE ROUNDUPS   One of the best ways to explore this beautiful and rugged mountain country is on the back of a horse. The **Spraddle Creek Ranch,** 100 Spraddle Creek Rd. (© **970/476-6941;** www.spraddlecreekranch.com), is especially geared to families, with rides for beginners to experts. A 1-hour ride costs $35. Also providing horseback rides are **Piney River Ranch** (see above), which offers guided horseback rides starting at $35 for 1 hour and 15-minute pony rides for kids for $15. **Triple G Outfitters** at 4 Eagle Ranch, 4 miles north of I-70 exit 157 (© **970/926-3372;** www. 4eagleranch.com), charges $35 and up for horseback rides, and also offers half-day cattle roundups for about $120.

LLAMA TREKKING   **Paragon Guides** (see "Backcountry Ski Tours," above) offers llama-trekking trips, from 3 to 6 days, July through September. They are limited to eight persons for camping, or slightly larger groups for hut trips, and start at $970 per person for 3 days. Custom treks are also available, from overnight to 1 week.

MOUNTAIN BIKING   Summer visitors can take their bikes up the Eagle Bahn Gondola to Adventure Ridge on Vail Mountain (all-day passes are $29 for adults, $22 for children 5–12) and cruise downhill on a series of trails. There are many other choices for avid bikers, both on backcountry trails and road tours. A popular trip is the 13-mile Lost Lake Trail along Red Sandstone Road to Piney Lake. The 30-mile Vail Pass Bikeway goes to Frisco, with a climb from 8,460 feet up to 10,600 feet. Pick up a trail list (with map) at an information center.

Mountain bike repairs and rentals are available at a number of shops, including **Vail Bike Tech,** 555 E. Lionshead Circle, Vail (© **800/525-5995** or 970/476-5995; www.vailbiketech.com), which also offers guided tours; and **Wheel Base,** 610 W. Lionshead Circle (© **970/476-5799**). Rental rates are about $20 to $30 for a half day, $28 to $40 for a full day, depending on the type of bike.

RIVER RAFTING   The Eagle River, just a few miles west of Vail, offers thrilling white water, especially during the May to June thaw. Families can enjoy the relatively gentle (Class II–IV) lower Eagle, west of Minturn; the upper Eagle, above Minturn, is significantly rougher (Class IV–V rapids). Area rafting companies also take trips on the Colorado River, which they access about 35 miles northwest via Colo. 131, at State Bridge. Rafting companies here include **Colorado River Runs** (© **800/826-1081** or 970/653-4292; www.coloradoriverruns.com); **Nova Guides** (see above); and **Lakota River Guides** (© **800/274-0636** or 970/845-7238; www.lakotariver.com). Rates usually run $50 to $80 per adult for a half-day trip, with slightly lower rates for youths (young children aren't usually permitted).

THE FESTIVAL SCENE

The summer season's big cultural event is the **Bravo! Vail Valley Music Festival,** from late June through early August. Established in 1988, the festival features a variety of classical music from orchestral to chamber music to vocal, with performers such as the New York Philharmonic, Rochester Philharmonic, and Dallas Symphony. Tickets range from $20 to $77; contact the festival office at P.O. Box 2270, Vail, CO 81658 (© **877/812-5700** or 970/827-5700; www. vailmusicfestival.org).

The **Vail International Dance Festival** features both classes and performances. The World Masters Ballet Academy at Vail teaches the Russian style of artistic expression and other techniques, and presents a series of performances each summer. For information, contact the Vail Valley Foundation, P.O. Box 309, Vail, CO 81658 (© **888/883-8245** or 970/949-1999; www.vvf.org).

The Vail Valley Foundation also hosts **Hot Summer Nights,** free concerts of contemporary rock, jazz, or blues, on Tuesday evenings at 6:30pm from mid-June through early August.

NEARBY MUSEUMS & OTHER ATTRACTIONS

Betty Ford Alpine Gardens ⭐   A wonderful place for a relaxing break from the rigors of an active vacation, these peaceful gardens offer a chance to see a variety of flowering alpine plants unique to the Rocky Mountains. At 8,200 feet, these are the highest public botanical gardens in North America. The alpine display, perennial garden, and mountain meditation garden together represent about 2,000 varieties of plants, demonstrating the wide range of choices to be grown at high altitudes. The gardens attract a variety of birds, and there is also a rock garden with a stunning 120-foot waterfall. Allow 1 to 3 hours.

Ford Park, east of Vail Village, Vail. © **970/476-0103**. www.bettyfordalpinegardens.org. Free admission. Snowmelt to snowfall daily dawn–dusk.

Colorado Ski Museum–Ski & Snowboard Hall of Fame   The history of more than a century of Colorado skiing—from the boards that mountain miners first strapped on their feet, to the post–World War II resort boom, to Coloradans' success in international racing and the Olympics—is depicted in this popular showcase. Also included is the evolution of snow boarding, plus the role of the U.S. Forest Service. There's one room devoted to the 10th Mountain Division, the only division of the military trained in ski warfare. A theater presents historical and current ski videos. The museum incorporates the Colorado Ski & Snowboard Hall of Fame with plaques and photographs honoring Vail founder Peter Seibert, filmmaker Lowell Thomas, Olympic skier Buddy Werner, and others. Allow 1 hour.

Vail Transportation Center, Level 3. © **970/476-1876**. www.skimuseum.net. Free admission. Tues–Sun 10am–5pm. Closed May and Oct, except by appointment.

SHOPPING

There are a wide variety of shops and galleries in Vail and Beaver Creek, but this is not a place for bargain hunters. Among art galleries of note are **Vail Fine Art Gallery,** Vail Village Crossroads Center, 141 E. Meadow Dr. (© **970/476-2900;** www.vailfineart.com), with beautiful sculptures and fine paintings. **Currents Fine Jewelers,** 285 Bridge St. (© **970/476-3322**), offers original designs in platinum, gold, and silver jewelry plus fine Swiss watches. Other interesting shops include **Noel the Christmas Shop,** in the Sitzmark Building, 183 Gore Creek Dr. (© **970/476-6544**), with unusual nutcrackers and exclusive ornaments, including the work of Christopher Radko; and **Kitchen Collage,** at

Riverwalk, the Crystal Building, Edwards (© **970/926-0400;** www.kitchen collage.com), which carries fine cookware, gourmet foods, linens, and a multitude of handy gadgets.

WHERE TO STAY

Like most of Colorado's ski resorts, Vail has an abundance of condominiums. Many are individually owned and available for rent when the owners aren't in town, so you'll find that they have more individuality and homey touches than you often find in a hotel. We discuss some of the better condominium developments below (along with other lodging choices), and there are scores more. Contact the **Vail Valley Chamber and Tourism Bureau** (p. 304), which can provide additional lodging information or make your reservations for you, as well as provide information on skiing and other activities.

As in most ski areas, rates are highest during peak ski season, particularly Christmas, and can sometimes be halved after the lifts close. During ski season, you'll find the lowest rates at the very beginning, from opening to about December 20. Unless otherwise noted, parking is free. Room taxes add almost 12% to lodging bills.

Skiers on a tight budget can probably save a few dollars by staying in the town of Eagle (zip 81631), just south of I-70 exit 147, about 18 miles west of Beaver Creek and 29 miles west of Vail. Here there is a **Comfort Inn**, 285 Market St., P.O. Box 668 (© **970/328-7878**), with rates for two of $69 to $119; and the **Best Western Eagle Lodge,** 200 Loren Lane, P.O. Box 128 (© **800/475-4824** or 970/328-6316), which charges double rates of $75 to $165 most of the time and $100 to $275 from December 21 to January 4.

IN VAIL

In addition to the properties reviewed below, another good choice in Vail, despite its ridiculous name, is the **Best Western The Fabulous Vailglo Lodge,** 701 W. Lionshead Circle, Vail, CO 81658 (© **800/541-9423** or 970/476-5506), with double rates of $270 to $280 from mid-November to late April, and $115 to $150 the rest of the year.

Expensive

Vail Cascade Resort & Spa ★★★ A wonderful choice for those who love pampering, the Vail Cascade gets better every time we visit. A $5-million room renovation project, completed in summer 2004, has resulted in a decor that we might call "upscale contemporary Rocky Mountain." It includes solid-wood furnishings and woodwork, leather chairs, large desks, granite double-sink vanities, stone tile floors, overstuffed pillows, and pillow-topped mattresses. Both the deluxe rooms (480 sq. ft.), which have the vanity outside the bathing area, and standard rooms (390 sq. ft.) feature bright, bold colors and wooden armoires concealing 27-inch TVs. Suites have 600 to 1,000 square feet in two rooms and most have a king-size bed plus a hide-a-bed. All units boast fabulous mountain or courtyard views; some units have outdoor balconies with tables and chairs.

The courtyard entrance is beautifully landscaped, with tall Colorado blue spruce, aspens, and an abundance of flowers in the summer. There are elevators accessing the four floors, and interior corridors everywhere so you never have to go outside until you're ready to ski—and the Cascade Village chairlift is just outside the door. Of course, there is also a ski concierge on hand to assist. The Cascade offers complimentary shuttle service, two movie theaters with first-run films, and a top-notch restaurant, Chap's Grill & Chophouse (see "Where to Dine," below).

And here is where the pampering gets really serious: The Aria Spa & Club (www.ariaspa.com) is a 78,000-square-foot spa and athletic club, offering a complete spa experience with 14 treatment rooms, a couple's spa suite, manicure/pedicure stations, aromatherapy steam rooms, and practically every treatment imaginable. There are also three squash courts, racquetball, and basketball; Cybex and free weights; cardiovascular equipment; an indoor track; and exercise classes. The resort offers a children's program and child-care service, too.

1300 Westhaven Dr., Vail, CO 81657. ℂ **800/420-2424** or 970/476-7111. Fax 970/479-7020. www.vail cascade.com. 292 rooms and suites, 72 condos and private residences. Winter $259–$519 double, $879–$1,300 suite, higher at Christmas; summer $129–$299 double, $750 suite. AE, DC, DISC, MC, V. Free underground parking available (7-ft. height limit). Take I-70 exit 173 for West Vail, head east on South Frontage Rd. to Westhaven Dr., and turn right. **Amenities:** Restaurant (chophouse); bar; 2 heated outdoor pools; tennis courts (4 indoor, 3 outdoor); state-of-the-art health club and spa; hot tubs (2 outdoor, 1 indoor); sauna; concierge; shopping arcade including sporting-goods stores with rentals and apparel; 24-hr room service; massage; babysitting. *In room:* TV w/pay movies, dataport (high-speed Internet access), minibar, coffeemaker, hair dryer, iron.

Moderate

Antlers at Vail ★★
This luxurious condominium property near the foot of the Lionshead Gondola has a well-deserved reputation for friendly service and unobstructed views of Vail Mountain. The comfortable, open, and airy units range in size from studios to four bedrooms, and each has a fireplace, private balcony, and fully equipped kitchen. There's also a sun deck and ski storage. A $20-million expansion project was completed in June 2002, adding 22 units and a new heated underground garage (free).

680 W. Lionshead Place, Vail, CO 81657. ℂ **800/843-8245** or 970/476-2471. Fax 970/476-4146. www. antlersvail.com. 88 units. Winter $270–$1,320 (higher during Christmas holidays); summer $160–$495. AE, DC, DISC, MC, V. Pets accepted in some units, fee $15 per pet per night. **Amenities:** Outdoor heated pool; exercise room; whirlpool; 2 saunas; basic business center; coin-op laundry. *In room:* TV/VCR, kitchen, hair dryer, iron.

Lion Square Lodge
A ski-in/ski-out property on Gore Creek at the base of the Lionshead Gondola, Lion Square offers deluxe lodge rooms and one-, two-, and three-bedroom condominiums. Many of the condo units have mountain views, and all have spacious living rooms with balconies, fireplaces, and fully equipped kitchens. Stop in the lobby for complimentary coffee and newspapers. There's a jogging trail, plus ski and bicycle storage.

660 W. Lionshead Place, Vail, CO 81657. ℂ **800/525-5788** or 970/476-2281. Fax 970/476-7423. www.lion square.com. 108 units. Winter $195–$450 double, $265–$1,850 condo; summer $89–$175 double, $115–$350 condo. Children under 17 stay free in parents' room. AE, DISC, MC, V. **Amenities:** Restaurant (Mediterranean/Italian); outdoor heated pool; small exercise room plus access to nearby health club and spa; 3 hot tubs; sauna; concierge; babysitting; coin-op and valet laundry. *In room:* TV, kitchen, coffeemaker, hair dryer, iron.

Vail's Mountain Haus
Nestled along Gore Creek at the Covered Bridge in the heart of Vail Village, the Mountain Haus offers guests a choice of lodging, ranging from handsome hotel rooms to luxury condos. Many units are Western or Southwestern in decor, and all are elegantly comfortable. Located just a few steps from world-class skiing, dining, and shopping, all have gas fireplaces, VCRs, private balconies, fully equipped kitchens, and a bathroom for every bedroom. There are men's and women's steam rooms and saunas, express checkout, and complimentary coffee and refreshments.

292 E. Meadow Dr., Vail, CO 81657. ℂ **800/237-0922** or 970/476-2434. Fax 970/476-3007. www. mountainhaus.com. 74 units. Winter $155–$310 double lodge room; $250–$2,725 condo. Summer $135 double lodge room; $160–$890 condo. Rates include continental breakfast in winter. AE, DC, MC, V. Parking

free in summer, $15 in winter. **Amenities:** Outdoor heated pool; exercise room; whirlpools (indoor, outdoor); 2 saunas; concierge; massage; coin-op and valet laundry service. *In room:* TV, kitchen, coffeemaker, hair dryer, iron.

Inexpensive

Park Meadows Lodge *Value*   Located in West Vail, adjacent to the bicycle path, and an 8-minute walk from the Cascade Village Lift and terminus of the free Vail shuttle, the Park Meadows is one of the few family-style economy lodges left in the Vail valley. A condominium property, units range from efficiency studios to one- and two-bedrooms, and each has a full kitchen and a hide-a-bed. There's a common area with a large fireplace, board games, and Ping-Pong table; and the hot tub's in a very nice courtyard.

1472 Matterhorn Circle, Vail, CO 81657. © **888/245-8086** or 970/476-5598. Fax 970/476-3056. www.park meadowslodge.com. 29 units. Winter $84–$270 double; summer $64–$99 double. $12 per additional person in room. Up to 2 children under 12 stay free in parent's room. DISC, MC, V. Take I-70 exit 173 for West Vail, head east on South Frontage Rd. to Matterhorn Circle and turn right. **Amenities:** Outdoor hot tub; coin-op laundry. *In room:* TV, kitchen, hair dryer, iron.

BEAVER CREEK AREA
Very Expensive

Park Hyatt Beaver Creek Resort and Spa ⛷⛷   An architecturally unique hotel at the foot of the Beaver Creek lifts, this luxurious ski-in/ski-out Park Hyatt blends features of medieval European alpine monasteries with Rocky Mountain styles and materials. The exterior is native stone, offset with stucco and rough timbers. The interior is of rough-hewn pine and sandstone; wall-size fireplaces enhance numerous cozy alcoves furnished with overstuffed chairs and sofas. Elk-antler chandeliers and works by contemporary artisans lend a Western ambience.

Guest rooms have a European country elegance, with knotty-pine furnishings and TVs hidden in armoires. The raised beds have dust ruffles, pillow shams, and quilted comforters; the bathrooms feature a marble-top vanity and heated towel rack; and most rooms have private balconies. Other amenities include high-speed Internet access, bathrobes and slippers, and refrigerators.

Named for one of the first settlers in the Vail Valley, Bivans is a family restaurant serving three meals daily in a relaxed, informal atmosphere. The outdoor dining terrace dazzles the eye with spectacular views year-round—wool blankets and heaters keep guests warm when temperatures drop. For an intimately romantic dinner, come to Vue and enjoy a gourmet French meal. The flip-side is Whiskey Elk lounge: high energy, lively entertainment, and choice single-malt scotch, small batch bourbons, and a wide selection of ports and wines by the glass. The Cafe has all manner of snacks and sandwiches, and prepares picnic baskets for mountain hikes and rides. The new $5.5-million Allegria Spa is a state-of-the-art facility that offers an array of treatments, as well as fitness and nutritional counseling.

50 W. Thomas Place (P.O. Box 1595), Avon, CO 81620. © **800/55-HYATT** or 970/949-1234. Fax 970/949-4164. www.beavercreek.hyatt.com. 273 units. Winter $259–$875 double, $525–$3,300 suite; spring, summer, and fall $135–$470 double, $575–$1,210 suite. Rates are for double occupancy. Children 18 or under stay free in parent's room. AE, DC, DISC, MC, V. Valet parking $18. **Amenities:** 3 restaurants (American, French, Southwestern); lounge; indoor/outdoor swimming pool; 6 outdoor tennis courts; health club; full-service spa; 6 outdoor whirlpools; sauna; children's programs; concierge; limited room service; massage; coin-op laundry. *In room:* TV w/pay movies, dataport, coffeemaker, hair dryer, iron.

Expensive

The Charter at Beaver Creek ⛷   This elegant European-style lodging offers the luxury of a world-class hotel and the convenience of condominiums, set in the magnificent Rocky Mountains. Lodge rooms, simply decorated, can accommodate up to four persons; most have two queen beds, though some have one king. All units have robes, and a few have grand views of the valley or surrounding mountains. The one- to five- bedroom condominiums have a full kitchen, fireplace—some of lovely river rock—and balcony or patio. All are decorated by the owners—some in Western motif, some more traditional. The property is ski-in/ski-out, with ski valet service. And there are nature trails and a jogging/walking trail.

The traMonti Restaurant offers northern Tuscan cuisine in an elegant setting for dinner; the more casual Terrace Restaurant serves an American-style breakfast.

120 Offerson Rd. (P.O. Box 5310), Beaver Creek, CO 81620. ☎ **800/525-6660** or 970/949-6660. Fax 970/949-6709. www.thecharter.com. Winter $185–$425 double, $270–$2,300 condo; summer $135–$175 double, $165–$645 condo. AE, MC, V. Underground parking, height limit 7 ft., 6 in.; valet parking available. Closed late Apr to late May. **Amenities:** 2 restaurants (Italian, American); indoor and outdoor heated pools, separate children's pool (seasonal); 18-hole golf course; large health club and spa; indoor and outdoor hot tubs; sauna; game room; concierge; full-service rental and retail sports shop; limited room service; coin-op laundry; valet laundry and dry cleaning;. *In room:* TV/VCR, kitchen (in condos), fridge, coffeemaker, hair dryer, iron, safe.

The Lodge & Spa at Cordillera ★★

Reminiscent of a Belgium mountain-style château, this luxurious hideaway nestles in 7,500 acres of private forest just 20 minutes west of Vail and Beaver Creek. Summer 2004 saw the completion of a $5-million renovation of all guest rooms, amenities, and common areas. Rocky Mountain timber and stone, along with elegant wrought iron, are prominent in the handsome, residential-style guest rooms. More than half the rooms feature wood-burning and gas fireplaces; all have king- or queen-size beds with down comforters, and most have private balconies or decks with views of the New York Range of the Rockies. Smoking is not permitted. The expanded spa includes two dedicated facial rooms, a hydrotherapy room, a dedicated manicure and pedicure salon, a meditation room, and several multipurpose treatment rooms. The resort offers 15 miles of mountain biking/cross-country ski trails, a Nordic ski center, and golf and ski shuttles.

Restaurant Mirador (formerly Picasso) is one of the Vail Valley's better dining options, with a cuisine that's hard to pin down. The chef draws from flavors around the world, creating dishes that produce an avant garde dining experience. The Chapparal offers steaks, chops, and seafood at lunch and dinner, and the Timber Hearth Grille serves contemporary American lunch and dinners. There's also a casual Irish pub, Grouse on the Green.

2205 Cordillera Way (P.O. Box 1110), Edwards, CO 81632. ☎ **800/877-3529** or 970/926-2200. Fax 970/926-2486. www.cordilleralodge.com. $150–$400 double; $275–$750 suite. Extra person $20; children under 12 stay free in parent's room. AE, DC, MC, V. Valet parking. **Amenities:** 4 restaurants (American, eclectic, Continental, global); 2 pools (outdoor, indoor lap); golf courses (2 18-hole and a 10-hole short course); 2 tennis courts; exercise room; full-service spa; indoor/outdoor whirlpool; steam room; sauna; bicycle rentals; concierge; limited room service (6:30am–10pm); massage; valet laundry and dry cleaning. *In room:* A/C, TV, coffeemaker, hair dryer, iron.

WHERE TO DINE

Vail and Beaver Creek have dozens of excellent restaurants, although few of them are what we would call bargains. Following are a few of our favorites. For other suggestions check the websites for the Vail Valley Chamber and Tourism Bureau (www.visitvailvalley.com) and Vail Mountain Resort (www.vail.com).

Beano's Cabin ★★ AMERICAN CONTINENTAL   A splurge that many Beaver Creek visitors consider one of the highlights of their stay is the sleigh-ride dinner trip (or in summer, on horseback) to Beano's. This isn't the log home-stead that Chicago lettuce farmer Frank "Beano" Bienkowski built on Beaver Creek Mountain in 1919—it's far more elegant. Diners board the 42-passenger, Sno-Cat–driven sleighs at the base of the Centennial Lift, arriving 20 minutes later for a candlelit five-course dinner around a crackling fire with musical enter-tainment. The menu varies, but entree choices might include selections such as grilled Colorado tenderloin of beef, balsamic-marinated ostrich, grilled Atlantic salmon, wood-grilled venison loin chop, and Colorado lamb loin. Vegetarian meals and a lower-priced children's menu are available.

Near Larkspur Bowl, Beaver Creek Resort. ✆ 970/949-9090. Reservations required. Fixed-price meal $89 and up. AE, DC, DISC, MC, V. Departures from Rendezvous Cabin (at Centennial Lift) 4:15–9:15pm winter daily; summer Wed–Sun. Closed several months in spring and fall.

Chap's Grill & Chophouse ★★ STEAKS/SEAFOOD   Real food for real appetites, expertly prepared and presented in an upscale mountain lodge setting, makes Chap's among our top dining choices in a town that's overflowing with excellent restaurants. The decor is casually elegant, with nicely-padded chairs and lots of rich wood, and large windows offering mountain views. The dinner menu includes prime-cut steaks, seafood, Colorado lamb, and game. Among our favorites here are the 12-ounce buffalo rib-eye, grilled with ancho-chile glazes; the grilled Colorado double lamb chops with a cucumber-garlic sauce; and the pepper-herb-crusted ahi tuna. Soups, salads, and sandwiches are served at lunch, and there is a delicious breakfast buffet including made-to-order omelets.

In summer you can dine outside on the patio. The Fireside Bar is a great place to relax in the evenings, with nightly entertainment—usually jazz, folk, country, or contemporary—by local musicians.

In Vail Cascade Resort & Spa, 1300 Westhaven Dr., Vail, CO 81657. ✆ 970/479-7014. www.vail cascade.com. Reservations recommended. Main courses $7–$14 lunch, $19–$44 dinner. AE, DC, DISC, MC, V. Daily 7–11am, 11:30am–5pm, and 5:30–10pm.

Montauk Seafood Grill ★★ SEAFOOD   Owner Gary Boris grew up around the harbors of Montauk Point, New York, but has abandoned Long Island to create what we consider one of the best seafood restaurants you'll find in landlocked Colorado. It's a busy, high-energy place, decorated in a sort of Colorado casual nautical theme. Boris flies fresh fish in daily from both coasts, Hawaii, and the Gulf of Mexico; and creates unique specialty presentations. Our top choice here is the Hawaiian ahi, seared rare, with a soy-ginger sauce. Steak, chops, chicken, and pasta are also available.

549 Lionshead Mall. ✆ 970/476-2601. Reservations recommended. Main courses $18–$28. AE, DC, DISC, MC, V. Daily 5–9:30pm.

Sweet Basil CREATIVE AMERICAN   Contemporary art and large win-dows complement the tasteful modern decor of this pleasant restaurant. A deck overlooks the Lodge Promenade in the center of Vail Village; diners sit at private tables or at the wine bar. Menus change seasonally but include items such as a tender slow-roasted rosemary pork with crispy polenta, our favorite; the grilled Colorado leg of lamb with white-bean ratatouille; grilled rib-eye steak; or pan-roasted Alaskan halibut with black-truffle risotto and asparagus. Sweet Basil's wine list has earned *Wine Spectator*'s Award of Excellence.

193 E. Gore Creek Dr. ✆ 970/476-0125. www.sweetbasil-vail.com. Reservations recommended. Main courses $9–$15 lunch, $24–$35 dinner. AE, DC, DISC, MC, V. Daily 11:30am–2:30pm and 5:30–10pm.

VAIL AFTER DARK

Vail's greatest concentration of late-night haunts can be found in a 1½-block stretch of Bridge Street from Hanson Ranch Road north to the covered bridge over Gore Creek. From mountainside to creek, they include **The Club** (© **970/479-0556**), the **Red Lion** (© **970/476-7676**), and **Vendetta's** (© **970/476-5070**), reportedly the hang-out for Vail's ski patrollers. Perhaps the hottest bars in town, at least according to some bar-hopping locals, are **The Tap Room,** 333 Bridge St. (© **970/479-0500**), which (not surprisingly) has an extensive selection of beers on tap, plus great martinis; and the **Sanctuary,** above The Tap Room at the same address and phone, a hip spot for a younger, with-it crowd who like the wild lights and sounds and want to work up a thirst on the dance floor.

Another popular hangout is **8,150,** 143 E. Meadow Dr. (© **970/479-0607**), so named for Vail's elevation, offering some of Vail's best live music in winter. **Altitude Billiards & Sports Club,** in the Evergreen Lodge, 250 S. Frontage Rd. (© **970/476-7810**), keeps sports fans busy with large screen TVs, video games, and pool tables. A piano bar draws quieter and somewhat older types to **Mickey's,** in the Lodge at Vail, 174 E. Gore Creek Dr. (© **970/476-5011**).

7 Leadville

38 miles S of Vail, 59 miles E of Aspen, 113 miles W of Denver

Not much more than a century ago, Leadville was the most important city between St. Louis and San Francisco. It was the stopping point for Easterners with nothing to lose and everything to gain from the promise of gold and silver. Today, Leadville is one of the best places to rediscover the West's mining heritage.

Founded in 1860 on the gold that glimmered in prospectors' pans, Leadville and nearby Oro City quickly attracted 10,000 miners who dug $5 million in gold out of a 3-mile stretch of the California Gulch by 1865. When the riches were gone, Leadville was deserted, although a smaller lode of gold-bearing quartz kept Oro City alive for another decade. Then in 1875 two prospectors located the California Gulch's first paying silver lode. Over the next 2 decades, Leadville grew to an estimated 30,000 residents—among them "the Unsinkable" Molly Brown, whose husband made his fortune here before moving to Denver, where the family lived at the time of Molly's *Titanic* heroism.

Now a town of about 2,800 residents, this isolated mountain town (elevation 10,152 feet) has managed to maintain its historic character. Many buildings of the silver boom (which produced $136 million from 1879–89) have been preserved in Leadville's National Historic Landmark District. So for those who want to take a break from playing outdoors to explore Colorado's frontier past, Leadville's just the place to do it.

ESSENTIALS

GETTING THERE   By Car   Coming from Denver, leave I-70 at exit 195 (Copper Mountain), and proceed south 24 miles on Colo. 91. From Grand Junction, depart I-70 at exit 171 (Minturn), and continue south 33 miles on U.S. 24. From Aspen, in the summer take Colo. 82 east 44 miles over Independence Pass (closed in winter), then turn north on U.S. 24 for 15 miles. There's also easy access from the south via U.S. 24.

By Plane The nearest airport with commercial service is the **Eagle County Regional Airport,** which offers car rentals and bus service to Leadville (see "Essentials," under Vail, earlier in this chapter).

VISITOR INFORMATION Contact the **Leadville/Lake County Chamber of Commerce,** 809 Harrison Ave. (P.O. Box 861), Leadville, CO 80461 (© **800/933-3901** or 719/486-3900; www.leadvilleusa.com), which operates a visitor center that's usually open daily from 9am to 5pm.

GETTING AROUND U.S. 24 is Leadville's main street. Entering Leadville from the north, it's named Poplar Street; then it turns west on Ninth Street for a block and then south on Harrison Avenue. The next 7 blocks south, to Second Street, are the heart of this historic town. A block north, Seventh Street climbs east to the old train depot and 13,186-foot Mosquito Pass, among America's highest, open to four-wheel-drive vehicles after the snow melts, usually in July.

   Dee Hive Tours, 506 Harrison Ave. (© **719/486-2339**), offers **taxi** service.

FAST FACTS There's a 24-hour emergency room at **St. Vincent's General Hospital,** 822 W. Fourth St. (© **719/486-0230**). The **post office** is at 136 W. Fifth St.; for hours and other information contact the U.S. Postal Service (© **800/275-8777**; www.usps.com). The Sheriff's office (© **719/486-1249**) provides **road reports.**

EXPERIENCING LEADVILLE'S PAST

A great many residences of successful mining operators, engineers, and financiers are preserved within the **Leadville National Historic Landmark District** 🌟🌟, which stretches along 7 blocks of Harrison Avenue and part of Chestnut Street, where it intersects Harrison at the south end of downtown. A self-guided walking tour of this district, with map, is available free at the visitor center. An informative 30-minute video, *The Earth Runs Silver: Early Leadville,* is shown at the visitor center (see "Visitor Information," above) on request, with free admission, and provides a good overview of Leadville's place in American mining history.

   Leadville has numerous historic buildings open to the public; allow 30 minutes to an hour for each of the following.

   You'll discover Leadville's colorful past at **The Heritage Museum,** corner of Ninth Street and Harrison Avenue (© **719/486-1878**), a historical museum loaded with exhibits on and artifacts from Leadville's early days, from mining dioramas to a scale model of the ice palace that Leadville residents created in 1896. There's also an art gallery displaying the work of local artists (most of it is for sale), and a gift shop with a good selection of books and mining-related souvenirs. Admission costs $3.50 for adults, $3 for seniors 62 and older, $2.50 for students 6 to 16, and free for children 5 and younger. It's open May through October, daily from 10am to 6pm.

   At the **National Mining Hall of Fame and Museum** 🌟🌟, 120 W. Ninth St. (© **719/486-1229**; www.leadville.com/miningmuseum), you'll find walk-through replica mines, models of mining machinery, and dioramas depicting the history of Colorado mining from coal to gold. Admission is $6 for adults, $5 for seniors 62 and older, $3 for children 6 to 12, and it's free for children under 6. Open May through October daily from 9am to 5pm, and November through April Monday through Friday from 10am to 2pm.

   Built in the 1870s, the **Tabor Home,** 116 E. 5th St. (© **719/486-2092** for information), is where mining magnate Horace Tabor lived with his wife,

Augusta, until 1881, when he moved into a local hotel to be closer to his mistress, Baby Doe, whom he eventually married. Here you'll see how a mining king lived in the 1800s, and discover that Horace Tabor did in fact end up paying for his sin. Admission costs $4 for adults, $2 for children 6 to 12, and free for children under 6. It's open from Memorial Day until Labor Day, daily from 10am to 4pm

Peer into Horace Tabor's **Matchless Mine,** 1¼-mile east up Seventh Street, and tour the **Baby Doe Tabor Museum** [tel] **719/486-4918;** www.matchless mine.com), where you'll see the cabin Tabor's widow, Baby Doe, spent the final 36 years of her life, hoping to strike it rich once more. Admission is $4 for adults, $1 for children 6 to 12, and free for kids under 6. Open Memorial Day to Labor Day daily from 9am to 5pm.

To get an up-close look at where a few fortunate miners were able to escape the rough-and-tumble atmosphere of the mines, if only for an evening, visit **Healy House and Dexter Cabin** ✪, 912 Harrison Ave. (© **719/486-0487;** www.coloradohistory.org). Healy House was built by smelter owner August Meyer in 1878, and later converted into a lavish boardinghouse by Daniel Healy. The adjacent rough-hewn log cabin was built by James Dexter and furnished in an elegant style. Admission is $4 for adults, $3.50 for seniors 65 and older, $2.50 for children 6 to 16, and free for children under 6. Open Memorial Day weekend through September, daily from 10am to 5pm.

The **Tabor Opera House,** 308 Harrison Ave. (© **719/486-8409;** www. taboroperahouse.net), is where Leadville's mining magnates and their wives kept up with cultural happenings back East. Opened in 1879, over the years it has hosted everything from the Ziegfeld Follies and the Metropolitan Opera to prizefighter Jack Dempsey (a Colorado native) and magician Harry Houdini (whose vanishing square is still evident on the stage floor). Visitors explore the 880-seat theater, backstage, and dressing rooms, or attend one of the musical or theater performances still held here (check the website for the current schedule and prices). Admission to tour the opera house is $4 for adults, $2 for children 12 and under. Open Memorial Day to Labor Day daily from 10am to 5pm.

Although opera and the other refinements of a cultured society may have been on the minds of some early Leadville residents, others were more interested in "pleasures of the flesh," and in the 1870s and 1880s Leadville was a pretty wild place, with a hundred or more saloons and a busy red-light district.

MORE TO SEE & DO

Leadville, Colorado & Southern Railroad ✪   This spectacularly scenic ride, in a 1955 diesel train, departs the 1893 C&S Depot, 3 blocks east of U.S. 24, and follows the old "high line" along the headwaters of the Arkansas River to a splendid view of Fremont Pass. The return takes you to the French Gulch Water Tower for a dramatic look at Mount Elbert, Colorado's tallest mountain, at 14,433 feet. The ride lasts about 2½ hours, and because of the high elevations, jackets or sweaters are recommended even on the hottest summer days.

326 E. Seventh St. at Hazel St. © 719/486-3936. www.leadville-train.com. Admission $27 adults, $15 children 4–12, free for children 3 and under. Daily Memorial Day to early Oct, call for schedule.

Leadville National Fish Hatchery   Established in 1889, this is the second-oldest hatchery operated by the U.S. Fish and Wildlife Service that's in existence today. Rainbow, brown, and cutthroat trout are raised here, at an elevation of 10,000 feet on the east side of Mount Massive. Visitors can also enjoy self-guided nature trails, with breathtaking views of the surrounding mountains and occasionally deer and elk. One trail passes by the remains of the Evergreen Hotel, a late-1800s resort, and several connect to the Colorado Trail. In winter, take cross-country skis or snowshoes. There are also picnic tables and two public fishing ponds. Allow 30 to 45 minutes.

2844 Colo. 300 (6 miles southwest of Leadville off U.S. 24). (*C*) **719/486-0189**. http://leadville.fws.gov. Free admission. Daily 7am–4pm.

SPORTS & OUTDOOR ACTIVITIES

Much of the outdoor recreation in this area takes place in nearby national forest lands, and you can get information at the **San Isabel National Forest** office, 2015 N. Poplar St. ((*C*) **719/486-0749;** www.fs.fed.us/r2), as well as the visitor center.

Adventurous **hikers** can attempt an ascent of Mount Elbert (14,433 ft.) or Mount Massive (14,428 ft.); either can be climbed in a day without technical equipment, though altitude and abruptly changing weather conditions are factors that should be weighed. One popular trail for hiking, walking, and mountain biking is the **Mineral Belt Trail,** a 12-mile loop that circles Leadville, passing through the mining district and the mountains in the process. A good access point for it is near the recreation center at Sixth Street and McWethy Drive.

There's good trout and kokanee **fishing** at Turquoise Lake, Twin Lakes, and other small high-mountain lakes, as well as at beaver ponds located on side streams of the Arkansas River. There's also limited stream fishing in the area.

Golfers head to 9-hole **Mount Massive Golf Course,** 3½ miles west of town at 259 C.R. 5 ((*C*) **719/486-2176**), which claims to be North America's highest golf course, at 9,700 feet. Greens fees are $28 for 18 holes, and views of surrounding mountain peaks are magnificent.

If snow sports are more to your liking, **Ski Cooper,** P.O. Box 896, Leadville, CO 80461 ((*C*) **800/707-6114** or 719/486-3684, 719/486-2277 for snow reports; www.skicooper.com), is the place to go, with 400 acres of lift-served skiable terrain and another 2,400 acres accessible by snowcat. It began as a training center for 10th Mountain Division troops from Camp Hale during World War II. Located 10 miles north of Leadville on U.S. 24 near Tennessee Pass, it offers numerous intermediate and novice runs, and hosts backcountry Chicago Ridge Snowcat Tours for experts (call for details). Four lifts serve 26 runs—rated 30% beginner, 40% intermediate, and 30% expert—and the mountain has a 1,200-foot vertical drop from the peak of 11,700 feet. Full-day tickets cost $34 for adults, $18 for children 6 to 14, $25 for seniors 60 to 69, $10 for seniors 70 and older, and are free for kids under 6. The **Piney Creek Nordic Center** ((*C*) **719/486-1750;** www.tennesseepass.com/skiing.htm), at the foot of the mountain, has 24km of groomed track and skating trails, plus rentals and lessons. Trail passes cost $8 for adults, $6 for children and seniors.

WHERE TO STAY

In addition to the properties listed below, Leadville has a **Super 8,** 1128 U.S. 24 ((*C*) **800/800-8000** or 719/486-3637), with rates of $50 to $90 double. Taxes add just under 9% for lodging bills.

Apple Blossom Inn   An 1879 Victorian on Leadville's historic millionaires' row, this inn features the house's original handcrafted woodwork, detailed mantels, and crystal light fixtures. Rooms range from warm and cozy to large and sunny; the atmosphere is resplendent with mining-era charm. Estelle's Room has a large fireplace, four-poster queen feather bed, and sitting area, while the

Library features a 14-foot ceiling, five stained-glass windows, a fireplace, parquet floor, and a king-size feather bed. Tea, coffee, and hot chocolate are provided free, there's a microwave for guest use, and guests have access to a stocked refrigerator of complimentary soft drinks. The hot tub resides in a lovely garden.

120 W. Fourth St., Leadville, CO 80461. ✆ 800/982-9279 or 719/486-2141. Fax 719/486-0994. www.the appleblossominn.com. 5 units. $89–$119 double; from $145 suite. Extra person $20 per night. Children under 10 incur a $25 surcharge. Rates include full breakfast. MC, V. **Amenities:** Outdoor hot tub.

Delaware Hotel   Built in 1886, this hotel was restored in 1985 and is once again a Victorian gem. The lobby is beautiful in the style of grand old hotels, with a turn-of-the-20th-century player piano, crystal chandeliers, and magnificent Victorian furnishings. Guest rooms have brass or iron beds, quilts, and lace curtains. Rooms have private bathrooms with showers but no tubs; the four suites have full bathrooms with tub/shower combos. The hotel restaurant serves a very good continental breakfast daily to both guests and the public, and there's an antique shop in the lobby. Smoking is not permitted.

700 Harrison Ave., Leadville, CO 80461. ✆ 800/748-2004 or 719/486-1418. Fax 719/486-2214. www.delawarehotel.com. 36 units. $70–$119 double; $109–$139 family room or suite. 15%–25% discounts Apr–May and Oct–Nov. Children 12 and younger stay free. Rates include continental breakfast. Inquire about special packages for skiing, golfing, and theme weekends. AE, DC, DISC, MC, V. **Amenities:** Restaurant (American, breakfast only); whirlpool. *In room:* TV.

WHERE TO DINE

Boomtown Brewpub BREWPUB   This breezy microbrewery, across the street from the Delaware Hotel, is housed in what was a church in the late 1800s, but more recently was a roller rink and tire store. It usually offers five to eight brews on tap, including the Mineral Belt Pale Ale and a Scottish ale. The menu is pretty typical brewpub: fish and chips, sandwiches, and burgers for lunch and dinner, plus pastas, steak, and fish dishes at dinnertime. The upstairs features pool tables and foosball. Smoking is not permitted.

115 E. Seventh St. ✆ 719/486-8297. Reservations not accepted. Main courses $6–$11 lunch; $6–$16 dinner. AE, DC, DISC, MC, V. Daily 11am–11pm.

Columbine Cafe AMERICAN/VEGETARIAN   This is a simple cafe with historic photos on the walls and inviting blue booths. Breakfasts range from traditional eggs and pancakes to more exotic dishes such as malted Belgian waffles and eggs Benedict, which can be prepared with avocados or tomatoes instead of meat. Lunches include basics such as home-style roast beef, sandwiches, burgers, veggie burgers, and other vegetarian dishes, plus more unique items such as the spicy Cajun burger.

Another Columbine Cafe is in the village at Copper Mountain Resort (172 Copper Circle; ✆ 970/968-2630).

612 Harrison Ave. ✆ 719/486-3599. Reservations not accepted. Main courses $5.75–$8.50. AE, DISC, MC, V. Daily 6am–2pm.

The Golden Burro Café AMERICAN   People have been enjoying good food in a comfortable Western setting at the Golden Burro since it opened in 1938. Old photos and drawings hang on the white walls above wainscoting, glass-and-brass chandeliers cast a warm glow, and the large front windows provide views of the mountains. The emphasis at the Burro is on food like Grandma used to make, such as a hot meatloaf sandwich (homemade meatloaf, served open-faced with brown gravy, mashed potatoes, and a vegetable), pork chops, chicken-fried steak, and liver and onions, plus burritos with your choice of red or green chile. The freshly baked cinnamon rolls are especially good.

710 Harrison Ave. © **970/486-1239.** Main courses $3.95–$9.95. MC, V. Sun–Thurs 6:30am–9:30pm; Fri–Sat 6:30am–10:30pm.

8 Aspen

172 miles W of Denver, 130 miles E of Grand Junction

Like Vail, Aspen's reputation precedes it. Anyone with a pulse knows that it's more than likely to wind up in the tabloids when two celebrities—who are married to other people—are captured on film sharing a chairlift together; and, yes, plenty of Hollywood stars and wannabe stars hang out here.

However, if you take the time to dig beneath the media hype, you may be surprised by what you find. Aspen, at an elevation of 7,908 feet, is a real town with a fascinating history, some great old buildings, and spectacular mountain scenery. If you're a serious skier, you owe yourself at least a few days' worth of hitting the slopes (as if you need us to tell you that); but if you've never strapped on boards and you're thinking of visiting in summer, you'll be doubly pleased: Prices are significantly lower, and the crowds thin out. Many of the fabulous restaurants are still open, the surrounding forests are teeming with great trails for hiking, biking, and horseback riding, and it becomes one of the best destinations in the country for summer music and dance festivals.

Aspen was "discovered" when silver miners from nearby Leadville wandered a bit further afield. When the Smuggler Mine produced the world's largest silver nugget (1,840 lb.), prospectors started heading to Aspen in droves. The city soon had 12,000 citizens—but just as quickly the population dwindled to one-tenth that number after the 1893 silver crash.

It took almost 50 years for Aspen to begin its comeback, which came as a result of another natural resource—snow. Shortly before World War II, a small ski area was established on the mountain now known as Ajax. During the war, 10th Mountain Division ski-soldiers training near Leadville spent weekends in Aspen and were enthralled with its possibilities. An infusion of money in 1945 by Chicago industrialist Walter Paepcke, who moved to Aspen with his wife, Elizabeth, resulted in the construction of what was then the world's longest chairlift. The Aspen Skiing Corporation (now Company) was founded the following year, and in 1950 Aspen hosted the alpine world skiing championships. Then came the opening in 1958 of Buttermilk Mountain and Highlands, and in 1967, the birth of Snowmass.

The Paepckes' vision of the resort was not exclusively commercial, however. They saw Aspen as a year-round intellectual and artistic community that would nourish the minds and spirits as well as the bodies of those who visited. Chief among their accomplishments was the establishment of the Aspen Music Festival. A love of ideas and high-minded discourse attracted the likes of Thornton Wilder and Albert Schweitzer to the community, and today a wide variety of intellectual types, artists, and writers (and yes, even those annoying Hollywood people) make this town of almost 6,000 their full- or part-time home.

ESSENTIALS
GETTING THERE   By Car   Aspen is located on Colo. 82, halfway between I-70 at Glenwood Springs (42 miles northwest) and U.S. 24 south of Leadville (44 miles east). In summer, it's a scenic 3½-hour drive from Denver: Leave I-70 West at exit 195 (Copper Mountain); follow Colo. 91 south to Leadville, where you pick up U.S. 24; turn west on Colo. 82 through Twin Lakes and over 12,095-foot Independence Pass. In winter, the Independence Pass road is closed,

so you'll have to take I-70 to Glenwood Springs, and head east on Colo. 82. In optimal winter driving conditions, it'll take about 4 hours from Denver.

By Plane   Visitors who wish to fly directly into Aspen can arrange to land at **Aspen/Pitkin County Airport,** 5 miles northwest of Aspen on Colo. 82 (② 970/920-5384; www.aspenairport.com). Operating year-round flights are **United Express** (② 800/241-6522) and **America West Express** (② 800/235-9292). Other airlines sometimes operate during ski season, and in summer, **Northwest** (② 800/225-2525) has daily flights from Minneapolis/St. Paul and Memphis.

Another option is the **Eagle County Regional Airport** near Vail (② 970/524-9490; www.eagle-county.com/airport). See section 6, earlier in this chapter.

By Airport Shuttle   Colorado Mountain Express (② **800/525-6363** or 970/926-9800; www.cmex.com) offers shuttle service from Denver International Airport starting at about $80 per person, one-way.

By Train   En route from San Francisco or Chicago, **Amtrak** (② **800/872-7245;** www.amtrak.com) stops in Glenwood Springs, 42 miles northwest of Aspen.

VISITOR INFORMATION   For information, contact the **Aspen Chamber Resort Association,** 425 Rio Grande Place, Aspen, CO 81611 (② **888/667-5666** or 970/925-1940; www.aspenchamber.org), which operates a **Visitor Center** at the same location (open Mon–Fri 8am–5pm), and another at the Wheeler Opera House, located at Hyman Avenue and Mill Street (usually open daily 10am–6pm). You can also get information from the **Snowmass Village Resort Association,** P.O. Box 5566, 38 Village Mall, Snowmass Village, CO 81615 (② **800/766-9627;** www.snowmassvillage.com).

GETTING AROUND   Entering town from the northwest on Colo. 82, the artery jogs right (south) 2 blocks on Seventh Street, then left (east) at Main Street. "East" and "West" street numbers are separated by Garmisch Street, the next cross street after First Street. Mill Street is the town's main north–south street. There are several pedestrian malls downtown, which throw a curve into the downtown traffic flow.

By Shuttle Bus   Free bus service is available within the Aspen city limits, beyond which you can get connections west as far as Glenwood Springs, at reasonable rates, usually less than $5. Exact fare is required. Information can be obtained from the Roaring Fork Transportation Authority's **Rubey Park Transit Center,** Durant Avenue between Mill and Galena streets, in Aspen (② **970/925-8484;** www.rfta.com). Schedules, frequency, and routes vary with the seasons; services include free ski shuttles in winter between all four mountains, shuttles to the Aspen Music Festival, and tours to the Maroon Bells scenic area in summer.

Free shuttle transportation within Snowmass Village is offered daily during ski season and on a limited schedule in summer, by the **Snowmass Transportation Department** (② **970/923-2543;** www.tosv.com).

By Taxi   Call **High Mountain Taxi** (② **970/925-8294;** www.hmtaxi.com).

By Rental Car   Car-rental agencies include **Alamo** (② **800/327-9633** or 970/920-2603), **Budget** (② **800/527-0700** or 970/925-2151), **Dollar** (② **800/800/800-4000** or 970/920-2008), **Eagle** (② **970/925-2128**), and **Thrifty** (② **800/367-2277** or 970/920-2305).

Aspen

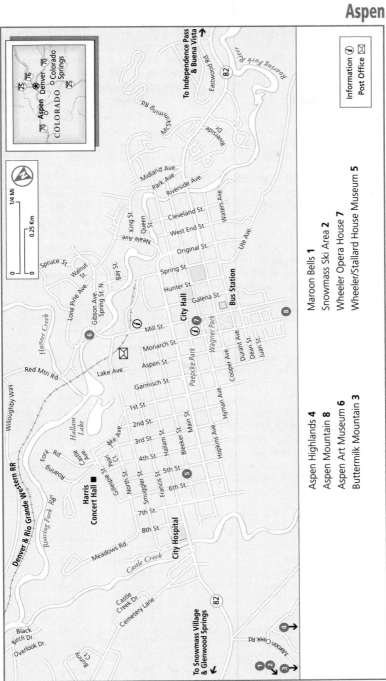

Information ⓘ
Post Office ✉

Maroon Bells **1**
Snowmass Ski Area **2**
Wheeler Opera House **7**
Wheeler/Stallard House Museum **5**

Aspen Highlands **4**
Aspen Mountain **8**
Aspen Art Museum **6**
Buttermilk Mountain **3**

FAST FACTS The **Aspen Valley Hospital,** 401 Castle Creek Rd., near Aspen Highlands (© **970/925-1120**), has a 24-hour emergency room. The **post office** is at 235 Puppy Smith St., off Mill Street north of Main; there's another in the Snowmass Center. For hours and other information contact the U.S. Postal Service (© **800/275-8777;** www.usps.com). For **road reports,** call © **970/920-5454.**

SPECIAL EVENTS Wintersköl Carnival, mid-January, in Aspen and Snowmass; Aspen Gay Ski Week, late January; Snowmass Mardi Gras, early March; *Food & Wine* Magazine Classic, in June, in Aspen; Aspen Arts Festival, August; Aspen Filmfest and Aspen Cocktail Classic, late September.

SKIING & OTHER WINTER ACTIVITIES

Skiing Aspen really means skiing the four Aspen area resorts—Aspen Mountain, Aspen Highlands, Buttermilk, and Snowmass. All are managed by Aspen Skiing Company, and one ticket gives access to all. Daily lift ticket prices during peak season are $74 for adults 18 to 64, $67 for youths 13 to 17, $45 for children 7 to 12, and $67 for seniors 65 and older. Children 6 and under ski free. For more information, contact **Aspen Skiing Company,** P.O. Box 1248, Aspen, CO 81612 (© **800/525-6200** or 970/925-1220; www.aspensnowmass. com). Call © **888/277-3676** or 970/925-1221 for snow reports.

ASPEN MOUNTAIN Named for an old miner's claim, Aspen Mountain is not for the timid. This is the American West's original hard-core ski mountain, with no fewer than 23 of its runs named double diamond—for experts only. One-third of the mountain's runs are left forever ungroomed—sheer ecstasy for bump runners. There are mountain-long runs for intermediates as well as advanced skiers, but beginners should look to one of the other Aspen/Snowmass mountains.

From the **Sundeck** restaurant at the mountain's 11,212-foot summit, numerous intermediate runs extend on either side of Bell Mountain—through Copper Bowl and down Spar Gulch. To the east of the Gulch, the knob of Bell offers a mecca for mogul mashers, with bump runs down its ridge and its east and west faces. To the west of the Gulch, the face of Ruthie's is wonderful for intermediate cruisers, while more mogul runs drop off International. Ruthie's Run extends for over 2 miles down the west ridge of the mountain, with an extension via Magnifico Cut Off and Little Nell to the base, and is accessed by the unique Ruthie's high-speed double chair.

Aspen Mountain has a 3,267-foot vertical drop, with 76 trails on 673 skiable acres. The resort rates its trails as follows: none easiest, 48% more difficult, 26% most difficult, and 26% expert. There are eight lifts—a high-speed gondola, one high-speed quad chair, two quad chairs, one high-speed double, and three double chairs. Average annual snowfall at the 11,212-foot summit is 300 inches (25 ft.). Aspen Mountain is usually open from late November to mid-April.

There are a total of five restaurants—three on-mountain and two at the base.

ASPEN HIGHLANDS A favorite of locals for its expert and adventure terrain—Highland Bowl—Aspen Highlands also has a good mix of terrain, from novice to expert, with lots of intermediate slopes. It also offers absolutely splendid views of the famed Maroon Bells (see the box "Natural Attractions," below).

It takes two lifts to reach the 11,675-foot Loge Peak summit, where most of the advanced expert runs are found in the Steeplechase area and 199 acres of glades in the Olympic Bowl. Kandahar, Golden Horn, and Thunderbowl give the intermediate skier a long run from top to bottom, and novices are best served midmountain on trails like Red Onion and Apple Strudel. There are also some fantastic opportunities for experts at Highland Bowl, which is a short walk from the top of the Loge Peak lift.

Freestyle Friday, a tradition at Highlands for almost 3 decades, boasts some of the best freestyle-bump and big-air competitors in Colorado every Friday from early January to mid-April. In this technical head-to-head contest, competitors bump their way down Scarlett's Run, and finish with a final jump that lands them within perfect view of lunchtime guests at the Merry-Go-Round Restaurant.

There are 130 trails on 790 acres, served by four lifts (three high-speed quads and a triple chair). Trails are rated 18% easiest, 30% more difficult, 16% most difficult, and 36% expert. Aspen Highlands also has a terrain park, appropriate for intermediate to expert snowriders.

There are seven restaurants, including three on the mountain. Highlands is usually open from mid-December to early April.

BUTTERMILK MOUNTAIN   Buttermilk is a premier beginners' mountain, one of the best places in America to learn how to ski. And it's also the home of the ESPN Winter X Games, at least through 2007.

The smallest of Aspen's four mountains, it has 42 trails, which the resort rates at 35% easiest, 39% more difficult, 26% most difficult, and none expert, plus a great terrain park. There are nine lifts (two high-speed quads, three double chairs, two handle tows, and two school lifts) on 420 acres, with a 2,030-foot vertical drop. Average annual snowfall at the 9,900-foot summit is 200 inches (16 ft., 8 in.). There's a restaurant on top and a cafe at the base. Buttermilk is usually open from mid-December to early April.

SNOWMASS   A huge, mostly intermediate mountain with something for everyone, Snowmass has 33% more skiable acreage than the other three Aspen areas combined! Actually four distinct self-contained areas, each with its own lift system, its terrain varies from easy beginner runs to the pitches of the Cirque and the Hanging Valley Wall, the steepest in the Aspen area.

Big Burn, site of a 19th-century forest fire, boasts wide-open advanced and intermediate slopes and the expert drops of the Cirque. Atop the intermediate Alpine Springs trails is the advanced High Alpine Lift, from which experts can traverse to the formidable Hanging Valley Wall. Elk Camp is ideal for early intermediates who prefer long cruising runs. Sam's Knob has advanced upper trails diving through trees, and a variety of intermediate and novice runs around its northeast face and base. All areas meet in the scattered condominium developments that surround Snowmass Village Mall. All told, there are 3,100 skiable acres at Snowmass, with a 4,406-foot vertical drop from the 12,510-foot summit. The mountain has 87 trails, rated 6% easiest, 50% more difficult, 12% most difficult, and 32% expert. There are 21 lifts (seven high-speed quad chairs, two triple chairs, six double chairs, two school platter-pulls, two handle tows, and two Magic Carpets). Average annual snowfall at the summit is 300 inches (25 ft.).

The renowned Snowmass ski school has hundreds of instructors, as well as programs for children 18 months and older. The area also has three terrain parks, one super pipe, and a rail yard. There are 12 restaurants.

Snowmass is usually open from late November to mid-April.

CROSS-COUNTRY SKIING   The Aspen/Snowmass Nordic Council operates a free Nordic trail system with nearly 60km of groomed double track extending throughout the Aspen-Snowmass area, and incorporating summer

> ⟨*Moments* **Natural Attractions**
>
> The two sheer, pyramidal peaks called **Maroon Bells,** on Maroon Creek Road 10 miles west of Aspen, are probably two of the most photographed mountains in the Rockies. During summer and into early fall, you can take a 20- to 30-minute narrated bus tour from Aspen Highlands up the Maroon Creek Valley (© **970/925-8484;** www.rfta.com). Cost for the bus trip is $6 adults, $3 for youths 6 to 16, $4 for seniors, and it's free for children under 6. There is also a 50¢ fee per person from the U.S. Forest Service.

bicycle paths. Instruction and rentals are offered along the trail at the **Aspen Cross-Country Center,** Colo. 82 between Aspen and Buttermilk (© **970/925-2145;** www.utemountaineer.com), and the **Snowmass Touring Center,** Snowmass Village (© **970/923-3148**), both of which provide daily condition reports and information regarding the entire trail system.

Independent backcountry skiers should consult **White River National Forest,** 806 W. Hallam St. (© **970/925-3445;** www.fs.fed.us/r2), and two hut systems provide shelter on multiday trips (see "Hiking & Mountaineering," below). Also, see the website **www.aspennordic.com.**

DOGSLEDDING For rides in winter or a kennel tour in summer, call **Krabloonik,** 4250 Divide Rd., Snowmass Village (© **970/923-2342;** www. krabloonik.com). Every day in winter, teams of Alaskan sled dogs pull guests into the Snowmass-Maroon Bells Wilderness Area. Half-day trips, at 8:30am and 12:30pm, include lunch at **Krabloonik** restaurant (see "Where to Dine," later in this chapter) and cost $225 per adult and $170 for children 3 to 8 years of age. Children under 3 are not permitted. One-hour kennel tours run from mid-June to Labor Day, Monday through Saturday, starting at 11am and 2:30pm. Cost is $6 for those over 12, $5 for 12 and under.

WARM-WEATHER & YEAR-ROUND ACTIVITIES

Your best source for information on a wide variety of outdoor activities in the mountains around Aspen, including hiking, mountain biking, horseback riding, four-wheeling, fishing, and camping, is the **White River National Forest** (see "Cross-Country Skiing," above).

There's no lack of guides, outfitters, and sporting-goods shops in Aspen. Among the best one-stop outfitters is **Blazing Adventures** (© **800/282-7238** or 970/923-4544; www.blazingadventures.com), which offers rafting, mountain-biking, hiking, four-wheeling, hot-air ballooning, and horseback-riding excursions.

BICYCLING There are two bike paths of note. One connects Aspen with Snowmass Village; it covers 13 miles and begins at Seventh Street south of Hopkins Avenue, cuts through the forest to Colo. 82, then follows Owl Creek Road and Brush Creek Road to the Snowmass Mall. Extensions link it with Aspen High School and the Aspen Business Park. The Rio Grande Trail follows the Roaring Fork River from near the Aspen Post Office, on Puppy Smith Street, 2 miles west to Cemetery Lane. See also "Mountain Biking," below.

FISHING Perhaps the best of a great deal of good trout-fishing in the Aspen area is to be found in the Roaring Fork and Frying Pan rivers, both considered gold-medal streams. The Roaring Fork follows Colo. 82 through Aspen from

Independence Pass; the Frying Pan starts near Tennessee Pass, northeast of Aspen, and joins the Roaring Fork at Basalt, 18 miles down valley.

Stop at **Taylor Creek Fly Shop** in Aspen Sports, 408 E. Cooper Ave., Aspen (© **970/920-1128;** www.taylorcreek.com), for your fishing needs. Guided fishing trips are offered by Taylor Creek and **Blazing Adventures** (see above).

GOLF   Public 18-hole championship courses in the Aspen valley include **Aspen Golf Course,** 9461 Colo. 82, 1 mile west of Aspen (© **970/925-2145**), one of the longer courses in Colorado at 7,165 yards, charging $80 for 18 holes; and **The Snowmass Club,** 239 Snowmass Club Circle (© **970/923-5600**), charging about $150 for 18 holes, including a cart.

HIKING & MOUNTAINEERING   Among the best ways to see the spectacular scenery here is on foot. You can get maps and tips on where to go from **White River National Forest** offices (see above). One popular trail is the route past the Maroon Bells to Crested Butte; the trek would take 175 miles by mountain road, but it's only about 30 miles by foot—14 miles from the end of Aspen's Maroon Creek Road.

Hikers can also make use of two hut systems for multiday trips—the 12-hut **10th Mountain Trail Association's** system toward Vail, and the six-hut **Alfred A. Braun and Friends Hut System** (© **970/925-5775** for both; www.huts.org) toward Crested Butte. Huts are basic, with bunk beds, but do have wood-burning stoves, propane burners, photovoltaic lighting, kitchen equipment, mattresses, and pillows. A bed in one of the huts costs about $26 per night. Association offices are at 1280 Ute Ave., Suite 21, in Aspen.

HORSEBACK RIDING   Several stables in the Aspen valley offer a variety of rides, and some outfitters even package gourmet meals and country-western serenades with their expeditions. A wide variety of adventures are offered; rates usually start at about $40 per person for a 1-hour ride. Inquire at **Aspen Wilderness Outfitters** (© **970/963-0211;** www.aspenwilderness.com), **Capitol Peak Outfitters** (© **970/963-0211;** www.capitolpeak.com), and **OutWest Guides** (© **970/984-3801;** www.outwestguides.net).

MOUNTAIN BIKING   There are hundreds of miles of trails through the White River National Forest that are perfect for mountain bikers, offering splendid views of the mountains, meadows, and valleys. Check with the Forest Service (p. 326) and local bike shops for tips on the best trails. Among full-service bike shops offering rentals are **Aspen Velo Bike Shop,** 465 N. Mill St. (© **970/925-1495;** www.aspenvelo.com), and **Aspen Sports,** 408 E. Cooper Ave. (© **970/925-6331;** www.aspensports.com). A half-day rental is $20 to $35.

RIVER RAFTING   Rafting trips are offered on the Roaring Fork, Arkansas, and Colorado rivers with several companies, including **Colorado Riff Raft** (© **800/282-7238** or 970/923-4544; www.riffraft.com), **Up Tha Creek Expeditions** (© **877/982-7335;** www.upthacreek.com), and **Blazing Adventures** (see above). Rates are usually about $75 to $90 for a half-day.

MUSEUMS, ART CENTERS & HISTORIC SITES

The **Aspen Historical Society,** 620 W. Bleeker St. (© **970/925-3721;** www.aspenhistory.org), offers a variety of guided tours of Aspen and the surrounding mining camps during the summer. One 2-hour walking tour of Aspen covers about 1 mile and begins on the grounds of the Wheeler/Stallard House Museum (see below), explores the West End residential area, and ends in the lobby of the historic Hotel Jerome (see "Where to Stay," below). The cost is $10

Aspen Music

Nestled in the picturesque Roaring Fork Valley is one of the top ski resorts in Colorado, and in summer, when the snows have (mostly) melted, the schussing of skis is replaced with the glorious sound of music.

The **Aspen Music Festival and School** originated in 1949, and is now considered one of America's top summer music programs. Lasting 9 weeks from mid-June to late August, it offers more than 350 events, including symphonic and chamber music, opera, choral, and children's programs. Most concerts take place in the state-of-the-art, 2,050-seat Benedict Music Tent and 500-seat Joan and Irving Harris Concert Hall, both at Third and Gillespie streets. The acoustics in the Tent are very good, but in Harris Hall they're awesome.

During the season, ensembles-in-residence—the American and Emerson string quartets, and the American Brass Quintet—give recitals; the Aspen Chamber Symphony and Aspen Festival Orchestra perform; and varied chamber groups are created from amongst the roster of professional musicians that make up the school's faculty. Plus, there are numerous open rehearsals and other programs offered. Events scheduled for 2005 include works by Bach, Beethoven, Chopin, Schumann, and Debussy, to name a few.

On top of Aspen Mountain—you'll have to ride the gondola—student groups perform free 1-hour concerts each Saturday at 1pm. This **"Music on the Mountain"** soars into the backdrop of the Elk Mountain range. Another special experience is the **intimate concerts in private homes,** on various afternoons. The **family events** include several programs geared to youngsters under 10, such as storytelling and music at the Pitkin County Library (free; most Thurs mornings), plus the annual family picnic and concert of short fun classical pieces. Certain **rehearsals** of the Aspen Chamber Symphony and Aspen Festival Orchestra are open to the public, giving visitors an inside look at how a concert is put together. And if you're a visiting musician, check out the master classes while you're in town.

Open rehearsals cost $10 to $15, master classes are $17, and most concert tickets run $18 to $58. Free programs include most of the family events plus the popular Saturday "Music on the Mountain" concerts atop Aspen Mountain. **Free tours** of the Tent and concert hall, a historic walking tour from the Hotel Jerome to the Tent, and a tour of the music school campus are available. Parking is limited, but there is free bus service from many points in town, Snowmass Village, and downvalley (© **970/925-8484** for schedule information).

For additional information contact **Aspen Music Festival and School,** 2 Music School Rd., Aspen, CO 81611 (© **970/925-9042;** www.aspenmusicfestival.com).

per person. Guided tours of the **Ashcroft ghost town** are offered several times daily, at a cost of $3 per person. Call for reservations and specific times. Self-guided tour brochures are also available.

Aspen Art Museum   This attractive museum presents rotating exhibits highlighting the work of nationally known contemporary artists, and hosts an annual exhibit showcasing local talent. Lectures and art education programs for adults and children are offered year-round, and there's a free wine-and-cheese reception most Thursdays from 5 to 7pm. Allow 30 minutes.

590 N. Mill St., Aspen. © 970/925-8050. www.aspenartmuseum.org. Admission $5 adults, $3 students and seniors 65 and older, free for children under 12; free general admission Fri. Tues–Sat 10am–6pm (until 7pm most Thurs); Sun noon–6pm.

Wheeler/Stallard House Museum   Silver baron Jerome B. Wheeler had this three-story Queen Anne–style brick home built in 1888, and its steeply pitched roofs, dormers, and gables have made it a landmark in Aspen's West End neighborhood. A museum since 1969, the exterior of this handsome house has been restored to its appearance in the heady days of silver mining. Exhibits describe Aspen's history from Ute culture through the mining rush, and from railroads and ranching to the founding of the skiing industry. Allow an hour.

620 W. Bleeker St., Aspen. © 970/925-3721. www.aspenhistory.org. Admission $6 adults, $5 seniors, $3 children 12 and younger. Tues–Sat 10am–4pm.

SHOPPING

To truly appreciate the Aspen experience, one must shop Aspen. Note that we say shop (meaning browse) rather than buy, because if you're not careful, you just might blow next month's mortgage payment on some Western fashion accessory. No one ever brags about the great bargain they snagged last season in Aspen.

On the other hand, quality is usually tops, shop clerks are friendly, and your neighbor probably doesn't already have one. Having said all that, we suggest you lock up your credit cards, put on some good walking shoes, and spend a few hours exploring the galleries and shops of Aspen. Following are a few of our favorites, and several are grouped together in a minimall at 525 E. Cooper Ave.

For **original art,** check out: **Aspen Grove Fine Arts,** 525 E. Cooper Ave., upper level (© **970/925-5151;** www.aspengrovefineart.com), featuring paintings, graphics, and sculpture; and **Duval Smart Gallery,** 525 E. Cooper Ave. (© **970/925-9044;** www.duvalsmartgallery.com), for contemporary American paintings, graphics, and glass. When it's time to pick up a gift, we like **Chepita,** 525 E. Cooper Ave. (© **970/925-2871;** www.chipeta.com), a toy store for adults, with jewelry, sculpture, and home accessories; and **Curious George Collectibles,** 426 E. Hyman Ave. (© **970/925-3315**), for silver buckles, belts, and Western artifacts that (allegedly) used to belong to notorious cowboys. For **clothing,** try **Kemo Sabe,** 434 E. Cooper Ave. (© **970/925-7878;** www.kemosabe.com), for wonderful hats and other Western wear; the **Freudian Slip,** 416 S. Hunter St. (© **970/925-4427;** www.thefreudianslip.com), for fine lingerie; and **Gorsuch, Ltd.,** 611 E. Durant St. (© **800/525-9808** or 970/920-9388; www.gorsuchltd.com), for outdoor clothing.

WHERE TO STAY

Occupancy rates run 90% or higher during peak winter and summer seasons, so it's essential to make reservations as early as possible (or avoid peak seasons, as we try to do). The easiest way to book your lodgings is to call **Aspen Snowmass** central reservations (© **888/649-5982;** www.stayaspensnowmass.com). You can also find lodging through **Aspen Resort Accommodations** (© **888/598-2005;** www.aspenreservations.net).

Many accommodations close during the spring and fall; if they're open, rates during those months are typically the lowest of any time during the year. Unless otherwise noted, parking is free. A tax of just under 10% is added to hotel bills.

VERY EXPENSIVE

Hotel Jerome ★★★   The historic ambience and superb service at the Hotel Jerome make it the best place to stay in Aspen—for those who can afford it. Jerome B. Wheeler built the Jerome during the peak of the silver boom. It opened in 1889 as Colorado's first hotel with electricity and indoor plumbing, and the first west of the Mississippi River with an elevator. The silver crash of 1893 ended Aspen's prosperity and the glory years of the Hotel Jerome, but a multimillion-dollar renovation has restored the Jerome to its original splendor. With its Eastlake Victorian architecture lovingly preserved, and furnished with period antiques, the Jerome is now on the National Register of Historic Places.

Each beautifully appointed guest room is spacious—even the smallest is more than 500 square feet—and unique, containing period antiques and reproductions, a desk, comfortable chairs, queen or king beds with down comforters, and plush terry bathrobes. Bathrooms, finished with white Carrera marble and reproduction 19th-century octagonal tiles, boast oversize tubs and separate showers.

The resort's signature Century Room offers savory Alpine-American fare served in classical Victorian elegance, with main courses in the $20 to $30 range. Guests with lighter appetites can get sandwiches and salads at the historic J-Bar (see "Aspen After Dark," below). In summer, the outdoor dining patio is delightful.

330 E. Main St., Aspen, CO 81611. (© **800/331-7213** or 970/920-1000. Fax 970/925-2784. www.hotel jerome.com. 91 units. Mid-Apr to late May and late Sept to mid-Nov $235–$415 double, $655–$865 suite; late May to late Sept and late Nov to mid-Dec $445–$605 double, $865–$1,015 suite; early Jan to mid-Apr $600–$760 double, $1,160–$1,310 suite; Christmas season $790–$995 double, $1,210–$1,360 suite. AE, DC, MC, V. Underground valet parking $18. Pets permitted ($75 fee). **Amenities:** 2 restaurants (American); 2 bars; heated outdoor pool; exercise room; 2 whirlpools; concierge; ski concierge; courtesy shuttle; secretarial services; 24-hr. room service; valet laundry. *In room:* A/C, TV/VCR or TV/DVD, dataport w/high-speed Internet, minibar, hair dryer, iron, safe.

The Little Nell ★★   Located just 17 paces (yes, it's been measured) from the base terminal of the Silver Queen Gondola, the Little Nell boasts the virtues of an intimate country inn as well as the personalized service and amenities of a grand hotel. No two guest rooms are alike, but each has a gas fireplace, Belgian-wool carpeting, down-filled lounge chairs or sofa, oversized bed with down comforter, and marble-finished bathroom with two vanities, separate shower and tub, and Crabtree & Evelyn toiletries. Some suites have separate Jacuzzi tubs and steam showers. All rooms have a view of either the town or the mountain.

The hotel's signature Montagna restaurant serves American Contemporary cooking by award-winning chef Paul Wade in an artsy atmosphere with large windows looking toward the hotel courtyard and Aspen Mountain. The elegant Greenhouse Bar boasts rich wood, a two-sided sandstone fireplace, historic photos of the Aspen ski scene, and outdoor terrace seating. The adjoining Montagna Bar offers a more relaxed atmosphere.

A ski technician is on staff, and there's also a complimentary shuttle.

675 E. Durant Ave., Aspen, CO 81611. (© **888/843-6355** or 970/920-4600. Fax 970/920-4670. www.the littlenell.com. 92 units. Early winter, early spring, and summer $405–$530 double, $1,050–$2,800 suite; winter $625–$875 double, $1,300–$4,600 suite; spring and fall $360–$385 double, $530–$1,800 suite. Call for holiday rates. AE, DC, DISC, MC, V. Valet parking $21 per day. Pets accepted. **Amenities:** Restaurant

(American regional); 2 bars; heated pool; health club and spa; outdoor whirlpool; concierge; shopping arcade; 24-hr. room service; massage; same-day valet laundry. *In room:* A/C, TV/VCR (video rental available), minibar, coffeemaker, hair dryer, iron.

The St. Regis Aspen ✦✦✦   The best keep getting better, and the St. Regis, already one of Aspen's top places to stay, completed the major portion of a $37-million project in the winter of 2004 that includes redesigning guest rooms, adding 20 new units, and constructing a 15,000-square-foot spa with lavish treatment rooms and therapies. Located at the base of Ajax Mountain, between the gondola and Lift 1A, the St. Regis Aspen offers luxurious comfort in a casual but definitely upscale Western atmosphere; the lobby is decorated with rich wood, muted earth tones, and original paintings by 19th- and 20th-century artists. The lobby also offers cozy seating, a large river-rock fireplace, and magnificent views of Aspen Mountain.

Most rooms have views of either the mountains or town, and a few on the ground floor offer views of the hotel's flower-filled courtyard. Each unit is richly decorated in a Rocky Mountain Western style, with overstuffed leather chairs, leather tabletops, handsome marble bathrooms, and sport such amenities as bathrobes, CD players, 30-inch flat-screen TVs, and portable phones. The Club Floor offers its own concierge, and five complimentary food and beverage servings throughout the day. In winter, a ski concierge coordinates ski rentals, lift tickets, and lessons. Olives Aspen Restaurant serves Mediterranean-inspired cuisine, and in summer the flower-filled courtyard is open to dining.

315 E. Dean St., Aspen, CO 81611. ✆ **888/454-9005** or 970/920-3300. Fax 970/925-8998. www.stregis aspen.com. 179 units. $465–$895 double; suites to $1,725. AE, DC, DISC, MC, V. 24-hr. valet parking $26. **Amenities:** Restaurant (Mediterranean); bar; outdoor heated pool; fitness center & spa; whirlpools (1 indoor, 1 outdoor); sauna; steam room; concierge; courtesy airport transportation; business center; 24-hr. room service, concierge-level rooms. *In room:* A/C, TV/DVD, fax (suites only), dataport (high-speed Internet), minibar, hair dryer, iron, safe.

EXPENSIVE & MODERATE

Hearthstone House   Small and sophisticated, the Hearthstone House is located just 2 blocks west of the Wheeler Opera House. Guests share a large, elegant living room with teak-and-leather furnishings and a wood-burning fireplace, dining room with bright flowers, and an extensive library. Rooms are bright and homey, with queen-size or twin beds, and two rooms have a king-size bed. Four units feature whirlpool tubs. Smoking is not permitted.

134 E. Hyman Ave. (at Aspen St.), Aspen, CO 81611. ✆ **888/925-7632** or 970/925-7632. Fax 970/920-4450. www.hearthstonehouse.com. 16 units. Summer $179–$229 double; winter $189–$320 double. Rates include breakfast plus afternoon wine and cheese. AE, DC, DISC, MC, V. **Amenities:** Access to Aspen Club & Spa; outdoor Jacuzzi; herbal steam room; bikes available (free); wireless Internet access. *In room:* TV/VCR, fridge, coffeemaker.

Hotel Lenado ✦   This small hotel—best described as a contemporary mountain lodge—feels right at home in this old mining town, with natural wood beams, wood floors, handsome wood furniture, and a comfortable but upscale feel. The Western-style rooms have a rustic appearance, with four-poster hickory or apple-wood beds, down comforters and pillows, excellent sound systems, shared balconies, and twice-daily maid service. Some units have wet bars, refrigerators, and wood-burning stoves. There's a red rock–and-concrete fireplace in the lobby that stands 28 feet tall, a hot tub on a second-floor deck that offers a spectacular view of Aspen Mountain, ski storage, and a heated locker for ski boots. An excellent gourmet breakfast is served daily.

200 S. Aspen St., Aspen, CO 81611. ℂ **800/321-3457** or 970/925-6246. Fax 970/925-3840. www.hotel lenado.com. 19 units. Winter $285–$495; summer $265–$295; spring and fall $125–$250. Rates include full breakfast. AE, DC, MC, V. **Amenities:** Bar; outdoor heated pool; hot tub; sauna; concierge; limited room service; in-room massage; valet laundry service. *In room:* A/C, TV/VCR or TV/DVD, hair dryer.

Limelite Lodge *(Value* Located within walking distance of practically everything in town, the lodge has two separate buildings facing each other across Cooper Avenue—one three stories, the other two—each with its own heated outdoor swimming pool and whirlpool. Rooms in both buildings are well kept, and offer what we consider a step-above-average lodging at a good value. Most units have queen beds with comforters, wood furnishings, refrigerators, and a small private bathroom on the other side of a walk-through closet/vanity. The nine apartments in the Deep Powder building have full kitchens; some also have fireplaces. Hot beverages are available 24 hours a day; there's also a 24-hour desk, sun deck, and ski lockers.

228 E. Cooper Ave. (at Monarch St.), Aspen, CO 81611. ℂ **800/433-0832** or 970/925-3025. Fax 970/925-5120. www.limelite-lodge.com. 72 units. Early/late ski season $89 double, $130 suite; holiday period $200–$215 double, $320 suite; Jan 180–$195 double, $240 suite; Feb–Mar $250–$265 double, $300 suite; May–June $125–$140 double, $150 suite; July–Aug $169–$184 double, $189 suite; Sept–Oct $139–$154 double, $169 suite. Rates include continental breakfast. AE, DC, DISC, MC, V. Pets accepted for $10 a night. **Amenities:** 2 outdoor heated pools; 2 whirlpools; in-room massage; coin-op laundry. *In room:* TV, fridge.

Snowflake Inn This is a comfortable ski lodge–style inn with a variety of accommodations. Rooms have painted rough-wood walls, overstuffed chairs and sofas, kitchens, and good lighting; some have gas fireplaces and some have skylights. There's complimentary coffee in the lobby. Centrally located just 1 block from downtown Aspen, it's within easy walking distance of the Aspen lifts and right in front of a stop for the free ski shuttle.

221 E. Hyman Ave., Aspen, CO 81611. ℂ **800/247-2069** or 970/925-3221. Fax 970/925-8740. www. snowflakeinn.com. 38 units. Early/late ski season $85–$155; holiday period $258–$343; Jan to mid-Feb $155–$215; mid-Feb to late Mar $196–$256; spring and fall $82–$136; summer $138–$195. Children 17 and under stay free with parent. Winter rates include continental breakfast. AE, DISC, MC, V. **Amenities:** Outdoor heated pool; whirlpool; sauna; coin-op laundry. *In room:* TV, kitchenette, safe.

INEXPENSIVE

In addition to the property discussed below, those on a budget might want to consider the **St. Moritz Lodge & Condominiums,** 334 W. Hyman Ave., Aspen, CO 81611 (ℂ **800/817-2069** or 970/925-3220; www.stmoritzlodge. com), which is one of the best deals in Aspen; small double rooms with shared bathrooms start at $42 in spring and fall, $58 in summer, and $84 in ski season. There are also hostel beds ($30–$44 per person), plus rooms with private bathrooms, units with kitchenettes, and one- and two-bedroom condominium units.

The Mountain Chalet You'll find a friendly, ski-lodge atmosphere here, just 1½ blocks from the lifts. There's a TV in the lobby (where complimentary wine and hors d'oeuvres are served on Mon nights in winter) and a piano and game room on the lower level. Rooms are light-colored, with wood furnishings and good-quality twin, double, queen, or king beds, plus a few trundle beds. There are even some bunk rooms with four beds, rented by the bed at greatly reduced rates in ski season. Most rooms have refrigerators; some have central air-conditioning. Ski lockers are available.

333 E. Durant Ave., Aspen, CO 81611. ℂ **888/503-9355** or 970/925-7797. Fax 970/925-7811. 59 units. Winter $90–$310 double, $420 apt., rates higher during holidays; summer $95–$180 double, $250 apt.; spring and fall $55–$110 double, $140 apt. Children 3 and under stay free. Rates include full breakfast in winter, continental breakfast in summer. DC, DISC, MC, V. Underground parking. **Amenities:** Outdoor heated

pool; exercise room; large indoor whirlpool; sauna and steam room; game room; coin-op laundry. *In room:* TV, fridge (most rooms).

WHERE TO DINE

Most restaurants in the Aspen-Snowmass area are open during the ski season (Thanksgiving to early Apr) and summer (mid-June to mid-Sept) seasons. Between seasons, however, some close their doors or limit hours. Call ahead if you're visiting at these times.

EXPENSIVE

Krabloonik ★★ *(Moments)* INTERNATIONAL   There's something very wild, something that hearkens back to Jack London, perhaps, about sitting in a log cabin watching teams of sled dogs come and go as you bite into a tender caribou loin or wild-boar chop. That's part of the pleasure of Krabloonik. A venture of the largest dog kennel in America's lower 48 states, this rustic restaurant has huge picture windows with mountain views and seating around a sunken fireplace. Skiers drop into the restaurant from the Campground Lift for lunch, and visitors can dine before or after an excursion on a dogsled (see "Dogsledding," earlier in this section). You might try a wild game burger or roasted loin of New Zealand elk for lunch. For dinner there's Krabloonik smoked trout with creamy horseradish for starters and a wide variety of game, beef tenderloin, lamb, and fish for the main course. Those with hearty appetites can choose between two combination game entrees: caribou, elk, and deer; or caribou, quail, and boar. Smoking is not permitted.

4250 Divide Rd., off Brush Creek Rd., Snowmass Village. ✆ **970/923-3953**. www.krabloonik.com. Reservations recommended at lunch, essential at dinner. 3-course prix-fixe lunch $28; dinner main courses $23–$50. AE, MC, V. Winter Mon–Fri 11am–2pm (daily during Christmas holidays), daily 5:30–9:30pm; summer Fri–Sat 6–9pm.

MODERATE & INEXPENSIVE

In addition to the restaurants discussed below, **The Big Wrap,** 520 E. Durant Ave., Aspen (✆ **970/544-1700**), prepares wraps such as the Hail Caesar (grilled chicken, black beans, lettuce, roasted red peppers, feta cheese, and toasted pumpkin seeds), plus salads and soups. It's open daily from 9am to 6pm, with most items from $4 to $6.

La Cocina ★ SOUTHWESTERN   Locals love this place, and we do, too. The menu, although somewhat limited, reminds us of some of our favorite stops in Santa Fe and Taos, and no lard is used. A basket of chips and spicy-hot salsa have greeted diners here since La Cocina opened in 1972. You might start with the green-chile soup, then slide into a platter of blue-corn chicken enchiladas with a side of posole, an assertive burrito, or, for those who prefer less spiciness, a seafood quesadilla. Top it off with a slice of chocolate velvet cake or bread pudding with whiskey sauce for dessert.

308 E. Hopkins Ave. ✆ **970/925-9714**. Reservations not accepted. Main courses $8–$15. MC, V. Daily 5–10pm. Closed Apr to early June and Oct–Nov.

Takah Sushi ★ JAPANESE/PACIFIC RIM   This lively sushi bar and Japanese restaurant serves some of the best sushi you'll find between the East and West coasts. A wide variety of raw fish, from halibut to octopus, is sliced and rolled by Takah's chefs, incorporating Japanese tradition into their own creative styles. For those not desiring sushi or sashimi, the menu also includes crisp Chinese duck, several vegetarian dishes, free-range chicken, and a teriyaki-tempura combination with beef, chicken, or salmon, as well as a savory selection of Pacific Rim cuisine.

420 E. Hyman Ave. (C) **877/925-8588** or 970/925-8588. www.takahsushi.com. Reservations recommended. Main courses $16–$32. AE, DC, DISC, MC, V. Winter daily 5:30–11pm; summer daily 6–11pm.

Woody Creek Tavern ★★ (Finds) AMERICAN/MEXICAN Woody Creek is a true local hangout. It is said that celebrities like to visit, too, but we didn't meet any on our last visit. Probably the only old-time, rustic tavern left in the Aspen area, its walls are covered with a variety of news clippings and other paraphernalia. You'll find a good selection of well-prepared tavern food, including barbecued pork ribs, thick steaks, and burgers (made with low-fat Colorado limousine beef); plus fresh talapia, organic salads, vegetarian (and organic when possible) soups, as well as excellent Mexican food, which goes well with the house-specialty drink—fresh-squeezed lime-juice margaritas made with 100% blue-agave tequila. Dine alfresco on the patio in summer.

Upper River Rd., Woody Creek. (C) **970/923-4585.** Reservations not accepted. Main courses $8–$18. No credit cards. Daily 11:30am–10pm, bar stays open later. Drive west on Colo. 82, ¾ mile past the Snowmass Village turnoff, turn right on Smith Rd. into Woody Creek Canyon, turn left at the first fork, and continue 1¼ miles. This road can be icy in winter.

ASPEN AFTER DARK

Aspen's major performing arts venue is the 1889 **Wheeler Opera House,** 320 E. Hyman Ave., at Mill Street ((C) **970/920-5770** box office; www.wheeler operahouse.com). Built at the peak of the mining boom by silver baron Jerome B. Wheeler, this meticulously restored stage hosts a year-round program of music, theater, dance, film, and lectures. The building itself is worth a visit, with brass wall sconces, crystal chandeliers, gold trim and stencils on the dark-blue walls, rich wood, red carpeting, and red velvet seats. The box office is open daily from 10am to 6pm.

Among Aspen's top nightspots, **Syzygy,** 520 E. Hyman Ave. ((C) **970/925-3700**), ranks high with young, high-energy types who appreciate live jazz. An equally young, energetic crowd makes its way to **The Double Diamond,** 450 S. Galena St. ((C) **970/920-6905**), for dancing to live music. Those who like to dance also head to **Club Chelsea,** 415 E. Hyman Ave. ((C) **970/920-0066**), for its DJ music with a big sound system, plus live music from local bands.

Aspen's oldest bar is the **Red Onion,** 420 E. Cooper Ave. ((C) **970/925-9043**), which opened in 1892 and today remains a noisy, popular hangout, with occasional live music. **Bentley's at the Wheeler,** 328 E. Hyman Ave. ((C) **970/920-2240**), is an elegant English-style pub, good for the older crowd. The **Lobby Lounge** at the St. Regis, at the base of Aspen Mountain ((C) **970/920-3300;** www.stregis.com), draws scores of après-skiers; and among our favorite Aspen bars is the quietly sophisticated and historic **J-Bar,** in the Hotel Jerome at Main and Mill streets ((C) **970/920-1000**).

The Western Slope

Separated from Colorado's major cities by the mighty Rocky Mountains, the communities along the state's western edge are not only miles, but also years away from the hustle and bustle of Denver and the California-style sophistication of Boulder. Even Grand Junction, the region's largest city, remains a sprawling Western town, and the rugged canyons and stark rocky terrain make you feel like you've stepped into a John Ford Western. The lifeblood of this semidesert land is its rivers—the Colorado, Gunnison, and Yampa—for not only have they brought life-giving water, but over tens of thousands of years their ceaseless energy has also gouged out stunning canyons that lure visitors from around the world. Colorado National Monument, west of Grand Junction, is remarkable for its land forms and prehistoric petroglyphs; Dinosaur National Monument, in the state's northwestern corner, preserves a wealth of dinosaur remains; and the Black Canyon of the Gunnison, a dark, narrow, and almost impenetrable chasm east of Montrose, challenges adventurous rock climbers and rafters.

But it's not all rocks and dinosaurs here. In the tiny community of Palisade, outside Grand Junction, some of the West's best wine is produced; and downtown Grand Junction boasts a continually changing and evolving outdoor art exhibit with its delightful Art on the Corner sculpture display.

1 Grand Junction & Colorado & Dinosaur National Monuments

251 miles W of Denver, 169 miles N of Durango

One of our favorite Colorado cities, Grand Junction is an excellent base camp for those who want to drive or hike through the awe-inspiring red-rock canyons and sandstone monoliths of Colorado National Monument, or explore the canyons at Dinosaur National Monument, about 2 hours north. Grand Junction is also the eastern entrance to one of the West's most scenic and challenging mountain-biking treks, Kokopelli's Trail, which ends in Moab, Utah. For the less athletically inclined, Grand Junction has an active visual arts community, good museums, and a fine botanical garden. Nearby you'll find more than a dozen wineries.

Located at the confluence of the Gunnison and Colorado rivers at an elevation of 4,586 feet, the city was founded in 1882 where the spike was driven to connect Denver and Salt Lake City by rail. It quickly became the primary trade and distribution center between the two state capitals, and its mild climate, together with the fertile soil and irrigation potential of the river valleys, helped it grow into an important agricultural area. Soybeans, and later peaches and pears, were the most important crops. The city was also a center of the western Colorado uranium boom in the 1950s and the oil-shale boom in the late 1970s, and today is a fast-growing trade center serving practically all of western Colorado and eastern Utah.

ESSENTIALS

GETTING THERE   By Car   Grand Junction is located on I-70. U.S. 50 is the main artery from the south, connecting with Montrose and Durango.

By Plane   On the north side of Grand Junction, **Walker Field,** 2828 Walker Field Dr. (© **970/244-9100;** fax 970/241-9103; www.walkerfield.com), is less than a mile off I-70's Horizon Drive exit. More than 20 commercial flights connect Grand Junction with the West's major cities.

Airlines serving Walker Field include **America West Express/Mesa Airlines** (© 800/235-9292 or 970/728-4868), **The Delta Connection/SkyWest** (© 800/ 453-9417), **Frontier** (© 800/432-1359), **Great Lakes Aviation** (© 800/554-5111), and **United Express/SkyWest** (© 800/241-6522).

By Train   Amtrak (© 800/USA-RAIL or 970/241-2733; www.amtrak.com) has a passenger station at 337 S. First St. The California Zephyr stops twice daily, once in each direction, on its main route from San Francisco and Salt Lake City to Denver and Chicago.

VISITOR INFORMATION   Contact the **Grand Junction Visitor & Convention Bureau,** 740 Horizon Dr., Grand Junction, CO 81506 (© **800/962-2547** or 970/244-1480; fax 970/243-7393; www.visitgrandjunction.com). There's a visitor center on Horizon Drive at I-70 exit 31 (open 8:30am–8pm in summer and 8:30am–5pm the rest of the year), and a Colorado Welcome Center at I-70 exit 19 (Fruita and Colorado National Monument), 12 miles west of Grand Junction, which is open daily from 8am to 5pm.

GETTING AROUND   Main Street and named avenues run east–west, and numbered streets and roads run north–south. Downtown Grand Junction lies south of I-70 and north of the Colorado River, encompassing 1 block on each side of Main Street between First and Seventh streets.

Car rentals are available in the airport area from **Alamo** (© 970/243-3097), **Avis** (© 970/244-9170), **Budget** (© 970/244-9155), **Enterprise** (© 970/242-8103), **Hertz** (© 970/243-0747), **National** (© 970/243-6626), and **Thrifty** (© 970/243-7556). **Sunshine Taxi** (© 970/245-8294) offers 24-hour service, and **Grand Valley Transit** (© 970/256-7433) operates buses in the Grand Junction area, including a shuttle service to and from Walker Field.

FAST FACTS   There's a 24-hour emergency room at **St. Mary's Hospital,** Patterson Road and Seventh Street (© **970/244-2273**). The main **post office** is at 241 N. Fourth St.; contact the U.S. Postal Service (© **800/275-8777;** www.usps.com) for hours and other information. For **weather conditions,** call © 970/243-0914; for **road conditions,** call © 877/315-7623.

SPECIAL EVENTS   Cinco de Mayo, early May; Dinosaur Days, mid-June in Fruita; Art & Jazz Festival, mid-June; Junior College Baseball World Series, starting Memorial Day weekend; Mesa County Fair, early August; Peach Festival, mid-August in Palisade; Colorado Mountain Wine Fest, late September.

COLORADO NATIONAL MONUMENT 🏵🏵

Just minutes west of Grand Junction, this relatively undiscovered national monument is a delight, offering a colorful maze of steep-walled canyons filled with an array of naturally sculpted spires, pinnacles, and other impressive sandstone rock formations. Easy to get to and easy to see, in many ways it's a miniature

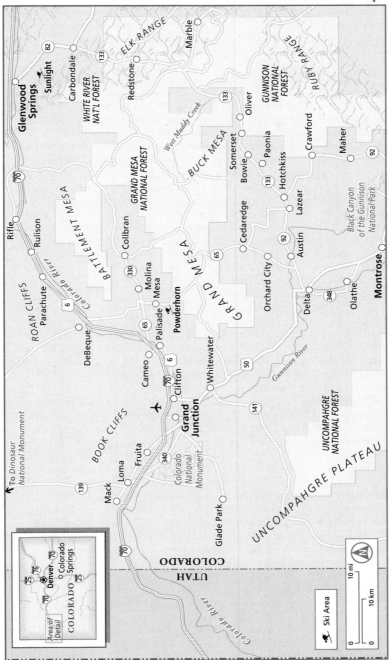

Grand Canyon, without the crowds. You can see much of the monument from your car on the 23-mile Rim Rock Drive, and there are ample opportunities for hiking, horseback riding, and cross-country skiing. Bighorn sheep, mountain lions, golden eagles, mule deer, and lizards are among the monument's residents. The monument ranges in elevation from 4,700 feet to 7,028 feet.

Carved by water and wind over millions of years, Colorado National Monument encompasses 32 square miles of red-rock canyons and sandstone monoliths, more than 1,000 feet above the Colorado River. A combination of upward lifts and erosion caused the chaos of formations here. Each layer visible in the striations of the canyon walls marks a time in the land's history. Fossils permit scientists to date these rocks back through the Mesozoic era of 225 million to 65 million years ago, and the Precambrian formation dates back 1.67 billion years.

The east entrance is only 5 miles west of Grand Junction, off Monument Road, but the best way to explore the monument is to follow the signs off I-70 from Fruita to the west entrance, 15 miles west of Grand Junction. It's here that **Rim Rock Drive,** built during the Great Depression, begins. Snaking up dramatic Fruita Canyon, it offers panoramic views of fanciful and bizarre natural stone monuments as well as the cliffs and mesas beyond. At 4 miles it reaches the national monument headquarters and **visitor center** (open 9am–5pm daily except Christmas). Exhibits on geology and history and an interactive video program introduce the park, and rangers can help you plan your visit. Guided walks and campfire programs are offered during the summer.

Rim Rock Drive—open to bicycles as well as motor vehicles—offers access to hiking trails varying in length from 400 yards to 8.5 miles. Many of the short, easy trails lead to spectacular canyon overlooks, while the longer backcountry trails head out across the mesas or down into the canyons. Strange formations such as Window Rock, the massive rounded Coke Ovens, the boulder-strewn Devils Kitchen, and the free-standing Independence Monument—all of which can be viewed from the road—are easily reached by foot.

If you're looking for an easy walk, try the 1-mile (round-trip) **Canyon Rim Trail,** which follows the edge of a cliff to spectacular views of the colorful rock formations in Wedding Canyon. Allow about an hour. An even shorter walk— the **Window Rock Trail**—also affords views of Wedding Canyon. Allow a half-hour for .3-mile loop.

Those who want to get down into the monument, rather than viewing it from above, should tackle one of the backcountry trails. The relatively difficult 12-mile round-trip **Monument Canyon Trail** drops 600 feet from the plateau into the canyon, among many of the monument's more dramatic rock formations, such as the aptly named Kissing Couple. The canyon is home to rattlesnakes and scorpions, so watch where you put your feet and hands. Also, it's hot and dry down there, so be sure to carry plenty of water. The **Black Ridge Trail,** the national monument's highest, offers panoramic views of the countryside that stretch to the canyons of Utah. Allow about 6 hours for the rugged, 11-mile round-trip hike, and again, carry plenty of water.

Winter visitors may want to take their skis along. Among your best choices here is **Liberty Cap Trail,** which meanders across gently sloping Monument Mesa through a piñon-juniper forest and sagebrush flatlands. The trail is 14 miles round-trip, but cross-country skiers may want to turn back before the last 1.5 miles, which drop sharply into the Grand Valley.

While the monument is worth visiting at any time of year, the best time to go is fall, when the air is crisp but not cold, the cottonwood trees turn a brilliant gold, and the summer crowds have departed. Those visiting in May and June should carry insect repellent to combat the clouds of gnats that invade at this time.

The monument's **Saddlehorn Campground,** located in a piñon-juniper forest near the visitor center, has 80 sites, some shady, and restrooms but no showers or RV hookups. Cost is $10 per night. Like most areas administered by the National Park Service, pets must be leashed and are not allowed on trails or in the backcountry.

The national monument is open year-round. The day-use fee is $5 per vehicle or $3 per person for cyclists and pedestrians. The visitor center is open daily from 9am to 5pm. To obtain a brochure and other information, contact **Colorado National Monument,** Fruita, CO 81521 (© **970/858-3617;** www.nps. gov/colm). Those who want more in-depth information can order topographic maps, books, and other materials from the nonprofit Colorado National Monument Association at the monument's address and phone number above.

DINOSAUR NATIONAL MONUMENT ⚐

This national monument, about 2 hours north of Grand Junction, is really two separate parks divided by the Utah-Colorado border. One side takes a close-up look at the world of dinosaurs, while the other opens onto a wonderland of colorful rock, deep river canyons, and a forest of Douglas firs.

About 150 million years ago a river and sufficient vegetation made this region a suitable habitat for dinosaurs. Most of their skeletons decayed and disappeared, but in at least one spot they were preserved under a layer of sediment, when the river dried up and they died of thirst.

This **Dinosaur Quarry** is accessible only from the Utah side of the park. From Dinosaur, Colorado, head 20 miles west on U.S. 40 to Jensen, Utah, and then go 7 miles north. This is the only place in the monument to see dinosaur bones. The quarry contains one of the world's most concentrated and accessible deposits of the fossils of dinosaurs, crocodiles, turtles, and clams. There's one section of bones you can touch, plus models that show what paleontologists believe these dinosaurs looked like when they had their skin.

But visitors who limit their Dinosaur National Monument trip to its namesake dinosaur quarry miss quite a bit. Encompassing 325 square miles of stark canyons at the confluence of the Yampa and Green rivers in Colorado, there are hiking trails to explore, spectacular panoramic vistas, and the thrill of whitewater rafting. Your first stop should be the small **visitor center** located about 2 miles east of the town of Dinosaur, Colorado, at the intersection of U.S. 40 and Harpers Corner Drive. (You have to return to U.S. 40 to get to the dinosaur quarry in the Utah section of the park.)

Allow about 4 hours for the scenic **Harpers Corner Drive.** This paved 62-mile round-trip drive has several overlooks offering panoramic views of the gorges carved by the Yampa and Green rivers, the derby-shaped Plug Hat Butte, and a variety of other colorful rock formations. The drive also offers access to the easy ¼-mile round-trip **Plug Hat Nature Trail,** and the moderately difficult 2-mile round-trip **Harpers Corner Trail,** highly recommended for a magnificent view of the deep river canyons. In addition to several developed trails, experienced hikers with the appropriate maps can explore miles of unspoiled canyons and rock benches.

A superlative way to see this rugged country is on the river, crashing through thrilling white water and gliding over the smooth, silent stretches. One of the best authorized companies running the Yampa and Green rivers through the monument is **Hatch River Expeditions** (© **800/342-8243** or 435/789-4316; fax 435/789-8513; www.hatchriver.com). Prices start at $66 for adults, $56 for kids ages 6 through 12 for a 1-day trip; multiday trips over longer stretches are also available. The season generally runs from mid-May through mid-September, depending on water levels. A complete list of authorized river-running companies is available from monument headquarters.

Rivers are not safe for swimming or wading; the water is cold, and the current is stronger than it may first appear.

Fishing in the Green and Yampa most often yields catfish, northern pike, and smallmouth bass, although there are also some trout. Several endangered species of fish—including the razorback sucker and humpback chub—must be returned unharmed to the water if caught. You'll need Utah and/or Colorado fishing licenses, depending on which side of the state line you're fishing.

There are **campgrounds** in both sections of the monument, but no showers or RV hookups, and camping fees range from $8 to $12 per night.

The national monument entrance near Dinosaur, Colorado, is about 110 miles north of Grand Junction. From Grand Junction, head west on I-70 about 12 miles to exit 15, turn right (north) onto Colo. 139 and go about 75 miles to Colo. 64, where you turn left, and follow it west for 20 miles to the town of Dinosaur. Then turn right onto U.S. 40 and go east about 2 miles to the monument entrance. The monument is open around the clock, and Quarry Visitor Center is open daily year-round, except Thanksgiving, Christmas, and New Year's Day; Headquarters Visitor Center is open daily in summer but closed weekends in winter. The admission fee, charged only at the Utah entrance as of this writing, is $10 per vehicle, and $5 per person for those on foot, motorcycles, or bicycles.

For information contact **Dinosaur National Monument,** 4545 East U.S. 40, Dinosaur, CO 81610-9724 (© **970/374-3000;** www.nps.gov/dino). In addition, the nonprofit **Intermountain Natural History Association,** 1291 E. U.S. 40, Vernal, UT 84078 (© **800/845-3466;** fax 801/781-1304; www.inhaweb.com), offers numerous publications, maps, posters, and videos on the park's geology, wildlife, history, and especially its dinosaur fossils.

SPORTS & OUTDOOR ACTIVITIES

In addition to activities in Colorado and Dinosaur national monuments, there are numerous opportunities for hiking, camping, mountain biking, off-roading, horseback riding, cross-country skiing, snowmobiling, and snowshoeing on other public lands administered by the federal government. Contact the **Bureau of Land Management,** 2815 H Rd., Grand Junction, CO 81506 (© **970/244-3000;** www.co.blm.gov), and the **Grand Valley Ranger District of Grand Mesa National Forest,** 2777 Crossroads Blvd., Ste. A (off Horizon Dr.), Grand Junction, CO 81506 (© **970/242-8211;** www.fs.fed.us/r2).

You'll also find plenty to do at **Colorado River State Park** (© **970/434-3388;** www.parks.state.co.us), which has two sections, both with campgrounds (see "Camping" under "Where to Stay," later in this section). **Island Acres** (© **970/464-0548**), on the east side of Grand Junction at I-70 exit 47, also offers hiking, picnicking, fishing, and just gazing out at the river. The newer section of the park, west of Grand Junction in **Fruita** (© **970/858-9188**), covers 81 acres and has all of the above, plus boating and a swimming lagoon.

The Grand Junction **Parks and Recreation Department** (© **970/254-3842;** www.gjcity.org) manages more than 30 parks and other facilities, covering about

467 acres, which offer picnicking, hiking, tennis, playgrounds, swimming pools, softball, playing fields, horseshoe pits, and golf courses.

A busy local shop where you can get information on the best spots for outdoor recreation is **Summit Canyon Mountaineering,** 461 Main St. (© **800/254-6248** or 970/243-2847; www.summitcanyon.com). In addition to information, it stocks a wide variety of outdoor-sports equipment, plus travel and outdoor clothing.

GOLF   Our favorite course here, in large part because of the views, is the 18-hole **Tiara Rado Golf Course,** 2057 S. Broadway (© **970/254-3830**), at the base of the Colorado National Monument canyons. Greens fees Monday through Thursday are $13 for 9 holes and $23 for 18 holes; Friday through Sunday $16 and $27, respectively. The **Chipeta Golf Course,** an 18-hole executive course at 222 29 Rd. (© **970/245-7177**), has weekday fees of $10 for 9 holes and $18 for 18 holes, with weekend rates of $12 and $22, respectively. The 27-hole **Adobe Creek National Golf Course,** 876 18½ Rd., Fruita (© **970/858-0521**), is 9 miles west of Grand Junction. On weekdays it charges $17 for 18 holes; on weekends the fee is $24.

HIKING   Hikers and walkers who want to stay close to town can explore the trails in the Colorado Riverfront Project. Collectively known as the **Colorado River Trails,** the system includes almost 20 miles of paved trails that meander along the Colorado and Gunnison rivers, offering the chance to see ducks, geese, blue heron, deer, and rabbits. They are open to walkers and hikers, runners, bikers, in-line skaters, and horseback riders, but are closed to all motorized vehicles (except wheelchairs). Dogs are permitted if leashed, but owners are asked to clean up after their dogs. Most of the trails are between .5 and 2 miles long, and they can be combined for longer hikes. Although all the trails tend to be busy on weekends, on weekdays you'll find they're very quiet. An excellent brochure with maps of the various river trails and directions to their trail heads is available free at the Grand Junction Visitor & Convention Bureau (see "Visitor Information," above).

You'll also find hiking trails at **Colorado River State Park** (see the introduction to this section, above).

HORSEBACK RIDING   Trail rides near the west entrance of Colorado National Monument are available through **Rimrock Adventures,** Box 608, Fruita, CO 81521 (© **888/712-9555** or 970/858-9555; www.rradventures.com). The stables are about a mile south of Fruita on Colo. 340. Rates for a 1-hour ride are $20 for adults and $15 for children 5 to 12, and a half-day ride into the wilderness of Devil's Canyon costs $50 for adults and $40 for children. Kids' pony rides, lasting about 15 minutes, cost $5. Those with their own horses will enjoy the 14-mile (round-trip) Liberty Cap Trail through Colorado National Monument, which winds through a scrub forest and over a sagebrush mesa before dropping steeply into a valley.

MOUNTAIN BIKING   Grand Junction has become important to mountain bikers as the eastern terminus of **Kokopelli's Trail** to Moab, Utah. Winding for 142 miles through sandstone and shale canyons, it has an elevation differential of about 4,200 feet. There are primitive campsites at intervals along the trail. The Colorado gateway is at the Loma Boat Launch, 15 miles west of Grand Junction off I-70.

For information on Kokopelli's Trail and several other area trails, contact the **Colorado Plateau Mountain-Bike Trail Association,** P.O. Box 4602, Grand

Wine Tasting & More Amid the Canyons

Colorado may not be the first location that comes to mind when wine-making is mentioned, but the state does have a growing wine industry and the heart of it is here in the fertile Grand Valley. Area wineries welcome visitors for tastings and sometimes tours, and they all have picnic areas so bring your lunch. Organized tours by van or limousine are also available. Most of the wineries are located in the community of **Palisade,** about 12 miles east of Grand Junction, up the Grand Valley along U.S. 6 (or I-70 exit 42).

The state's oldest existing winery, **Colorado Cellars Winery,** 3553 E Rd., Palisade (© **800/848-2812** or 970/464-7921), produces an excellent selection of award-winning wines, including chardonnays, merlots, Rieslings, fruit wines, and port. Tastings are given year-round, Monday through Friday from 9am to 4pm, and Saturday from 11am to 4pm.

Carlson Vineyards, 461 35 Rd., Palisade (© **888/464-5554** or 970/464-5554; www.carlsonvineyards.com), is a winery with a sense of humor, as well as a good product. Its wines have names such as Prairie Dog Blush and Tyrannosaurus Red, and are made with Colorado grapes. Visitors are welcome year-round, daily from 11am to 6pm.

Rocky Mountain Meadery, 3701 G Rd., Palisade (© **800/720-2558;** 970/464-7899; www.rocky-mountain-meadery.com), produces honey wine—also known as mead. Popular in medieval times, mead was known as "the drink of the gods," and is often served at Shakespearean festivals. It contains no grapes, but is made from orange-blossom honey from citrus groves in Arizona, and ranges from very sweet to quite dry. Rocky Mountain Meadery also produces blends of honey wine and fruit, as well as hard apple and pear cider, and a port-style wine. The tasting room is open daily from 10am to 5pm.

Other local wineries include **Grande River Vineyards,** 787 Elberta Ave., Palisade (© **800/264-7696** or 970/464-5867; www.granderiverwines.com), which produces a variety of wines including a merlot and chardonnay. The tasting room is open daily from 9am to 6pm from spring through fall, and daily from 10am to 5pm in winter. **Plum Creek Cellars,** 3708 G Rd., Palisade (© **970/464-7586**), produces a wide variety of wines, including chardonnays, cabernet sauvignons, merlots, Rieslings, and pinot noirs, using only Colorado grapes. The tasting room is open daily from 9:30am to 6pm April through November, and from 10am to 5pm the rest of the year. **Garfield Estates Winery,** located on a 100-year-old homestead at 3572 G Rd., Palisade (© **970/464-0941;** www.garfield estates.com), produces several fine wines made from Palisade-area

Junction, CO 81502 (www.copmoba.com). There's also a bike route through and around Colorado National Monument (earlier in this chapter). Covering 33 miles, it follows Rim Rock Drive through the park and 10 additional miles on rural South Camp Road and South Broadway at the base of the canyons. Rim Rock Drive does not have a separate bike lane, or shoulders, so be alert for motor traffic. The national monument publishes a free brochure.

grapes—merlot, cabernet sauvignon, sauvignon blanc, shiraz, and port. The tasting room is open daily from noon to 5pm, and they welcome picnickers.

Canyon Wind Cellars, 3907 North River Rd., Palisade (© **970/464-0888;** www.canyonwindcellars.com), produces three big-bodied wines: chardonnay, merlot, and cabernet sauvignon. Its tasting room is open daily from 10am to 5pm. **St. Kathryn Cellars,** 785 Elberta Ave., Palisade (© **877/464-4888** or 970/464-9288; www.St-Kathryn-Cellars.com), produces a chardonnay, a merlot, blends, fruit wines, and port. Its tasting room is open daily from 10am to 5pm. At **Two Rivers Winery,** 2087 Broadway, Grand Junction (© **866/312-9463** or 970/255-1471; www.two riverswinery.com), 11 acres of vineyards surround the French château-style winery and tasting room. Two Rivers produces a cabernet sauvignon, chardonnay, and shiraz. The tasting room is open from 10:30am to 6pm Monday through Saturday and from noon to 5pm Sunday. **Confre Cellars,** 785 Elberta Ave., Palisade (© **970/464-1300**), offers a variety of grape, honey, and fruit wines plus hard ciders. The tasting room is open daily from 10am to 5pm.

The **Debeque Canyon Winery,** 3943 U.S. 6, Palisade (© **970/464-0550**), produces a wide range of wines including chardonnays and cabernets, merlots and shiraz, fruit wines and port. The tasting room is open daily from 8am to 6pm in summer and 8am to 5pm in winter. **Amber Ridge Vineyards,** 3820 G ¼ Rd., Palisade (© **970/464-5314;** www. corleyvineyards.com), produces chardonnay, cabernet sauvignon, and merlot, and is open Thursday afternoons only, from 1pm to 5pm. South of Grand Junction about 7 miles is **Reeder Mesa Vineyards,** 7799 Reeder Mesa Rd., Whitewater (© **970/242-7468;** www.reedermesawines.com) offering cabernet sauvignon, merlot, shiraz, Riesling, and port. They're open Friday through Sunday, from 10am to 6pm.

Maps to the wineries and additional information can be obtained from the Grand Junction Visitor & Convention Bureau (p. 336) and online at **www.coloradowinecountry.com**.

Palisade is just as famous for its fruit orchards as it is for its vineyards and wineries. Most fruit is picked between late June and mid-September, when it's available at roadside fruit stands. For a fruit directory, harvest schedule, and map, contact the **Palisade Chamber of Commerce,** 319 Main St., Palisade, CO 81526 (© **970/464-7458;** www. palisadecoc.com).

There are also several short mountain bike rides in the area. Inquire at the Visitor & Convention Bureau (see "Visitor Information," earlier in this chapter) for their brochures.

RIVER RAFTING   For our money, one of the best ways to see this area's beautiful red sandstone canyons is from the river, in a big old rubber raft. Colorado river-rafting trips are provided by **Rimrock Adventures** (see "Horseback

Riding," above). Cost for a 1½-hour trip about 5 miles down the Colorado is $20 for adults and $15 for children 12 and under; a 30-mile full-day float trip costs $90 per adult and $65 per child. An exciting 17-mile white-water trip through Westwater Canyon costs $130 per person. The company also rents rafts ($60–$100 per day), canoes ($35 per day), and inflatable kayaks ($30–$40 per day) for those who want to explore the river on their own.

    Adventure Bound River Expeditions, 2392 H Rd., Grand Junction, CO 81505 (Ⓒ **800/423-4668** or 970/245-5428; www.raft-colorado.com), offers 1- to 7-day trips. Rates for 1-day trips start at $95 per person and 2-day trips cost about $290 per person; call for additional rate information.

SKIING & SNOWBOARDING   **Powderhorn Resort** ★, Colo. 65, 7 miles south of Mesa (Ⓒ **800/241-6997** for reservations only, or 970/268-5700; www. powderhorn.com), is located 35 miles east of Grand Junction on the north face of the Grand Mesa. A favorite among local skiers and snowboarders of all ability levels, this pleasant resort offers 510 acres of skiable terrain with an average annual snowfall of 250 inches. Powderhorn has one quad lift, two doubles, and a surface lift serving 27 trails, which are rated 20% beginner, 50% intermediate, 15% advanced, and 15% expert. Elevation at the top is 9,850 feet, and there's a vertical drop of 1,650 feet. Lift-ticket prices (highest Fri–Sun and holidays) are $35 to $45 for adults age 26 to 54, $28 to $38 for young adults age 19 to 25, $25 to $35 for students 7 to 18 and seniors 55 to 69; $10 for those 70 and older; and $5 for children 6 and younger. The resort has a ski school, a rental shop, and repair center. It is usually open from early December through early April.

    Located at Powderhorn is a slope-side lodge, the **Inn at Wildewood,** P.O. Box 370, Mesa, CO 81643 (Ⓒ **970/268-5170**). It has 27 rooms with double rates from $65 to $119 and fully equipped two- and three-bedroom condominium units that sleep from 8 to 10 people with rates of $199 to $299. The **Wildewood Restaurant** serves lunch and dinner in a casually elegant atmosphere, with an American/Continental cuisine of sandwiches, salads, exotic pizzas, and pasta dishes.

SNOWMOBILING   A trail connects Powderhorn Resort to Sunlight Mountain Resort, running 120 miles from Grand Junction's local ski area to Glenwood Springs, the longest multiuse winter recreational trail in Colorado, traversing White River and Grand Mesa national forests. It is fully marked and continuously groomed. Other trails can be accessed from the parking areas along Colo. 65, between Mesa Lakes and Grand Mesa.

SWIMMING   Centrally located **Lincoln Park,** at 12th Street and North Avenue, has a 50m outdoor heated pool with a 351-foot water slide, along with lighted tennis courts, playgrounds, picnic areas, and a 9-hole golf course. The **Orchard Mesa Community Center,** 2736 C Rd., has an indoor pool, open year-round, with a diving area and shallow-water section. For hours, fees, and other specifics, contact park offices (Ⓒ **970/254-3886**) or the Grand Junction Parks and Recreation Department (Ⓒ **970/254-3842;** www.gjcity.org).

THE MUSEUM OF WESTERN COLORADO ★★

For a huge step through time—from 150 million years ago all the way up to the present—you'll want to visit the various facilities of the **Museum of Western Colorado** (Ⓒ **888/488-3466** or 970/242-0971; fax 970/242-3960; www. wcmuseum.org). These include the **History Museum/Smith Educational Tower, Dinosaur Journey,** and **Cross Orchards Historic Farm** (each of which is discussed below).

In addition, the Museum of Western Colorado manages three **natural resource areas** (free admission, open 24 hr.), where you can get a firsthand look at the geology and paleontology of western Colorado. **Rabbit Valley Research Natural Area,** located at I-70 exit 2, about 30 miles west of Grand Junction, encompasses a working dinosaur quarry. The "Trail Through Time," a 1½-mile self-guided walking tour, offers a close-up view of dinosaur fossils preserved in ancient stream channels. **Riggs Hill,** located off South Broadway in Grand Junction, is the site of the first official dinosaur excavation in western Colorado. It's named for paleontologist Elmer S. Riggs of Chicago's Field Museum of Natural History, who discovered huge fossilized bones of the previously unknown dinosaur Brachiosaurus altithorax here in 1900. The site has a .8-mile self-guided interpretive trail, as well as stupendous panoramic views from the top of Riggs Hill. **Dinosaur Hill,** south of Fruita, off Colo. 340 near Colorado National Monument, is western Colorado's second excavated site, also dug by Riggs. It contains a 1-mile self-guided interpretive trail.

Cross Orchards Historic Farm   With over 22,000 apple trees covering 243 acres, Cross Orchards was one of the largest apple orchards in western Colorado during the first quarter of the 20th century. Today, the remaining 24 acres of the historic site preserve the feel of an old working farm and orchard, where blacksmiths and woodworkers continue to ply their trades, and visitors often smell ginger cookies baking in wood-burning stoves. Costumed guides lead tours through the original barn and packing house, workers' bunkhouse, and farm owner's gazebo. The site contains an extensive collection of vintage farm and road construction equipment, plus rail cars and a reconstructed depot. There's also a gift shop. Each year in mid-October visitors enjoy the **Apple Jubilee,** a harvest festival that includes plenty of fresh apple cider and other apple goodies. Allow 1½ to 2 hours.

3073 F Rd. ℂ **970/434-9814.** Admission $4 adults, $3 seniors 60 and over, $2.50 children 12 and under; immediate family rate $10. May to mid-Oct Tues–Sat 10am–3pm. Closed Nov–Apr except for special events (ℂ 970/242-0971 for schedule).

Dinosaur Journey *Kids*   Enter a virtual time machine to journey back to the age of dinosaurs, where you'll encounter the 18-foot forelimb of a Brachiosaurus. There are cast skeletons of dinosaurs such as Allosaurus and Stegosaurus, as well as real bones and robotic reconstructions. The cleverly designed and constructed full-size models move, bellow, and occasionally spit water. Hands-on, interactive exhibits allow kids of all ages to learn about and experience the forces that created the lands around us, and to feel the earth shake on an earthquake simulator. There is also a working paleontology lab, where you can see scientists prepare dinosaur bones for study. Visitors can join in a real dinosaur dig at one of the museum's quarries with advance registration (ℂ **888/488-3466**). Allow 1 to 3 hours.

550 Jurassic Ct., Fruita (just south of I-70 exit 19). ℂ **970/858-7282.** Admission $7 adults, $6 seniors 60 and over, $4 children 12 and under; immediate family rate $20. May–Sept daily 9am–5pm; Oct–Apr Mon–Sat 10am–4pm, Sun noon–4pm.

History Museum/Smith Educational Tower   This extensive museum offers a step back into the history of the American West, with "immersive" exhibits that remove the glass between visitor and exhibit, allowing you to literally step into history. Listen to the antique siren as you inspect the 1921 LaFrance fire truck; or examine a superb collection of Southwestern pottery in an adobe villa. You can explore an 1890s schoolhouse and a 1930s post office, as well as venture inside a full-size uranium mine, where the sounds of blasting and drilling continue to echo, and even "fly" a computer-controlled 1950 Cessna and learn about Colorado aviation history. The museum also boasts one of the finest firearms collections in the region, and has a display on the life of Alferd Packer, Colorado's notorious cannibal. From the upper levels of the six-story Smith Tower you'll get impressive 360-degree views of Grand Junction and the surrounding countryside. Connect to a wealth of historical, genealogical, and natural history materials in the Loyd Files Research Library. Allow 1½ to 3 hours.

5th St. and Ute Ave. ℂ 970/242-0971. Admission $5.50 adults, $4.50 seniors 60 and over, $3 children 12 and under; immediate family rate $16. May–Sept Mon–Sat 9am–5pm, Sun noon–4pm; Oct–Apr Tues–Sat 10am–3pm.

MORE TO SEE & DO

In addition to the attractions discussed here, those interested in art might check out the **pottery classes** offered at The Gallery bed-and-breakfast inn (see "Where to Stay," below).

Art on the Corner ⚅   This outdoor sculpture exhibit, with more than 100 works, helps make Grand Junction's Downtown Shopping Park one of the most attractive and successful in the country. About half of the sculptures are on loan by the artists for 1 year, during which time they are for sale, while the rest are on permanent display. The sculptures were created in a variety of styles in bronze, chrome, iron, and other materials. We particularly like the large bronze pig named *Sir,* located on the east side of Sixth Street at Main, and *Greg La Rex,* a sculpture in steel that depicts a dinosaur skeleton atop a bicycle, at the corner of Third and Main. The shopping park has art galleries, antiques shops, restaurants, and a variety of retail stores, with wide, tree-lined pedestrian walkways. Allow at least an hour.

Main St., from Second to Seventh sts. ℂ 970/245-2926. Free admission. Daily 24 hr., with shops and restaurants open usual business hours.

Banana Fun Park *Kids*   A fun place for kids of all ages (and the adults who are lucky enough to have their kids take them), this amusement park has a great miniature golf course—with waterfalls, fountains, and ponds—plus an arcade, go carts, bumper boats in a small "bay," and a cafe. Allow 2 hours or more.

2469 River Rd. ℂ 970/243-0070. Tickets for individual activities vary; packages start at $11 per person. Sun–Thurs 10am–10pm; Fri–Sat 10am–midnight.

Western Colorado Botanical Gardens ⚅⚅ *Kids*   This botanical garden along the Colorado River offers a delightful escape into the natural world. Located on 12⅓ acres, the facility includes a butterfly house, greenhouse, paved trails, and outdoor gardens and demonstration areas.

In the butterfly house, visitors stroll through a lush forest of flowering plants, ferns, and ponds. But don't let the butterflies land on your palms—oil from your hands will clog their taste buds, which are located on their feet, and prevent them from finding food. The adjacent greenhouse contains hundreds of plants, including orchids and other colorful tropical varieties. Also in the greenhouse are fishponds and several whimsical metal sculptures of animals, including one of the friendliest-looking snakes you've ever seen. The sculptures are for sale, along with numerous other botanically related items, in the well-stocked gift shop. Walkways connect the botanical gardens with the Colorado River Trails system, which is discussed under "Hiking" on p. 341. Allow 2 to 4 hours.

655 Struthers Ave. © **970/245-9030.** Fax 970/245-9001. www.wcbotanic.org. Admission $3 adults, $2 students and seniors, $1.50 children 5–12, free for kids 4 and under. Feb–Oct Tues–Sun 10am–5pm; Nov–Jan Tues–Sun 10am–4:30pm. Located at the south end of Seventh St.

Western Colorado Center for the Arts   This art center has hundreds of works of art, many with Western themes, as well as traveling exhibits. The collection includes lithographs by Western artist Paul Pletka and more than 50 Navajo weavings dating from the early 1900s. There's also a gift shop featuring unique handcrafted items. Classes, changing exhibitions, and other events are scheduled throughout the year (call for a schedule).

1803 N. Seventh St. © **970/243-7337.** Fax 970/243-2482. www.gjartcenter.org. Admission $2 adults, free for children under 12. Tues–Sat 9am–4pm.

Western Colorado Math & Science Center ★★ *Kids*   This incredible, hands-on facility is designed to "create enthusiasm and excitement for math and science" for kids of all ages—right on up to seniors. It's the brainchild of physicist John McConnel, who decided to turn from research to education and started a mentoring program in math and science for western Colorado K through 12 students. With sophisticated hands-on experiments and interactive presentations packed in the trunk of his car, McConnel traveled from school to school; eventually, the popular program outgrew the car's trunk and morphed into the Western Colorado Math & Science Center. Somewhere along the way it acquired the acronym SITHOK, or Science In The Hands Of Kids. And that's it in a nutshell: The basic elements of science and math are presented with explanations, and kids (and adults) are invited to "touch, turn, look, listen, feel, pull, adjust, try out, and question." The staff of volunteers are continually adding and changing exhibits. Be sure to schedule your visit around school hours, since schools from a 160-mile radius make field trips to the center. Allow 1 to 4 hours.

2660 Unaweep Ave. © **970/254-1626.** www.sithok.org. Admission $1. Wed–Sat 10am–3pm.

SHOPPING

For Colorado's most artful shopping experience, head to Grand Junction's **Downtown Shopping Park,** where you'll find a variety of shops, art galleries, and restaurants set amid an outdoor sculpture garden that runs some 7 blocks along Main Street. (See "Art on the Corner," above.) Our favorite gallery is **Working Artists Studio,** 520 Main St. (© **970/256-9952**), with a wonderful variety of hand-thrown pottery, delightful sculptures, weavings, wind chimes; large—and expensive—wondrous things and quite affordable smaller items. In addition, there is an area in the back where you can usually watch an artist at work. There's also a resident cat, though he doesn't always show himself.

The western slope's largest indoor shopping mall, **Mesa Mall,** is located at 2424 U.S. 6 and 50 (© **970/242-0008;** www.shopmesamall.com). It's anchored by Sears, Mervyn's, JCPenney, Target, and Herberger's, and contains more than 100 specialty shops, services, and eateries.

WHERE TO STAY

Major chains offering reasonably priced lodging in Grand Junction, all conveniently lined up along Horizon Drive, include **Adam's Mark Grand Junction,** 743 Horizon Dr., Grand Junction, CO 81506 (© 800/444-2326 or 970/241-8888), with rates of $63 to $129; **Best Western Sandman Motel,** 708 Horizon Dr., Grand Junction, CO 81506 (© 800/937-8376 or 970/243-4150), with rates of $52 to $77; **Comfort Inn,** 750 Horizon Dr., Grand Junction, CO 81506 (© 800/228-5150 or 970/245-3335), with rates of $59 to $98; **Days Inn,** 733

Horizon Dr., Grand Junction, CO 81506 (© 800/329-7466 or 970/245-7200), with rates of $60 to $80; **Holiday Inn,** 755 Horizon Dr., Grand Junction, CO 81506 (© 888/489-9796 or 970/243-6790), with rates of $84 to $109; and **Super 8,** 728 Horizon Dr., Grand Junction, CO 81506 (© 800/800-8000 or 970/248-8080), with rates of $49 to $86. Those desiring larger rooms and their own kitchen facilities might consider **Hawthorn Suites,** 225 Main St., Grand Junction, CO 81501 (© 800/922-3883 or 970/242-2525), with rates from $99. All rates listed above are for two people, with the highest rates during the summer. Room tax adds almost 11% to lodging bills.

The Gallery *★★*   Are you the arty type? Then this small bed-and-breakfast inn might be just what you want. The Gallery is the home of local artist Damian Radice, who has made two comfortable bedrooms available for guests, along with two private bathrooms. Each room has a queen-sized bed, plush robes, and a TV/VCR (videos are available). The attractive home also has a large living area with a fireplace for guests' use, and a ceramics studio where guests can often see local artists at work. Pottery lessons are offered at $35 per hour, with a minimum of 2 hours, for 1 to 4 people. The rate includes all materials plus domestic shipping charges for your finished work. The full breakfasts include a hot entree, in-season fruits, and coffee brewed from locally roasted beans; afternoon refreshments are also served. Also on the property is a separate house with two bedrooms that can be rented nightly, ideal for a family or two couples traveling together (call for rates and other details).

547 30 Rd., Grand Junction, CO 81504. © **970/243-2501.** www.thegallerybb.com. 2 units. $65 double, or both rooms for $120. Rates include full breakfast. MC, V. *In room:* A/C, TV/VCR, no phone.

Grand Vista Hotel *★★*   The aptly named Grand Vista does indeed have grand views, especially from the upper floors of its six stories. On the south side of the building you'll be looking out over Colorado National Monument with its majestic canyons, while guests on the building's north side see the Book Cliffs and Grand Mesa. Units here are very quiet, with good lighting, comfortable seating, complimentary wireless hi-speed Internet, and a table and two uphol-stered chairs even in the smallest rooms. The minisuites are especially spacious, and come with a king bed, recliner, modem dataport, and whirlpool tub. All king rooms have pillow-top mattresses

Bailey's Lounge is a handsome Old English–style pub with great deals on drinks and appetizers on weekday evenings. Golf and rafting packages are available. Four floors are designated completely nonsmoking.

2790 Crossroads Blvd., Grand Junction, CO 81506. © **800/800-7796** or 970/241-8411. Fax 970/241-1077. www.grandvistahotel.com. 158 units. Apr–Oct $69–$79 double, lower at other times. AE, DC, DISC, MC, V. Small pets accepted for a $10 fee. **Amenities:** Restaurant (American); bar; large heated indoor pool; 24-hr. hot tub; complimentary airport/train/bus shuttle. *In room:* A/C, TV w/on-demand movies and video games, coffeemaker, hair dryer, iron.

CAMPING

In addition to campgrounds at **Colorado National Monument** (see earlier in this chapter), **Colorado River State Park** (www.parks.state.co.us) has two campgrounds. The **Island Acres** unit (© **970/464-0548**), 10 miles east of Grand Junction at I-70 exit 47, has 80 campsites, ranging from tent only ($12) to electric ($16) to full RV hookups ($20). The **Fruita** unit *★★* (© **970/ 858-9188**), off I-70 exit 19 and about 10 miles west of Grand Junction, has 57 campsites, a group site, and the same rates. This is our choice of where to camp—it's well laid out and very conveniently located just a few miles from the west entrance of Colorado National Monument. Both campgrounds have showers and laundry facilities, a playground, naturalist programs, picnicking, fishing, and hiking. The Fruita unit also boasts a swimming lagoon and boating.

There are also several commercial campgrounds in the Grand Junction area, complete with full RV hookups, hot showers, and all the usual niceties. We like **Junction West R.V. Park,** 793 22 Rd., Grand Junction (© **970/245-8531**), which not only has about the cleanest bathhouses we've seen anywhere, but is also quiet and conveniently located. There are 61 large, somewhat-shaded sites, a store, coin-operated laundry, and game room. Our only complaint is that the park is open to RVs only—no tents or even tent trailers—which we find a bit elitist. Rates are in the $23 to $25 range. Registrations are not accepted after 9pm. To get there, take U.S. 6 and 50 to 22 Road (or I-70 exit 26), and go north half a mile.

WHERE TO DINE
MODERATE

The Winery Restaurant ★★ STEAK/SEAFOOD   Fine dining in an atmosphere of Western elegance is what you'll experience at the Winery, which we rate as one of the best restaurants in Grand Junction. The dining room, of redbrick and weathered barn wood, is decorated with lots of plants, stained glass, and wine barrels and bottles. It's hard to go wrong here, especially if you choose from the Winery Favorites section of the menu. We recommend the prime rib (get there early—it often sells out) and the salmon filet. The salmon and catch of the day are always fresh. You can also get a variety of steaks, steak and seafood combos, rack of lamb, or pork chops. For a real treat, order the 14-ounce Australian lobster tail.

642 Main St. © **970/242-4100.** Reservations recommended. Main courses $9.50–$30. AE, DC, DISC, MC, V. Sun–Thurs 5–9pm, Fri–Sat 5–10pm; closed major holidays.

INEXPENSIVE

Crystal Cafe and Bake Shop *Finds* AMERICAN   You may have to wait for a table at this local favorite, especially for breakfast and lunch, but the food here is worth waiting for. The simple, modern decor includes hardwood tables and bentwood cafe-style chairs, with woven place mats and napkins. Selections are mostly innovative variations on standard American dishes, highlighted by the cafe's own fresh-baked breads, rolls, pastries, and desserts. For breakfast there's a variety of pancakes, as well as egg dishes that include a Greek omelet—a two-egg omelet with fresh tomatoes, black olives, red onions, oregano, and feta cheese. Lunch and dinner items include plenty of salads, hot and cold sandwiches, and a quiche of the day. Sandwiches often include uniquely seasoned mayonnaise. We particularly enjoyed the smoked turkey with red onion and basil mayonnaise.

314 Main St. © **970/242-8843.** Breakfast $3–$7.50; lunch and dinner $6–$11. MC, V. Mon–Fri 7am–1:45pm, Thurs–Fri 5–9pm, Sat 8am–noon and 5–9pm; bakery open until 3pm Mon–Fri and until 1pm Sat.

Main Street Café AMERICAN   The '50s are back at the Main Street Café, with an old-fashioned soda fountain (there's also seating at tables), photos of Marilyn and Elvis, and 45-rpm records. In addition to the shot of nostalgia, you'll find good diner food at reasonable prices. Breakfasts include bacon and eggs, pancakes, and, for the more adventurous, several spicy combinations. For lunch there are several vegetarian items, numerous sandwiches and salads, excellent hand-packed Black Angus burgers, and blue-plate specials including

Italian-style meat loaf, brisket, and chicken-fried steak, all with real mashed potatoes and fresh vegetables. Leave room for the praiseworthy banana split or hot-fudge sundae.

504 Main St. ⓒ **970/242-7225**. Breakfast $2.95–$6.95; lunch $3.25–$11. AE, DISC, MC, V. Daily 7am–4pm.

Pablo's Pizza 🐾 *Kids* PIZZA   Inspired by Pablo Picasso, who forever changed the art world with his revolutionary creations, Pablo's Pizza strives for the same sort of impact on our taste buds. And it succeeds. Being purists, we had a simple pepperoni pizza, which was delicious. But for the adventuresome spirit, there are specialty pizzas such as Dracula's Nemesis—garlic white sauce, roasted garlic, roasted red onion, chicken, green onions, and cheese; or Big Daddy's Rajun Cajun—spicy hot tomato sauce, andouille sausage, shrimp, red and green bell peppers, and cheese. Or you can build your own, beginning with one of their eight sauces, and adding cheese, meats, vegetables, and even fruits. You can watch them make your pizza from the tossing of the crust to when they take it from the oven on a wooden paddle. The redbrick-and-white walls are decorated with Picasso-style original artwork, and the ceiling is of pressed tin. All in all, the place has a 1960s Greenwich Village–coffeehouse atmosphere. Pablo's also offers beer and wine; soups, salads, and desserts; take-out and delivery service.

319 Main St. ⓒ **970/255-8879**. Pizza $7.50–$22; by the slice $1.85–$2.60. DISC, MC, V. Sun–Thurs 11am–8:30pm; Fri–Sat 11am–9pm.

2 Glenwood Springs

84 miles E of Grand Junction, 41 miles NW of Aspen, 169 miles W of Denver

Scenic beauty and hot mineral water are the lures here. Members of the Ute tribe visited the Yampah mineral springs on the banks of the Colorado River for centuries. Calling it "big medicine," they came from miles around to heal their wounds or use nearby vapor caves as a natural sauna. But it wasn't until the 1880s that the springs were commercially developed. The three Devereux brothers, who had made a small fortune in silver at Aspen, built what was at the time the largest hot-springs pool in the world, then added a red-sandstone bathhouse and built the Hotel Colorado. Soon everyone from European royalty to movie stars to President Theodore Roosevelt made their way to Glenwood Springs.

The springs supported the town until the Great Depression and World War II caused a decline in business. After the war, with the growth of the ski industry at nearby Aspen, Glenwood Springs began to reemerge as a resort town, but on a smaller scale. Today, this city of 8,200, at an elevation of 5,746 feet, is a popular recreational center. The hot-springs complex underwent a total renovation in the 1970s, and additional improvements were made in 1993, as it celebrated its centennial.

Also completed that year was a 12-year, $490-million project to build a four-lane interstate through the 18-mile Glenwood Canyon. One of the most expensive roadways ever built—as well as one of the most beautiful interstate highway drives in America—the road offers a number of trail heads and raft-launching areas as well as viewpoints from which travelers can safely gaze at the Colorado River and its spectacular canyon.

ESSENTIALS
GETTING THERE   By Car   I-70 follows the Colorado River through Glenwood Springs. Colo. 82 (the Aspen Hwy.) links the city with Aspen, 42 miles southeast.

By Bus   Roaring Fork Transit Agency (© **970/920-8484;** www.rfta.com) offers service between Glenwood Springs and Aspen, with numerous stops along the route, daily from 6am to midnight, at a cost of $6 each way, less for inter-mediate stops.

By Shuttle Van   Transportation from Denver to Glenwood Springs and Aspen is provided by **Colorado Mountain Express** (© **800/525-6363;** 970/926-9800; www.cmex.com). Call for rates and times.

By Train   There's **Amtrak** service (© **800/USA-RAIL;** www.amtrak.com) to Glenwood Springs daily aboard the California Zephyr, direct from Denver and Salt Lake City. The depot is at Seventh Street and Cooper Avenue.

VISITOR INFORMATION   The **Glenwood Springs Chamber Resort Association,** 1102 Grand Ave., Glenwood Springs, CO 81601 (© **970/945-6589;** www.glenwoodchamber.com), maintains a visitor center on the south side of downtown, on the southeast corner of 11th and Grand. Brochures are available 24 hours a day.

GETTING AROUND   The confluence of the Roaring Fork and Colorado rivers forms a T in the heart of Glenwood Springs, and streets follow the valleys carved by the two streams. Downtown Glenwood is south of the Colorado and east of the Roaring Fork.

The city-run bus service, **Ride Glenwood Springs,** operates daily, providing rides to and from hotels, motels, restaurants, shopping areas, and the Hot Springs Pool. Passes cost $2 per person per day for unlimited rides (exact change required), and can be obtained from bus drivers. Schedules are available at the Chamber Resort Association office (see above).

FAST FACTS   Valley View Hospital, providing 24-hour emergency care, is at 1906 Blake Ave. (© **970/945-6535**), a block east of Colo. 82 at 19th Street. The **post office** is at 113 Ninth Street; contact the U.S. Postal Service (© **800/275-8777;** www.usps.com) for hours and additional information.

SPECIAL EVENTS   Ski Spree Winter Carnival, from late January to early February; Summer of Jazz, June and July; the Strawberry Days Festival, third full week of June; and the Fall Art Festival, late September.

SPORTS & OUTDOOR ACTIVITIES

There are plenty of outdoor recreation opportunities in and around Glenwood Springs. Stop at the **chamber** office (see "Visitor Information," above), the **White River National Forest,** Ninth Street and Grand Avenue (© **970/945-2521;** www.fs.fed.us/r2), or the **Bureau of Land Management (BLM),** 50629 U.S. 6 and 24 (© **970/947-2800;** www.co.blm.gov), for maps, recreational sug-gestions, and other information.

A busy local shop where you can get information on the best spots for hiking, mountain climbing, rock climbing, kayaking, camping, and cross-country ski-ing is **Summit Canyon Mountaineering,** 732 Grand Ave. (© **800/360-6994** or 970/945-6994; www.summitcanyon.com). In addition to selling a wide vari-ety of outdoor-sports equipment, it also sells travel and outdoor clothing, with an especially good selection of women's travel apparel. The shop also rents cross-country ski gear, tents, sleeping bags, and backpacks.

Logging onto **www.glenwoodactivities.com** will connect you to **Rock Gar-dens,** a company that offers guided jeeping, rafting, kayaking, fishing, and bik-ing trips. It's located in Glenwood Canyon along the Glenwood Canyon Recreational Trail at I-70 exit 119.

An Underground Fantasy & an Above-Ground Vision

Billed as the Eighth Wonder of the World, guided tours of Glenwood Springs' **Fairy Caves** ☞☞ were a major tourist attraction in the late 1890s and early 1900s. Located on Iron Mountain, a half mile north and 1,300 feet above the town, the caves attracted visitors from around the world until the onset of World War I shut down the operation. They were a sight to see—numerous stalactites and stalagmites, needles, gypsum flowers, bacon, soda straws, and other delicate and colorful formations, illuminated by electric lights—all for the 1897 price of 50¢. Visitors would either walk to the caves' entrance or ride a burro.

Formed in limestone that was deposited some 325 million years ago, the cave system is believed to be one of the largest in the state, with one room—the barn—over five stories tall. These caves are also significant because, unlike a number of other caves, they're live, meaning that they remain moist and continue to produce new formations.

Closed since 1917, the Fairy Caves were reopened to the public in 1999, along with a section of the caves that remained undiscovered until more recent times. The cave temperature remains a constant 52°F (11°C) year-round, so you'll probably want a light jacket even on the hottest summer day. Since you'll also be traversing some 127 stairs, be sure to wear comfortable walking shoes. New trails, hand rails, and lighting have been installed for the 1-hour guided **Cave Tour,** which covers a half mile.

Because of the combination of the elevation (7,100 feet) and the exertion required, the tour is not recommended for pregnant women

BICYCLING   A paved bike trail runs from the Yampah Vapor Caves into Glenwood Canyon, and trails and four-wheel-drive roads in the adjacent White River National Forest are ideal for mountain bikers (see "Hiking," below). You'll find bike rentals (about $6 per hr. or $19–$25 per day), plus repairs and accessories, in town at **Canyon Bikes,** at the Hotel Colorado, 526 Pine St. (✆ **800/ 439-3043** or 970/945-8904; www.canyonbikes.com), which also offers a shuttle service ($13 per person), and **Sunlight Mountain Ski & Bike Shop,** 309 Ninth St. (✆ **970/945-9425;** www.sunlightmtn.com). Also offering bike rentals is **Rock Gardens,** 1308 C.R. 129 (✆ **800/958-6737** or 970/945-6737; www. rockgardens.com; also see above).

FISHING   Brown and rainbow trout are caught in the Roaring Fork and Colorado rivers, and fishing for rainbow and brook trout is often good in the Crystal River above the community of Redstone. Get licenses, equipment, and advice from **Roaring Fork Anglers,** 2114 B Grand Ave. (✆ **970/945-0180;** www. rfanglers.com), who have offered guided fly-fishing trips since 1975. Rates for one or two people on a full-day float trip are $395, including lunch; a full-day wading trip, including lunch, is $280 for one and $330 for two. Half-day trips are available, and Roaring Fork also has 4 miles of private waters. Another local company offering guided fishing trips, at similar rates, is **Blue Sky Adventures** (see "River Rafting," below).

nor those with heart or respiratory problems. Wheelchairs, baby back-packs, and strollers are not allowed in the cave, due to the stairs and narrow passageways. Very young children can be carried in arms or a front pack.

Most of the caves have been left in as natural a state as possible for the guided 3- to 4-hour **Wild Tour,** which is for small groups of physically fit individuals who don't mind crawling on their stomachs through dirty narrow passages wearing knee pads and helmet lights. Participants must be at least 13 years old, and a parent or guardian must accompany each youth from 13 to 17. Reservations are required. Cost is $50 per person.

And now there's an easy and entertaining way to get to these won-drous caves: Ride the tram! The **Glenwood Caverns Adventure Park** opened in April 2003, with eight six-person gondolas rising the 1,400 feet from the valley floor up the side of Iron Mountain. You'll have panoramic views all the way to the top, where there's a visitor center, gift shop, moderately difficult nature trail, good food at Exclamation Point Restaurant & Bar (open daily 11am to 9pm), plus Discovery Rock (extra fee)—a place for kids to pan for jewels and unearth fossils.

The tram operates daily (8:30am to 10pm in summer, call for winter hours) from the **Iron Mountain Tramway Station** at 51000 Two Rivers Plaza Rd. Combination tram and cave tour tickets cost $17 for adults, $15 for seniors 65 and older, and $12 for children 3 to 12; tram-only tickets are $10, $9, and $7 respectively. Reservations are suggested (© **800/530-1635** or 970/945-4228; www.glenwoodcaverns.com).

GOLF   Glenwood Springs Golf Club, 193 Sunny Acres Rd. (© **970/945-7086**), is a 9-hole course, with fees of $19 for 9 holes and $29 for 18 holes. Some 27 miles west of Glenwood Springs, near Rifle, is the championship 18-hole **Rifle Creek Golf Club,** at 3004 Colo. 325, off I-70 exit 90 (© **888/247-0370** or 970/625-1093), which charges $18 for 9 holes and $35 for 18 holes.

Fans of miniature golf will discover two beautifully landscaped 18-hole water-obstacle courses at **Johnson Park Miniature Golf,** 51579 U.S. 6 and 24, in West Glenwood Springs (© **970/945-9608**). Open April through October, rates for 18 holes are $5 for adults and $4 for children under 12 and seniors over 60. The **Glenwood Hot Springs Pool** (see "Taking the Waters," below) also has a miniature golf course, with rates of $5.25 for adults and $4.25 for kids under 12.

HIKING   **There are plenty of hiking opportunities in the area. Stop at the national forest office (see above) for free **Recreational Opportunity Guide (ROG) sheets for many local trails. The office sells detailed forest maps and has other information, too. The BLM (see above) also has maps and information.

One convenient walk is the **Doc Holliday Trail** ⚐, which climbs about .5 mile from 13th Street and Bennett Street to an old cemetery that contains the grave of notorious gunslinger Doc Holliday (see "Exploring Glenwood Springs's Frontier Past," below).

Hikers will also find numerous trail heads along the **Glenwood Canyon Recreation Trail** 🦌 in Glenwood Canyon, with some of the best scenery in the area. Among them, **Hanging Lake Trail,** 9 miles east of Glenwood Springs off I-70, is especially popular. The trailhead is accessible from eastbound I-70; westbound travelers must make a U-turn and backtrack a few miles to reach the parking area. The trail climbs 1,000 feet in 1 mile—allow several hours for the round-trip—and just beyond Hanging Lake is Spouting Rock, with an underground spring shooting out of a hole in the limestone cliff. Dogs, swimming, and fishing are forbidden. The **Grizzly Creek Trail** is in the Grizzly Creek Rest Area, along I-70 in Glenwood Canyon, where there is also a launching area for rafts and kayaks. The trail climbs along the creek, past wildflowers and dogwood trees.

The **Glenwood Springs Chamber Resort Association** offers a free map showing a variety of trails in the area with trail heads marked.

JEEP TOURS   Explore the high country around Glenwood Springs in an open-air jeep. The knowledgeable and friendly guides at **Rock Gardens** (see above) will show you some breathtaking views—don't forget your camera—and share with you some of the natural history and wildlife of the area. Half-day trips cost $44 for adults, $39 for youths; full-day trips, which include lunch, cost about $85 and $75, respectively.

RIVER RAFTING   Bouncing down the rapids through magnificent **Glenwood Canyon** 🦌🦌 is, to our way of thinking, one of the best ways to see this spectacular country. Companies offering raft trips include **Rock Gardens,** 1308 C.R. 129, at I-70 exit 119 (© **800/958-6737** or 970/945-6737; www.rockgardens.com). Half-day trips cost about $43; full-day trips, which include lunch, cost about $69. Shorter trips of about 1½ hours, which usually cover mostly calm stretches of river, are also offered, at about $28. These are adult rates; children's rates are usually 20% to 30% less.

Blue Sky Adventures, in the Hotel Colorado (© **877/945-6605** or 970/945-6605; www.blueskyadventure.com), offers rafting on the Colorado and Roaring Fork rivers. The popular half-day Adventure Trip costs $43 for adults, $31 for youths 15 and under; the half-day Mild Trip costs $32 and $27 respectively. A popular full-day trip through the white water of Shoshone Rapids costs $69 and $53, respectively, including a cold lunch; for the hot barbecue lunch you'll have to pay $74 and $58 respectively.

SKIING & SNOWBOARDING   **Sunlight Mountain Resort,** 10901 C.R. 117, Glenwood Springs, CO 81601 (© **800/445-7931** or 970/945-7491; www.sunlightmtn.com), is located 10 miles south of Glenwood Springs in the White River National Forest. Geared toward families, Sunlight has 470 skiable acres and a 2,010-foot vertical drop from its 9,895-foot summit; it's served by one triple and two double chairlifts and a ski-school surface lift. There are 67 runs, rated 20% beginner, 55% intermediate, 20% advanced, and 5% expert. There's also a special area for snowboarders. The ski area is usually open from early December to early April. A full-day lift ticket runs $28 to $35 for adults, $22 to $25 for children 6 to 12 and seniors 60 to 69, and is free for kids under 6 and seniors 70 and over. For equipment rentals and repairs, see the **Sunlight Ski Shop,** 309 Ninth St., in downtown Glenwood Springs (© **970/945-9425**).

Sunlight's Cross-Country and Nordic Center has 16km of groomed Nordic trails, available free, with rentals and lessons available. Information and equipment are also available at **Summit Canyon Mountaineering,** 732 Grand Ave. (© **800/360-6994** or 970/945-6994; www.summitcanyon.com).

SNOWMOBILING   The **Sunlight to Powderhorn Trail,** running 120 miles from Glenwood's local ski area to Grand Junction's, on the Grand Mesa, is the longest multiuse winter recreational trail in Colorado, traversing White River and Grand Mesa national forests. It is fully marked and continuously groomed. Other trails can be accessed from the end of C.R. 11, 2 miles beyond Sunlight Mountain Resort and 12 miles south of Glenwood Springs. For information and rentals, contact the resort.

TAKING THE WATERS

There may be no better or more luxurious way to rejuvenate the dusty, tired traveler than by soaking in a natural hot spring. In Glenwood Springs, there are two places to experience this ancient therapy.

Glenwood Hot Springs Pool ★★   Named Yampah Springs—meaning "Big Medicine"—by the Utes, this pool was created in 1888 when enterprising developers diverted the course of the Colorado River and built a stone bathhouse. The springs flow at a rate of 3½-million gallons per day, and, with a temperature of 122°F (50°C), they're one of the world's hottest springs. The content is predominantly sodium chloride, but there are significant quantities of calcium sulfate, potassium sulfate, calcium bicarbonate, and magnesium bicarbonate, plus traces of other therapeutic minerals.

The two open-air pools together are nearly 2 city blocks in length. The larger pool, 405 feet by 100 feet, holds more than a million gallons of water, and is maintained at 90°F (32°C). The smaller pool, 100 feet long, is kept at 104°F (40°C). There's also a children's pool with water slides, plus a deli, sport shop, and miniature golf course. The red-sandstone administration building overlooking the pools was the Hot Springs Lodge until 1986, when the new Hot Springs Lodge and Pool (see "Where to Stay," below) and bathhouse complex were built, and an athletic club opened (day passes are $22).

Suit and towel rentals and coin-operated lockers are available, as are massages, starting at $39 for a half-hour. Allow from 1 to 4 hours.

401 N. River Rd. (C) **800/537-7946** or 970/947-2955. Fax 970/945-6683. www.hotspringspool.com. Admission summer $14 adults, $8.50 children 3–12; rest of year $12 and $7.50 respectively; free for children 2 and under year-round. Reduced evening rates. Water slide summer $4.25 for 4 rides or $5.50 for 8 rides; rest of year $4 and $5.25 respectively. Summer daily 7:30am–10pm; rest of year daily 9am–10pm.

Yampah Spa and Vapor Caves   The hot Yampah Spring water flows through the floor of nearby caves, creating natural underground steam baths. Once used by Utes for their curative powers, today the cave has an adjacent spa where such treatments as massages, facials, herbal wraps, body muds, and salt glow rubs are offered. There's also a full-service beauty salon on the premises. Allow at least 1 hour.

709 E. Sixth St. (C) **970/945-0667**. www.yampahspa.com. Admission to caves $9.75; spa treatments start at about $45. Daily 9am–9pm.

EXPLORING GLENWOOD SPRINGS'S FRONTIER PAST

Although most Colorado visitors tend to think of Telluride or Cripple Creek when the subject of the Wild West comes up, Glenwood Springs had its share of desperados and frontier justice. The Ute tribe first inhabited the area, using it as a base for hunting and fishing, and also making use of its mineral hot springs. When whites finally arrived in the mid- to late 1800s, the growing community—then called Defiance—was little more than a muddy street lined with saloons, brothels, and boardinghouses, where miners from nearby Aspen and Leadville could be relieved of their newfound wealth. The hot springs began to attract mine owners and other prominent businessmen to Defiance, and in 1885 the town's name was changed to the more refined Glenwood Springs. However, it wasn't until 1886 that civilization finally arrived, along with the railroad. The following year, notorious gunfighter Doc Holliday arrived, and although he is said to have practiced his card-playing skills (and even a bit of dentistry), there is no record that he was involved in any gunplay in the town. By 1888, the lavish Hot Springs Pool and Hotel Colorado opened, and Glenwood Springs— now dubbed the "Spa in the Rockies"—began to attract the rich and famous.

Much of the grandeur of Glenwood Springs in the late 19th and early 20th centuries remains, and can be seen on a walk through the downtown area. The self-guided **Historic Walking Tour** guide and map is available for $1 at the Chamber Resort Association's visitor center (see earlier in this chapter) and the Frontier Historical Museum (see below). The guide describes more than 40 historic buildings and sites, including the 1884 Mirror Saloon, the oldest existing building in downtown Glenwood Springs; the site of the 1884 Hotel Glenwood (only a small portion remains), where Doc Holliday died; the 1893 Hotel Colorado, which was used by President Theodore Roosevelt as his "Western White House" in the early 1900s; and the 1885 Kamm Building, where gangster Al Capone is said to have been a jewelry customer in the 1920s.

Doc Holliday's Grave   After the famous shootout at the OK Corral, Doc Holliday began a final search for relief from his advanced tuberculosis. But even the mineral-rich waters of Glenwood Springs could not dissipate the ravages of hard drinking and disease, and Doc died in 1887 at the Hotel Glenwood. Although the exact location of Doc's grave is not known, it is believed he was buried in or near the Linwood Cemetery, on Lookout Mountain overlooking the city. Also in the cemetery are the graves of other early citizens of Glenwood.

From the chamber office on Grand Avenue, walk or drive uphill on 11th to Bennett and turn right. Not far on the left is the sign marking the trail to the cemetery. The trail is a .5-mile uphill hike, and you'll have a grand view of the city along the way. In the cemetery, near the flagpole, is a tombstone with the inscription, "Doc Holliday 1852–1887 He Died in Bed," and in front of it is another monument that reads, "This Memorial Dedicated to Doc Holliday who is Buried Someplace in the Cemetery." Allow about a half-hour.

Linwood Cemetery.

Frontier Historical Museum   Highlights of this museum, which occupies a late Victorian home, include the original bedroom furniture of Colorado legends Horace and Baby Doe Tabor, brought here from Leadville. The collection also includes displays on famed dentist-turned-gunfighter Doc Holliday, plus other pioneer home furnishings, including a complete kitchen. There are also toys, historic photos and maps, American-Indian artifacts, and a mining and minerals display. The museum contains an extensive archive of historic documents and photographs from the early days of Glenwood Springs. Allow an hour.

1001 Colorado Ave. © 970/945-4448. Fax 970/384-2477. www.glenwoodhistory.com. Admission $3 adults, $2 seniors 60 and older, free for children under 12. May–Sept Mon–Sat 11am–4pm; Oct–Apr Mon and Thurs–Sat 1–4pm.

WHERE TO STAY

Rates are usually highest in summer, although busy ski times, such as Christmas week, can also be high. You can book a wide variety of lodgings throughout the area with **Glenwood Springs Central Reservations** (© 888/445-3696).

Among the reliable moderately priced chains and franchises are the **Best Value Inn & Suites,** 51871 U.S. 6 and 24, at I-25 exit 114 (© **888/315-2378** or 970/945-6279), with rates of $52 to $140; the **Best Western Antlers,** 171 W. Sixth Ave. (© **800/626-0609** or 970/945-8535), with rates from $79 to $229 double; the **Hampton Inn,** 401 W. First St. (© **800/426-7866** or 970/947-9400), charging $89 to $139; the **Holiday Inn Express,** 501 W. First St. (© **800/465-4329** or 970/928-7800), charging from $89 to $199; and **Ramada Inn,** 124 W. Sixth St. (© **800/332-1472** or 970/945-2500), with rates from $69 to $149. All the above are in Glenwood Springs, zip 81601, and rates for all of hotels are for two people; taxes add close to 12% to lodging bills.

EXPENSIVE

Hot Springs Lodge & Pool ☆   Heated by the springs that bubble through the hillside beneath it, this handsome modern hotel overlooks the Glenwood Hot Springs Pool complex. Three-quarters of the rooms have private balconies or patios. Rooms are spacious, with one king or two queen beds, cherry- or light-wood furnishings; some have hide-a-beds, refrigerators, and double vanities.

415 Sixth St. (P.O. Box 308), Glenwood Springs, CO 81602. © **800/537-7946** or 970/945-6571. Fax 970/947-2950. www.hotspringspool.com. 107 units. Mid-Mar to Sept and Christmas $145–$275 double; rest of year $109–$275. Rates include continental breakfast. AE, DC, DISC, MC, V. **Amenities:** Unlimited admission to the hot springs pool and discounts at the health club (see "Taking the Waters," above); whirlpool; basic business center; coin-op laundry. *In room:* A/C, TV, dataport, coffeemaker, hair dryer, safe.

MODERATE

Four Mile Creek Bed & Breakfast ☆☆   A lovely spot for a romantic get-away or a peaceful base from which to explore the area, this B&B has both antique charm and modern conveniences. The historic log home was the head-quarters of the Four Mile Ranch, homesteaded in 1885 and listed on the National Registry of Historic Places, and the surrounding grounds boast aspen groves and gardens of herbs and flowers, a handsome red barn built in 1919, and a variety of animals, including llamas and goats.

In the main log house is a cozy living room with an imposing rock fireplace, a sunroom overlooking the creek, and a porch along the front. There are two rooms in the main house which share a bathroom: the Blackbird Room boasts wrought-iron blackbirds (what else?) perched on the queen bed, and its elegant furnishings are reminiscent of the mining boom era; the nearby Star Room sets a totally different mood, with whimsical folk art and celestial symbols. The B&B's two cabins, with kitchens and private bathrooms, can accommodate up to four persons each. The aptly named Garden Cabin offers the pleasant ambi-ence of several nearby perennial gardens plus a gas fireplace. The charming Creekside Cabin—so named because Four Mile Creek gurgles its way along one side of the cabin—boasts log beams and barnwood walls plus an unusual brightly colored bird chandelier.

6471 C.R. 117, Glenwood Springs, CO 81601. © **970/945-4004.** Fax 970/945-2820. www.fourmilecreek. com. 4 units, 2 with private bathroom. Room $85 double; cabin $140 (up to 4 people). Rates include evening refreshments and full breakfast. AE, MC, V. *In room:* No phone.

Hotel Colorado ☆   Want to step into the not-so-wild West of the late 19th century? This is the place. The stately Hotel Colorado, constructed of sandstone and Roman brick in 1893, was modeled after Italy's Villa de Medici. Among the most impressive hotels of the region in its day, the Hotel Colorado attracted all the VIPs of the era. Two American presidents—William Howard Taft and Theodore Roosevelt—spoke to crowds gathered beneath the orators' balcony in a lovely landscaped fountain piazza. There are claims (disputed by some) that this is the birthplace of the teddy bear: The story goes that when a disappointed Roosevelt returned to the hotel in May 1905 after an unsuccessful bear hunt, hotel maids made him a small bear from scraps of cloth and the president's daughter Alyce named it Teddy.

The attractive guest rooms are individually decorated, most with firm double beds and the usual hotel furnishings; suites are more spacious, with upgraded decor and period antiques. Fifth-floor penthouse suites also have wet bars and refrigerators, as well as outstanding views. Two bell-tower suites, reached by stairs only, have double Jacuzzis and private dining balconies. They also have private staircases into the ancient bell towers, where 19th-century graffiti can still be deciphered. There's a full bar and a large outdoor dining and cocktail area, with gardens and a fountain for summer use. There's also a specialty coffee and juice bar; a chiropractor; and seasonal rental shops for rafting, biking, or skiing.

526 Pine St., Glenwood Springs, CO 81601. ℂ 800/544-3998 or 970/945-6511. Fax 970/945-7030. www.hotelcolorado.com. 126 units. $129–$169 double; $189–$495 suite. Children under 18 stay free in parent's room. AE, DC, DISC, MC, V. Pets accepted with a $10 fee. **Amenities:** Restaurant; bar; exercise room and spa; massage. *In room:* TV, coffeemaker, hair dryer, iron.

INEXPENSIVE

Glenwood Springs Hostel 🏃 Active travelers will find the bargain sports packages this hostel offers a real plus. Featured activities include downhill and cross-country skiing, rafting, kayaking, mountain biking, and caving. There's a large record library, free coffee or tea in the mornings, and two fully equipped kitchens for guests' use. Like most hostels, there are dormitory bunks, common toilets and showers, guest laundry, and other common areas. Linen is available ($2), and it's just a 5-minute walk from the train and bus. The individual rooms are great for couples and others who prefer more privacy, although they still share bathrooms.

1021 Grand Ave., Glenwood Springs, CO 81601. ℂ 800/946-7835 or 970/945-8545. http://hostelcolorado. com. 42 beds including dorm and 5 private rooms. Dorms $14 per person per night (or $44 for 4 nights); private rooms $21 single, $29 double. No private bathrooms. Rates include tax. AE, MC, V. *In room:* No phone.

Red Mountain Inn *Value* This bright, cheery, modern motel lives up to its advertising as "Glenwood's best value." Rooms are spacious, with better-than-average lighting, firm mattresses, and comfortable seating. Most rooms have 10-foot ceilings. The dozen cabins are essentially larger motel units, with sleeping for two to eight, plus complete kitchens. Some cabins have fireplaces, while a few have private patios with picnic tables. There's a delightful shaded grassy picnic area away from the road; and several restaurants and a miniature golf course are within easy walking distance.

51637 U.S. 6 and 24, Glenwood Springs, CO 81601. ℂ 800/748-2565 or 970/945-6353. Fax 970/928-9432. www.redmountaininn.com. 40 units. Summer $68–$94 motel units, $90–$210 cabins; winter $49–$71 motel units, $64–$160 cabins. AE, DISC, MC, V. On I-70 north Frontage Rd. between exits 114 and 116. Pets accepted with a $100 refundable deposit. **Amenities:** Outdoor heated pool (seasonal); outdoor hot tub (year-round); coin-op laundry. *In room:* A/C, TV.

CAMPING

Rock Gardens Campground & RV Resort On the banks of the Colorado River in beautiful Glenwood Canyon, this campground is a great home base for those exploring this scenic terrain. The Glenwood Canyon Recreational Trail passes the campground on its way into Glenwood Springs, and hiking trails into the White River National Forest are nearby. Bathhouses are clean, showers are

hot, and there's a dump station, but no sewer hookups. There's also a store selling groceries, firewood, and ice, as well as bike and yahoo (sit-on-top kayaks)
rentals, jeep tours, and raft trips (see "Sports & Outdoor Activities," earlier in
this chapter).

1308 C.R. 129 (I-70 exit 119), Glenwood Springs, CO 81601. © 800/958-6737 or 970/945-6737. Fax
970/945-2413. www.rockgardens.com. 75 sites. $23–$29 tent sites; $27–$38 RV sites, with electric and water
hookups. Rates are for 2 people; additional persons 5 years and up are $4 each. AE, MC, V. Closed Nov to
mid-Apr.

WHERE TO DINE

To stock up for a camping trip or picnic, or to get food to take back to your
room or RV, we recommend **City Market Food & Pharmacy,** 1410 S. Grand
Ave. (© **970/945-8207**), which is open daily from 5am to 1am. The store not
only has all the usual supermarket departments, including a deli and bakery with
seating area, but it also has an excellent buy-by-the-pound salad bar.

The Bayou ★★ CAJUN/CREOLE   This delightful New Orleans–style eatery
might not be the best choice for those who take themselves very seriously, but if
you're looking for a good time along with excellent food, the Bayou is worth a
trip. A move to Glenwood Springs' downtown in late 2004 may have put The
Bayou in a historic building, but the decor is still fun and funky, with harlequin
masks on the walls. Come for down-home Cajun cuisine—such as seafood
gumbo, shrimp Creole, chicken étouffée, or swamp and moo (redfish and
rib-eye)—and stay for the staff-provided entertainment, including "dumb
server tricks," birthday specials (ask if you dare), and the Frog Leg Revue. The
Bayou has the largest selection of hot sauces in the valley, rated from "spicy" to
"hurt me." There are also a few vegetarian dishes. Live music is scheduled most
Friday and Saturday nights, and possibly other times. The entire restaurant is
smoke-free.

919 Grand Ave. © **970/945-1047.** Main courses lunch and dinner $6.25–$16. AE, DC, DISC, MC, V. Daily
11am–10pm; bar open later Fri–Sat.

Daily Bread Cafe & Bakery ★ CAFE/BAKERY   Try not to be in a hurry
when you go to the Daily Bread—the service isn't slow, but this is such a popular spot that you're likely to find yourself waiting behind a line of locals for your
table or booth. Decor here is strictly American cafe: storefront windows with
lace curtains, a high ceiling, oak floor, and local art on the walls. For breakfast
you might try one of the many egg dishes, such as Terry's Delight—an English
muffin topped with eggs, shaved ham, and melted cheese—or perhaps the
healthful Fresh Fruit Special—a carved-out half cantaloupe stuffed with fresh
fruit, covered with fat-free vanilla yogurt and granola, and served with a fat-free
muffin. The lunch menu lists dozens of sandwiches, burgers, and salads, including a number of low-fat offerings. Favorites include the Grand Avenue Deli—
roast beef, turkey breast, Swiss cheese, lettuce, tomato, sprouts, and Thousand
Island dressing on your choice of the bakery's own bread.

729 Grand Ave. © **970/945-6253.** $3.50–$9.95. DISC, MC, V. Mon–Fri 7am–2pm; Sat 8am–2pm; Sun
8am–noon.

Glenwood Canyon Brewing Company BREWPUB   There are two dining
rooms in this busy and popular brewpub—one that's particularly noisy with a
long bar and an under-30 crowd, and the other one, slightly more sedate, for the
rest of us. The decor for both is standard brewpub: brick walls, historic photos,
wood tables, TVs with sporting events, and a view of the brewing equipment.

Served at all times are a selection of half-pound burgers, several sandwiches (such as a hot smoked-turkey Philly), salads, pasta, and bread bowls (filled with soup or stew). Dinner entrees are a bit more elaborate, and include a grilled salmon filet and soft tacos made of Maine lobster. There are always eight hand-crafted beers on tap plus homemade root beer, and half-gallon growler jugs are available for takeout. This brewpub is entirely smoke-free, and boasts four regulation-size billiard tables.

402 Seventh St. (in the Hotel Denver). ✆ 970/945-1276. $5.95–$18. AE, MC, V. Daily 11am–10pm (bar open later).

Italian Underground 𝒦 *Value* ITALIAN   A favorite of locals, the Italian Underground offers good Italian food at excellent prices. Get here early and expect to wait. Located in a basement along busy Grand Avenue, the restaurant has stone walls, brick floors, red-and-white-checked tablecloths, candlelight, and exceedingly generous portions of fine food. Try the lasagna, linguine with pesto, or spaghetti with tomato and basil sauce. All entrees come with salad, bread, and ice cream. Smaller portions of most items are available at 15% off the regular price, and be sure to ask about the daily specials. There's an excellent selection of Italian wines by the glass and a full bar; espresso and cappuccino are also served. Smoking is not permitted.

715 Grand Ave. ✆ 970/945-6422. Reservations not accepted. Main courses $8.95–$14; pizzas $8.95–$15. AE, DISC, MC, V. Daily 5–10pm.

Sopris 𝒦𝒦 *Moments* CONTINENTAL   This is the spot for those celebrating wedding anniversaries or other special events, or if you simply want to impress that someone special with your good taste. Swiss chef Kurt Wigger opened the Sopris in 1974, and it has been a favorite of locals ever since. Amid red-lit Victorian decor, accented by reproductions of classic oil paintings, Wigger serves generous portions of veal and seafood dishes, as well as steak, lamb, and vegetarian dishes. House specialties include the pepper steak flambé—New York strip with cracked pepper, shallots, and red-wine sauce; and Swiss veal—minced veal and mushrooms served in a cream sauce. There's an extensive wine list and a full bar.

7215 Colo. 82, 5 miles south of Glenwood Springs. ✆ 970/945-7771. Reservations recommended. Main courses $10–$35. AE, DISC, MC, V. Daily 5–10pm.

3 Montrose: Gateway to Black Canyon of the Gunnison National Park

61 miles S of Grand Junction, 108 miles N of Durango

Although at first glance this quiet city of just over 12,000 is little more than a commercial center for area ranchers and farmers, Montrose is rapidly being discovered as an ideal base camp for hikers, mountain bikers, anglers, and others who want to explore western Colorado. Located at an elevation of 5,794 feet, Montrose is surrounded by the Uncompahgre, Gunnison, and Grand Mesa national forests, and it's within a short drive of Black Canyon of the Gunnison National Park and Curecanti National Recreation Area.

Ute Chief Ouray and his wife, Chipeta, ranched in the Uncompahgre Valley here until the government forced the tribe to migrate to Utah in 1881. Once the Utes were gone, settlers founded the town of Pomona, named for the Roman goddess of fruit. Later the town's name was changed to Montrose, for a character in a Sir Walter Scott novel. The railroad arrived in 1882, providing relatively reliable transportation and a means to ship out potatoes, beets, and other crops; and Montrose began in earnest its role as one of Colorado's major food producers, which continues today.

ESSENTIALS

GETTING THERE   By Car   Montrose is an hour's drive southeast of Grand Junction via U.S. 50, a 2½-hour drive north of Durango via U.S. 550, and a 5½-hour drive west of Colorado Springs via U.S. 50 through Salida and Gunnison.

By Plane   The **Montrose Regional Airport,** 2100 Airport Rd. (© **970/249-3203**), is off U.S. 50, 2 miles northwest of town. Regional airlines serving the town include **American** (© **800/433-7300**), **Continental** (© **800/525-0280**), **SkyWest** (© **800/433-7300**), and **United** (© **800/241-6522** or 970/249-8455).

GETTING AROUND   Montrose lies along the east bank of the Uncompahgre River. Townsend Avenue (U.S. 50 and U.S. 550) parallels the stream; Main Street (U.S. 50 and Colo. 90) crosses Townsend in the center of town. Numbered streets extend north and south from Main.

   Western Express Taxi (© **970/249-8880**) provides local cab service. Car-rental agencies with outlets at the airport include **Budget** (© 970/249-6083), **Dollar** (© 970/249-3770), **National** (© 970/252-8898), and **Thrifty** (© 970/249-8741).

VISITOR INFORMATION   Contact the **Montrose Visitors & Convention Bureau,** 433 S. First St. (P.O. Box 335), Montrose, CO 81402 (© **800/873-0244** or 970/240-1414; www.visitmontrose.net), or stop at the **visitor center** (© **970/249-1726**) in the **Ute Indian Museum,** 17253 Chipeta Dr., on the south side of town off U.S. 550, which is open daily from 9am to 4:30pm in summer, and the same hours Monday through Saturday the rest of the year. Information is also available from the **Montrose Chamber of Commerce,** 1519 E. Main St., Montrose, CO 81401 (© **800/923-5515** or 970/249-5000).

FAST FACTS   Montrose Memorial Hospital, with a 24-hour emergency room, is at 800 S. Third St. (© **970/249-2211**). The **post office** is at 321 S. First St. Call the U.S. Postal Service (© **800/275-8777;** www.usps.com) for hours and other information. For **road conditions,** call © **970/249-6282.**

SPECIAL EVENTS   Lighter Than Air Balloon Affaire, early July; Montrose County Fair, early August; Parade of Lights, early December.

WHAT TO SEE & DO

Those wanting to step back into Montrose's past should ask at the visitor center, chamber of commerce, or city hall (433 S. First St.) for a free copy of the self-guided **Historic Montrose Downtown Walking Tour** brochure. It contains a map to help you locate numerous historic buildings and interpretative signs.

Montrose County Historical Museum   Pioneer life in western Colorado is highlighted at this museum, housed in a historic Denver & Rio Grande Railroad Depot. The museum features a furnished 1890s homesteader's cabin, log cowboy cabin, railroad memorabilia including a Union Pacific caboose, farm equipment, antique dolls and toys, old musical instruments, a country store, and American-Indian artifacts. Historical photos and Montrose newspapers from 1896 to 1940 depict the town's history. Allow at least an hour.

W. Main St. and Rio Grande Ave. © 970/249-2085. stepbackintime@Montrose.net. Admission $4 adults, $3 seniors over 55, $1 children 13–18, 50¢ children 5–12, free for children under 5. Mid-May to Sept Mon–Sat 9am–5pm.

Ute Indian Museum ✮   Located on the site of the final residence of southern Ute Chief Ouray and his wife, Chipeta, the Ute Indian Museum offers one of Colorado's most complete exhibitions of Ute traditional and ceremonial artifacts, including clothing, baskets, and household items. Several dioramas depict mid-19th-century lifestyles, and historic photos are displayed. Also on the grounds are Chipeta's grave, bubbling Ouray Springs, a native plants garden, and an outdoor display on Spanish explorers who passed this way in 1776. The museum sponsors various festivals and programs throughout the year (call for details). It also has a store that specializes in Ute pottery and other handcrafted American-Indian arts and crafts, and houses the Montrose Visitor Center. Allow about 1½ hours.

17253 Chipeta Dr. ℂ 970/249-3098. Admission $3 adults, $2.50 seniors over 64, $1.50 children 6–16, free for children under 6. Mon–Sat 9am–4:30pm; first Sun each month 1–4pm. Located 2 miles south of downtown off U.S. 550.

SPORTS & OUTDOOR ACTIVITIES

In addition to boating and other outdoor recreational activities available in Black Canyon of the Gunnison National Park (discussed below) and nearby Curecanti National Recreation Area (see "Gunnison & Curecanti National Recreation Area," in chapter 13), there are plenty of opportunities for hiking, mountain biking, horseback riding, off-roading, fishing, camping, cross-country skiing, and snowmobiling on other federal lands in the area. Information is available at the **Public Lands Center,** 2505 S. Townsend Ave. (ℂ **970/240-5300**).

BIKING   There are more than 9 miles of paved off-street walking and biking trails in Montrose, plus numerous areas for mountain biking in nearby lands administered by the U.S. Forest Service and Bureau of Land Management. A free map of **city trails** is available at the visitor center, chamber of commerce, and city hall (433 S. First St.); stop at the Public Lands Center (see above) for information on where to ride on BLM and Forest Service lands. You can also obtain maps, information, bike repairs, and accessories at **Cascade Bicycles,** 25 N. Cascade Ave. (ℂ **970/249-7375**), and **Grand Mesa Cyclery,** 223 N. First St. (ℂ **970/249-7515**). As of this writing there were no bike rentals available in town.

The Tabeguache Trail—142 miles from Shavano Valley near Montrose, to No Thoroughfare Canyon near the Colorado National Monument west of Grand Junction—is a popular and challenging route for mountain bikers. Send a self-addressed, stamped envelope for a free trail map to the **Colorado Plateau Mountain-Bike Trail Association,** P.O. Box 4602, Grand Junction, CO 81502. Bikers can also use the Uncompahgre Riverway; it's eventually scheduled to connect Montrose with Delta (21 miles north) and Ouray (37 miles south).

FISHING   For starters, you can drop a line into the Uncompahgre River from Riverbottom Park, reached via Apollo Road off Rio Grande Avenue. Most anglers seek rainbow trout here and at Chipeta Lake, behind the Ute Indian Museum, south of Montrose. About 20 miles east via U.S. 50 is the Gunnison River, which produces trophy-class brown and rainbow trout.

GOLF   The 18-hole **Montrose Golf Course,** 1350 Birch St. (ℂ **970/249-4653**), is open year-round, weather permitting. Greens fees are $18 for 9 holes and $28 for 18 holes. The **Links at Cobble Creek,** 669 Cobble Dr. (ℂ **970/249-9542**), is another 18-hole course with fees of $20 for 9 holes and $32 for 18 holes.

HIKING   The best hiking in the area is in the Black Canyon of the Gunnison National Park (p. 364), but there are also paved paths in town (see "Biking," above) and plenty of trails on nearby national forest and BLM lands. These include the 4.5-mile Ute Trail along the Gunnison River, 20 miles northeast of Montrose; and the 17-mile Alpine Trail from Silver Jack Reservoir in Uncompahgre National Forest, 35 miles southeast of Montrose via Cimarron on U.S. 50. Contact the Public Lands Center (see above) for information.

WHERE TO STAY

In addition to the properties discussed below, Montrose (zip 81401) has a **Best Western Red Arrow Motor Inn,** 1702 E. Main St. (© **800/468-9323** or 970/249-9641) with rates for two from $69 to $109, **Comfort Inn,** 2100 E. Main St. (© **800/424-6423** or 970/240-8000), with rates for two from $59 to $99; **Days Inn,** 1655 E. Main St. (© **800/329-7466** or 970/249-3411), with double rates from $37 to $66; **Holiday Inn Express Hotel & Suites,** 1391 S. Townsend Ave. (© **800/465-4329** or 970/240-1800), with rates for two from $89 to $149; and **Super 8,** 1705 E. Main St. (© **800/800-8000** or 970/249-9294), with double rates from $47 to $80. Rates here are usually highest in July and August, and lowest November through April. Room tax is about 8.5%.

Western Motel   A one-story white stucco building with a two-story annex, this attractive independent motel offers clean, comfortable rooms that are a tad larger than average, with some homey touches, and beds that range in size from full to king. The bathrooms are basic but kept scrupulously clean. A few family rooms are available, and most units have door-front parking. This is a good choice for those on a budget who want something a bit more interesting than a chain motel. VCRs are available for rent.

1200 E. Main St. (at Stough Ave.), Montrose, CO 81401. © 800/445-7301 or 970/249-3481. Fax 970/249-3471. www.westernmotel.com. 28 units. $57–$66 double; $85–$125 family unit. Lower rates available in winter. Rates include continental breakfast May–Sept. AE, DC, DISC, MC, V. Pets are accepted. **Amenities:** Outdoor heated pool (seasonal); hot tub; sauna. *In room:* A/C, TV, fridge (some), coffeemaker.

CAMPING

In addition to the campgrounds in Black Canyon of the Gunnison National Park discussed below, we recommend **The Hangin' Tree R.V. Park** at 17250 U.S. 550 S. (© **970/249-9966** or 970/249-1462), with rates from $16 to $24. Conveniently located within walking distance of Chipeta Lakes and open year-round, the Hangin' Tree has grassy tent sites, large pull-through RV sites, and very clean bathhouses.

DINING

A good bet for those seeking groceries, deli sandwiches, a bakery, or a buy-by-the-pound salad bar is one of the two **City Market** grocery stores in Montrose. There's one at 128 S. Townsend Ave. (© **970/249-3405**) and another at 16400 S. Townsend Ave. (© **970/249-3236**).

Glenn Eyrie Restaurant *Finds* CONTINENTAL/AMERICAN   This small, cozy restaurant is lodged in a colonial farmhouse on the south end of town. In summer, guests dine inside or outdoors in the garden; in winter, folks seek tables near the cozy central fireplace. Just about everything is made in-house, including rolls, jams, and sauces; and many items, such as fruits, herbs, and greens, are grown on the grounds. Owner-chef Steve Schwathe changes the menu frequently to reflect the seasons and availability of fresh ingredients, but if you're lucky you might be able to choose between our favorites—whole rack of lamb, which is grilled, then slow-baked, and served with a sauce of tomato, rosemary, and garlic; or steak Diane, a butterflied beef tenderloin steak that is flamed tableside in a mustard, applejack brandy, and cream sauce, with mushrooms and artichoke hearts. There are also fresh seafood selections, vegetarian dishes, and a full bar.

2351 S. Townsend Ave. ℂ **970/249-9263**. Reservations recommended. Main courses $12–$30. AE, DISC, MC, V. Mon–Sat 5–9pm.

4 Black Canyon of the Gunnison National Park

The **Black Canyon of the Gunnison** 🌟🌟, which had been a national monument since 1933, became a national park on October 21, 1999. In a statement issued after the bill-signing ceremony, President Bill Clinton called the Black Canyon a "true natural treasure," and added, "Its nearly vertical walls, rising a half-mile high, harbor one of the most spectacular stretches of wild river in America."

> ## Impressions
>
> *No other canyon in North America combines the depth, narrowness, sheerness, and somber countenance of the Black Canyon.*
> —Geologist Wallace Hansen, who mapped the canyon in the 1950s

The canyon was avoided by early American Indians and later Utes and Anglo explorers, who believed that no human could survive a trip to its depths. The entire canyon measures 48 miles long, and the 14 miles that are included in the national park (which at 30,385 acres is among America's smallest) range in depth from 1,730 to 2,700 feet. Its width at its narrowest point (cleverly called "The Narrows") is only 40 feet. This deep slash in the earth was created by 2 million years of erosion, a process that's still going on—albeit slowed by the damming of the Gunnison River above the park.

Most visitors view the canyon from the South Rim Road, site of the visitor center, or the lesser-used North Rim Road. Short paths branching off both roads lead to splendid viewpoints with signs explaining the canyon's unique geology.

The park also has hiking trails along both rims, backcountry-hiking routes down into the canyon, and excellent trout fishing for ambitious anglers willing to make the trek to the canyon floor. It also provides an abundance of thrills for the experienced rock climbers who challenge its sheer canyon walls. In winter, much of the park is closed to motor vehicles, but it's a delight for cross-country skiers and snowshoers.

The Black Canyon shares a portion of its south boundary with Curecanti National Recreation Area, which offers boating and fishing on three reservoirs, as well as hiking and camping.

JUST THE FACTS
ENTRY POINTS

The park is located northeast of Montrose. To reach the south rim, head east on U.S. 50 for 8 miles to the well-marked turnoff, where you will turn north (left) onto Colo. 347 for 6 miles. To reach the north rim from Montrose, drive north 21 miles on U.S. 50 to Delta, east 31 miles on Colo. 92 to Crawford, then south on an 11-mile access road.

FEES & REGULATIONS

Admission for up to 7 days costs $8 per vehicle. Camping costs $10 to $15 per night. Required backcountry permits are free. Visitors are warned not to throw anything from the rim into the canyon, since even a single small stone thrown or kicked from the rim could be fatal to people below; and to supervise children very carefully because many sections of the rim have no guard rails or fences.

Unlike at most national parks, leashed pets are permitted on some trails (check with rangers), but they are specifically prohibited from wilderness areas.

VISITOR CENTERS & INFORMATION

The **South Rim Visitor Center** is open daily year-round, except winter federal holidays, with hours from 8am to 6pm in summer and from 8:30am to 4pm the rest of the year. The **North Rim Ranger Station** is open intermittent hours during the summer but closed at other times. For information on both the national park and the adjacent Curecanti National Recreation Area, contact **Black Canyon of the Gunnison National Park/Curecanti National Recreation Area,** Park Headquarters, 102 Elk Creek, Gunnison, CO 81230 (© **970/641-2337,** or the South Rim Visitor Center at 970/249-1914, ext. 423; www.nps.gov/blca).

SEASONS

Temperatures and weather conditions often vary greatly between the canyon rim and the canyon floor, and it gets progressively hotter as you descend into the canyon. Average summer temperatures range from highs of 60° to 100°F (16°C–38°C), with summer lows dropping to 30° to 50°F (–1°C to 10°C). During winter, highs range from 20° to 40°F (–7°C to –4°C), with lows from –10° to 20° F (–23°C to –7°C). Brief afternoon thunderstorms are fairly common in the summer. The South Rim Road usually remains open to the visitor center through the winter, but the North Rim Road is often closed by snow between December and March. The elevation at the South Rim Campground is 8,320 feet.

RANGER PROGRAMS

Ranger-conducted **nature walks, geology talks,** and **evening campfire programs** are presented daily from Memorial Day through late September on the South Rim (a schedule is posted at the visitor center). During the winter, guided **snowshoe walks** and **moonlight cross-country ski tours** are offered on the South Rim when snow conditions are right (stop at the visitor center or call ahead for information and reservations).

SEEING THE HIGHLIGHTS

It's fairly easy to see a great deal here in a short amount of time, especially if you stick to the South Rim. First stop at the visitor center to see the exhibits and get an understanding of how this phenomenal canyon was created. Then, drive the 7-mile (one-way) **South Rim Drive,** stopping at the overlooks. There are about a dozen overlooks along the drive, and in most cases you'll be walking from 140 feet to about 700 feet to reach the viewpoints from your vehicle. Among the not-to-be-missed overlooks are **Gunnison Point,** behind the visitor center, which offers stunning views of the seemingly endless walls of dark rock; and the **Pulpit Rock Overlook,** which provides a splendid view of the rock walls and about 1½ miles of the Gunnison River, some 1,770 feet down. Further along the drive is **Chasm View,** where you can see the incredible power of water, which here cuts through over 1,800 feet of solid rock. Near the end of the drive, be sure to stop at **Sunset View,** where there's a picnic area and a short (140 ft.) walk to a viewpoint, which offers distant views beyond the canyon as well as of the river, now 2,430 feet below your feet. And, if your timing is right, you might be treated to a classic Western sunset, in all its red and orange glory. Finally, take off on one of the **rim hiking trails,** such as the easy Cedar Point Nature Trail or the somewhat more challenging Warner Point Nature Trail (see "Hiking & Backpacking," below). If you'll be camping in the park or staying nearby, you might plan to attend the evening ranger program.

SPORTS & OUTDOOR ACTIVITIES

CLIMBING   The sheer vertical walls and scenic beauty of the Black Canyon make it an ideal and popular destination for rock climbers, but, and we cannot emphasize this too strongly, this is no place for on-the-job training. These cliffs, known for crumbling rock, dizzying heights, and very few places to put protective gear, require a great deal of experience and the best equipment. Free permits are required, and prospective climbers should discuss their plans first with park rangers.

FISHING   Dedicated anglers can make their way to the Gunnison River at the bottom of the canyon in a quest for brown and rainbow trout. The Gunnison within the park has been designated as Gold Medal Waters. Only artificial lures are permitted, and other special rules apply (check with park rangers). A Colorado fishing license is required.

HIKING & BACKPACKING   Trails on the park's rims range from short, easy walks to moderate-to-strenuous hikes of several miles. Hiking below the rim is mostly difficult and not recommended for those with a fear of heights. Permits are not needed for hiking rim trails, but are required for all treks below the rim.

Trails along the **South Rim** include the easy **Cedar Point Nature Trail.** From the Cedar Point trailhead, along South Rim Road, this .7-mile round-trip walk has signs along the way describing the plants you'll see, and provides breathtaking views of the Gunnison River, 2,000 feet down, at the end. The moderately rated **Rim Rock Nature Trail,** which is 1 mile round-trip, is accessed near the entrance to the campground's Loop C. Following the rim along a relatively flat path, this trail leads to an overlook, providing good views of the Gunnison River and the canyon's sheer rock walls. A pamphlet available at the trailhead describes plant life and other points of interest.

The moderate **Warner Point Nature Trail** begins at High Point Overlook at the end of South Rim Road. It's 1.5 miles round-trip and offers a multitude of things to see, from flora such as mountain mahogany, piñon pine, and Utah juniper, to distant mountains and valleys, as well as the Black Canyon and its creator, the Gunnison River. A trail guide is available at the trailhead. The trailhead for the 2-mile round-trip **Oak Flat Loop Trail,** rated moderate to strenuous, is near the visitor center. Dropping slightly below the rim, this trail offers excellent views into the canyon, while also taking you through a grove of aspen, past Gambel oak, and finally through a forest of aspen, Gambel oak, and Douglas fir. Be aware that the trail is narrow in spots, and a bit close to steep drop-offs.

Trails along the **North Rim** include the moderate **Chasm View Nature Trail,** .3 miles round-trip, with a trailhead at the end of the North Rim campground loop. Beginning in a piñon-juniper forest, this trail heads to the rim for good views of the canyon and the river; you'll also have a good chance of seeing swallows, swifts, and raptors here.

A longer North Rim trail is the 5-mile round-trip **Deadhorse Trail,** rated easy to moderate, which begins at the Kneeling Camel Overlook. Actually an old service road, this trail offers a good chance of seeing various birds, plus views of Deadhorse Gulch and the East Portal area at the southeast end of the park. The 7-mile **North Vista Trail,** which begins at the North Rim Ranger Station, is moderate to strenuous. It offers some of the best views into the Black Canyon and also rewards hikers with a good chance of seeing red-tailed hawks, white-throated swifts, Clark's nutcrackers, and ravens.

Experienced **backcountry hikers** in excellent physical condition may want to hike down into the canyon. Although there are no maintained or marked trails, there are several routes that rangers can help you find. Free permits are required. There are also a limited number of campsites available for backpackers. The most popular inner canyon hike is the strenuous **Gunnison Route,** which branches off the South Rim's Oak Flat Trail and heads down to the river. Eighty feet of chain help keep you from falling on a stretch about a third of the way down. This hike has a vertical drop of 1,800 feet and takes 4 to 5 hours.

WATERSPORTS   Although the river may look tempting, our advice for watersports enthusiasts is **don't do it!** The Gunnison River through the park is **extremely dangerous,** for both swimmers and rafters (it's considered **unraftable**). There are sections of the river west of the park that are more suitable; information is available from the **Public Lands Center** office, 2505 S. Townsend Ave., Montrose, CO 81401 (© **970/240-5300**). The only exception is for **experienced kayakers,** who find the river an exhilarating challenge. Free permits are required.

WILDLIFE VIEWING   The park is home to a variety of wildlife, and you're likely to see chipmunks, ground squirrels, badgers, marmots, and mule deer. Although not frequently seen, there are also black bear, cougars, and bobcats; and you'll probably hear the lonesome high-pitched call of coyotes at night. The peregrine falcon can sometimes be spotted along the cliffs, and you may also see red-tailed hawks, turkey vultures, golden eagles, and white-throated swifts.

WINTER SPORTS   When the South Rim Road is closed by winter snows, the park service plows only to the South Rim Visitor Center, leaving the rest of the park the domain of cross-country skiers and snowshoers.

CAMPING

There are campgrounds on both rims, usually open April through September, with a limited water supply hauled in by truck. They have pit toilets, and no showers; but there are electric hookups available on Loop B of South Rim Campground. Sites are available on a first-come, first-served basis, and cost per site is $10, $15 with electric hookups. The **South Rim Campground,** which is rarely packed, has 88 sites, but the **North Rim Campground,** with only 13 sites, does occasionally fill up.

12

Southwestern Colorado

A land apart from the rest of the state, southwestern Colorado is set off by the spectacular mountain wall of the San Juan Range. The Ancestral Puebloans (also called the Anasazi) who once lived here created cliff dwellings that more closely resemble structures found in New Mexico and Arizona than anything you might expect to see in Colorado. The ancient cliff dwellings of Mesa Verde National Park are a case in point, and there are similar but less well-known sites throughout the area, primarily around Cortez.

Durango is the area's major city. Its vintage main street (ca. 1880) and narrow-gauge railroad hearken back to the Old West days of the late 19th century, when it boomed as a transportation center for the region's silver and gold mines. Telluride, at the end of a box canyon surrounded by 14,000-foot peaks, has capitalized on its highly evident mining heritage in its evolution as a major ski and summer resort. And those who drive the Million Dollar Highway—down U.S. 550 from Ouray, over 11,008-foot Red Mountain Pass through Silverton, and on to Durango—can't miss the remains of turn-of-the-20th-century mines scattered over the mountainsides.

1 Durango

332 miles SW of Denver, 169 miles S of Grand Junction, 50 miles N of Farmington, New Mexico

Born as a railroad town more than a century ago, Durango remains a railroad town to this day, as thousands of visitors take a journey back in time aboard the Durango & Silverton Narrow Gauge Railroad. Durango was founded in 1880 when the Denver & Rio Grande Railroad line was extended to Silverton to haul precious metals from high-country mines. Within a year, 2,000 new residents had turned the town into a smelting and transportation center. Although more than $300 million worth of silver, gold, and other minerals rode along the route over the years, the unstable nature of the mining business gave the town many ups and downs. One of the "ups" occurred in 1915, when southern Colorado boy Jack Dempsey, then 20, won $50 in a 10-round boxing match. Dempsey went on to become the world heavyweight champion.

Durango remained a center for ranching and mining into the 1960s. In 1965, with the opening of the Purgatory ski resort (now Durango Mountain Resort), 25 miles north of Durango, a tourism boom began. When the railroad abandoned its tracks from Antonito, Colorado, to Durango in the late 1960s, leaving only the Durango–Silverton spur, the town panicked. But from that potential economic disaster blossomed a savior. The Durango & Silverton Narrow Gauge Railroad is now Durango's biggest attraction, hauling more than 200,000 passengers each summer. Durango also attracts mountain-biking enthusiasts from all over the country—in fact, opportunities abound for outdoor activities of all kinds, from river rafting to trout fishing.

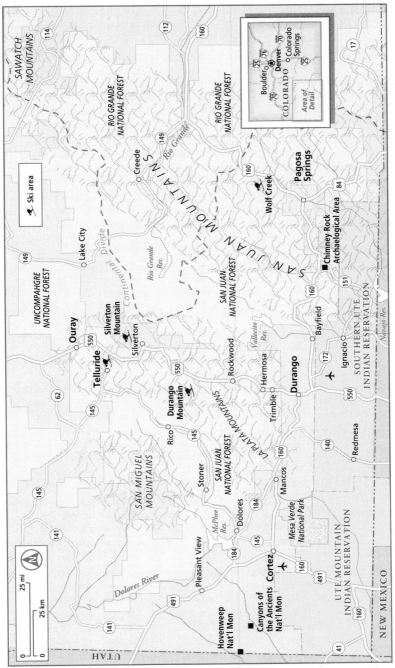

Area of Detail

COLORADO

Boulder
Denver
Colorado Springs
76
70
70
25
25

Ski area

SAWATCH MOUNTAINS

RIO GRANDE NATIONAL FOREST

RIO GRANDE NATIONAL FOREST

114
112
160
17

Rio Grande

149

Creede

Pagosa Springs

160

Wolf Creek

84

SAN JUAN MOUNTAINS

Chimney Rock Archeological Area

UNCOMPAHGRE NATIONAL FOREST

Lake City

Continental Divide

Rio Grande Res.

149

SAN JUAN NATIONAL FOREST

151

SOUTHERN UTE INDIAN RESERVATION

Navajo Res.

Ouray

Silverton Mountain

Silverton

550

Rockwood

Vallecito Res.

Bayfield

160

Telluride

62

550

Hermosa

Durango

172

Ignacio

145

Durango Mountain

550

Trimble

SAN JUAN MOUNTAINS

Rico

145

LA PLATA MOUNTAINS

140

Redmesa

SAN MIGUEL MOUNTAINS

Stoner

SAN JUAN NATIONAL FOREST

160

145

Dolores

184

Mancos

141

McPhee Res.

Mesa Verde National Park

UTE MOUNTAIN INDIAN RESERVATION

Pleasant View

184

145

Cortez

160

491

Dolores River

Canyons of the Ancients Nat'l Mon

160

141

491

Hovenweep Nat'l Mon

41

NEW MEXICO

UTAH

25 mi
25 km

ESSENTIALS

GETTING THERE   By Car   Durango is located at the crossroads of east–west U.S. 160 and north–south U.S. 550.

By Plane   Durango/La Plata County Airport, 14 miles southeast of Durango off Colo. 172 (© **970/247-8143;** www.durango.com), has direct daily nonstop service from Denver, Houston, Albuquerque, and Phoenix, with connections to cities throughout North America. The airport is served by **America West Express** (© 800/235-9292), **Mesa** (© 800/775-4922), and **United Express** (© 800/241-6522).

VISITOR INFORMATION   Contact the **Durango Area Tourism Office,** P.O. Box 2321, Durango, CO 81302 (© **800/463-8726;** www.durango.com). The **Durango Visitor Center** is just south of downtown, on U.S. 160/550 opposite the intersection of East Eighth Avenue. June through October, it's open Monday through Saturday from 8am to 5pm, and Sunday from 10am to 4pm; the rest of the year, hours are from 8am to 5pm Monday through Friday.

GETTING AROUND   The city is on the banks of the Animas River. U.S. 160 lies along the southern edge, and is joined by U.S. 550 about 5 miles east of Durango. Just before U.S. 160 crosses the river, U.S. 550 branches north as Camino del Rio, and junctions with Main Avenue at 14th Street. Downtown Durango is built around Main Avenue from 14th Street south to Fifth Street. College Drive (Sixth St.) is the principal downtown cross street.

Transportation throughout Durango is provided by **The Durango Lift** (© **970/259-5438;** www.durangogov.org/resident/services/transit.html). The **city bus** has three fixed-route loops that operate weekdays, from about 7am to 7pm, year-round (does not operate on major public holidays), and there are also some evening schedules. The fare is $1 per ride one-way. Also part of the Durango Lift is the **Durango Trolley,** which runs along Main Avenue every 20 minutes. In summer it operates from 7am to 10:40pm daily; winter hours are 7am to 7pm weekdays and 10am to 7pm Saturdays. Cost is 50¢. Bus and trolley schedules and route maps are available at the visitor center (see above), and all are fully accessible for those with handicaps.

Taxi service is provided 24 hours a day by **Durango Transportation** (© 800/626-2066 or 970/259-4818; www.durango.com). Car-rental agencies include **Avis** (© 970/247-9761), **Budget** (© 800/527-7000), **Dollar** (© 970/259-3012), **Enterprise** (© 970/385-6860), **Hertz** (© 800/654-3131), **National** (© 970/259-0068), and **Rent-A-Wreck** (© 970/259-5858).

FAST FACTS   There's a 24-hour emergency room at **Mercy Medical Center,** 375 E. Park Ave. (© **800/345-2516** or 970/247-4311; www.mercydurango. org). For **road conditions,** call © **877/315-ROAD,** and for a **weather forecast** and ski conditions, call © **970/247-0930.**

SPECIAL EVENTS   Snowdown!, late January; Iron Horse Bicycle Classic, Memorial Day weekend; Animas River Days, June; Music in the Mountains, at Durango Mountain Resort, July; La Plata County Fair, August; the Durango & Silverton Narrow Gauge Railroad Railfest, August; the Durango Cowboy Gathering, late September or October; and the Durango Christmas Tree Lighting Ceremony, November.

THE TOP ATTRACTION

The Durango & Silverton Narrow Gauge Railroad ✸✸✸   Colorado's most famous train has been in continual operation since 1881. In all that time, its route has never varied: up the Río de las Animas Perdidas (River of Lost Souls), through 45 miles of mountain and San Juan National Forest wilderness to the historic mining town of Silverton, and back. The coal-fired steam locomotives pull strings of gold-colored Victorian coaches on the 3,000-foot climb, past relics of mining and railroad activity from the last century.

A summer trip takes 3¼ hours each way, with a 2-hour stopover in the picturesque town of Silverton before the return trip. You can also overnight in Silverton and return to Durango the following day. (For information on what to see and do during your layover, see "A Side Trip to Silverton," later in this chapter.) Stops are made for water, and also for hikers and fishermen at remote trail heads inaccessible by road. Refreshments and snacks are available on all trains; the first-class parlor car has a bar. Several private cars are available for charter, including an 1886 caboose, the 1887 *Cinco,* and the 1878 *Nomad*—believed to be the oldest operating private railroad car in the world, host of U.S. presidents from Taft to Ford.

The summer schedule runs from early May through October, making the full trip to Silverton and back to Durango, with several trains daily during the peak season, from early June through mid-August, and fewer trains at other times. From the last week in November through early May (except Christmas) there's a daily train to Cascade Canyon and back, 52 miles round-trip. Call or check the website for information on special excursions and events.

479 Main Ave., Durango, CO 81301. ✆ **888/872-4607** or 970/247-2733. www.durangotrain.com. Advance reservations advised. Summer round-trip fare $60 adults, $30 children 5–11; $99 for the parlor car (minimum age 21). Winter round-trip fare $45 adults, $22 children 5–11; $89 for the parlor car. Parking $7 per day per car, $9 for RVs and buses.

OTHER DURANGO HIGHLIGHTS

While taking a steam-train trip on the Durango & Silverton Narrow Gauge Railroad is undeniably the area's top attraction, there are other things to do here. Those interested in a close-up view of the city's numerous historic buildings will want to pick up free copies of several **walking tour** brochures from the visitor center (see above). Along Main Avenue you'll see the handsome **Strater Hotel,** the building that housed the region's first bank, and the sites of saloons and other businesses of the late 1800s and early 1900s; while walking down Third Avenue you'll pass several stone churches and some of the finest homes in Durango from the same period, including the house where silent movie star Harold Lloyd lived during part of his childhood.

Animas Museum   A 1904 stone schoolhouse in north Durango is the home of the La Plata County Historical Society museum, so it's appropriate that a turn-of-the-20th-century classroom is one of its central displays. The museum, which makes a good first stop for those interested in the history of the area, also contains a restored 1870s log cabin from the early days of Animas City, the town that predated Durango. There are also changing exhibits depicting local history, American Indians, and the American West. The museum shop has a good selection of new and used books on regional history and culture, Indian arts and crafts, and unique gifts; the museum houses an excellent research library and photo archives. Allow a minimum of 1 hour.

31st St. and W. Second Ave. ✆ **970/259-2402.** www.frontier.net/~animasmuseum. Admission $2.50 adults, free for children under 12. May–Oct Mon–Sat 10am–6pm; Nov–Apr Tues–Sat 10am–4pm.

Center of Southwest Studies Museum   This museum, located on the Fort Lewis College campus northeast of downtown Durango, contains a variety of

Southwestern Colorado on the Silver Screen

This is John Wayne country, where the Duke slugged it out, shot it out, and sometimes yelled it out as he tamed the American West on movie screens from the late 1920s through the 1970s. It was the location shoot for the multi-Oscar-winning 1969 hit *Butch Cassidy and the Sundance Kid,* starring Robert Redford and Paul Newman. It also hosted *City Slickers,* the 1991 comedy starring Billy Crystal as a hapless city dweller on an Old West–style cattle drive.

Movie critics may argue the point, but to many Americans, the king of them all was the Duke—this bigger-than-life symbol of American manhood made numerous films in and around Gunnison, Ridgway, Delta, Durango, and Pagosa Springs, where you can still find the exact spots certain scenes were filmed.

The classic, if bleak, 1956 John Ford film *The Searchers,* with Wayne, Jeffrey Hunter, Vera Miles, and Ward Bond, used a ranch near Gunnison as a military outpost. To reach the ranch, go north from Gunnison for 3 miles on Colo. 135, then turn left onto Ohio Creek Road and drive for about 8 miles, where you'll see a barn and several other buildings off to the left. Ford's later Western *How the West Was Won* (which, to the great disappointment of Wayne fans, didn't include the Duke) shows a wagon train crossing the Gunnison River west of Delta along 1800 Road, as well as scenes of the Durango & Silverton Narrow Gauge Railroad.

As real John Wayne aficionados know, in 1969 he teamed with Glen Campbell and Kim Darby to make one of his most famous films, *True*

Southwestern artifacts, including excellent exhibits of textiles, woven over 800 years by Navajo, Puebloan, and Hispanic weavers. Allow 45 minutes.

1000 Rim Dr., Fort Lewis College. ☎ 970/247-7494. Free admission. Mon–Fri 1–4pm and by appointment.

Children's Museum of Durango *Kids*   Hands-on activities for children from preschool through preteen make a nice break for vacationing kids who have seen a few too many Victorian homes. Parents stay with and supervise their children while the kids enjoy the changing exhibits, which might include a wood shop, mini-grocery store, puppet theater, dress-up area, and a variety of physics demonstrations with items such as magnets and optical illusions. There are also computer games, arts and crafts, and an archaeology section. Allow 2 hours. *Note:* A move to a new location is scheduled for summer 2006, so call first.

802 E. Second Ave., upstairs at the Arts Center. ☎ 970/259-9234. www.childsmuseum.org. Admission $5.50 adults, $4 children, free for seniors and children under 2. Wed–Sat 9:30am–4:30pm; Sun 1–5pm.

Durango Fish Hatchery and Wildlife Museum *Kids*   A pleasant change from the usual attractions, this fish hatchery offers an opportunity to see and feed trout and also see mounted birds and other wildlife native to Southwestern Colorado. The hatchery, operated by the Colorado Division of Wildlife, also has a short video presentation on fish hatchery operation. Allow 1 hour.

151 E. 16th St. ☎ 970/247-4755. Free admission. Open mid-May to mid-Sept Mon–Sat 10am–4:30pm, Sun noon–4pm.

Grit. The town of Ridgway becomes Fort Smith in the movie, and nearby is the ranch where Wayne jumps his horse over a river. *The Cowboys,* filmed in 1972 outside Pagosa Springs, finds Wayne as a cattleman who hires a group of schoolboys to drive his herd of 1,500 cattle after the gold rush lures away his crew. There are several location shoots from this film in the area; ask for directions at the Pagosa Springs Chamber of Commerce.

But Wayne wasn't the only one shooting up Colorado's southwest corner. Several movie companies have made use of the area, particularly the classic Durango & Silverton Narrow Gauge Railroad. The best train scene has to be the one in *Butch Cassidy and the Sundance Kid,* where Butch, Sundance, and their gang attempt to blow open the train's safe and instead blow up the entire mail car, sending money flying in all directions. Reportedly, the extent of this explosion was a surprise to everyone, even the special-effects technicians who apparently were a bit too liberal with their use of black powder. You can see the train at the depot at 479 Main Ave. in Durango, or in summer hop aboard for a ride to Silverton and back. There's a plaque commemorating the filming about 10 miles east of Durango; ask at the chamber of commerce for directions.

For additional information on films made or being made in Colorado, check with the **Colorado Film Commission,** 1625 Broadway, Suite 1700, Denver, CO 80202 (© **800/SCOUTUS** or 303/620-4567; www.colorado film.org).

Durango & Silverton Narrow Gauge Railroad Museum   The glory days of steam trains come alive here, where you can climb up into a full-size locomotive, a caboose, parlor car, and other rolling stock to get a close-up view. The large museum, located in the Durango & Silverton rail yard, also houses a vast amount of railroad memorabilia, from conductors' uniforms, watches, and belt buckles to lanterns, railroad art, and historic photos. Allow 1 hour.

479 Main Ave. © **888/872-4607** or 970/247-2733. Admission $5 adults, $2.50 children under 12; free with a train ticket. Summer daily 8am–6pm; call for off-season hours.

SPORTS & OUTDOOR ACTIVITIES

In addition to contacting the various companies listed below, you can arrange for most activities through the **Durango Area Tourism Office** (© **800/463-8726;** www.durango.org).

Durango is surrounded by public land, with numerous opportunities for hiking, mountain biking, fishing, and winter sports. For information contact the **Public Lands Center** (© **970/247-4874**) at 15 Burnett Ct., off U.S. 160 west in the Durango Tech Center, which offers information on activities in the San Juan National Forest (www.fs.fed.us/r2/sanjuan) and on lands administered by the Bureau of Land Management (www.co.blm.gov).

The **Durango Parks and Recreation Department** (© **970/385-2950**) operates about 20 parks throughout the city, where you'll find picnic areas, free tennis courts, and other facilities. The department also operates the **Durango Community Recreation Center,** 2700 Main Ave., which has an indoor swimming pool, climbing wall, weights and other workout equipment, and other facilities. A recreation center day pass, which includes all the facilities at the center, costs $4 for adults 18 to 54, $3 for kids 4 to 17 and adults 55 and up, and is free for children under 4.

ALPINE SLIDE   The **Durango Mountain Resort Alpine Slide** (✆ 970/247-9000) is open from Father's Day to Labor Day, weather permitting (call for hours). You ride the chairlift up, then come down the mountain in a chute on a self-controlled sled. Cost is $8 per ride or $49 for an all-day Total Adventure Ticket, which also includes miniature golf, a maze, and other activities.

FISHING   Six-mile-long **Vallecito Lake,** 23 miles northeast of Durango via C.R. 240 and C.R. 501, is a prime spot for rainbow trout, brown trout, kokanee salmon, and northern pike; for information, contact the Vallecito Lake Chamber of Commerce, P.O. Box 804, Bayfield, CO 81122 (✆ **970/247-1573;** www.vallecitolakechamber.com). There are also numerous streams in the Durango area. To buy Colorado fishing licenses and supplies, get information on the best fishing holes, rent equipment, or arrange for a guided fly-fishing trip, stop in at **Duranglers,** 923 Main Ave. (✆ **888/347-4346** or 970/385-4081; www.duranglers.com). Full-day float trips for two people cost about $325; wading trips for two cost about $295. Lunch is included. Similar guide services are offered by **Anasazi Angler** (✆ **970/385-HOOK;** www.sanjuantrout.com).

GLIDER RIDES   For a quiet, airborne look at Durango and the San Juan Mountains, take a glider ride with **Durango Soaring Club** (✆ **970/247-9037;** www.soardurango.com), located 3 miles north of Durango on U.S. 550. Rides are conducted daily from 9am to 6pm from mid-May through mid-October; soaring is smoother in the morning but there is greater thermal activity, offering the opportunity for longer rides, in the afternoon. Rates are about $95 for 25 minutes and $175 for 50 minutes, and individuals cannot weigh less than 50 pounds or more than 260 pounds.

GOLF   Two public 18-hole golf courses open in early spring, weather permitting, in Durango. There's **Hillcrest Golf Course,** 2300 Rim Dr., adjacent to Fort Lewis College (✆ **970/247-1499**), with fees of $13 for 9 holes and $25 for 18 holes; and **Dalton Ranch and Golf Club,** 589 Trimble Lane (C.R. 252), 6 miles north of Durango via U.S. 550 (✆ **970/247-8774;** www.daltonranch.com), charging $32 for 9 holes and $55 for 18 holes.

HIKING & BACKPACKING   Durango is at the western end of the 500-mile Colorado Trail to Denver. The trail head is 3½ miles up Junction Creek Road, an extension of 25th Street west of Main Avenue. There are numerous other trails in the Durango area, including paths into the Weminuche Wilderness Area reached via the Durango & Silverton railroad. For information on area trails contact the **Public Lands Center** (see above).

HORSEBACK RIDING & CATTLE DRIVES   To see this spectacular country as the pioneers did, arrange for a short horseback ride or a 2- to 6-day expedition into the San Juan National Forest or Weminuche Wilderness. Our choice for a licensed outfitter here is **South Fork Stables & Outfitters, Inc.,** a working ranch 5 miles south of Durango at 28481 U.S. 160 E. (✆ **970/259-4871;** www.durangohorses.com). Rides are available year-round, but most are offered in warm weather, with prices of $25 for a 1-hour ride, $45 for a 2-hour ride, $65 for a 3-hour ride, and $110 for an all-day ride. A sunset steak ride, which includes a 1½-hour ride plus a steak dinner costs $45. In winter, 1-hour rides at $30 and 2-hour rides at $50 are offered.

Perhaps the ultimate Old West experience is to join in a South Fork Stables' **cattle drive,** where you help round up and brand the cattle. Two-hour cattle drives run $65 per person, and multiday cattle drives, where you get your grub at the chuck wagon and sleep in teepees, start at $795 per person for a 3-day trip.

LLAMA TREKKING   Guided llama trips, overnight pack trips, and llama leasing are the specialty of **Buckhorn Llama Co.** (© **800/318-9454** or 970/667-7411; www.llamapack.com). Guided pack trips for one to three people cost $300 per person per day and include all equipment, meals, and necessary supplies, except for sleeping bags.

MOUNTAIN BIKING   The varied terrain and myriad trails of San Juan National Forest have made Durango a nationally known mountain-biking center. The Colorado Trail (see "Hiking & Backpacking," above), Hermosa Creek Trail (beginning 11 miles north of Durango off U.S. 550), and La Plata Canyon Road (beginning 11 miles west of Durango off U.S. 160) are among our favorites. For information contact the **Public Lands Center** (see above).

You can also get information and rent mountain bikes at **Mountain Bike Specialists,** 949 Main Ave. (© **970/247-4066;** www.mountainbikespecialists. com), with rental rates of $22 to $37 for a half-day and $30 to $45 for a full day. Rentals are also available, at slightly lower rates, at **Hassle Free Sports,** 2615 Main Ave. (© **800/835-3800** or 970/259-3874; www.hasslefreesports.com).

Guided tours are available from **Durango Mountain Bike Camp** (© **970/385-0411;** www.durangomountainbikecamp.com), with rates (not including bikes) of $50 for a half-day and $90 for a full day.

MOUNTAINEERING & ROCK & ICE CLIMBING   A variety of terrain offers mountaineering and rock- and ice-climbing opportunities for beginners as well as advanced climbers. Guided tours and instruction are offered by **Southwest Adventures** (© **800/642-5389** or 970/259-0370; www.mtnguide.net), with group rates starting at $95 for a half-day rock-climbing course and $570 per person (minimum two people) for a 3-day mountaineering course. Two-day waterfall ice-climbing courses, with a minimum of two people, cost $395 per person.

RIVER RAFTING   The three stages of the Animas River provide excitement for rafters of all experience and ability levels. The churning class IV and V rapids of the upper Animas mark its rapid descent from the San Juan Range. The 6 miles from Trimble Hot Springs into downtown Durango are an easy, gently rolling rush. Downstream from Durango, the river is mainly classes II and III, promising a few thrills but mostly relaxation.

Most of the many outfitters in Durango offer a wide variety of rafting excursions, such as 2- to 4-hour raft trips that cost $25 to $45 for adults and $17 to $30 for kids, and full-day river trips, which include lunch, costing $50 to $200 for adults and $40 to $175 for kids. Trips in inflatable kayaks are also offered at slightly higher rates. Among our favorite companies here are **Durango Rivertrippers** (© **800/292-2885** or 970/259-0289; www.durangorivertrippers.com), **AAM's Mild to Wild Rafting** (© **800/567-6745** or 970/247-4789; www.mild 2wildrafting.com), and **Mountain Waters Rafting** (© **800/748-2507** or 970/259-4191; www.durangorafting.com).

RODEO   From late June through the third weekend in July, the **Durango Pro Rodeo** series takes place most Monday, Wednesday, Friday, and Saturday nights starting at 7:30pm at the La Plata County Fairgrounds, Main Avenue and 25th

Street (© **602/237-3000;** www.durangoprorodeo.com). Admission costs $12 for adults and $5 for kids 12 and under. A Western barbecue ($7 per plate) is served from 6pm.

SWIMMING & MINERAL BATHS   **Trimble Hot Springs** ✦, 7 miles north of Durango just off U.S. 550 (© **970/247-0111;** www.trimblehotsprings.com), at the junction of C.R. 203 and Trimble Lane, is a national historic site more than 100 years old, where you'll often find Mom and Dad relaxing in the soothing mineral pools or getting a massage while the kids have fun in the adjacent swimming pool. Facilities include two natural hot-springs therapy pools, a separate Olympic-size swimming pool (heated by the hot springs but not containing hot-springs water), massage and therapy rooms, a snack bar, picnic area, and gardens. Water from the natural hot springs comes out of the ground at 118° to 120°F (48°C–49°C), and the therapy pools are kept at a more comfortable temperature of 102° to 108°F (39°C–42°C). The swimming pool is usually about 85°F (29°C). The complex is open daily from 8am to 11pm in summer, and in winter from 9am to 10pm Sunday through Thursday and until 11pm Friday and Saturday. From June through August day passes cost $11 for adults and $7.50 for children 12 and younger; the rest of the year the cost is $9 for adults and $6.50 for children 12 and younger. Day passes cover use of the therapy mineral pools and the swimming pool. The Trimble Hot Springs Spa is open daily from 9am to 9pm year-round, providing expanded body treatments and a quiet relaxing atmosphere for therapeutic massage, herbal oil wraps, face and scalp treatments, dry body brush, and radiant salt glow. Massages start at about $50 for a half-hour. Reservations are recommended but walk-ins are welcome.

WINTER SPORTS   Some 25 miles north of Durango on U.S. 550, **Durango Mountain Resort** ✦✦, 1 Skier Place, Durango, CO 81301 (© **800/525-0892** or 970/247-9000; www.durangomountainresort.com), has bragging rights to more sunshine than any other Colorado resort. Surprisingly, the sun doesn't come at the expense of snow—average annual snowfall is 260 inches—so you really get the best of both snow and sun. The resort, which has a laid-back friendly atmosphere that we particularly enjoy, contains 1,200 acres of skiable terrain, with 85 trails rated 23% beginner, 51% intermediate, and 26% advanced, and 11 lifts (one high-speed six, one high-speed quad, four triples, three doubles, one surface lift, and one Magic Carpet). The mountain has a vertical drop of 2,029 feet from a summit elevation of 10,822 feet.

Snowboarders are welcome on all lifts and trails, and two snowboard parks offer jumps, slides, and a half-pipe. The Durango Nordic Center has 16km of trails for Nordic skiers for both classic and skate skiing.

Three on-mountain restaurants complement the facilities, which include a hotel, condominiums, several restaurants and taverns, shops, and equipment rentals. All-day lift tickets are about $55 for adults, $28 for children 6 to 12, $40 for seniors 62 to 69 and students, $15 for seniors 70 and older, and free for kids 5 and younger. The resort is usually open from Thanksgiving to early April, daily from 9am to 4pm.

SHOPPING

You'll find some of your best shopping opportunities in southwest Colorado in downtown Durango, along Main Avenue from the Durango & Silverton Railroad Depot north to 10th Street. Here, interspersed among restaurants and historic hotels, are shops selling a wide variety of items—ranging from custom-made

Western hats to kitchen gizmos to fine porcelain and imported gifts. And yes, there are plenty of tacky T-shirts, as well.

Those seeking the region's premier art gallery will have to leave Main Avenue, but it's not far to the **Toh-Atin Gallery,** 145 W. Ninth St. (© **800/525-0384** or 970/247-8277; www.toh-atin.com). Specializing in original Southwestern and American-Indian art, the gallery stocks Navajo weavings, bronze and alabaster sculptures, original paintings, pueblo pottery, and handcrafted jewelry.

WHERE TO STAY

Durango has a definite lodging season. When the Durango & Silverton Narrow Gauge Railroad runs most of its trains in midsummer, expect to pay top dollar for your room, and expect higher rates during the Christmas holidays and in peak ski seasons as well. But go in the off season—late spring and fall—and you'll find much more reasonable rates. An easy way to book accommodations is to contact the **Durango Area Tourism Office** (© **800/525-8855;** www. durango.org). Room taxes add about 9% to lodging bills.

Among chain and franchise motels offering moderately priced rooms are the **Best Western Mountain Shadows,** 3255 N. Main Ave. (© 800/521-5218 or 970/247-5200), charging $59 to $129 double; the **Comfort Inn,** 2930 N. Main Ave. (© 800/532-7112 or 970/259-5373), with rates for two from $59 to $129; **Days Inn,** 1700 C.R. 203 (© 800/338-1116 or 970/259-1430), with double rates of $59 to $109; **Econo Lodge,** 2002 Main Ave. (© 877/883-2666 or 970/247-4242), charging $59 to $109 double; **Rodeway Inn,** 2701 Main Ave. (© 800/752-6072 or 970/259-2540), with rates for two from $39 to $109; and **Super 8,** 20 Stewart Dr. (© 800/800-8000 or 970/259-0590), with rates for two from $46 to $86. All are in Durango, CO 81301.

VERY EXPENSIVE

The Wit's End Guest Ranch & Resort ★★ *Kids*   A delightful dude ranch some 24 miles northeast of Durango at 8,000 feet elevation, the Wit's End is located on 550 acres in a narrow valley at the head of Vallecito Lake. Surrounded by the 12,000- to 14,000-foot peaks of the Weminuche Wilderness, the Wit's End offers a unique combination of rustic outdoors and sophisticated luxury, with numerous activities ranging from guided horseback rides and boating to a summer kids' program. The one- to four-bedroom log cabins, some dating from the 1870s, have retained their rustic outer appearance, but the knotty-pine interiors have been fully renovated. All have stone fireplaces, queen beds, full bathrooms with tub/shower combos, robes, porches (with porch swings), and striking views.

Most meals are served in the beautiful log lodge, dating from the 1870s, with a huge stone fireplace and walls mirrored with cut glass from London's 1853 Crystal Palace. Filet mignon, roast duckling, chicken Culbertson, and other hearty American dishes are served, with fine dining 3 evenings each week and outdoor Western cookouts the other nights. The game room, on the second floor, has an antique billiards table.

254 C.R. 500, Bayfield, CO 81122. © **800/236-9483.** Fax 970/884-3261. www.witsendranch.com. 34 cabins. From $4,722 per week for 2 guests. Extra adult $2,973, extra child (4–12) $1,963, nannies $1,738. Rates include all meals and activities. These rates effective Memorial Day to Labor Day, with 7-day minimum stay. Off-season cabin-only rates available. AE, DISC, MC, V. **Amenities:** Restaurant (Western/American); bar; large outdoor pool (summer only); 2 outdoor tennis courts; exercise room; 2 hot tubs; mountain biking; extensive summer children's program for ages 4–17; game room; airport transportation; limited room service; massage; horseback riding (private lessons available); fishing (Orvis-endorsed instruction available); hiking; boating; trap shooting; winter-sports equipment. *In room:* TV/VCR (videos available), kitchen.

EXPENSIVE

Purgatory Village Condominium Hotel   This ski-in/ski-out hotel at Durango Mountain Resort, 23 miles north of Durango, is located at the base of the mountain, surrounded by a village offering shops, bars, restaurants, and just about everything skiers want. Summer visitors use the hotel as their base for hiking, mountain biking, and other outdoor activities.

A variety of room types is available, both in the hotel building itself and in adjacent condominiums. Most rooms, regardless of size, have a fireplace, and private deck, as well as a "snow room" with a ski locker. Standard one- and two-bedroom condominiums have whirlpool baths and/or steam showers, and classic furnishings. Efficiency units make ultimate use of space with a Murphy bed that doubles as a dining table.

The hotel restaurant serves dinner only, but the pub adjacent to the hotel serves all three meals daily, as well as offering live music for dancing.

Purgatory Village Condominium Hotel, 1 Skier Place, Durango, CO 81301. ℭ **800/982-6103** or 970/259-2000. www.durangomountainresort.com. 155 units. Summer $119–$144 double, $179–$264 1- or 2-bedroom condo; winter $119–$184 double, $189–$384 condo; higher for holidays. AE, DISC, MC, V. **Amenities:** Restaurant (Continental); outdoor heated pool; 3 hot tubs; concierge; activities desk; babysitting; coin-op laundry. *In room:* TV, kitchen (most).

Strater Hotel ✶✶✶   Durango's most famous hotel is a wonderful place to relax and soak up the ambience of the real Old West (at least the real Old West for those who had money). An exceptional example of American Victorian architecture, the four-story redbrick Strater was built in 1887 by Henry H. Strater, a prominent druggist of the mining-boom era. It boasts the original ornamental brickwork and white-stone cornices, embossed ceiling designs, and intricately carved columns. Crystal chandeliers and a variety of ornate woodworking styles grace the public areas. The hotel has been in the Barker family (Rod Barker is the current CEO) since 1926.

Spread throughout the guest rooms is one of the world's largest collections of American Victorian walnut antiques, and even the wallpaper is authentic to the 1880s. One of the most popular units is no. 222, a corner room directly over the Diamond Belle Saloon, where prolific author Louis L'Amour gave life to many of his Western heroes. The bathrooms are modern, with tub/shower combos in most, but showers only in 16 of the 93 units. The hotel also boasts a Victorian-style hot tub, available by reservation only.

Employees—many of whom have been with the Strater for years—seem to take a personal interest in the happiness of each guest, and manage to be attentive and friendly without falling into the trap of becoming too chummy. Guests of the Strater from Thanksgiving through New Year's are treated to a display of Victorian Christmas decorations, plus complimentary homemade cookies. The Diamond Belle Saloon has live ragtime piano, the Office Spiritorium is a refined martini bar with exquisite charm, and the hotel's theater presents summer melodrama (see "Durango After Dark," below).

699 Main Ave. (P.O. Drawer E), Durango, CO 81302. ℭ **800/247-4431** or 970/247-4431. Fax 970/259-2208. www.strater.com. 93 units. Mid-May to mid-Oct and Christmas holidays $149–$225 double; mid-Oct to mid-May $89–$179 double. AE, DC, DISC, MC, V. **Amenities:** Restaurant (Mahogany Grillle, p. 379); 2 bars; hot tub; concierge; limited room service; valet laundry. *In room:* A/C, TV.

MODERATE

The Leland House Bed & Breakfast Suites ✶✶   Built as an apartment house in 1927 and handsomely restored in 1993, the Leland House offers an intriguing mix of lodging types in a comfortable inn with early-20th-century decor. Owned by the Komick family, who also own the historic Rochester Hotel across the street (see below), the Leland House contains six suites with sitting rooms and full kitchens, plus four studios with kitchenettes. All have private bathrooms with showers (no tubs), and are decorated with a compatible combination of good-quality beds, antiques, near-antiques, and contemporary furniture. The Pittman Suite is a large family suite with two full bedrooms, two bathrooms, a full kitchen, and a large living area. Rooms are named for historic figures associated with the Leland House and its neighbors, such as Max Baer, world heavyweight boxing champion in the 1930s. Throughout the house are photos, memorabilia, and framed biographies of these individuals, many of whom played significant roles in the development of early Durango.

In B&B style, you'll find the friendly staff to be service oriented. Breakfasts, which are served across the street at the Rochester, include a selection of fresh-baked goods, fruit, cereals, juice and coffee, plus a hot entree. Fresh-baked cookies and other refreshments are served in the evening, and like the Rochester, the Leland House has a great close-to-downtown location. Smoking is not permitted.

721 E. Second Ave., Durango, CO 81301. ℭ **800/664-1920** or 970/385-1920. Fax 970/385-1967. www.leland-house.com. 10 units. $109–$149 studio; $159–$199 1-bedroom suite; $299–$340 2-bedroom suite. Rates include full breakfast. AE, DC, DISC, MC, V. *In room:* A/C, TV.

Rochester Hotel ★★   Among our favorite places to stay in Durango, the 1892 Rochester retains the feel of an Old West hotel with high ceilings, original trim and hardware, antiques, historic photos and original Western art, and 1890s-style furnishings. Completely renovated in the mid-1990s the hotel offers 15 spacious rooms, each with its own bathroom (two have whirlpool tubs with showers, and the rest have large walk-in showers). Rooms have good, firm queen or king beds; one unit has a king bed and a kitchen and another, a king and a separate living room. The hotel's hallways are lined with posters and photos from many of the films shot in the area, including *City Slickers, Butch Cassidy and the Sundance Kid, How the West Was Won,* and *The Cowboys.*

Although technically a hotel, the Rochester is run more like a large bed-and-breakfast inn, with an innkeeper on hand to act as concierge. The wonderful breakfasts include fresh-baked muffins, scones, or breads; a selection of fruit; oatmeal; cold cereals; yogurt; and beverages; plus a hot entree such as havarti-dill scrambled eggs with potato chive cake. Fresh-baked cookies and other refreshments are also provided in the evening. Another plus is the location—within easy walking distance of Durango's downtown restaurants and attractions. Smoking is not permitted.

726 E. Second Ave. (write to 721 E. Second Ave.), Durango, CO 81301. ℭ **800/664-1920** or 970/385-1920. Fax 970/385-1967. www.rochesterhotel.com. 15 units. $109–$199 double, $179–$229 suite (called King Deluxe). Rates include full breakfast. AE, DC, DISC, MC, V. Pets accepted in 2 units with $20 per night charge. *In room:* A/C, TV.

WHERE TO DINE
EXPENSIVE

Mahogany Grille ★★ NEW AMERICAN   This fun upscale restaurant, attached to the Strater Hotel, is a lively spot serving cutting-edge dishes to the sounds of jazz. Serving only dinner, the Mahogany Grille boasts award-winning Chef Rustin Newton's sinfully delicious and visually distinctive creations—primarily new American cuisine with definite international influences. We suggest the pepper steak Herbert, a brandy-flamed filet mignon with a mango-chutney sauce; the oven-roasted pistachio-crusted halibut with a lemon-and-garlic sauce; and the broiled elk tenderloin in a blackberry-sage sauce for the adventurous.

Vegetarians should especially enjoy the portobello mushroom stack—charbroiled portobello mushrooms, spinach, asparagus, and caramelized onions piled on a bed of couscous. Save room for the decadent chocolate avalanche—a huge homemade brownie loaded with other chocolate treats plus strawberries; or the much more refined Grand Marnier–soaked tangerine crème brûlée. There's also an extensive menu of specialty martinis—the restaurant's signature Mahogany Cheer contains vodka and a bunch of other stuff they won't talk about—plus there's a good international wine list.

Adjacent to the Strater Hotel, 699 Main Ave. (C) **970/247-4433.** www.mahoganygrille.com. Main courses $13–$28. AE, DISC, MC, V. Summer daily 5–10pm; the rest of the year daily 5–9pm.

MODERATE

Cyprus Cafe ★★ MEDITERRANEAN   This tiny restaurant a block from Durango's busy Main Avenue offers a delightful alternative to the basic American and Southwestern cuisine that dominates southwestern Colorado, and gets our vote as the place to go when we feel adventurous. Located in what was once the living room of a modest home, the dining room has a simple cafe atmosphere, with 10 wood tables, a stained-glass window, and a few pieces of original art. In summer, there's also outdoor patio seating, which more than doubles the restaurant's capacity, with live music several evenings a week. Waits of up to a half-hour are not uncommon on weekends year-round. The emphasis is on freshness, with produce from local farms when available, and the restaurant serves only natural meats, free-range chicken, and sustainable seafood. The menu changes seasonally, but dinner entrees might include spanakopita, spinach and feta cheese wrapped in phyllo dough; various Colorado lamb dishes; fresh seafood; and at least one vegetarian item. Those new to Mediterranean cuisine might try the combination appetizer plate that includes hummus, baba ganoush, olives, feta, spanakopita, and grilled pita, which can easily serve several people as an appetizer or one for dinner.

725 E. Second Ave. (C) **970/385-6884.** www.cypruscafe.com. Lunch $6.95–$11; dinner $12–$24. AE, DISC, MC, V. Mid-May to Sept daily 11:30am–3pm and 5–10pm; Oct to mid-May Tues–Sat 11:30am–2:30pm and 5–9pm.

The Palace Restaurant STEAK/SEAFOOD/PASTA   Adjacent to the Durango & Silverton Narrow Gauge Railroad terminal, the Palace Restaurant, which also contains the Quiet Lady Tavern, has a Victorian drawing-room atmosphere, with Tiffany lamps hanging over the tables, historical photos and classic oil paintings on the walls, and a large fireplace. House specialties at lunch include the lemon-thyme chicken sandwich with thinly sliced apples and grilled Rocky Mountain trout. At dinner, try the slow-roasted duck in a honey-almond sauce or the steak McMahon—a 12-ounce New York cut served on crisp hash browns with a roasted-garlic sauce. Available at lunch and dinner, and great at either meal, is the chicken and dumplings with cranberry compote. A variety of seafood and pasta dishes are also offered. The Quiet Lady Tavern, by the way, is named for the headless female sculpture at its entrance.

505 Main Ave. (C) **970/247-2018.** www.palacerestaurants.com. Main courses $7–$12 at lunch, $16–$28 at dinner. AE, MC, V. Daily 11am–2:30pm and 5:30–10pm. Closed Christmas.

Steamworks Brewing Co. BREWPUB   Situated in a 1920s building, formerly a car dealership, this brewpub has made the most of the funky, warehouselike structure with huge wooden rafters and pipes of all sizes running in all directions. The brewing vats are in the middle of everything, behind glass. There's also patio dining. The food matches the decor: large, substantial portions to satisfy any appetite. Half-pound burgers come in a variety of choices, such as Southwestern, with green chile, pepper jack cheese, and a chipotle sauce. There's also a spicy Cajun chicken sandwich, and a grilled Reuben. Entrees include enchiladas and burritos, steak, chicken, and pasta selections such as the Roman Pasta—fresh spinach, pine nuts, diced tomatoes, garlic, and artichoke hearts with feta cheese and tossed with penne pasta. The tasty side salad with Italian vinaigrette dressing practically overflows the plate, and along with a pepperoni pizza is a perfect (and inexpensive) dinner for two. Close to a dozen of the brewer's beers are usually on tap, including a delightfully bitter pale ale.

801 E. Second Ave. at Eighth St. © 970/259-9200. www.steamworksbrewing.com. Main courses $6.95–$18; pizza $7.95–$12 (serves 1 or 2). AE, DISC, MC, V. Daily 11am–10pm; bar open until 2am.

INEXPENSIVE

Carver Brewing Co. AMERICAN   Carver's was a popular breakfast spot for years, in large part because of its wonderful baked goods. But that wasn't enough, so the restaurant jumped into another niche when it opened Durango's first brewpub. Breakfast selections include French toast prepared with the bakery's own brioche, plus buttermilk or blueberry pancakes and eggs of all sorts, including a number of Mexican-style specialties. For lunch or dinner there are soups and stews—including really good chicken stew served in a bread bowl—plus sandwiches, beef and buffalo burgers, and Navajo tacos. Especially good are the salads, such as the San Juan Salad—mixed greens with red onions, green peppers, and tomatoes, with grilled portabella, chicken, salmon, or ahi. Available after 5pm, dinner entrees include chipotle-grilled salmon, bison bratwurst (we especially recommend that one), and several steaks. The brewery produces a variety of ales, ranging from fairly light golden ales to hearty stouts.

1022 Main Ave. © 970/259-2545. www.carverbrewing.com. Main courses $5.25–$15. AE, DISC, MC, V. Mon–Sat 6:30am–10pm; Sun 6:30am–1pm.

Durango Diner AMERICAN   Locally famous for good basic grub at reasonable prices, the Durango Diner has been going strong since 1965. Serving breakfast and lunch only, the diner is a skinny storefront with a long counter and a table or two looking out on busy Main Avenue. Breakfasts include standard American egg choices, huge hotcakes, and a variety of specials such as excellent homemade green chili, chile rellenos, and breakfast burritos. Lunch here means sandwiches and burgers—the half-pound burger with Swiss cheese and green chili is great—plus turkey and roast beef dinners. The Durango Diner also does a booming business selling its green chile, salsa, and enchilada sauce by the pint, quart, and gallon.

957 Main Ave. © 970/247-9889. www.durangodiner.com. Most items $3–$7. No credit cards. Mon–Sat 6am–2pm; Sun 6am–1pm.

Olde Tymer's Cafe AMERICAN   This popular local hangout is a busy, noisy place in a historic building, complete with the original tin ceiling and decorated with antique bottles and tins from the early-20th-century drugstore that was once located here. The food is primarily burgers, sandwiches, and finger food—the 8-ounce burger in an onion roll is especially good. The menu also features homemade chili, nachos, and hearty salads such as the chicken salad and Cobb salad, and there are daily specials. Service is fast, friendly, and efficient. The patio out back, open in warm weather, is especially pleasant (and quieter than inside).

100 Main Ave. (corner of 10th St. and Main Ave.) © 970/259-2990. Reservations not accepted. Most items $3.50–$9. AE, DISC, MC, V. Daily 11am–10pm.

DURANGO AFTER DARK

During summer, the highly acclaimed **Diamond Circle Melodrama,** in the Strater Hotel, 699 Main Ave. (© **877/325-3400** or 9770/247-3400; www. diamondcirclemelodrama.com), presents authentic late 1800s melodrama—hiss the evil villain and cheer the beautiful heroine—plus a vaudeville review of singing, dancing, and comedy Monday through Saturday evenings at 7:45pm. Tickets are $20 for adults, $15 for children under 12.

You'll get a tasty meal and a live Western stage show at **Bar D Chuckwagon Suppers,** 8080 C.R. 250 (© **888/800-5753** or 970/247-5753; www.bard chuckwagon.com), 9 miles north of Durango via U.S. 550 and Trimble Lane (C.R. 252). Open from Memorial Day weekend through Labor Day weekend, Bar D offers a traditional chuckwagon-style meal with a tasty choice of roast beef, barbecued chicken breast, both beef and chicken, or flame-broiled 12-ounce rib-eye steak, served with potato, beans, biscuits, applesauce, spice cake, and coffee or lemonade. There are usually seconds available, but most people get plenty the first time.

The ranch complex, which includes an Old West town of shops and a minia-ture train (from 5:30–7:15pm, $1 per person per ride), opens at 5:30pm. By 7:30pm you should be in the open-air dining area (yep, there's a portable roof in case of rain), to go through the chow line for your grub, piled onto big metal plates, before taking your seat at a long picnic table. After dinner comes the show—fine Western music with fiddle, flatpick guitar, mandolin, bass, and great singers; plus some really hokey comedy.

Reservations are required. Cost includes supper and show and is $19 for those 9 and older and $9 for children under 9 for the beef or chicken supper. The beef-chicken combination platter costs $20 per person and the rib-eye steak costs $26.

For a variety of entertainment, ranging from avant-garde films to live music, check out the current schedule at the historic **Abbey Theatre,** 128 E. College Dr. (© **970/385-1711;** www.abbeytheatre.com).

A SIDE TRIP TO SILVERTON

For a look at the real Old West, without the need for a time machine, head to the town of Silverton. At an elevation of 9,318 feet at the northern terminus of the Durango & Silverton Narrow Gauge Railroad, the town has a year-round population of about 500 and plenty of things to see and do for the more than 250,000 people who visit each year.

Founded on silver production in 1871, today the entire town is a National Historic Landmark District. In its heyday, Blair Street was such a notorious area of saloons and brothels that no less a character than Bat Masterson, fresh from taming Dodge City, Kansas, was imported to subdue the criminal elements. Today the original false-fronted buildings remain—some in better shape than others—but they now house restaurants and galleries, and are occasionally used as Old West movie sets. There are some fascinating shops and galleries here, along with plenty of places to buy tacky T-shirts, and we strongly recommend that you spend at least an hour just wandering around.

From Memorial Day through Labor Day the Silverton Gunfighters Association stages gunfights at the corner of 12th and Blair streets Thursday, Friday, Saturday, and holidays at 5:30pm. On Sundays from June through September the Silver-ton Brass Band performs at 6pm on one of Silverton's street corners—don't worry, you won't have any trouble finding them, just follow the music and the crowds.

You can get walking-tour maps of the historic downtown area; information on local shops, restaurants, and lodgings; plus details on the numerous outdoor activities in the surrounding mountains from the **Silverton Chamber of Commerce,** 414 Greene St. (Colo. 110) off U.S. 550 (P.O. Box 565), Silverton, CO 81433 (© **800/752-4494** or 970/387-5654; www.silvertoncolorado.com). From July through September the chamber's visitor center is open daily 9am to 6pm; in May, June, and October it's open daily 9am to 5pm; and from November through April it's open daily from 10am to 4pm.

The **San Juan County Historical Society Museum,** in the 1902 county jail at Greene and 15th streets (© **970/387-5838;** www.silvertonhistoricalsociety org), displays memorabilia of Silverton's boom days, including mining equipment and minerals, a collection of Derringer handguns, and railroad collectibles. Altogether, there are three floors of historic displays, including the most popular stop—the original jail cells, a good place to snap a photo of that would-be convict you're traveling with. A shop sells books on area history. The museum is open daily, from Memorial Day weekend through September from 9am to 5pm; and from 10am to 3pm in October. Admission is $3.50 for adults and free for children under 12. The adjacent **San Juan County Courthouse** has a gold-domed clock tower, and the restoration of the **Town Hall,** at 14th and Greene streets, after a devastating 1993 fire, has won national recognition.

The **Old Hundred Gold Mine** (© **800/872-3009** or 970/387-5444; www. minetour.com) is located about 5 miles east of Silverton via Colo. 110, offering an underground guided tour that starts with a ride 1,500 feet underground in an electric mine train, and continues with a walk through lighted tunnels where you see drilling and mucking demonstrations. There's gold panning aboveground, plus a gift shop, snack bar, and picnic area. Cost is $15 for adults 13 to 59, $7.95 for children 5 to 12 (children under 5 held on a lap are free), and $14 for seniors 60 and older. Reservations are not necessary; the temperature in the mine is about 48°F (9°C), so a sweater or jacket is recommended. The mine is open from early May through mid-October, daily from 10am to 4pm, with tours on the hour.

The self-guided **Mayflower Gold Mill Tour** (© **970/387-0294;** www. silvertonhistoricalsociety.org) takes place in the old Sunnyside Mill, about 2 miles northeast of Silverton via Colo. 110. Former miners are sometimes on hand to demonstrate the process of milling, and you can see the historic mill and its original milling equipment, much of it still operational. A video explains the mill's history. There's also gold panning and a gift shop. Cost for a self-guided tour is $6.50 for those 13 to 59, $5.50 for those 60 and older, and free for children 12 and younger. Guided tours for groups of eight or more are available with advance reservations for an additional $2.50 per adult and senior. The mill is open Memorial Day weekend to mid-September daily from 10am to 5pm.

Expert and advanced skiers and snowboarders have discovered Silverton's newest attraction, **Silverton Mountain Ski Area,** which opened in early 2002 and has been booked solid ever since. Located almost 7 miles north of Silverton, the ski area has one double chairlift that accesses more powder than most skiers have ever seen. Base is at 10,400 feet, with a peak lift-served elevation of 12,300 feet and a fairly easy hike to 13,300 feet elevation. The area's steepest run is 55 degrees and its easiest runs are 25 to 30 degrees, what most other ski areas call a really steep run. In summer the area offers scenic chairlift rides Fridays, Saturdays, and Sundays. The area also has a difficult mountain bike trail for experienced riders. For current hours, rates, required equipment, and other details, contact **Silverton Mountain,** P.O. Box 654, Silverton, CO 81433 (© **970/387-5706;** www.silvertonmountain.com).

WHERE TO STAY

The Wyman Hotel & Inn ★★★   Our top choice for overnight lodging in Silverton, the Wyman fits in beautifully with the historic ambience of this Old West mining town, but then it ought to—the hotel's been here almost as long as the town. Built in 1902 and now listed on the National Register of Historic Places, this handsome red-sandstone building has arched windows, high ceilings, Victorian-style wallpaper, and rooms and common areas furnished with antiques dating from the 1870s to the early 1900s—mostly Renaissance and East Lake styles. Rooms are individually decorated and range in size. The hotel offers a two-room suite, a three-room suite, and a very large family room. In addition to the rooms in the hotel, a Southern Pacific Railroad caboose has been converted to a honeymoon suite, with a hand-carved antique bed from Spain and a two-person whirlpool tub (four other units also have two-person whirlpool tubs). Ten rooms have showers only, and all have top-quality king- or queen-size feather beds with down pillows and down duvets. Telephones have dataports.

Although the rooms are wonderful, it would be well worth coming here simply for the food, which is truly a gourmet experience. Breakfasts include fresh-baked muffins, fresh fruit, beverages, and an entree such as quiche with rosemary potatoes; and those who opt for the dinner package enjoy a four-course candlelight meal. A wine-and-cheese social hour is included in the rates. The hotel also contains a small art gallery featuring the work of Colorado artists. Honeymoon packages are available, and the Wyman is popular for weddings and elopements. The entire hotel is nonsmoking.

1371 Greene St., Silverton, CO 81433. (C) **800/609-7845** or 970/387-5372. Fax 970/387-5745. www.the wyman.com. 17 units. B&B rates $129–$210 double; B&B plus dinner $229–$310 double. AE, DISC, MC, V. Rates include full breakfast and afternoon wine and cheese or tea and homemade cookies. Pets accepted ($25 per stay) in a few rooms. **Amenities:** Guest computer. *In room:* TV/VCR, hair dryer.

2 A Spectacular Drive Along the San Juan Skyway

The **San Juan Skyway** ★★, a 233-mile circuit, crosses five mountain passes and takes in the magnificent San Juan Mountains, as well as the cities and towns of the region. It can be accomplished in a single all-day drive from Durango or divided into several days, incorporating stops in Cortez, Telluride, and Ouray—all of which are discussed later in this chapter. Check for closed passes in winter and early spring.

The route can be driven either clockwise (heading west from Durango on U.S. 160) or counterclockwise (heading north from Durango on U.S. 550). We'll describe the clockwise route.

Eleven miles west of Durango you'll pass through the village of Hesperus, from which a county road runs 10 miles north into **La Plata Canyon,** with its mining ruins and ghost towns.

Farther west, U.S. 160 passes the entrance road to **Mesa Verde National Park.** About 45 miles west of Durango, just before Cortez, turn north on Colo. 145, which traverses the historic town of Dolores, site of the **Anasazi Heritage Center** (see section 4 of this chapter), then proceeds up the **Dolores River Valley,** a favorite of trout fishermen.

Sixty miles from Cortez, the route crosses 10,222-foot **Lizard Head Pass,** named for a startling rock spire looming above the roadside alpine meadows. It then descends 13 miles to the resort town of **Telluride,** set in a beautiful box canyon 4 miles off the main road.

Follow Colo. 145 west from Telluride down the San Miguel River valley to **Placerville.** Then turn north on Colo. 62, across 8,970-foot Dallas Divide, to Ridgway, a historic railroad town and home of **Ridgway State Park (℗ 970/ 626-5822)**, with a sparkling mountain reservoir, trout fishing, boating (there's a full-service marina), swimming, hiking, mountain biking, horseback riding, and camping.

From Ridgway, turn south, and follow U.S. 550 to the scenic and historic town of **Ouray.** Here begins the remarkable **Million Dollar Highway,** so named for all the mineral wealth that passed over it.

The 23 miles from Ouray over 11,008-foot **Red Mountain Pass** to Silverton is an unforgettable drive. It shimmies up the sheer sides of the Uncompahgre Gorge, through tunnels and past cascading waterfalls, then follows a historic toll road built in the 19th century. Mining equipment and log cabins are in evidence on the slopes of the iron-colored mountains, many of them over 14,000 feet in elevation. Along this route you'll pass a monument to snowplow operators who died trying to keep the road open during winter storms.

From Silverton, U.S. 550 climbs over the Molas Divide (elevation 10,910 ft.), then more or less parallels the track of the Durango & Silverton Narrow Gauge Railroad as it follows the Animas River south to Durango, passing the **Durango Mountain Resort** (p. 376) en route.

3 Cortez

45 miles W of Durango, 203 miles S of Grand Junction

An important archaeological center, Cortez is surrounded by a vast complex of ancient villages that dominated the Four Corners region—where Colorado, New Mexico, Arizona, and Utah's borders meet—1,000 years ago. Mesa Verde National Park, 10 miles east, is certainly the most prominent nearby attraction, drawing hundreds of thousands of visitors annually (see section 4 of this chapter). In addition, archaeological sites such as those at Canyons of the Ancients and Hovenweep national monuments as well as Ute Mountain Tribal Park are an easy drive from the city. San Juan National Forest, just to the north, offers a wide variety of recreational opportunities. Most visitors to Cortez won't be spending much time in the city, but will use it as a home base. Elevation is 6,200 feet.

ESSENTIALS

GETTING THERE   By Car   Cortez is located at the junction of north–south U.S. 491 and east–west U.S. 160.

As it enters Cortez from the east, U.S. 160 crosses Dolores Road (Colo. 145, which goes north to Telluride and Grand Junction), then runs due west through town for about 2 miles as Main Street. The city's main thoroughfare, Main Street intersects U.S. 491 (Broadway) at the west end of town.

By Plane   Cortez Airport, off U.S. 160 and 491, southwest of town (℗ **970/ 565-7458;** www.cityofcortez.com), is served by **Great Lakes Airlines** (℗ **800/ 554-5111** or 970/565-9510), with direct daily flights to Denver.

Budget (℗ 800/527-0700 or 970/564-9012) and **Enterprise** (℗ 800/325-8007 or 970/565-6824) provide car rentals at the airport.

VISITOR INFORMATION   Stop at the **Colorado Welcome Center at Cortez,** Cortez City Park, 928 E. Main St. (℗ **970/565-4048;** www.swcolo.org), open daily from 8am to 6pm in summer and from 8am to 5pm the rest of the year; or contact the **Mesa Verde Country Visitor Information Bureau,** P.O.

Box HH, Cortez, CO 81321 (© **800/253-1616;** www.mesaverdecountry.com), or the **Cortez Area Chamber of Commerce,** P.O. Box 968, Cortez, CO 81321 (© **970/565-3414;** www.cortezchamber.org).

FAST FACTS The local hospital is **Southwest Memorial Hospital,** 1311 N. Mildred Rd. (© **970/565-6666**), which has a 24-hour emergency room. The **post office** is at 35 S. Beech St.; contact the U.S. Postal Service (© **800/275-8777;** www.usps.com) for hours and additional information.

SPECIAL EVENTS American Indian Dances and Storyteller Programs, mid-May to Labor Day; Mancos Old Time Fiddlers' Contest, first weekend in June; Ute Mountain Round-Up and Rodeo, early June; Arts and Crafts Fiesta, mid-June; Parade of Lights, early December.

WHAT TO SEE & DO

In addition to the area's excellent archaeological sites, discussed in section 4 of this chapter, attractions here include the **Four Corners Monument,** the only place in the United States where you can stand in four states at once. Operated by the Navajo Parks and Recreation Department (© **928/871-6647;** www.navajo na tionparks.org), there's a flat monument marking where Utah, Colorado, New Mexico, and Arizona meet, and visitors perch for photos. The official seals of the four states are displayed, along with the motto, "Four states here meet in free-dom under God." Surrounding the monument are the states' flags, flags of the Navajo Nation and Ute tribe, and the U.S. flag.

A visitor center has crafts demonstrations by Navajo artisans, and jewelry, pottery, sand paintings, and other crafts are for sale. In addition, traditional Navajo food, such as fry bread, is available. The monument is located half a mile northwest of U.S. 160, about 40 miles southwest of Cortez. It's open daily from 7am to 7pm in summer, with shorter hours in winter. Admission costs $3 per person. Allow 30 minutes.

WHERE TO STAY

Summer is the busy season here, and that's when you'll pay the highest lodging rates. Among the major chains providing comfortable, reasonably priced lodging in Cortez (zip code 81321) are **Best Western Sands,** 1120 E. Main St. (© 800/937-8376 or 970/565-3761), with double rates of $60 to $92; **Best Western Turquoise Inn & Suites,** 535 E. Main St. (© 800/547-3376 or 970/565-3778), with rates for two from $69 to $149; **Comfort Inn,** 2321 E. Main St. (© 800/424-6423 or 970/565-3400), which charges $69 to $119 double; **Econo Lodge,** 2020 E. Main St. (© 800/553-2666 or 970/565-3474), with double rates of $49 to $99; **Super 8,** 505 E. Main St. (© 800/800-8000 or 970/565-8888), with rates of $49 to $79 double; and **Travelodge,** 440 S. Broadway (© 800/578-7878 or 970/565-7778), with rates for two from $45 to $79. Room tax adds about 8% to lodging bills.

Anasazi Motor Inn This standard, well-kept motel offers spacious South-west-decorated rooms with either one king-size bed or two queens; many of the ground-floor rooms have patios. There's also a sand volleyball court, horseshoe pits, a short walking trail, and free shuttle service to downtown.

640 S. Broadway, Cortez, CO 81321. © **800/972-6232** or 970/565-3773. Fax 970/565-1027. www.anasazi motorinn.com. 87 units. $55–$75 double. AE, DC, DISC, MC, V. Pets accepted. **Amenities:** Restaurant (American); bar; pool (outdoor heated); hot tub; airport shuttle. *In room:* A/C, TV.

Rio Grande Southern Bed & Breakfast ✮ Although the Rio Grande Southern Railroad folded in 1893 after just 2 years in business, the hotel built for its customers has endured to become a charming National Historic Landmark. You'll check in at the old front desk, climb carpeted stairs to the second floor, then pass Norman Rockwell prints and a tiny library on your way to the guest rooms. All the units here are multiroom suites, so although the individual rooms are small, you'll have plenty of room. If you're lucky, you'll be in Room 4, where Zane Gray is said to have stayed while writing *Riders of the Purple Sage.* Guest rooms are decorated with Victorian antiques and have queen-size and double beds; many have claw-foot tubs. A fine Southwestern-style breakfast is served downstairs in a small cafe. The entire property is nonsmoking.

101 S. Fifth St. (P.O. Box 516), Dolores, CO 81323. ✆ **800/258-0434** or 970/882-7527. www.riogrande bandb.com. 4 units. $75 double for 1-bedroom suite; $130 for 4 people in 2-bedroom suites. Rates include full breakfast. DISC, MC, V. Closed mid-Dec to Feb. *In room:* No phone.

WHERE TO DINE

Homesteaders Restaurant 🌟 AMERICAN/MEXICAN A rustic, Old West atmosphere pervades this popular family restaurant, which is decorated with historic photos and pioneer memorabilia. The menu has a good selection of home-style American basics, with charbroiled beef, including burgers, T-bones, and top sirloins. Those wanting a bit more zip might try the Southwestern steak—top sirloin smothered with salsa, green chile, and cheese. We also suggest the barbecued baby back ribs and the old-fashioned dinners, such as thin-sliced roast beef or deep-fried catfish filet. Several Mexican standards are also offered, as well as salads and vegetarian items. Smoking is not permitted.

45 E. Main St. ✆ **970/565-6253.** Fax 970/564-9217. www.thehomesteaders.com. Main courses $4.50–$6 lunch, $7–$17 dinner. AE, DISC, MC, V. Mon–Sat 11am–10pm; summer also Sun 5–10pm.

Main St. Brewery and Restaurant 🌟 AMERICAN Fans slice the air under a stamped-tin ceiling, and fanciful murals splash color above subdued wood paneling. The pleasant contrasts found in the decor carry over to the menu. In addition to brewpub staples such as fish and chips, pizza, and bratwurst, this brewery and restaurant offers steaks and prime rib—dry aged Angus beef from its own herd of Angus cattle, raised with no artificial growth stimulants or antibiotics—plus a vegetarian skewer plate and Rocky Mountain trout. The beers brewed here go well with everything. We especially recommend the hoppy, slightly bitter Pale Export and the Munich-style Pale Bock.

21 E. Main St., Cortez. ✆ **970/564-9112.** Reservations not accepted. Main courses $6.95–$18. AE, MC, V. Daily 3pm–midnight.

Nero's 🌟🌟 ITALIAN/AMERICAN Our top choice in this area when we're craving something a bit different. The innovative entrees, prepared by Culinary Institute of America chef Richard Gurd, include house specialties such as the Cowboy Steak (a charbroiled 12-ounce sirloin seasoned with a spicy rub and served with pasta or fries); our favorite, the mushroom ravioli served with an Alfredo sauce, sautéed spinach, sun-dried tomatoes, and pecans; and shrimp Alfredo—sautéed shrimp with spinach served over fettuccine with Alfredo sauce and Romano cheese. There's an excellent selection of beef, plus seafood, fowl, pork, veal, and lots of homemade pasta. A small, homey restaurant with a Southwestern art-gallery decor, Nero's also offers pleasant outdoor seating in warm weather.

303 W. Main St. ✆ **970/565-7366.** http://subee.com/neros/home.html. Reservations recommended. Entrees $10–$22. AE, MC, V. Daily 5–9:30pm. Closed Sun in winter.

4 Mesa Verde National Park & Other Archaeological Sites of the Four Corners Region

MESA VERDE NATIONAL PARK

Mesa Verde is the largest archaeological preserve in the United States, with some 4,000 known sites dating from A.D. 600 to 1300, including the most impressive cliff dwellings in the Southwest.

The earliest known inhabitants of Mesa Verde (Spanish for "green table") built subterranean pit houses on the mesa tops. During the 13th century they moved into shallow caves and constructed complex cliff dwellings. Although a massive construction project, these homes were only occupied for about a century; their residents left in about 1300 for reasons as yet undetermined.

The area was little known until ranchers Charles and Richard Wetherill chanced upon it in 1888. Looting of artifacts followed their discovery until a Denver newspaper reporter's stories aroused national interest in protecting the site. The 52,000-acre site was declared a national park in 1906—it's the only U.S. national park devoted entirely to the works of humans.

Fires have plagued the park in recent years, and burned, dead trees and blackened ground are very evident today. Two lightning-induced fires blackened about 40% of the park during the summer of 2000, closing the park for about three weeks. Officials said that although the park's piñon-juniper forests were severely burned, none of the major archaeological sites were damaged, and in fact the fires revealed some sites that they were not aware existed. Then a lightning-induced fire struck again in the summer of 2002, closing the park for about 10 days. It destroyed several employees' homes, a sewage treatment plant, and phone and power lines, and also damaged a water storage tank. Officials said that the only damage to archaeological sites was the scorching of the wall of one ruin.

JUST THE FACTS

ENTRY   The park entrance is located on U.S. 160, 10 miles east of Cortez and 6 miles west of Mancos.

FEES & REGULATIONS   Admission to the park for up to 1 week costs $10 per vehicle. Tours of Cliff Palace, Balcony House, and Long House are $2.75; ranger-guided tours of other areas are free. To protect the many archaeological sites, the Park Service has outlawed backcountry camping and off-trail hiking. It's also illegal to enter cliff dwellings without a ranger present. The Wetherill Mesa Road cannot accommodate vehicles longer than 25 feet. Cyclists must have lights to pedal through the tunnel on the entrance road.

VISITOR CENTERS & INFORMATION   **Chapin Mesa,** site of the park headquarters, museum, and a post office, is 20 miles from the park entrance on U.S. 160. The **Far View Visitor Center,** site of Far View Lodge, a restaurant, gift shop, and other facilities, is 15 miles off U.S. 160. For a park brochure, contact Mesa Verde National Park, P.O. Box 8, Mesa Verde, CO 81330-0008 (© **970/529-4465;** www.nps.gov/meve).

HOURS & SEASONS   The park is open daily year-round, but full interpretive services are available only from mid-June to Labor Day. In winter, the Mesa Top Road and museum remain open, but many other facilities are closed. The **Far View Visitor Center** is open from mid-April through mid-October only, from 8am to 5pm daily. The **Chapin Mesa Archeological Museum** is open daily from 8am to 6:30pm from mid-April through mid-October, daily from 8am to 5pm the rest of the year.

AVOIDING THE CROWDS   With close to half a million visitors annually, Mesa Verde seems packed at times, but the numbers are much lower just before and after the summer rush, usually from June 15 to August 15. Another way to beat the crowds is to make the 12-mile drive to Wetherill Mesa, which attracts only a small percentage of park visitors.

RANGER PROGRAMS   In addition to guided tours to the cliff dwellings (see below), rangers give nightly campfire programs at Morefield Campground in summer.

SEEING THE HIGHLIGHTS IN A DAY

If you have only a day to spend at the park, stop first at the Far View Visitor Center to buy tickets for a late-afternoon tour of either Cliff House or Balcony House—visitors are not allowed to tour both on the same day. Then travel to the Chapin Mesa archeological museum for a look at the history behind the sites you're about to see. From here, walk down the trail behind the museum to Spruce Tree House. Then drive the Mesa Top Loop Road. Cap your day with the guided tour.

EXPLORING THE PARK

The **Cliff Palace,** the park's largest and best-known site, is a four-story apartment complex with stepped-back roofs forming porches for the dwellings above. Accessible by guided tour only, it is reached by a quarter-mile downhill path. Its towers, walls, and kivas (large circular rooms used for ceremonies) are all set back beneath the rim of a cliff. Another ranger-led tour takes visitors up a 32-foot ladder to explore the interior of **Balcony House.** Each of these tours is given only in summer and into fall (call for exact dates). Guided tours are also offered by Far View Lodge (see "Where to Stay & Dine in the Park," below).

Two other important sites—**Step House** and **Long House,** both on Wetherill Mesa—can be visited in summer only. Rangers lead free tours to **Spruce Tree House,** another of the major cliff-dwelling complexes, only in winter, when other park facilities are closed. Visitors can also explore Spruce Tree House on their own at any time.

Although none of the trails to the Mesa Verde sites is strenuous, the 7,000-foot elevation can make the treks tiring for visitors who aren't used to the altitude. For those who want to avoid hiking and climbing, the 12-mile **Mesa Top Road** makes a number of pit houses and cliff-side overlooks easily accessible by car. **Chapin Mesa Archeological Museum** houses artifacts and specimens related to the history of the area, including other nearby sites.

⟮*Tips*⟯ Keeping Fido Safe & Happy

While there's plenty to do for human visitors to Mesa Verde National Park, the U.S. Park Service is not very welcoming to our canine friends, and prohibits them on all trails (the only exceptions are for service dogs, such as Seeing Eye dogs). This means that if you want to explore the park you'll need to leave your dogs behind. Fortunately, there are several kennels in the area, including **The Dog Hotel,** 33350 Colo. 184, Mancos (© **970/882-5416**), which is a well-run facility that also offers accommodations for cats. Appointments are necessary, and pet owners must have proof of current vaccinations.

(*Fun Fact* **What's in a Name?**

The prehistoric inhabitants of the ancient villages of the Four Corners region have long been known as the Anasazi. That word is being phased out, however, in favor of "Ancestral Puebloans" or "ancient Pueblo people," because modern American Indians who trace their roots to the Ancestral Puebloans consider the word Anasazi demeaning. "Anasazi" is a Navajo word meaning "enemy of my people," as the Navajos considered the Ancestral Puebloans their enemies.

OUTDOOR ACTIVITIES Though this isn't an outdoor recreation park per se—the reason to come here is to see the cliff dwellings and other archaeological sites—you'll find yourself hiking and climbing to get to the sites. Several longer hikes into scenic Spruce Canyon let you stretch your legs and get away from the crowds. Hikers must register at the ranger's office before setting out.

CAMPING Open from mid-April to mid-October, **Morefield Campground** (© **800/449-2288** or 970/533-1944; www.visitmesaverde.com), 4 miles south of the park entrance, has 435 sites, including 15 with full RV hookups. The campground is set in rolling hills in a grassy area with scrub oak and brush. The attractive sites are fairly well spaced, and are mostly separated by trees and other foliage. Facilities include modern restrooms, coin-operated showers (not within easy walking distance of most campsites), picnic tables, grills, and an RV dump station. Programs on the area's human and natural history and other subjects are presented nightly at the campground amphitheater from Memorial Day weekend through Labor Day weekend. Campsites cost $19, $25 with hookups. If you're hoping to snare one of the 15 full hookup sites, try getting to the park by late morning; there are almost always nonhookup sites available. There are also several commercial campgrounds along U.S. 160, just outside the park entrance.

WHERE TO STAY & DINE IN THE PARK

We like to be where the action is, and recommend staying overnight at either the Morefield Campground (see "Camping," above) or the Far View Lodge (see below); both are operated by park concessionaire Aramark, which also operates several restaurants in the park. There are numerous lodging and dining possibilities in Cortez, too (see "Cortez," above).

Far View Lodge ★ Located in the heart of Mesa Verde National Park, Far View Lodge offers not only the most convenient location for visiting the park, but also the best views of any accommodations in the area. The facility lodges guests in 17 separate buildings spread across a hilltop. Rooms aren't fancy and they're a bit on the small side, but they are well maintained and more than adequate, with Southwestern decor. In fact, many of the units have recently been renovated and upgraded. New in 2003 were the "Kiva" rooms with handcrafted furniture, one king- or two queen-size beds, bathrobes, CD players, and other upscale amenities. Most standard rooms have one queen-size bed or two doubles, although a variety of bed combinations are available. For a couple, we prefer the rooms with one bed—they seem less cramped than rooms with two beds. There are no TVs, but each unit has a private balcony, and the views are magnificent in all directions.

There's a 24-hour front desk, complimentary morning coffee and newspaper, and gift shop. Half- and full-day guided tours of the park embark from the lodge and campground daily during the warmer months. Rates for full-day tours to Cliff Palace and Spruce Tree House, including lunch, are $56 adults, $44 children 5 to 17, and free for children under 5. The cost for the half-day tours to Spruce Tree House is $36 adults, $25 children 5 to 17, and free for those under 5; half-day tours to Balcony House cost $39 adults, $28 children 5 to 17, and free for those under 5.

Mesa Verde National Park (P.O. Box 277), Mancos, CO 81328. (©) **800/449-2288** or 970/533-1944. Fax 970/ 533-7831. www.visitmesaverde.com. 150 units. Open Apr–Oct only. $82–$122 double. AE, DC, DISC, MC, V. Pets accepted with a deposit. **Amenities:** 2 restaurants (Southwestern American). *In room:* Fridge (some), coffeemaker.

NEARBY ARCHAEOLOGICAL SITES
CORTEZ CULTURAL CENTER
The center, 25 N. Market St., Cortez (© **970/565-1151;** www.cortezcultural-center.org), includes a museum with exhibits on both prehistoric and modern American Indians, an art gallery with displays of regional art, a good gift shop offering crafts by local tribal members, and a variety of programs including American-Indian dances during the summer. From June through August the center is open daily from 10am to 10pm, and the rest of the year it is open daily from 10am to 5pm. Admission is free and you should plan to spend at least an hour. Call or check the website for the schedule of Indian dances and other programs, which are also free.

UTE MOUNTAIN TRIBAL PARK 🐾🐾
If you liked Mesa Verde, but would have enjoyed it more without the company of so many fellow tourists, you'll *love* the Ute Mountain Tribal Park (P.O. Box 109, Towaoc, CO 81334; © **800/847-5485** or 970/565-3751 ext. 330; www. utemountainute.com/tribalpark.htm). Set aside by the Ute Mountain tribe to preserve its heritage, the 125,000-acre park—which abuts Mesa Verde National Park—includes wall paintings and ancient petroglyphs as well as hundreds of surface sites and cliff dwellings that are similar in size and complexity to those in Mesa Verde.

Access to the park is strictly limited to guided tours. Full- and half-day tours begin at the Ute Mountain Museum and Visitor Center at the junction of U.S. 491 and U.S. 160, 20 miles south of Cortez. Mountain-biking and backpacking trips are also offered. No food, water, lodging, gasoline, or other services are available within the park. Some climbing of ladders is necessary on the full-day tour. There's one primitive **campground** ($12 per vehicle; reservations required).

Charges for tours in your vehicle start at $20 per person for a half-day, $40 for a full day; it's $8 extra to go in the tour guide's vehicle, and reservations are required.

ANASAZI HERITAGE CENTER
When the Dolores River was dammed and the McPhee Reservoir was created in 1985, some 1,600 ancient archaeological sites were threatened. Four percent of the project costs were set aside for archaeological work, and over two million artifacts and other prehistoric items were rescued. Most are displayed in this museum. Located 10 miles north of Cortez, it is set into a hillside near the remains of 12th-century sites.

Operated by the Bureau of Land Management, the center emphasizes visitor involvement. Children and adults are invited to examine corn-grinding implements, a loom and other weaving materials, and a re-created pit house. You can touch artifacts 1,000 to 2,000 years old, examine samples through microscopes, use interactive computer programs, and engage in video lessons in archaeological techniques.

A half-mile trail leads from the museum to the **Dominguez and Escalante Ruins,** atop a low hill, with a beautiful view across the Montezuma Valley.

The center also serves as the visitor center for Canyons of the Ancients National Monument (see below). It is located at 27501 Colo. 184, Dolores (© **970/882-5600;** www.co.blm.gov/ahc). It's open March through October, daily from 9am to 5pm; November through February, daily from 9am to 4pm; and is closed Thanksgiving, Christmas, and New Year's Day. An admission fee of $3 for adults is charged March through October only; admission is free for those 17 and under. Allow 2 hours.

CANYONS OF THE ANCIENTS NATIONAL MONUMENT

Among the country's newest national monuments, Canyons of the Ancients was created by presidential proclamation in June 2000. The 164,000-acre national monument, located west of Cortez, contains thousands of archaeological sites—what some claim is the highest density of archaeological sites in the United States—including the remains of villages, cliff dwellings, sweat lodges, and petroglyphs at least 700 years old, and possibly as much as 10,000 years old.

Canyons of the Ancients includes **Lowry Pueblo,** an excavated 12th-century village that is located 26 miles from Cortez via U.S. 491, on C.R. CC, 9 miles west of Pleasant View. This pueblo, which was likely abandoned by 1200, is believed to have housed about 100 people. It has standing walls from 40 rooms plus 9 kivas (circular underground ceremonial chambers). A short, self-guided interpretive trail leads past a kiva decorated with geometric designs and continues to the remains of a great kiva, which, at 54 feet in diameter, is among the largest ever found. There are also a picnic area, drinking water, and toilets.

Canyons of the Ancients is managed by the Bureau of Land Management, and as yet has no visitor center or even a contact station. Those wishing to explore the monument are strongly advised to contact or preferably stop first at the **Anasazi Heritage Center** (see above) for information, especially current road conditions and directions. Information is also available online at www.co.blm.gov/canm. Allow at least 2 hours.

HOVENWEEP NATIONAL MONUMENT

Preserving some of the most striking and isolated archaeological sites in the Four Corners area, this national monument straddles the Colorado-Utah border, 40 miles west of Cortez.

Hovenweep is the Ute word for "deserted valley," appropriate because its inhabitants apparently left around 1300. The monument contains six separate sites, and is noted for mysterious, 20-foot-high sandstone towers, some square, others oval, circular, or D-shaped. Archaeologists have suggested their possible function as everything from guard or signal towers, celestial observatories, and ceremonial structures to water towers or granaries.

A ranger station, with exhibits, restrooms, and drinking water, is located at the **Square Tower Site,** in the Utah section of the monument, the most impressive and best preserved of the sites. The **Hovenweep Campground,** with 30 sites, is open year-round. Sites are fairly small—most appropriate for tents or small pickup truck campers—but a few sites can accommodate RVs up to 25 feet long. The campground has flush toilets, drinking water, picnic tables, and fire pits, but no showers or RV hookups. Cost is $10 per night; reservations are not accepted, but the campground rarely fills.

From Cortez, take U.S. 160 south to C.R. G (McElmo Canyon Rd.), and follow signs into Utah and the monument. The other five sites are difficult to find, and you'll need to obtain detailed driving directions and check on current road conditions before setting out. Summer temperatures can reach over 100°F (38°C), and water supplies are limited—so take your own and carry a canteen, even on short walks. Bug repellent is advised, as gnats can be a nuisance in late spring.

The visitor center/ranger station is open daily from 8am to 5pm year-round, and trails are open from sunrise to sunset. Admission for up to a week costs $6 per vehicle or $3 per person on bike or foot. For advance information, contact Hovenweep National Monument, McElmo Route, Cortez, CO 81321 (📞 970/ 562-4282 or 435/719-2100; www.nps.gov/hove).

5 Telluride

126 miles N of Durango, 127 miles S of Grand Junction

This was one seriously rowdy town a century ago—in fact, this is where Butch Cassidy robbed his first bank, in 1889. Incorporated with the boring name of Columbia in 1878, the mining town assumed its present name the following decade. Some say the name came from tellurium, a gold-bearing ore, while others insist the name really means "to hell you ride," referring to the town's boisterous nature.

Telluride became a National Historic District in 1964, and in 1968 entrepreneur Joe Zoline set to work on a "winter recreation area second to none." The Telluride Ski Company opened its first runs in 1972, and Telluride was a boomtown again. Telluride's first summer festivals (bluegrass in June, film in Sept) were celebrated the following year. Today, the resort, at 8,745 feet elevation, is a year-round destination for mountain bikers, skiers, anglers, and hikers.

ESSENTIALS

GETTING THERE   By Car Telluride is located on Colo. 145. From Cortez, follow Colo. 145 northeast for 73 miles. From the north (Montrose), turn west off U.S. 550 at Ridgway, onto Colo. 62. Proceed 25 miles to Placerville, and turn left (southeast) onto Colo. 145. Thirteen miles ahead is a junction—a right turn will take you to Cortez, but for Telluride, continue straight ahead 4 miles to the end of a box canyon. From Durango, in summer take U.S. 550 north to Colo. 62, and follow the directions above; in winter it's best to take the route through Cortez and avoid Red Mountain Pass above Silverton.

By Plane   Telluride Airport (📞 **970/728-5051**), 5 miles west of Telluride atop a plateau at 9,078 feet, is served year-round by **Great Lakes Airline** (📞 800/ 554-5111) from Denver and **America West** (📞 800/235-9292) from Phoenix. In winter, **American Airlines** (📞 800/433-7300) provides flights from Dallas and Chicago; and **Continental Airlines** (📞 800/525-0280) provides service from Los Angeles, Newark, and Houston.

VISITOR INFORMATION Contact **Telluride & Mountain Village Convention & Visitors Bureau,** 630 W. Colorado Ave. (P.O. Box 1009), Telluride, CO 81435 (📞 **888/605-2578;** www.visittelluride.com). The **Telluride Visitor Information Center,** open daily from 9am to 6pm, can be found at the corner of West Colorado Avenue and Davis Street, on the west side of town.

GETTING AROUND The city is located on the San Miguel River, where it flows out of a box canyon formed by the 14,000-foot peaks of the San Juan Mountains. Colo. 145 enters town from the west and becomes Colorado Avenue, the main street.

With restaurants, shops, and attractions within easy walking distance of most lodging facilities, many visitors leave their cars parked and use their feet. However, if you do want to ride there's a free town shuttle in winter and summer. Telluride Mountain Village, at 9,500 feet, can be reached in winter and summer by a free gondola, operating daily from 7am to midnight. Motorists can take Mountain Village Boulevard off Colo. 145, a mile south of the Telluride junction.

Budget (© 800/527-0700 or 970/728-4642) and **National** (© 800/227-7368 or 970/728-9380) provide car rentals, including vans and four-wheel-drive vehicles.

FAST FACTS   The hospital, **Telluride Medical Center,** with a 24-hour emergency room, is at 500 S. Pacific Ave. (© **970/728-3848**). The **post office** is at 150 S. Willow St.; call the U.S. Postal Service (© **800/275-8777;** www. usps.com) for hours and other information. For **road conditions,** call © **877/315-7623.**

SPECIAL EVENTS   Telluride Wine Festival, late June; Chamber Music Festival, mid-August; Mushroom Festival, fourth weekend in August; Imogene Pass Run, early September; Oktoberfest, early Oct. See also "The Festival Scene," below.

DOWNHILL SKIING & SNOWBOARDING

The elegant European-style Mountain Village, built in 1987, offers a fascinating contrast to the laid-back community of artists, shopkeepers, and dropouts in the 1870s Victorian mining town of Telluride below. Located midmountain at an elevation of 9,450 feet, the Mountain Village offers ski-in/ski-out accommodations; a variety of slope-side restaurants including Gorrono Ranch, a historic homestead; spectacular scenery; and—of course—great skiing.

The mountain's **South Face,** which drops sharply from the summit to the town of Telluride, is characterized by steep moguls, tree-and-glade skiing, and challenging groomed pitches for experts and advanced intermediates. **Lift 4,** which rises from the Mountain Village Resort, caters to intermediate skiers. The broad, gentle slopes of the **Meadows** stretch to the foot of Sunshine Peak. This part of the mountain, with trails over 2½ miles long devoted entirely to novice skiers, is served by a high-speed quad chair. Average annual snowfall is 325 inches (27 ft.). The gently rolling slopes of **Ute Park** (Lift 11) serve as the beginner training area, while **Prospect** (Lift 12) accesses intermediate and expert terrain. **Gold Hill** (Lift 14) offers intermediate and expert skiers an expanse of steep terrain as well as breathtaking views.

In all, Telluride offers more than 1,700 acres of skiable terrain. The lift-served vertical drop is an impressive 3,530 feet from the 12,255-foot summit. The mountain has 84 trails served by 16 lifts (two high-speed gondolas, seven high-speed quads, two triples, two doubles, two surface lifts, and one Magic Carpet). Of the trails, 24% are rated for beginners, 38% for intermediates, and 38% for experts. The longest run here, at 4½ miles, is **Galloping Goose,** but for some of the most spectacular views in Colorado, ski the aptly-named run **See Forever.** Helicopter skiing is also available (© **970/835-5050**), and Telluride has one of the top **snowboarding parks** in Colorado, offering more than 13 acres of terrain.

Full-day lift tickets cost about $70 for adults, $40 for children 5 to 12, $50 for seniors 65 and older, and are free for children under 6. Rates over the Christmas holidays are higher. Ski and snowboarding lessons are offered, as well as child care. The resort is usually open daily from Thanksgiving to early April.

For additional information, contact **Telluride Ski and Golf Company,** 565 Mountain Village Blvd., Telluride, CO 81435 (© **800/801-4832** or 970/728-6900; www.tellurideskiresort.com).

OTHER WINTER ACTIVITIES

In addition to skiing at Telluride Ski Resort, there are plenty of other opportunities for cold-weather adventures in the Telluride area. Much of it takes place at **Town Park,** at the east end of town (© **970/728-3071;** www.town.telluride. co.us), where there are groomed cross-country trails, daytime sledding and tubing at Firecracker Hill, and free ice skating. There's also free ice skating at the outdoor rink in the Mountain Village (© **970/728-8000**). Skate rentals are available at local sporting-goods stores. The **River Corridor Trail** follows the San Miguel River from Town Park to the valley floor. Popular with bikers and hikers in warm weather, it's perfect for cross-country skiing and skate-skiing after the snow falls.

The Mountain Village at Telluride Ski Resort (see above) has 30km of **Nordic trails,** which connect with 20km of groomed trails at Town Park and River Corridor Trail, giving cross-country skiers a total of 50km. **Cross-country and snowshoe tours** are offered by Skyline Guest Ranch in Mountain Village (© **888/754-1126**) at a cost of $45 per person. For Nordic skiers who really want to put some miles behind them, there's the **San Juan Hut System,** providing backcountry huts with bunks, wood stoves and wood, and kitchens. Hut rental is $25 per night (see "Mountain Biking," below).

Guided snowmobile tours ranging from 2 hours to all day, with rates starting at about $125 for one rider on one machine, are offered by several local companies including **Dave's Mountain Tours** (© **970/728-9749;** www.telluridetours. com). Those who want to (and can afford to) take a helicopter to some of the best powder skiing available should contact **Telluride Helitrax** (© **866/435-4754** or 970/728-8377; www.helitrax.net), with rates for a five- or six-run day of about $795 per person.

WARM-WEATHER & YEAR-ROUND ACTIVITIES

Telluride isn't just a ski town—there's a wide variety of year-round outdoor activities. **Town Park** (see above) is home to the community's various festivals. It also has a public outdoor pool, open in summer, plus tennis courts, sand volleyball courts, a small outdoor basketball court, a skateboarding ramp, playing fields, picnic area, and fishing pond (see "Fishing," below). A campground for tent and car campers, open from May 15 to October 15, has 34 sites, showers ($2) but no RV hookups, and costs $12 to $15 per night.

There are a number of outfitting companies in the Telluride area. Our favorite for summer adventures is **Telluride Outside,** 121 W. Colorado Ave. (© **800/831-6230** or 970/728-3895; www.tellurideoutside.com). Equipment rentals are available throughout Telluride and Mountain Village. You'll find mountain bikes, fishing gear, camping equipment, and inflatable kayaks at a number of locations operated by **Telluride Sports** (© **800/828-7547;** www.telluride sports.com). Additional choices are listed in the Telluride Visitor Guide and online at **www.visittelluride.com**.

FISHING   There's excellent fishing in the San Miguel River through Telluride, but it's even better in nearby alpine lakes, including Silver Lake, reached by foot in Bridal Veil Basin, and Trout and Priest lakes, about 12 miles south via Colo. 145. At Town Park there's the Kids Fishin' Pond for children 12 and under, which is stocked Memorial Day to Labor Day.

Equipment, licenses, and fly-fishing instruction are offered by **Telluride Outside** (see above), which offers a walk-and-wade trip for two costing about $225 for a half-day and $425 for a full day.

FOUR-WHEELING To see old ghost towns, mining camps, and spectacular mountain scenery from the relative comfort of a bouncing four-wheel-drive vehicle, join **Telluride Outside** (see above) or **Dave's Mountain Tours** (see "Other Winter Activities," above). A variety of trips are offered, including rides over the 13,000-foot Imogene Pass jeep road, with prices for full-day trips about $100 for adults and $80 for children 12 and younger. Half-day trips are about $70 and $50, respectively.

GOLF The 18-hole par-71 **Telluride Golf Course** is located at Telluride Mountain Village (© 970/728-2606 or 970/728-6157). Greens fees with the required cart are $165 from July through Labor Day, $145 at other times.

HIKING & MOUNTAINEERING The mountains around Telluride offer innumerable opportunities for hiking, mountaineering, and backpacking. Sporting-goods stores and the visitor center have maps of trails in the Telluride area. Especially popular are the easy 4-mile (round-trip) **Bear Creek Canyon Trail** ☆, which starts at the end of South Pine Street and leads to a picturesque waterfall; the **Jud Wiebe Trail** that begins at the north end of Aspen Street and does a 2.7-mile loop above the town, offering views of Bridal Veil Falls, the town, and ski area; and the 1.8-mile (one-way) hike to the top of **Bridal Veil Falls,** which starts at the east end of Telluride Canyon.

HORSEBACK RIDING One of the best ways to see this spectacular country is by horse. **Roudy's Telluride Horseback Adventures** (© 800/828-7547 or 970/728-9611; www.ridewithroudy.com) has "gentle horses for gentle people and fast horses for fast people, and for people who don't like to ride, horses that don't like to be rode." Another good company is **Many Ponies Outfit** (© 970/728-6278;** www.manyponiesoutfit.com). Rates are about $60 to $70 for a 2-hour ride, $85 to $95 for a half-day ride, and $110 to $130 for a full day in the saddle.

MOUNTAIN BIKING Telluride is a major mountain-biking center. The **San Juan Hut System** links Telluride with Moab, Utah, via a 206-mile-long network of backcountry dirt roads. Every 35 miles is a primitive cabin, with bunks, a wood stove, propane cooking stove, and cooking gear. The route, open to mountain bikers from June through September, is appropriate for intermediate level riders in good physical condition, and an advanced technical single track is found near the huts for more experienced cyclists. Cost for riders who plan to make the whole trip is about $475, which includes use of the six huts, three meals daily, sleeping bags at each hut, and maps and trail descriptions. Shorter trips, guide services, and vehicle shuttles are also available. For information contact San Juan Hut System, P.O. Box 773, Ridgeway, CO 81432 (© 970/626-3033; www.sanjuanhuts.com).

Several companies, including **Telluride Outside,** offer guided downhill tours, with rates starting at about $75 per person, including a bike. Mountain-bike rentals are available throughout town, with rates of about $25 per day for basic 21-speed bikes, going up to about $40 per day for full-suspension and racing bikes.

SEEING THE SIGHTS

The best way to see the Telluride National Historic District, examine its hundreds of historic buildings, and get a feel for the West of the late 1800s is to take to the streets. Either follow the **walking tour** described in the *Telluride Visitor's Guide,* available at the Telluride Visitor Information Center (see "Visitor Information," above), or rent a mini-disk player with a disk and accompanying map at the Telluride Historical Museum (see below) for one of the recorded **audio walking tours** of Telluride. Cost of the audio tour rental is $7, and there are five tours available, each concentrating on a different part of the community.

Among the buildings you'll see are the **San Miguel County Courthouse,** Colorado Avenue at Oak Street, built in 1887 and still in use today. A block north and west, at Columbia Avenue and Aspen Street, is the **L. L. Nunn House,** home of the late-19th-century mining engineer who created the first high-voltage alternating-current power plant in the world. Two blocks east of Fir Street, on Galena Avenue at Spruce Street, is **St. Patrick's Catholic Church,** built in 1895, whose wooden Stations of the Cross figures were carved in Austria's Tyrol region. Perhaps Telluride's most famous landmark is the **New Sheridan Hotel** and the **Sheridan Opera House,** opposite the County Courthouse at Colorado and Oak. The hotel, built in 1895, rivaled Denver's famed Brown Palace Hotel in service and cuisine in its early days. The exquisite Opera House, added in 1914, boasts a Venetian scene painted on its roll curtain.

Colorado's highest waterfall (365 ft.) can be seen from the east end of Colorado Avenue. **Bridal Veil Falls** freezes in winter, then slowly melts in early spring, creating a dramatic effect. Perched at the top edge of the falls is a National Historic Landmark, a hydroelectric power plant that served area mines in the late 1800s. Recently restored and once again supplying power to the community, it's accessible by hiking or driving a switchback, four-wheel-drive road.

Telluride Historical Museum ★★   This fine museum should be the first stop in Telluride for anyone interested in learning about the history of the Old West and seeing its fascinating Victorian architecture. Built in 1896 as the community hospital, this beautifully restored facility contains a collection of some 9,000 artifacts and 1,400 historic photos that show what Telluride was like when the likes of Butch Cassidy stalked the streets. Exhibits include hard rock mining, with displays of mining equipment and models of mines and mills; the narrow-gauge railroad; the area's Ute Indian heritage; the history of medical facilities and treatments in Telluride (this was the town hospital, after all); and the development of the town's AC electric power—the world's first AC-generating plant was built here in the 1890s. There is also a replica of a local mining family's cabin in the early 1900s, plus exhibits on the town's Victorian architecture and Telluride's emergence as a major outdoor recreation destination. You'll learn about train and bank robber Cassidy and other historic figures from Telluride's past, and see some of the fancy dresses worn by Big Billie, one of the community's leading madams during the town's red-light days. The museum store is a good source for books on the area's history—an especially good local read is *Tomboy Bride* by Harriet Backus—and you can rent equipment for a self-guided audio tour of Telluride (see above). Allow 1 to 2 hours.

201 W. Gregory Ave., at the top of Fir St. (ℂ) **970/728-3344.** www.telluridemuseum.com. Admission $5 adults, $3 seniors and students, free for children under 5. Tues–Sat 11am–5pm.

THE FESTIVAL SCENE

Telluride must be the most festival-happy town in America, and visitors come from around the world to see the finest new films, hear the best musicians, and even pick the most exotic mushrooms. In addition to the phone numbers listed, you can get additional details and often tickets from **Telluride Visitor Services** ((ℂ) **800/525-3455;** www.visittelluride.com).

The **Telluride Film Festival** ✯✯, an influential festival within the film indus-try that takes place over Labor Day weekend, has premiered some of the finest films produced in recent years (*The Crying Game, The Piano,* and *Sling Blade* are just a few examples). What truly sets it apart, however, is the casual interaction between stars and attendees. Open-air films and seminars are free to all. Call (② **970/728-4640**) for further information.

MountainFilm, which takes place every Memorial Day weekend, brings together filmmakers, writers, and outdoor enthusiasts to celebrate mountains, adventure, and the environment. Four days are filled with films, seminars, and presentations; recent guests have included Sir Edmund Hillary. Call ② **970/ 728-4123** for tickets and information.

The **Telluride Bluegrass Festival** ✯✯ is one of the most intense and renowned bluegrass, folk, and country jam sessions in the United States. Held over 4 days during mid- to late June in conjunction with the Bluegrass Academy, recent lineups have featured Mary Chapin Carpenter, Mark O'Connor, Shawn Colvin, and James Taylor. Call ② **800/624-2422** for details.

Telluride Jazz Celebration, a 2-day event in early August, is marked by day concerts in Town Park and evening happenings in downtown saloons. Recent performers have included Leon Russell, Marleena Shaw, Stanley Jordan, and Terence Blanchard. Call ② **970/728-7009** for information.

Telluride Mushroom Festival draws fungophiles in late August for a week-end of wild mushroom forays into the surrounding forests, plus lectures on edi-ble, psychoactive, and poisonous mushrooms, and plenty of mushroom tasting. There's even a mushroom parade! Call ② **303/296-9359** for details.

Nothing Fest, a nonevent begun in the early 1990s, is just that—nothing special happens, and it doesn't happen all over town. It's usually scheduled in mid- to late July. When founder Dennis Wrestler was asked how long the festi-val would continue, he responded, "How can you cancel something that doesn't happen?" Admission is free, and you can get all the noninformation you need from Telluride Visitor Services (see above, or don't).

WHERE TO STAY

Telluride's lodging rates probably have more different "seasons" than anywhere else in Colorado. Generally speaking, you'll pay top dollar for a room over the Christmas holidays, during the film and bluegrass festivals, and at certain other peak times. Nonholiday skiing is a bit cheaper, summertime lodging (except for festival times) is cheaper yet, and you may find some real bargains in spring and fall. The key to finding inexpensive lodging and avoiding crowds is timing; unless you particularly want to attend the Bluegrass Festival, plan your trip another time. You're also much more likely to find attractive package deals on skiing and other activities if you go during quieter times, and not on weekends.

Telluride has a wide variety of lodging options, including B&Bs, hotels, con-dominiums, and private homes. Many are managed by **Resort Quest** (② **877/ 826-8043;** www.telluridelodging.com) and **Alpine Lodging** (② **800/376-9769;** www.alpinelodging.com). Perhaps the best way to book lodging, however, is with **Telluride Visitor Services** (② **888/605-2578;** www.visittelluride.com), which represents all accommodations in the area.

EXPENSIVE

Camel's Garden Resort Hotel ✯✯   This luxury property, with 30 rooms and suites plus six condo units, has a perfect location—it's ski-in/ski-out, only steps from the town gondola, and also within 2 short blocks of the main shopping and dining section of historic Telluride. The hotel rooms—even the smallest, least expensive ones—are spacious, with the feel of upscale condo units, and all have high-speed Internet and two-line phones with voice mail. All units have cherry-oak furnishings, Italian marble bathrooms with oversized tubs, CD players, and gas fireplaces. All the condos and suites and all but four of the hotel rooms have balconies, with views of either the town or mountains. Rooms have quality beds (mostly kings) on pedestals (step stools are available on request). The simple but tasteful decor includes nature prints and black-and-white photos of the area. The one-, two-, three-, and four-bedroom condos are huge, with complete kitchens, washer/dryers, jetted tubs and showers, and heated towel racks.

The continental breakfast includes the usual fresh fruit, juices, coffee, tea, and cereals, plus excellent baked goods from an on-site bakery. Afternoon refreshments are served during ski season. Other amenities include a 25-foot outdoor jetted hot tub that offers great views of the nearby mountains, a sporting goods store, and ski storage and ski valet services. The entire property is nonsmoking.

250 W. San Juan Ave. (P.O. Box 4145), Telluride, CO 81435. ℂ **888/772-2635** or 970/728-9300. Fax 970/728-0433. www.camelsgarden.com. 36 units. Ski season and festivals $245–$490 double hotel room and suite, $460–$1,164 condo; other times $155–$250 double hotel room and suite, $380–$765 condo. Rates include continental breakfast. AE, DC, DISC, MC, V. Free underground heated parking, height limit 6 ft. 4 in. (outside parking available for larger vehicles). **Amenities:** Restaurant (Continental); spa; Jacuzzi; steam room; laundry. *In room:* TV/VCR, dataport, safe deposit boxes available on request.

Hotel Telluride ⭐⭐   An upscale lodging choice for those who want pampering, the Hotel Telluride combines elements of the American West with fine European hotels to give it the look and feel of a refined hotel of the Victorian-era American West. Rooms are elegantly decorated, with plush seating, refrigerators, two phones and a large desk, bathrobes, CD players, and other amenities, and boast extremely comfortable and luxurious feather beds. All units have balconies or patios with magnificent views of the surrounding mountains, and there's a splendid spa offering aromatherapy treatments and other services. The two suites have gas fireplaces, large-screen televisions, and wet bars, and can be configured as one, two, or three bedroom units. The cooked-to-order breakfast buffet includes eggs, omelets, Belgian waffles, pancakes, and crepes.

199 N. Cornet St. (P.O. Box 1740), Telluride, CO 81435. ℂ **866/468-3504** or 970/369-1188. Fax 970/369-1292. www.thehoteltelluride.com. 59 units. Winter holidays $379–$459 double; other times $209–$279 double; suites from $499. Rates include buffet breakfast. AE, DC, DISC, MC, V. Small pets accepted ($25 fee). **Amenities:** Restaurant (tavern); spa; steam room; laundry. *In room:* TV w/pay movies, dataport, fridge, hair dryer, iron, bathrobes.

Inn at Lost Creek ⭐⭐⭐   This luxurious boutique inn at the base of the slopes in Mountain Village offers the best of both worlds—all the amenities of an upscale resort hotel with the charm and intimacy of a small inn. Staying here is certainly not for those pinching pennies, but when you consider all that you get for your money, it's really quite a good deal. The overall theme is rustic elegance, which begins in the lobby, with its massive timbered beams and handsome two-sided stone fireplace, and continues throughout the restaurant and into the rooms. Each unit is individually decorated, with an Old World feel, and all boast hand-textured walls, fine art photography, marble baths, jetted tubs, steam showers, clothes washers and dryers, and high speed Internet. Units range from studios—with one queen-sized bed and a fully-equipped kitchenette—to two-bedroom suites, with a full kitchen, two bathrooms, and two TVs. In between are several one-bedroom styles. All except the studios have stone fireplaces.

It would be difficult to find some service that is not provided at the Inn at Lost Creek, from pre-arrival trip planning with the concierge to complimentary boot warming and waxing and de-burring of skis. There is twice-daily maid service, turn-down service, bell service, a ski and golf valet, and airport transportation. Two eight-person whirlpool tubs are perched on the inn's roof, offering spectacular mountain views. The excellent restaurant serves three meals daily.

119 Lost Creek Lane, Telluride, CO 81435. © **888/601-5678** or 970/728-5678. Fax 970/728-7953. www. innatlostcreek.com, 32 units. Mid-Dec through Mar $415–$1,360; the rest of the year $205–$695 double. AE, DC, DISC, MC, V. Valet parking $15 per night; free self-parking nearby. **Amenities:** Restaurant (New American/Regional), bar; golf course nearby; health club & spa; sports equipment rentals/sales; concierge; limited room service; *In room:* A/C, TV/VCR, dataport, kitchen/kitchenette, hairdryer, iron, safe, bathrobes/slippers, washer/dryer.

MODERATE

Ice House Lodge and Condominiums   A full-service lodging just half a block from the Oak Street chairlift, the Ice House offers casual and comfortable accommodations in a European alpine style. Stairs and an elevator ascend from the ground-floor entrance to the lobby, which is furnished with simple Southwestern pieces. The decor carries to the guest rooms, which contain a king-size bed and sleeper sofa or two full-size beds, European comforters, custom-made light wood furniture, and great mountain views from private decks. Thirty-nine of the rooms have shower/tub combos with oversized tubs; three rooms have showers only. The one-, two-, and three-bedroom condominium units have full kitchens, washers and dryers, two bathrooms, and a large deck. Guests also have access to the Atmosphere Spa nearby in Ice House's sister property, the Camel's Garden Resort Hotel. VCRs are available on request.

310 S. Fir St. (P.O. Box 2909), Telluride, CO 81435. © **800/544-3436** or 970/728-6300. Fax 970/728-6358. www.icehouselodge.com. 42 units. Ski season and festivals $215–$495 double lodge room and suite, $400– $1,050 condo; other times $145–$260 double lodge room and suite, $330–$515 condo. Higher rates on some festival weekends. Rates include continental breakfast and afternoon refreshments. AE, DC, DISC, MC, V. **Amenities:** Pool (half indoors and half outdoors); hot tub; steam room; limited room service; massage; laundry service. *In room:* TV, minibar.

New Sheridan Hotel ☆   The pride of Telluride when it was built in 1895, the New Sheridan reached the peak of its fame in 1902 when presidential candidate William Jennings Bryan delivered a speech from a platform outside. Completely renovated in 1995, the decor of this delightful historic hotel, located a few blocks from the slopes, still proclaims its Victorian heritage while introducing the comforts of the modern age. Rollaways or day beds are available; some units have whirlpool tubs. The suites, in a separate building, are condominium-style units, with a full kitchen, living room, and bedrooms. The Sheridan lounge, with an Austrian-made cherrywood bar, is on the hotel's first floor. Smoking is not permitted.

231 W. Colorado Ave. (P.O. Box 980), Telluride, CO 81435. © **800/200-1891** or 970/728-4351. Fax 970/728-5024. www.newsheridan.com. 32 units (24 with private bathroom). $90–$300 double; $200–$425 suite. Rates include full breakfast. AE, DC, MC, V. **Amenities:** Lounge. *In room:* TV, dataport.

INEXPENSIVE

The Victorian Inn ☆ *Value*   Built in 1976, in keeping with the turn-of-the-20th-century flavor of the town, the well-maintained and service-oriented Victorian offers a pleasant alternative to the seemingly hundreds of condos that populate Telluride. The spacious and recently renovated rooms, decorated with Victorian-style furnishings, are fully carpeted and have individually controlled heating, one or two queen beds, and refrigerators. Two units have kitchenettes, and there is also a honeymoon suite and a cottage. The continental breakfast includes fresh-baked pastries, coffee, juice, assorted teas, and hot cocoa. The inn is located a half block from Main Street, the free gondola, and ski lift no. 8. Smoking is not permitted.

401 W. Pacific Ave. (P.O. Box 217), Telluride, CO 81435. ℂ 800/611-9893 or 970/728-6601. Fax 970/728-3233. www.tellurideinn.com. 32 units. $89–$249 double (10% discount for mentioning Frommer's). Children 12 and under stay free in parent's room. Rates include continental breakfast. AE, DC, DISC, MC, V. **Amenities:** Hot tub; dry sauna; coin-op laundry. *In room:* TV, dataport, fridge, hair dryer.

WHERE TO DINE

Telluride lives by its seasons, and some restaurants will close for a few weeks in the slow seasons, generally spring and fall. Restaurant information is available online at **www.diningintelluride.com**. A local ordinance prohibits smoking in restaurants and other public buildings.

EXPENSIVE

Cosmopolitan ★★ CREATIVE AMERICAN   An elegant fine-dining restaurant, the Cosmopolitan is also casual enough for a relaxing meal after a hard day on the slopes. The decor is modern and comfortable, and there's a delightful enclosed patio. The dinner menu includes a variety of dishes—beef, fish, lamb, duck, and vegetarian—all prepared with an innovative flair by chef/owner Chad Scothorn. Recommended dishes are the barbecued salmon with crispy corn-potato ravioli, and the grilled dry-aged rib-eye served with chive-horseradish mashed potatoes. The Cosmopolitan's Tasting Cellar offers guests an intimate six-course dinner in their wine cellar. The wine list—there are more than 200 wines—has received the "Award of Excellence" from *Wine Spectator* magazine.

300 W. San Juan Ave. ℂ 970/728-1292. www.cosmotelluride.com. Reservations recommended. Main courses $19–$28. AE, MC, V. Daily 6pm–close.

MODERATE

Eagles Bar & Grille CREATIVE AMERICAN   This busy restaurant/bar is a favorite gathering spot for locals, who get there in time for the happy-hour drink specials and grab a chair near the floor-to-ceiling windows that look out onto Colorado Avenue. Or maybe they just gaze up at the two carved wooden life-size eagles. Lunch offerings include half-pound burgers, entrees such as spicy chicken fettuccine, and a variety of creative sandwiches, such as fajita cheese steak. Dinner entrees run the gamut from an 8-ounce filet mignon with burgundy demi-glace and garlic mashed potatoes to pad Thai rice noodles in a spicy peanut, ginger, and garlic sauce. Brick-oven pizzas—including Thai chicken, barbecued chicken, and goat cheese—are available all day.

100 W. Colorado Ave. ℂ 970/728-0886. Lunch items $6.50–$15; dinner main courses $10–$22. AE, DISC, MC, V. Daily 11:30am–10pm (lunch until 3pm, happy hour 3–5pm, dinner from 5pm).

Fat Alley Barbecue *Value* BARBECUE/AMERICAN   A favorite of local ski bums with big appetites and near-empty wallets, Fat Alley offers a variety of hickory-smoked meats, sandwiches, burgers, and vegetarian items. In a small, simply decorated, cafe-style restaurant, it delivers spicy pork spare ribs or beef ribs by the rack or half rack, and whole, half, or quarter roast chicken. Sandwiches include smoked brisket, chicken, or pork shoulder; and vegetarian entrees include a ziti and black-bean plate. Free in-town delivery is available.

122 S. Oak St. ℂ 970/728-3985. Reservations not accepted. Main courses $5.75–$19. AE, MC, V. Daily 11am–10pm.

INEXPENSIVE

Maggie's Bakery & Cafe ✦ AMERICAN   The atmosphere here is simple, with oak tables and antique cookie jars, and the cuisine is geared toward those who appreciate home-baked breads and pastries, and hearty sandwiches. Breakfast dishes include traditional bacon and eggs with potatoes and fresh-baked bread, pancakes, biscuits with sausage gravy, and fresh fruit. Lunch possibilities include large burgers on home-baked buns, a variety of deli and vegetarian sandwiches, pizzas, and soups.

217 E. Colorado Ave. ℭ **970/728-3334.** Reservations not accepted. Breakfast and lunch $3.50–$7.75. No credit cards. Daily 7:30am–3:30pm.

6 Ouray

73 miles N of Durango, 96 miles S of Grand Junction

Named for the greatest chief of the southern Ute tribe, whose homeland was in this area, Ouray, at an elevation of 7,760 feet, got its start in 1876 as a gold- and silver-mining camp. Within 10 years it had 1,200 residents, a school, a hospital, dozens of saloons and brothels, and even a few churches. Today Ouray retains much of its 19th-century charm, with many of its original buildings still standing. It offers visitors a restful getaway while serving as home base for exploring the beautiful San Juan Mountains, with peaks rising to over 14,000 feet.

ESSENTIALS

GETTING THERE   By Car   U.S. 550 runs through the heart of Ouray, paralleling the Uncompahgre River, and connecting it with Durango to the south and Montrose to the north. As you enter town from the north, the highway becomes Main Street. Above Third Avenue, U.S. 550 begins its climb up switchbacks to the Million Dollar Highway.

VISITOR INFORMATION   Stop at the **Ouray Visitor Center** beside the Ouray Hot Springs Pool, on U.S. 550 at the north end of town, open from 9am to 6pm daily; or contact the **Ouray Chamber Resort Association,** P.O. Box 145, Ouray, CO 81427 (ℭ **800/228-1876** or 970/325-4746; www.ouraycolorado.com). If you're planning a winter visit, be sure to ask about half-price skiing at Telluride when you stay in Ouray.

SPECIAL EVENTS   Ouray Ice Festival, mid-January; Evenings of History Lecture Series, early June; the Alpine Artists' Holiday, August; Ouray County Fair, early September; Oktoberfest, early October.

WHAT TO SEE & DO

The main summertime outdoor activity here is exploring the spectacularly beautiful mountains and forests by foot, mountain bike, horse, or four-wheel-drive vehicle. Our favorite local outfitter, which can arrange for a variety of outdoor adventures, is **Switzerland of America,** 226 Seventh Ave. (ℭ **800/432-5337** or 970/325-4484; www.soajeep.com), which also rents four-wheel-drive jeeps for about $130 per day. The company leads jeep tours into the high country ($50 per person half-day, $100 full day), and arranges horseback rides (starting at $60 per person for 2 hours), raft rides (about $65 per person for a half-day on the San Miguel River), and balloon rides ($175 for adults and half price for children 12 and under). Guided fishing trips are also available, along with shuttle service for hikers and mountain bikers; call for rates. Another local company offering jeep rentals and tours at similar rates is **Colorado West,** 701 Main St., Ouray (ℭ **800/648-5337** or 970/325-4014; www.coloradowesttours.com).

At the southwest corner of Ouray, at Oak Street above Third Avenue, the **Box Canyon Falls** *★★* (*©* **970/325-4464**) are among the most impressive in the Rockies. The Uncompahgre River tumbles 285 feet through—not over, *through*—a cliff: It's easy to get a feeling of vertigo as you study the spectacle. The trail to the bottom of the falls is easy; to the top it is moderate to strenuous. Admission to the area is $3 for adults and $1.50 for children 5 to 12. It's open daily 8am to 8pm or dark, whichever comes first.

Winter visitors will likely be basing themselves in Ouray to ski at Telluride or head out into the mountains on cross-country skis or snowshoes, but Ouray's main claim to winter fame is the **Ouray Ice Park,** located in the southwest corner of town off U.S. 550 (*©* **970/325-4288;** www.ourayicepark.com), which Ouray folks claim is the world's first park devoted exclusively to the sport of ice climbing. Climbing in the park is free and it's open at any time during the winter. Ice-climbing courses are offered by **San Juan Mountain Guides** (*©* **970/ 325-4925;** www.ourayclimbing.com); a 2-day basic ice-climbing course costs $305 and includes all equipment.

Bachelor-Syracuse Mine Tour *★★*

For a fun time where you'll actually learn something, we heartily recommend this trip into the underworld. A mine train takes visitors 3,350 feet inside Gold Hill, to see where some $8 million in gold, $90 million in silver, and $5 million in other minerals have been mined since silver was discovered here in 1884. Guides, many of them former miners, explain the mining process and equipment and recount the various legends of the mine. Also on the property is an operating blacksmith shop, plus streams where you can learn the technique of gold panning ($6.95 extra). An outdoor cafe serves an all-you-can-eat breakfast until noon ($6 adults, $4 children under 12) and Texas-style barbecue all day ($4.50–$8). The mine temperature is a cool 50°F (10°C), so jackets are recommended, even in summer. Allow about 1½ hours.

2 miles from Ouray via C.R. 14. *©* **800/227-8545** or 970/325-0220. www.bachelorsyracuse.com. Admission $16 adults, $7.95 children 3–11, free for children under 3. Mid-May to mid-Sept 9am–5pm; shorter hours at the beginning and end of this period. Closed July 4th. Reservations recommended, especially July–Aug.

Ouray County Museum

Lodged in the original Miners' Hospital, which was completed in 1887 and operated by the Sisters of Mercy, this large three-story museum is packed to the rafters with fascinating exhibits from Ouray's past. There are more than two dozen exhibit rooms, each having a different theme, plus many small displays and changing exhibits. You'll see pioneer and mining-era relics, items relating to railroad and other transportation modes of the 19th century, ranch artifacts, memorabilia of Chief Ouray and the Utes, early hospital equipment including some scary-looking medical devices, Victorian artifacts, and historic photos. Allow about an hour, and ask here for a walking-tour guide to the town's many historic buildings.

420 Sixth Ave. *©* **970/325-4576.** www.ouraycountyhistoricalsociety.org. Admission $5 adults, $1 children 6–12. June to mid-Sept daily 10am–noon and 2–6pm; shorter hours (call) Mar–May and mid-Sept through Nov. Closed Dec–Feb.

Ouray Hot Springs Pool & Fitness Center

This oval outdoor pool, 120 feet by 150 feet, holds nearly a million gallons of odorless mineral water. Spring water is cooled from 150°F (66°C) and there are three separate soaking sections, with temperatures ranging from 88° to 105°F (31°C–41°C). Also on the property is a fitness center, with aerobic exercise equipment including treadmills, a stair climber, a stationary bicycle, free weights, leg-press machines, and an

abdominal board. There's a picnic area and playground in an adjacent municipal park. Allow 1 to 2 hours.

U.S. 550, at the north end of Ouray. (📞 970/325-7076 or 970/325-7073. Pool only $8 adults, $6 students
7–17 and seniors 65 and over, and $3 children 3–6, free children under 3; fitness center only $8 for everyone
except $6 seniors 65 and older; both pool and fitness center $10 everyone. June–Aug daily 10am–10pm;
Sept–May daily noon–9pm.

WHERE TO STAY

Rates here are usually highest during summer and at Christmastime. A good
chain motel is the **Comfort Inn,** 191 Fifth Ave., Ouray, CO 81427 (📞 **800/
228-5150** or 970/325-7203), with rates for two from $97 to $128 in summer
and lower rates at other times. Room tax is 7% plus $2 per night lodging fee.

Columbus House Bed & Breakfast   This handsome Victorian building was
constructed in 1898 as a saloon with what was then called a "female rooming
attachment" on the second floor, and almost immediately neighboring businesses and citizens began complaining about the women's line of work. Things
have changed, and today this former house of sin is a well-kept budget bed-and-
breakfast inn, where those who don't mind sharing a bathroom can spend the
night in a small but delightfully decorated room, with a good firm queen bed
and Victorian-style wallpaper and furnishings, including some genuine antiques.
Guests share a sitting room with a TV, and breakfast is served downstairs at the
Silver Nugget Cafe (see "Where to Dine," below). All rooms are on the second
floor, accessible by stairs only. Smoking is not permitted.

746 Main St. (P.O. Box 31), Ouray, CO 81427. (📞 970/325-4551. Fax 970/325-7388. www.colorado-bnb.com/
columbus. 6 units, all share bathroom with shower only. $59–$69 double. Rates include full breakfast. MC, V.
Closed mid-Oct to mid-May. Children over 12 accepted. *In room:* No phone.

Ouray Victorian Inn   Located in Ouray's National Historic District, this
handsome Victorian-style inn, completely remodeled in spring 2002, offers spacious rooms with outstanding views and lots of historic charm, plus a sun deck
and playground. There's a variety of choices, including rooms with one king-size
bed, units with two queen beds, and lavish two-room suites. In addition, the
management rents privately owned cabins, town houses, and apartment-type
units with full kitchens (call for rates).

50 Third Ave. (P.O. Box 1812), Ouray, CO 81427. (📞 800/846-8729 or 970/325-7222. Fax 970/325-7225.
www.ouraylodging.com. 38 units. $65–$100 double; $80–$120 suite. Rates include buffet breakfast in winter. AE, DC, MC, V. Amenities: 2 outdoor hot tubs; playground. *In room:* TV, coffeemaker.

St. Elmo Hotel ★★   An 1898 town landmark restored to Victorian splendor,
the St. Elmo has an old-fashioned lobby that's a meeting place for locals and
guests alike. All the units here ooze historic charm, and contain many original
furnishings. Each of the six standard rooms has one queen-size bed. They're
average size for a historic hotel, which means they're a bit small compared to a
modern chain; some have shower/tub combos and a few have showers only. The
suites are larger, with separate sitting areas and stained glass, polished wood, and
brass trim throughout; the Cascade Suite has a king-size bed plus a second bedroom with a double bed. There's a TV in the parlor and the well-regarded Bon
Ton Restaurant (see "Where to Dine" below) is on the premises. Smoking is not
permitted.

426 Main St. (P.O. Box 667), Ouray, CO 81427. (📞 866/243-1502 or 970/325-4951. Fax 970/325-0348. www.
stelmohotel.com. 9 units. $85–$120 double; $100–$140 suite. Rates include full breakfast buffet and afternoon wine-and-cheese social hour. AE, DC, DISC, MC, V. Not suitable for children under 10. **Amenities:**
Restaurant (steak/Italian); hot tub; sauna. *In room:* No phone.

WHERE TO DINE

Bon Ton Restaurant ★★ STEAK/ITALIAN   A fixture in Ouray for more than a century—it was in another location before moving into the St. Elmo Hotel basement in 1898—the Bon Ton is one of Ouray's finest restaurants. With stone outer walls, hardwood floors, and reproduction antique furnishings, it carries a Western Victorian appeal. The menu, which varies nightly, includes a variety of pasta dishes, such as our choice, the lasagna Luciano—a classic seven-layer, four-cheese lasagna with spinach and either marinara or meat sauce. We also recommend the beef, including the charbroiled 8-ounce Colorado beef tenderloin, wrapped in bacon and served with a Bordelaise sauce and herb butter; and the veal piccata—thinly sliced veal sautéed with butter, shallots, mushrooms, capers, white wine, and lemon juice, and served with pasta and garden vegetables. There's an exceptionally good wine list, along with a children's menu and an elaborate brunch offered each Sunday.

In the St. Elmo Hotel, 426 Main St. ℂ **970/325-4951**. www.stelmohotel.com. Reservations recommended. Main courses $10–$28. AE, DC, DISC, MC, V. Sun 9:30am–1pm; daily 5:30–9:30pm.

Silver Nugget Cafe AMERICAN/MEXICAN   A busy, contemporary eatery, the Silver Nugget occupies a historic building at the north end of Ouray. You can get a Denver omelet or huevos rancheros for breakfast, and good burgers and a wide variety of deli-style sandwiches for lunch. The dinner menu runs the gamut from liver and onions and spaghetti with meat sauce to deep-fried Rocky Mountain rainbow trout and top sirloin steak; most dinner choices are under $10.

746 Main St. ℂ **970/325-4100**. Lunch $5.95–$9.95; dinner $6.95–$20. DC, MC, V. Summer daily 7am–9pm; call for winter hours.

7 Wolf Creek Ski Area

75 miles E of Durango, 65 miles W of Alamosa

Wolf Creek is famous throughout Colorado as the area that consistently has the most snow in the state—an annual average of 465 inches (almost 39 ft.).

One of the state's oldest ski areas, Wolf Creek has terrain for skiers of all ability levels, but especially intermediates. Expert skiers often leave the lift-served slopes to dive down the powder of the Water Fall Area. The Alberta Peak area offers extremely steep skiing and one of the most spectacular views of the peaks and pristine wilderness. Slopes are rated 20% beginner, 35% intermediate, 25% advanced, and 20% expert. Snowboarders are welcome in all areas of the resort.

In all, the area has 1,600 acres of terrain with 50 miles of trails, and a vertical drop of 1,604 feet from the 11,904-foot summit. The mountain has 50 trails served by six lifts (one quad, two triple chairs, two doubles, and a Magic Carpet). Wolf Creek Lodge is a day lodge with restaurant and bar service. The Sports Center offers ski sales and rentals.

Contact **Wolf Creek Ski Area,** P.O. Box 2800, Pagosa Springs, CO 81147 (ℂ **970/264-5639** for information, or 800/775-9653 or 970/264-5629 for a ski report; www.wolfcreekski.com). Lift tickets cost $43 for adults, $25 for children 12 and under and seniors 65 and over. The resort is usually open from early November through mid-April, daily from 8:30am to 4pm.

WHERE TO STAY   Among nearby communities with lodging, dining, and other services is Pagosa Springs (zip 81147), 25 miles southwest of the ski area via U.S. 160. Lodging choices include the **Best Western Oak Ridge Lodge,** 158 Hot Springs Blvd. (ℂ **866/472-4672** or 970/264-4173), with rates of $62 to

$124 double; and **Super 8,** 34 Piedra Rd. (© **800/800-8000** or 970/731-4005), with double rates of $48 to $106. Room tax in Pagosa Springs is just under 9%.

For additional lodging choices and other area information, consult the **Pagosa Springs Area Chamber of Commerce,** P.O. Box 787, Pagosa Springs, CO 81147 (© **800/252-2204** or 970/264-2360; www.pagosaspringschamber. com). The chamber operates a **visitor center** on the south bank of the San Juan River at Hot Springs Boulevard, across from Town Park, which has picnic tables and a river walk. It's open from 8am to 5pm Monday through Friday, 10am to 2pm Saturday, and 1 to 5pm Sunday.

13

The Southern Rockies

If Colorado is the rooftop of America, then the southern Rockies are the peak of that roof. Some 30 of Colorado's fourteeners—14,000-plus-foot peaks—ring the area, and from Monarch Pass, at 11,312 feet, rivers flow in three directions.

Isolated from the rest of Colorado by its high mountains and rugged canyons, this region has historically bred proud, independent-minded people. In the 18th century, settlers came from Taos, New Mexico, and built some of the region's striking Spanish architecture. To this day, the influence of these Spanish settlers remains strong, particularly in the San Luis Valley.

Today these mountain and river towns have earned reputations as recreational capitals: Gunnison for fishing and hunting, Crested Butte for skiing and mountain biking, and Salida and Buena Vista for white-water rafting. Alamosa is within easy reach of numerous scenic attractions, including the remarkable Great Sand Dunes National Park and Preserve. In the foothills of the San Juan Range are the historic mining towns of Creede and Lake City, and in the tiny community of Antonito you can hop a narrow-gauge steam train for a trip back to a simpler (though smokier) time. This is a rugged and sparsely populated land, with numerous opportunities for seeing the wilds of mountain America at their best.

1 Gunnison & Curecanti National Recreation Area

196 miles SW of Denver, 161 miles W of Pueblo, 65 miles E of Montrose

A rough-and-ready Western town, Gunnison is where you go to get a hot shower and a good meal after a week of camping, hiking, boating, or hunting in the rugged mountains and canyons in the surrounding area.

Utes began hunting here about 1650, and although Spanish explorers probably never penetrated this isolated region, mountain men, who were pursuing pelts, arrived by the 1830s. First mapped by U.S. Army captain John Gunnison in 1853, the town was established in 1874, soon growing into a ranching center and transportation hub for nearby silver and gold mines. Established in 1911, Western State College now has an enrollment of 2,400. In 1987 it became the first college in the United States with a certified technical-evacuation mountain-rescue team, and it maintains its certification with the Mountain Rescue Association into the 21st century. Ninety percent of the all-volunteer team is made up of college students, with the remainder coming from the community. Gunnison sits at an elevation of 7,681 feet and its population is about 5,400.

ESSENTIALS
GETTING THERE By Car Gunnison is located on U.S. 50, midway between Montrose and Salida. From Denver, the most direct route is U.S. 285

southwest to Poncha Springs, then west on U.S. 50. From Grand Junction, follow U.S. 50 through Montrose.

By Plane   The **Gunnison–Crested Butte Airport,** 711 Rio Grande Ave. (© **970/641-2304**), is just off U.S. 50, a few blocks south of downtown Gunnison. **United Express** (© **800/241-6522**) provides daily year-round service from Denver.

Alpine Express (© **800/822-4844** or 970/641-5074) provides shuttle service from the airport to Crested Butte, frequently in ski season, call to check on availability at other times. Reservations are required.

VISITOR INFORMATION   Contact the **Gunnison Country Chamber of Commerce,** 500 E. Tomichi Ave. (P.O. Box 36), Gunnison, CO 81230 (© **800/274-7580** or 970/641-1501; www.gunnisonchamber.com), which operates a visitor center at the same location, open Monday through Friday from 8am to 5pm. Another good source of information is the **Gunnison–Crested Butte Tourism Association** (© **800/215-2266**).

GETTING AROUND   The town lies along the southeast bank of the west-flowing Gunnison River. Tomichi Avenue (U.S. 50) runs east–west through town. Main Street (Colo. 135) intersects Tomichi Avenue in the center of town and proceeds north to Crested Butte.

Car-rental agencies include **Avis** (© 970/641-0263), **Budget** (© 970/641-4403), and **Hertz** (© 970/641-2881).

FAST FACTS   **Gunnison Valley Hospital,** with a 24-hour emergency room, is at 711 N. Taylor St. (© **970/641-1456**), 2 blocks east of Main Street and 6 blocks north of U.S. 50. The **post office** is located at 201 N. Wisconsin St. at Virginia Avenue; for hours and other information contact the U.S. Postal Service (© **800/275-8777;** www.usps.com). For **road conditions** (winter only) call © **877/315-7623** (in-state only).

SPECIAL EVENTS   Winter Carnival, late February; Annual Fireman's Concert, March; Cattlemen's Days, Colorado's oldest continually held rodeo, late July; Art in the Park, late July; Classic Car Show, late August; Sugar Plum Festival, late November; and the Parade of Lights, early December.

CURECANTI NATIONAL RECREATION AREA

Dams on the Gunnison River, just below Gunnison, have created a series of three very different reservoirs, extending 35 miles to the mouth of the Black Canyon of the Gunnison (see "Black Canyon of the Gunnison National Park," in chapter 11). **Blue Mesa Lake** (elevation 7,519 ft.), the easternmost (beginning 9 miles west of Gunnison), is the largest lake in Colorado when filled to capacity, and a watersports paradise popular for fishing, motorboating, sailboating, board sailing, and other activities. Fjordlike **Morrow Point Lake** (elevation 7,160 ft.) and **Crystal Lake** (elevation 6,755 ft.) fill long, serpentine canyons accessible only by precipitous trails and thus are limited to use by hand-carried boats. These lakes offer some of Colorado's best boating (permits cost $4 for 2 days, $10 for 14.)

There are two full-service marinas, offering fuel, supplies, and boat rentals. **Elk Creek Marina** is on Blue Mesa Lake, 16 miles west of Gunnison off U.S. 50 (© **970/641-0707;** www.bluemesalake.com). Rental rates are $14 to $16 per hour, $45 to $50 half-day, and $65 to $70 full day for small fishing boats with outboard motors. Pontoon boats cost $35 per hour, $135 half-day, and $185 full day. There's also a restaurant, Pappy's, at Elk Creek Marina, serving three meals

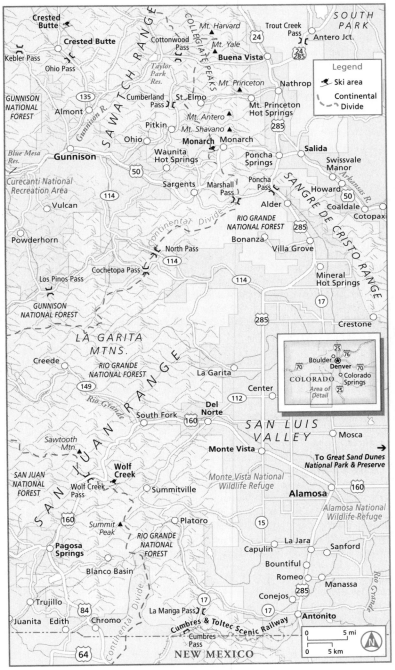

daily, with American and Italian cuisine, and lunch and dinner prices in the $8 to $12 range. A second marina, under the same management, is at Lake Fork, 25 miles west of Gunnison, at the reservoir's west end (© **970/641-3048;** www.bluemesalake.com). It offers boat rentals at similar rates.

Both Elk Creek and Lake Fork marinas also offer a fishing guide service, at $14 per hour. A boat tour, offered by the park service, leaves the Pine Creek Trail boat dock on Morrow Point Lake twice daily, Memorial Day through Labor Day, to explore the Upper Black Canyon of the Gunnison. *Be forewarned:* There is a .8-mile hike followed by 232 steps down to get to the dock; all of which has to be repeated in reverse after the boat ride. Rates are $12 adults, $6 ages 2 through 12 and 62 and up. Reservations are required (© **970/641-2337,** ext. 242).

Hikers find a variety of trails, often with splendid views of the lakes. Those who want to see birds can't go wrong with the **Neversink Trail,** a 1-mile round-trip hike on the north shore of the Gunnison River, near a great blue heron rookery. Also watch for warblers, redwing blackbirds, and great horned owls, plus an occasional mule deer among the cottonwoods and willows that shade the river. The trail is flat and relatively easy, and also provides fishing access. A moderately strenuous hike where you might see a golden eagle or two, and possibly some bighorn sheep, is the 4-mile round-trip **Dillon Pinnacles Trail,** which is open to horseback riders as well as hikers. It provides spectacular views of the strangely eroded volcanic formations called the Dillon Pinnacles. The visitor center has a free brochure that describes these and several other hikes.

Anglers visit Curecanti year-round—there's ice fishing in winter—but the main season is May to October, when rainbow, brown, and Mackinaw trout and kokanee salmon are caught in large numbers. **Hunting,** especially for elk and deer, is popular in the adjacent West Elk Mountains.

The recreation area has 10 developed **campgrounds,** with about 350 sites. Showers are available for a small fee at Elk Creek (179 campsites) and Lake Fork (87 campsites). Elk Creek is open year-round, but water is turned off in winter. The other campgrounds are open until blocked by snow. Camping costs $10 per night, $15 with electric. Several campgrounds have marinas, boat ramps, and RV dump stations; Loop D at Elk Creek has electric hookups. Backcountry and boat-in camping is also permitted, at no charge; check with rangers.

The **Elk Creek Visitor Center,** 16 miles west of Gunnison off U.S. 50, has exhibits and audiovisual programs, as well as maps and publications. It's open daily from mid-May through November, and weekends and occasional weekdays the rest of the year, except for federal holidays in winter. Nature hikes and evening campground programs are presented throughout the summer. At **Cimarron,** 35 miles west of Gunnison, there's a visitor center open daily from Memorial Day through September, with a historic train exhibit, book sales, and a road to **Morrow Point Dam** power plant. The **Lake Fork Visitor Center,** 25 miles west of Gunnison off U.S. 50, near Blue Mesa Dam, is open daily from mid-May through September.

For a brochure and other information before your trip, contact Curecanti National Recreation Area, 102 Elk Creek, Gunnison, CO 81230 (© **970/641-2337** or 970/641-2337, ext. 205; www.nps.gov/cure).

OTHER SPORTS & OUTDOOR ACTIVITIES

In addition to activities in the recreation area, there are opportunities for hiking, mountain biking, hunting, fishing, camping, and four-wheeling on other nearby public lands under the jurisdiction of the U.S. Forest Service and Bureau of

Land Management. For maps and other information, contact the offices of the **Gunnison Ranger District** and the **Bureau of Land Management Resource Area** at 216 N. Colorado St. (© **970/641-0471;** www.fs.fed.us/r2 or www.co.blm.gov).

A good base for exploring this area is **Three Rivers Resort and Outfitting,** 11 miles north of Gunnison at 130 C.R. 742 (P.O. Box 339), Almont, CO 81210 (© **888/761-3474** or 970/641-1303; www.3riversresort.com). Located between Gunnison and Crested Butte, close to the national forest, Three Rivers offers fishing and rafting trips (see below), and also has fully equipped and furnished cabins ($45 and up) and an RV park ($22 including hookups).

FISHING   The Gunnison River, both above and below town, and the tributary Taylor River, which joins the Gunnison at Almont, 11 miles north of town, are outstanding trout streams. In addition, the region's lakes are also rich in fish. **Willowfly Anglers,** located at Three Rivers Resort, Almont (© **970/641-1303**), offers fly-fishing instruction, rentals, and guide service. Full-day float fishing trips cost $225 for one person and $275 for two, and walking trips are also available, starting at $135 for one person, half-day.

GOLF   The 18-hole **Dos Rios Golf Club,** off U.S. 50 about 2 miles west of town (© **970/641-1482**), charges $75 for 18 holes, including a cart.

HORSEBACK RIDING   One of the best ways to see this beautiful area is from a saddle. **Ferro's Ranch Resort,** P.O. Box 853, Gunnison, CO 81230 (© **800/617-4671** or 970/641-4671; www.coloradodirectory.com/ferrosbluemesa), offers horseback rides into remote areas of Curecanti National Recreation Area and to nearby national forests from late April through mid-November, weather permitting. Rates are $18 for 1 hour, $35 for 2 hours, $50 for a half-day, and $85 for a full day, including lunch. Pack trips are also available, including food and all equipment, starting at $100 per day. Ferro's is located on Soap Creek Road, about 26 miles west of Gunnison, overlooking Blue Mesa Reservoir. In addition to horseback rides, Ferro's has a general store with fishing licenses and supplies, plus six lodging units, including several historic cabins, with rates from $30 to $85. There are also 33 campsites, 8 of which can accommodate RVs although only 2 have hookups (water and electric only); the cost is $10 to $16.

RIVER RAFTING & KAYAKING   For trips on the Taylor and other rivers, check with **Three Rivers Resort and Outfitting** (see above). Rates for 3-hour raft trips over relatively calm stretches are $22 to $25 for adults and $14 to $20 for children under 12. Three Rivers also offers guided white-water trips with rates from $45 per person.

SKIING   The two major winter-sports centers in the area are **Crested Butte,** 32 miles north on Colo. 135 (see section 2 of this chapter) and **Monarch,** 44 miles east on U.S. 50 (see section 3 of this chapter).

DISCOVERING GUNNISON'S PAST

Founded in the 1870s, the town of Gunnison has a number of historic buildings, ranging from log cabins to fancy 1880s homes—many in Gothic revival and Italianate styles—plus the 1882 stone Episcopal Church. A free walking-tour brochure is available at the chamber of commerce visitor center (see above).

Gunnison Pioneer Museum   A Denver & Rio Grande narrow-gauge steam train and depot are highlights at this local historical society museum, which includes eight buildings from the area's past. There's an emphasis on ranching

The Bizarre Tale of Alferd Packer

The winter of 1873 to 1874 was bad in southwest Colorado's San Juan Mountains—deep snow, staggeringly strong winds, and below-zero temperatures. But among the many miners who found themselves there, drawn by the hope of staking a claim among the region's newly discovered silver deposits, the temptation to change their fortunes in a day was just too powerful to resist. In February, six eager miners, led by Alferd Packer, set out from a Ute encampment near the present-day town of Delta, ignoring warnings from Ouray, chief of the Ute people. They took only 10 days' worth of food and weren't heard from for over 2 months, until Packer arrived alone at Los Piños Indian Agency, about 25 miles south of the present town of Gunnison.

Packer told Indian Agency officials that after he became ill, his companions abandoned him, and he survived on roots and bushes while making his way through the mountains. Curiously, he refused food upon his arrival. After resting, Packer traveled to the nearby community of Saguache, where he went on a drinking binge, paying with money from several wallets.

Since Packer had been penniless when the six men left the Ute encampment, and was the only one to return, Indian Agency officials became suspicious. When strips of what appeared to be human flesh were discovered along the path Packer had taken he changed his story, claiming that others in the party had killed their companions one by one, until only he and fellow miner Wilson Bell remained. Finally Packer was forced to kill Bell in self-defense. After admitting to eating the remains of his companions, Packer was arrested and jailed.

Packer escaped from jail that August, at just about the time that five partially decomposed bodies were discovered along the northeast side

and homemaking equipment from the late 1800s and early 1900s, and exhibits include a rural schoolhouse (ca. 1905), a home with 19th-century furnishings, a dairy barn (ca. 1880), minerals and arrowheads, wagons, toys, and Gunnison's first post office (1876); plus over 40 antique and classic motor vehicles on display, from a Model A Ford tanker truck to an old Cadillac hearse. Allow an hour. East U.S. 50 at the corner of S. Adams St. and Tomichi Ave. ℂ 970/641-4530. Admission $7 adults, $1 children 6–12, free for children under 6. Memorial Day to Labor Day Mon–Sat 9am–5pm; Sun 1–4pm.

WHERE TO STAY

Lodging rates are at their highest in Gunnison in summer and during the Christmas holidays. You'll usually find the lowest rates in late winter and early spring. Major chain and franchise motels that provide reasonably priced lodging in Gunnison include the **Best Western Tomichi Village Inn,** on U.S. 50, 1 mile east of Gunnison (ℂ **800/641-1131** or 970/641-1131), charging double rates of $70 to $150 in summer and $55 to $90 the rest of the year; **Comfort Inn,** 911 N. Main St. (ℂ **800/424-6423** or 970/642-1000), with rates of $90 to $100 double in summer and $70 to $90 at other times; **Days Inn,** 701 W. U.S. 50 near the airport (ℂ **800/329-7466** or 970/641-0608), with rates of $50 to of Lake San Cristobal, a few miles south of the present town of Lake City. Four of the men had apparently been murdered in their sleep, their heads split open with an ax, while a fifth had been shot. Chunks of flesh had been cut from at least two of the men's chests and thighs, and one was decapitated.

The search was now on in earnest, but Packer was nowhere to be found. About 9 years later, he was discovered living in Wyoming, using the name John Schwartz, was arrested, and in April 1883 was convicted of premeditated murder and sentenced to hang. That should have been the end of Packer, but the trial was declared unconstitutional on a technicality.

Retried in 1886, Packer was convicted on five counts of manslaughter, and sentenced to 45 years in prison. However, due to poor health, he was pardoned by Governor Charles Thomas after only 5 years behind bars. Packer died of natural causes in the Denver area in 1907, at the age of 64, and was buried in the Littleton Cemetery. As an interesting aside, all through his life, Packer's first name, Alferd, had been misspelled. Apparently, it was a problem that followed him into death, since today the name "Alfred" is prominently displayed on his tombstone.

Though many at the time considered it an open-and-shut case, some have questioned whether Packer was really guilty of murder, or if he was simply convicted because of the public's revulsion at his admission of cannibalism. In 1989, the bodies were exhumed, and it was determined that they had likely been victims of cannibalism—but no evidence has shown definitively that Packer killed them. The site where the bodies were found, near the town of Lake City (see "A Side Trip to Lake City," below), is now known as Cannibal Plateau.

$80; and **Super 8,** 411 E. Tomichi Ave. (© **800/800-8000** or 970/641-3068), with double rates from $45 to $85 in summer and $40 to $70 at other times.

Room tax adds just under 9% to lodging bills.

Mary Lawrence Inn   Built in 1885 in Italianate style, this attractive bed-and-breakfast offers personal service and historic flavor. The inn is named for Illinois widow Mary Axtell Lawrence, who bought it in 1908 and operated a boardinghouse in the home while serving as teacher and school administrator in Gunnison. Now owned and operated by Janette McKinny, the inn is located in a quiet neighborhood near Western State College. Rooms are individually decorated with antique furnishings, colorful quilts, stenciled walls, and original artwork; some have four-poster beds. Five units have shower/tub combos and two have showers only; two suites have TVs. The shared parlor contains a fireplace, books, and games. There's a large outdoor deck, a gazebo, and a cozy sunroom. Creative country-style breakfasts are served, and fresh-baked snacks are available throughout the day. Smoking is not permitted.

601 N. Taylor St., Gunnison, CO 81230. © **888/331-6863** or 970/641-3343. www.commerceteam.com/mary.html. 7 units. $69–$135 double; from $120 suite. Rates include full breakfast. AE, MC, V. **Amenities:** Outdoor hot tub. *In room:* No phone.

Wildwood Motel Built in 1928 as a summer refuge for members of the Chicago underworld, today the Wildwood is a favorite hideaway for budget-conscious outdoor sports lovers. The rooms are quaint, quiet, and cozy, and all have a full kitchen. Units were recently remodeled with all new soft goods, upgraded plumbing, flooring, and kitchens. Five units have shower/tub combos and the rest have showers only. The property boasts a playground, swings, horseshoe pits, shady picnic tables, a fish-cleaning station, and two duck ponds, where Tasmanian rainbow trout are raised for release into the Gunnison River.

Summer 2004 saw the addition of two cabins, both with two bedrooms, two bathrooms, a washer and dryer, and private deck. Call for rates. Also on the property is a campground for fully self-contained RVs (no tents). Open May through September, weather permitting, it has 20 large sites, with complete hookups including cable TV ($23). Reservations are recommended.

1312 W. Tomichi Ave., Gunnison, CO 81230. ℭ **970/641-1663.** www.wildwoodmotel.net. 18 units. $52–$75 double. Fishing, hunting, and ski packages available. MC, V. From downtown, continue straight on Tomichi Ave. when U.S. 50 curves to the left and you see the motel's blue sign; from the west turn left on New York Ave. (1st traffic light), then right on 8th and left onto Tomichi. The motel is ahead on the right. **Amenities:** Outdoor hot tub, laundry. *In room:* TV, kitchen.

CAMPING

In addition to the campgrounds in Curecanti National Recreation Area (see above), you'll find dozens of sites scattered throughout the Gunnison National Forest and lands administered by the Bureau of Land Management (ℭ **970/ 641-0471**). Wildwood Motel (see above) also offers RV sites.

Mesa Campground A good base camp for fishing, hunting, or sightseeing trips, this campground caters mostly to RVs but does accept tents. The campground has large pull-through sites to accommodate big RVs, and 50-amp electric service is available. Facilities include clean bathhouses with plenty of hot water, a dump station, self-service laundry, gas pumps, a playground, a recreation room, and a store with propane and a limited selection of groceries and RV supplies.

36128 W. U.S. 50, Gunnison, CO 81230. ℭ **800/482-8384** or 970/641-3186. www.coloradodirectory.com/ mesacamp. 135 sites. $20–$30. MC, V. Closed Dec through Mar. Located 3 miles west of Gunnison.

WHERE TO DINE

Blue Iguana *(Value* MEXICAN Homemade Sonoran-style Mexican food is the fare at the Blue Iguana, a better-than-average fast-food restaurant in the Elk Horn Building, 2 blocks east of Main Street—look for the big chrome sculpture of an elk out front. Inside, the decor is simple: picnic tables with red plastic coverings, and light-colored walls with bright red trim and red chile designs. Order at the counter and pick up your taco, burrito, enchilada, or combo plate when your name is called. We recommend either the burrito (it's huge) or the house specialty, a chimichanga—a deep-fried flour tortilla stuffed with your choice of five fillings (shredded beef, beans, chicken, rice, green chile, red chile, and on and on), and topped with sour cream and guacamole. Locals consistently declare the Blue Iguana the best place for Mexican food—and we agree!

303 E. Tomichi Ave. ℭ **970/641-3403.** Reservations not accepted. Most items $3–$7.95. DISC, MC, V. Summer Mon–Sat 11am–10pm; closes 9pm in winter.

Josef's Restaurant ★★ AMERICAN/EUROPEAN A European old-world atmosphere pervades this fine restaurant adjacent to the Best Western Tomichi Village Inn. The menu features a variety of steaks, poultry, pasta, and fresh seafood, but we recommend the house specialties, all true European favorites such as traditional Wiener schnitzel, Hungarian-style goulash (slowly braised beef tips with onions, mushrooms, paprika, and cabernet sauvignon demi-glace sauce), and hickory smoked rib-eye steak with a Gorgonzola cheese cream sauce. Try Josef's fresh-baked pastries for a special treat.

41883 E. U.S. 50, 1 mile east of Gunnison. ✆ **970/641-5032.** Main courses $8–$24. AE, DC, DISC, MC, V. Daily 5–9pm.

A SIDE TRIP TO LAKE CITY ✿✿

The historic mining town of Lake City is 55 miles southwest via Colo. 149 (turn south off U.S. 50, 9 miles west of Gunnison). Founded in 1874, this former silver and gold town is set at 8,671 feet elevation against a backdrop of 14,000-plus-foot peaks in three different national forests—the Gunnison, Uncompahgre, and Rio Grande. Although the year-round population is a bit under 400, that figure quintuples in summer.

One of Colorado's largest national historic districts, Lake City has more than 75 buildings that date from the 19th century. Visit the renovated **Hinsdale County Courthouse,** 317 N. Henson St., built in 1877 and still the home of county government. You'll see exhibits on the trial of the notorious Alferd Packer and the courtroom where his trial took place (see "The Bizarre Tale of Alferd Packer," above). History buffs will also enjoy the **Hinsdale County Museum,** 130 Silver St., at the corner of Silver and Second streets (✆ **970/944-2050** in summer, or 970/944-9515 at other times), with exhibits about the Packer trial, of course, plus the area's silver-mining heritage. Next door is the 1870s **Smith-Grantham House,** a small, furnished Victorian home where you can see how people here lived in the late 1800s. The museum and Smith-Grantham House are open from mid-June until Labor Day, daily from 10am to 5pm; and irregular hours the rest of the year. Admission, which includes both the museum and the Smith-Grantham House, costs $2 for adults, $1 for children 8 to 12, and is free for children 7 and younger.

For those intrigued with mining, visit the **Hard Tack Mine Tour & Museum,** about 3 miles west of town, via C.R. 20. George and Beth Hurd of Lake City own the property and, with the help of their daughter Buffy, developed the tour and museum. The 40-minute tour will take you back more than 100 years and show you how the miners lived and worked. Be aware that the temperature underground is a constant 45° (7°C), so take a jacket even on the hottest summer day. There's also a gift shop open Tuesday through Saturday from 10am to 5pm, Memorial Day through Labor Day (✆ **970/944-2506;** www.hardtack mine.com).

Surrounded by some 600,000 acres of public land, Lake City is an important recreational center, offering hiking, mountain biking, horseback riding, jeep rides, camping, and fishing in summer; and ice fishing, cross-country skiing, snowshoeing, and snowmobiling in winter. Lake San Cristobal, just south of town via C.R. 30, is Colorado's second-largest natural lake and is particularly popular with fishermen. Also nearby you'll find several ghost towns and historic sites, most of which will require a four-wheel-drive vehicle, horse, mountain bike, or a good pair of hiking boots.

For information, including lists of boat and jeep rentals, outfitters, stables, accommodations, and restaurants, contact the **Lake City Chamber of Commerce,** P.O. Box 430, Lake City, CO 81235 (✆ **800/569-1874** or 970/944-2527; www.lakecity.com). The chamber operates a visitor information center at 800 Gunnison Ave., on the north side of town, which is usually open from 9am to 5pm Monday through Saturday and from 11am to 3pm Sunday.

2 Crested Butte (★(★

A delightful little gem of a town, Crested Butte is a year-round destination resort, with wonderful skiing in winter, and hiking, mountain biking, and other outdoor recreational activities in warmer weather. In fact, Crested Butte has the best mountain biking in the state, and boasts of having some of the most colorful displays of wildflowers you'll see anywhere.

The town of Crested Butte was born in 1880 as the Denver & Rio Grande line laid a narrow-gauge rail track from Gunnison to serve the gold and silver mines in the area. But it was coal, not the more precious minerals, which sustained the town from the late 1880s until 1952, when the last of the mines closed. The economy then languished until Mt. Crested Butte ski area was developed in 1961.

An influx of newcomers began renovating the old buildings in the 1970s, and in 1974 the entire town was designated a National Historic District—one of the largest in Colorado. Crested Butte is as different from those other overcrowded interstate highway resorts as you can get. A guest really has a sense of having gotten away from it all after a vacation here.

ESSENTIALS

GETTING THERE   By Car   Crested Butte is 28 miles north of Gunnison on Colo. 135, the only year-round access. In summer, the gravel-surface Kebler Pass Road links Crested Butte with Colo. 133 at Paonia Reservoir, to the west.

By Plane   The **Gunnison–Crested Butte Airport,** serves Crested Butte (see section 1 of this chapter). **Alpine Express** (© **800/822-4844** or 970/641-5074) provides shuttle service from the airport to Crested Butte, frequently in ski season; call to check on availability at other times. Reservations are required.

VISITOR INFORMATION   Consult the **Crested Butte–Mt. Crested Butte Chamber of Commerce,** P.O. Box 1288, Crested Butte, CO 81224 (© **800/ 545-4505** or 970/349-6438; www.crestedbuttechamber.com). Another good source is the **Gunnison–Crested Butte Tourism Association** (© **800/215- 2266**); and an excellent website with numerous links is **www.visitcrestedbutte. com**. An **information center** is located downtown at the four-way stop at the corner of Elk Avenue and Sixth Street.

GETTING AROUND   There are actually two separate communities here: the old mining town of Crested Butte and the modern resort village of Mt. Crested Butte, 3 miles away. Colo. 135 enters Crested Butte from the south and is intersected by Elk Avenue, which runs east–west as the town's main street.

Mountain Express (© **970/349-7318**) provides free shuttle-bus service between Crested Butte, Mt. Crested Butte, and area condominiums. Call for schedules. Local taxi service is available from **Town Taxi** (© **970/349-5543**).

FAST FACTS   The **Crested Butte Medical Center,** in the Ore Bucket Building in downtown Crested Butte (© **970/349-0321**), can handle most health needs; the medical center also operates a clinic at the ski area during winter (© **970/349-4370**). The **post office** is on the north side of Elk Avenue between Second and Third streets; contact the U.S. Postal Service (© **800/275-8777;** www.usps.com) for hours and other information. For local **road conditions,** call © **877/315-7623** (in-state only).

SPECIAL EVENTS   Fat Tire Bike Week, late June; Black and White Ball at the Heritage Museum, early July; Wildflower Festival, early July; Festival of the

Arts, early August; Rubber Duckie Race, early August; Vinotok Slavic Fall Festival, mid-September.

SKIING & OTHER WINTER SPORTS

Crested Butte may be Colorado's best-kept secret. Situated at the intersection of two overlapping winter storm tracks, it's guaranteed to have outstanding snow. Offering abundant opportunities for beginners and intermediate skiers, Crested Butte also has what many experts consider the most challenging runs in the Rockies.

The resort has 1,434 acres of skiable terrain, including 448 acres of "extreme limits" skiing—double black diamond ungroomed terrain for experts only. Altogether, trails are rated 15% beginner, 44% intermediate, 10% advanced, and 31% expert. The vertical drop is 3,062 feet from a summit of 12,162 feet. There are 85 trails served by 15 lifts (three high-speed quads, three triples, three doubles, four surface lifts, and two Magic Carpet rolling conveyors). Average annual snowfall is 240 inches, and there's snow making on trails served by all but two of the resort's lifts. The resort also has an easily accessible snowboard terrain park, half-pipe terrain, and offers snowboarding lessons.

Crested Butte offers both a ski and snowboard program (plus year-round recreation) for visitors with disabilities, with specially trained and certified instructors, at the Adaptive Sports Center, located at the base of the ski area in the Treasury Center Building. The resort's Kid's Ski & Snowboard World provides lessons, day care, and nursery services. Private and group lessons are available in half- or all-day packages. The resort offers rentals of skis, snowboards, helmets, snowshoes, ski boards, and telemark equipment, in single- and multiday prices, with overnight storage included. A full-service repair shop is available also. All children 12 and under who participate in lessons are required to wear a helmet (included in the lesson price and available at the rental shop). Equipment rental is also available at several other shops in the base area and around town.

Don't forget to keep an eye out for Bubba and Betty Bear, the beloved mascots of Crested Butte Mountain Resort, who will gladly stop for a warm, fuzzy hug, and a picture.

For more information, contact **Crested Butte Mountain Resort,** 12 Snowmass Rd. (P.O. Box 5700), Mt. Crested Butte, CO 81225 (© **800/544-8448** or 970/349-2390; 888/44-BUTTE or 970/349-2323 for snow reports; www.crestedbutteresort.com). Lift tickets are $63 for adults, 25 percent off for seniors 65 to 69, youths ages 13 to 16 pay $20 to $38, children 5 to 12 pay their age (no blackout dates apply), children 4 and under and seniors 70 and older ski free. Discounted lift ticket, lodging, and air packages are available year-round through **Crested Butte Vacations** (© **800/544-8448**). The resort is open from mid-December to early April, daily from 9am to 4pm.

CROSS-COUNTRY SKIING, SNOWSHOEING, SLEDDING & ICE SKATING   The **Crested Butte Nordic Center,** based at Big Mine Park, Second Street and Whiterock Avenue in downtown Crested Butte (P.O. Box 1269), Crested Butte, CO 81224 (© **970/349-1707;** www.cbnordic.org), maintains 25km to 40km of marked and groomed trails and organizes backcountry tours over more than 100 miles of wilderness trails. It's open in winter daily from 9am to 4pm. A 1-day trail pass costs $12 for adults, $10 for seniors 60 to 69, $8 for students 12 to 20, and $6 for children under 12. Dogs of any age are free on select trails. Nordic ski rentals (skis, boots, and poles) cost $16 per day for adults and $10 for children; high-performance rental equipment costs $28 per day.

The center also maintains a free lighted ice-skating rink and a free sledding hill, plus skate and sled rentals. In addition, it offers snowshoe tours and rentals.

WARM-WEATHER SPORTS & OUTDOOR ACTIVITIES

This is rugged country, surrounded by **Gunnison National Forest,** three wilderness areas, and towering 12,000- to 14,000-foot peaks. For maps and tips on the many activities available, contact the Gunnison Ranger District office at 216 N. Colorado St. in Gunnison (© 970/641-0471; www.fs.fed.us/r2). The lifts at Crested Butte Mountain Resort don't stop just because the snow's gone, but operate daily from late June through early August for hikers or those who simply want to enjoy the beautiful mountain scenery without effort. Single trips cost $15 for adults, $8 for children 7 to 17 and seniors 65 and older; all-day passes cost $17 and $10, respectively. Kids 6 and younger ride free (one per paying adult).

There are numerous area outfitters and guide services that will help you with practically any outdoor activity. **Alpine Outside** (© **800/833-8052** or 970/349-5011), located at the four-way stop in downtown Crested Butte, works with a number of local guides and can book a wide variety of outdoor adventures.

GOLF   The 18-hole course at **The Club at Crested Butte,** 2 miles south of Crested Butte off Colo. 135 (© **800/628-5496** or 970/349-6131), is one of Colorado's best mountain courses. It's usually open from mid-May through October. The fee for 18 holes, including the mandatory cart, is $120 in summer, lower in the off season.

HIKING   There are practically unlimited opportunities for hiking and backpacking in the Crested Butte area. Ask the chamber of commerce for trail suggestions, or contact the Gunnison National Forest office (see above).

HORSEBACK RIDING   Guided rides are offered year-round by **Fantasy Ranch Horseback Adventures,** P.O. Box 236, Crested Butte, CO 81224 (© **888/688-3488** or 970/349-5425; www.fantasyranchoutfitters.com), ranging from 1½ hours to weeklong pack trips. Trips go into three different mountain wilderness areas, at elevations from 7,000 feet to 12,700 feet, including the incredibly scenic Maroon Bells. Prices per person are $45 for the 1½-hour ride and $65 for the half-day rides. Call for rates for overnight pack trips. Fantasy Ranch also offers supper barbecue rides and hay rides, and has lodging available as well.

MOUNTAIN BIKING   **Crested Butte** has established a firm reputation as the place to mountain bike in Colorado. From single-track trails to jeep roads, there's something here to please every ability level. You can get information from the Crested Butte Visitor Center or the Forest Service (see above). Among local shops where you can get trail information, maps, and mountain-bike rentals (from about $25 per day), we recommend **Flatiron Sports** (© **800/821-4331** or 970/349-6656; www.flatironsports.net) and **Christy Sports** (© **970/349-6601**) in the Treasury Center at Mt. Crested Butte, and **Crested Butte Sports** (© **970/349-7516**) and **The Alpiner** (© **970/349-5210**) in the town of Crested Butte.

Popular choices include the **Strand Hill** route, which runs for 18 miles and is considered intermediate. It climbs to 10,255 feet elevation, through wooded areas, and includes several miles on downhill single-track. Advanced mountain bikers will love **Trail no. 401,** one of the best trails in the area. This 26-mile round-trip route climbs to 11,500 feet and offers incredible mountain scenery, including views of the magnificent Maroon Bells (p. 326) as it passes through aspen groves and meadows of wildflowers.

Guided mountain-bike tours are offered by several companies, including **Pioneer Mountain Bike Guides** and **Crested Butte Mountain Guides,** both at 416 Sopris Ave. (*©* **970/349-5430**), and **Expedition International,** located at 117 White Rock Ave. (*©* **970/349-5430**). Half-, full-, and multiday-plus custom tours can be arranged. Prices start around $50 for a half-day.

OTHER HIGHLIGHTS

The chamber of commerce provides a free brochure on a **self-guided walking tour** of more than three-dozen historic buildings in Crested Butte, including the picturesque 1883 Town Hall, 1881 railroad depot, numerous saloons and homes, and a unique two-story outhouse.

Downtown Crested Butte is home to a half-dozen or so **art galleries,** mostly along or just off Elk Avenue. The **Paragon Galley,** at the corner of Second Street and Elk Avenue (*©* **970/349-6484**), is a cooperative, displaying the works of more than a dozen local artists and craftspersons.

Crested Butte Mountain Heritage Museum   This museum, located in a historic building, concentrates on the area's mining, ranching, and skiing heritage, with interactive exhibits, historical photos, and a wide array of memorabilia from local settlers' cabins. There are also vintage mountain bikes and an exhibit on the local Ute tribe. You can pick up a free copy of the Crested Butte walking-tour map here, and borrow (also free) an audio tour with player. Allow about an hour.

331 Elk Ave. *©* 970/349-1880. Admission $3, children under 12 free. Ski season and summer daily noon–8pm; call for hours spring and fall.

WHERE TO STAY

Lodging properties listed below with Mt. Crested Butte addresses are at or near the ski slopes, while those in Crested Butte are about 3 miles away. However, free transportation from Crested Butte to the slopes is available with the Mountain Express (see "Getting Around," above).

Rates in Crested Butte are highest during ski season, and lowest in what locals call "mud season," after the ski area closes and before summer.

The Claim Jumper   A huge log home packed with antiques and family heirlooms, this B&B easily qualifies as Crested Butte's most unique accommodation. Each guest room has a particular theme: The Rough and Ready Room is dedicated to cowboys, Prospector's Gulch to miners, and Commodore Corrigan's Cabin to seafarers. Ethyl's Room, complete with restored gas pump, appeals to 1950s nostalgia buffs; and the Sports Room contains a putting green built into the floor. There are several hundred video movies available for guest use. One unit has a claw-foot tub only, two have showers only, and four have shower/tub combos. The inn also features a redwood hot tub and a sauna. Hearty five-course breakfasts include fresh fruit, fresh-baked items, and entrees such as bacon and eggs or pancakes.

704 Whiterock Ave. (P.O. Box 1181), Crested Butte, CO 81224. *©* 970/349-6471. www.visitcrestedbutte. com/claimjumper. 7 units. $99–$139 double. Rates include full breakfast. AE, DISC, MC, V. Dogs and well-behaved children over 10 are welcome. **Amenities:** Hot tub; sauna. *In room:* TV/VCR.

Crested Butte International Lodge & Hostel ⚡   This handsome, three-story hostel is among the nicest you'll find in Colorado; and it's just 100 feet from the free ski shuttle. Dorm rooms have four, six, or eight single beds, so a family can have a private room by renting all its beds. Of course, in the hosteling tradition, they'll share the large bathrooms and other facilities. Each bunk has its own reading light and a lockable drawer, and all rooms have a desk. Sleeping bags, sheets, and towels can be rented. The large shared living room has a stone fireplace and comfortable sitting areas; and guests have use of a fully equipped kitchen. Ski and other outdoor recreation packages are available. There are three private rooms for two, a family room that sleeps five, and an apartment that sleeps six; linens are provided for these. They offer high-speed Internet, and use of copy and fax machines. Smoking and alcoholic beverages are not permitted.

615 Teocalli Ave. (P.O. Box 1332), Crested Butte, CO 81224. ⓒ 888/389-0588 or 970/349-0588. Fax 970/349-0586. www.crestedbuttehostel.com. 5 total beds; 4 private rooms; 1 apt. All but one private room share bathrooms. Bunk rooms summer $20–$22 per bed, winter $28–$32 per bed, half price for children 3–8, free for babies under 2; private rooms $55–$100 double; apt. $145–$225. $2 discounts for Hostelling International members. DISC, MC, V. **Amenities:** Coin-op laundry. *In room:* No phone.

Elk Mountain Lodge   Built in 1919 as a miners' hotel, this historic three-story lodge has been beautifully renovated, and is a good choice for those seeking both a good night's sleep and a bit of historic ambience. Located near the center of town, it offers individually decorated, basic rooms with twin, queen, or king beds. Third-floor units have spectacular views of the town and surrounding mountains, and many have balconies. There's also ski storage.

Second and Gothic sts. (P.O. Box 148), Crested Butte, CO 81224. ⓒ 800/374-6521 or 970/349-7533. Fax 970/349-5114. www.elkmountainlodge.net. 19 units. Summer $90–$120 double; winter $90–$130 double. Rates include full breakfast. AE, DISC, MC, V. No children under 10 years of age. **Amenities:** Bar; indoor hot tub. *In room:* TV, dataport.

The Historic Pioneer Guest Cabins   Located 10 minutes from Crested Butte ski area, the Pioneer is a great escape for those seeking a rustic (but not too rustic) log cabin in the woods. Although these historic cabins lack TVs and in-room phones, they have modern bathrooms (showers only); fully furnished and equipped kitchens; handmade wood furniture; and cozy down comforters on the beds. In addition to propane heaters, the cabins have either fireplaces or antique wood-burning stoves, and outside each cabin is a fire pit and picnic table.

The four small cabins, each with two double beds, were built as part of a historic ski resort that closed in the early 1950s. The four larger cabins, built in the late 1960s and early 1970s, have three double beds, are more open, and have more of a modern feel than the historic cabins. Located in the Gunnison National Forest, the cabins provide easy access to fishing, hiking, mountain biking, cross-country skiing, and snowshoeing. All units are nonsmoking.

Cement Creek Rd., Crested Butte, CO 81221. ⓒ 970/349-5517. Fax 970/349-9697. www.thepioneer.net. 8 units. $90–$110 double. Free for children 5 and under. MC, V. Most breeds of dogs accepted with deposit and at management discretion. From Crested Butte, take Colo. 135 south 7 miles to Cement Creek Rd., turn left and go 2 miles. *In room:* Kitchen, no phone.

The Nordic Inn *Kids*   Among the first lodges built at the foot of the Crested Butte ski slopes, this well-kept, family-owned inn is still going strong. The big fireplace in the lobby is the focus of attention at breakfast, and the whirlpool tub on the sun deck is open year-round. Guest rooms have Scandinavian decor; most have two double beds, although a few contain either one king- or two queen-size beds. Each also has a bathroom with a tub/shower combo and a separate vanity. Especially good for families are the kitchenette and full-kitchen units, which sleep from four to eight people. The entire inn is nonsmoking.

14 Treasury Rd. (P.O. Box 939, Crested Butte, CO 81224), Mt. Crested Butte, CO 81225. ⓒ 800/542-7669 (reservations only) or 970/349-5542. Fax 970/349-6487. www.nordicinncb.com. 28 units. $93–$305 double.

Rates include continental breakfast. AE, MC, V. Closed from the end of ski season through May. **Amenities:** Whirlpool tub. *In room:* TV, hair dryer.

WHERE TO DINE

In addition to the restaurants recommended here, you'll find information on a number of dining choices, some with menus, on the Internet at **www.visit crestedbutte.com**.

Le Bosquet COUNTRY FRENCH   Green plants peek through the lace curtains of this popular restaurant, which is our choice for a quiet, intimate dinner. Under the same ownership since 1978, the restaurant's menu changes seasonally, but always includes fresh seafood, beef, lamb, and vegetarian entrees. Typical entrees might include a roast Colorado rack of lamb in a red wine–and–garlic butter sauce or fresh filet of salmon in a ginger glaze. Le Bosquet also serves what it calls classic French bistro items, such as the 10-ounce Black Angus New York strip served with a side of horseradish mayo and french fries. Available from 5:30 to 6:30pm only, the Twilight Menu offers, for $19, soup or salad, a choice of several entrees such as filet of salmon or grilled rack of pork, and a choice of desserts. There's also an excellent wine list. Smoking is not permitted.

Attached to the restaurant is an upscale take-out service called **Why Cook?** (© **970/349-5858**). Call for current selections and prices.

Sixth St. at Belleview Ave. (in Majestic Plaza). © **970/349-5808.** Reservations recommended. Entrees $14–$30. AE, DISC, MC, V. Daily 5:30–10pm. May be closed 1 month in spring and 2 weeks in fall.

The Slogar Bar & Restaurant AMERICAN   If you do something right, why mess around with anything else? That's the way the Slogar feels about its skillet-fried chicken and we couldn't agree more. The fixed-price menu offers chicken every night—the best in the region—accompanied by tangy coleslaw, mashed potatoes and gravy, biscuits with honey butter, creamed corn, and ice cream. Also available is a family-style steak dinner, which is fine, but we still prefer the chicken. The atmosphere here is 1880s Victorian, somewhat elegant but not so highbrow as to scare off families.

517 Second St., at Whiterock Ave. © **970/349-5765.** Reservations recommended. Fixed-price dinner $15–$22. AE, MC, V. Daily 5–9pm.

3 Salida: White-Water Rafting Center of the Rockies

138 miles SW of Denver, 96 miles W of Pueblo, 82 miles N of Alamosa

With a strategic location on the upper Arkansas River, it was natural that Salida (elevation 7,080 ft.) should become an important farming, ranching, and transportation center in its early days, and a major river-rafting and kayaking center today. Zebulon Pike opened the area for Americans in the early 19th century; he was followed by trappers, then miners after the discovery of gold in 1859. When Leadville boomed on silver in the late 1870s, the Denver & Rio Grande Railroad built a line up the Arkansas from Pueblo, and the town of Salida was founded at a key point on the line. The downtown core has kept its historic ambience alive, and now has a growing arts community while it serves as a base camp for outdoor recreation enthusiasts.

ESSENTIALS

GETTING THERE   By Car U.S. 50 connects Salida with Gunnison, 66 miles west, and Pueblo, 96 miles east on I-25. Colo. 291 heads north from Salida, providing a vital 9-mile link between U.S. 50 and U.S. 285, which runs north–south 5 miles west of Salida (through Poncha Springs).

By Plane   The nearest airport with commercial service is at **Gunnison,** 65 miles west (see "Gunnison & Curecanti National Recreation Area," earlier in this chapter).

VISITOR INFORMATION   Consult the **Heart of the Rockies Chamber of Commerce,** 406 W. Rainbow Blvd. (U.S. 50), Salida, CO 81201 (© **877/772-5432** or 719/539-2068; www.salidachamber.org), which operates an information center daily in summer from 9am to 5pm; it's open the same hours on Monday through Saturday only in winter.

GETTING AROUND   Salida sits on the southwestern bank of the Arkansas River, just above its confluence with the South Arkansas. U.S. 50 (Rainbow Blvd.), which follows the north bank of the South Arkansas, marks the southern edge of town. At the eastern city limit, Colo. 291 (Oak St.) turns north off U.S. 50, and 6 blocks later, turns northwest as First Street through the historic downtown area.

FAST FACTS   The **Heart of the Rockies Regional Medical Center,** 448 E. First St. (© **719/539-6661**), has a 24-hour emergency room. The **post office** is at 310 D St. Contact the U.S. Postal Service (© **800/275-8777;** www.usps.com) for hours and other information.

SPECIAL EVENTS   Continental Divide Auto Hill Climb, early June; FIBArk Whitewater Festival, mid-June; Art Walk, late June; Collegiate Peaks Stampede Rodeo, mid-July; Crest Crank Mountain Bike Ride, early September; Angel of Shavano Car Show, mid-September; Lighting of Christmas Mountain USA, Thanksgiving weekend, late November.

RIVER RAFTING

Considered the white-water rafting center of the Rockies, Salida is the perfect base for enjoying the **Arkansas Headwaters Recreation Area,** a 148-mile stretch of river from Leadville to Pueblo Lake. With headquarters off Colo. 291 in downtown Salida at 307 W. Sackett Ave. (P.O. Box 126), Salida, CO 81201 (© **719/539-7289;** www.parks.state.co.us), the recreation area includes about 20 developed sites along the river, offering raft and kayak access, fishing, hiking, camping, and picnicking. There are also undeveloped areas that offer access to the river, but be careful to avoid trespassing on private property.

The busiest stretch of the river is Browns Canyon, a granite wilderness between Buena Vista and Salida, with class III and IV rapids (moderately difficult to difficult) along a 10-mile stretch of river from Nathrop to Stone Bridge. User fees are $2 per person per day (free for kids 15 and under), plus $10 per night for camping.

Most people explore Colorado's rivers with experienced rafting companies, which provide trips on stretches of river that range from practically calm and suitable for everyone to extremely difficult, with long, violent rapids that are recommended only for skilled white-water boaters. For a full listing of dozens of rafting companies approved to run the Arkansas, contact the recreation area office (see above). Leading outfitters include **Dvorak's Rafting & Kayak** ⊛⊛⊛ (© **800/824-3795** or 719/539-6851; www.dvorakexpeditions.com), which offers half- and full-day trips, plus multiday excursions. (*Note:* Dvorak's also offers rafting trips elsewhere in Colorado, plus Utah, Arizona, and New Mexico.) Other major rafting companies here include **Whitewater Encounters** (© **800/530-8362** or 719/530-0937; www.weraft.com), **American Adventure Expeditions** (© **800/288-0675** or 719/539-4680; www.americanadventure.com), and **River Runners, Ltd.** (© **800/332-9100;** www.riverrunnersltd.com).

Generally, adult rates for half-day raft trips are $38 to $60; full-day trips including lunch are in the $69 to $95 range, and multiday excursions start at about $200. Prices for children are about 20% less, and trips through Royal Gorge are usually higher.

OTHER SPORTS & OUTDOOR ACTIVITIES

FISHING   The Arkansas River is considered by many to be the finest fishing river in Colorado. There's also trout fishing in numerous alpine lakes, including Cottonwood Lake, Twin Lakes, and O'Haver Lake. For tips on the best fishing spots, plus licenses, supplies, and equipment sales and rentals, stop at **Arkansas River Fly Shop,** 7500 W. U.S. 50, Salida (© **719/539-4223;** www.arkanglers. com), which also offers a guide service. Cost for a guided half-day wading trip for one person is $110, and a half-day float-fishing trip on the Arkansas River for two costs $195. The company also offers fly-fishing and fly-tying lessons.

GOLF   The **Salida Golf Club,** a municipal course that opened in 1926, is at Crestone Avenue and Grant Street (© **719/539-1060**). Greens fees are $23 for 18 holes.

HIKING   There are outstanding trails for all experience levels throughout the region, particularly in the San Isabel National Forest, along the eastern slope of the Continental Divide west of Salida. Of particular interest are hikes into the Collegiate Range (mts. Harvard, Columbia, Yale, Princeton, and Oxford) off Cottonwood Creek Road west of Buena Vista, and trips from the ghost town of St. Elmo up Chalk Creek Road from Mount Princeton Hot Springs.

For maps and other information, stop at the **Salida Ranger District** office, 325 W. Rainbow Blvd. (© **719/539-3591;** www.fs.fed.us/r2).

MOUNTAIN BIKING   There are numerous trails suitable for mountain biking throughout the area, and many provide stupendous views of the surrounding 14,000-plus-foot peaks. **Absolute Bikes,** 330 W. Sackett St. (© **888/539-9295** or 719/539-9295; www.absolutebikes.com), rents, sells, and services mountain bikes and can provide information on nearby trails. Ask for a free copy of the *Mountain Bike Guide,* which gives details, including maps, for 15 area rides. Rentals—from three-speed townies to full-suspension, plus kid bikes, tandems, and road bikes—are available. Prices start at $30 per day for mountain bikes; $10 for kid bikes; and $15 for town bikes.

ROCKHOUNDING   The richest mineral and gem beds in Colorado are found in the upper Arkansas River valley and the eastern slope of the Continental Divide, just west of Salida. For a free brochure on rockhounding locations, stop at the chamber of commerce office. Those wanting hammers, eye protection, and other equipment will find it at **The Rock Doc** at Prospector's Village, 17897 U.S. 285, north of Salida (© **719/539-2019**).

SKIING & SNOWBOARDING   Among the finest of Colorado's small ski resorts, **Monarch Ski & Snowboard Area** ★★, 20 miles west of Salida at Monarch Pass on U.S. 50, serves all levels of ability with 55 trails, with 21% rated beginner, 37% intermediate, and 42% advanced. The longest run is one mile. Backcountry skiing is available via Sno-Cat.

Covering 670 acres, the mountain has a vertical drop of 1,171 feet from its summit of 11,961 feet. It gets about 350 inches of snow annually, and has no snow-making equipment. It has one fixed quad and four double chairs. All-day tickets are $39 to $41 for adults, $17 for juniors 7 to 12, $26 for seniors 62 to 69, free for those under 7 or over 69. The area is usually open from mid-Novembe through mid-April, daily from 9am to 4pm. For information, contact the resort at 1 Powder Place, Monarch, CO 81227 (© **888/996-7669** or 719/539-3573; www.skimonarch.com). You'll find comfortable accommodations and dining at the 100-room **Monarch Mountain Lodge,** 22720 W. U.S. 50, Monarch, CO 81227 (© **800/332-3668** or 719/539-2581; www.monarchmountainlodge.com). Room rates are $59 to $99 double; $195 to $230 suites.

SEEING THE SIGHTS

Monarch Crest Tram   Climbing from 11,312-foot Monarch Pass to the Continental Divide at an altitude of 12,012 feet, this tram offers views of five mountain ranges—up to 150 miles away—when skies are clear. The tram includes six four-passenger gondolas. At the top is a large gift shop. Allow about 2 hours.

Monarch Pass, U.S. 50, 22 miles west of Salida. © 719/539-4091. Admission $7 adults, $6 seniors over 55, $4 children 12 and under. Mid-May to mid-Sept, weather permitting, daily 8:30am–5:30pm.

Mt. Shavano Fish Hatchery   This state-run fish hatchery, about a half mile northwest of town off Colo. 291, produces some four million trout each year, used to stock Colorado's numerous streams and lakes. Visitors can see how the hatchery operates, walk among the fish raceways and ponds, and feed the fish (food provided from coin-operated machines). Guided tours are provided daily from June until Labor Day, and self-guided tours are available at other times. Allow 30 minutes to an hour.

7725 C.R. 154. © 719/539-6877. Free admission. Daily 7:30am–4pm.

Salida Hot Springs   Colorado's largest indoor hot springs have been in commercial operation since 1937, when the Works Progress Administration built the pools as a Depression-era project. Ute tribes considered the mineral waters, rich in bicarbonate, sodium, and sulfate, to be sacred and medicinal. Today, the main 25m (82-ft.) pool, with two lap lanes available at all times, is kept at a refreshing 82°F (28°C), and a 4-foot-deep leisure pool, with a ramp entrance, is kept at about 100°F (38°C). European-style private hot baths, at 114° to 120°F (46°C–49°C), are available for adults only ($6 per person per hr.). Also available are aquasize and arthritis classes, and swimming lessons for all ages. Adjacent Centennial Park has a picnic pavilion, playground, and tennis and volleyball courts. Allow 1 to 3 hours.

410 W. Rainbow Blvd. (U.S. 50). © 719/539-6738. www.salidapool.com. Admission $6 adults, $4 students 6–17, $2 children 5 and under. Memorial Day to Labor Day daily 1–9pm; call or check website for winter hours.

Salida Museum   The Salida Museum provides a look at the history of this part of Colorado, with a wide selection of pioneer, mining, and railroad exhibits, plus displays on the lives of the American Indians who lived here. You'll see lots of arrowheads, plus exhibits that explain how baskets and pots were made. The museum also contains rocks, fossils, and shells from the area, plus petrified wood and dinosaur bones and teeth. You can learn about Laura Evans, a local madam who operated a brothel in Salida from the late 1800s until 1953, and see a replica of a lady's bedroom of the late 1800s, bizarre-looking medical equipment, and bone baskets—used to transport corpses in the early 1800s. Allow 30 minutes.

406½ W. Rainbow Blvd. (U.S. 50). © 719/539-4602 for information. Admission $3 adults, $1 children 6–12, free for kids under 6. Memorial Day to mid-Sept Mon–Sat 9am–5pm. *Note:* Hours may vary based on availability of volunteer staffing. Located just behind the chamber of commerce.

WHERE TO STAY

Rates are highest here during summer, and lowest in late winter and early spring (before rafting season begins). Among reliable chain motels in the area are the **Best Western Colorado Lodge,** 352 W. Rainbow Blvd./U.S. 50 (© 800/777-7947 or 719/539-2514), with double rates from $45 to $112; **Comfort Inn,** 315 E. Rainbow Blvd./U.S. 50 (© 800/424-6423 or 719/539-5000), with rates from $70 to $100 for two; **Days Inn,** 407 E. Rainbow Blvd./U.S. 50 (© 800/329-7466 or 719/539-6651), with double rates from $45 to $89; **Econo Lodge,** 1310 E. Rainbow Blvd./U.S. 50 (© 800/553-2666 or 719/539-2895), with rates for two from $49 to $119; **Super 8,** 525 W. Rainbow Blvd./U.S. 50 (© 800/800-8000 or 719/539-6689), with rates for two from $55 to $120; and the **Travelodge,** 7310 U.S. 50 (© 800/234-1077 or 719/539-2528), with double rates from $39 to $95. Room tax adds just under 9% to lodging bills.

Aspen Leaf Lodge *(Value)*   This small family-owned and -operated motel has a friendly feel, from the forest of large evergreens and aspens surrounding the hot-tub pavilion to the coffeepot that's on in the office each morning. Remodeled in 2000, it's managed to keep its rates very reasonable. The one-story motel has simply but attractively decorated rooms with king or queen beds; some rooms have microwaves and refrigerators. Rollaways are available. Guests also have use of a secluded deck overlooking a peaceful horse pasture, and there are restaurants within walking distance.

7350 W. U.S. 50, Salida, CO 81201. © 800/759-0338 for reservations only, or 719/539-6733. Fax 719/539-6304. 18 units. $35–$69 double. Children under 12 stay free in parent's room. AE, DC, DISC, MC, V. Small pets accepted with $5 fee. *In room:* A/C, TV.

River Run Inn ⭐   Built by Chaffee County in 1895 as a home for the indigent, this building—about 3 miles northwest of town—served that purpose for half a century. Since 1983, however, it has functioned as a charming bed-and-breakfast, and is listed on the National Register of Historic Places. A wide front porch leads into a large sitting room and library, and the back porch looks out over a small pond and to the rolling hills and mountains beyond. The lovely guest rooms, most with mountain views, are decorated with period furnishings, including brass or four-poster beds and have either all new showers or tubs (not both). The king room bathroom has its own whirlpool tub. The dormitory, available to parties of 5 to 13 people (twin beds and one bathroom), covers the entire third floor. Full breakfasts include a hot entree, such as a specialty rolled oven omelet or stuffed French toast, fresh baked goods, and fresh fruit. The grounds include a section of the Arkansas River that provides private fishing access (a Colorado fishing license is required). Smoking is not allowed.

8495 C.R. 160, Salida, CO 81201. © 800/385-6925 or 719/539-3818. Fax 801/659-1878. www.riverruninn.com. 6 units (5 with private bathroom). $100–$125 double with private bathroom; $150 up for dormitory. Rates include full breakfast, afternoon and evening refreshments. AE, MC, V. Children over 12 welcome. *In room:* No phone.

WHERE TO DINE

Country Bounty Restaurant & Gift Shoppe AMERICAN   This combination gift shop and restaurant gives diners plenty to look at while waiting for their meals. The gift shop seems to spill over into the restaurant with all manner of country-style crafts, Southwestern jewelry, and other items. The lunch menu offers cheeseburgers, sandwiches and wraps, some great salads—try the spinach Cobb salad: fresh spinach, egg, crumbled bacon, red onion, fresh mushrooms, tomatoes, and avocado, topped with a grilled lemon chicken breast and crumbled

Gorgonzola cheese. For dinner you might choose the traditional pot roast (slowly braised beef with carrots, onions, celery, and yellow and red potatoes, in a rich gravy) or opt for the fresh Atlantic salmon filet, seasoned with lemon, roasted garlic, virgin olive oil, capers, and dry white wine. The Country Bounty is also locally famous for its pies and cobblers. The entire restaurant is smoke-free.

413 W. U.S. 50. ☎ **719/539-3546.** Lunch items $5.50–$9; dinner entrees $8–$15. AE, DISC, MC, V. Summer daily 7am–9pm; winter daily 7am–8pm.

First St. Café ⭐ AMERICAN/MEXICAN   In the heart of historic downtown Salida, First St. Café occupies an 1880 two-story brick building, with hardwood floors and regional paintings. Among the town's most popular restaurants, it's a focal point for artists, musicians, and other creative types. The kitchen turns out excellent home-style cooking such as pepper steak, made with either a New York strip or filet mignon, plus fresh cracked pepper and a burgundy-mushroom sauce. Another plus: The steaks are hand cut in-house, and the hamburgers are prepared from fresh, extra-lean ground beef. The spicy Colorado burrito is cooked the proper way—with shredded beef (ground beef is acceptable only in cheap fast-food joints) plus beans, all smothered with red chile and cheese. The restaurant also serves vegetarian casseroles, fish and chips, burgers, a variety of sandwiches, a daily quiche, and fish. The soup and salad bar is included with all dinners.

137 E. First St. ☎ **719/539-4759.** Lunch items $5.95–$9.95; dinner main courses $8.95–$21. AE, DISC, MC, V. May–Sept Mon–Thurs 11am–9pm, Fri–Sat 11am–10pm; closes 1 hour earlier the rest of the year. Closed during the fall; call in advance.

4 Alamosa & Great Sand Dunes National Park & Preserve

212 miles SW of Denver, 149 miles E of Durango, 173 miles N of Santa Fe, New Mexico

If you're looking for Colorado's largest sandbox, here it is: Just 35 miles from Alamosa are the tallest sand dunes in North America.

Founded in 1878 with the extension of the Denver & Rio Grande Railroad into the San Luis Valley, the town was named for the cottonwood *(alamosa)* trees that lined the banks of the Rio Grande. Soon rails spread out in all directions from the community, and it became a thriving transportation center for farmers and a supply depot for miners. Farming remains important today, but Alamosa has also become an educational center with Adams State College, a 4-year institution founded in 1921. Elevation is 7,544 feet, and the population is a bit under 8,000.

ESSENTIALS

GETTING THERE   By Car   Alamosa is at the junction of U.S. 160, which runs east 73 miles to I-25 at Walsenburg and west to Durango; and U.S. 285, which extends south to Santa Fe, New Mexico, and north to Denver. Because of a jog in U.S. 285, however, a more direct route into the city from the north is to take Colo. 17 the last 50 miles.

By Plane   The **Alamosa San Luis Valley Regional/Bergman Field Airport** (☎ **719/589-6444**), 2500 State St., 3 miles off U.S. 285 South, has service to and from Denver with **Great Lakes Airlines** (☎ **800/554-5111**).

VISITOR INFORMATION   The **Alamosa County Chamber of Commerce,** Cole Park (Chamber Dr. at Third St.), Alamosa, CO 81101 (☎ **800/258-7597** or 719/589-4840; www.alamosa.org), operates a visitor information center, with summer hours from 8am to 6pm Monday through Friday and from

9am to 4pm Saturday and Sunday; and winter hours from 8am to 5pm Monday through Friday.

FAST FACTS   The **San Luis Valley Regional Medical Center,** with a 24-hour emergency room, is at 106 Blanca Ave. (© **719/589-2511**). The **post office** is at 505 Third St., off State Avenue. Contact the U.S. Postal Service (© **800/275-8777**; www.usps.com) for hours and other information.

SPECIAL EVENTS   Crane Festival, mid-March, in Monte Vista; Pro Rodeo, early July; Early Iron Festival (classic cars and hot rods), Labor Day weekend.

GREAT SAND DUNES NATIONAL PARK & PRESERVE ✦

Just 35 miles northeast of Alamosa, on Colo. 150, is Colorado's fourth—and newest—national park. Since 2000, when Congress passed the law approving park status pending the acquisition of "sufficient land having a sufficient diversity of resources," we have been waiting for this moment. It came on Monday September 13, 2004, when the U.S. Secretary of the Interior arrived at Great Sand Dunes to publicly announce the designation of Great Sand Dunes National Park and Preserve. The necessary property was acquired with the help of the Nature Conservancy.

Far from any sea or major desert, this 39-square-mile expanse of sand seems incongruous here. The dunes are the tallest on the continent, piled nearly 750 feet high against the western edge of the Sangre de Cristo Mountains—a startling sight. The dunes were created over thousands of years by southwesterly winds blowing across the valley. They formed when streams of water from melting glaciers carried rocks, gravel, and silt down from the mountains. In addition, as the Rio Grande changed its course, it left behind sand, silt, and debris.

Even today the winds are changing the face of the dunes. So-called "reversing winds" from the mountains pile the dunes back upon themselves, building them higher and higher. Though it's physically impossible for sand to be piled steeper than 34 degrees, the dunes often appear sheerer because of deceptive shadows and colors that change with the light: gold, pink, tan, sometimes even bluish. Climbing dunes is fun, but it can be tiring at this 8,200-foot altitude. *Beware:* The sand's surface can reach 140°F (60°C) in summer.

Among the specialized animals that survive in this weird environment are the Ord's kangaroo rat, a creature that never drinks water, plus four insects found nowhere else on earth: the Great Sand Dunes tiger beetle and three other beetle varieties. These animals and the flora of the adjacent mountain foothills are discussed in evening programs and guided walks during summer.

For orientation, walk the easy .5-mile self-guided nature trail that begins at the visitor center. If you want more of a challenge, hike the dunes—you can get to the top of a 750-foot dune and back in about 90 minutes. Those who make it all the way to the top are rewarded with spectacular views of the dunes and the surrounding mountains.

Pinyon Flats Campground, with 88 sites, is open year-round. It has picnic tables, fire grates, flush toilets, and drinking water, but no showers or RV hookups. Campsites are assigned on a first-come, first-served basis, and cost $12 per night. Admission to the monument for up to a week is $3 per person (free for those under 17). The **visitor center** (© **719/378-6399**) is open daily year-round (closed on winter holidays). For further information, contact Great Sand Dunes National Park and Preserve, 11999 Colo. 150, Mosca, CO 81146-9798 (© **719/378-2312**; www.nps.gov/grsa).

From Alamosa, there are two main routes to Great Sand Dunes: east 14 miles on U.S. 160, then north on Colo. 150; or north 14 miles on Colo. 17 to Mosca, then east on Six Mile Lane to the junction of Colo. 150.

SPORTS & OUTDOOR ACTIVITIES

Many of the best outdoor activities in this part of the state take place in the **Rio Grande National Forest,** with the Supervisor's Office at 1803 W. U.S. 160, Monte Vista, CO 81144 (*©* **719/852-5941;** www.fs.fed.us/r2). For equipment for a variety of outdoor activities (including mountain bike and ski rentals), visit **Kristi Mountain Sports,** Villa Mall, 3217 Main St., Alamosa (*©* **719/589-9759**).

FISHING   The Rio Grande is an outstanding stream for trout, walleye, and catfish; and there are numerous high mountain lakes and streams throughout the Rio Grande National Forest where you're apt to catch rainbow, brown, brook, cutthroat, and Rio Grande cutthroat trout. For information, contact the Forest Service office (see above). You can get licenses, tackle, and advice at **Wal-Mart,** 333 Clark St., off U.S. 160 about 3 miles east of downtown Alamosa (*©* **719/589-9071**).

Moments   **The Cumbres & Toltec Scenic Railroad**

This is our idea of the best way to see this country. Built in 1880 to serve remote mining camps, the **Cumbres & Toltec Scenic Railroad** ★★ follows a spectacular 64-mile path through the San Juan Mountains from Antonito, Colorado, to Chama, New Mexico. This narrow-gauge steam railroad weaves through groves of pine and aspen and past strange rock formations before ascending through the spectacular Toltec Gorge of the Los Piños River. At the rail-junction community of Osier, passengers picnic or enjoy a catered lunch while the *Colorado Limited* exchanges engines with the *New Mexico Express*. Round-trip passengers return to their starting point in Antonito, while onward passengers continue a climb through tunnels and trestles to the summit of 10,015-foot Cumbres Pass, then drop down a precipitous 4% grade to Chama. A joint venture by the states of Colorado and New Mexico, the train is a registered National Historic Site.

A through trip from Antonito to Chama (or vice versa), traveling one-way by coach, runs $70 for adults, $37 for children 11 and under. A regular round-trip to Osier, without transfers, is $55 for adults and $30 for children 11 and under, but this omits either the gorge or the pass. Either way, it's an all-day adventure, leaving between 8 and 10:30am, and returning between 4:30 and 6:30pm. All fares include a hot lunch at Osier. *Note:* In especially dry conditions a $2 surcharge per ticket may be added for extra fire-prevention measures. The train operates daily from Memorial Day weekend to mid-October. For reservations and information, contact the Cumbres & Toltec Scenic Railroad, P.O. Box 668, Antonito, CO 81120 (*©* **888/286-2737** or 719/376-5483; www.cumbrestoltec.com). The depot is 28 miles south of Alamosa, just off U.S. 285.

GOLF   The **Cattails Golf Club,** 6615 N. River Rd. (© **719/589-9515**), is an 18-hole course along the Rio Grande on the north side of Alamosa. Generally open March through November, the cost is $30 for 18 holes. The 9-hole **Monte Vista Country Club,** at 101 Country Club Dr. in the town of Monte Vista (© **719/852-4906**), 17 miles west of Alamosa, is a particularly challenging course due to its small greens. Open April through October, the course is on the migratory path of sandhill and whooping cranes. The fee is $18 for 18 holes.

HIKING   The best opportunities in the region are found in the surrounding **Rio Grande National Forest,** with nearly 2 million acres. One of the most popular hikes, with easy access, is **Zapata Falls,** reached off Colo. 150 about 20 miles northeast of Alamosa and south of Great Sand Dunes. This cavernous waterfall on the northwest flank of 14,345-foot Mount Blanca freezes in winter, turning its cave into a natural icebox that often remains frozen well into summer. More challenging hikes include trails into the **Wheeler Geologic Area,** known for its unique rock formations. Obtain directions from the Forest Service (see above).

MOUNTAIN BIKING   There are plenty of opportunities for mountain biking on local federal lands. Stop at the visitor center to pick up a copy of the *San Luis Valley Mountain Bike Guide* for $2.50. Get additional information from the Forest Service (see above), or stop at **Kristi Mountain Sports** (see above) for tips on the best places to go, rentals (starting around $20 per day), repairs, and accessories.

SWIMMING   **Splashland Hot Springs,** 5895 S. Colo. 17 (© **719/589-6307**), 1 mile north of Alamosa via U.S. 160, has a geothermally heated outdoor pool (94°F/34°C average temperature) measuring 150 feet by 60 feet, with both high dive and low dive, and a popular mini-water slide. There's also an 18-inch-deep wading pool. Bathing suits, towels, and pool paraphernalia can be rented; there's a snack bar and public showers. It's open Memorial Day to Labor Day, Thursday through Tuesday. Weekday hours are from 10am to 6:30pm; Saturdays and Sundays from noon to 9pm. Pool passes cost $2 to $5; nonswimmers pay $1.

OTHER HIGHLIGHTS

Adams State College–Luther E. Bean Museum   Located on the second floor of Richardson Hall in room 256, this museum has an excellent fine-art gallery featuring works by local artists. Also on display is the Woodard Collection, a sampling of artifacts from around the world. Allow about an hour.

208 Edgemont Blvd. © **719/587-7827**. Free admission. Mon–Fri 1–4:30pm. Closed Dec 23–Jan 1 and other major holidays.

Colorado Gators 🔆 *Kids*   Alligators in Colorado? Yep, they're here! Geothermal wells keep the temperature a cozy 87°F (31°C) at this fish and alligator farm and wildlife habitat, located 17 miles north of Alamosa off Colo. 17. There are more than 400 alligators at the farm—some up to 11 feet long and weighing about 600 pounds. Kids should love watching the alligator feedings, which happen several times each day. The farm also raises fish, desert tortoises, turtles, and iguanas. Allow about an hour.

9162 C.R. 9 North, Mosca. © **719/378-2612**. www.gatorfarm.com. Admission $6 adults, $4 children 6–12 and seniors 65–79, free for those under 6 and over 80. June–Aug Mon–Sat 9am–7pm; Sept–May Mon–Sat 9am–5pm.

NATURAL HIGHLIGHTS

The **Alamosa–Monte Vista National Wildlife Refuges** (℗ **719/589-4021;** http://refuges.fws.gov) together have preserved nearly 25,000 acres of vital land for a variety of marsh birds and waterfowl, including many migrating and wintering species. Sandhill and whooping cranes visit in early to mid-October and early March; at other times of the year there may be egrets, herons, avocets, bitterns, and other avian species. A wide variety of ducks are year-round residents, and waterfowl numbers are at their peak March through May.

The refuges have self-guided driving tours with a number of viewpoints, and also several hiking trails. Bring binoculars, since they'll be useful. To get to the Alamosa refuge, which contains the visitor center and refuge headquarters, go 4 miles east of Alamosa on U.S. 160 and then south 3 miles on El Rancho Lane. Monte Vista refuge is located 6 miles south of the community of Monte Vista on Colo. 15. Admission is free. The refuges are open daily from sunrise to sunset; the visitor center is open Monday through Friday from 7:30am to 4pm.

WHERE TO STAY & DINE

Your base camp for exploring this area will likely be Alamosa, where there are a number of typical chain motels and a variety of restaurants.

Some reliable chain properties include the **Best Western Alamosa Inn,** 2005 Main St. (℗ **800/459-5123** or 719/589-2567), with a restaurant that serves three meals daily and double rates of $70–$107; **Comfort Inn,** 6301 U.S. 160 (℗ **800/228-5150** or 719/587-9000), charging $50 to $120 double; **Days Inn,** 224 O'Keefe Pkwy. at the junction of U.S. highways 160 and 285 (℗ **800/329-7466** or 719/589-9037), with rates of $40 to $65 for two; and **Super 8,** 2505 W. Main St. (℗ **800/800-8000** or 719/589-6447), with double rates of $40 to $80.

You'll find a number of restaurants along Main Street. We especially like the Mexican food at **Oscar's Restaurant,** 710 Main St. (℗ **719/589-9230**), open from 11am to 8pm Sunday through Thursday and from 11am to 9pm Friday and Saturday, with prices from $4.95 to $9.95. We also recommend the restaurant at the **Best Western Alamosa Inn** (see above).

Room tax adds just over 9% to lodging bills.

The Cottonwood Bed & Breakfast and Gallery

This delightful bed-and-breakfast has a distinctly artsy orientation. Innkeeper Deborah Donaldson has decorated the common areas and bedrooms as a gallery of regional art, much of which is for sale. The Cottonwood is composed of two main buildings and a carriage house. The 1908 neocolonial two-story bungalow has five guest rooms, furnished largely in Arts and Crafts style. Each room is unique: The Rosa Room has queen and single beds to accommodate small families, along with children's books and stuffed animals, while the Blanca Room weds a nice airy white decor with Art Deco motifs. Bathrooms in three of these units have showers only; the others have shower/tub combos. Adjacent to the bungalow is a 1920s fourplex with four apartment suites, each with a kitchen and claw-foot tub with shower conversion. These are perfect for families with children or pets. Located between the two main buildings is a cobblestone courtyard with a hot tub, and the carriage house, perfect for those who prefer being off by themselves. Full homemade breakfasts often feature regional specialties, such as fresh fruit crepes with Mexican chocolate and whipped cream. Smoking is not permitted.

123 San Juan Ave., Alamosa, CO 81101. ℗ **800/955-2623** or 719/589-3882. Fax 719/589-6437. www.cottonwoodinn.com. 10 units. $55–$125 double, $15 per extra adult, $10 per child. Rates include full breakfast. AE, DC, DISC, MC, V. Located 3 blocks north of Main St. Pets accepted in 2 apt suites with $60 deposit. **Amenities:** Outdoor hot tub.

5 A Side Trip to Creede: A Slice of Colorado's Mining History

Among the best preserved of all 19th-century Colorado mining towns, Creede had a population of 10,000 in 1892 when a balladeer wrote, "It's day all day in the daytime, and there is no night in Creede." Over $1 million in silver was mined every day, but the Silver Panic of 1893 eclipsed Creede's rising star. For most of the next century, area mines produced just enough silver and other minerals to sustain the community until the 1960s, when tourism and outdoor recreation became paramount. Today this mountain town, at an elevation of 8,838 feet, has a population of about 400. It's fairly easy to see most of the town in a day, and be sure to include a stop at the Creede Museum, drive the Bachelor Historic Tour route, and if at all possible take in a show at the Creede Repertory Theatre.

To get to Creede from Alamosa, drive west on U.S. 160 about 48 miles to South Fork, and turn north on Colo. 149, which follows the Rio Grande about 23 miles to Creede.

You can obtain information on what to see and do, as well as lodging and dining options, from the **Creede/Mineral County Chamber of Commerce,** in the County Annex building at the north end of Main Street (P.O. Box 580), Creede, CO 81130 (© **800/327-2102** or 719/658-2374; www.creede.com). The office is staffed Monday through Friday from 9am to 5pm, and brochures and other information are available on a self-serve basis 24 hours daily. There's also a visitor information booth on Main Street in the middle of town, open daily from 9am to 6pm from Memorial Day to mid-September. Another good source for information is the **Divide Ranger District office** of the U.S. Forest Service, located at the corner of 3rd Street and Creede Avenue (© **719/658-2556;** www.fs.fed. us/r2), which can provide maps and information on hiking, mountain biking, horseback riding, four-wheeling, fishing, cross-country skiing, and all sorts of other outdoor activities in the nearby San Juan and Rio Grande national forests. May through August the Forest Service office is open daily from 8:30am to 5pm; from September to mid-October it's open the same hours Monday through Friday only. Hours are cut back dramatically the rest of the year; call for the current schedule.

The **Creede Repertory Theatre** ★★, P.O. Box 269, Creede, CO 81130 (© **866/658-2540** or 719/658-2540; www.creederep.org), was established in 1966 by a small troupe of young actors from the University of Kansas. Now nationally acclaimed, it has matinee and evening performances from mid-June to late September in its 243-seat theater and a separate 90-seat theater, both at 124 North Main St. The company usually presents four full-length productions, a family show, and sometimes shorter plays, in repertory. Productions vary, but might be musicals, comedies, contemporary or classic dramas. Recent productions have included Larry Shue's comedy *The Foreigner,* Noel Coward's *Hay Fever,* and a family show, *The Magic of Roald Dahl,* storytelling with puppets. Tickets for full-length productions run from $16 to $24, and family shows are $5 to $8. In addition to its repertory theater productions, the company presents a variety of concerts and other special events year-round. Advance reservations are strongly recommended.

Stop at the chamber office, visitor information booth, or the Divide Ranger District office (see above) for directions to the **Wheeler Geologic Area,** a region of volcanic rock formations accessible only by jeep, horseback, or a 5-hour hike; and **North Creede Canyon,** where remnants of the old town of Creede still stand near the **Commodore Mine,** whose workings seem to keep a ghostly vigil over the canyon.

The former Denver & Rio Grande Railroad depot is now the **Creede Museum,** behind City Park (© **719/658-2004**), which tells the story of the town's wild-and-woolly heyday. There were dozens of saloons and gambling tables, and shootouts were not uncommon. Bob Ford, the killer of Jesse James, was murdered in his own saloon, and Bat Masterson and "Poker Alice" Tubbs were other notorious residents. Photographs and exhibits on gambling and other activities are included in the museum's collection, and you can obtain a walking-tour map of the town here. It's usually open daily from 10am to 4pm in summer, with free admission. The **Underground Mining Museum,** on the north edge of town (© **719/658-0811**), is contained in a series of rooms and tunnels blasted into a cliff face. Inside this subterranean world are exhibits that trace the history of mining, along with displays of mining memorabilia and gemstones. It's always 51°F (11°C) down here, so bring a jacket. Guided tours are offered ($10, reservations required), and there's also a gift shop. The museum is open daily from 10am to 6pm in summer, with shorter hours the rest of the year. Admission costs $6 for adults, $5 for seniors 60 and over, and $4 for children 12 and under.

The 17-mile **Bachelor Historic Tour** is described in a booklet available from the chamber of commerce ($1). The route follows a Forest Service road through the mountains, past abandoned mines, mining equipment, the original Creede cemetery, and 19th-century town sites. The road is fine for passenger cars in dry weather, but may be closed by winter snow. Allow 1 to 2 hours.

14

Southeastern Colorado

Colorado's southeastern quadrant owes its life to the Arkansas River, which forges one of the world's most spectacular canyons—the deep, narrow Royal Gorge. On the river's trek through Pueblo it supplies water for a major steel industry. Then it rolls across the Great Plains, providing life-giving water to an arid but soil-rich region that produces a wide variety of vegetables and fruits. Bent's Old Fort, a national historic site that has re-created one of the West's most important frontier trading posts, also rests beside the river, east of the community of La Junta. South of Pueblo, the town of Trinidad is the center of a century-old coal-mining district.

1 Pueblo

111 miles S of Denver, 42 miles S of Colorado Springs, 317 miles N of Albuquerque, New Mexico

Don't trust your first impressions. As you drive through Pueblo along the interstate, it might appear that this bland but industrious city—with its railroad tracks, warehouses, and factories—doesn't warrant a stop. But take the time to get off the superslab and discover the real Pueblo. You'll find handsome historic homes, fine Western art, a well-run zoo, and a number of outdoor recreational opportunities.

Although Zebulon Pike and his U.S. Army exploratory expedition camped at the future site of Pueblo in 1806, there were no white settlements here until 1842, when El Pueblo Fort was constructed as a fur-trading outpost. It was abandoned following a Ute massacre in late 1854, but when the Colorado gold rush began 5 years later, the town of Pueblo was born on the site of the former fort.

In the early 20th century, the city grew as a major center for coal mining and steel production. Job opportunities attracted large numbers of immigrants, especially from Mexico and eastern Europe. Pueblo today is home to high-tech industries as well as the University of Southern Colorado. As the largest city (pop. a bit over 100,000) in southeastern Colorado, it is the market center for a 15-county region extending to the borders of New Mexico, Oklahoma, and Kansas. Elevation is 4,695 feet.

ESSENTIALS

GETTING THERE By Car I-25 links Pueblo directly with Colorado Springs, Denver, and points north; and Santa Fe, Albuquerque, and other New Mexico cities to the south. U.S. 50 runs east to La Junta and west to Cañon City, Gunnison, and Montrose.

By Plane Pueblo Memorial Airport, 31201 Bryan Circle, Keeler Parkway off U.S. 50 East (© **719/948-9088**), is served by **Great Lakes Airlines** (© **800/ 554-5111** or 719/948-9462) with daily flights to Denver and other locations. Agencies providing rental cars at the airport include **Avis** (© **800/831-2847** or 719/948-9665) and **Hertz** (© **800/654-3131** or 719/948-3345).

VISITOR INFORMATION   Contact the **Greater Pueblo Chamber of Commerce,** 302 N. Santa Fe Ave. (P.O. Box 697), Pueblo, CO 81003 (✆ **800/ 233-3446** or 719/542-1704; www.pueblochamber.org), for most travel-related needs. The **Visitor Information Center** is located at the chamber office, which is open year-round Monday through Friday from 8am to 5pm, and some Saturdays from 10am to 2pm.

GETTING AROUND   Pueblo lies on the eastward-flowing Arkansas River at its confluence with Fountain Creek. The downtown core is located north of the Arkansas and west of the Fountain, immediately west of I-25. Santa Fe Avenue and Main Street, 1 block west, are the principal north–south thoroughfares; the cross streets are numbered (counting northward), with Fourth and Eighth streets the most important. Pueblo Boulevard circles the city on the south and west, with spurs leading to the nature center and Lake Pueblo State Park.

Public transportation is provided by **Pueblo Transit** (✆ **719/553-2727**). For taxi service, call **City Cab** (✆ **719/543-2525**). In addition to the rental-car agencies at the airport (see above), there is also an outlet for **Enterprise** in Pueblo (✆ **800/325-8007** or 719/542-6100).

FAST FACTS   Medical services are provided downtown by **Parkview Medical Center,** 400 W. 16th St. (✆ **719/584-4000**). The main **post office** is located at 1022 Fontino Blvd.; call the U.S. Postal Service (✆ **800/275-8777;** www.usps. com) for hours and locations of other post offices.

SPECIAL EVENTS   Bluegrass on the River, at the Greenway & Nature Center, early June; Boats, Blues & BBQ on the Historic Arkansas Riverwalk, mid-June; the Colorado State Fair, late August into early September; the Chile and Frijoles Festival, late September; Holiday on Parade and Christmas at Rosemount Museum, November; and the Christmas Posada, December.

WHAT TO SEE & DO

Historic Pueblo runs along Union Avenue north from the Arkansas River to First Street, a distance of about 5 blocks. More than 40 buildings in the **Union Avenue Historic District** (www.puebloonline.com/unionave) are listed on the National Register of Historic Places, including the **Vail Hotel** (217 S. Grand Ave.), headquarters of the **Pueblo County Historical Society** museum and library (✆ **719/543-6772;** www.pueblohistory.org), with railroad memorabilia, locally made saddles, and some 8,000 books, historical maps, and photographs depicting Pueblo's history. **Union Depot,** with its mosaic-tile floors and beautiful stained-glass windows, houses retail stores and offices, yet still serves rail freight lines. **Walking-tour maps** can be obtained at the Visitor Information Center (see "Visitor Information," above), as well as from Union Avenue businesses.

El Pueblo History Museum ★★   Replacing the former El Pueblo Museum (demolished in 2001), this beautiful museum, which opened during the city's 2003 Chile and Frijoles Festival, is a splendid introduction to this region. Located at the intersection of West First Street, Union Avenue, and Grand Avenue, the museum also serves as the Scenic Byways Visitor Center and as a gateway to the Arkansas Riverwalk (see "Outdoor Activities," below) and the historic district.

Evocative of a mid-1800s trading post, the museum's design replicates a square adobe building with a central plaza, reminiscent of Bent's Old Fort. The museum showcases the traditions of the numerous cultural and ethnic groups in the area, utilizing maps and photos plus displays specific to each era. It begins with such items as beaded garments, pouches, American-Indian baskets and stonework; then, it moves into the Spanish, French, and American exploration of the area, highlighting the fur traders and Bent's Fort. The founding of the city through farming, ranching, and the early steel and mining industries comes next, followed by early-20th-century labor issues.

The museum also explores the area's continued industrial expansion, which brought a tremendous influx of immigrants, resulting in a rich cultural mix. Other exhibits explain how outdoor activities drew visitors to the area in the 20th century, and will likely tempt visitors outside to explore the Riverwalk. Allow at least an hour and a half.

301 N. Union Ave. © 719/583-0453. www.coloradohistory.org. Admission $4 adults, $3 seniors, students, and children 6–12; under 6 free; Saturdays 12 and under free. Tues–Sat 10am–4pm.

The Greenway & Nature Center ✿
A major recreation and education center, this area provides access to more than 36 miles of paved biking and hiking trails along the Arkansas River and around Lake Pueblo. There's also a 150-foot fishing dock, volleyball courts, horseshoe pits, an amphitheater, nature trails, picnic areas, and a large children's playground. Boats and canoes can be put into the Arkansas River here. Bikes and recreational equipment are available for rent (call for rates). An interpretive center displays exhibits on the flora and fauna of the area, there are demonstration gardens along the river, and the Cafe del Rio serves American and Southwestern dishes. At the Raptor Center, injured eagles, owls, and other birds of prey are nursed back to health and released into the wild. The center also houses several resident birds of prey. Allow at least an hour.

5200 Nature Center Rd. © 719/549-2414. www.gncp.org. Free admission, but donations welcome. Grounds open daily sunrise–sunset; Raptor Center Tues–Sun 11am–4pm; Interpretive Center and gift shop Tues–Sat 9am–5pm.

Pueblo Weisbrod Aircraft Museum
Twenty-six historic aircraft—World War II and postwar—are on display, as well as numerous exhibits and photographs depicting the B-24 bomber and its role in World War II. It's hard to miss the restored Boeing B-29 Superfortress, with its 141-foot wingspan, which dominates a large hangar. Also on display are a Douglas A-26 Invader, a Grumman F-9 Cougar, a Douglas C-47 Skytrain (or, as the G.I.'s dubbed it, a Gooney Bird), a Boeing Stearman training plane, and a McDonnell Douglas F-101A Voodoo. There's a well-stocked souvenir shop, offering hard-to-find military and general aviation-related items. Allow 1 to 2 hours.

31001 Magnuson Ave. © 719/948-9219. www.pwam.org. Admission $6, free for children under 10. Mon–Fri 10am–4pm; Sat 10am–2pm; Sun 1–4pm. At Pueblo Memorial Airport, 6 miles east of downtown via U.S. 50.

Pueblo Zoo (Kids)
More than 350 animals (representing about 110 species) reside in this 25-acre zoo, listed on the National Register of Historic Places for several buildings and other structures (including a moat) that were constructed of native sandstone during the Depression by WPA workers. Attractions include a Northern River Otter exhibit, a tropical rainforest, and a black-footed penguin underwater exhibit. You'll find all sorts of reptiles and insects in the herpetarium; kangaroos and emus in the Australia Station; an excellent African lion exhibit; and endangered species such as cottontop tamarins, prehensile tail skinks, and maned wolves. You'll also see zebras, Malayan sun bears, and Lar gibbons. Kids in a participatory mood should flock to Pioneer Farm, where they can feed a variety of rare domesticated animals, and to the Discovery Room, which features hands-on exhibits for all ages. Stop by the Watering Hole snack bar or the Wild Things gift shop, which boasts a better-than-average selection of animal-related items, if you need a rest between exhibits. Allow 2 to 4 hours.

City Park, 3455 Nuckolls Ave. © 719/561-9664. www.pueblozoo.org. Admission $6 adults, $5.50 seniors 65 and older, $3.50 children 3–16, free for children 2 and under. Memorial Day weekend through Labor Day daily 10am–5pm; rest of year daily 9am–4pm.

Rosemount Museum 🍴 This 37-room mansion, completed in 1893 for the pioneer Thatcher family, is considered one of the finest surviving examples of late-19th-century architecture and decoration in North America. The three-story, 24,000-square-foot home was constructed entirely of pink rhyolite stone. Inside you'll find handsome oak, maple, and mahogany woodwork; remarkable works of stained glass; hand-decorated ceilings; exquisite Tiffany lighting fixtures; period furniture; and 10 fireplaces. Also on the property is a restaurant, serving lunch Tuesday through Saturday from 11am to 2pm. Allow 1 to 2 hours.

419 W. 14th St. (at Grand Ave.) © 719/545-5290. Fax 719/545-5291. www.rosemount.org. Admission $6 adults, $5 seniors 60 and over, $4 youths 6–18, free for children 5 and under. Tues–Sat 10am–4pm. Closed major holidays and Jan. Take the I-25 exit for 13th St.

Sangre de Cristo Arts & Conference Center 🍴 (Kids) Pueblo's cultural hub is a three-building complex that houses a 500-seat theater, two dance studios, four art galleries (including one with a fine collection of Western art), a gift shop, and the state-of-the-art Buell Children's Museum, which covers 12,000 square feet with a wide variety of hands-on arts and science exhibits. The high-tech, multisensory "Sensations" exhibit has some 50 sensors in the floors and walls, which activate lights, sound clips, or videos. The "Artrageous Studio" provides visitors with paper, ribbon, mylar, and other wonderfully sparkly and gooey materials to use while creating their own masterpieces. The center also hosts concerts and other performing arts events, including a children's theater program (call for details). Allow 2 to 3 hours.

210 N. Santa Fe Ave. © 719/295-7200. www.sdc-arts.org. $4 adults, $3 children 15 and under. Tues–Sat 11am–4pm.

OUTDOOR ACTIVITIES

Pueblo's mild climate makes it a popular destination for boating, fishing, and other outdoor recreation, with several major stops for the region's outdoor enthusiasts.

Watersport aficionados are drawn to **Lake Pueblo State Park** 🍴 (also called Pueblo Reservoir), which boasts some 4,500 surface acres of water and 60 miles of shoreline. There's boating of all kinds, plus swimming, hiking, biking, and horseback riding. The park's **North Marina** (© 719/547-3880) provides a gas dock, boating and fishing supplies, groceries, and a restaurant. The **South Marina** (© 719/564-1043; www.thesouthshoremarina.com) provides the same services and also rents pontoon boats ($120–$160 for 4 hours and $240–$320 for 9 hours, plus fuel) and fishing boats ($80–$100 for 4 hours and $160–$200 for 9 hours, plus fuel), April through October.

The **Rock Canyon Swim Beach** (© 719/564-0065) at the east end of the park is open Memorial Day through Labor Day daily from 11am to 7pm, and has lifeguards on duty. There's a five-story, three-flume water slide, plus rentals of bumper boats and paddle boats, and a snack bar. Entrance to the beach costs $1 in addition to the general park admission fee (see below).

Pueblo Lake is popular among **anglers** trying for rainbow trout, brown trout, crappie, black bass, and channel catfish, and there's a free fish-cleaning station.

Lake Pueblo State Park has about 400 **campsites,** some with electric and water hookups. A dump station and showers are available, and camping rates are $14 to $22 May 1 through Labor Day; $12 to $20 the rest of the year. Camping reservations are available for an extra charge of $8 by calling ℭ **800/678-2267,** or through the state parks website listed below. Day use costs $5 per vehicle, and campers must pay this in addition to camping fees. From Pueblo, take U.S. 50 west for 4 miles, turn south onto Pueblo Boulevard and go another 4 miles to Thatcher Avenue, then turn west and go 6 miles to the park. For information, contact the park office at ℭ **719/561-9320,** or go to **www.parks.state.co.us**.

Pueblo's $28-million **Historic Arkansas Riverwalk of Pueblo (HARP)** covers some 26 acres (which, as you may have noticed, brings the cost to just over $1 million per acre). This beautifully landscaped waterfront park has pedestrian and bike paths, benches, sculptures, gardens, and natural areas that provide good wildlife-viewing opportunities. Pedal-boat rentals are available from early April through late September on a small lake along the Riverwalk, daily in summer and weekends only at the beginning and end of the season. Rates are $6 per half-hour for a one-person boat and $10 per half-hour for a two-to-four-seater boat. Excursion boat rides along the Arkansas take place on weekends in April, and operate daily from May through late September. Rates for the narrated 25-minute tours are $5 adults, $4 for seniors and members of the military, and $3 for children 3 to 12. Hours for both pedal-boat rentals and the excursion-boat rides vary throughout the season; call the boathouse (ℭ **719/595-1589**) for the schedule. The Riverwalk is located near the south end of the Union Avenue Historic District (see "What to See & Do," above), and is easily accessed via Main Street. For information, contact HARP Authority, 200 W. First St., Suite 303, Pueblo, CO 81003 (ℭ **719/595-0242;** www.pueblohatp.com).

Also in town, stop at **City Park,** northeast of the intersection of Pueblo Boulevard (Colo. 45) and Thatcher Avenue. The park, home to the Pueblo Zoo (see above), covers some 200 acres, and offers 2 fishing lakes, 17 tennis courts, a swimming pool (open in summer), and playgrounds. There's also a beautiful hand-carved antique carousel built in 1911, with music provided by a 1920 Wurlitzer Military Band Organ. The carousel is open evenings and Sunday afternoons in summer; the park is open daily year-round. For information, call the Pueblo Parks and Recreation Department (ℭ **719/566-1745**).

For information on hiking, backpacking, mountain biking, and fishing in nearby lands under the jurisdiction of the U.S. Service, contact the headquarters of the **Pike and San Isabel National Forests and Comanche and Cimarron National Grasslands,** 2840 Kachina Dr., Pueblo, CO 81008 (ℭ **719/553-1400;** www.fs.fed.us/r2).

Local **golf courses** open to the public include **Walking Stick,** 4301 Walking Stick Blvd. (ℭ **719/584-3400**), at the northwest corner of the University of Southern Colorado. Rated among Colorado's best courses and best values, this 18-hole course has a driving range and charges $26 to $28 for 18 holes. Other local courses include **Elmwood** at City Park, 3900 Thatcher Ave. (ℭ **719/561-4946**), with an 18-hole regulation course plus executive 9-hole course. Greens fees for 18 holes are $24 to $26. **Desert Hawk Golf Course at Pueblo West,** 251 S. McCulloch Blvd. (ℭ **719/547-2280**), is an 18-hole regulation course with greens fees for 18 holes from $25 to $32.

SPECTATOR SPORTS

MOTOR SPORTS   Stock-car races are held from mid-April through September on the quarter-mile paved oval track at **Beacon Hill Speedway,** 400 Gobatti Place (ℭ **719/542-2277**). Nationally sanctioned drag racing and other motor sports take place at the **Pueblo Motorsports Park,** U.S. 50 and Pueblo Boulevard in Pueblo West (ℭ **719/543-7747**), April through September.

RODEO Those visiting Pueblo from mid-August to early September can take in the **Colorado State Fair** (© 800/876-4567; www.coloradostatefair.com), which includes a professional rodeo, carnival rides, food booths, industrial displays, horse shows, animal exhibits, and top-name entertainers.

WHERE TO STAY

There are numerous lodging possibilities in Pueblo, with many of the national franchises and chains represented. Rates are highest in summer, and most motels in Pueblo also charge higher rates during the State Fair (mid-Aug to early Sept). Among the reliable major chains are the **Best Western Town House Motor Hotel,** 730 N. Santa Fe St. (© 800/WESTERN or 719/543-6530), with double rates of $52 to $85; **Comfort Inn,** 4645 N. Freeway (© 800/424-6423 or 719/542-6868), charging $50 to $85 double; **Super 8,** 1100 U.S. 50 W. (© 800/800-8000 or 719/545-4104), charging $40 to $90 double; **Hampton Inn,** 4703 N. Freeway, just west of I-25 exit 102 (© 800/HAMPTON or 719/544-4700), with double rates from $75 to $90; and **Days Inn,** 4201 N. Elizabeth St. (© 800/325-2525 or 719/543-8031), with rates from $50 to $89 double. Room tax adds about 12%.

Abriendo Inn ★★ This delightful B&B, built in 1906 as a mansion for brewing magnate Martin Walter, his wife, and their eight children, is the best place to stay for those who want to soak up some of the region's history without sacrificing modern comforts and conveniences. A traditional four square-style house listed on the National Register of Historic Places, the Abriendo Inn has won a deserved number of awards. It's also very conveniently located in Pueblo's historic district, close to shops, the Riverwalk, and other attractions.

The comfortable guest rooms are decorated with antique furniture and period reproductions, plus king- or queen-size brass or four-poster beds. Four units have showers only; the rest have shower/tub combos or whirlpool tubs for two. Delicious homemade breakfasts, which might include egg-sausage soufflé or baked apricot French toast, are served in the oak-wainscoted dining room or on the outdoor patio. Smoking is permitted on the veranda only.

300 W. Abriendo Ave., Pueblo, CO 81004. © 719/544-2703. Fax 719/542-6544. www.abriendoinn.com. 10 units. $69–$165 double. Rates include full breakfast and 24-hr. refreshments. AE, DC, MC, V. *In room:* A/C, TV, VCR (some units), dataport.

CAMPING

There are two KOA campgrounds in the Pueblo area, both open year-round and with all the usual commercial campground amenities, including seasonal swimming pools. The **Pueblo KOA** is 5 miles north of the city at I-25 exit 108 (© 800/562-7453 for reservations, or 719/542-2273) and charges $16 to $19 for tent sites and $23 to $29 for RV hookup sites. The **Pueblo South KOA,** about 20 miles south of Pueblo at I-25 exit 74 (© 800/562-8646 for reservations, or 719/676-3376), charges $17 to $20 for tent sites and $25 to $31 for RV hookup sites. There are also some 400 campsites at **Lake Pueblo State Park** (see "Outdoor Activities," above).

WHERE TO DINE

Ianne's Whiskey Ridge ITALIAN/STEAK/SEAFOOD Serving Pueblo for well over 50 years, this family-owned and -operated restaurant prepares everything from scratch and warns evening diners that because each meal is cooked to order, they may have to wait—perhaps as long as a half-hour. But we think it's worth it. Pasta dishes are the specialty here; our favorites are the lasagna and ravioli. There's also a large selection of fresh seafood, chicken, veal, and certified Angus steaks. The atmosphere is casual but attractive, with dark-wood accents— what we think of as upscale family dining.

4333 Thatcher Ave. ✆ **719/564-8551.** Reservations recommended. Main courses $9–$25. AE, DISC, MC, V. Mon–Thurs 4:30–9pm; Fri–Sat 4–10pm; Sun 11am–9pm.

La Renaissance STEAK/SEAFOOD   Housed in an historic 1880s Presbyterian church, La Renaissance, a favorite of locals since it opened in 1974, offers casual dining in a unique atmosphere. The decor includes stained-glass windows, high vaulted ceilings, and oak pews, which provide some of the seating. Dinners begin with a tureen of soup and finish with dessert, which might be the delightful cream puffs. Although the menu changes periodically, entrees might include the tender slow-roasted prime rib, Alaskan king crab legs, or breast of chicken stuffed with broccoli and cheese. There's a wide variety of domestic and imported wine and beer, and service is attentive and friendly.

217 E. Routt Ave. ✆ **719/543-6367.** Reservations recommended. 5-course dinner $9.95–$36. AE, DC, DISC, MC, V. Tues–Sat 5–9pm. From I-25 exit 97B, take Abriendo Ave. northwest for 4 blocks, turn left onto Michigan St., and go 2 blocks to the restaurant.

2 Royal Gorge & Cañon City

The Royal Gorge, one of the most impressive natural attractions in the state, lies 8 miles west of Cañon City off U.S. 50, at the head of the Arkansas River valley.

This narrow canyon, 1,053 feet deep, was cut through solid granite by 3 million years of water and wind erosion. When Zebulon Pike saw the gorge in 1806, he predicted that man would never conquer it. But by 1877, the Denver & Rio Grande Railroad had laid a route through the canyon and it soon became a major tourist attraction.

The gorge is spanned by what is said to be the world's highest suspension bridge and an aerial tramway, built for no other reason than to thrill tourists. The quarter-mile-long bridge was constructed in 1929, suspended from two 300-ton cables, and reinforced in 1983. An incline railway, believed to be the world's steepest, was completed in 1931; it plunges from the rim of the gorge 1,550 feet to the floor at a 45-degree angle, giving passengers a view from the bottom as well as the top. Added in 1968, the 35-passenger tram provides views of the gorge and the bridge from a height of 1,178 feet above the Arkansas River.

Owned by Cañon City, the park also includes a 260-seat multimedia theater (where visitors can see a video presentation on the area's history and construction of the bridge), miniature railway, trolley, old-fashioned carousel, various thrill rides and children's attractions, restaurants, gift shops, a petting zoo with free burro rides, and herds of tame mule deer. Live entertainment and a variety of special events are presented throughout the year.

The park is open year-round, daily from 8:30am to dusk. Admission—$20 for adults, $18 for seniors, $16 for children 4 to 11, free for children under 4— includes crossing the bridge and all other park rides and attractions. For information, contact **Royal Gorge Bridge,** P.O. Box 549, Cañon City, CO 81215 (✆ **888/333-5597** or 719/275-7507; www.royalgorgebridge.com).

An interesting way to view the canyon is from the **Royal Gorge Route Railroad,** 401 Water St. (south of U.S. 50 on Third St.), Cañon City, CO 81212 (✆ **888/RAILS-4U** or 303/569-2403; www.royalgorgeroute.com). The train takes passengers on a 2-hour 24-mile trip through the canyon. From late May to early September, the train departs daily at 9:30am and 12:30pm; departures are less frequent the rest of the year. Tickets cost $27 for adults and $17 for children 3 to 12, and are free for children under 3 who sit on a guardian's lap. Reservations are recommended.

To see this beautiful gorge looking up from the river, while also enjoying some thrills, consider a raft trip. Rates for adults run $90 to $100 for a full-day trip, including lunch; a half-day trip is about $40 to $60. Most Royal Gorge raft trips include rough white-water stretches of the river, but those preferring calmer sections should inquire about such excursions with local rafting companies. Major outfitters include **Arkansas River Tours** (© **800/321-4352** or 719/942-4362; www.arkansasrivertours.com), **Echo Canyon River Expeditions** (© **800/748-2953;** www.raftecho.com), and **Wilderness Aware Rafting** (© **800/462-7238** or 719/395-2112; www.inaraft.com).

OTHER AREA ATTRACTIONS

Cañon City was a popular setting for filmmakers during the industry's early days, and it was a special favorite of silent screen actor·Tom Mix, who reputedly worked as a cowboy in the area before becoming a film star. The drowning death of a prominent actress temporarily discouraged film companies from coming here, but the area's beautiful scenery and Old West heritage lured the industry back in the late 1950s with the creation of Buckskin Joe, a Western theme park and movie set where dozens of films have been shot, including *How the West Was Won, True Grit,* and *Cat Ballou.*

While movies are rarely shot here nowadays, **Buckskin Joe Frontier Town & Railway** (© **719/275-5149;** www.buckskinjoes.com), located about 8 miles west of Cañon City on U.S. 50, remains a popular tourist attraction and is a great place to take kids. The authentic-looking Old West town was created from genuine 19th-century buildings relocated from across the state. Visitors can watch gunfights, pan for gold, see a magic show, ride horseback (or a horse-drawn trolley), and wander through a Western maze. **The Scenic Railway** (© **719/275-5485**) offers a 30-minute trip through rugged Royal Gorge country, where you're likely to see deer and other wildlife, to the rim of the Royal Gorge for a panoramic view of the canyon and bridge.

Frontier Town is open 9am to 6:30pm daily May to August, and 9am to 6:30pm Thursday to Tuesday in September. The railway runs 8am to 6:20pm Memorial Day to Labor Day; call for hours during May and September. Combination admission tickets, which include the Scenic Railway, horse-drawn trolley, and all the Frontier Town attractions and entertainment, are $16 for adults, $14 for children 4 to 11, and free for children under 4. Railway-only tickets are $8 for adults and $7 for children. Expect to spend 2 to 4 hours here.

Other Cañon City attractions include the **Museum of Colorado Prisons** ⊛, 201 N. First St. (© **719/269-3015;** www.prisonmuseum.org), just the thing for those with an appreciation of the macabre. Housed in the state's former women's prison, just outside the walls of the original territorial prison that opened in 1871, this museum contains an actual gas chamber, historic photos of life behind bars, weapons confiscated from inmates, the last hangman's noose used legally in the state, a simulation of a lethal-injection system, a simulation of the "Old Gray Mare" (a cruel apparatus used to punish obstreperous prisoners), and other artifacts and exhibits showing what prison life was like in the Old West, and even in more modern times. There's even a gift shop selling arts and crafts made by inmates housed at a medium-security prison next door. The museum is open May through September, daily from 8:30am to 6pm; October through April, Friday through Sunday from 10am to 5pm. Admission is $6 for adults, $5 for seniors 65 and older, $4 for ages 6 to 12, and free for those 5 and under. Allow about an hour.

Those interested in Colorado history might also enjoy stopping at the **Royal Gorge Regional Museum and History Center,** 612 Royal Gorge Blvd. (© **719/ 276-5279**), which has displays of American-Indian artifacts, guns, gems, minerals, wild-game trophies, historic photos, old dolls, pioneer household items, and other memorabilia. These are pretty much the kinds of things you'll find in most small-town museums in the American West, but what sets this museum apart somewhat are several renovated and authentically furnished buildings out back. Here are the 1860 log cabin built by Anson Rudd, local blacksmith and first warden of the Colorado Territorial Prison, and the Rudd family's three-story stone house built in 1881, which contains a collection of Victorian furniture and Western artifacts. Although the museum is closed for renovation until late 2005, it's typically open from 9:30am to 5pm Tuesday through Friday and Mondays 11am to 7pm. It's closed December 24 plus all state and federal holidays. Admission is free. Allow a half-hour.

Another local attraction, especially fascinating for young would-be dinosaur hunters, is **Dinosaur Depot** ⭐, 330 Royal Gorge Blvd. (© **800/987-6379** or 719/269-7150; www.dinosaurdepot.com). The depot's main claim to fame is the dinosaur lab, where paleontologists are working to remove various dinosaur fossils from the rock that has encased them for the last 150 million years. There are also several interpretive dinosaur exhibits, including fossilized bones that visitors can hold in their hands, a fossilized tree, a children's Discovery Room with plenty of hands-on exhibits, and a gift shop. Dinosaur Depot also arranges tours of the internationally renowned **Garden Park Fossil Area** just north of town, which is the source of many of the museum's exhibits, and to see some 90-million-year-old dinosaur tracks nearby. The museum is open daily from 9am to 6pm June to September; there are shorter hours the rest of the year. Admission is $3 for adults, $1.50 for children 4 to 12, and free for children under 4. Allow 45 minutes at Dinosaur Depot, and another 1 to 2 hours at Garden Park Fossil Area.

There are several midpriced lodging options in Cañon City, including the **Best Western Royal Gorge Motel,** 1925 Fremont Dr., Cañon City, CO 81212 (© **800/231-7317** or 719/275-3377), with double rates ranging from $50 to $100 in summer and $40 to $90 the rest of the year; **Quality Inn & Suites** (formerly the Cañon Inn), 3075 E. U.S. 50, Cañon City, CO 81212 (© **800/ 525-7727** or 719/275-8676; www.canoninn.com), which has six indoor hot tubs, with rooms priced from $68 to $99 double in summer, and about $20 less in winter. The **Barquero Restaurant** at the Quality Inn features Mexican and American food, and the hotel's **True Grit Lounge** has a John Wayne theme. Most dinner entrees cost $8 to $16. Another good dining option is **Merlino's Belvedere,** 1330 Elm Ave. (© **719/275-5558;** www.belvedererestaurant.com), specializing in gourmet Italian cuisine, steaks, and seafood at lunch and dinner daily. Dinner main courses run $10 to $30.

For more information on where to stay and eat, a walking tour of historic downtown Cañon City, and details on scenic drives and other attractions, contact the **Cañon City Chamber of Commerce,** 403 Royal Gorge Blvd., Cañon City, CO 81212 (© **800/876-7922** or 719/275-2331; www.canoncitychamber.com).

3 Trinidad

197 miles S of Denver, 247 miles N of Albuquerque, New Mexico

History and art are two reasons to stop in Trinidad when traveling along I-25 through southern Colorado. Bat Masterson was sheriff in the 1880s, Wyatt Earp drove the stage, Kit Carson helped open the trade routes, and even Billy the Kid passed through. Many historic buildings—handsome structures of brick and sandstone—survive from this era. Plains tribes roamed the area for centuries before the 17th- and 18th-century forays by Spanish explorers and settlers. Later, traders and trappers made this an important stop on the northern branch of the Santa Fe Trail.

German, Irish, Italian, Jewish, Polish, and Slavic immigrants were drawn to the area starting in the late 1800s for jobs at area coal mines and cattle ranches, and agriculture and railroading were also important economic factors. Ranching remains a cornerstone of the economy today, and the tourism industry is growing. Today the population is slightly above 9,000; elevation is 6,019 feet.

ESSENTIALS

GETTING THERE By Car If you're traveling from north or south, take I-25: Trinidad straddles the interstate, halfway between Denver and Santa Fe, New Mexico. From the east, take U.S. 50 into La Junta, then turn southwest for 80 miles on U.S. 350; or from southern Kansas follow U.S. 160 to Trinidad. From Durango and points west, follow U.S. 160 to Walsenburg, then travel south 37 miles on I-25.

By Train The **Amtrak** Southwest Chief passes through Trinidad twice daily— once eastbound, once westbound—on a run between Chicago and Los Angeles. The depot is on Pine Street just off North Commercial Street, next to Pizza Hut (© **800/872-7245;** www.amtrak.com).

VISITOR INFORMATION The **Colorado Welcome Center,** 309 N. Nevada Ave. (I-25 exit 14A), Trinidad, CO 81082 (© **719/846-9512**), open daily from 8am to 5pm in winter and from 8am to 6pm in summer, has information not only on Trinidad and southeastern Colorado, but also on the entire state. The **Trinidad–Las Animas County Chamber of Commerce** is in the same building (© **719/846-9285;** www.trinidadco.com).

GETTING AROUND Main Street (U.S. 160/350) parallels El Rio de Las Animas en Purgatorio (The River of Lost Souls in Purgatory), better known as the Purgatoire River, which flows south to north through the center of town. The historic downtown area is focused around Main and Commercial streets on the south side of the river. Main Street joins I-25 on the west side of downtown.

Car rentals are available from **J&J Motors** (© **719/846-3318**) and **Pioneer Motors** (© **719/846-4100**). Taxi service is provided by **Your Ride Transportation Services** (© **719/859-3344**).

The **Trinidad Trolley,** operating Memorial Day to Labor Day, provides an excellent—and free—way to see this historic city. Running daily from 10am to 3pm, you can board the trolley at the Colorado Welcome Center (see above), and get on and off at the various museums and other attractions. Pick up a schedule at the Welcome Center.

FAST FACTS Medical services, including a 24-hour emergency room, are provided at **Mt. San Rafael Hospital,** 410 Benedict Ave. off Main Street (© **719/ 846-9213**). The **post office** is at 301 E. Main St. Contact the U.S. Postal Service (© **800/275-8777;** www.usps.com) for hours and other information.

SPECIAL EVENTS Santa Fe Trail Festival, in June; fireworks display over Trinidad Lake on the Fourth of July; Las Animas County Fair and Rodeo, late August; and Las Posadas, Los Pastores, and other Christmas events in December.

WHAT TO SEE & DO

Main Street was once part of the Mountain Route of the Santa Fe Trail, and many of the streets that cross it are paved with locally made red brick. The Trinidad Historical Society distributes a booklet titled *A Walk Through the History of Trinidad* ($2), available at several shops, the library, and local museums. Among the buildings it singles out for special attention are the Trinidad Opera House (1883) and Columbian Hotel (1879), which are across from each other on Main Street, as well as the Trinidad Water Works (1879), on Cedar Street at the Purgatoire River.

A. R. Mitchell Memorial Museum of Western Art ✪ The Old West lives again here, at least on canvas and photographic paper. More than 250 paintings and illustrations by Western artist Arthur Roy Mitchell (1889–1977) are displayed, along with works by other nationally recognized artists and a collection of early Hispanic folk art including bultos, retablos, and tinwork plus Penitente artifacts. The museum also contains an historic collection of photographs, taken by Oliver E. Aultman, Benjamin Wittick, and Almerod Newman from the late 1800s through much of the 20th century; plus early cameras, darkroom equipment, and studio props. The museum gift shop sells a wide variety of jewelry, pottery, prints, and some original works of art, at fairly reasonable prices. The huge building, originally a department store, is a 1906 Western-style structure with the original pressed-tin ceiling, wood floors, and a horseshoe-shaped mezzanine. Allow 1 to 1½ hours.

150 E. Main St. ✆ **719/846-4224.** Admission $2 adults, free for children under 12. Mid-Apr through Sept Tues–Sun 10am–4pm; off season by appointment.

Louden-Henritze Archaeology Museum Millions of years of southern Colorado history are displayed here, including fossils, casts of dinosaur tracks, arrowheads, pottery, petroglyphs, and other prehistoric-man artifacts discovered during area excavations. Watch for the fossilized partial skeleton of a mosasaur (a sea reptile) that lived in the area some 80 million years ago. There's also a gift shop. Allow 1 to 2 hours.

Freudenthal Memorial Library, Trinidad State Junior College, near the intersection of Park and Prospect sts. ✆ **719/846-5508.** www.trinidadstate.edu/museum. Free admission. May–Sept Mon–Fri 10am–4pm; call for off-season hours.

Old Firehouse No. 1 Children's Museum *(Kids)* On exhibit here are a historic fire truck, Trinidad's original 1930s-era alarm system, a model train diorama, and a restored turn-of-the-20th-century schoolroom. Kids will enjoy the hands-on displays, including Grandma's trunk for dress-up and Trinidad's original jail cells (a good place to leave that pain-in-the-neck brother or sister). Allow 30 minutes to an hour.

314 N. Commercial St. ✆ **719/846-8220** or 719/846-2024. Free admission. June–Aug Mon–Fri 11am–3pm. Closed Sept–May and July 4th.

Trinidad History Museum ✪✪ Together, the Baca House, Bloom Mansion, and Santa Fe Trail Museum—known collectively as the Trinidad History Museum—rank as Trinidad's principal attraction, and serve as an excellent introduction to the history and culture of southern Colorado. The 1870 Baca House, along the Mountain Route of the Santa Fe Trail, is a two-story Greek

Revival–style adobe. Originally owned by sheep rancher Felipe Baca, the house contains some of the Baca family's original furnishings. Nearby stands the 1882 Bloom Mansion, a Second Empire–style Victorian manor embellished with fancy woodcarving and ornate ironwork. The Colorado Historical Society operates both homes as well as the Santa Fe Trail Museum, located behind the homes in a building that was originally living quarters for Baca's hired help. Both the Baca House and Santa Fe Trail Museum are certified sites on the Santa Fe National Historic Trail.

On the grounds are shade trees and gardens of hollyhocks, grapevines, and cacti. The museum bookstore sells books on local history, the Santa Fe Trail, Hispanic culture, area recreation, and children's books. Allow 2 to 3 hours.

312 E. Main St. © 719/846-7217. www.coloradohistory.org. Admission $5 adults, $2.50 children 6–16, $4.50 seniors, free for children under 6. May–Sept daily 10am–4pm; off season by appointment for large groups only.

SPORTS & OUTDOOR ACTIVITIES

Located 3 miles west of town on Colo. 12, **Trinidad Lake State Park** (© 719/ 846-6951; www.parks.state.co.us) is the place to go for all sorts of outdoor recreational possibilities, and it's also a good base for campers who want to explore southern Colorado and northern New Mexico. Its 800-acre reservoir on the Purgatoire River is popular for powerboating, water-skiing, sailboating, and sailboarding. Swimming is prohibited, however. There's a boat ramp and dock, but no boat rentals or supplies. Fishermen go after largemouth bass, rainbow and brown trout, channel catfish, walleye, crappie, and bluegills. Ten miles of hiking and mountain-biking trails here include the Levsa Canyon Nature Trail, a 1-mile self-guided loop that also branches off for another 4 miles to the historic town of Cokedale (see the description of Cokedale in "A Drive Along the Scenic Highway of Legends," below). For those with their own horses, there are 4 miles of equestrian trails on the south side of the lake. The Long's Canyon Watchable Wildlife Area offers viewing blinds in a wetlands area. Commonly seen in the park are great blue herons, Canada geese, red-tailed hawks, great horned owls, hummingbirds, mule deer, cottontail rabbits, and ground squirrels. An attractive 62-unit campground, with fees of $12 to $16, has some electric hookups, a dump station, and coin-operated showers. Reservations are available through the state parks website (see above) or by calling © 800/678-2267 for an extra charge of $8. Day-use admission costs $5 per vehicle, which is also tacked onto camping fees. During the winter there's cross-country skiing, ice skating, and ice fishing.

BICYCLING, ROLLER BLADING & SKATEBOARDING   Since opening in May 2003, the **Trinidad Skate Park** has provided hundreds of bikers, bladers, and boarders with a great space to hone their skills. The 15,000 square feet of park has a terrific layout with the snake leading into the two bowls, offering long runs with plenty of speed and opportunity for tricks. Use of safety equipment (helmets, knee and elbow pads, wrist supports, proper shoes) is required at all times, and users are responsible for the proper maintenance of their gear. Summer hours are daily, 8am to 10pm. For additional information, check the website (www.trinidadskatepark.com), or contact the City of Trinidad (© 719/846-9843 or the chamber of commerce (© 719/846-9285). From I-25 take exit 13B onto Main Street east, turn right (south) onto Santa Fe Trail Drive, then left onto Jefferson Street. Take the second right (follow the community center sign) and continue straight to the park.

GOLF   The 9-hole **Trinidad Golf Course,** off the Santa Fe Trail adjacent to I-25 at exit 13A (✆ **719/846-4015**), is considered among the best 9-hole courses in the state, with fees of $15 for 9 holes and $20 for 18 holes.

WHERE TO STAY

Several national chains provide most of the lodging in Trinidad. Rates here are for two people in summer; rates at other times are usually 10% to 20% lower. Among your choices are the **Best Western Trinidad Inn,** 900 W. Adams St., I-25 exit 13A (✆ **800/955-2215** or 719/846-2215), charging $59 to $109 double; **Super 8,** 1924 Freedom Rd., I-25 exit 15 (✆ **800/800-8000** or 719/846-8280), charging $50 to $79 double; **Budget Host Derrick Motel,** just off I-25 exit 11 (✆ **800-BUD-HOST** or 719/846-3307), with double rates of $59 to $64. Taxes totaling about 8% are added to lodging bills.

Those looking for lodging with more character, along with a bit of pampering, should consider **The Stone Mansion Bed and Breakfast** ✿, 212 E. Second St., Trinidad, CO 81082 (✆ **877/264-4279** or 719/845-1625; www.stone mansionbb.com), an elegant home built in 1904 that combines Victorian and Arts and Crafts styles. Located 2 blocks from downtown, the inn has three rooms, decorated with mostly Victorian antiques. Summer rates for two, which include a full breakfast with entrees such as peach puff pancakes, are $95 to $110 with a private bathroom and $86 for a shared bathroom; November through April rates are discounted 10%. Smoking is not permitted inside, and children 8 and older are welcome.

WHERE TO DINE

El Capitan Restaurant & Lounge MEXICAN/ITALIAN/AMERICAN This attractive but simply decorated restaurant, with a relaxing, comfortable atmosphere, serves some of the best margaritas in southern Colorado. It's known for its Mexican and Italian dishes, although you can also get steaks, seafood, barbecued ribs, burgers, and sandwiches. Mexican items include green or red chili, bean or beef burritos, enchiladas, chimichangas, and a vegetable quesadilla. On the Italian side of the menu you'll find gnocchi, beef ravioli, and spaghetti with meatballs, meat sauce, or sausage. Whatever entree you pick, be sure to top off your meal with the tasty fried ice cream for dessert.

321 State St. ✆ **719/846-9903.** Sandwiches and a la carte Mexican items $2–$6.25; dinners $3–$12. AE, DISC, MC, V. Mon–Fri 11am–9pm; Sat 4:30–9pm.

Nana & Nano Monteleone's Deli & Pasta House ITALIAN The Monteleone family takes pride in the Italian specialties served here, each cooked to order (expect a 20-min. wait), and served with salad, bread, and butter. Daily specials include rigatoni, mostaccioli, and ravioli, and the regular menu offers a good selection of pasta, sandwiches, and fish. Many pasta selections are available with a choice of meatballs or Italian sausage, and there is also a "Smaller Appetite" menu for all ages. Monteleone's Deli, located in the restaurant, offers traditional deli sandwiches to eat in or take out, plus deli meats and cheeses.

418 E. Main St. ✆ **719/846-2696.** Main courses $5.50–$11; deli sandwiches $3.75–$5.95. AE, DISC, MC, V. Tues–Sat 10:30am–7pm.

4 A Drive Along the Scenic Highway of Legends

Unquestionably the most fascinating day trip from Trinidad is the appropriately named Scenic Highway of Legends, which runs some 80 miles west, north, then northeast, mostly on Colo. 12, from Trinidad to Walsenburg.

Traveling west about 7 miles from Trinidad, past Trinidad Lake State Park, the first site of special note is **Cokedale,** just north of the highway. The best existing example of a coal camp in Colorado, **Cokedale** was founded in 1907 by the American Smelting and Refining Co. as a self-contained company town, and by 1909 was a thriving community of 1,500. When the mine closed in 1947, residents were offered the company-owned homes at $100 per room and $50 per lot. Some stayed, incorporating in 1948, and in 1984 Cokedale was placed on the National Register of Historic Places. Many of today's 120 or so residents are descendants of those miners, or retired miners themselves. As you drive in, you'll see some of the 350 coke ovens, used to convert coal to hotter-burning coke, for which the town was named. Walking through the community, you'll see the icehouse, schoolhouse, mining office, Sacred Heart of Jesus and Mary Church, Gottlieb Mercantile Company, and other buildings, including a boardinghouse where bachelors could get room and board for $25 a month.

Proceeding west, you'll pass several old coal towns, including Segundo, Weston, and Vigil, and two coal mines—the Golden Eagle, where underground mining is still done, and New Elk Mine, now a processing plant—before entering **Stonewall Valley,** 33 miles west of Trinidad. Named for a striking rock formation—a vertical bed of lithified sandstone—Stonewall is both the site of a small timber industry and the location of many vacation homes.

From Stonewall, Colo. 12 turns north past **Monument Lake,** part of Trinidad's water-supply system, named for a rock formation in the middle of the lake that some say resembles two American Indian chiefs. Several miles past Monument Lake is **North Lake,** a state wildlife area and home to rainbow, cutthroat, kokanee, and brown trout.

The highway continues north across 9,941-foot **Cucharas Pass.** Overlooking the pass are the **Spanish Peaks,** eroded remnants of a 20-million-year-old volcano. The native Arapaho believed them to be the home of the gods, and they served as guideposts to early travelers. Legends persist about the existence of a treasure of gold in this area, but none has been found. Several miles north of Cucharas Pass is **Cucharas River Recreation Area,** home of Blue Lake, named for its spectacular color.

Numerous geologic features become prominent as the road descends toward Walsenburg. Among them are the **Devil's Stairsteps,** one of a series of erosion-resistant igneous dikes that radiate out like spokes from the Spanish Peaks; **Dakota Wall,** a layer of pressed sandstone thrust vertically from the earth; and **Goemmer Butte,** sometimes called "Sore Thumb Butte," a volcanic plug rising 500 feet from the valley floor. At this point, about 65 miles from Trinidad, is the foothills village of **La Veta** (pop. just over 900), founded in 1862 by Colonel John M. Francisco, who reportedly said after seeing the pretty valley, "This is paradise enough for me."

Continuing east, Colo. 12 joins U.S. 160, which goes by **Lathrop State Park** (✆ **719/738-2376;** www.parks.state.co.us), the state's oldest state park, with two lakes for boating (no rentals), swimming, and fishing (rainbow trout, channel catfish, tiger muskie, bass, walleye, bluegill, and crappie). There's also a 3-mile paved trail around the lake for hikers and bikers; plus the 2-mile Hogback Trail, a self-guided nature hike (free brochures available at the visitor center). Also available at the visitor center are a list of birds sighted in Lathrop, and the wildflowers found here, with descriptions and blooming times noted. In winter, there's cross-country skiing, ice skating, and ice fishing. There are 100 campsites, about 40 with electric hookups, plus showers and a dump station. Camping costs $12 to $16 per night, and reservations are available for an extra charge of $8 by calling ℂ **800/678-2267** or through the state park website (see above). The park's day use fee is $5 per vehicle, which is also added to camping fees. Located at the park but managed independently is the 9-hole **Walsenburg Golf Course** (ℂ **719/738-2730**), with a fee of $16 to $18.

From the park it's about 2 miles to Walsenburg on U.S. 160, and then just under 40 miles south down I-25 to return to Trinidad.

5 La Junta

81 miles NE of Trinidad, 64 miles E of Pueblo, 274 miles NW of Amarillo, Texas

Situated in one of Colorado's pockets of fruit growing, this busy little town has several surprises for visitors, including some of the best American-Indian art in the country, and a nearby handsome reconstruction of a historic fort.

Once the hunting and fishing grounds of the Arapaho, Cheyenne, and Ute tribes, and visited briefly by Spanish soldiers in the 17th and 18th centuries, this area did not become known to white Americans until Zebulon Pike led his exploratory expedition into the Arkansas River valley in 1806. Trappers and traders followed, creating the Santa Fe Trail; brothers William and Charles Bent then built Bent's Fort in 1833 as a trading post and the first American settlement in the region.

La Junta was founded in 1875 as a railroad camp. First called Manzaneras, then Otero, it was renamed La Junta—Spanish for "the junction"—on completion of rail links to Pueblo and Trinidad in 1877. The town flourished as a farming and ranching center. Today, it produces a wide variety of fruits, vegetables, and wheat. The population is a bit over 7,500, and the town sits at an elevation of 4,052 feet.

ESSENTIALS

GETTING THERE   By Car   La Junta is easily reached via U.S. 50, which comes into town from Kansas in the east, and continues west to I-25 at Pueblo. From New Mexico, exit I-25 at Trinidad and take U.S. 350; from Durango and southwestern Colorado, take U.S. 160 to Walsenburg, and continue on Colo. 10 to La Junta.

By Train   Passenger service is available aboard **Amtrak** (ℂ **800/872-7245;** www.amtrak.com), with a depot on First Street at Colorado Avenue. The Southwest Chief passes through twice daily (once in each direction) on the main line between Chicago and Los Angeles.

VISITOR INFORMATION   Contact the **La Junta Chamber of Commerce,** 110 Santa Fe Ave., La Junta, CO 81050 (ℂ **719/384-7411;** www.lajuntaco chamber.com).

GETTING AROUND   La Junta is located on the Arkansas River, and U.S. 50, which runs through town as First Street, follows the river's south bank. Highways from Trinidad and Walsenburg join it just west of town. The downtown core focuses on First, Second, and Third streets, crossed by north–south Colorado and Santa Fe avenues. At the east edge of town, Colo. 109 (Adams Ave.) crosses the Arkansas into north La Junta (where it becomes Main St.); 6 blocks past the river, Colo. 194 (Trail Rd.) forks to the right and leads 5 miles to Bent's Old Fort.

FAST FACTS   Health services are provided by the **Arkansas Valley Regional Medical Center,** 1100 Carson Ave. at 10th Street (ℂ **719/384-5412**), which has a 24-hour emergency room. The **post office** is located at 324 Colorado Ave. (at Fourth St.); contact the U.S. Postal Service (℡ **800/275-8777;** www. usps.com) for hours and other information.

SPECIAL EVENTS Santa Fe Trail Encampment, at Bent's Old Fort, July; Kid's Rodeo, August; Early Settlers Day, Saturday after Labor Day; Traditional Holiday Celebration, at Bent's Old Fort, early to mid-December.

WHAT TO SEE & DO

To see a number of buildings from the late 1800s and early 1900s that are listed on the National Register of Historic Places, take the self-guided Historic Homes of La Junta walking/driving tour, described in a free packet available from the La Junta Chamber of Commerce.

Bent's Old Fort National Historic Site ★★   Once the most important settlement on the Santa Fe Trail between Missouri and New Mexico, Bent's Old Fort has been reconstructed as it was during its reign as a major trading post from 1833 to 1849. Located 7 miles east of modern La Junta, this adobe fort on the Arkansas River was built by brothers Charles and William Bent and partner Ceran St. Vrain. It was the hub of trade for eastern U.S. merchants, Rocky Mountain fur trappers, and plains tribes (mainly Cheyenne, but also Arapaho, Ute, Apache, Kiowa, and Comanche).

As American settlement increased, driving off the buffalo that were the lifeblood of the tribes, the Bents were caught between two cultures. Serious hostilities began in 1847, and trade rapidly declined during a cholera epidemic in 1849. Part of the fort burned that year, and was not rebuilt until modern times. Reproductions furnish the 33 rooms, which include a kitchen with adjoining pantry, a cook's room, and a dining room; a trade room with robes, pelts, and blankets; blacksmith and carpenter shops; William Bent's office and bedroom; quarters for Mexican laborers, trappers, and soldiers; a billiards room; and the quarters of a merchant's wife (who kept a meticulous diary).

It's a quarter-mile walk on a paved path from the historic site's entry station to the fort itself, where hosts in period costume greet visitors during the summer. You'll see demonstrations of frontier life, such as blacksmithing, adobe making, trapping, cooking, and medical and survival skills. In summer, 45-minute guided tours begin on the hour daily; a 20-minute film on the fort is shown year-round. There's also a gift and bookshop. Allow 1 to 4 hours.

35110 Colo. 194 E. ℡ **719/383-5010.** www.nps.gov/beol. Admission (including optional guided tour) $3 adults, $2 children 6–12, free for children under 6. June–Aug daily 8am–5:30pm; Sept–May daily 9am–4pm. Closed Thanksgiving, Christmas, and New Year's Day.

Koshare Indian Museum and Kiva ★★★   American-Indian art—featuring Pueblo and plains tribal members both as artists and subjects—is the focus of this excellent museum, which gets our vote as a must-see for anyone even remotely interested in the art of the American West. On display are Western paintings and sculptures, including one of the finest collections of works by early Taos, New Mexico, artists we've seen—watch for the painting *Relics of His Ancestors,* considered one of the best works by Bert Phillips, one of the founding artists of the Taos art colony in 1898. Other exhibits here include authentic American-Indian clothing, jewelry, and baskets. In operation since 1949, the museum is housed in an adobe-style building resembling a northern New Mexico pueblo. It underwent a million-dollar renovation in 2001, and is on the Colorado Register of Historic Sites.

The Koshare Dancers, a nationally acclaimed troop of Boy Scouts, have been honing their dancing skills since 1933. They perform an average of 60 times a year, primarily in their own great *kiva,* a circular chamber traditionally used for religious rites by Southwestern tribes. Dances are held at least weekly in summer, and the Koshare Winter Ceremonials are a December tradition. Plus, on the first Sunday of each month an artist gives a demonstration. Allow at least 2 hours.

Otero Junior College, 115 W. 18th St. ⓒ **800/693-5482** or 719/384-4411. Fax 719/384-8836. www.koshare. org. Museum admission $4 adults, $3 students 7–17 and seniors 55 and older, free for children 6 and under; free the first Sun of each month; dance performance & museum admission $5 adults, $3 students and youths. Daily 10am–5pm (Mon and Wed until 9pm), extended hours during ceremonials. Dancers perform throughout June and July, call for schedule; Dec 27–30 at 7pm; Dec 31 at 4pm. Located 1 block west of Colorado Ave.

Otero Museum   One of the more interesting small town museums we've run across, this museum complex—there are several historic buildings—provides a look at what life was like in eastern Colorado between the 1870s and 1940s. Although lighting could be a bit better and exhibits tend to be a bit dusty, there's a good collection here, and anyone who likes old stuff is bound to find something of interest. There's a genuine 1865 Concord stagecoach, an 1880s-type reaper, a well-stocked grocery store from the early 20th century, a fully restored and working windmill, an early 1900s blacksmith shop, a replica of the community's first school, railroad equipment and memorabilia, and items from both world wars plus the Civil War. Being fans of classic cars, we especially like the 1905 Reo Sidewinder, and the 1954 fire engine, purchased by the Rural Fire Department after its formation in 1953. Allow 1 ½ to 2 hours.

Third and Anderson sts. ⓒ 719/384-7500 or 719/384-7406. www.rootsweb.com/~cootero/museum. Free admission, donations welcome. June–Sept Mon–Sat 1–5pm; off-season tours by appointment.

OUTDOOR ACTIVITIES
Colorado's newest state park, **John Martin Reservoir** ★★★, is a delight, a welcome oasis in the plains of southeastern Colorado. The entrance is off C.R. 24 out of Hasty, about 35 miles east of La Junta, although the reservoir stretches along the south side of U.S. 50 for some 10 miles before you reach it. That's just to whet your appetite for the many recreational opportunities that await you.

The park's namesake reservoir is very popular with those who love to windsurf, water-ski, or zip around in personal watercraft. There are three boat ramps, some great fishing, picnic areas scattered about, two campgrounds, plus birding and a little swimming.

On the back side of the dam that forms John Martin Reservoir is the much smaller Lake Hasty, where only small watercraft with electric motors—no gas—are permitted. Lake Hasty also boasts a wheelchair-accessible fishing pier and small swimming area; plus there are several picnic areas and the developed Hasty Campground lies on its north side. This is where you'll find coin-op showers, laundry facilities, and a dump station; and all sites have electric hookups. The many cottonwood and Russian olive trees provide shade and shelter numerous birds—we saw about a dozen turkey vultures resting in a group of trees not far from our campsite—and you'll see cottontail and jack rabbits all over the place. Point Campground is on a peninsula on the north side of the reservoir, with vault toilets, no electricity or water, but stupendous views of the reservoir and surrounding plains. It's closed in winter.

Anglers try for walleye, wiper, large and small mouth bass, crappie, catfish, bluegill, and perch in the main reservoir. Lake Hasty has those plus rainbow and cutthroat trout, and nearby is a fish-cleaning station. A portion of the reservoir is usually closed to all public access from November through mid-March. That's the nesting and brooding season of the threatened piping plover and endangered interior least tern, and the shores of the reservoir are one of their few remaining nesting areas in Colorado. The threatened bald eagle also likes to winter here, in the large trees in Hasty Campground, so some of the campsites there are closed from November through March.

A 4.5-mile graveled hiking trail circles Lake Hasty and leads to a Santa Fe Trail Marker overlooking the reservoir. In 2002 a beautiful new visitor center, several restrooms, plus numerous improvements to handicapped access points and camping facilities were completed.

There are 109 electric sites in Hasty Campground and 104 basic sites in the Point. Camping rates are $7 to $16; reservations are available for an extra charge of $8 by calling ℭ **800/678-2267,** or through the state parks website listed below. Day use costs $5 per vehicle, and campers must pay this in addition to camping fees. From La Junta, take U.S. 50 east for 35 miles, then turn south on C.R. 24 to the park. For information, contact the park office at ℭ **719/829-1801,** or go to **www.parks.state.co.us**.

WHERE TO STAY

Among the national chain motels in La Junta is **Holiday Inn Express,** 27994 U.S. 50 Frontage Rd. (ℭ **800/HOLIDAY** or 719/384-2900), with rates from $79 to $99 double; and **Super 8,** 27882 U.S. 50 Frontage Rd. (ℭ **800/800-8000** or 719/384-4408), charging $48 to $58 double. In Las Animas, about 20 miles east of La Junta, there is the **Best Western Bent's Fort Inn,** 10950 E. U.S. 50 (ℭ **877/236-8738** or 719/456-0011), with rates of $57 to $69 double. Room tax of just over 7% is added to lodging bills.

Mid-Town Motel ✦ *Value*   A great little mom-and-pop motel off the main highway, the Mid-Town offers clean, quiet, and comfortable rooms with good-quality beds and linens, and standard, well-kept bathrooms. Rooms have desks and one or two beds; several have couches or love seats, and the rooms with one bed also have recliners. Owners Jack and P. J. Culp are an invaluable source of information for area visitors. Free morning coffee is served in the lobby.

215 E. Third St., La Junta, CO 81050. ℭ **719/384-7741.** Fax 719/384-7323. pjnjack@centurytel.net. 26 units. $34–$44 double. AE, DC, DISC, MC, V. Pets accepted. *In room:* A/C, TV.

Appendix:
Colorado in Depth

The Rocky Mountains are the backbone of North America, and Colorado is their heart, with more than 50 peaks that soar above 14,000 feet. The Rockies—with their evergreen and aspen forests, racing streams and rivers, and wealth of wildlife—are perfect for recreation year-round, from summer hiking, mountain biking, and rafting, to winter skiing through deep powder snow.

But Colorado isn't just mountains. It's also the wheat and cornfields of the vast eastern prairies, the high plateau country of the west, numerous historic towns and American-Indian communities, and the modern, sophisticated cities of the Front Range.

1 The Natural Environment

First-time visitors to Colorado are often awed by the looming wall of the Rocky Mountains, which come into sight a good 100 miles away, soon after drivers cross the line from Kansas. East of the Rockies, a 5,000-foot peak is considered high—yet Colorado has 1,143 mountains above 10,000 feet, including 54 over 14,000 feet! Highest of all is Mount Elbert at 14,433 feet, southwest of Leadville.

The Rockies were formed some 65 million years ago by pressures that forced hard Precambrian rock to the earth's surface, breaking through and pushing layers of earlier rock up on end. Then millions of years of erosion eliminated the soft surface material, producing the magnificent Rockies of calendar fame.

An almost-perfect rectangle, Colorado measures some 385 miles east to west, and 275 miles north to south. The ridge of the Continental Divide zigzags more or less through the center of the 104,247-square-mile state, eighth largest in the nation.

2 Geography

Colorado's basic topography can be visualized by dividing the state into vertical thirds: The eastern part is plains; the midsection is high mountains; and the western third is mesa land.

That's a broad simplification, of course. The central Rockies, though they cover six times the mountain area of Switzerland, are a series of high ranges running roughly north–south. East of the Continental Divide, the primary river systems are the South Platte, Arkansas, and Rio Grande, all flowing toward the Gulf of Mexico. The westward-flowing Colorado River system dominates the western part of the state, with tributary networks including the Gunnison, Dolores, and Yampa-Green rivers. In most cases, these rivers are not broad bodies of water like the Ohio or Mississippi, but streams heavy with spring and summer snowmelt, which are reduced to mere trickles during much of the year by the demands of farm and ranch irrigation. Besides agricultural use, they provide life-giving water to wildlife and offer wonderful opportunities for rafting and fishing.

The forested mountains are essential to retaining precious water for the lowlands. Eleven national forests comprise 15 million acres, and there are 8 million acres controlled by the Bureau of Land Management; these are also open for public recreation. Another half million acres are within national parks, monuments, and recreation areas managed by the National Park Service. In addition to all this, Colorado has more than 40 state parks.

Colorado's name, Spanish for "red," derives from the state's red soil and rocks. Some of the sandstone agglomerates have become attractions in their own right, such as Red Rocks Amphitheater west of Denver and the startling Garden of the Gods in Colorado Springs.

Of Colorado's 4.3 million people, more than three-quarters of them live along the Front Range, the I-25 corridor, where the plains meet the mountains. Denver, the state capital, has a population just over 550,000, with another million in the metropolitan area. Colorado Springs has the second largest population, with just over 360,000 residents.

3 Colorado Today

Ask any Coloradan what makes the state unique, and the response most likely will be its mountains. It is almost impossible to exaggerate the spectacular beauty here, or the influence it has had on the development and present-day character of the state. Colorado has been a prime tourist destination practically since the day the first pioneers arrived. Particularly in the 19th century, those attracted to this rugged land tended to be independent types—sometimes downright ornery and antisocial—who sought wide-open spaces, untamed wilderness, and plenty of elbow room. Of course, the dream of riches from gold and silver mines helped, too.

These early transplants established the state's image as the domain of rugged individualists—solitary cowboys, prospectors, and others—who just wanted to be left alone. Much of that feeling still survives, and today's Coloradans have a deserved reputation as a feisty, independent lot. Colorado has the distinction of being home to some of the most politically active liberals and conservatives in the country. They don't follow trends; they make them. It's where some of the country's first municipal gay-rights ordinances were passed; yet it's also home to the vanguard of the family values movement: Focus on the Family, one of the most powerful lobbying organizations for the Christian right's political agenda, is based in Colorado Springs.

Somewhat understandably, such a diversity of political perspectives doesn't exactly engender accord. In the early 1990s, the rest of the country got a quick lesson in Colorado-style politics during the controversy surrounding Amendment 2, a state constitutional amendment aimed at prohibiting certain antidiscrimination laws.

Although the successful 1992 ballot measure was vaguely worded, its intent was clear: to eliminate local gay-rights ordinances that Aspen, Boulder, and Denver had passed, and to prevent other communities, or the state legislature, from creating laws that would specifically protect gays and lesbians from discrimination in employment and housing.

A high-profile nationwide boycott of the state was launched in 1993, and although it scared off some convention business and kept a few tourists away, the end result was a bit of a wash, and the 1992–93 ski season was among the best in the state's history. The boycott was called off when the amendment was declared unconstitutional by the state Supreme Court later that year. The state appealed, but the ruling was upheld by the U.S. Supreme Court in the spring of 1996.

After the controversy died down, further proof of Colorado's maverick streak came just a few months later, when former three-term governor Richard

Lamm—known as "Governor Gloom" for his philosophy of fiscal conservatism and individual sacrifice—announced he would seek the presidential nomination from Ross Perot's Reform Party, virtually ensuring a showdown with the megalomaniacal Perot, but also broadening the appeal of Perot's creation. Not surprisingly, he lost to Perot, but in true Colorado spirit, he went down fighting. Lamm described the toe-to-toe experience with Perot as akin to drinking water out of a fire hydrant, but also admitted he wouldn't have missed it for the world.

An issue on which almost all Coloradans agree, pretty much regardless of other differences, is the need to control tourism. While the industry's financial benefits to the state are well understood, it's generally acknowledged that if tourism is allowed to grow unchecked, the cost to the state's natural resources will be tremendous.

To that end, town officials in Vail reached an agreement with resort management in 1995 to limit the number of skiers on the mountain and alleviate other aspects of overcrowding in the village. The word from Vail and other high-profile Colorado tourist destinations is that visitors will be given incentives, such as discounts, to visit at off-peak times. Ski area officials also have not ruled out turning away skiers after a set number of passes are sold.

Conflicts between environmentalists and the ski industry came to a head in October 1998, when militant environmental activists set fires at a Vail resort that caused more than $12 million in damage. A group called Earth Liberation Front claimed credit for the arson, although investigators said they could not prove the group was responsible. The organization wanted to halt an expansion project at Vail that it said would harm a potential habitat for the lynx, a threatened member of the cat family that is similar to a bobcat.

Another issue that has wide support across the state is controlling growth. The rugged mountains and scenic beauty that lure tourists and outdoor recreation enthusiasts have also fueled an influx of transplants—a modern version of the gold-seekers and pioneers who settled the state. Since 1990, Colorado has gained new residents at the staggering rate of three times the national average.

Many of these new residents are active, outdoorsy types who relish the idea of riding their bikes to work and escaping the pollution, crime, and overcrowding of the coasts. But perhaps inevitably, many native and long-term Coloradans have begun to complain that these newcomers are changing the character of the state, and bringing with them the very problems from which they sought escape.

The challenge for Coloradans in the 21st century is to solve the twin riddles of tourism and growth that are plaguing much of the American West: How do we achieve a balance between preserving a state's unique character and spectacular natural resources for future generations, while still enjoying all it has to offer today?

4 History 101

To explore Colorado today is to step back into its history, from its dinosaur graveyards, impressive stone and mud cities of the Ancestral Puebloans, reminders of the Wild West of Doc Holliday, and elegant Victorian mansions, to today's science and technology. The history of Colorado is a

Dateline

- **12,000 B.C.** First inhabitants of Colorado include Folsom Man.
- **3000 B.C.** Prehistoric farming communities appear.
- **A.D. 1000** Ancestral Puebloan cliff-dweller culture peaks in Four Corners region.

continues

testimony to the human ability to adapt and flourish in a difficult environment.

The earliest people in Colorado are believed to have been nomadic hunters, who arrived some 12,000 to 20,000 years ago following the tracks of the now-extinct woolly mammoth and bison. Then, about 2,000 years ago, the ancestors of today's Pueblo people arrived, living in shallow caves in the Four Corners area, where the borders of Colorado, Utah, Arizona, and New Mexico meet.

Originally hunters, they gradually learned farming, basket making, pottery making, and the construction of pit houses. Eventually they built complex villages, such as can be seen at Mesa Verde National Park. For some unknown reason, possibly drought, they had deserted the area by the end of the 13th century, probably moving southward into present-day New Mexico and Arizona.

EXPLORATION & SETTLEMENT

Spanish colonists, having established settlements at Santa Fe and Taos in the 16th and 17th centuries, didn't immediately find southern Colorado attractive for colonization. Not only was there a lack of financial and military support from the Spanish crown, but the freedom-loving, sometimes-fierce Comanche and Ute also made it clear that they would rather be left alone.

Nevertheless, Spain still held title to southern and western Colorado in 1803, when U.S. President Thomas Jefferson paid $15 million for the vast Louisiana Territory, which included the lion's share of modern Colorado. Two years later the Lewis and Clark expedition passed by, but the first official exploration by the U.S. government occurred when Jefferson sent Capt. Zebulon Pike to the territory. Pikes Peak, Colorado's landmark mountain and a top tourist attraction near Colorado Springs, was named for the explorer.

- **Late 1500s** Spanish explore upper Rio Grande Valley, colonize Santa Fe and Taos, New Mexico, and make forays into what is now southern Colorado.
- **1776** U.S. declares independence from England.
- **1803** The Louisiana Purchase includes most of modern Colorado.
- **1805** The Lewis and Clark expedition sights the Rocky Mountains.
- **1806–07** Captain Zebulon Pike leads first U.S. expedition into the Colorado Rockies.
- **1822** William Becknell establishes the Santa Fe Trail.
- **1842–44** Lieutenant John C. Frémont and Kit Carson explore Colorado and the American West.
- **1848** Treaty of Guadalupe-Hidalgo ends the Mexican War, adds American Southwest to the United States.
- **1858** Gold discovered in modern Denver.
- **1859** General William Larimer founds Denver. Major gold strikes in nearby Rockies.
- **1861** Colorado Territory proclaimed.
- **1862** Colorado cavalry wins major Civil War battle at Glorieta Pass, New Mexico. Homestead Act is passed.
- **1863–68** Ute tribe obtains treaties guaranteeing 16 million acres of western Colorado land.
- **1864** Hundreds of Cheyenne and Arapahoe killed in Sand Creek Massacre. University of Denver becomes Colorado's first institution of higher education.
- **1871** General William Palmer founds Colorado Springs.
- **1876** Colorado becomes 38th state.
- **1877** University of Colorado opens in Boulder.
- **1878** Little Pittsburg silver strike launches Leadville's mining boom, Colorado's greatest.
- **1879** Milk Creek Massacre by Ute warriors leads to tribe's removal to reservations.
- **1890** Sherman Silver Purchase Act boosts price of silver. Gold discovered at Cripple Creek, leading to state's biggest gold rush.
- **1893** Women win right to vote. Silver industry collapses following repeal of Sherman Silver Purchase Act.

As the West began to open up in the 1820s, the Santa Fe Trail was established, cutting through Colorado's southeast corner. Bent's Fort was built on the Arkansas River between 1828 and 1832, and the reconstructed fort is a national historic site near La Junta.

Much of eastern Colorado, including what would become Denver and Colorado Springs, was then part of the Kansas Territory. It was populated almost exclusively by plains tribes until 1858, when gold seekers discovered flakes of the precious metal near the junction of Cherry Creek and the South Platte, and the city of Denver was established, named for Kansas governor James Denver.

The Cherry Creek strike was literally a flash in the gold-seeker's pan, but two strikes in the mountains just west of Denver in early 1859 were more significant: Clear Creek, near what would become Idaho Springs, and in a quartz vein at Gregory Gulch, which led to the founding of Central City.

THE TERRITORY Abraham Lincoln was elected president of the United States in November 1860, and Congress created the Colorado Territory 3 months later. Lincoln's Homestead Act brought much of the public domain into private ownership, and led to the platting of Front Range townships, including Denver.

Controlling the American-Indian peoples was a priority of the territorial government. A treaty negotiated in 1851 had guaranteed the entire Pikes Peak region to the nomadic plains tribes, but that had been made moot by the arrival of settlers in the late 1850s. The Fort Wise Treaty of 1861 exchanged the Pikes Peak territory for 5 million fertile acres of Arkansas Valley land, north of modern La Junta. But when the Arapaho and Cheyenne continued to roam their old hunting grounds, conflict became inevitable. Frequent rumors and rare instances of hostility against settlers led the

- **1901–07** President Theodore Roosevelt sets aside 16 million acres of national forestland in Colorado.
- **1906** U.S. Mint built in Denver.
- **1913** Wolf Creek Pass is first highway to cross Continental Divide in Colorado.
- **1915** Rocky Mountain National Park established.
- **1934** Direct Denver–San Francisco rail travel begins. Taylor Grazing Act ends homesteading.
- **1941–45** World War II establishes Colorado as a military center.
- **1947** Aspen's first chairlift begins operation.
- **1948–58** Uranium "rush" sweeps western slope.
- **1955** Environmentalists prevent construction of Echo Park Dam in Dinosaur National Monument.
- **1967** Colorado legalizes medically necessary abortions.
- **1972** Colorado voters reject a chance to host the 1976 Winter Olympics.
- **1988** Senator Gary Hart, a front-runner for the Democratic presidential nomination, withdraws from the race after a scandal involving a Miami model.
- **1992** Colorado voters approve Amendment 2, a controversial state constitutional amendment barring any measures to protect homosexuals from discrimination.
- **1995** The $4.2-billion state-of-the-art Denver International Airport and $2.16-million Coors Field baseball stadium open. Denver goes sports-crazy with its fourth major professional sports team, the Avalanche, a member of the National Hockey League.
- **1996** The U.S. Supreme Court strikes down Amendment 2, saying it denies gays and lesbians constitutional rights afforded to all Americans.
- **1996** The Avalanche win the Stanley Cup, giving Colorado its first championship in any major league.
- **1997** Weather wreaks havoc across the state. First, a summer rainstorm turns a small creek that runs through Fort Collins into a roaring river that floods parts of the town, killing five residents

continues

Colorado cavalry to attack a peaceful settlement of Indians—who were flying Old Glory and a white flag—on November 29, 1864. More than 150 Cheyenne and Arapaho, two-thirds of them women and children, were killed in what has become known as the Sand Creek Massacre.

Vowing revenge, the Cheyenne and Arapaho launched a campaign to drive whites from their ancient hunting grounds. Their biggest triumph was the destruction of the northeast Colorado town of Julesburg in 1865, but the cavalry, bolstered by returning Civil War veterans, managed to force the two tribes onto reservations in Indian Territory, in what is now Oklahoma—a barren area that whites thought they would never want.

Also in 1865, a smelter was built in Black Hawk, just west of Denver, setting the stage for the large-scale spread of mining throughout Colorado in years to come. When the first transcontinental railroad was completed in 1869, the Union Pacific went through Cheyenne, Wyoming, 100 miles north of Denver, but 4 years later the line was linked to Denver by the Kansas City–Denver Railroad.

STATEHOOD Colorado politicians had begun pressing for statehood during the Civil War, but it wasn't until August 1, 1876, that Colorado became the 38th state. Occurring less than a month after the United States' 100th birthday, it was natural that Colorado would become known as "the Centennial State."

The state's new constitution gave the vote to blacks, but not to women, despite the strong efforts of the Colorado Women's Suffrage Association. Women finally succeeded in winning the vote in 1893, 3 years after Wyoming became the first state to offer universal suffrage.

At the time of statehood, most of Colorado's vast western region was still

and causing some $200 million in damage. Then, in late October, a 24-hour blizzard, the worst October storm in Denver since 1923, piles snow across the Front Range, virtually shutting down I-25 from Wyoming to New Mexico and stranding thousands of passengers at Denver International Airport.

■ **1997** Gary Lee Davis, convicted of the 1986 abduction and murder of a Colorado farm wife, is executed by lethal injection, the state's first execution in 30 years.

■ **1998** The Denver Broncos win the Super Bowl, defeating the Green Bay Packers (the defending champs) 31–24. The stunning victory saves the Broncos the indignity of becoming the first team to lose five Super Bowls.

■ **1998** Militant environmental activists set fires that cause more than $12 million in damage in an effort to stop expansion at a Vail resort.

■ **1999** The Broncos win the Super Bowl again, this time defeating the Atlanta Falcons.

■ **1999** The worst school shooting in United States history takes place in suburban Denver when two students open fire inside Columbine High School, killing 13.

■ **2000** Colorado ski resorts report that the 1999–2000 season was the worst in history due to poor snowfall and potential skiers' fears about Y2K problems.

■ **2001** The Avalanche win the Stanley Cup again, beating the New Jersey Devils 3–1; also, a California couple give the University of Colorado $250 million, the largest gift ever to a public university in the United States.

■ **2002** One of the worst wildfire seasons in history hits Colorado, with about 1,000 fires burning some 364,000 acres across the state. The biggest fire—considered the largest forest fire in the state's history—burned 138,000 acres and destroyed 133 homes southwest of Denver. Other major fires were near Durango, in Mesa Verde National Park, near Colorado Springs, and near Glenwood Springs.

occupied by some 3,500 members of a half-dozen Ute tribes. Unlike the plains tribes, their early relations with white explorers and settlers had been peaceful. Chief Ouray, leader of the Uncompahgre Utes, had negotiated treaties in 1863 and 1868 that guaranteed them 16 million acres—most of western Colorado. In 1873, Ouray agreed to sell the United States one-fourth of that acreage in the mineral-rich San Juan Mountains in exchange for hunting rights and $25,000 in annuities.

- **2003** Scandal hits the U.S. Air Force Academy in Colorado Springs when dozens of female cadets came forward claiming that they had been victims of sexual assaults by male cadets and that academy officials had mostly ignored their complaints and sometimes blamed the victims.
- **2004** Colorado obtains its fourth national park when Great Sand Dunes gains national park status, after getting additional land with help from the Nature Conservancy.

But a mining boom that began in 1878 led to a flurry of intrusions into Ute territory and stirred up a "Utes Must Go!" sentiment. Two years later the Utes were forced onto small reserves in southwestern Colorado and Utah, and their lands opened to white settlement in 1882.

THE MINING BOOM   Colorado's real mining boom began on April 28, 1878, when August Rische and George Hook hit a vein of silver carbonate 27 feet deep on Fryer Hill in Leadville. Perhaps the strike wouldn't have caused such excitement had not Rische and Hook, 8 days earlier, traded one-third interest in whatever they found for a basket of groceries from storekeeper Horace Tabor, the mayor of Leadville and a sharp businessman. Tabor was well acquainted with the Colorado "law of apex," which said that if an ore-bearing vein surfaced on a man's claim, he could follow it wherever it led, even out of his claim and through the claims of others.

Tabor, a legend in Colorado, typifies the "rags-to-riches" success story of a common working-class man. A native of Vermont, he had mortgaged his Kansas homestead in 1859 and moved west to the mountains, where he worked as a postmaster and storekeeper in several towns before moving to Leadville. He was 46 when the silver strike was made. By age 50, he was the state's richest man and its Republican lieutenant governor. His love affair with and marriage to Elizabeth "Baby Doe" McCourt, a young divorcée for whom he left his wife, Augusta, became a national scandal, the subject of numerous books, and even an opera. Today the town of Leadville is among the best places to relive the West's mining days.

Although the silver market collapsed in 1893, gold was there to take its place. In the fall of 1890, a cowboy named Bob Womack found gold in Cripple Creek, on the southwestern slope of Pikes Peak, west of Colorado Springs. He sold his claim to Winfield Scott Stratton, a carpenter and amateur geologist, and Stratton's mine earned a tidy profit of $6 million by 1899, when he sold it to an English company for another $11 million. Cripple Creek turned out to be the richest gold field ever discovered, ultimately producing $500 million in gold.

Unlike the flamboyant Tabor, Stratton was an introvert and a neurotic. His fortune was twice the size of Tabor's, and it grew daily as the deflation of silver's value boosted that of gold. But he invested most of it back in Cripple Creek, searching for a fabulous mother lode that he never found. By the early 1900s, like silver, the overproduction of gold began to drive the price of the metal down.

ENVIRONMENTALISM & TOURISM   Another turning point for Colorado occurred just after the beginning of the 20th century. Theodore Roosevelt had visited the state in September 1900 as the Republican vice-presidential nominee. Soon after he acceded to the presidency in September 1901 (following the assassination of President McKinley), he began to declare large chunks of the Rockies as forest reserves. By 1907, when an act of Congress forbade the president from creating any new reserves by proclamation, nearly one-fourth of Colorado was national forestland—16 million acres in 18 forests. Another project that reached fruition during the Roosevelt administration was the establishment in 1906 of Mesa Verde National Park, the first national park to preserve the works of humans.

Tourism grew hand in hand with the setting aside of public lands. Easterners had been visiting Colorado since the 1870s, when General William J. Palmer founded a Colorado Springs resort and made the mountains accessible via his Denver & Rio Grande Railroad.

Estes Park, northwest of Boulder, was among the first of the resort towns to emerge in the 20th century, spurred by a visit in 1903 by Freelan Stanley. With his brother Francis, Freelan had invented the Stanley Steamer, a steam-powered automobile, in Boston in 1899. Freelan Stanley shipped one of his steamers to Denver and drove the 40 miles to Estes Park in less than 2 hours, a remarkable speed for the day. Finding the climate conducive to his recovery from tuberculosis, he returned in 1907 with a dozen Steamers and established a shuttle service from Denver to Estes Park. Two years later he built the luxurious Stanley Hotel, still a hilltop landmark today.

Stanley developed a friendship with Enos Mills, a young innkeeper whose property was more a workshop for students of wildlife than a business. A devotee of conservationist John Muir, Mills believed tourists should spend their Colorado vacations in the natural environment, camping and hiking. As Mills gained national stature as a nature writer and lecturer, he urged that the national forestland around Longs Peak, outside Estes Park, be designated a national park. In January 1915, the 400-square-mile Rocky Mountain National Park was created by President Woodrow Wilson, and today it is one of America's leading tourist attractions, with more than 2 million visitors each year.

The 1920s saw the growth of highways and the completion of the Moffat Tunnel, a 6¼-mile passageway beneath the Continental Divide that in 1934 led to the long-sought direct Denver–San Francisco rail connection. Of more tragic note was the worst flood in Colorado history. The city of Pueblo, south of Colorado Springs, was devastated when the Arkansas River overflowed its banks on June 1, 1921; 100 people were killed, and the damage exceeded $16 million. The Great Depression of the 1930s was a difficult time for many Coloradans, but it had some positive consequences. The federal government raised the price of gold from $20 to $35 an ounce, reviving Cripple Creek and other stagnant mining towns.

World War II and the subsequent Cold War were responsible for many of the defense installations that are now an integral part of the Colorado economy, particularly in the Colorado Springs area. The war also indirectly caused the other single greatest boon to Colorado's late-20th-century economy: the ski industry. Soldiers in the Tenth Mountain Division, on leave from Camp Hale before heading off to fight in Europe, often crossed Independence Pass to relax in the lower altitude and milder climate of the 19th-century silver-mining village of Aspen. They tested their skiing skills, which they would need in the Italian Alps, against the slopes of Ajax Mountain.

In 1945, Walter and Elizabeth Paepcke—he the founder of the Container Corporation of America, she an ardent conservationist—moved to Aspen and established the Aspen Company as a property investment firm. Skiing was already popular in New England and the Midwest, but had few devotees in the Rockies. Paepcke bought a 3-mile chairlift, the longest and fastest in the world at the time, and had it ready for operation by January 1947. Soon, Easterners and Europeans were flocking to Aspen—and the rest is skiing history.

THE MODERN ERA Colorado continued its steady growth in the 1950s, aided by tourism and the federal government. The $200-million U.S. Air Force Academy, which opened to cadets in 1958, is Colorado Springs's top tourist attraction today. There was a brief oil boom in the 1970s, followed by increasing high-tech development and even more tourism.

Weapons plants, which had seemed like a good idea when they were constructed during World War II, began to haunt Denver and the state in the 1970s and 1980s. Rocky Mountain Arsenal, originally built to produce chemical weapons, was found to be creating hazardous conditions at home by contaminating the land with deadly chemicals. A massive cleanup was begun in the early 1980s, and the arsenal is now well on its way to accomplishing its goal of converting the 27-square-mile site into a national wildlife refuge.

The story of Rocky Flats, a postwar nuclear-weapons facility spurred on by the Cold War, is not so happy. Massive efforts to find a solution to contamination caused by nuclear waste have been largely unsuccessful. Although state and federal officials announced early in 1996 that they had reached agreement on the means of removing some 14 tons of plutonium, their immediate plan calls for keeping it in Denver until at least the year 2010, and Department of Energy officials don't know what they'll do with it then. In the meantime, plans are under way to build storage containers that will safely hold the plutonium for up to 50 years.

As the state enters the 21st century, thoughts have turned to controlling population growth. With a growth rate of three times the national average—the state grew by 1 million people during the 1990s—residents and government leaders are questioning how this unabated influx of outsiders can continue without causing serious harm to the state's air, water, and general quality of life.

Index

FROMMER'S® COMPLETE TRAVEL GUIDES

FROMMER'S® DOLLAR-A-DAY GUIDES

FROMMER'S® PORTABLE GUIDES

FROMMER'S® NATIONAL PARK GUIDES

Algonquin Provincial Park
Banff & Jasper
Family Vacations in the National
  Parks

Grand Canyon
National Parks of the American
  West
Rocky Mountain

Yellowstone & Grand Teton
Yosemite & Sequoia/Kings
  Canyon
Zion & Bryce Canyon

FROMMER'S® MEMORABLE WALKS

Chicago
London

New York
Paris

San Francisco

FROMMER'S® WITH KIDS GUIDES

Chicago
Las Vegas
New York City

Ottawa
San Francisco
Toronto

Vancouver
Walt Disney World® & Orlando
Washington, D.C.

SUZY GERSHMAN'S BORN TO SHOP GUIDES

Born to Shop: France
Born to Shop: Hong Kong,
  Shanghai & Beijing

Born to Shop: Italy
Born to Shop: London

Born to Shop: New York
Born to Shop: Paris

FROMMER'S® IRREVERENT GUIDES

Amsterdam
Boston
Chicago
Las Vegas
London

Los Angeles
Manhattan
New Orleans
Paris
Rome

San Francisco
Seattle & Portland
Vancouver
Walt Disney World®
Washington, D.C.

FROMMER'S® BEST-LOVED DRIVING TOURS

Austria
Britain
California
France

Germany
Ireland
Italy
New England

Northern Italy
Scotland
Spain
Tuscany & Umbria

THE UNOFFICIAL GUIDES®

Beyond Disney
California with Kids
Central Italy
Chicago
Cruises
Disneyland®
England
Florida
Florida with Kids
Inside Disney

Hawaii
Las Vegas
London
Maui
Mexico's Best Beach Resorts
Mini Las Vegas
Mini Mickey
New Orleans
New York City
Paris

San Francisco
Skiing & Snowboarding in the
  West
South Florida including Miami &
  the Keys
Walt Disney World®
Walt Disney World® for
  Grown-ups
Walt Disney World® with Kids
Washington, D.C.

SPECIAL-INTEREST TITLES

Athens Past & Present
Cities Ranked & Rated
Frommer's Best Day Trips from London
Frommer's Best RV & Tent Campgrounds
  in the U.S.A.
Frommer's Caribbean Hideaways
Frommer's China: The 50 Most Memorable Trips
Frommer's Exploring America by RV
Frommer's Gay & Lesbian Europe
Frommer's NYC Free & Dirt Cheap

Frommer's Road Atlas Europe
Frommer's Road Atlas France
Frommer's Road Atlas Ireland
Frommer's Wonderful Weekends from
  New York City
The New York Times' Guide to Unforgettable
  Weekends
Retirement Places Rated
Rome Past & Present

Travel Tip: He who finds the best hotel deal has more to spend on facials involving knobbly vegetables.

Hello, the Roaming Gnome here. I've been nabbed from the garden and taken round the world. The people who took me are so terribly clever. They find the best offerings on Travelocity. For very little cha-ching. And that means I get to be pampered and exfoliated till I'm pink as a bunny's doodah.

Travel Tip: Make sure there's customer service for any change of plans — involving friendly natives, for example.

One can plan and plan, but if you don't book with the right people you can't seize le moment and canoodle with the poodle named Pansy. I, for one, am all for fraternizing with the locals. Better yet, if I need to extend my stay and my gnome nappers are willing, it can all be arranged through the 800 number at, oh look, how convenient, the lovely company coat of arms.

travelocity®